Chennai

Also by V. Sriram

A Guide to Fort St George
Four Score and More: History of the Music Academy, Madras
Historic Residences of Chennai
The Devadasi and the Saint: Life and Times of Bangalore Nagarathnamma
Carnatic Summer: Lives of Twenty Two Exponents

Chennai

A Biography

V. SRIRAM

ALEPH

ALEPH

ALEPH BOOK COMPANY
An independent publishing firm
promoted by ***Rupa Publications India***

First published in India in 2021
by Aleph Book Company
7/16 Ansari Road, Daryaganj
New Delhi 110 002

ISBN: 978-93-90652-98-3

To

R. Venkatakrishnan—who opened my eyes to Chennai's history

S. Muthiah—who guided me through it

N. Krishnan—who encouraged me to wander through it

this book is dedicated in eternal gratitude.

CONTENTS

INTRODUCTION
A CITY DIVIDED

Our city officially declared itself Chennai in 1996 but, to some, it remains Madras. 'Chennai is a city; Madras is an emotion' is a Facebook post that is liked and disliked in equal measure. But then this is an era where you have to take a stand on everything and condemn anyone who dares to hold a different view. The debate on the city's name has followed likewise—those who cling to Madras are branded elitist and Raj apologists. They, in turn, consider the Chennai lobby to be renegade and fuelled by political considerations, with scant respect for history. There are large chunks of truth on both sides of the debate.

The battle on the name of the city is taken up with fresh vigour each August when Madras Week is celebrated. The event came about innocently when three men—S. Muthiah, the city's indefatigable Anglophile chronicler, to whom it was always Madras; Vincent D'Souza, the editor of *Mylapore Times*, a tabloid dedicated to the eponymous suburb; and Sashi Nair, a journalist—got together and decided that it was high time that the city's birth was celebrated. Muthiah, of course, had the details of Madras' birth at his fingertips and said that since the city was founded in August, it would be best that the celebrations took place that particular month.

But was the city founded in August? That has remained a subject of doubt ever since historians began documenting the city's past. The British were the first to evince interest and perhaps the best researcher among them was Colonel Henry Davison Love of the Royal Engineers. He served as the principal of the College of Engineering (now located in the southern suburb of Guindy and a part of the Anna Technological and Research University) between 1880 and 1907. After retirement he went back to England and there penned an exhaustive history of our city, in four volumes. Published in 1913, the work titled *Vestiges of Old Madras* spans the period 1639 to 1800 and remains the best documentation of Madras/Chennai's past. A great reference volume, its index is its crowning feature and with its help you can mine some real gems of Madras—scandal, intrigue, or just some plain facts.[1]

Love and other historians of the time have it that Madras was founded in 1639, by Francis Day, chief of the settlement at Armagaon (present-

[1]Henry Davison Love, *Vestiges of Old Madras 1640-1800*, London: John Murray, 1913.

day Durgarayapatnam in Andhra Pradesh). He had been asked to scout for a suitable site on which a factory (chiefly a warehouse) could be built, and which would serve as a base for purchasing and exporting textiles for which the region was famous. Day negotiated with the nayak (chieftain) who ruled the part of the coast that lay between the salt lake of Pulicat, around which the Dutch had a thriving settlement doing business in cloth, and the town of San Thome, now a part of Madras but then a Portuguese stronghold. The ruler, whose name is variously given as Damarla Venkatadri/ Venkatappa/Venkatapati/Vincatadra/Vintutedra/Vinkatedro/Venkatapate was happy enough to grant the British permission. He confirmed this by way of a deed or firman and that carried within it the seeds of all the confusion that followed.

'Whereas Mr Francis Day, Captain of the English at Armagaon, upon great hopes by reason of our promises often made unto him, hath repaired to our port of Medrasapatam...'[2] begins this document. From this it appears that Madraspatnam or Madras was already in existence when Francis Day came to these parts. If so, what is he really credited with founding?

Second, was August 1639 really the month that Madras was founded, if founded it was at all? The document referred to above is dated 22 July, on which date, as East India Company (EIC) correspondence shows, Day was nowhere near Madras. He arrived only on 27 July. It was therefore inferred by Love that July was an erroneous entry and the correct date was probably 22 August.[3] It is on these tenuous grounds that the birth date of Madras was decided.

Up until 1947, none of this was disputed. All government publications carried this information as a matter of routine for many years afterwards as well. In 1939, a Madras Tercentenary Celebration Committee was formed under the presidentship of Sir Samuel Ebenezer Runganadhan, the then vice chancellor of the University of Madras. A commemoration volume, brought out by a sub-committee under the chairmanship of Rao Sahib C. S. Srinivasachari, was released on 4 August.[4] The chairman also published an independent work, *History of the City of Madras*,[5] for the same occasion.

---

[2]Love, *Vestiges of Old Madras*, Vol. 1, p. 17.

[3]Ibid.

[4]*The Madras Tercentenary Commemoration Volume*, Madras: Madras Tercentenary Commemoration Committee, 1939.

[5]Rao Sahib C. S. Srinivasachari, *History of the City of Madras*, Madras: P. Varadachary & Company, 1939.

Both of these remain important works of reference.

In 1939 these texts went unchallenged. Not so in 2014, when Madras, going by the above works, ought to have completed 375 years. The celebrations were marked by the complete absence of any governmental involvement. The *Times of India* queried officials on this and was told that the government was not in the habit of promoting colonial heritage.[6]

Debates such as those on Madras Week and attitudes on celebrations that are deemed colonial have sharpened since 1996, when the Dravida Munnetra Kazhagam (DMK), then in power in the state, decided to rename Madras as Chennai, deeming the latter name to be Tamil, while Madras, it declared, was a colonial remnant the city could do without. The DMK had in fact been a pioneer of the name change, a practice it instituted when it first came to power in 1967. But then it was restricted to correcting obvious English corruptions—Tinnevelly went back to being Tirunelveli and Madura to Madurai, for instance. Madras was perhaps the first in the state to have a complete change of name. First, the state, which shared the city's name, became Tamil Nadu in 1969. And then, in 1996, the city became Chennai.

There were arguments for and against, with Muthiah leading the latter. Why not change the name to Mylapore, he queried, for, after all, that was one of the oldest parts of the city which had a record of existence from at least the second century CE.[7] He continued to cling to the name Madras till he passed away in 2019, prefacing each of his well-known talks on the city with the sentence, 'Before the British, there was no Madras. There was no Chennai either.' This raised the hackles of scholars such as A. R. Venkatachalapathy, prolific author, historian, speaker, and professor at the Madras Institute of Development Studies. As if to counter the claims of Muthiah and his ilk, Venkatachalapathy brought out a compilation of writings on the city titled *Chennai, Not Madras* in 2006. It had been ten years since the name change but then this is a city that always takes its time and, moreover, will rarely allow a controversy to die. The book's flyleaf said it all:

> Books on the city that are available are written from a somewhat elite perspective, epitomised by the opposition to the renaming of Madras a few years ago. But the fact is that in Tamil literature it has always been referred to as Chennai. Thus the tussle revolves around the cultural views of colonial Madras and the Chennai of wider democratic populace. This somewhat provocatively titled book seeks to highlight

[6]'Madras Week celebrations begin, govt won't join in', *Times of India*, 14 August 2014.

[7]S. Muthiah, 'A Letter to the CM', *Madras Musings*, Vol. VI, No. 8, 1–15 August 1996.

> the vernacular character of Chennai. Many of the contributors have not been visible to a non-Tamil audience before, others are academics who have been researching aspects of the city. Their writings are reflective and impressionistic and describe the changing character of the metropolis.[8]

In short, Madras is colonial; Chennai is democratic. Madras is English; Chennai is Tamil. Madras is ossified; Chennai reflects the changing character of the metropolis. This, in a nutshell, summed up the pro-Chennai argument. Significantly, all those who appealed for retaining the name Madras, spoke, wrote, and thought in English.

But where did Chennai come in? That, it is claimed, is a shortened version of Chennapattanam or the town of Chenna. It gets its name from Chennappa Nayaka, the father of Damarla Venkatapathy, the nayak referred to above. From a detailed write-up by Diwan Bahadur S. Krishnaswami Aiyangar in the tercentenary volume referred to above, it would appear that Chennapattanam was the larger town. This, according to him, is evident from the renewal of the grant to the British in 1645. That document 'makes it quite clear that the main town was Chennapattanam; that Madraspatnam was but a small southern suburb', he concludes. He goes on to add that Sriranga Raya, the nominal ruler of the region in 1645 had stipulated that a southern suburb of Madraspatnam, itself the southern suburb of Chennapattanam, ought to be named Srirangarayalupattinam, after himself. But this did not bear fruit and the city developed between Chennapattanam and Madraspatnam, names that gradually shortened to Chennai and Madras.[9]

The origins of these two names have spawned their own debates and it is likely that each historian of the city has his or her pet theory. Of these, the etymology of Chennai or Chennapattanam is clear. Named after the father of the local chieftain, it was either an existing settlement or one that came up in the area surrounding the place where the British built their enclosure, which they rather grandiosely called Fort St George. The irony is that old Chennappa was Telugu and so the name that the Tamil Nadu government chose to confer on the city in 1996 was not Tamil at all. But that it was vernacular cannot be denied.

What then of Madras? Sadly, there is no clear-cut answer. A popular take

---

[8]A. R. Venkatachalapathy (ed.), *Chennai, Not Madras: Perspectives on the City*, Mumbai: Marg Publications, 2006.

[9]Diwan Bahadur S. Krishnaswami Aiyangar, 'The Character and Significance of the Foundation of Madras', *The Madras Tercentenary Commemoration Volume*, Madras: Madras Tercentenary Commemoration Committee, p. 39.

is that the land on which the English built Fort St George belonged to a village of fishermen, all of whom were Christians. The fact that San Thome, now a Chennai suburb, was a Portuguese settlement for long is quoted in favour of the village belonging to that faith. The chief was a Madarasan, it is said, and the area takes its name after him. There is, however, no documentary evidence for this.[10] Another theory is that the place takes its name from the Madra family. A tombstone discovered in 1927 at the St Lazarus Church in San Thome is dedicated to Manuel Madra, son of Vicente Madra and Lucy Brague, and dates to the 1600s.[11] This Portuguese family was wealthy and owned much of the land in the vicinity. It is, therefore, argued that they gave their name to the settlement. Another Portuguese family, that of the de Madeiros, was also a powerful one and even till the 1750s, a Mrs de Madeiros was considered the wealthiest woman in the city, with her house being rented to the governor when he felt the need to move out of the narrow confines of Fort St George. There is, besides, a church, that of Madre de Deus, now known as Dhyana Ashram in the Mandaveli area, which dates to Portuguese times. Some believe that it lent its name to the region, and hence, Madras.[12]

Those then are the facts on which we base our city's history. It would appear that both Madraspatnam and Chennapattanam were in existence when the British came, thereby negating the belief that Francis Day was the city's founder. They may have, however, at best, been small settlements, perhaps mere hamlets, for there are no records of a teeming metropolis or even of families that trace their origins to a time before 1639. But celebrating Chennai as Tamil would be wrong, for it is of Telugu origin, though it cannot be denied that from the early days of the city, its name was always Chennai in vernacular writing. The English and the Western-educated Indian elite preferred Madras, which contributed to the divide that has continued till now. The theory that Madras is colonial while Chennai is not cannot be taken with anything but a pinch of salt, for the name appears to predate the British, as does Chennai. In short, one is no better than the other. Lastly, the government branding Madras Week as colonial is laughable if you consider that the elected governments of Tamil Nadu have their offices in Fort St George, that most colonial of all edifices. In fact, parts of the chief

---

[10]Love, *Vestiges of Old Madras*, Vol. 1, p. 86. Love quotes Bundala Ramaswamy Nayudu's note dated 1820 on this and then dismisses it as unreliable.

[11]Rao Bahadur R. Krishna Rao Bhonsle, 'Origin of the Name Madras', *The Madras Tercentenary Commemoration Volume*, p. 35.

[12]Love, *Vestiges of Old Madras*, Vol. 1, p. 87.

minister's chamber date back to the 1690s.[13] But then politics is always the art of presenting one perspective over another, with a view to appeal to public sentiment.[14] And, let us face it, changing the name has not made any palpable difference to the way the city is administered. Interestingly, the continued celebration of Madras Week has had at least one fallout—the Vanniya community has begun putting up posters on 22 August celebrating the memory of Chennappa Nayaka. These offer salutations to 'the founder of Chennai', above which is an artiste's impression of how the chieftain must have looked—turban with diadem, a moustache (but of course, how can any Dravidian leader be clean shaven?), and rippling muscles. Madras Week has given the man who lent his name to Chennai cult status.[15] And now comes the surprise—there probably was never a Chennappa! Historian Jean-Baptiste Prashant More, who, in recent years, has been at pains to establish that Madras is indeed a Tamil name, points out that in the genealogical list of rulers from Kalahasti as prepared by Colonel Colin Mackenzie in 1800, there is no Chennappa at all.

More brings in a new theory himself, based on Krishnaswami Aiyangar's writings—the English were given land between the Cooum and Elambore rivers and this was known as Nari Medu (the mound of jackals). The new city was named Medu Rasa Pattinam (the city on the mound given by a king)[16] but this has no historic backing—not that any of the other theories have any. It is interesting that the various explanations for the two names have religious endorsement as well. Thus, according to Dr V. Raghavan, the great Sanskrit scholar, Chennai got its name from the Chenna Kesava Perumal Temple, now located at Devaraja Mudali Street.[17] But the temple was built only in 1646 while the name finds reference from an earlier date. The Madra/Madeiros/Madarasan theory finds favour with the Christians. Then in 1939, came an Islamic theory—that this was once Marakkayarkuppam, named after a wealthy

---

[13]V. Sriram, *A Guide to Fort St George*, Chennai: Palaniappa Bros, 2017.

[14]In 2021 however, Chief Minister M. K. Stalin greeted residents of the city on the occasion of Chennai Day and the corporation put out its greetings for Madras Day. The government it would seem is as confused as all of us.

[15]'Cashing in on Madras Week, Short and Snappy', *Madras Musings*, Vol. XXIX, No. 10, 1–15 Sep 2019.

[16]See Review of J. B. P. More, *Origin and Foundation of Madras*, Chennai: Saindhavi 2014, available here: http://jbprashantmore.com/books/origin-and-foundation-of-madras-saindhavi-chennai-2014/.

[17]Dr V. Raghavan, 'Notices of Madras in Two Sanskrit Works', *Madras Tercentenary Commemoration Volume*, p. 112.

clan called Marakairs who made their fortune in shipping. No trace of such a family has ever been found but the Marakkayarkuppam to Makhraskuppam to Madras theory has its adherents. There are others who believe that Fort St George is located where a madrasa once stood.[18] But that again is nothing but a figment of someone's imagination. The theory that Madras is derived from the word Mandarajya—the kingdom of the benighted[19]—has also been circulated, probably by someone who disliked the city.

If that be the history of the city's name, the stories behind the names of the various localities within it, particularly the older areas, are a mix of fact and legend. In recent times, it has become fashionable to invent histories to justify many names, the origins of which are lost in the mists of time. Take, for instance, the village of Mambalam. Mombalon, Marmalon, Marmalong, and Mamelon are some of the names by which this ancient village was known to the British.[20] In the 1640s when Madras was in its infancy, this was a village known for its painters and printers—those who did Kalamkari work and block printing on cloth.[21] The village, however, did not come under British rule till 1750 or thereabouts. It used to remain outside the municipal limits of Madras till the 1950s. The etymology of the name is obscure but that has not prevented anonymous self-proclaimed experts from circulating WhatsApp stories of how this was once Maha Bilva Vanam, the forest of sacred bilva trees, which was corrupted to Mambalam. Historically, there is no proof of this. Similarly, the first planned colony of the city, Chintadripettah, set up by the British in the 1730s, traces its name to Chinna Tari Pettah—the small village of looms, for it was intended as a weavers' settlement.[22] But Christians today claim that it was St Andrews Pettah which was corrupted to Chintadripettah. This is despite the fact that the Scottish church of St Andrews came up nearly a century after Chintadripettah was created. More laughable is the attempt to give ancient Tamil roots to the very English name of Kellys, an area that takes its name from a doctor from Madras who, in the eighteenth century, was the first to try and get something done about the city's drainage system,[23] a task that still daunts the civic administrators. That area is now known as Killiyur, linking it to the Chola prince, Ilam

[18]Love, *Vestiges of Old Madras*, Vol. 1, p. 86.
[19]Ibid.
[20]Ibid., p. 77.
[21]Ibid.
[22]Love, *Vestiges of Old Madras*, Vol. 2, pp. 258–261.
[23]V. Sriram, 'Kelly's Bottle, Where Was It?', *Madras Musings*, Vol. XXI, No. 4, 16–30 June 2011.

Killi who is said to have ruled this region in the first century CE.

The nawabs of Arcot who ruled the Madras region in the seventeenth and eighteenth centuries, before the English took away their kingdom by foul means, have added to the confusion. Kodambakkam, which gives its name to Kollywood, the moniker of the Tamil film industry, is said to be a corruption of Ghoda Bagh, the horse garden where the nawabs stabled their horses. Given that the rulers had their residence at Chepauk, which was 7.6 kilometres away, it appears to be quite some distance for a dismounted nawab to have trekked each day. The fact is that the name Kodambakkam has no logical explanation to offer and was spelt in EIC records as Quodumbauca as early as in 1708, when the nawabs were still in Arcot and had not yet moved to the city. The nawab's home at Chepauk too is a mystery. It is convenient to explain that this was Cheh Bagh or six gardens but there was never a mention of these in any historic text. The northern, once aristocratic but now depressed, suburb of Tondiarpet has its name attributed to a Muslim Sufi, Kunangudi Mastan Sahib, who is buried here. This eighteenth-century musical mystic came from the southern Tamil Nadu area of Tondi and so it is believed that the place became Tondiarpet (the place of the person from Tondi). How then can we explain that a hundred years before Mastan Sahib came here, the English were referring to the place as Tandore?[24] Avadi, where a number of defence-related industries set up base during and after World War II, is said to be an acronym for Armoured Vehicles and Defence Industries but the railways have had a station by that name in this locality since 1873.[25] The rather culinary sounding name of Egmore has been explained away in several tales—that it was that part of Madras where the sun rose first is perhaps the most outlandish, for it is a western and not eastern suburb! What is forgotten, however, is that it is an area that has been in existence from Palaeolithic times, and its name is at least from the eleventh century CE.[26] Inscriptions refer to it as Ezhumoor.

The fact is that much of what makes up Madras today is a set of villages of considerable antiquity and the explanations behind their names are lost forever, leaving behind much speculation. The English only added to the confusion, mutilating perfectly good names to suit their tongues. Nungambakkam, that upmarket neighbourhood, for instance, appears variously in their records as

[24]Love, *Vestiges of Old Madras*, Vol. 1, p. 10.

[25]*Memoirs of the Geological Survey of India*, Vol. X, p. 31.

[26]K. V. Raman, *Early History of the Madras Region*, Madras: Amudha Nilayam, 1957, p. 51.

Nimynbacka,[27] Lamgabawca, Lungumbaca,[28] Loongombauk,[29] Lingumbauca,[30] and Moongumbaukum![31]

In sharp contrast to these, there are some areas that have very clear histories of their names and development over centuries. These include localities such as Mylapore, Thiruvottiyur, Padi, Thiruvanmiyur, Thiruvallikeni, and Thiruneermalai. All of them trace their origins to shrines located in their midst, all of which have survived to tell the tale. Most have been immortalized in ancient Tamil verse, which tell us something about their past glory. There are also inscriptions and edicts left behind by rulers, chieftains, and munificent donors.

As this chapter is being written, further renaming is going on, thereby adding to the confusion. Fraser's Bridge Road is now Tamil Nadu Public Service Commission Road, whatever that means. Halls Road is now Tamizh Salai. There will, no doubt, be more changes in the years to come. Chennai, however, is fast losing creativity when it comes to place names. One survey revealed the following:[32]

Names	**Times repeated**
Anna Nagar	16
Anna Salai	56
Indira Nagar	23
Kamaraj Nagar/puram	24
Kamaraj Salai	54
Kalaignar Karunanidhi Nagar	7
MGR Puram/Nagar/Colony	19
Ambedkar Nagar/Colony	21
Ambedkar Road	36

But let us leave these names aside, for they can change at any time based on political will. There are, however, some aspects of the city that will never change. These make up what is quintessentially Madras or Chennai—the city's character that has built up over the years and defines it today. Many of these are taken for granted; most are brushed aside and, worse, forgotten. But these

[27]Love, *Vestiges of Old Madras*, Vol. 1, p. 352.
[28]Ibid., Vol. 2, p. 22.
[29]Ibid.
[30]Ibid., p. 153.
[31]Ibid., Vol. 1, p. 352.
[32]Eicher City Map, 2008.

are what make for a great city. A casual glance at Wikipedia will roll out the standard Chennai statistics—fourth most populous agglomeration and sixth most populous city of India, named in several international magazines as the most liveable Indian city, one among fifty-two top tourist destinations in the world,[33] and the food capital of India as per yet another publication.[34] Such lists and rankings are ephemeral in the face of Chennai's essence. That quality is a little hard to define. Are we laidback as a city? No. Are we conservative? Well, no longer. Are we backward? No, certainly not. Are we then progressive? Well...you see, it is like this...we do progress, but at our own pace. We do move forward, but for every two steps forward, we turn back to see if that which was worthwhile from our past has come along with us.

This sense of connection to the past is very important. We always expect our children to specialize in STEM subjects and go global but nothing satisfies us more than their coming home to marry someone of their parents' choice. We will begin the day with coffee as M. S. Subbulakshmi's 'Venkateswara Suprabhatam' plays in the background, then go on to attend conference calls with international centres, go to office in western attire while sporting vibhuti and kumkumam on our forehead, start our workday after praying to a couple of gods, do back-end work for some multinational somewhere in the world, listen to a bewildering variety of music including Carnatic classical, the latest in rock or jazz, and some Tamil folk songs, go out to dinner and no matter what we order, always finish with curd rice, and go home for a quick prayer before going to bed. And yes, though we pray to a multitude of gods, we will vote for our very own local Dravidian parties who, in their initial days at least, questioned our modes of worship. In our view, someone local who knows local issues is far better than a leader who promises the moon and speaks an alien language. But we do like the suffix 'ji' and use it liberally. There are parts of Chennai where you can get away with no knowledge of Tamil, by the way. If you are in the upper-class shopping district of Khader Nawaz Khan Road you can get by with English; Hindi can see you through in Sowcarpet, and Telugu in parts of T. Nagar! Near Apollo Hospitals and Sankara Nethralaya, Bengali is the medium of

---

[33]Chennai was named one among the fifty-two destinations to visit in the world for the year 2014 by *New York Times*. See 'Chennai among "52 places to Go in 2014" list', *India Today*, 11 Jan 2014. Lonely Planet did the same in 2015.

[34]National Geographic featured Chennai in 2015 as one among the top ten food destinations of the world. See Zubeda Hamid, 'Food puts city on top of the world', *The Hindu*, 8 February 2015.

communication with signboards bearing words in that script. Talking about language, we imagine we speak in Tamil but our lingua franca is actually an amalgamation of words from a variety of tongues, slapped onto a base of Tamil. We call it Madras bhashai, don't you know? It is colourful, rich, and has more expletives in it than a sailor's lexicon. And though we speak Tamil, or think we do, we give our children the most Sanskrit of names and often, outlandish ones.

Idli and dosa (and for heaven's sake the 'd' in dosa is soft like the one in Modi, though we in Chennai insist on pronouncing his name the hard way) still define our food and we are rather proud of them, for they have now become internationally known. And did you know that dosa was served at the White House when Prime Minister Manmohan Singh visited in 2010?

Speaking of politicians, Modiji could have made inroads here had he spent some time acting in movies rather than serving with the Rashtriya Swayamsevak Sangh (RSS). We like our leaders to be what our heroes are in films, and our heroes too would like to be chief ministers. Even those who have no flair for politics keep testing the waters and, in turn, keep us guessing.

Muthiah always referred to Chennai (oops, Madras!) as the first city of modern India. It was his view that almost every modern institution we can think of began here. A few were disputed—for instance, the State Bank of India's official history does not begin with the Madras Bank founded in Fort St George in the 1640s—but it cannot be denied that there was much in what Muthiah claimed. The Indian Army began here, for the Madras Regiment is the oldest among the constituent units, founded in the 1750s by Major Stringer Lawrence.[35] The civic body, the Corporation of Chennai, is the oldest in India, begun in 1688.[36] The Tamil Nadu Archives, once the Madras Records Office, established in 1672, is the oldest such facility in the world.[37] The second oldest eye hospital in the world is in Egmore, begun in 1819.[38] The oldest bookshop in India and the oldest railway station (the older ones elsewhere have been demolished and so ours was promoted) are here—Higginbothams and the Royapuram Railway Station, respectively. What most people don't know is that long before the railway line from Bombay to Thane, laid in 1853 and said to be India's first, our Chintadripet had one

[35]S. Muthiah, *Madras Rediscovered: A Historical Guide to Looking Around, Supplemented with Tales of Once Upon A City*, Chennai: EastWest, 2018, p. 33.

[36]See *The Official Handbook of the Corporation of Madras*, 1950.

[37]Muthiah, *Madras Rediscovered*, pp. 491–492.

[38]Ibid., pp. 421–422.

as early as the 1830s.[39] The first recognized 'industrial enterprise' in India, a tannery, began in San Thome in 1805.[40] By the early 1900s, Madras had a Department of Industries, long before the rest of India had one.[41] The English began the Great Trigonometrical Survey of India here,[42] and the marker for it still survives inside the Meteorological Department's campus. For that matter, we had the oldest colonial observatory in India, and until 1947, this is where time was kept for India. At 8 p. m. a time gun would fire in Fort St George. Though Bombay (now Mumbai) and Calcutta (now Kolkata) had their own time zones from 1882, it was Madras Time that the railways followed, making it India's mean time till the observatory was shifted in 1947 to Allahabad. By the 1930s, the city had a woman chartered accountant, India's first, in Ramasamy Sivabhogam.[43]

And our achievements are not just from the past. Accepting the 'Madras was British and Chennai is Indian' argument for a minute, we find that the latter keeps notching up one achievement or the other. This is no tired beldame as Kipling wrote but a dynamic metropolis. The country's first green corridor, to transport a 'live' organ from a recently dead donor to a patient, was done by the city's police in 2014[44] and the rest of India followed. We produce one vehicle every three minutes, beating Detroit at its game.[45] And that achievement is one of several in engineering over the years—the oldest technical institution in the country (now the College of Engineering, Guindy, which began from the Survey School of the 1790s), the first automotive component manufacturer of India (India Pistons, 1949), and the country's second oldest industrial estate (Guindy, 1958). We remain at the top of the charts in the medical profession, accounting for anywhere up to 30 to 40 per cent of India's medical tourism industry.[46] We pride ourselves on our record in leather—more than 35 per cent of India's export is from here.[47] And, as

---

[39]S. Muthiah, 'India's First Railway Line', *The Hindu*, 7 Dec 2014.

[40]N. S. Ramaswami and S. Muthiah, *Parrys 200: A Saga of Resilience*, Madras: Affiliated East-West Press Private Limited, 1988, p. 36.

[41]V. Sriram, *Championing Enterprise, 175 years of the Madras Chamber of Commerce and Industry*, MCCI, 2008.

[42]Muthiah, *Madras Rediscovered*, p. 522.

[43]V. Sriram, 'India's First Woman Auditor', *The Hindu*, 3 June 2016.

[44]Green Corridor System, Donate Life, https://www.donatelife.org.in/green-corridor-system.

[45]'Chennai makes three cars each minute', *Deccan Herald*, 9 July 2015.

[46]Zubeda Hamid, 'The medical capital's place in history', *The Hindu*, 20 August 2012.

[47]'Mega Gains For Micro Biz; Leg Up For Leather, Textiles', *Times of India*, 2 February 2018.

for textiles, let us not forget that it was for this that the Dutch and the British came here. And after they left, Chennai still remained a textile centre.

Outsiders may have branded us conservative, but we are, in reality, progressive. Our social reformers had fought for representation and equality for the most depressed classes much before such a movement gained ground elsewhere in India. When we legislated for reservation in government jobs, and that was as early as 1921, long before Independence, we kick-started India's long journey to social inclusivity. This was the land of Ayothi Das Pandithar, Rettamalai Srinivasan, and Rao Bahadur M. C. Rajah, leaders who fought for Dalit rights long before Periyar E. V. Ramasamy Naicker came on the scene. In today's world, Kanshi Ram and Mayawati may be seen as the first crusaders in that battle but we have been at it, chipping away at upper-caste hegemony for over a century. True, the headway that has been made is precious little, but we are far ahead of the rest of the country, except perhaps the states of Kerala and West Bengal.

At a time when the rest of India was rejoicing over Independence, we were considering secession.[48] Chennai was at the forefront of demanding federalism[49] and even now, its political leadership at least pays lip service to that ideal. We opposed the idea of Hindi being a common language for all states. And yet, our Muslim citizens remained ours—they did not ever think of leaving for Pakistan in 1947, for they were happy here (may they continue to add colour to our city). 'I am an Indian Muslim,' declares His Highness Ghulam Muhammed Abdul Ali Khan Bahadur, the nawab of Arcot. 'My ancestors chose to live here and so have I. I am first an Indian and then a Muslim. Then where else am I supposed to go?'[50] Historian Kombai S. Anwar has been leading heritage walks to sensitize people about the Islamic heritage of Chennai for over seven years now. Each year, during the month of Ramzan, his walk ends at the Big Mosque, just as the evening prayers end and people break their fast. The non-Muslims who follow him are made welcome and given nombu kanji—the traditional dish first partaken while breaking the fast.

'To the people of Chennai, Allah is yet another Sami or God,' says Anwar, citing the presence of a hill near Meenambakkam named Allahsami Malai. 'Muharram is known here as Allahsami Pandigai—the ritual of the

---

[48]R. Kannan, *Anna: Life and Times of C. N. Annadurai*, New Delhi: Penguin Viking, 2010, p. 56.

[49]Ibid., p. 216.

[50]Interview with the author, Chennai, 13 February 2020.

God called Allah.'[51] Deep in Mylapore, there is a Mosque Street which draws huge crowds—what draws them there is a temple to Veera Anjaneya. Not far from there is a mosque at the intersection of Mandaveli and Mylapore. Early in the morning, Hindu mothers line up here with their ailing children. At the conclusion of the morning prayer, the elders come out of the mosque and pray for the well-being of the infants, each prayer concluding with a ceremonial blowing of air over the head to remove the evil eye. In North Chennai, each Tuesday, hundreds line up to light candles at the altar of St Anthony, in St Mary's Co-Cathedral. Not everyone here is a Christian and, for years, the most regular visitor was Valliammal, the traditional yet fiercely independent wife of Muthiah. It was in this city that a church displaced a temple, following which the latter moved to a site where its tank was dug on land donated by Muslims. This is where a cave shrine has been functioning as a mosque for years.

Our inter-religious record does us proud but not so our intra-religious past and, sadly, our present. Chennai is forever riven by caste distinctions, which a century of struggle for social equality has not been able to efface. Thus identities here are forever on the basis of Iyer, Iyengar, Nadar, Thevar, Chettiar, Mudaliar, and countless divisions within each—something that the scholar, IAS officer V. Sundaram once branded as subliminal sub-communalism Each group has been unable to overcome its hatred for the other, and today, manifests itself in political speeches, community events, and posts on social media. Will we ever overcome these prejudices? Perhaps not. Therein lies another division, like Madras vs Chennai. And this is not just intrinsic to the Hindus. Muslims and Christians have the same splits in the city, with converts, in particular, carrying their caste baggage wholesale into their new faith.

Our struggle for water has made us internationally renowned. 'The southern Indian city of Chennai is in crisis, after the four main water reservoirs ran completely dry,' Leonardo DiCaprio posted on Instagram sometime in June 2019 when the city appeared to be racing inexorably towards day zero. 'The acute water shortage has forced the city to scramble for urgent solutions and residents have to stand in line for hours to get water from government tanks.'[52] We, of course, knew all of this beforehand but an international celebrity posting about us somehow jolted many into new awareness. We have had water crises since 1639. We know we can survive, somehow. Just

---

[51] Heritage walk conducted by Kombai Anwar on 20 August 2011.

[52] 'Leonardo DiCaprio's Instagram post on Chennai's water crisis brings global attention to the issue', *The Hindu*, 26 June 2019.

as we have survived floods, which come once in a decade, leading to water being let into the sea.

Chennai is a city with a high literacy rate. Education is important to us. This is probably why so much of printed matter floods us on a daily basis—magazines, books, dailies, and, above all, posters. You can see the last named everywhere—on bus shelters, on buses, on the walls of private buildings, and government institutions. And what cannot be conveyed by posters is taken care of by hoardings. We invented these giant cut-outs of our film heroes during the heyday of Kollywood. When our actors made it to politics, the cut-outs migrated with them. Activists have cried foul and judges have concurred but the cut-outs, flex banners, and posters have survived. Some may detest them, but others seem to accept them as part of the scenery. Recently, it was even argued in court and accepted that such flex boards and banners are Chennai's traditional way of welcoming dignitaries.[53] Here too lies a divide.

We are also a city of appalling economic divisions. There are the uber rich, with private aircrafts and sprawling residences, as well as teeming slums, snaking along the three rivers that long ago turned into drains. You can always identify the slum dweller—they smile more often than the rich, and they are more resilient in times of adversity. The poor more or less have an idea of how the rich live in Chennai; the reverse may not always be true. And we have a political class that needs the votes of the less well-off to win elections but chooses to cosy up to the rich.

We need to also look at how the city is divided geographically. There are 200 wards or divisions, divided into fifteen zones and grouped into three regions—North, Central, and South. The North is by and large forgotten—it is the old historic quarter. All the old institutions and industries began there. It is what the scholar M. S. S. Pandian once referred to as the backyard—a convenient place to dump just about anything while starving it of all possible amenities. And yet, North Chennai survives, or just about. Central Madras is what Pandian spoke of as a museum—it cannot be neglected, for this is where much of old Madras' money is. Maintenance is what the museum zone specializes in—the old infrastructure just about keeps this part going. It has not changed much over time; indeed, it may not have scope to change at all. That this is the museum zone is also reinforced by the fact that this is the area that receives the attention of all heritage activists—walks, talks, and celebrations of old Madras happen here.

---

[53]'Modi-Xi summit: Madras HC allows Tamil Nadu government to erect banners from Chennai to Mamallapuram', *Scroll.in*, 3 October 2019.

And then we have what Pandian called exhibition—the new South Chennai which stretches beyond Thiruvanmiyur and goes almost up to Mamallapuram. This is our new city that we perpetually boast about. This is where the two new roads of the city—the ECR (East Coast Road) and OMR (Old Mamallapuram Road, also known as Rajiv Gandhi IT Expressway) snake their way out of Chennai. They are both recent creations and lining them are the symbols of the new world—IT parks, gated communities and villas, cutting-edge factories, five-star hotels. This part of Chennai has no connect with old Madras and once you are inside one of those offices or housing complexes, you could be anywhere in the world.[54]

Lastly, we come to the old and new numbers. It is almost a decade and more since the Corporation of Chennai embarked on an enumeration exercise of properties in the city and began giving them new door numbers. The Opposition, whichever party it was then, screamed itself hoarse that this was all to change the electoral voter list in favour of the party in power. Whatever be the truth behind the whole move, it was never taken to its logical conclusion. People were never officially notified and all they knew was that there was a new number next to the old one, painted on their doors The citizens solved it their own way—by an unspoken consensus, people began giving out their addresses as new number/old number and so it has remained. The whole city now gets by on an oblique. The confusion does not end here. The registrar of properties has an entirely different system of identifying where you live—by survey numbers, classified based on district, taluk, and village—taking you back to a time when Madras was nothing more than a collection of semi-rural hamlets. The land, measured for commercial purposes in square feet (Chennai is unique in that it maintains land measures in grounds—2,400 square feet make a ground and 18 grounds make an acre), suddenly switches over to square metres at the survey office.

In short, life is never dull in Chennai/Madras—there are enough splits in the city to justify two or perhaps more names and identities. Imagine if it were a well-administered, homogenous city, filled with the same kind of people, quietly going about their work. How boring that would be.

[54]M. S. S Pandian, A. Srivathsan, Mahesh Radhakrishnan, and Deepti Adlakha, *Project on Mega Cities: Chennai—Museum, Exhibition, Backyard,* Indian National Trust for Art and Cultural Heritage, 2006.

1 | LONG, LONG AGO

I am standing in the courtyard of the tiny temple to Shiva as Chidambaresvara. This is in the northern district of Choolai, an area that once supplied many of the bricks that went into building homes and, more importantly, the grand Indo-Saracenic edifices in which the Raj housed its offices and institutions. It is a Sunday morning and I have located the temple with much difficulty, even though it was on the very street that I criss-crossed many times, all the while asking the locals for it. Nobody knew of this historic shrine, built in the eighteenth century by Dubash Thotikalai Kumarappa Mudali as a miniature version of the Chidambaram Temple. Having walked in and offered my prayers, I make a systematic study of the commemorative stones and plaques and remark to the priest that while the shrine was constructed around 300 years ago, most markers are only from the last century.

'300 years?' he reacts in shock. 'My dear sir, this is 2,000 years old, having been constructed by Raja Raja Chola.' I did not want to challenge him on the many errors in that one sentence.

Modern Madras successfully hides much of its antiquity. The temples are perhaps the most visible reminders and, even here, there is very little of the old, subjected as these shrines are to much misguided modernization. The average Chennaiite, if asked the age of a temple, is likely to say that it is 2,000 years old. This is considered a safe figure, beyond any questioning. The surprising thing is that when it comes to the age of the city, such an answer may not be too far wrong, give or take a century or two.

Chennai and Madras may have been inchoate settlements, if at all they were in existence prior to the coming of the British, but what cannot be denied is that the area that the city now spans is of very great antiquity, dating to pre-historic times. An excellent work that covers the region's past before the city came to dominate it is *The Early History of the Madras Region* by K. V. Raman and much of what follows in this chapter is paraphrased from that book. Excavations in the late nineteenth and early twentieth centuries by archaeologists such as Dr Robert Bruce Foote revealed that the military-dominated suburb of Pallavaram, which takes its name from the Pallava dynasty that ruled from Kanchipuram between the third and ninth centuries CE, was rich in Palaeolithic relics. In fact, Pallavaram is where the first Palaeolithic tool was found in the whole of India. That was in 1863 and it was discovered in a ballast pit of the Brigade Ground. More tools surfaced in localities in the immediate vicinity, leading to Madras and its neighbouring district of Chingleput being declared classic grounds of early Palaeolithic culture in South India. According to Raman, the reason this area alone is particularly rich in Palaeolithic finds is the presence of a large number of quartzite yielding rocks. These were used to make stone tools for hunting. The Neolithic period seems to have passed relatively lightly over the region but came into its own once again in the Iron Age. Excavations in the present-day ever-busy Halls Road (now Tamizh Salai), in the area of Egmore, revealed a complete private cemetery, a sarcophagus, burial urns, and several iron tools of that period. In addition, burial urns and tombs that are referred to as megaliths have continued to surface periodically in various parts of the city, particularly in the newer areas, and their discovery has not exactly been welcomed by the local residents, for they fear that their properties will be confiscated in the name of historic preservation. Occasionally, earthenware sarcophagi, of designs that are similar to the ones that were used in Baghdad, have also been unearthed. These have been cited as proof that this region had extensive trade with countries in the West.

Immediately after the Iron Age follows the Sangam Era—a nomenclature that is unique to Tamil Nadu. Spanning the period between fourth century BCE and second century CE, it takes its name from three poetry conclaves from which some works have survived. These poems describe the region that is now Chennai as having been dominated by hunter-tribes known as the Kurumbas who were renowned for their courage. The Kurumbas built a chain of impregnable forts in the area and had their headquarters either at Puzhal (where the Chennai prison is) or Madhavaram (a place famed in the early twentieth century for its milk farm). There are some who claim that the Kurumbas were subjugated by Emperor Ashoka but this is disputed by others. There is, however, no denying that the Kurumbas are still commemorated here by place names. This community divided the region into administrative units termed kottams and each had a name. Of these, some have survived to the present time—Puzhal, Puliyur (which is much of present-day Kodambakkam), and Ekkaduthangal, which is a relatively new suburb to be incorporated into the city. But, of the history of these places, there is not much information.

Coastal Tamil Nadu is very clearly documented from the time of the successors to the Kurumbas. In the second century CE there was a powerful ruler here—Thondaiman Ilam Tiraiyan—and it is said that the area came to be known as Thondaimandalam or Thondai Nadu after him, a nomenclature that still survives. His antecedents are obscure; some believe he was of Chola blood but there isn't enough evidence to say one way or the other. The Sangam Era work *Perumpanatrupadai* mentions him and states that he ruled from Kanchi. Other Sangam creations such as the *Purananuru*, *Pattinappalai*, and *Manimekalai* refer to him as a poet and scholar. What happened immediately after his rule is somewhat obscure though there are references to the Chola prince Ilam Killi ruling from here. The Andhra-based Satavahanas came to control the area towards the end of the second century CE and one of the rulers appears to have appointed a local viceroy, Bappaswami, who some claim was the progenitor of the Pallavas.

The Satavahana Empire collapsed in the third century, leading to the rise of the Pallavas, who ruled from Kanchi. The Madras region came under their control and remained that way till the ninth century. It was during this time that several religions came to hold sway over the area—Buddhism and Jainism, immediately followed by the two dominant forms of Vedic Hinduism—Shaivism and Vaishnavism. This was also when these two branches established their canon of saints, the former recognizing sixty-three—the Nayanmars—and the latter twelve—the Azhwars. Of these, some were from the Madras region. They left their impressions and descriptions by way of poems that are hugely helpful in forming an idea as to how the place was in their time.

The Cholas made a comeback after the Pallava dynasty lost power and between the ninth and thirteenth centuries ruled the region from their capitals at Thanjavur and Gangaikondacholapuram. In the early years of Chola control, there was a brief interregnum when what we know as Madras/Chennai and its surroundings came under the control of the Rashtrakutas. That was following the Battle of Takkolam, in 949 CE. This village is near Arakkonam, the railway junction just preceding Chennai as you approach from the north. It took the Cholas till the early eleventh century to decisively eject the Rashtrakutas from this region. Thereafter, the area remained under Chola rule till the thirteenth century.

The closing years of this great empire, which began in the twelfth century, saw several feudatories to the Cholas controlling Thondaimandalam. These included the Telugu-speaking Chodas, the Kadavarayas, and the Yadavarayas. But by the thirteenth century, the Pandyas had emerged all-powerful. In 1279 CE, Jatavarman Sundara Pandya defeated the last of the Cholas, and Tondai Nadu, along with much else of what is Tamil Nadu today, came under his rule. The Pandya Empire was much weakened by internecine strife and the arrival of Muslim forces from the north in the fourteenth century. The Sambuvarayas, feudatories to the erstwhile Cholas, gained control of Tondai

Nadu for a while but were no match for the might of the Vijayanagar Empire, which took over the region around 1361 CE.

This empire waxed powerful under its three dynasties and various kings, including the mighty Krishna Deva Raya. Even today, a lot of Vijayanagar's influence is evident in Thondaimandalam. The empire needed horses to counter the Bahmani and other sultanates immediately to the north of it. The finest of these animals came from Arabia and the supply was controlled by the Portuguese who dominated the seas. The Vijayanagar rulers were, therefore, very close to the Portuguese and when the latter, attracted by the legend of Saint Thomas the Apostle, wanted to settle near Mylapore, they were granted permission to build a fort. This became San Thome, a name that still persists, even though there is no evidence of the fort.

The Vijayanagar Empire suffered a grievous blow in 1565 when its army was defeated by that of the five confederate states of Berar, Bidar, Ahmednagar, Golconda, and Bijapur at Talikota. The capital at Vijayanagar was sacked and the ruling family fled to Penugonda from where some semblance of control could be established. The days of the empire were, however, numbered and it was completely destroyed in 1652 or thereabouts. Its capital, during its final years, was at Chandragiri near Tirupati.

Right through the times of the Vijayanagar Empire, there are continued references to the excellence of cloth produced in the Thondaimandalam region. It was this industry that attracted the Dutch, who, with the permission of the Vijayanagar ruler, established a base at Pulicat, the saltwater lagoon just north of what would become Madras. Permission was given in 1608 to build a stronghold, and this was named Fort Geldria. The Dutch soon established a series of trading posts all along the coast from Andhra down to Nagapattinam and business boomed. That brought the English in 1639.

But, even while the Europeans were laying the foundations of their empires here, the earlier dynasties had not yet resolved their differences. In 1642, the combined forces of Bijapur and Golconda under General Mir Jumla laid siege to what was left of the Vijayanagar Empire. By 1642, San Thome, Pulicat, Madras, and much of what lay between and around had come under their control. Kutchery Road in Mylapore takes its name from an old Golconda courthouse that once stood on it.[1] Some of the earliest mosques of Madras are in this area and Jonahan Street takes its name from a Tamil word for Arabs—Sonahar. The region remained under its European traders while being controlled by Golconda until that kingdom fell to the

[1]Love, *Vestiges of Old Madras*, Vol. 1, p. 309.

Mughals in 1687. Thereafter, Madras and the surrounding areas became Mughal territory. In reality, of course, the English had come to stay and it was from here that they fanned out to conquer the rest of India, some of it by warfare and much of it by plain treachery and deceit, in which act of chicanery many Indians played a very willing part.

The EIC rule followed by that of the British Raj added considerably to the history of Madras. It cannot be denied that the city, as we know of it today, is essentially a colonial and post-colonial creation. It was during these years that a set of scattered villages coalesced to form the city. Economic prosperity by way of trading, printing, later manufacturing and, still later, information technology and its allied businesses, came about. The city acquired railways, a harbour, which was principally instrumental in providing the first big boost, telecommunications and, above all, a network of educational institutions. All of these made Madras, that is Chennai, a powerful city. But before we get there, we need to know what exactly was written about the older parts of Madras, long before the city absorbed them.

The best sources of information about these places are temple inscriptions. It may perhaps be sufficient to take up two—one Shaivite and the other Vaishnavite—to trace the city's antiquity. Thiruvottiyur is a northern suburb of Madras, better known today for two aspects—the industries in the vicinity and the continuing incursion of the sea, which, for over 150 years now, has been steadily eroding the land here, in sharp contrast to the way it is receding in South Madras. Tucked away in a quadrangle behind an impressive tank that is now sadly dry is the large temple of Adipureeswarar. The principal deity here is Shiva, in the form of a linga that is an ossified anthill. It is unlike any other linga, for it is square in shape and encased in silver; this covering is removed only on certain days of the year. This settlement has had a continuous history from at least the second century CE, for the temple here is attributed in its original form to Thondaiman Ilam Tiraiyan. Various kinds of Shiva and Devi worship appear to have been practised here—a stone slab in one of the side streets depicts in bas-relief human sacrifices as well. There is an idol of Shiva as Gauliswara near the main sanctum, which is not seen in any other temple of India. After the time of Thondaiman Ilam Tiraiyan, we see the Pallavas, Cholas, Pandyas, and Rashtrakutas offering worship and endowments here, as is evident from the numerous inscriptions that abound in the temple. The Cholas also rebuilt the sanctum for Lord Shiva here, and when they did so, gave it an apsidal form. Known as a Gajaprishta (the rear of an elephant), this design authentically dates the present structure to the twelfth century. Several additions were made to the temple over the centuries, with the Vijayanagar rulers or their local representatives constructing a strikingly beautiful multi-pillared pavilion for a processional icon of Shiva known as Tyagaraja.

Thiruvottiyur is rich in its poetic history as well. Of the sixty-three Nayanmars of the Shaivite canon, the three most prominent members—Appar, Sambandar, and Sundarar—all of whom lived between the seventh and eighth centuries CE, have visited the shrine and sung of it. Their verses depict a prosperous settlement by the sea. Sundarar states that the air here is moisture-laden owing to its proximity to the sea and that the waves bring rare forms of conches, shells, precious stones, and even gold and deposit them on the shores.[2] That the place was a favourite among Shiva followers who practised harsh austerities is evident from Sundarar's verses. He also mentions the presence of charming bangle-wearing maidens.[3] He should know, for it was here that he fell in love with and married Sangili, a woman dedicated to the temple.[4] That this was a harbour of some kind is evident from Sundarar's description of various vessels that dotted the sea here.[5] Appar reinforces this maritime connection when he prays to the Lord that he be granted the ability to remember the Almighty when the rock of passion strikes the vessel of desire in which he, with ego as his oar and anger as his cargo, sets sail.[6]

The reformer Adi Sankara, too, is said to have prayed to the goddess here and changed the way she was worshipped, weaning the faithful away from human sacrifices and other tantric forms. A small sanctum in an ambulatory corridor of the main shrine has the Vattaparai Amman—a goddess who was propitiated by animal (and it is rumoured, human) sacrifice, whose mode of worship was made Vedic by Sankara. The principal goddess at this temple complex, who goes by the name of Tripurasundari, has a separate sanctum to herself and worship here is conducted even today by families descended of Namboodiris from Kerala. Sankara is believed to have established this practice in the seventh century. But independent of him, there was a Kerala connection to this temple. One of the Chola kings married a Chera princess and she endowed a monastery here, to be run by a certain Niranjana Guru. This establishment appears to have flourished here for centuries, with the royal preceptors of the Cholas visiting it as well. Several other monasteries

---

[2]Sundarar Tevaram, Verse 3 of the decad 'Azhukku Meykodun', 7th *Tirumurai.*

[3]Sundarar Tevaram, Verse 8 of the decad 'Pattum Padi', 7th *Tirumurai.*

[4]V. Sriram, 'When the Lord Played Cupid', *The Hindu*, 13 February 2015.

[5]Sundarar Tevaram, Verse 1 of the decad 'Pattum Padi', 7th *Tirumurai.*

[6]Appar Tevaram, 'Manamenum Toni Patri', *4th Tirumurai.*

surrounded the temple and over time became separate shrines themselves. An instance of this is the Mekekattu Nandikeshwara Temple, which can be found in a side street. Once a monastery, it is a regular temple now.[7]

In the fifteenth century, Arunagirinatha, the composer of verses called the *Thiruppugazh,* dedicated some of his pieces to this shrine. Pattinathar, a patron saint of the business community of Chettiars, settled here, sang of the deity, and is buried in the vicinity. His verse on Shiva compares the Lord to a sugarcane (dark-hued in the throat, with three eyes/leaves, tall as the heavens, full of sweetness that melts the heart of devotees, this is the sugarcane that grows by the sea at Ottriyur).[8] Throughout its long history, the Thiruvottiyur Temple had a strong courtesan tradition. The women were graded based on the deity to whom they were attached as well as the skills they possessed. There are records of some of them receiving royal honours and of spirited disputes between them over seniority.[9] Like most historic temples, and it must be admitted here, several modern ones, the Thiruvottiyur complex never stopped growing. As late as the nineteenth century, it acquired a magnificent central shrine to Thiruvotteeswarar, thanks to the munificence of a family that made its fortune in liquors and spirits. In the twentieth century, several smaller shrines were added along the periphery, all of them of very poor artistry. Despite their detracting presence, visiting Thiruvottiyur is akin to going back several centuries in time.

Arguably the best-known Vaishnavite shrine in Madras city is the Parthasarathy Temple located in the busy Thiruvallikeni area. The name means 'sacred lily tank', of which there is no trace today. The temple, however, has a large tank which, following a misguided renovation in the 1980s, when concrete slabs were laid in its bed,[10] has very low level of water. But, until the early 1920s, this was a water body that was quite full and claimed at least one life each year.[11] The main deity here is a striking Pallava idol, of around eight feet—a magnificent standing image of Lord Krishna as he set out to be charioteer to Arjuna during the Kurukshetra war. In keeping with this, the deity is two-armed, carries a conch and, most importantly, sports a

---

[7]V. Sriram, 'Once a Centre of Learning', *Madras Musings*, Vol. XXIX, No. 12, 1–15 October 2019.

[8]A. Mahadeva Yogi, *Pattinathar Padal Mulamum Thattuvartha Vilakka Uraiyum*, Chennai: B. Rathina Nayakar & Sons, 1932, p. 255.

[9]Raman, *Early History*, pp. 162–163

[10]Sekhar Raghavan, 'A Note on Temple Tanks', *Madras Musings*, Vol. XXX, No. 19, 1–15 February 2021.

[11]M. A. Sreenivasan, *Of the Raj, Maharajahs and Me*, Delhi: Ravi Dayal Publisher, 1991.

handlebar moustache (made of camphor) that was not on the original idol.

What establishes the antiquity of the shrine indubitably is two verses, the first composed sometime before Christ and the second in the eighth century. The former, by Budathazhwar, one of the twelve saints of the Vaishnavite canon, describes the village of Thiruvallikeni as being on the seashore where waves deposit pearls and corals.[12] A few centuries later, when Thirumangai Azhwar, the last of the twelve, visited the place, this was a full-fledged temple, with all its present sub-shrines—to Narasimha, Parthasarathy, Rama, Padmanabha, and Vardaraja. Thirumangai, who sang of all the deities mentioned above, accredits the construction to a Pallava king, thereby enabling us to date the shrine as well.[13] Subsequent rulers and patrons added to the complex but the core is evidently still what Thirumangai saw. In recent years, further evidence has surfaced—a piece of cement plaster fell off during renovations in 2015 to reveal a Pallava period mural of the Kurukshetra war. It depicts several fiercely moustachioed warriors going off to battle on robust horses.[14]

There are inscriptions from the Chola period in this temple and from that point on we have a continuous record right up to the period of the British, who named the area Triplicane, a corruption that has, unfortunately remained. The Parthasarathy Temple is an instance of a Pallava shrine that has undergone changes over time. But if you need to see what that dynasty was really capable of, you need to go to Mamallapuram, a seaside settlement 56 kilometres to the south. The exact details of the historic evolution of the place are vague but historians have arrived at a broad consensus that it depicts Pallava might, by which we mean the seventh and eighth centuries CE. The kings that it is most closely associated with are Narasimhavarman (630–668 CE) and his great-grandson Narasimhavarman II (700–728 CE), who was also known as Rajasimha Pallava. The former king was also a great wrestler and, hence, known as Maha Malla. One school of thought believes this is why the town became Mamallapuram. The other claim is that 'mallal' in Tamil meant prosperity and given that this was a port town to which Romans and the ancient Chinese came, as evident from the coins excavated here, this explanation too is equally plausible. Visiting the Vishnu temple that stood by the sea in his time, and which was later reconstructed inland during the Vijayanagar era, Thirumangai Azhwar of the eighth century

[12]Budathazhwar, 'Vandudaitta Ventiraigal'.

[13]Thirumangai Azhwar, 'Periya Thirumozhi 2-3'.

[14]T. S. Subramaniam, 'Chennai Temple Yields More History', *The Hindu*, 8 June 2015.

described the town as a place where ships laden with elephants and nine kinds of gems called frequently.[15]

Today all that is a matter of history but what stands out are the sculptures that the Pallavas left behind. One of the largest bas-reliefs in India is a wonderful medley of gods, demons, humans, and animals in the middle of which, a natural cleft in the rock has been imaginatively used to depict a river in descent. This is known as the Descent of the Ganges and could well be that episode from Hindu mythology. It is also referred to as Arjuna's Penance, for some interpret this to be a scene from the Mahabharata.[16] More important are the temples—some free-standing, others hewn into rock faces that depict the earliest attempts at making temples out of stone in Tamil Nadu. The Pallavas were traditional enemies of the Chalukyas at Vatapi (present-day Badami in Karnataka) and during one of their wars had seen what the latter had done by way of carvings in the sandstone cliffs of that town. Mahendravarman, the father of Narasimhavarman I, declared that he was the first to build a temple without using brick, mortar, metal, or wood. This was at Mandagapattu in Villupuram District of Tamil Nadu, where he had a cave temple made for the trinity of the Hindu pantheon. This is considered the first stone shrine to a Hindu deity in Tamil Nadu.[17] Mahendravarman's son, Narasimhavarman, carried on the experiment at Mamallapuram. Here we see not only cave shrines, but also free-standing temples carved from single rocks. A variety of styles were experimented with. A cluster of five is most famous, erroneously named rathas or chariots by the British, and because of the number believed to depict shrines to the five Pandavas and their wife, Draupadi. The cave shrines too are fascinating, with beautiful bas-reliefs depicting various scenes from Hindu mythology. There are also monolithic carvings of bulls, elephants, and lions. By the sea stands a shrine made of dressed stone. This, known as the Shore Temple, is a thing of beauty. There is a persistent myth that this is the last of seven such structures, the others having been swallowed by the sea—a tale created by European sailors. The tsunami of 2004 revealed several submerged stone carvings but of six other temples, there was no sign. For all its grandeur, Mamallapuram is also a puzzle. The exact purpose of these carvings and the reasons behind abandoning the town are both unknown. Now a UNESCO World Heritage Site, Mamallapuram is well worth a visit,

---

[15] Thirumangai Azhwar, 'Periya Thirumozhi 2-6-6'.

[16] Michael D. Rabe, *The Great Penance at Mamallapuram*, Chennai: Institute of Asian Studies, 2001.

[17] K. A. Nilakanta Sastri, *The Colas*, Madras: University of Madras, 1935.

despite the state government's best efforts to beautify the place with ugly statuary of the twentieth century.

The patterns of the Thiruvottiyur and Thiruvallikeni temples are repeated in several other locations across the city. The origins of most are unknown but they display the styles of the Pallavas, Cholas, Pandyas, and the Vijayanagar Empire. Sometimes there is too much history in the temples and any attempt at renovation or modernization affects something. Those in charge simply go ahead and sandblast or demolish, resulting in the destruction of precious heritage. Sometimes the temples are lucky. The Parthasarathy Temple, for instance, had, for years, a stone pavilion near the tank, covered in corrugated sheets. These were removed a few years ago to reveal a stunningly beautiful multi-pillared mandapam, meant for the ceremonial anointing of the processional icon of Andal, the only woman Azhwar.[18]

We have other shrines in the city praised by the Azhwars at places such as Thiruninravur, Thirmazhisai, and Thiruneermalai. Of these, the last named now in the midst of a thriving industrial centre was, till a couple of decades ago, a hillock surrounded by water bodies and fields. It was as described by Thirumangai in the eighth century. It has changed a great deal from those descriptions but the temple is a must visit for its depictions of Vishnu in four postures—reclining, sitting, standing, and walking!

The Shaivite Nayanmars also came to Thiruvanmiyur, Mylapore, and Thirukazhugukunram, as did the fifteenth-century savant Arunagirinatha. Among these temples, the one at Mylapore is perhaps the city's best-known shrine. It has been sung of repeatedly from the seventh century onwards and, if modern histories of the second-century Tamil poet and philosopher Thiruvalluvar are to be believed, this was the area where he lived and wrote his very thoughtful couplets known as the *Kural*. In form, if not in content, they are very much akin to the tweets of today.

And yet, despite all this hoary history, this is a temple in whose story there is a gap of several centuries. The present shrine is no older than the eighteenth century and it has no vestiges of what it was like earlier. And yet, we know the temple did exist in Mylapore from at least the seventh century, by which time it was obviously a well-established religious centre with a calendar of festivals. This is inferred from a decade of verses that Sambandar the Nayanmar composed here.[19] Each verse describes one festival of the

---

[18]J. V. Siva Prasanna Kumar, 'Parthasarathy Swami Temple reverts to tradition', *Deccan Chronicle*, 1 June 2015.

[19]Sambandar, 'Poompavai Pathigam'.

temple—that those events are conducted even today is a matter of wonder. The ten-day annual festival, celebrated in March/April, in particular, draws hundreds of thousands of devotees, the third, fifth, seventh, eighth, and tenth days being hugely popular. And to imagine that someone in the seventh century had seen them! Sambandar describes the temple festival as being full of noise and music. The same atmosphere prevails even now, especially on the afternoon of the eighth day when several thousand devotees spill into the four streets as Lord Shiva, with his wife, Karpagambal, sons Ganesha and Karthikeya, courses down, preceded by bronze icons of his sixty-three favoured devotees. Sambandar is one of them. Another is Vayila Nayanar, who is the local saint. In the hagiography of the sixty-three Shaivite savants, in a twelfth-century work known as the *Periya Puranam*, he epitomizes the Vedantic truth about God. Desiring to build a temple for his deity, he chose to do so in his mind. There, he illuminated the structure with the light of self-realization, anointed it with the waters of bliss, and fed it the elixir of love.[20] Not many care to visit the sub-shrine of Vayila Nayanar inside the Kapaliswarar Temple, and, perhaps, he too prefers it that way.

Arriving here in the fifteenth century, Arunagirinatha described Mylapore as a beautiful and convenient place that had tall buildings that appeared to pierce the sky, dark groves, streams, fields, and tanks filled with lotuses. After a dark period between the fifteenth and eighteenth centuries, there is no doubt that the Kapaliswarar Temple in Mylapore has resurrected itself. It sees pilgrims, worshippers, and tourists lining up every day of the year. In its sub-shrine to Singaravelar, the deity sung of by Arunagirinatha, is a stone slab that has curious lettering and numbers on it. This was a Portuguese tombstone, which no doubt during the reconstruction made its happy way into a sanctum!

What happened to the temple in the intervening years before it was rebuilt where it stands today remains a mystery. There is a strong opinion that the temple originally stood where the San Thome Basilica is today and that the Portuguese razed it to make way for their shrine. This is buttressed by a fleeting reference in Robert Sewell's *A Forgotten Empire*, which is a chronicle of Vijayanagar, the kingdom that was destroyed in 1565. According to this, the Brahmins of Mylapore invited Aliya Rama Raya, the all-powerful son-in-law of Krishna Deva Raya, in 1558, to check the spread of Christianity. The Order of St Francis had destroyed many temples, they complained. Rama Raya did come, but 'on finding that the inhabitants were loyal to him', went

[20]G. Vanmikinathan, *The Periya Puranam of Sekkizhar*, Madras: Sri Ramakrishna Math, 1984.

away without taking any action.[21] In any case, the relationship between the Portuguese and the Vijayanagar rulers was very close and Rama Raya was probably unwilling to sacrifice that for a temple or two.

Christianity was, however, not new to Madras. The Roman Catholics firmly believe that St Thomas, the doubting apostle of Jesus, came to this region immediately after the crucifixion and preached at Mylapore. Meeting with stiff resistance, he moved to the hill in the south of the city and preached from there. This became St Thomas Mount; the smaller hillock next to it came to be known Little Mount. The apostle is said to have walked to Mylapore every day and wherever he rested, a church came up. It is significant that an old church in the Mandaveli area, just south of Mylapore, goes by the name of Descanso, which means 'breathing space' in Portuguese. It is believed that St Thomas met with a violent end in Madras and was buried where the San Thome Cathedral came up over his remains. His body, if it was indeed his body, is no longer here, for the relics were shipped off to Edessa in Mesopotamia in the third century and from there made a journey in the thirteenth century to Ortona in Italy. What Madras has is a small hand bone and a lance, the latter being the instrument that is said to have killed the apostle. Certainly, by the time of the traveller Marco Polo, the legend of St Thomas in Madras had gained ground.[22]

St Thomas' arrival, stay, and passing away here is strongly disputed and as historian K. V. Raman notes, 'a vast literature, not always free from the personal prejudices of the writers, has grown around the subject'.[23] But the Vatican recognizes only three basilicas as having been built over an apostle's remains—St Peter's in Rome, Santiago de Compostela in Spain, and San Thome in Madras. If the legend of St Thomas' coming here is true, it is yet another proof of the antiquity of our city. The Portuguese had no doubts about St Thomas having once been buried at Mylapore, and by the early sixteenth century, were attracted to the place and had built San Thome. Several churches came up within and immediately outside this walled city and a few survive, giving their names to the localities where they are situated. Luz in Mylapore, for instance, is named after the Portuguese word for light. It is believed that a ship full of Portuguese sailors that was being tossed about by a storm off the coast was guided to safety by a light on the shore. The

---

[21]Robert Sewell, *A Forgotten Empire (Vijayanagar)*, A Contribution to the History of India, London: Swan Sonnenschein & Co. Limited, 1900, p. 193.

[22]Muthiah, *Madras Rediscovered*, pp. 239–241.

[23]Raman, *Early History*, p. 30.

sailors, on landing, followed it to a spot where it vanished and decided to build a shrine there for Our Lady of the Light as a gesture of gratitude. The Luz Church, as it is known, came up in 1516, though this date too is a matter of debate. Nevertheless, the shrine celebrated 500 years in 2016 and also commemorated the half-a-millennium-old strong Portuguese connection with the place![24] San Thome Fort has vanished, the Dutch, the Golconda forces, and the English destroying it completely over a century and a half.[25] But if you walk behind San Thome Basilica towards the ocean, you will realize it is necessary to climb down a long flight of steps to reach it. This then was the height of the San Thome Fort. At the top of this stairway is a battered wooden post. This marks the spot where the French erected a flagstaff during the two years (1672–1674) when they had wrested San Thome from Golconda. For some reason, it became known as the Dutch flagstaff and survived for years before being removed in the twentieth century.[26] Post the tsunami of 2004 a new flagstaff with a distressed appearance has been put up. It now goes by the name of St Thomas' staff. It reinforces a legend that the apostle drove his staff into the ground and declared that the sea would rise no further than that spot. On Boxing Day, 2004, the sea obeyed him. Below the San Thome Basilica is a crypt that has since expanded to become a museum dedicated to the apostle, designed rather unfortunately in a cinematic tradition. This construction has put paid to any further excavation in the area, which, in turn, closes any further investigation into Mylapore's past. According to old-timers from the area, bits and pieces of Hindu shrines used to keep surfacing here.

If San Thome's history is that of a temple making way for a church, Pallavaram is even more interesting, for it has a cave shrine that has since become a mosque! This area, as we have seen earlier, is an ancient part of Madras and around the sixth century CE was Pallava territory. It was here that Mahendravarman, the Pallava king, excavated yet another of his cave temples. There is an inscription about Mahendravarman on the upper and lower beams of the structure[27] and the shrine has five chambers fronted by

---

[24]Muthiah, *Madras Rediscovered*, p. 261.

[25]V. Sriram, 'The Ghosts of Fort San Thome', *Madras Musings*, Vol. XXVII, No. 24, 1–15 April 2018.

[26]N. S. Ramaswami, *Political History of the Carnatic Under the Nawabs*, Delhi: Abhinav Publications, 1984, p. 117.

[27]C. R. Krishnamacharlu, A. R. No. 369 of 1908, South Indian Inscriptions, Vol. 12, Madras: Government Press, 1943.

classic Pallava-era pillars, all of which are part of the same rock. It is not known as to what deities once adorned the sanctum but the number of chambers linked the place to the Pandavas and so it became Pancha Pandava Malai (Hill). Over the years, the rock and cave became identified with a Muslim saint.[28] Now known as the Moula Ali Dargah, it has been heavily modernized but has still not shed its cave origins. The rock is known as Moula Ka Pahad!

Madras is often described as having been a fishermen's village before the British made a city out of it. These original inhabitants lived by the sea in a series of scattered settlements. Sambandar, in his verses on Mylai, describes the Lord as having seated himself in a dense grove by a seaside hamlet whose residents use sharp spears to capture fish.[29] The community was divided between those following their traditional religion and Christianity. The former had their own deities, most of whom have been absorbed into the Vedic pantheon. These include Angala Parameswari, for whom there are a number of temples by the sea. One of the most famous is in Mylapore itself. Not far from here is yet another shrine to a local goddess—Mundagakanni Amman, she of the lotus eyes. This deity, worshipped in the form of an ossified snake hill, is said to predate Vedic practices. The goddess is in a sanctum that brooks no permanent roof. A thatch shelter covers the small triangular stone, which is the deity itself. Government records maintain that the temple is of uncertain antiquity though they do concede that it is ancient. Popular legend links it to Korravai, the Sangam-age war goddess who feasted on the flesh of slain enemies and drank their blood. By the time of the *Shilappadikaram*, a second-century CE work, Korravai was in the process of being absorbed into the Vedic pantheon and made synonymous with Durga. If Mundagakanni is Korravai, it makes the temple a very old one indeed. There were also guardian goddesses at various places, each marking the boundaries of villages that later merged with Madras. One of these is Kolavizhi Amman of Mylapore, who is ceremoniously worshipped and whose permission is sought before the Kapaliswarar Temple begins its annual festival.

Long before the Nayanmars of the seventh and eight centuries CE successfully drove the Jains out of Tamil country, the latter were a powerful presence here. Indeed, the development of the Tamil script owes much to the Jains. The Pallava and Pandya rulers became Jains for some time in their respective eras and it was then that the religion waxed powerful. In keeping

[28]Raman, *Early History*, p. 47.

[29]Sambandar, 'Oor Thirai Velai', *Poompavai Pathigam*.

with Jain philosophy, education became widespread and even today, the term for school in Tamil is 'palli', which is the same as a Jain monastery. The first five classics of Tamil—the *Shilappadikaram*, *Manimekalai*, *Jivakachintamani*, *Valayapathi*, and *Kundalakesi*—all display Jain influence. Parts of what would become Madras were centres of Jainism. Mylapore was definitely one, for there are plenty of Jain works between the twelfth and fourteenth centuries CE that describe the presence in Mylapore of a temple dedicated to the Tirthankara Neminatha.[30] It is said that the idol was later shifted to Mel Sithamur near the historic fortress of Gingee, where it is still worshipped. Statues of Tirthankaras have been unearthed at San Thome near Mylapore and are now in the Government Museum. Similar figurines have been excavated from Villivakkam, Puzhal, and Pallavaram.

That Buddhism co-existed here with Jainism is evident from Sambandar's decad on Mylapore. He was invited here by Sivanesan Chettiar, a businessman who was sternly opposed to both Buddhism and Jainism. Chettiar's daughter, Poompavai, had died from a snakebite and her ashes were preserved in a pot in the hope that Sambandar could do something when he visited. Sure enough, when the boy saint finished his ten verses, Poompavai emerged from the pot, just as a 'baby comes out from a mother's womb at the end of nine months'. In his last verse in the set, Sambandar states that the Jains and Buddhists watched in open-mouthed wonder as the miracle unfolded. Similarly, Thirumazhisai Azhwar, who takes his name from Thirumazhisai, a Chennai suburb, was first a Buddhist, later a Jain, and finally became an ardent Vaishnavite.

This was Madras well before the arrival of the English—a set of scattered villages, each with its history and temples. Many place names have the suffix Pakkam/Vakkam, Puram or Pettai, indicating that they were settlements big enough to be recognized as towns. Some places have names that seem to indicate a pastoral past—Ayanavaram, for instance, is a corruption of Ayanpuram, the area of the shepherd.

There are also a number of places that were named after natural features. Was Purasawalkam really a grove of Purasu (Flame of the Forest/ *Butea monosperma*)? There is one solitary representative in that area's Gangadeeswarar Temple, which has inscriptions from the thirteenth century onwards. Thiruvottiyur was as per Appar, a grove of Punnai (Alexander Laurel/ *Calophyllum innophyllum*) trees. Mylapore was known as Mylappu or Mylarpil—the place that resounded with the cries of peacocks. Only stone

[30]Raman, *Early History*, pp. 175, 209.

representations of these birds survive today. Mangadu—for long a forgotten village with a temple dedicated to Goddess Kamakshi—is now a part of Madras. As the name indicates, it was a forest of mango trees. During the mango season, it is part of daily worship to place a mango in the hands of the principal deity. This is not plucked off a tree, for there are none, but is bought from one of the many shops lining the place.

There are also countless places named after hereditary professions. Kosapettai indicates potters' settlements. Sarhang is a word that means boatswain, and this was corrupted to syrang. There are streets in North Madras commemorating men who bear that surname, indicating the seafaring nature of that area. Oil mongers, washers, headmen, priests, masons, and native doctors all get their share of honours.

The big mystery of course is Madras—what was the original village like? Did it not have at least one temple to speak of its antiquity? Or was it just a tiny hamlet populated by fishermen? Why are there no inscriptions that speak of the place? There may just be—a couple of years ago, a stone inscription in the village of Penneswara Matam, Krishnagiri taluk, was finally deciphered three decades after it was excavated. Dating to 1367, it lists a series of places that came under the sway of the Vijayanagar Empire. Pudupattanam, Madarasapattanam, Nilankaraiyanpattanam, and Kovalam feature in it. Since all of these names pertain to areas in and around Chennai, it is likely that Madarasapattanam became the Madras of later years.[31] In which case, Madras is, by itself, at least 650 years old. Not at all a bad record for a city that had repeatedly been given up as a bad idea because of its weather, water, and much else.

---

[31]M. T. Saju, 'Stone Inscriptions are the original documents of a city', *Times of India*, 6 November 2018.

2 | TOWN, CITY, METROPOLIS

In July 1639, an Englishman came down the Coromandel Coast. He was looking for a place to set up business on behalf of the British East India Company. The earlier settlements at places such as Surat and Masulipatnam were unprofitable and the pressure to find a better site to settle in and trade from was intense. Francis Day was his name and he found just such a spot. It was a sandy wasteland by the sea, with a few fishing hamlets dotting the skyline. He reported that cloth, which was the principal item of trade for the EIC, was 20 per cent cheaper here than in any other place on the coast.[1] His superior at Masulipatnam, Andrew Cogan, was most impressed and negotiations were begun immediately for acquiring some land.

The nominal ruler of the area was the raja of Chandragiri, a descendant of the great Vijayanagar rulers, whose empire had long since been fragmented. Under him ruled local chieftains or nayaks. The spot that Day fancied was under the control of Damarla Venkatapathy Nayak, whose territory extended from Pulicat—the Dutch settlement to the north of Chennai, to San Thome—the Portuguese settlement that abutted Mylapore in what would eventually become South Chennai. The nayak's headquarters were at Poonamallee. The discussions were carried on through the good offices of Day's dubash or translator, Beri Thimmappa of Palacole, who negotiated chiefly with Venkatapathy's brother, Ayyappa Nayak. Sometime in August 1639, a deal was struck and the English had their first overseas possession,[2] which went by the name Madras and/or Chennai. In the heart of this new settlement, they began constructing a fort—Fort St George, which, so many years later, continues to be the seat of power for the state of Tamil Nadu. It is interesting that Chennai still develops and grows along four principal thoroughfares radiating from the Fort—First Line Beach/Rajaji Salai and beyond to the north, Beach Road/Kamaraj Salai and further towards the south, Poonamallee High Road to the west where the nayak lived, and finally, Mount Road leading to where the British troops were stationed, at St Thomas Mount.

The nearest town to the English settlement was San Thome, then a flourishing urban centre, with a population exceeding 10,000. Initially, there

[1]Love, *Vestiges of Old Madras*, Vol. 1, p. 20.

[2]What set apart Madras from other settlements such as Surat and Masulipatnam was that it was transferred to the Company which, therefore, collected revenue from it.

was bad blood between the English and the Portuguese.[3] But many Portuguese women began leaving San Thome for the largely bachelors' establishment of Fort St George.[4] Children born out of such unions were brought up in the Catholic faith. It was only after eligible women, known as the Fishing Fleet, chiefly because they were sent to Madras to look for husbands, began arriving from England in the late 1600s[5] that these liaisons with the Portuguese women ceased. But San Thome and its abutting town of Mylapore would remain outside the purview of the British till 1749, when the area became a part of Madras.

While the English lived within the fort, a thriving native town came up under its walls. This was named Black Town, for the Indians who served Fort St George lived here. The population comprised Indian businessmen and agents, translators (dubashes who knew two languages), moneylenders, shopkeepers, soldiers, musicians, and dancers. Just behind Black Town were two older hamlets–Muthialpet and Peddanaikpet that over time were absorbed into it. These four areas—Fort St George, Black Town, Muthialpet, and Peddanaikpet—formed the core of what would become the Madras that is now Chennai. Thomas Salmon came to Madras in 1739. He describes Old Black Town as being inhabited by 'Portuguese, Indians, Armenians, and a great variety of other people.' The precinct was a square, 'better than a mile and a half in circumference, being surrounded with a brick wall seventeen feet thick, with bastions at proper distances; it also has a river on the west and a sea on the east; and to the northward a canal is cut from the river to the sea, which serves for a moat on that side.' The river was no doubt the Elambore, which flowed where NSC Bose Road is at present. Salmon had great praise for the town: 'The streets are wide, and trees planted in some of them; and having the sea on one side and the river on the other, there are few towns so pleasantly situated.'[6]

In sharp contrast, however, are several other accounts that speak of the crowded and insanitary conditions of the place and, even today, you would agree with the latter. The streets are narrow and prone to tremendous

---

[3]One of the episodes that best reflect this was the kidnapping of Father Ephraim de Nevers, the Capuchin priest at the Fort, by his detractors at San Thome. The English retaliated by kidnapping the chief padre governor of San Thome. For further details see V. Sriram, *A Guide to Fort St George*, p. 110.

[4]Ibid.

[5]For further details on the activities of the Fishing Fleet, see Henry Dodwell, *The Nabobs of Madras*, London: Williams and Norgate Limited, 1926, p. 190.

[6]Love, *Vestiges of Old Madras*, Vol. 1, p. 71.

congestion with houses, residents, shops, retailers, wholesalers, and itinerant vendors competing for space. The area has, however, changed its name—in 1906, it became George Town in honour of King George V, who had, as Prince of Wales, visited Madras a year earlier. In commemoration of that visit and the name change, a statue of King George V was erected at the entrance to George Town. It still remains there, a forlorn relic of the British Raj. The statue's pedestal, complete with the epitaph 'Honi Soit Qui Mal Y Pense' (May he be shamed who thinks badly) is a convenient urinal by day and a site for some serious drinking by evening. The king gazes disapprovingly, no doubt reflecting on past glory. Every once in a while, he suffers more insults—his hand holding the sceptre is a convenient place to fix party flags, and political bunting are usually stretched from his crown to the opposite end of the street. George Town, today, is an area that the government has forgotten, but it teems with history.

In 1676, the EIC formally rented from the sultan of Golconda the village of Triplicane, though it appears to have been in possession of the place from at least 1658.[7] The settlements of Egmore, Purasawalkam, and Tondiarpet were leased from the Mughal emperor Aurangzeb in 1693.[8] Fifteen years later, in 1708, Nawab Daud Khan Panni gave the EIC the villages of Tiruvottiyur, Nungambakkam, Vyasarpadi, Ennore, and Sathangadu.[9] All of these became the property of the EIC by 1720.[10]

The EIC was principally a trading entity during this time. Cloth was the principal commodity being exported from here and, over time, it became important to settle weavers close to the fort. In 1718, the village of Colletspettah was built, named after Governor Joseph Collet and now referred to as Kaladipettai.[11] The first planned colony of the city was created shortly thereafter. This was for the settling of weavers in an exclusive area demarcated for them—Chinna Tari Petta or Chintadripet. Nestling in the arms of the Cooum, it was selected because of the presence of several trees, carefully tended by Dubash Sunkurama, who is commemorated in a street name here after land was forcibly taken away from him.[12] Chintadripet is laid out in a fishbone pattern—a straight spine that cuts across the peninsula, the

---

[7]Love, *Vestiges of Old Madras*, Vol. 1, pp. 349–352.

[8]Ibid., p. 578.

[9]Love, *Vestiges of Old Madras*, Vol. 2, p. 21.

[10]Ibid., pp. 192–196.

[11]Ibid., p. 169.

[12]Ibid., p. 258.

river Cooum going around on three sides, with streets branching away from it. All the streets slope down to the river, thereby ensuring natural drainage or, at least, they did at one time. Unlike Black Town and the other villages in the area, segregation based on caste was strictly forbidden in Chintadripet, a first step towards cosmopolitan life.[13]

In 1742 the EIC acquired Vepery, Perambur, Pudupakkam, and Sadayankuppam.[14] The twin settlements of Mylapore and San Thome were added in 1749. The countryside was still unsettled and very few of the English ventured to live outside Fort St George. But Madras was a British stronghold and so the nawab of Arcot, who, with the decline of the Mughal Empire, had emerged as the local ruler with the help of the British, decided to move in. It was all technically his territory but the nawab still thought it fit to request the English for space within Fort St George to build a suitable residence. This was given in the 1760s, but the nawab's advisers were against his moving into a British enclave. And so, while an alternative location was being identified, he, with his entourage, lived in a vast camp just outside Mylapore. A street leading to it became Deorhi (the doorway of) Sardar-ul-mulk Dilawar Jung Bahadur (all of which were the nawab's titles), now shortened to Devadi Street.[15] The English were kind enough to grant him hundred acres of his own land by the seaside, in a place called Chepauk. And there, in 1768, the nawab planned a magnificent palace for himself, to be built by the notoriously corrupt Paul Benfield, a British contractor. India's first British-built Indo–Saracenic structure is what emerged from this, though the nawab and his descendants did not have long to live in it. The British managed to diddle them out of the palace and the kingdom by 1855, for which act of chicanery, the nawabs were as much to blame.[16] Post the First War of Indian Independence in 1857, there was a rethink on the part of the British. Had they after all not been unfair to the nawab? There was, of course, no question of returning what had been taken. To make amends, Queen Victoria bestowed the title of Prince of Arcot on the head of the family in 1867. A former police court, renovated to resemble the Queen-Empress's Osborne House on the Isle of Wight, was renamed Amir Mahal and given to the prince and his family to live in, in perpetuity. A pension

[13]Ibid., p. 259.

[14]Ibid., p. 285.

[15]V. Sriram, 'Doorway to Mohammedan Mylapore', *The Hindu*, 26 2013.

[16]Shanti Jayewardene Pillai, *Imperial Conversations, Indo-Britons and the Architecture of South India*, New Delhi: Yoda Press, 2007.

was also settled on the family. This, the title, and the rank of a cabinet minister were recognized by the Constitution of India after Independence as well.[17] The nawabi presence in Chepauk, just abutting Triplicane, meant a strong Islamic influence in that area and its surroundings, adding to the already mixed heritage of Madras.

Even as Chepauk Palace was nearing completion in the 1760s, the English had begun losing interest in the city. Calcutta, with the promise of rich pickings, beckoned, and by the 1770s, it, along with the western metropolis of Bombay, was to be the favoured destination. Madras chugged along, with its share of developments, but these no longer excited colonial interest. The city was capital to a vast presidency that stretched all the way from Orissa down to Kanyakumari, with parts of present-day Kerala, Karnataka, Telangana, and Andhra thrown in, but in terms of revenue, which was all that the British were interested in, it lagged. Rudyard Kipling dismissed the city as a 'withered beldame dreaming of ancient fame'.[18]

Development activities, therefore, suffered, much to the chagrin of mercantile interests in the city. Madras, which gave its name to the entire presidency that it lorded over, was referred to as the benighted province, and as a business leader from the city was to famously remark in the nineteenth century: it was the Cinderella among all the Presidencies of the British Empire.[19]

The circumstances during the late eighteenth century did not exactly help the city. With most of the colonial minds focusing on Calcutta and Bombay, there was not much assistance forthcoming for Madras. Added to this was the relative insecurity in the city. It was only from the 1760s onwards that the French in Pondicherry ceased to be a threat. As soon as they were neutralized, the father and son duo of Hyder Ali and Tipu Sultan from Mysore took over and threatened Madras and its immediate neighbourhood at least twice. The British did what they could to protect themselves, and some vestiges of those days still remain. The eastern face of Fort St George had the sea to protect it anyway. To strengthen the defences on the north, south, and west, all housing in the immediate vicinity was cleared, and a vast esplanade, an empty stretch, was created. Boundary pillars were erected to prevent the

---

[17]Ibid.

[18]Rudyard Kipling, *The Song of the Cities*, available here: https://archive.org/stream/rudyardkiplingsvkipl/rudyardkiplingsvkipl_djvu.txt/.

[19]Comment made by Sir George Gough Arbuthnot, in 1898.

town from spilling over onto this green. One of these pillars still stands.[20] When peace came in the 1800s (after the death of Tipu Sultan), the green was put to good use, making way for the High Court of Madras and the Law College (now called Dr B. R. Ambedkar Government Law College).

It was only with the death of Tipu Sultan in 1799, in a battle that was engineered and foisted on him from our city, that the English became bold enough to move out of the narrow confines of the fort with business houses shifting out and settling north of it. The first to move was Parry & Company, today a constituent of the Murugappa Group, an industrial conglomerate of South India. The space it shifted to was no man's land, with the sea actually lapping its walls. This became Parry's Corner, a name that has remained in vogue for over two centuries, with Parry continuing to function from where it was, albeit in a magnificent art-deco structure dating to the 1930s.

Mount Road, whose present contours had come into shape by 1799, was till then essentially the Great Choultry Plain, taking its name from a small charitable rest house or choultry that stood near the present-day Thousand Lights Mosque. But the habitable part of this great artery was only till where the Gemini flyover now begins. After that, it was all one sheet of water—the Long Tank of Mylapore with fields and cultivation around it. The village of Mambalam was on the other side of this tank and, if you went further, you came to Saidapet, which was a separate district by itself, outside the city boundary. Between the city and Saidapet lay the Adyar and on its other bank lay the vast wooded estate that was the governor's weekend retreat. Guindy Lodge, as it was known, became the Raj Bhavan post-Independence, with the city residence of the governor, known as Government House and set in the midst of Government Estate at the beginning of Mount Road, being put to several uses before its eventual demolition to make way for the new assembly-cum-secretariat that was later transformed into a multi-speciality referral hospital run by the government.

Residences began to be constructed in what, at that time, were far off areas—Kilpauk, Chetpet, Nungambakkam, Egmore, and places close to the Adyar. Each home was set in a vast compound with plenty of trees. Some of these bungalows gave their names to entire housing colonies that came up in later years in the same spaces—Andersons Gardens, Moores Road, Wallace Garden, Wheatcrofts Road, and Mackays Gardens are but a few instances. Most of the houses were named after villages in England or Scotland, by

[20]For further details on the growth of old Madras, see V. Sriram, 'How Tiny Was My City', *Frontline*, 5 September 2014.

some homesick resident or the other. With so many people leaving the fort, attendance at prayers on Sunday in the Church of St Mary's, the oldest Anglican church to be built east of the Suez Canal, began to dwindle. A new cathedral was required for the city and so St George's, designed like St Martin-in-the-Field in London, came up in 1815, just off Mount Road, giving rise to a new thoroughfare named Cathedral Road. Two years later, the same architect—Thomas Fiott de Havilland—built a kirk for the Scots, based on the same design once again. This was St Andrews and it is still a landmark in Egmore.

Between the 1630s and the 1800s, the dubashes evolved from being mere interpreters to consummate businessmen, who battened on the waxing power of the British. Many were notoriously corrupt and at the same time put their wealth to good use, building temples and extending patronage to courtesans, poets, scholars, and musicians, thereby planting the seeds for Madras to become a cultural capital. The early dubashes gave their names to many streets in the older parts of the city such as George Town and Mylapore. With the English moving to newer areas, the dubashes followed suit, as did many prosperous Indian businessmen, all of whom had, till then, lived close to the fort. Nungambakkam, Egmore, and Kilpauk became their residential areas of choice, where they built palatial houses aping their colonial masters. Inside, however, life went on in the most orthodox fashion. Many, in fact, retained their erstwhile residences in town, for conducting all their religious rites. Several of these men also constructed community halls for the benefit of less well-to-do families of their sects. These were meant for weddings, funerals, and other observances. Most of these structures have now vanished, though some remain, their beautiful woodwork and masonry standing testimony to what we were capable of creating till a century or so ago. The dubashes also endowed the city with plenty of temples in the seventeenth and eighteenth centuries. Perhaps the oldest of these is the Chenna Kesava Perumal Temple dating to just after the founding of Black Town and, according to some sources, the reason for the city being named Chennai. This was endowed by Beri Thimmappa, the first of the dubashes. By the 1750s, when a large swathe of Black Town had to be cleared for security purposes, the temple was shifted. The EIC gave some money for the purchase of a new site, the rest coming from an early instance of crowdfunding, one of the largest donors being the most powerful dubash of that era—Manali Muthukrishna Mudali. In the process, the temple acquired a twin, the Chenna Malleeswara Swami Temple, dedicated to Shiva and the two shrines co-exist side by side with a door connecting them, on Devaraja Mudali Street in George Town. The concept of building twin temples, to Vishnu and Shiva, thereby placating the devotees of the two principal deities in Hinduism, however, appears to have taken birth at Chintadripet, where Vennala Adi Narayana Nayak built the first of these in 1735—the Adipuriswara and Adi Kesava temples. There are, besides these, plenty of other shrines built by the dubashes, in areas such as George Town, Triplicane, Komaliswaranpet, and Nungambakkam. Dubashi munificence would spill over to more historic temples of the city, for instance, in places such as Mylapore, Triplicane, Thiruvottiyur, and Kovur. It would benefit temples in the hinterland as well, with one of the most generous donors being Pachaiyappa Mudaliar, whose wealth would also fund many educational institutions.

By the early nineteenth century, Madras city was 'a conurbation' comprising several diversely populated district towns and a 'loose agglomeration of villages'. Ever since its inception, the city had an uneven spread of population. Some areas had a density of less than fifteen people to an acre while others were horribly overcrowded. In 1871, the first Census of Madras city was conducted and recorded a population of just 397,852. But the construction of the harbour, on which work began in 1875, followed by industrialization, the expanding railway network, and the establishment of the high court, led to population growth. The 1931 Census showed the population to be 647,232, not even double that of 1875. And yet, it was at this time that the city added a new area—the suburb of Theyagaraya Nagar, known locally as T. Nagar. At this time, it was one of the most significant developments in the area.

Difficult though it may be to believe now, a large section of what is now T. Nagar was once a lake—the Long Tank of Mylapore, which spanned around 70 acres. The Boat Club, now lending its name to an upmarket area by the Adyar, once functioned on this tank and the annual regattas were big events in the social calendar of Madras. Sadly, by the early 1900s, land was considered more important and the tank was acquired for development as a township. By 1924, more land, from Mambalam, Puliyur, and Government Farm[21] villages and a portion of the Mylapore division, comprising a total of 540 acres, was acquired. Modelled very much on the lines on which New Delhi had been developed, it followed the Beaux Arts pattern, with a large park as its focus from which radiated four arterial

---

[21]This quaint name comes from a vast tract of 350 acres where in 1865 the government began a model farm. A Farm School, later College, was begun here in 1868 and was India's first. This moved to Coimbatore in 1906 and later became the Tamil Nadu Agricultural University. For further details see Muthiah, *Madras Rediscovered*, p. 121.

roads, all connecting to Mount Road. The land between these roads was made over for development, 410 acres earmarked for private use and the rest being given to open spaces that would be developed as parks, and for the construction of public buildings—police stations, electric sub-stations, markets, bazaars, fruit stalls, hospitals, dispensaries, pumping stations, model schools, places of worship, industrial buildings, and government offices. Housing plots were divided into one, half, quarter, one eighth, one twelfth, and one eighteenth of an acre. The total cost of acquisition of land was ₹4.90 lakh!

Though the plan was ready by 1924, work on the area only began ten years later. By then, the Justice Party had long been in power and several of its stalwarts were to be commemorated in street names in the area. The focal park was named after the raja of Panagal, the second prime minister of Madras. His statue adorns the park even now. The entire development, known initially as the Mambalam Town Planning Scheme, Eastern Section, was named Theagaraya Nagar, after Sir Pitti Theagaraya Chetty—the first Indian to become president (equivalent to the present-day mayor) of the city's civic body. And there were tributes to corporation workers as well. Nathamuni and Govindu were humble drain-diggers who were killed when the land caved in on them. Streets commemorate them too. T. Nagar subsumed within itself the eastern part of Mambalam village. What remained was cut off by a railway line and became West Mambalam, thereby giving rise to one of Chennai's eternal quiz questions—where is East Mambalam?

The population boom came during World War II, though it must also be acknowledged that right in the middle of it there was a brief period when the numbers shrank to an all-time low. Both boom and (near) bust were direct consequences of the war. During World War I, Madras was the only city in British India to be bombed—the German cruiser *Emden*, in September 1914, lobbed a few shells and sailed away. Dr K. N. Kesari, noted Ayurvedic practitioner, wrote his memories of that day:

> It happened on 22 September 1914 during World War I. The German cruiser, *Emden*, dropped bombs on Madras. I was on the verandah of my house after dinner at 9 p.m. Suddenly, I noticed a huge flame and sound from the sea. People rushed to see what was happening. I too followed them but when I saw that the Burmah Shell oil storage tanks were falling down, I beat a retreat. After the *Emden* left, Indian Armed Forces fired bombs into the sea. That night lakhs of people were in utter distress and confusion. Those who could not leave their homes

remained there itself. My wife was sick at that time and hearing the loud sound of the bomb she fainted.[22]

The flames from the burning oil tanks that stood off the harbour could be seen for miles around and a young R. K. Narayan, who would go on to become a beloved writer, would see it from his family home: 1, Vellala Street, Purasawalkam.[23] The next morning, people, Dr Kesari included, scoured the beach for spent shells to have as keepsakes. The compound wall of the high court, which took a direct hit, has a plaque to commemorate the attack. Back in Germany, the kaiser was jubilant that a city of the British Empire was hit. He gave orders that the crew could add the name *Emden* to their surnames thereafter. The ship, considered unsinkable, met with a most unforeseen end—long after it had thwarted several veterans, the Australian vessel HMAS *Sydney* sank it on 9 November 1914.[24] It was the latter warship's maiden voyage! The *Emden* created a month or so of terror in the city and left behind its name as a new word in the Tamil vocabulary, becoming synonymous with a bully.

In World War II, Madras, by some quirk of fate, became the only harbour on the eastern side to escape bombing. But that did not prevent the government from losing its nerve in April 1942 and instructing everyone who did not have essential business in the city to evacuate. Shops and offices closed, the high court shifted to Coimbatore,[25] and the Port Trust moved to Ooty,[26] as far away as possible from the sea. People abandoned Madras and the city became a ghost town. The wilder animals in the zoo were shot dead.[27] From his safe confines in the summer capital of Ooty, the governor of Madras, Sir Arthur Hope, appealed for calm, but to no avail. And then, as suddenly as it had begun, the scare ended and people trickled back. Madras resumed life, with a sheepish look, but in the meanwhile much real estate had been sold at throwaway prices. Those who stayed back and invested made a killing.

---

[22]Vasantha N. Menon, *Life and Times of Dr K N Kesari (1875-1953)*, Manipal: Manipal Technologies Limited, 2013, p. 44.

[23]R. K. Narayan, *My Days*, Chennai: Indian Thought Publications, 1979, p. 36.

[24]K. R. A. Narasiah, 'The Emden refuses to vanish', *Madras Musings*, Vol. XVII, No. 13, 16–31 October 2007.

[25]V. C. Gopalratnam, *A Century Completed, A History of the Madras High Court, 1862-1962*, Madras: Madras Law Journal Office, 1962, p. 140.

[26]S. Muthiah and K. R. A. Narasiah, *Overcoming Challenge, The 125 Year Saga of a Harbour Men Made*, Chennai: The Chennai Port Trust, 2007, p. 108.

[27]A. Srivathsan, 'October, 69 years ago, when Madras was bombed', *The Hindu*, 2 October 2012.

Several accounts of the city emptying have survived. The lawyer and diarist N. D. Varadachariar stayed on and recorded each day as it happened. It is unmatched for the sheer drama of what came to be known as the evacuation of Madras.[28]

> 7 April 1942—An air raid alert was sounded, lasting for an hour—the first of its kind. Wildest rumours going around—fortunately untrue. Large numbers of people are leaving the city.
>
> 8 April 1942—Exodus of all classes from the city. The Central Station railway enquiry office man said that 15,000 passed through the station yesterday and there is no abatement of rush today. The government offices cannot also function properly as most clerks, depending on hotel food, have not been able to get their meals.
>
> 9 April 1942—Lots of people still clearing out of the city. I brought down my things from the town office, which I closed today.
>
> 12 April 1942—Government offices and High Court have closed down to open at various mofussil places. In the evening drove to Central Station with friends. No evidence of life in the town except in the station where hundreds are leaving. The greatest rush I have ever seen. This is how danger does come when it comes, suddenly and as a bolt from the blue.
>
> 17 April 1942—Today's estimate of the city's population is 1.5 lakhs against the normal 8.5 lakhs

The pioneering aviator Captain V. Sundaram has left behind another account:

> By April 1942, World War II had escalated. The Japanese were taking over one country after another. They marched into Burma, which fell without any resistance. Their next target was India. Speculation was rife that they would land on the Madras coast. The British defences were weak, and they had their scorched earth policy ready to go into action. Railway stations, the harbour, Fort St George and important rail and road bridges were wired with dynamite. All essential services, including the flying club, were moved to Bangalore.
>
> The city looked ghostly. Houses, roads, and shops were all deserted.

---

[28] N. V. Sampath, Rangaswami Malathi, and N. V. Kasturi, *The Kasi Diaries, Excerpts from the diaries of N. D. Varadachariar*, Madras: East West Books, 2004, pp. 274–276.

The roads were unswept. At night the entire city was blacked out. Petrol bunks were closed. Hotels had their shutters down. People were selling off their homes and cars for a song. Looting and pilfering were the order of the day. On more than one occasion, Japanese planes flew overhead, and once one of the planes even dropped a few bombs near the overbridge at the Fort Station. Luckily there were no casualties.[29]

Sir Arthur Hope, the governor, was not of great help. Varadachariar records that 'the governor concedes there is absolutely no means of defending the city now. The police have been asked to disperse and make themselves scarce. The officers are to disappear to their homes in the villages in case invasion should occur and our forces are unable to hold. It is instructions like these, which appear to have frightened officials thoroughly—they fled for their dear lives.'[30]

Delhi was not amused with such pusillanimity. The viceroy, Lord Linlithgow sent Sir Reginald Maxwell, Member for Home, Viceroy's Executive Council, to administer a personal rebuke and stiffen the governor's spine. Sir Arthur Hope, an inveterate gambler and who, in Raj parlance, was prone to bending his elbow rather too often, did not survive long in Madras, thereafter. It was found that he frittered around 4,000 pounds intended for the Red Cross on horse racing. By 1944, his position became untenable and he had to resign, citing the face-saver of failing health.[31]

In the event, the war never came to Madras and neither did the horrors of Partition. Its relative safety allowed for the setting up of numerous defence establishments here and also the arrival of troops meant for the Eastern Front. With all of this requiring more people, a large-scale migration to the city began. Adding to the numbers from the hinterland were people from up north, refugees from lands that had become Pakistan. Sikh and Hindu Punjabis arrived by trains to be received here by their kinsmen who had already settled in the city working in the auto parts, sports goods, and pharmaceuticals businesses, among other things. The population doubled between 1941 and 1951, from 7.77 to 14.16 lakhs. The city expanded to handle this new load by adding 19 square miles to itself.[32]

In 1944, J. P. L. Shenoy, took over as commissioner of the Corporation of Madras and on him fell the task of ensuring proper development of these

---

[29]Captain V. Sundaram, *An Airman's Saga*, Bharatiya Vidya Bhavan, 1998, p. 57.

[30]Sampath et. al., *Varadachariar*, p. 276.

[31]S. Muthiah, 'A Scandal of Hope', *The Hindu*, 20 April 2019.

[32]Muthiah, *Madras Rediscovered*, p. 29.

spaces. Shenoy conceived the idea of a big housing colony in the Aminjikarai area. He, however, chose to leave the corporation in 1947 before the plans were finalized. It was left to Challagalla Narasimham, who succeeded him as commissioner, to see the scheme through and also ensure that it was named Shenoy Nagar, 'a rich and proper tribute to his services'.[33]

Narasimham was to oversee another development—that of Gandhi Nagar. The city which had always had the Adyar as its municipal boundary, extended beyond it for the first time in 1945. The minister for Local Administration, Daniel Thomas, felt that the area immediately south of the river would be ideal for a middle-class housing colony. The 150-acre space belonged to the Bishopric of Madras. The negotiations were conducted by Narasimham who settled on a price of ₹17 lakh for 136 acres. The foundation stone was laid by the premier of Madras, Omandur Ramasamy Reddiar, on 23 January 1948, and the proposed housing colony was named Gandhi Gram, later changed to Gandhi Nagar. A year later, with Gandhi Nagar becoming a popular destination, the city extended further. Kasturba Nagar came up on 130 acres purchased from Sir Benegal Rama Rau and his brothers, Sir Benegal Narasinga Rau and B. Shiva Rau.[34]

The 1960s saw some of the land between Mylapore and Adyar filling up, with the development of Abhiramapuram, Mandaveli, and Raja Annamalaipuram. One important development in the 1960s was the Boat Club area. Located along the Adyar, this area was taken up for residential housing, chiefly for the top bosses of the British-run companies. The neighbouring presence of the Madras Club, India's second oldest of its kind, founded in 1832, which was till then only for whites, must have been an added attraction. The textile company, Binny's, which had earlier developed Poes Gardens (of Rajinikanth and Jayalalithaa fame) in the 1950s, began the shift, constructing six bungalows in the Boat Club area.[35] Others soon followed—ICI, Parry, the Mercantile Bank (now HSBC), and many more. To prevent outsiders from coming in and spoiling what was a sylvan locality, the companies formed a real estate entity in which each of them were shareholders.[36] The Adyar Property Holdings Private Limited has seen its owners change over time. As the English-run companies either folded up or were acquired by Indian

[33]C. Narasimham, *Me and My Times*, Hyderabad: Radha Printers, 1986, pp. 114–115.

[34]Ibid., pp. 130–132.

[35]S. Muthiah, 'An End to Binny's Beginning', *The Hindu*, 23 October 2017.

[36]S. Muthiah, *Down by the Adyar, The Story of the Madras Boat Club*, Chennai: Madras Boat Club, 2010, p. 45.

business houses, the residents of the houses changed too. More bungalows came up and today there are blocks of flats as well. There were shudders and groans when a prominent political family moved in during the 1990s. But nothing could be done, for their wealth is also corporate today—they control one of India's largest media houses. But Boat Club Road is still an aspirational location for many. This is where much of Madras walks in the morning and evening, casting envious glances at the high compound walls, the swanky cars that go in and out of these, and the name plates that glisten at the gateposts. The names of the houses are a throwback to a colonial past—Waterside, Coleroon, Kent House, and Deerhurst are some of them.

In 1964, the area to the west of T. Nagar saw a new colony coming up. A pillar topped with the Ashokan emblem of four lions marked the commencement of work and the area came to be named Ashok Nagar. A contiguous space was earmarked for several flats constructed in the 1970s by the Tamil Nadu Housing Board and this became Kalaignar Karunanidhi Nagar or K. K. Nagar, after the then chief minister. Burmese repatriates came in the 1960s and were given shops near the harbour as a means of livelihood. Quickly becoming the hub for all smuggled goods before India liberalized its economy, Burma Bazaar was where you went if you wanted imported whiskey, cassettes, and music systems. The place has since lost its glamour but in the alleys nearby you can still get authentic Burmese food—atho, bejo, mohinga, and khow suey. These refugees were all settled in Vyasarpadi, Ennore, and the Red Hills areas—on lands once occupied by water bodies that had since run dry.

The next big development was Anna Nagar, named after former chief minister, C. N. Annadurai. Developed in the early 1970s by the Tamil Nadu Housing Board, it spans an area of 5 square kilometres and is located on the site of the erstwhile Naduvakkarai and Mullam villages. Its success had much to do with the neighbouring industrial areas of Padi and Ambattur. It was earlier mentioned that business establishments moved out of Fort St George and settled along what was known as North Beach Road/First Line Beach, now Rajaji Salai. By 1836, these British-owned entities had become powerful enough to form a representative body, the Madras Chamber of Commerce, now the Madras Chamber of Commerce and Industry (MCCI) and the second oldest such organization in the country, being just one week younger than the Bombay Chamber. The MCCI lobbied hard for several developments including the harbour, railway services, and communications. As a consequence, all these amenities, when they came, were located close to where the business houses were functioning. The oldest railway station, operational from 1856, was set up in Royapuram, just north of First Line Beach. The harbour opened on the same thoroughfare and the General Post Office too came upon the opposite side.[37]

When these companies ventured forth into setting up industries, most of their factories and plants came up on the northern side of the city. Thiruvottiyur, Pulianthope, and Perambur became the sites where industrial establishments came up, a trend that was followed by the post-Independence Indian entrepreneurs. The Government of Madras (renamed Tamil Nadu in 1969) was most welcoming of private initiative, especially during the years when K. Kamaraj was chief minister (1954–1963). Vast tracts of land, and, sadly, some water bodies, were converted into industrial estates. Padi, Ambattur, and Guindy became home to many small- and large-scale industries. Thus, when the World Trade Fair came to be organized in Madras in 1968, the village of Naduvakkarai, owing to its proximity to Ambattur, became the site of choice. A modernist tower, named after the pioneering engineer of Mysore State, Sir M. Visvesvaraya, was erected for the fair. When the expo concluded, the area was made over to what was named the West Madras Neighbourhood Plan. A year later, Chief Minister Annadurai was dead and the new colony was named Anna Nagar.[38]

Thiruvanmiyur, just south of the Adyar area, remained outside city limits till well into the 1980s. The eponymous bus terminus was the back of beyond as far as city-dwellers were concerned, which may appear most surprising to present-day residents who live in daily dread of traffic snarls at that intersection. The historic temple to Shiva as Marundeeswarar (master of all medicines) saw hardly any visitors. Houses, when they came to be constructed here were few and far between, like in several suburban areas. This gave rise to many jokes in Tamil magazines, and the play 'Crazy Thieves in Palavakkam', written and acted in by the city's humourist 'Crazy' Mohan, became a runaway success. It dealt with a house in Palavakkam whose occupants are forced by a gang to keep a rich man's child as hostage. The child is eventually restored to its parents only to have another gang kidnap it and bring it back to the same house! The upmarket residential neighbourhood of Valmiki Nagar takes its name from a temple to Valmiki, author of the Ramayana, which stands just outside the Marundeeswarar shrine. Valmiki Nagar and takes its name from

---

[37]V. Sriram, *Championing Enterprise, 175 Years of the Madras Chamber of Commerce and Industry*, Chennai: The Madras Chamber of Commerce and Industry, 2011.

[38]Tripurasundari Sevvel, 'From Naduvakkarai to Anna Nagar', *Madras Musings*, Vol. XXVI, No. 8, 1–15 August 2016.

Justice P. V. Balakrishna Iyer, retired judge of the Madras High Court, who owned much of the land in the area.

The land to the south of the Adyar is today's IT hub, with its famed OMR (Old Mahabalipuram Road) now renamed Rajiv Gandhi Expressway. This was, as the name suggests, how people went to Mamallapuram, the historic Pallava port with its magnificent rock carvings, just 56 kilometres away from the centre of the city. In the old days, those wishing to make the journey had two options—a leisurely overnight boat journey on the Buckingham Canal that runs along the OMR or by the road itself. In the 1920s, as evident from H. A. Newell's trip by car, documented in his *Topee and Turban*, it took five hours.[39] Today, the same journey is accomplished in 90 minutes though river rides are no longer possible, what with the canal having been allowed to degrade into a gutter.

The OMR's present status as an IT corridor owes much to the shifting of the Engineering College from Chepauk Palace to Guindy, in 1920. The Alagappa College of Technology (AC Tech) came up next to it in 1944 followed by the School of Planning and Architecture in 1957. Thus, when Madras was selected for establishing an Indian Institute of Technology (IIT) in 1959, the land given for it was just opposite these institutions and carved out of the wooded estate of the Raj Bhavan. Until the 1970s, there was just one bridge linking Adyar to the city and that was the old Elphinstone, named after a colonial governor, which still stands, alongside the later Thiru Vi Kalyanasundaranar Bridge, which takes its name from a Tamil scholar, reformer, and labour leader. Students of IIT initially stayed in the hostels of AC Tech and were ferried across by boats.[40] In the 1980s came the Kotturpuram Bridge, breathing new life into what was just a flood-prone tract of land, once belonging to the nawabs of Arcot and, later, to two well-to-do Chettiar families from the city.[41] The bridge enabled the development of Kotturpuram into an upmarket residential locality, but the locality still floods anyway.

Other institutions came up further south—the Central Polytechnic moved here in 1958, as it was felt that proximity to the Guindy Industrial Estate

---

[39]Lt Col H. A. Newell, *Topee and Turban or Here and There in India*, London: John Lane, 1921, p. 160.

[40]For further details on the development of Guindy as a technical, education hub, see Kumaran Sathasivam and Ajit Kumar Kolar, *Campaschimes, IITM Through IITian Eyes*, Chennai: The Indian Institute of Technology, 2011.

[41]S. Muthiah, *Looking Back from Moulmein: A Biography of A. M. M. Arunachalam*, Chennai: East West Books, 2000, pp. 34–36.

would benefit both.[42] Its various departments became independent institutions specializing in printing, cinematography, chemicals, leather, and textiles. Not far from here is the Central Leather Research Institute. By the 1970s, several other institutions had set up base here, making this a knowledge corridor of sorts, and when the IT Revolution came, it gravitated here. Today, the IT corridor extends all the way to Sholinganallur. Interspersed among the various IT offices are some age-old temples too, showcasing Chennai's mixed heritage.

The addition of Anna Nagar, K. K. Nagar, Velacheri, and Thiruvanmiyur in the 1980s doubled the area of the city from 1871 but the population had grown nine times! The space available has been more than challenged since, the IT boom only adding to the city's numbers and infrastructure woes.[43] The area has not kept pace with the demand leading to land prices and rentals skyrocketing in upmarket residential and commercial areas and school districts. The city does have a master plan, chiefly on paper. Issued after great deliberation by the Chennai Metropolitan Development Corporation (CMDA) with a level of confidentiality normally maintained for nuclear codes, these are immediately trashed by independent architects, town planners, and former personnel of the CMDA who become activists after retirement. The first master plan was released in 1975 and not much attention was paid to it. One good outcome was the creation of the Chennai Mofussil Bus Terminus at Koyambedu. The frighteningly congested wholesale vegetable market which had been at Kotwal Chavadi in George Town for 300 years also shifted to Koyambedu as part of this plan. Thereafter, the city grew in leaps and bounds, leaving the master plan in tatters. A second one was released in 2008 and was expected to hold good till 2026. The plan was considered outdated even when it was prepared. A third one is expected sometime soon. One common feature among all the plans is that they are beyond the comprehension of the common man or woman, whose lives are nevertheless impacted by such documents. Public consultations on such plans prior to or immediately after release are essentially farcical exercises. Another issue with such plans is that there is very little area-wise detailing or study. One-solution-fits-all localities is the attitude with which these plans are created. Thus, a historic and congested district such as George Town will have the same guidelines as an aristocratic and expansive neighbourhood like Boat Club Road. The plans are also very South Chennai-focused, which is where

[42] V. Sriram, *Nurturing Music and Fine Arts: A Historical Perspective*, Chennai: The Tamil Nadu Dr J. Jayalalithaa Music and Fine Arts University, 2021, pp. 159–178.
[43] Muthiah, *Madras Rediscovered*, p. 29.

the interests of the real-estate lobby lie. The industrial north is neglected and is a planner's nightmare.

In the interim, expanding the limits of the city has been a sporadic exercise, done with not much planning in mind. In October 2011, the expansion process was once again initiated. In this move, forty-two small local bodies, including nine municipalities, eight town panchayats, and twenty-five village panchayats were merged with the Chennai Corporation, taking the area up by 140 per cent to 426 square kilometres from the earlier 176 square kilometres.

Outside of what falls within the Corporation limits is Chennai Metropolitan Area (CMA). In 2007, this extended from Minjur to Sholinganallur, an urban agglomeration of 1,177 square kilometres with a population of 7 million. Considered the feeder districts to the city, these were to gradually upgrade themselves to urban levels. Included here are places such as Tambaram, Chromepet, and beyond. These were all fairly old settlements, with Chromepet taking its name from Chrome Leather Works, a large factory that once stood here and whose stench was a byword for miles around. But all of these made no difference to the congestion of the city whose population had long gone out of control. In 2018, the state government announced an eight-fold expansion of the CMA, making it 8,878 square kilometres and bringing into its ambit Thiruvallur and Kanchipuram districts in full, apart from parts of Arakkonam taluk.[44] This makes CMA the second largest urban agglomeration in India, after the National Capital Region. That record is of dubious value since maintaining civic infrastructure over such a large area is going to be quite a challenge.

---

[44]Ibid.

3 | CHINGAPORE

Chennai is a functioning anarchy like all other Indian metros. And yet, the average Chennaiite will say: 'Well, we are at least not as bad as Bangalore.' Rivalry with the closest metropolis is long-standing but, for a city that according to its political leaders is forever en route to becoming another Singapore, being better off than Bangalore is setting a low bar.

A corporation administers Chennai and takes care of civic life in general. Like similar bodies elsewhere in the country, it is not the most efficient of organizations but it gets along. Referred to as CheMa (Chennai Managaratchi) in Tamil, its name, at least, does not allow for any unfortunate jokes at its expense, unlike Coimbatore's, which is known as CoMa and is said to be indicative of how it works.

In one way, however, the Corporation of Chennai is special—it is the country's oldest, founded in 1688. Its formation had some inspired thought behind it; Sir Josiah Child, the chairman of the EIC, decreed that the mayor and aldermen would constitute a committee of thirteen and that this should comprise three Englishmen, three Portuguese, seven Moors, and Gentoos (Muslims and Hindus, respectively).[1] This was somewhat watered down in reality but three Indians did make it.[2] The first mayor was Nathaniel Higginson, born in North America and the then governor was another American by birth—Elihu Yale. The two did not see eye to eye and Yale emasculated the corporation by denying funds to it.[3] This would set in motion a trend that has lasted till date—the city's corporation thrives only when the political party in majority in its council is also in power in the state legislature. When this is not so, the corporation suffers and so does the city.

The civic body's most visible symbol is its neo-classical headquarters, completed in 1913 and named after Lord Ripon, a viceroy for whom Indians had a lot of affection and who made the country take its first steps in local area administration.[4] Ripon Buildings, for some reason named in the plural, has always been painted pristine white, perhaps indicative of an aspiration to provide good, clean administration. In keeping with those rather high ideals,

[1] *Madras, the Official Handbook of the Corporation of Madras*, 1950, p. 93.

[2] Ibid., p. 95.

[3] Love, *Vestiges of Old Madras*, Vol. 1, p. 501.

[4] V. Sriram, *In Memory of Father Ripon*, *Madras Musings*, Vol. XXVII, No. 9, 16-31 August 2017.

the traditions and ceremonial occasions of the corporation too are throwbacks to an earlier era. The mayor has robes of office, more in keeping with the weather in England, though it must be said that when Sir Josiah Child first conceptualized them in 1688, he did make allowances for the Madras heat:

> The habit of the Aldermen in that hot country, we think ought to be thin scarlet silk gowns; their number twelve, besides the Mayor, that they may be allowed to have Kettysols (umbrellas) over them. The Burgesses to wear black silk gowns; their number to be limited to 60, 80 or 100 as you shall find most convenient. The Sergeants attending them, to bear silver maces gilt, not exceeding one yard in length...[5]

By 1933, the apparel had undergone some changes, but not all that much:

> At the time the Mayor attends the Council meetings, he shall wear the ordinary gown made of black silk or material with gold lace border, one inch broad, and white bands.
>
> The Mayor shall wear on special and ceremonial occasions a gown made of velvet or other suitable material of fuschia shade, with a gold lace border of two inches breadth.[6]

There was more to the Mayoral get up:

> The gold Mayoral Chain and Badge is to be worn on special and ceremonial occasions. The Chain consists alternatively of the Corporation Monogram and Shield raised in relief, and the top plaque of the pendant is beautifully enamelled with a picture of Ripon Buildings and surrounded by a wreath of thistles.
>
> The Mayor's mace is 4 feet and 6 inches in length, consisting of a highly chased spiral design surrounded by a Crown bearing on one side an embossed view of Ripon Buildings, and on the other the monogram of the Corporation, while on the top of the crown, there is the City Coat of Arms. A grand and massive canopied chair serves as the mayor's seat.
>
> The Mayor has always been preceded by the mace-bearer and ushered in by the Secretary when he enters the Council Chamber with all the members standing till he occupies the chair, after bowing to all sides of the House.[7]

---

[5]Rao Saheb C. S. Srinivasachari, 'A History of the Mayoralty of Madras', *Madras Tercentenary Commemoration Volume,* p. 183.

[6]*Madras, the Official Handbook of the Corporation of Madras*, p. 100.

[7]Srinivasachari, 'A History of the Mayoralty of Madras', pp. 192–193.

Such rituals, while they add to the ceremony of the office, do not sit well with the actual proceedings of the council. The Corporation of Chennai is one of the most politics-ridden institutions of the city and much of the fireworks traditionally witnessed in the legislative assembly of the state find their echo in the council chamber. A single report from *The Hindu* dating to 30 August 2005, when the AIADMK was in power in the Corporation, will suffice to illustrate this:

> CHENNAI: The opposition and ruling party members were locked in a wordy duel at the Corporation council meeting on Monday leading to the eviction of almost the entire opposition. AIADMK member (ward 39) T. Panneerselvam also walked out stating that people's problems were not being discussed.
>
> After the councillors observed silence as tribute to former Deputy Mayor Gopalasami, Opposition leader C. V. Malayan (DMK) unsuccessfully attempted to raise a point of order to discuss what he termed was an 'unnatural state of affairs'. He was frequently interrupted by ruling party leader V. Sukumar Babu, who suggested the discussion take place after question hour. The debate on allowing Mr Malayan to raise the point of order stalled the council proceedings for more than 20 minutes. When more than one DMK councillor stood to raise the issue, the Deputy Mayor asked the watch and ward staff to evict them, one by one. At one stage, when most of the opposition was on its feet, he ordered the eviction of the entire DMK barring a lone councillor. The AIADMK members accused the DMK of coming to the meetings with the sole intention of stalling it; the DMK members accused the Deputy Mayor of stifling the voice of the Opposition. When Congress floor leader R. Mano tried to speak regarding the eviction of the DMK, Deputy Mayor ordered his eviction too. Mr. Mano said that the Opposition councillors had a right to present public grievances at the meeting but were consistently denied the opportunity and were being thrown out. He attempted to stage a dharna in front of the Mayor's chair but was forcibly evicted. After they were evicted, the DMK and Congress members squatted outside the council hall and raised slogans against the ruling party. They also conducted a mock proceeding of what was happening inside. The few opposition councillors, who were not evicted, raised a slew of civic problems ranging from stray dog menace to declining garbage clearance in North Chennai and urged the officials to pay more

attention. CPM councillor Devi said people suffering from dog bites had to stay overnight at the Government Hospitals due to a shortage of medicines.[8]

And so it is that the problem of garbage and the menace of stray dogs receive short shrift in the face of political standoffs.

The interesting point is that the city is quite used to getting along without an elected Corporation Council. The biggest such break happened in 1973 when the muster rolls scandal broke. The cause célèbre came to light when advertisements for a film in the making began appearing in local magazines. This by itself was a routine matter unlikely to attract attention but what made the advertisements stand out was the photograph of the producer, E. Kannappan, who was a lowly clerk in the corporation. Subsequent developments are best described in the memoirs of Eric L. Stracey, then Director of Vigilance, Government of Tamil Nadu:

> Now producing a film takes a great deal of money, and curiosity was naturally aroused as to its source. Enquiries soon revealed that a huge, simple and successful stratagem had been going on for a long time to defraud the Electricity Department of the Corporation of Madras. Here, for several months past, a number of City Fathers and municipal employees had together been helping themselves from the public till with a lavishness which, as we discovered as the case unfolded, would only be described as vast. Their mode was simple. Muster rolls bearing the signatures or thumb impressions of hundreds of non-existent labourers had been used each month to draw large sums from the Corporation treasury, and the money shared among more than a hundred odd persons who formed this merry conspiracy.[9]

Even the deputy mayor had affixed his own thumb impression against the names of several bogus workers! The modus operandi had been so successful that it had spread to several other departments in the corporation—conservancy, health, and others.[10] Kannappan, the mastermind, very conveniently turned approver. A spate of arrests followed including of some councillors, ex-mayors, and officials. The DMK, which was the party in power, found its image

---

[8]'Bedlam in Council', *The Hindu*, 30 August 2005.

[9]Eric L. Stracey, *Odd Man In: My Years in the Indian Police*, New Delhi: Vikas Publications, 1981, p. 262.

[10]G. V. Rama Rao, 'Muster Rolls Case, Madras Corporation Officials Face Corruption Charges', *India Today*, 31 May 1978.

severely tarnished and, according to Stracey, the party high command did its best to stall action. But a scandal of this size could not just be brushed under the carpet. The trial began and went on in various courts of law till 1994, when the Supreme Court finally confirmed the convictions. It was said that the total value of monetary loss to the corporation was ₹126 lakh[11] and the trial, which went on for over twenty-two years, had cost a further ₹45 lakh! Of the seventy-seven accused, several had died by the time the final judgement was delivered.[12]

One of the biggest fallouts of the scam was the suspension of the Corporation Council in 1973. The administration was placed in the hands of a special officer of the IAS cadre. With the AIADMK coming to power in 1977, nothing was done to revive the corporation. This was chiefly because M. G. Ramachandran, popularly known as M. G. R, the new chief minister, knew that the city was a DMK bastion and that if elections were to be held, the council could end up in the hands of that party. The corporation functioned under bureaucrats, funded by revenue collections and grants from the government till 1996, when with the DMK once again in power, civic polls were announced. An entire generation had grown up with no idea of how a municipal body ought to function.

In the 1996 elections, the DMK swept to power in the council. M. K. Stalin, the son of M. Karunanidhi, the DMK supremo and chief minister, was voted in as mayor. This was the first time that this office had been subject to election by adult franchise. Thereafter, the council has run on political lines, with the city's electorate being careful to vote the same party to power in civic and legislature elections. Corruption has, however, not declined, as is evident from a famous emergency meeting of AIADMK party councillors called in 2012 by the then chief minister, J. Jayalalithaa. She warned them to mend their ways and even threatened to dissolve the council and run the corporation with special officers once again.[13] Rather ironically, that was to come true. In 2016, the term of the AIADMK-dominated Corporation Council ended and elections were due. But with Jayalalithaa's death, her party did not have the will to hold elections. There was a great fear that the corporation would once again fall into the hands of the DMK. The city was back to being administered by special officers.

There are many who don't have a problem with that. They argue, 'Is it

---

[11]Ibid.

[12]Supreme Court of India, *T. Thulasingam vs State of Tamil Nadu*, 13 May 1994.

[13]'Jayalalithaa warns corrupt councillors', *The Hindu*, 19 June 2012.

not better to be governed by a few officers than a set of corrupt councillors?' What is overlooked is that considerable funding from the Finance Commission of the Government of India for local development projects have been withheld because the city has not had a local body poll. As a consequence, the city's administration and civic upkeep suffers. The councillors, when in office, have not been helpful. Chennai's corporation has, in the last two decades, been more a vehicle for implementing the schemes of the party in power. If at all any civic amenity work, such as widening of sidewalks or doing away with large outdoor advertising, has come about, it is because of public interest litigation (PIL) and not due to any enlightened leadership. Our mayors have generally been happier approving schemes that never take off or spending time renaming roads. You need to just look at the plan to segregate garbage at source to get the idea. It has been hanging fire since 1996!

The city has also expanded sporadically as mentioned in the last chapter and the corporation, never fully in control of even the oldest parts of Chennai, has struggled to keep up with the additions. It has also not helped that the powers of the corporation too have steadily reduced. The planning aspect of the city is with the CMDA.[14] The water supply and drains are the responsibility of the Chennai Metropolitan Water Supply and Sewerage Board (CMWSSB). Many of the arterial roads are defined as highways and come under the purview of the Highways Department, with repair work being undertaken by the Public Works Department. The slums are the responsibility of the Tamil Nadu Slum Clearance Board. With no real power to administer and with many of its arms becoming independent entities, the corporation is toothless.

And yet, it is the most visible among the agencies responsible for the city and often gets abused for matters outside its purview. Thus, while it does lay many of the roads, it cannot quite control their being dug up. Hardly would a road be tarred afresh when along will come the CMWSSB and embark on a long and leisurely dig. Once that agency finishes, having left behind a pitted and scarred surface, it is the turn of the Department of Telephones or the Tamil Nadu Generation and Electricity Distribution Company (TANGEDCO) that is responsible for electric supply. If none of these are active, political parties, whose representatives invariably sit on the Corporation Council, dig up roads to erect flex banners and hoardings extolling their leaders. The high court has screamed itself hoarse over these banners and hoardings but to no avail.[15] They keep coming up on all roads

---

[14]About CMDA, available here: http://www.cmdachennai.gov.in/aboutcmda.html/.

[15]Mohammed S. Imranullah, 'Death by Flex Boards', *The Hindu*, 14 September 2019.

and street corners with the tacit approval of the officers at ground level. Finally, in 2018, the Madras High Court imposed a blanket ban on political banners. But when Prime Minister Narendra Modi arrived here for his summit with the Chinese President Xi Jinping, the Tamil Nadu government approached the court, requesting permission to erect banners as this was the 'traditional way of greeting dignitaries'.[16] This was granted and since then, efforts are on in the corporation to get the ban on hoardings lifted for all non-political events.

If at all there was someone who made everyone—from political parties to ward councillors to local area officers and also the highest in the land—nervous when it came to the city's administration, it was a diminutive old man by the name K. R. Ramaswamy, popularly referred to by the media as 'Traffic' Ramaswamy. Having lived well into his 80s, this former mill worker shot to fame in the 1990s when he volunteered to direct traffic at Parry's Corner, one of the city's traffic hotspots. The police was pleased and gave him an identity card. They were not so pleased when he began questioning them about their tacit encouragement of hawkers in the area, which only added to the congestion. They liked him even less when he asked why they allowed political banners that blocked traffic lights to be erected.[17] The corporation hated him because he began questioning the handing over of public spaces for political flagposts and kiosks and turning a blind eye when walls of private and public properties were covered with posters. Ramaswamy became a thorn in the administration's flesh as he went about fearlessly tearing down banners and posters minutes before the chief minister's convoy passed that way, thereby throwing black cat commandos, supplicants, ministers, officials, and the general public into a tizzy.[18] He was not deterred by murderous attacks on him, one of which left his vision permanently impaired. Even when his family disowned him he never relented. Ramaswamy became a familiar figure in the Madras High Court where he was a frequent public interest litigant.[19] There are times when it appears that the administration moved only because of Ramaswamy.

Not everyone agrees with all that he did or the causes he espoused.

---

[16]Mohammed S. Imranullah, 'Follow rules while putting up banners for Modi-Xi summit, HC tells Govt.', *The Hindu*, 4 October 2019.

[17]Dennis S. Jesudasan, 'Onus is on police, not politicians to crack down on illegal hoardings: Traffic Ramaswamy', *The Hindu*, 16 September 2019.

[18]Arun Janardhanan, 'There is no stopping Traffic', *New Indian Express*, 29 March 2015.

[19]Ibid.

Ramaswamy's solution to the problem of hawkers, for instance, was to get them out of the way. This had been questioned by those with more pro-poor leanings. For years the administration has turned a blind eye to hawkers who have come to proliferate. With repeated pressure from the likes of Ramaswamy, the high court, and some of the city's more influential people, the corporation rather half-heartedly attended to the problem. In areas such as T. Nagar, buildings dedicated to hawkers have been constructed, but these are so badly ventilated that nobody, hawkers and shoppers included, really wants to go there.[20] As a consequence, many of the hawkers have come back to the footpath, after renting out their allotted shops to others![21] This is where the administration is really weak, for it is unable to enforce adherence to the law. It has also been unable to restrict the entry of new hawkers who occupy the footpath spaces vacated by those who have opted to move into the buildings.

Problems of a similar kind pertain to slums. As in most Indian cities, the most affluent areas of Chennai have a slum abutting them and it is from where the former draw their steady supply of domestic help. The banks of Chennai's three famed and decrepit waterways—the Cooum, Adyar, and Buckingham Canal are the favoured areas of settlement, the proximity to water dictating their choice. Slums are not new to the city. As it rapidly urbanized, the agglomeration of villages that became Madras acquired vast stretches of shanty towns, the slums of today, and the cheris of yesteryears. That their condition was at all highlighted and made the responsibility of the corporation was due to the efforts of Sanitary Inspector Charles Edward Gover, who from 1869 'devoted the greatest portion of his attention, out of doors, to the improvement of these hovels.'[22]

Gover was a dynamic man and much of the work he did—widening of streets, the creation of the first sewage farms, and the first census of the city—have become the subjects of legend. But perhaps his most heart-warming work was in the slums. Gover was apparently the first to take up the study of these areas, and in 1869, he identified that although 'drainage and the provision of pure water are the great requirements of the city, neither can exert more than a portion of their true power while their influence is neutralised by (the) filthy and uncleanable collections of thatched huts,

---

[20]Evelyn Ratnakumar, 'Business dull for Pondy Bazar's relocated hawkers', *The Hindu*, 22 May 2014.

[21]'Encroachments on footpaths leave pedestrians in peril', *The Hindu*, 13 May 2019.

[22]For much of Gover's work, see Reports of the Administration of the Madras Municipality, 1869 to 1872.

hitherto deemed beyond the pale of all public effort or expenditure.' Gover enumerated the slums to be one hundred within city limits and noted that they had neither roads nor drains and no scavengers' cart could enter them. 'Language fails me to describe fully the abominations and conditions of these places,' he wrote.

The worst of these, according to him, were at Royapuram and Choolai and he noted that smallpox, cholera, and fevers of every kind were always present. At his first inspection of the Royapuram slum, he found 'one woman lying dead and eight other persons in various stages of small-pox. Pigs wandered everywhere and found their chief food in the adjacent latrine. Filth abounded.'

Gover took it upon himself to educate the slum-dwellers about a better quality of life. He convinced them to pull down the shanties in stages and rebuild them, with the commitment that the corporation would construct the mud walls up to 4 feet and also give a bonus of ₹2-8 for every house rebuilt according to the civic body's directives. At the end of the 'weary task to all concerned' the success gained 'was worth waiting and working for'. There arose a neat little settlement that could accommodate 1,000 people.

Gover then took on the task of reorganizing seventeen other slums. But sadly, he was dead within two years, dying of an infection he contracted in the very slums he was renovating, but not before publishing a translation of sections of the *Thirukkural*.[23] With his passing, the city lost a true friend. The death of Gover in 1872 appears to have put the development of slums on the backburner. A record in the early 1900s noted that 'about 80 percent live in rented buildings, mostly the poorest of the community, living in what are called "cheris", crowded places which hatch most of the diseases which spread over the whole population with great rapidity.'[24] Though the corporation, in 1918, launched a scheme of tenement construction to house the poorer classes, it did not meet with much success.[25]

The corporation pursued a definite policy of effective slum improvement from 1932. A survey revealed that Gover's hundred slums had ballooned to 158 by then, with an additional twenty-eight not making it to the official list. In all, 40,500 families were living in them. A Special Housing Committee of the corporation was appointed in 1933 and estimated that 200,000 or 30 per cent of the total population lived in slums. When the City Improvement

---

[23]Charles E. Gover, *Folksongs of South India*, Madras: Higginbothams, 1872.

[24]Shobha Menon, 'Municipal Services', in S. Muthiah (ed.), *Madras: Services, Education & The Economy*, Chennai: Palaniappa Bros., 2012, p. 112.

[25]Ibid.

Trust was constituted, the complete reconstruction of a few fairly large slums and quite a number of smaller ones was undertaken. The old huts and houses were demolished and the sites cleared for the erection of new houses, the municipality making itself responsible for the entire reconstruction. The largest of these schemes was at Cemetery Road, where 178 houses were erected; others were at Kasimode (147 houses), Conran Smith Nagar (106), and Bogipalayam (75). By the end of 1933, there were two other fairly large re-housing schemes under construction; at Bogipalayam and in the Harbour Division, blocks of two-storeyed tenements were being erected—110 tenements in each place.[26]

A pioneering effort was the complete relocation and rebuilding of Ayodhyakuppam, one of the historic fishing villages along the beach. In 1933, the fishermen were convinced by the corporation to form a co-operative to fund the exercise. Leading businessmen of the city, such as Ramnath Goenka and Jaisingh Lal (of Surajmal, the jewellers) sponsored the scheme and the entire village moved to the north of the Lady Willingdon Institute, on land leased to it by the corporation. Within a year, the new development was complete and in 1934 it was formally declared open by Governor Sir George Stanley with an unveiling of his portrait. Not so lucky was neighbouring Parthasarathykuppam recorded in 1938 as 'one of the most wretched and insanitary in the city'. It was proposed that the site should be cleared and 300 houses or tenements created to replace the existing huddle of miserable huts. But disputes over the land held up the project indefinitely.[27]

In 1950 came the next major exercise, Commissioner Narasimham leading the battle. And he documented what was done.

> When I was Commissioner, there were in all about 252 slums covering roughly a population of nearly 1.8 lakhs. I urged the council to take up improvement and not clearance of slums. I preferred to remove slum conditions in each slum and create appropriate sanitary conditions for healthy living. The officers concerned with the problem were, the Health Officer, the Engineer (General), the Water Works engineer, the Drainage Engineer (General), the Water Works Planning Officer. We as a team visited some slums, met the residents and saw the appalling conditions ourselves. We found to our satisfaction that the residents were quite willing and ready to give their cooperation to us in our effort to improve their living conditions. We selected 52 slums in all

[26]Ibid., p. 113.

[27]*Administrative Reports of the Madras Municipality, 1931 to 1938.*

for carrying out the improvements.

> The officers' meeting decided to have the huts removed and to provide accommodation to the up-rooted families in a plot of land nearest to the slum; otherwise they would not vacate. The officers identified vacant lands nearest to the 52 slums and considered most suitable for settling the excess slum dwellers. Some belonged to the corporation, but many were privately owned. By negotiation we purchased the private sites, we made roads, provided plinths for putting up huts, extended water supply and sewerage to those areas and provided in each hut a water tap, a flush-out latrine, a washing place and an electric light. The dwellers took possession of the plinths allotted to them, constructed huts there with the assistance given by the Corporation and occupied them willingly and happily. In all the 52 slums which were cleared of the congestion, underground sewers and water supply mains were laid and the streets were paved with cement and many reconstructed their huts with the monetary help given by the Corporation. Each hut was provided with all the amenities referred to above. One could wash all the paved streets in each slum with a few buckets of water. The slum dwellers were happy. After the improvements were carried out, these areas were completely free from small-pox, cholera, and malaria.[28]

A decade later, attention shifted to more cosmetic issues—in 1960, the corporation deemed the suffix 'cheri', which is how all slums were referred to, as derogatory and by a resolution dated 26 July, renamed them all as Nagars.[29] By the 1960s, the slum clearance schemes of the corporation were transferred to the Madras Housing Unit of the State Housing Board. In 1970, the government formulated a phased programme to eliminate slums over a period of time and the Tamil Nadu Slum Clearance Board (TNSCB) was constituted 'to clear slums within a specified period, to prevent further springing up of slums, to rehabilitate slum dwellers in multi-storeyed tenements'.[30] Thereafter, it became fashionable to declare that the city would become free of slums within a few years. The last such target was 2013.

The formation of the TNSCB saw a major policy shift and an unfortunate one at that. The emphasis became one of slum clearance and not rehabilitation. Efforts have been made ever since to drive out slum dwellers and get them

---

[28]Narasimham, *Me and My Times,* p. 158.

[29]Resolution passed by the Council of the Corporation on 26 July 1960. Puram also became an acceptable replacement with effect from 26 October 1964.

[30]Menon, 'Municipal Services', in S. Muthiah, *Madras*, p. 113.

to live elsewhere. None of them want to shift to these new locations, chiefly because they will be far removed from where their jobs are. Several crores have been spent under schemes such as the Jawaharlal Nehru National Urban Renewal Mission (JNNURM) and Rajeev Awas Yojana (RAY) to move the slum dwellers, but to no avail. It is ironic that the city administration has come to abandon the enlightened schemes of people such as Gover and Narasimham. In recent years, there has been some rethink but not enough. An instance of the blinkered view is the bringing in of fishing hamlets into the purview of slums. The occupants are, in reality, the original dwellers of Chennai, having been around when Day came along. Yet there have been attempts to get them to shift inland to places far removed from the sea![31]

The official number of slums in Chennai is 1,219. But unofficially, there are 444 more. What is being done for the residents of these slums? Very little, apart from persistent and misguided attempts to relocate them to the periphery of the city, thereby simply shifting the problem out of sight of the upper-class citizenry. All this and more are some of the highlights of a study done by an NGO, Transparent Chennai, in 2013. Excerpts from this study were published in *The Hindu* and the figures quoted here are from there. The TNSCB had under its purview only the officially recognized slums at the time of its formation (1970), which then were 1,202 in number. In 1985, a further seventeen were added to the list. And the tally stopped there. The unlisted ones do not have any form of governance, as the TNSCB claims it can only handle the approved ones. Some of the statistics quoted are truly frightening. As many as half a million people reside in the unofficial slums which occupy just 4.8 square kilometres of Greater Chennai—the congestion can only be imagined. Periodic eviction drives are the only strategy that the city's administration has towards these slums. The residents return after a while and the cycle continues. What is often forgotten is that it is this fringe population that provides most of the services in the city.[32]

An oft-repeated argument against slums and their inhabitants is that they occupy public space ('poromboke' in Tamil, also a term of abuse in Chennai colloquial language) that could be put to better (read pro-affluent) use. The land under slums, however, is a mere fraction compared to what has been encroached upon by the rich. The statistics there are truly staggering. In

---

[31]Srivathsan, 'Fishermen oppose move to relocate slum tenements', *The Hindu*, 12 January 2011.

[32]For further detail, see Nithya V. Raman and Priti Narayan, 'India's Invisible Population', *The Hindu*, 19 October 2013.

response to a PIL filed by 'Traffic' Ramaswamy, the Commissioner of the Corporation of Chennai admitted in court that around 90 per cent of the buildings in the congested and oldest quarter of George Town were illegal—in the sense that they violated building permits in one way or the other and therefore encroached upon someone else's right to land, light, water, and air. There are an estimated 100,000 illegal structures in Chennai today.[33]

The Consumer Action Group, an NGO that has espoused several public causes in the city, was the first to take this matter up seriously and bring it to the notice of the high court. This was in 1999, when the government declared a one-time amnesty to the violators whereby all defaults would be condoned after the payment of a fine. This, in itself, was questionable, as money can never set right the harm done to the environment, but what was ironic was that the government repeatedly sought to extend the deadline for the amnesty. And when the high court struck this down, the government sought to issue an ordinance whereby status quo would be maintained on all illegal structures.[34] If this was not an instance of government protecting law-breaking builders, what else can be? Despite several judgements by the Madras High Court and the Supreme Court, all in favour of sealing and demolishing the illegal structures, no action has been taken under one pretext or the other. One of the most laughable excuses given by the government has been that the interests of hawkers would be affected. This despite the fact that no judgement even mentioned hawkers, and the violators were all big names in business. Yet another argument was that those employed by the establishments operating from these illegal buildings would be thrown out of jobs. Whoever comes up with these excuses clearly knows the way our governments indulging in populist schemes work. There is also a fear that immediate action would further depress the recession-prone construction industry. Certainly, none in the administration would be willing to take any decisive action on demolition. As a consequence, illegal structures have proliferated in the city. The issue of illegal structures and encroachment on public land has also impacted water bodies, which is discussed in the next chapter.

One of the worst examples of violations of building permits is T. Nagar. In its time, it was the first properly planned district of the city in the modern

---

[33]'How can Courts get authorities to act?' *Madras Musings*, Vol. XXVI, No. 16, 1–16 December 2016.

[34]Jayaraj Sivan, 'Ordinance to prevent CMDA from demolishing 1.7L illegal buildings', *Times of India*, 29 July 2010.

sense. And yet, Theyagaraya Nagar or T. Nagar, the showpiece of Madras in the 1930s, is today a classic example of how faulty planning, poor implementation of building regulations, the real-estate-builder-government nexus and rampant exploitation of land with no concern for anything else can create an urban disaster. The area had become notorious for its ambient air having the highest particulate matter, far beyond what is permissible. The illegal structures were never inspected while construction was in progress. Technically, no electricity or water connections can be given unless the buildings are certified to be as per plan. Everyone of course happily ignored this. While the businesses flourished, the area went to seed. Residential streets became parking lots and rubbish tips, arterial roads were choked with traffic, and poor safety norms resulted in fires and stampedes causing loss of life. But with those in power turning a blind eye, business, and violation of norms continued merrily. After all, the place is a shoppers' paradise and draws thousands of people to it every day. Come the festival season, traffic in the area slows to a perpetual crawl.

Every once in a while, corporation officials and others visit these structures and enact an elaborate drama of sealing them. The owners then approach the courts and obtain a stay on the closure. Business continues as usual. When in 2017, a fire swept through seven floors of a popular retailer dealing in silk, a minister went on record to say that the building had been in gross violation of all permits ever since it was built in 2000. The original sanction had been for ground plus four floors; what came up was a seven-storey structure. This was constructed in full public view and yet the authorities remained oblivious to the violations. Thereafter, there ensued the usual process of going to court over the extra floors. Here again, despite orders for demolition of the additional and unapproved levels, the builder obtained a stay and merrily carried on business for a decade and more. That was until the fire came along.

There was a wave of self-righteousness in the immediate aftermath. Bureaucrats decried the way buildings had violated norms in T. Nagar and elsewhere. The Fire Department bemoaned the fact that such structures cut off all access in the event of any major disaster. It was a wonder that no lives were lost in the fire, they said. The storeowner said that he had violated norms and so would bring down the structure (there was not much of it left standing anyway). The public, many of them regular customers of this violator, wrote long posts on social media on how such businessmen thrive. A newspaper cynically reported that shoppers were back in full strength in the area a day after the fire. Clearly, nobody was worried about personal safety or, for that matter, environmental hazards.

Everyone had agreed that the retailer, if he did construct a new building, would put up a model structure in full compliance of all regulations. Little did they know what a builder-bureaucrat nexus could achieve. All of a sudden, a nine-floor structure, including a basement, came up in the same place. And, what is more, work began on the construction even before the builder filed for approvals, so sure was the retailer that everything would fall into place. The papers were submitted in May and the authorities, with an alacrity that they do not display when more humble citizens apply for permissions, immediately gave the go-ahead. That was in June. And immediately thereafter, the builder announced that he had completed 40 per cent of the work—within a month of obtaining approval! Anyone would think that Chennai was a foreign city if this efficiency is anything to go by.

The residents of T. Nagar were up in arms. First, how was it that a structure, permitted to have four floors in 2000 could have nine in 2018? In what way had the area become less congested or less at risk for those living nearby? Second, given the manner in which the fire raged and consumed many kilolitres of water for being extinguished, how was it that approval was given so readily? No damages or fines were inflicted on the retailer. The residents went to court but after a couple of stays being granted, the case was dismissed on technicalities. There is a lot that can be achieved by hiring the right legal counsel.[35]

Having turned a blind eye during the time T. Nagar transformed into a byword for chaos, efforts are now on to decongest the place. Unfortunately, nothing has worked. One of these measures was an aerial walkway between several of the high-rises (most of them in violation) and another has been a multilevel parking lot by the side of Panagal Park, which is the green lung of T. Nagar. Both have remained in the planning stage with no interest being displayed by bidders for the projects. The truth is that implementing anything in T. Nagar may just not be possible given the congestion that prevails there. And the same applies in different degrees to the rest of the city.

Violations in T. Nagar have become common but building collapses are still, thankfully, a rarity. But one such event did shake Chennai out of its usual indifference to such matters. On 28 June 2014, in the midst of a heavy downpour, an eleven-storeyed building under construction at Moulivakkam, a new suburb, collapsed, killing sixty-one workers from Tamil Nadu, Andhra Pradesh, and Odisha. It was one of two towers, the other one also of eleven storeys and under construction. The two were named Faith and Belief, the

[35]'Ground + 4 becomes 7, heads for 9', *Madras Musings*, Vol. XXVIII, No. 8, 1–5 August 2018.

entire complex rejoicing in the nomenclature of Trust Heights, all very ironic names given the project's eventual fate. It was Faith that had collapsed. It took with it the investment and probably the entire life savings of seventy-six prospective buyers.

The builders promptly blamed it on natural causes—their argument was that lightning, thunder, and rain had caused their building to collapse. But with so many deaths, the public was not buying the idea. The government appointed R. Reghupathi, a retired judge, as a one-man panel to investigate the causes of the collapse. What emerged was a sordid tale of plain greed and open connivance with the authorities. The builders had used substandard materials and had deviated considerably from the plan they had submitted to the CMDA and obtained approval for. This was, of course, quite a common practice in the city, with most builders squaring up the officials who come on inspection tours and thereby obtaining a compliance certificate. It was all right as long as no building fell and no one was caught in the act. Now with the full-fledged collapse and several lives to answer for, the rot was exposed. It was said that the CMDA itself did not have the expertise to review plans and detect serious lapses. But some of the violations were basic—the site was 'within a stone's throw' of the Porur Lake and so the soil was subject to dampness and subsidence. This was not factored into the construction at all. The permit granted for such a high-rise in proximity to the water body was also questionable. The Directorate of Town and Country Planning (DTCP) ought to have never countenanced such a construction. The builder was consistently violating the National Building Code of India when it came to the quality of materials. Lastly, in order to increase car parking space, the structure had too few columns at the basement level, in sharp deviation from the plan. This too had gone unchecked or perhaps was conveniently overlooked.[36]

In his report, Justice Reghupathy recommended that 'a special unit be established to deal with the "hidden and underground transactions" between officials concerned at various levels and realtors/promoters.' He also called for the reconstitution of the CMDA at the base level, so that such disasters did not occur again.[37] The report was tabled in the Tamil Nadu Legislative Assembly but very little action was taken, especially against the officials. Those

---

[36]Janyala Sreenivas, '11 floors went up on wetland in Chennai, until one fell, killing 60', *New Indian Express*, 4 July 2014.

[37]B. Kolappan, 'Moulivakam tragedy exposed dark side of construction business', *The Hindu*, 25 August 2015.

who bought flats in the building are still running from pillar to post seeking compensation. The matter is sub judice and the promoter has said he has no money. The authorities had cleared several houses in the neighbourhood that had been damaged when Faith fell. The owners of these homes were desperate to get back to their normal lives, having been uprooted for no fault of theirs. They never got any compensation.

The story does not end there. Faith may have collapsed but Belief was still standing as a shell. The district collector of Kanchipuram, under whose jurisdiction Moulivakkam fell, gave orders for the demolition of Belief. The promoter challenged this in the Madras High Court and a stay was granted. The Supreme Court however vacated this, based on a panel of experts that opined the structural design of the building to 'be so grossly inadequate that it can never be used for housing/habitation'.[38] Belief was eventually brought down, with explosives, two-and-a-half years after Faith fell. Rather appropriately, the CMDA supervised the demolition.[39]

There was just one positive outcome—trust, faith, and belief in real estate promoters decreased considerably. The tendency to rush in and invest in just about any project that was announced in the city and its outskirts also dropped drastically. And fly-by-night real-estate promoters began to fade away.[40]

The debris of the two buildings remained in situ until 2018, chiefly because Chennai has no mechanism to dispose of construction waste. The site became a den of stray dogs and snakes and the local residents were up in arms. The promoter finally began work on clearance, the steel rods being sold and the sintered concrete being used to fill pits elsewhere.[41] In a way, the Moulivakkam collapse also exposed the administration's inability to deal with garbage and waste disposal, of which more in a later chapter.

All these issues, and more, are often overlooked when it comes to elections to the city's corporation. The votes are garnered more on the basis of freebies, in line with what happens during elections to the legislative assembly and the parliament. All these civic problems, however, pale into insignificance when compared with the water crisis the city faces in perpetuity.

---

[38]'Moulivakkam Building Collapse', *New Indian Express*, 7 February 2019.

[39]'Belief Tower in Chennai's Moulivakkom razed two years after 61 died in building collapse', *NewsMinute*, 2 November 2016.

[40]'Homeless in Moulivakkam', *The Hindu*, 11 November 2016.

[41]'Debris of Moulivakkam building yet to be cleared', *New Indian Express*, 14 June 2018.

4 | 'A PERPETUAL GROPING FOR WATER...'

Chennai's history can be summed up as one long search for water. It is rather surprising that the city has thrived for so long despite the continuing scarcity of such an essential commodity. That the metropolis has grown in leaps and bounds in spite of this is a tribute to the crisis-management capability of its administration and the ability of its populace to make do with less. In that we cannot include the affluent and the establishments that cater to them—hotels, malls, swank offices, and upmarket residential apartments and houses—most of which waste water, despite claims to the contrary. Lines of people queuing up to fill plastic pots in financially disadvantaged areas is a common sight and tempers can run high. 'Fighting by a water tap' is a Tamil expression that is roughly equivalent to the English fish market. The mental image it conjures up is that of two women shouting abuse or at times clawing each other over who is next in line to fill their pot. Yes, water makes people desperate.

'Madras has never been, and probably never will be, a great industrial centre. Two things are lacking; coal within easy reach, and a sufficient water supply on the spot.'[1] That was J. C. Molony, writing in 1926. We did disprove him on the first count but the second is still true. Entire residential colonies housing the less affluent survive on water supplied by tankers. Men cycling along with pots of water precariously balanced on both sides of the vehicle can be seen all over the city. Some of the better-off do the same on other two-wheelers—scooters, motorcycles. It is very dangerous for those on the vehicle and those anywhere in the vicinity.

There are several slums that collectively hire what are known as fish carts, to collect water in pots and bring them to their homes. The term 'fish cart' needs an explanation, for it is a uniquely Chennai entity. These are, in essence, motorized carts that are mounted on three wheels. A creation of the 1970s, they came to stay, fulfilling a great role in transporting commodities in the more congested areas of the city. They were known as mini carts and the word 'mini' soon became 'meen', which is Tamil for fish. That, in turn, was translated into English—hence making them fish carts. They have been seen transporting everything from iron rods to bricks but never have they carried fish! Over the years, they became a byword for traffic

[1]J. Chartres Molony, *A Book of South India*, London: Methuen & Co., 1926, p. 19.

violations and emerged as a prime cause of accidents—their design was not meant for overloading them or for plying at great speeds, but these became the worst traits of these vehicles. They became the subject of several PILs, with the one by 'Traffic' Ramaswamy garnering the maximum publicity.[2] After being bitterly fought in the courts over a long and leisurely period of time, unregistered fish carts were banned.[3] But this happened only on paper. They are still a common sight all over the city and no doubt set 'Traffic' Ramaswamy's teeth on edge. He was known to frequently complain about them to the courts and the police.[4] One of the principal uses of the fish carts is the transportation of water.

The CMWSSB is the official agency responsible for the two functions that the name includes. Data released by Consumer Action Group has it that Chennai needs 1,009 million litres of water per day (MLD). In the best of times, when the rains are good, the supply is 766 MLD. In 2018, with the monsoons having come a cropper, it was around 550 MLD, supplied on alternate days. The ideal supply ought to be 135 to 150 litres per capita per day (LPCD). It is around 114 LPCD in the core city while the suburbs get 40 LPCD. The slums are doled out a meagre 25 LPCD![5] The CMWSSB supplies water via pipelines in the older and, therefore, better-managed parts of the city, and via water tankers elsewhere. There are entire housing colonies that get neither from the CMWSSB. And this category is a great democratic leveller—some of the swankiest and most of the poorest areas do not get a drop of water from the official agency. They depend on private suppliers who operate water tankers that fill up at the wells in the agricultural hinterland and supply to the city. These vehicles make the accident statistics of the fish carts pale in comparison. Deaths caused by speeding water tankers regularly make it to the news but are no longer headline-worthy. They are mere statistics in the growth of a modern city. In 2019, the Madras High Court demanded statistics on deaths caused by water tankers.[6] There has been no response simply because they have not been considered a problem. The tanker drivers are also a stressed lot—subject to harassment by the police and the notorious water mafia that has, over the years, tightened its hold on

[2]Writ Petition No. 19524 of 2002 before the Madras High Court.

[3]High Court's Order dated 25 January 2008.

[4]Contempt Petition 2447 of 2015.

[5]Bharath Kumar K. 'Is Chennai Water Secure?', Citizen Consumer and Civic Action Group, available here: https://www.cag.org.in/blogs/chennai-water-secure/.

[6]'Chennai police chief asked to share details of tanker deaths', *The Hindu*, 11 December 2019.

the villages and wells on the outskirts and extracted the water there. The ground water in most of these places is fast running out but as long as it can still be accessed, everyone turns a blind eye. IT companies, hospitals, and educational institutions take on lease large swathes of land that encompass wells, in the outskirts of the city. They extract the groundwater from here and have them transported via tankers to their locations. Once in a while, tanker operators go on strike. That brings the entire IT corridor in upmarket Rajiv Gandhi Expressway to its knees. The whole area has been planned sans underground piped water supply.[7]

Chennai was not built by a river. Yes, to be sure, Fort St George was. When in 1639, Francis Day came here, he selected the location for a future settlement very carefully. The sea was on the eastern side and on the south of the future fort was the Cooum River. On the western side, where NSC Bose Road is, was the Elambore River, now forgotten and lost, with what little of it remains being amalgamated into the Buckingham Canal, another waterway with a tragic history.[8]

When it came to security, Day had done what he could. As for water, the concept of piped supply did not exist in his time. People tapped groundwater by sinking wells. In addition, there were plenty of lakes and tanks all around the area. Day could never have imagined that what he was starting off was no mere warehouse and fort but a megapolis that would one day be home to millions. Can we then blame him for lack of foresight in planning a settlement with no large river in sight? Nevertheless, architect V. D. Krishnaswami rather aptly summed it up in the *Madras Tercentenary Commemoration Volume*: 'The location of the English settlement of 1639 cannot be described from the health point as anything but a blind one that has resulted in a perpetual groping for water, which has not yet found its goal.'[9] Eighty years on, the situation has only worsened.

The problem of water manifested itself shortly after the British settled at Fort St George. The Elambore to the rear of the fort was brackish and Alexander Hamilton, writing in 1718, says it 'obstructs all springs of fresh water, so that the Fort has no drinkable water within a mile'.[10] In the initial years, the fort and its inhabitants depended on water from wells in Black

[7]'BYOF/BYOC/BYOW', *Madras Musings*, Vol. XXIX, No. 6, 1–16 July 2019.

[8]V. Sriram, *A Guide to Fort St George*, p. 24.

[9]V. D. Krishnaswami, 'The Problem of Water in Madras' *Madras Tercentenary Commemoration Volume*, p. 283.

[10]Love, *Vestiges of Old Madras*, Vol. 2, pp. 86–88.

Town. This was transported in pots on cattle and carts by water-bearers and sold to the residents of the fort.[11] It is ironic that much of Chennai still relies on water being brought in pots, the only change being that plastic has replaced clay as the material. Huge cisterns of timber and masonry stored water for the garrison in the fort.[12] Today, it is commonplace to see synthetic tanks erected at street corners. These store water for the locality.

It is interesting to note, however, that the native population was far more aware of where good water could be found. The historic settlements of Mylapore, Thiruvallikeni, Thiruvottiyur, and much of what became Madraspatnam (the Black Town area), were all located on sand dune ridges and had good quality water. This is one reason why practically all the old thoroughfares were named as High Roads in the city, a practice unique to Chennai. The EIC, when it began settling its weavers here, evidently relied on local advice and chose Colletspet, near Thiruvottiyur and Chintadripet near Black Town chiefly because of good quality water.[13] There was no question of relocating the fort of course and so life went on there as usual, with water arriving in pots. Outings to St Thomas Mount, where the army was located, were looked forward to, one of the reasons being the excellent water that was to be had there.[14]

The French were aware of all this and one of the reasons why their siege of 1746 was so successful was that they cut off the water supply to the fort from Black Town. The English capitulated and returned only in 1749 when they got back the city, owing to the Treaty of Aix-la-Chapelle. The problem of water supply to the fort was addressed in right earnest once they were firmly in control. The principal challenge was that with no pumping technology available, water had to flow through gravity in a city that was largely flat. Then we have the entry of George Baker.

A naval captain, he was in charge of the sloop *Cuddalore*, and rendered service to the British at Fort St George when the French laid siege to Madras for a final time in 1758. A pleased board of directors appointed him Master Attendant of the Port. Baker, however, is chiefly remembered for another service of his, albeit one that he did with a commercial motive—piped water supply, perhaps the first in the city. Having returned to England in 1771, he addressed the board of directors of the EIC with a proposal for piped

[11]Love, *Vestiges of Old Madras*, Vol. 3, p. 42.

[12]Krishnaswami, *The Problem of Water*, p. 284.

[13]Ibid.

[14]Ibid.

water to Fort St George, to be drawn by gravitational force from seven wells, commemorated in Seven Wells Street in Peddanaikenpettah. This was agreed to, and Baker came once again to Madras, where he began the work. The lead pipes arrived a year later and were laid within a span of two months. Then came the task of building cisterns to hold water inside Fort St George and these were ready by 1776. Thereafter, Baker proposed a more ambitious scheme—laying pipes under the sea to ensure fresh water reaches the ships that, in the absence of a proper harbour, were anchored two miles from the shore.[15] This was, however, never implemented.

By 1780, Baker wanted to return to England. His offer to sell his waterworks to the EIC includes a note of warning about the civic sense of the people of Madras—nothing much has changed over the years. Then, as it is now, people cared very little about public spaces—they dug cess pits on the roads so that foul water from their houses flooded streets; heaps of bricks and construction debris were stored outside homes, thereby reducing space for movement; filth was thrown out of houses on to the streets, and there were structures that encroached. The EIC bought the waterworks for a sum of 35,000 pagodas[16] on 5 April 1780 and Baker returned home, a rich man.[17]

Seven Wells (in reality ten) remained for long the principal source of water supply to the fort. One of these wells still works and is part of the city's waterworks. Hyder Ali knew how important they were and, during one of his raids, tried to get his men to poison them. Sylvester Nicholas, an Irishman, managed to fob this attempt. The EIC, in gratitude, conferred on him the title of Custodian of the Seven Wells. The responsibility was given to the family for 125 years, with an allowance of ten pagodas a month and rent-free living on the premises. Nicholas fathered a family with a native woman and subsequent generations took pride in the title.[18] In recent years, city-based architect Zhayynn James, who is a descendant of the Nicholases, has kept the memory alive.

By 1791, water to the fort was no longer free, ₹1 being charged per month. The rest of the city (this is the native quarters) managed with open wells where the water, owing to the porous nature of the soil, was subject to serious pollution. Eighty years later, it was found to be so appalling that

---

[15]Love, *Vestiges of Old Madras*, Vol. 3, p. 42.

[16]A pagoda was the most commonly used currency within Madras Presidency. Its value in exchange to the British pound and Mughal rupee varied over time and the most valuable, the star pagoda, was around 3.5 rupees in 1780.

[17]Love, *Vestiges of Old Madras*, Vol. 3, p. 280.

[18]Molony, *A Book of South India*, p. 22.

the Indian Sanitary Commission declared that the water pronounced 'fit for drinking purposes by the Chemical Engineer in Madras would utterly be condemned at Home'.[19] It was in 1859 or so that the first steps were taken to provide the Indian sections of the city with potable water. Governor Sir Charles Trevelyan had a large basin dug at the northern end of the city and it was designed to drain much of the rainwater into itself.[20] The scheme was soon abandoned but certain remnants have survived. Trevelyan's Basin is an area in George Town and running close by is Water Works Street. To the north of Royapuram is Basin Bridge Railway Junction.

In 1866, work began on a much larger scheme, one that is in a sense in progress even now. This was to tap the waters of the neighbouring areas. The first of these was the Kosasthalaiyar (Kortaliyar in English parlance), a river that runs to the north of the city. A masonry weir built across this river diverted the waters via a channel to the Cholavaram Tank, which, in turn, was connected to the Red Hills Tank by another channel. It took eight years to get this done and when completed, supply began from the Red Hills Reservoir to the Kilpauk Water Works from where water was distributed to the city. Cisterns and fountains were built from where residents could collect the water. But even then there was a problem of plans keeping up with technology. The scheme of 1866 was hardly complete when J. A. Jones, municipal engineer, and after whom the Jones Tower in the Red Hills Reservoir is named, came up with another plan. This allowed water to be pumped and supplied to Kilpauk where it could be filtered and treated before supply to the city. But the corporation was in need of funds and raising it took time. In the meanwhile, many houses began laying water pipes from the city's mains. But water was even then in short supply and the public cisterns and fountains dried up.[21] Moreover, it was dirty. Dr K. N. Kesari writes thus of the water position at this time:

> Piped water came into vogue but it still contained germs and insects. So rich people would get their water supplied from Villivakkam. Even doctors advised that this water was good for health. It was carried by Brahmins and sold at one anna per pot.[22]

---

[19]Report on Military Sanitation in the Presidency of Madras, 1869.

[20]Srinivasachari, *History of the City of Madras*, p. 256.

[21]Much of the history of the piped water supply to Madras city as chronicled here is sourced from the *Golden Jubilee Souvenir of the Madras City Waterworks*, published by the Waterworks Department, Corporation of Madras, 1965.

[22]Menon, *Life and Times of Kesari*, p. 39.

It was to overcome this problem that the Jones Scheme was repeatedly revived, only to be shelved each time. In 1904, it was, however, resurrected and modernized, now becoming the responsibility of J. W. Madeley, special engineer in-charge, Water and Drainage. He is commemorated in a subway connecting Mambalam and T. Nagar which, given his designation, is rather ironically notorious for flooding each time it rains. Madeley began work on the Madras Water Works at Kilpauk, with a magnificent Indo-Saracenic structure being built to house it. A state-of-the-art filtration and pumping station came up within two years, being inaugurated in 1914. It works even now.

The waterworks may have promised filtered water to the entire city but ground reality was far different. It is best to tell that story in the words of Molony:

> To supply each day this (fifty million gallons) amount of filtered water the engineer in charge of the scheme considered twenty-one filter beds necessary. The Corporation constructed fourteen, and then, owing to financial stringency, was forced to stay its hand. There were three courses open and possible; the first, a voluntary restriction by the citizens of their consumption to the amount of filtered water that could be supplied; the second, an intermittent daily supply; the third, an admixture of unfiltered with filtered water. The Corporation finally elected for the third course. With this mixing of filtered and unfiltered water my name is likely to remain long and unhappily associated owing to Sir P Rajagopalachari, then Member of Government in charge of Local and Municipal Administration. He christened the brew 'Molony's Mixture' and the name stuck.[23]

Whatever be its faults, the Madeley system worked and by the time he retired in 1926, he had augmented it by providing a bacteriological lab for water analysis and installing metres to monitor consumption. But he could have never foreseen the population explosion during World War II. The scheme, planned for a population of 660,000 in 1961, had to contend with 770,000 in 1941 itself! Talks had already begun on the need for a new reservoir and, in 1939, the idea received an impetus with patriot S. Satyamurti becoming mayor of the city. He lobbied hard and ensured that the government released the funds required. The foundation stone was laid on 8 August 1940.[24] The

[23]Molony, *A Book of South India*, p. 143.

[24]P. G. Sundararajan, *The Life of S. Satyamurti*, New Delhi: South Asian Publishers, 1988,

Congress, of which Satyamurti was a member, largely stoked by arch-rival C. Rajagopalachari, raised a hue and cry when the former, as mayor, attended the foundation stone-laying ceremony where the Governor of Madras, Sir Arthur Hope presided. But Satyamurti would have none of it. Given a choice between country and city, he said he would plump for the latter and went ahead. In a separate letter to Maulana Abul Kalam Azad, he pointed out that the 'reservoir was not meant to strengthen British imperialism but to help quench the growing thirst of Madras'.[25]

The Poondi Reservoir was completed in 1944, by which time Satyamurti was long dead, having fallen victim to the harsh conditions of his imprisonment following the Quit India Movement. After Independence, K. Kamaraj, Satyamurti's protégé, lent his weight to the idea of naming the reservoir after him which is how it came to be called Satyamurti Sagar.[26] The increase in population, however, meant that the city was back to square one as far as water supply was concerned. 'In 1949 also the position is the same,' lamented Dr Kesari.

'After coming to Madras I have seen several changes but some things are still the same as before—the impurities in piped water, the bad odour from the River Cooum and the dirty water in the temple tanks. I doubt very much whether these will ever improve or not in the future.'[27] Not that water from the wells was any better. Writing about it in 1955 when he moved from Hyderabad and settled in the lower-middle-class colony of West Mambalam, author Ashokamitran recalls that the water in most houses was of a deep brown colour. 'There were only one or two residences in Mambalam that had good water in their wells. People would go there and get one or two pots full.'[28]

Dr Kesari ends his memoirs on a note of hope, stating that 'there would be relief only if the Krishna–Pennar project is implemented.'[29] That was in 1949, when Madras was a composite state, comprising much of coastal Andhra and the present-day state of Tamil Nadu. Four years later, with linguistic division taking place, the Telugu-speaking regions of Madras State were linked with the erstwhile Princely State of Hyderabad to form Andhra Pradesh.

---

p. 168.

[25]Ibid., p. 169.

[26]Ibid.

[27]Menon, *Life and Times of Kesari*, p. 40.

[28]Ashokamitran, *Oru Parvayil Chennai Nagaram*, Chennai: Kavitha Veliyidu, 2002, p. 14.

[29]Menon, *Life and Times of Kesari*, p. 39.

This was not a peaceful division and the Andhraites were left with much heartburn. All talk of linking the Krishna with the Pennar was abandoned for the nonce. To compound matters, Madras city faced a prolonged failure of monsoons between 1947 and 1951 and this may be a good point to dwell on the metro's dependence on rainfall.[30]

Chennai is rather uniquely placed, for it hardly receives any rainfall when the southwest monsoon is active over the rest of the country, between June and September. The bulk of its rainwater comes from the relatively weaker northeast monsoon between October and December. Cyclonic storms are quite frequent during this period and though most have been known in recent times to bypass the city, the seventeenth, eighteenth, and nineteenth centuries have seen a lot more havoc caused by these wind systems. The city, on an average, gets around 140 cm of rainfall in a year, of which 65 per cent comes from the northeast monsoon. When that fails, there is certain to be great water scarcity.

Between 1947 and 1951, as mentioned earlier, there was a prolonged drought. By the last year, C. H. Sibghatullah, who was the mayor, became frantic. Having failed in every effort to get water, he organized a prayer meeting. Strangely enough, at the end of it, the heavens opened up and the water crisis was averted.[31] The skies have not been so responsive in subsequent years.

Music has also been tried, the most publicized efforts in this direction being those of the maverick violin maestro Kunnakudi Vaidyanathan. In 1982, he famously waded into the Red Hills Reservoir and played the Raga Amrithavarshini, which is said to induce rain. At the same time, Muslims prayed at mosques and Hindus at temples. This was at the behest of the then chief minister, M. G. Ramachandran. The city, and for that matter, the rest of Tamil Nadu was facing one of its worst crises. The music did not move the rain gods. In later years, Kunnakudi would repeat his attempt, changing the venue to the Kapaliswarar Temple in Mylapore. These became mega events, with several musicians participating. The results were mixed at best.[32]

The drought of 1982, when Vaidyanathan made his first attempt to woo the rains with his violin, stretched to 1983. This time the MGR government brought in Thomas Jacob, a bank employee from Changanasserry, Kerala, who claimed to be able to electronically induce rain. He came as an official

---

[30]Narasimham, *Me and My Times*, p. 140.

[31]Ibid., p. 141.

[32]Prabhu Chawla, 'Tamilnadu: Waiting for Water', *India Today*, 15 November 1982.

invitee of the water and sewerage board and was escorted to the Red Hills Reservoir where, using a handheld transmitter, he claimed to send out electronic impulses that would generate a low-pressure system. It did not work, but the government was willing to try anything, except the IIT's suggestion that the water in the Red Hills Reservoir be covered with a layer of cetyl alcohol to prevent evaporation loss of almost 15 million litres a day. Years later, in 2017, to be precise, the government and its officials would be alacrity personified in implementing a variant of this idea near Madurai. Sellur Raju, a minister, suggested that the lake in question be covered with thermocol sheets!

But to go back to 1983: the crisis was intense; water being supplied once in five days via pipes. Tankers, introduced during the drought of 1951, were pressed into service and all the hostels were closed, students being sent home owing to lack of water. The Thomas Jacob experiment made the M (now C) MWSSB the butt of several jokes and he was kept incommunicado throughout his stay in Madras. After a week of chasing him, a journalist remarked that the rainmaker was as elusive as the rain. The IIT suggestion was finally accepted but by the time it was put into action, most of the water had evaporated.[33] Cloud seeding was tried though this was not the first time it was attempted—the maiden run was in 1975, during a similar drought. An American company was engaged on both occasions and it did produce some results.

But with no rains in sight, it was time to think out of the box. Someone remembered the Krishna–Pennar scheme and it emerged once again, this time to see a happy conclusion. MGR was chief minister in Tamil Nadu and his Telugu equivalent, the matinee idol turned politician N. T. Rama Rao, was chief minister of Andhra. The project had actually been agreed upon in 1976, the last time Chennai had seen a massive drought. In 1983, with two friends in power in neighbouring states, it was time to go ahead. A high-profile agreement ceremony took place in April 1983 followed by the foundation stone-laying event in May. The three Krishna River riparian states of Andhra, Karnataka, and Maharashtra agreed to each give up 5 billion cubic feet of water from their respective shares to Madras. It was a rare instance when a few states of India forgot their differences to help a city in yet another state. You only need to see the perennial disputes over water between Karnataka and Tamil Nadu to appreciate the difference.

---

[33]S. H. Venkataramani, 'Metrowater Board invites miracle rainmaker to parched city of Madras', *India Today*, 15 April 1983.

The scheme, known as the Telugu Ganga project, harnessed the surplus waters of the Krishna at the Srisailam Reservoir and channelled them via a series of interlinked canals and checkpoints to Uthukottai, the Zero Point where the water entered Tamil Nadu. The waters of the Pennar river join the canals at Somasila. They enter the Satyamurti Sagar and from there get distributed to Red Hills, Sholavaram, and Chembarampakkam.[34] All looked good on paper but when implemented, there were huge problems.[35] Less than 500 million cubic feet of water reached Madras, the rest having vanished owing to seepage, leakage, and evaporation. Matters languished thus till 2002 when the religious leader Sathya Sai Baba undertook to relay the pipelines as a private initiative. A massive property in Chennai belonging to his trust was sold and the money used to partially cover the costs.[36] The work was completed in 2006 and water came in its entirety to Chennai. It is just that the volume has never been anywhere close to the 15 billion cubic feet promised. With the demand for water in the riparian states going up too, Chennai has rarely got more than 4 billion cubic feet in any year and this is after buying all the water, including whatever was meant to be diverted for agricultural purposes along the route to the city.

With the population skyrocketing in the new millennium, it was time to come up with new plans, dust off old schemes, and score political points in the process. Jayalalithaa emerged an absolute winner on all these counts. Having been voted back to power in 2001, she was faced with acute water scarcity in Chennai. The AIADMK had in its manifesto promised making rainwater harvesting compulsory and this was made law in 2002. The chief minister went on television to appeal to the public to cooperate and this saw good results. Much of the groundwork was, however, done by Sekhar Raghavan.

Chennai sat up and took notice of this scientist who had lived quietly in the leafy suburb of Besant Nagar for decades. His eureka moment had come when one morning he discovered that the water in his taps had turned brackish. And yet, Besant Nagar was known for years for the good quality of its groundwater. 'Spurred by this I began studying the way ponds and tanks in rural areas were protected, and rainwater was channelled into these reservoirs for future use,' says Raghavan, seated in a large room at the Rain Centre's office in Gandhi Nagar.

---

[34]Telugu Ganga project, see here: https://en.wikipedia.org/wiki/Telugu_Ganga_project.

[35]Amarnath K. Menon, 'Telugu Ganga Project turns out to be a financial sink hole', *India Today*, 31 May 1985.

[36]'Chennai benefits from Sai Baba's initiatives', *The Hindu*, 1 December 2004.

'That Chennai had worked with a vengeance to be rid of all its water bodies was a well-known fact and one that could not be wished away. What I realized was that with most garden houses had given way to apartment blocks and office complexes, the open spaces surrounding the buildings were all being paved or covered with concrete. The rainwater that ran off these structures never managed to percolate into the ground and instead filled the storm water drains from where it ran into the sea.'

Raghavan therefore began propagating the idea of rainwater harvesting (RWH). He walked from building to building, only to be chased away by watchmen. But he did not give up. Sure enough, a few enquiries began coming in for his advice. An NRI gave the seed money for the setting up of an office and he operated in a small way. But the situation was to change. In the build-up to the 2001 assembly elections, Jayalalithaa had made RWH an important part of her party's manifesto. She had also vowed to get adequate water supply to the city. The AIADMK swept the polls following one of those complete swings in the mood of the electorate for which Tamil Nadu is famous. The chief minister did not forget her promise. The scramble began for suitably qualified persons and someone mentioned Raghavan.

When in 2002 the government legislated on RWH, he became the perfect choice. The following year, Raghavan set up the Rain Centre, which offered advice on how to set up RWH facilities in buildings. This was inaugurated by the chief minister herself. 'I was advised on what distance I was to maintain from her, where I was to stand, etc.,' he recalls with a twinkle in his eye. 'Several government departments descended on the Rain Centre and on inspection declared that the chief minister could never come to such a simple place. They spruced it up and we had a couple of working models of RWH systems. Madam came and was graciousness personified. She gave us a donation and encouraged by this, some other government departments did so too.'[37]

Work began, thereafter, to implement RWH in the city. In 2005, Chennai witnessed copious rains and the effect of RWH was there for all to see. The groundwater table went up by 20 feet in many places and the Kapaliswarar Temple Tank in Mylapore, bone dry for years, filled up, much to the delight of devotees and the eternal disappointment of at least one temple trustee who had been campaigning for years to cement the ground over and use the space for a laser show highlighting the heritage of the area. The benefits of RWH helped the city survive for a decade. Water tankers became less common as did

[37]Sekhar Raghavan, Interview with the author, Rain Centre, Chennai, 3 March 2020.

plastic pots and fights by the tap. There was no doubt that Chennai, which was racing towards Day Zero, when its groundwater would be exhausted had suddenly applied the brakes. But unfortunately, the initial momentum was lost—the driveways of most buildings were never harvested and these contributed significantly to surface runoffs. The authorities, with the talent they possess for converting any scientific solution into mere ritual, did not bother to ensure that new buildings implemented RWH. As a consequence much of the rainwater still makes its way to the sea.

When asked as to how many buildings seriously implement RWH in the city, Sekhar Raghavan says it is still a measly 20 per cent. 'The rest don't care even after all the demonstrated benefits. And I blame corruption for this. Whether a builder provides for RWH or not, he is expected to pay a bribe to get the certification that it is done. Most prefer to not go to the extent of getting the RWH in place. They prefer to save on that and pay the bribe instead.' He is also of the view that politicians prefer it this way. Most of the water supply by means of tankers is controlled by a mafia owing allegiance to various political overlords. This ensures that much of the new areas of the city don't get either piped water or drainage. The cleaning of septic tanks by means of tankers is controlled by the same mafia. Sekhar Raghavan fairly bristles when storm water drains are mentioned. 'They ought to be restricted to main roads, with the others being encouraged to tap run offs. Now all of it is drained and let into the nearest canal. They could have at least rejuvenated the lakes by getting the rainwater to drain into them. Even that is not done.'

Having made a success out of RWH, Jayalalithaa decided to revive the Veeranam Scheme. There was an element of altruism to this, of course, but it was also meant to show that she could achieve what arch-rival Karunanidhi could not. Veeranam or the Veeranarayanapuram Tank is a reservoir of 1,465 million cubic feet of water, around 235 kilometres south of Chennai. This reservoir is truly a tribute to the ancient Cholas. In the tenth century, crown prince Rajaditya was camping with a vast army near the village of Kattumannarkoil. The enemy did not come as anticipated and the men had to be kept in battle preparedness. The prince got them to excavate a lake, 11.2 kilometres in length and 4 kilometres in width, to hold the surplus waters of the Kollidam River, itself a floodwater channel of the Kaveri. The tank, when completed, was named Veeranarayana, after the local deity, and also commemorated one of the many names of Rajaditya's father, Parantaka I. It became a lifeline for several thousand acres of agricultural land in the Cuddalore district. In the 1830s, Arthur Cotton, the engineer who later harnessed the waters of the Krishna and Godavari, studied the tank in detail. He noted that there was no serious defect in it (this, 900 years after it was constructed) apart from the narrowing of the mouth of the Vadavar River that connected the lake to the Kollidam River and the tendency of the bund to breach when filled to the brim. In 1967, Annadurai, then freshly elected chief minister of the state, mooted the idea of supplying water to the capital city from Veeranam. He died in 1969 and it was left to his successor, Karunanidhi, to execute the plan. The project, estimated at ₹21 crore, was then the biggest to be sanctioned in independent India. The contractor put up a plant at Thirukazhukundram in collaboration with a Greek firm for making the pre-stressed concrete pipes.

What happened next did not reflect well on any of the parties involved. There were allegations of corruption, delays in sanctioning foreign exchange, and quality issues. With the DMK government being dismissed in 1976, the matter was taken to court. In the middle of it all, the contractor suddenly died, the cause of his death remaining a mystery. The pipes were abandoned all along the Cuddalore-Madras route and were put to good use—entire families lived in them and some others became latrines. In 2001, Jayalalithaa, after asking a number of uncomfortable questions about what happened in the 1970s, and as to how the contractor died, revived the Veeranam Scheme. The local farmers were none too happy that their water was being diverted to Chennai but then you did not defy Jayalalithaa. Water came to Chennai in 2004 and today the lake supplies anywhere between 50 to 180 MLD of water to the city.[38]

At the end of the decade, the shortage of water was still around 400 MLD. It was estimated that by 2030, the city would have a demand of 2,700 MLD.[39] Desalination was the next scheme. India's largest such facility, exclusively meant to cater to industrial establishments, came up at Minjur, near Chennai, using Spanish technology. Seawater is pumped in and by a process of reverse osmosis becomes fresh water. It is just that the process is energy intensive and the cost of the conversion is ₹49 per kilolitre. The CMWSSB purchases the water from the plant and distributes it. A second plant was commissioned at Nemmeli, also near Chennai, with Israeli technology. This produces 100 MLD of fresh water, at a lower cost.[40] A third plant of

[38]V. Sriram, 'A Chola gift to Chennai', *The Hindu*, 10 April 2015.

[39]Avilash Roul, 'Who will provide water security to Chennai?', *Down to Earth*, 31 May 2019.

[40]Brief details of these plants can be found on the CMWSSB website, available here: https://chennaimetrowater.tn.gov.in/.

150 MLD is in the offing, at Nemmeli.[41] The locations of these plants have come in for sharp criticism from environmental activists who are of the view that a 'rain-rich' area like Chennai does not need such facilities. Brine and backwash from the plants have also played havoc with the aquaculture of the sea, thereby ruining fishermen's prospects.[42]

Is Chennai really rain-rich? That may be an overstatement but the sad truth is that it does receive sufficient rain most years and sometimes gets it in excess as well. Until the 1940s, all this water was channelled into natural sinks such as lakes, ponds, reservoirs, and the vast Pallikaranai Marsh—one of Tamil Nadu's three natural (and the city's only) wetlands. It connects thirty-one water bodies and had, in its heyday, a catchment area of 235 square kilometres, much of it now converted into residential localities. Velachery is one of the largest of these.[43] Apart from the marsh, in 1893, Chennai had sixty water bodies, covering an area of 12.8 square kilometres. Today, we have twenty-eight of them, occupying 3.2 square kilometres.[44] What happened to the rest? The Long Tank of Mylapore became T. Nagar. The Nungambakkam Tank was given to Loyola College. The Villivakkam Tank was made over to the TVS Group of companies to build their factories in the 1960s. Names such as Tank Bund Road, Lake View Road, and Erikarai Mariamman (the goddess on the bank of a lake) Temple, now nowhere near any water, give us an idea of what wealth we once had by way of storage spaces.

At least, all of these were legal transfers, at a time when environmental awareness was non-existent. What has happened since then by way of systematic encroachment on lake areas and dumping of garbage on living water bodies to convert them into real estate is really unforgivable. That this malpractice still continues is what makes it doubly sad. It all begins innocuously—local residents begin dumping garbage along the tank. This is followed by construction debris. A builder, usually in cahoots with a politician, then engineers the overnight appearance of a slum. All of these activities gradually restrict the span of the water body and also cut off all feeder channels. The lake, deprived of fresh supply of water, begins to fester. The neighbourhood

---

[41]K. Lakshmi, 'Work on a third desalination plant at Nemmeli to begin by October end', *The Hindu*, 18 October 2019.

[42]K. Lakshmi, 'Chennai water crisis: Are desalination plants the answer?', *The Hindu*, 28 June 2019.

[43]S. T. Mahesh Kumar, 'With three rivers and five wetlands, why is Chennai staring at ecological collapse?', *Citizen Matters*, 6 February 2017.

[44]'Time to restore vanishing waterbodies', *Madras Musings*, Vol. XXVIII, No. 2, 1–15 May 2018.

complains of stench and mosquitoes. One day, the slum vanishes. The area is plotted out in what is colloquially known as an Eri (lake) Scheme. The land is sold and soon buildings begin coming up, with the official sanction of every civic agency that needs to give permission. And when it rains, these areas are flooded. The residents complain and the media gives them extensive coverage. Crores are spent in preventing the recurrence of flooding. 'There are still enough and more water bodies around the city,' says Sekhar Raghavan. 'But they are all systematically neglected.'

As mentioned earlier, once every few years, Chennai receives excess rainfall, and makes it to the news. During the 1943 rains, parts of Mount Road flooded.[45] In 1985, with a large section of the Adyar riverbed made over to slum tenements constructed by the government, the river overflowed its banks following heavy rains. The neighbourhood of Kotturpuram, which was low-lying to begin with, became increasingly flood-prone following the construction of the tenements and has since then been inundated each time it rains heavily. But what made headlines in 1985 was chief minister M. G. Ramachandran's Ramavaram Gardens' residence being marooned by the floodwaters in the Adyar. He and his wife, Janaki, were rowed in a boat up to a point and then made it by car to Hotel Connemara.[46] There was heavy flooding in 2005 too. But what happened in 2015 was the worst as we shall see later. That year, on one day in December, Chennai received 49 cm of rain.

But did we manage to store some of the water? Sadly no. The city's hugely faulty drainage system, the concretization of the Pallikaranai Marsh, the spate of illegal constructions over water bodies that were subsequently regularized, and the lack of any steps to build new reservoirs (the last being Satyamurti's), meant that despite heavy flooding in the city for over a week, very little was saved. The existing reservoirs had not been de-silted for years, reducing their storage capacity. As early as November that year, all of them were full, the combined capacity being 9,000 million cubic feet. A total of 13,000 million cubic feet was let out into the sea even before the December deluge came along, and when the latter happened, water was once again drained to the sea.[47] The net result was that by December 2016, the

---

[45]O. Pulla Reddy, *Autumn Leaves*, Bombay: Bharatiya Vidya Bhavan, 1978, p. 57.

[46]Raj Chengappa, 'Heavy Rain lashes Tamil Nadu incessantly', *India Today*, 15 December 1985.

[47]Abdullah Nurullah, 'Chennai emptied a year's drinking water into the sea', *Times of India*, 20 November 2015.

city was once again desperate for water. But it did serve as a wakeup call for Chennai. The four existing reservoirs have since been de-silted. A fifth, of 1,000 million cubic feet at Theravoy Kandigai has been completed.[48] A sixth storage facility, this of 1,300 million cubic feet has been planned in Sriperumbudur, one of the worst hit areas in the 2015 floods.[49]

Serendipity has also helped—all along the outskirts of the city are abandoned quarries that once supplied granite. In 1956, when these quarries were hills, the author Monica Felton records seeing them as she drove down with Rajaji, the last governor general of India, to the Madras Christian College at Tambaram.

> He looked at the hills on our left where quarry workers were sending up clouds of dust.
> 'Those hills,' he remarked, 'are the only beauty in the landscape near Madras, and soon they will disappear.'
> I asked, 'Has the Government no power to prevent it?'
> 'Oh yes. The power is to determine which hill shall be destroyed first. I suppose they will last my lifetime but not much longer.'[50]

Rajaji was correct and today, as flights descend, it is possible to see what looks like a moonscape just south of the airport. These are all deserted quarries and their shafts have now turned into water reservoirs. Better known for claiming a life or two each year when misguided people attempt swimming in them, they have turned lifelines for the city, with the CMWSSB tapping these too in its attempts to quench Chennai's thirst.[51]

The agency also taps wells in the hinterland beyond Chennai. These areas, largely farmlands, have of late begun to protest, as they too begin to face water shortage. To overcome this, the government has hit upon a simple stratagem. It expands what is known as the CMA each time there is a drought. The reasons given are noble—the expansion is done 'taking into account transport, basic infrastructure, environment protection, and protection of fertile agricultural lands'. The sole purpose in actual intent is to lay hands on the water sources, around 4,200 of them that still exist around the city.

---

[48]'A New Reservoir after 76 years', *Madras Musings*, Vol. XXX, No. 15, 1–15 December 2020.

[49]'New Rservoir coming up at Sriperumbudur to quench Chennai's thirst', *New Indian Express*, 10 February 2019.

[50]Monica Felton, *Rajaji*, New Delhi: Katha, 2003, p. 110.

[51]Press Release no 40/2017 dated 8 June 2017 from the CMWSSB on water from stone quarries.

The new CMA encompasses all of Thiruvallur and Kanchipuram districts apart from Arakonam taluk. It spans 8,878 square kilometres, making it the second largest urban agglomeration in India, after the National Capital Region![52]

Will all these measures mean that Chennai will become water-sufficient? There is some doubt. For a city that is so dependent on the benevolence of the clouds, there is also a widespread fear of the rain here, particularly after 2015. Chennai is no Mumbai or Kolkata, both cities with long monsoons that the local populace enjoys. Here, when it does come, the monsoon is short, lasting no more than four weeks, at most. But you should see the grumbles and groans that manifest. Television channels immediately begin beaming interviews with people in low-lying areas. Schools are closed as soon as a couple of clouds are sighted on the horizon. Traffic comes to a complete halt and all kinds of tardiness is attributed to the rain. The city's unpreparedness to cope with even a few showers is a matter of surprise, especially for those who come from other parts of India used to heavy rains for prolonged periods of time. Fear reigns supreme, fuelled these days by a plethora of panic messages on social media. Chennai would prefer to be blessed with plenty of water without any rain.

[52]'Proceeding insidiously with City expansion', *Madras Musings*, Vol. XXVIII, No. 4, 1–15 June 2018.

5 | MANY COOUMS

According to the average Chennaivasi, there are no rivers in and around the city. Point out the three streams that snake their way around the metro and the standard answer you will get is that these are all called the Cooum and that it is no river but a canal that smells to the high heavens. In fact, the term Cooum itself is now synonymous with gutter. Probe further and ask as to why this is so and the response will be that makkal (the people) have made it that way. As to who these mysterious makkal are, nobody has a clue. But the respondent will make it clear that he or she is in no way connected with those who degraded the waterways. Chennai's rivers are always someone else's problem and have remained that way for ages.

There are in reality three rivers, one principal canal, and forty-four minor drain channels in the city.[1] All of them are in pitiable condition. The collective stench from all these waterways is the first smell of the city you normally get, whether you fly in or arrive by train. Historically, the most significant was the Cooum, known at various times as the Triplicane River.[2] It runs a mere 72 kilometres, of which roughly half is within the city. Like its southern counterpart, the Adyar, it is filled more by tidal action, though it does have a source of freshwater at Thiruvirkolam aka Koovaram aka Koopam, near Vellore. The site is closely associated with the Cholas and the tank from which the river emerges was known as the Tribhuvana Mahadevi Pereri, after a queen of that dynasty.[3] The Adyar is even shorter, at 42 kilometres, fed by tanks and streams in the hinterland and storm water drains in the city.[4] It is an important part of the vast estuarine system that is Chennai. Neither river is perennial and depends on the rains to fill the tanks in the catchment areas. And yet, at one time, most of these were lifelines—to a much smaller city and a far smaller population.

It would be no exaggeration to state that modern Madras or Chennai

[1]Yogesh Kabirdoss, 'Canals that protect Chennai from floods clogged with sewage, weeds and waste', *Times of India*, 27 August 2018.

[2]Susheela Raghavan and Indira Narayanan, 'Geography, Madras: The Land, The People & Their Governance', in Muthiah, *Madras Rediscovered,* p. 11.

[3]Pradeep Chakravarthy, 'The Gods of the Holy Koovam', *Madras Musings*, Vol. XXVI, No. 23, 16–31 March 2017.

[4]Raghavan and Narayanan, 'Geography, Madras' in Muthiah, *Madras Rediscovered,* p. 11.

grew around the Cooum. The river ran just south of the fort. In the 1650s, the Roman Catholic Church, recognizing that Madras would probably outstrip San Thome in importance, made the areas north of the river into the separate diocese of Madras, as opposed to the diocese of Mylapore that lay south of it. They remained separate till 1952 when they merged together to form the Archdiocese of Madras-Mylapore.[5] The river also played an important role in the commerce of the region—not by way of navigation, for there are no records of any shipping or boating on it—but by way of being an important source of water. When in the 1730s it became necessary to settle weavers close to the fort, it was a peninsula in the Cooum that was selected to form the colony of Chintadripet. To the immediate west of this area was the aristocratic Indian quarter of Komaleeswaranpet. This was considered a particularly holy spot, for the river suddenly turns northward here, becoming an Uttaravahini, a feature much cherished as a suitable location for a shrine. A temple for Shiva as Komaleeswara was built sometime in the seventeenth or eighteenth centuries here.[6] Local lore has it that flowers for worship were brought to the temple by means of coracles, though there are no vestiges of steps leading to the water here. It is from the biography of Pachaiyappa Mudaliar, one the rich dubashes who lived here in the eighteenth century, that we find out that the river was not always known as the Cooum. Its old Sanskrit name was Vriddha (old) Ksheera (milk) Nadi (river). It, however, is in no way connected to the Palar (Milk River in Tamil) which presently runs south of the city and whose water is relentlessly tapped for the southern suburbs of Chennai.[7] But a theory persists that the Cooum is a remnant of an earlier course of the Palar, which is a river that has been continuously shifting its course over the centuries.[8] As many as 140 temples, many of them dating to the era of the Cholas, survive in various degrees along the river, speaking for its antiquity.[9] Two temples, sanctified by the verses of the seventh-century saint Sambandar, straddle the source of the Cooum. Of these, the ten verses on Thiruvirkolam have repeated mention of the place

[5]Muthiah, *Madras Rediscovered*, p. 437.

[6]Srinivasa Pillai, *Pachaiyappa Mudaliar Charittiram*, Chennai: Sethuselvi Pathippagam, 2015, p. 44.

[7]Ibid.

[8]This theory has been researched to quite an extent by S. Singanenjam, former Director of the Geological Survey of India.

[9]Sudha Umashanker, 'The temples of the Cooum', *Madras Musings*, Vol. XXV, No. 15, 16–30 November 2015.

as Koogam, which gives a clue about the river's present name.[10] The verses on Ilambiyankottur speak of a beautiful grove fed by a stream–our Cooum.[11] It is ironic that what was considered a holy river in ancient times is today a mere drain in popular memory.

The Cooum, at least, exists, but not so the Elambore or North River. In the seventeenth century, it ran along what is today N. S. C. Bose (China Bazaar) Road and suddenly turned east near the present site of the General Hospital and flowed that way for about a mile before abruptly turning south and merging with the Cooum close to where the latter river enters the Bay of Bengal.[12] Its point of origin is somewhat obscure. Towards the end of the seventeenth century, the narrow strip of land that separated the mouths of the Cooum and Elambore was cut by the British and the two joined[13] to form an island immediately south of the fort. The Island, as it is known today, became home to the military, the Gymkhana Club, and the magnificent equestrian statue of Sir Thomas Munro, governor of Madras between 1814 and 1827. The Island is also known for its exhibition grounds where fairs are held regularly.

The creation of the Island, however, marked the beginning of the end as far as the Elambore or North River was concerned. The EIC gave employment to a number of washers, bleachers, and dyers of calico and these had to be accommodated in wide-open spaces close to clean water. The banks of the Elambore were ideal for such a settlement and a colony came up on what was then a thoroughfare by the river. This was known as Washing, and is now Mint Street,[14] and there is no sign of a river nearby. By 1717, continued dyeing and bleaching operations had ruined the waterway and the weavers were all moved north, to a place with plenty of freshwater springs.[15] This became Washermanpet and, as for the Elambore, it was left to its own devices. The river flowed down the western rampart of Fort St George and that meant its course was continuously tampered with. For some time, it ran into the fort, flowing along Charles Street. Later, it served to fill water in the moat. Over time, it just disappeared. Parts of its bed were incorporated into the Buckingham Canal, of which more later, and as for the remaining,

---

[10]Sambandar, Verse 5 of the decad *Uruvinar Umaiyodum.*

[11]Sambandar, decad *Malaiyinar Paruppathan.*

[12]Love, *Vestiges of Old Madras*, Vol. 1, p. 26.

[13]Ibid.

[14]Ibid., Vol. 3, p. 568.

[15]Ibid., Vol. 1, p. 284.

they were tarred over and made into roads.[16]

The Elambore's death was a quick and painless one when compared with the fate of the Cooum. We have noted earlier that a peninsula carved by it became a weavers' colony and another landmass became an aristocratic residential area. Here, in the late eighteenth and early nineteenth centuries, lived rich dubashes such as Pachaiyappa Mudaliar and the chief medical practitioner in the Department of Vaccination, Dr Woodayagiri Singadivakkam Swamy Naik.[17] It is said that these men considered bathing in the Cooum to be a good practice. Crocodiles lived in the river, the last of these being sighted and captured in 1971.[18] One is part of a stuffed display in the Government Museum and is looked at with wonder by those who take the time to go and see it.[19] Could a crocodile have really lived in this polluted river? It did, like several others of its kind, as also varieties of fish. 'In 1949, there were forty-nine species, in the 1970s around twenty-one. Today, there may be none,' write Susheela Raghavan and Indira Narayanan.[20]

The river's bad days began in the nineteenth century. A stream of its size was probably not meant to handle the requirements of a metropolis, both as a source of water and a convenient drain. Its mouth getting blocked with sand became a regular occurrence and this was chiefly because of discharge of untreated sewage into the river. Sludge formed at the mouth and gradually erected a wall of sorts. In 1815, the sand bar blocking its exit into the sea near Flagstaff House was dredged and opened up. This had a terrible side effect—the arrival of a large number of deadly sea snakes upstream, resulting in eighteen deaths within the next two months. With the bar closing up once again, the only water in the river was sewage. By then, the river was referred to as the Cloaca Maxima, comparing it to the principal drain of ancient Rome. A newspaper report in 1861 noted that the sewers at Vepery and Triplicane had discharged so much solid waste over the years that the river had begun sloping backwards![21]

The following is an extract from a medical journal dating to 1849, much of it reading like reportage of today.

---

[16]Sriram, *A Guide to Fort St George*, p. 24.

[17]Historicus, *Sawmy Naick and his Family*, Madras: The Caxton Press, 1951, p. 19.

[18]'Crocodiles in the Cooum', *The Industrial Economist*, Vol. IV, No. 16, 1 November 1971.

[19]Zubeda Hamid, 'When Crocodiles swam free in the Cooum', *The Hindu*, 18 August 2015.

[20]Raghavan and Narayanan, 'Geography, Madras' in Muthiah, *Madras Rediscovered*, p. 11.

[21]V. Sriram, 'Cooum, Cleaned by the British', *The Hindu*, 9 May 2014.

> The river was made a necessity of by hundreds of natives daily throughout the year, and when the monsoon was heavy, and the bottom of this augean stable was thoroughly cleansed, no ill resulted from it; but if the monsoon failed, and the river remained uncleansed, when the hot weather returned, the water became low, and the filth at the bottom was exposed to the heat of the sun, the smell was most offensive and an attack of cholera was the certain result, its only victims being the inhabitants within a short distance of its banks.[22]

Cholera has since been dealt with owing to advances in medical science but not so the Cooum problem. The water is now permanently at an all-time low and so the stench is perpetual.

The river's gift of infectious diseases claimed some high-profile victims as well. Those living close to the river included the governor of Madras, who resided, as noted earlier, on Government Estate, at the head of Mount Road Sure enough, at least two incumbents died within a short time span—Sir Henry George Ward died of cholera in 1860 and Lord Hobart of typhoid in 1875. In both instances, the Cooum was blamed. The latter death was to have some interesting consequences for Madras, as we shall see later in this chapter.

By the 1870s, the Cooum was a 'foul and noisome cesspool'[23] receiving more drainage. 'The neglected and unwholesome state of the Cooum is a reproach to the city of Madras,' thundered a sanitary commissioners' report dated 1871.[24] The same document ended on a note of hope—plans are afoot, it noted, for the diversion of sewage from the river, the cleaning up of the banks, and the deepening of the riverbed. The language could well be that of a report from the twenty-first century, for plans to clean the Cooum are legion. As early as in 1901, *The Hindu* remarked that schemes to improve the river were as old as the fetid odours that emerged from it.[25]

Madrassi Madrigals is a slim book of verses on the city, published by Higginbothams, the country's oldest bookshop, in 1928. It has a poem on the Cooum and is worth quoting from:

> Of dirt and smell your sources make
> No promise; of the latter

[22] *The Monthly Journal of Medical Science*, London: January 1849, p. 472.

[23] Report on Measures Adopted for Sanitary Improvements in India, June 1870 to June 1871, p. 153.

[24] Ibid.

[25] A. Srivathsan, 'Down the Drain', *The Hindu*, 1 April 2013.

Chetput has no complaints to make,
Nor Egmore for that matter;
But thence each step accumulates
Some smell, that strongly carries
An odour that asphyxiates
The air round Bridge of Harris
Chintadripet has ceased to fret
Or fight against the doom
That wraps the Island in a stench
Peculiar to the Cooum
And near the sea, where one would think
Your water might be cleaner
It forms a cess-pit
Oh viscid stream! Oh, smelling flood!
Oh green and beastly river!
In short you are the emblem of
A real Madrassi Liver![26]

The poem may poke fun at the river but it also shows that even in the 1920s, the problem was someone else's. The administration, worried more about the World Wars, the freedom struggle, and the non-cooperation movement had ceased caring about the Cooum. It is also interesting to note that in the 1920s, the water did not smell at Egmore and Chetput. Now it stinks all over the city.

The floods of 1943, mentioned in an earlier chapter, led to a serious study of the river. The corporation engineer, A. R. Venkatachary, came up with the suggestion that a pump be installed at the mouth to prevent the build-up of sand.[27] But the main problem, of course, was the discharge of untreated sewage into the river and the blockage of water flow. The second problem was chiefly due to the insatiable thirst of Chennai. The Cooum is a distributary of the Kosasthalaiyar. The latter's waters are diverted at Tamaraipakkam to the Poondi Reservoir, which feeds much of the city. As a consequence, the Cooum gets almost nothing and whatever water it has is due to sewage and rain. Politicians were quick to see the advantage of such a filthy river. Promises to clean the Cooum were part of everyone's election manifesto. Those in power also saw another benefit—large-budget projects could be announced. But J. P. L. Shenoy, when he was commissioner of the

[26]V. H. Shipley, *Madrassi Madrigals*, Madras: Higginbothams & Co., 1928.
[27]'When cities went under water', *The Hindu*, 10 December 2015.

corporation, did get some improvements done. The first was to straighten the course of the river, especially at places where it was zigzagging. He also had the banks shored and strengthened. Arrangements were made to get seawater pumped in order to get the sludge in the river moving, especially during the summer months. Lastly, plenty of public toilets were constructed in the slums abutting the river. All of this ensured that the Cooum improved somewhat in the late 1940s.[28]

A government committee was set up to study the river in 1953.[29] Nothing much came out of it, though by 1960 the committee itself was upgraded into a 'high-powered committee', chiefly remembered today for its firm refusal to give assent to a scheme for diverting the Cooum at Chetpet so that it could connect to the Adyar, and the rest of its bed to be filled up.[30] This was when the DMK, led by Annadurai, was rapidly gaining public support. Anna and his close associate Karunanidhi were quite passionate about cleaning up the river, with Anna famously declaring that the waterway was a blot on the face of the city. Cleaning up the Cooum was very much part of the DMK's manifesto for the 1967 elections, which saw it capturing power for the first time in the state.

Largely at Karunanidhi's prodding, the first phase of the project was launched by Anna, in his capacity as chief minister, on 19 September 1967. 'On completion of the improvement scheme, the Cooum will bring Madras city pride of place like the Thames of London,' declared Anna. He then went on to add that his 'younger brother Karunanidhi has been pressurising me for financial provision when our first budget was under preparation. He could not rest assured on my statement till he himself saw the finance allocation.' Karunanidhi was then minister for Public Works. Budgeted at ₹118 lakh, the scheme was launched with much fanfare by Anna.

Karunanidhi as PWD minister was most enthusiastic about the project. The river, he declared, would be maintained consistently at a minimum depth of 8 feet and soon big cargo boats and, motorboats would sail on it. The project became a talking point for him and in most press conferences and assembly sessions of the time, he would repeatedly bring up the subject with great enthusiasm. The scheme involved narrowing the width of the river and casing its sides with concrete, this being a necessity for increasing the depth of the water.

---

[28]Narasimham, *Me and My Times*, p. 119.

[29]Srivathsan, 'Down the Drain'.

[30]Ibid.

Certain proposals made by earlier governments were also made part of the project. Noteworthy among these was the construction of several facilities just off the Marina—a gymnasium, a swimming pool, canteen facilities, and, most importantly, a boat club. Eight boating jetties were built all along the river. These were in the best PWD style—modernist with concrete pillars holding up a roof comprising several small arches. The Boat House on the Marina was far more grandiose. It had more than one floor, large verandas that afforded a grand view of the mouth of the river, and a boating jetty. It was completed by 1973. Most significantly, the plan did not envisage cleaning the water in the river or plugging the various outlets of untreated sewage that emptied into the water body.

The entire project received a further fillip when, following the demise of Annadurai in 1969, Karunanidhi became the chief minister. The Corporation of Madras began issuing enthusiastic reports of the progress in the river improvement scheme. Dredging of the river had already been taken up as Phase I of the project, this being flagged off by Karunanidhi in 1967. In 1970, steps were taken to evict all slum dwellers, this being necessary to carry out strengthening work on the banks. This was followed by the installation of a regulator and a sand pump at the mouth of the river. This was an absolute must, given that the Cooum lay south of the harbour and so was a victim of littoral drift, the phenomenon that causes accretion of sand.

The regulator and pump were in place by 1970. A vast team of workers descended on the Cooum to clean the river of rubbish. Rowing boats, power boats, and paddle boats were procured. A gala inauguration of the Cooum Pleasure Boat Service took place in February 1973 with the chief minister and his cabinet getting into the boats and sailing on the river. But, alas, nobody had contended with the volume of sand accumulating at the mouth. Technical difficulties soon arose with the pump. The boat rides that took place between Napier Bridge and Chetpet had to be stopped.

The project may have received due attention if the DMK government had not been dismissed during the Emergency. The rival AIADMK did not want to focus on a project so closely associated with its bête noire. Thereafter, with no functioning Corporation Council owing to the muster roll scandal, and the newly formed Madras Water Supply and Sewerage Board working on other pressing issues, the Cooum project was given up. There were several schemes to improve the river but none caught the public imagination like the boat service. Since then, we have had several politicians declare that they will not rest until boats once again sail down the Cooum.[31]

Thereafter, budgets have become bigger and bigger. In 1987, a major scheme of ₹194 crore was announced and this was followed in 1995 by one estimated at ₹80 crore. The new millennium demanded mega projects and so the next Cooum scheme was for ₹490 crore. The one in 2009 was estimated at ₹1,200 crore.[32] On 15 September 2015, the then chief minister Jayalalithaa launched the Cooum River Restoration Project budgeted at ₹2,000 crores.[33] It has remained mired in bureaucratic tangles, with multiple departments of the government fighting over the clean-up. The river has probably become worse as time has gone by.

In comparison to this, the Adyar presents a picture of being somewhat cleaner. Writing in the 1870s, Sir Mountstuart Elphinstone Grant Duff, who would later become governor of Madras, noted that of the two rivers in the city, 'Adiar is pretty', implying that the Cooum was not.[34] *Madrassi Madrigals* too gave it full marks in a verse dedicated to the Madras sunset, accompanied by a sketch of the Adyar:

When the palms and casuarina trees are thrown into relief
By the wizardry of evening, in her reign so badly brief,
As the cloud-flecked sky is gloried in a myriad-tinted light,
And the voice of day is merging in the whispers of the night;
Only then, Madras, you capture for a golden hour at least,
Just that fleeting, all-elusive mystic wonder of the East!

But that is just an illusion. If the Cooum has problems of poverty, flowing as it does through several less affluent neighbourhoods, the rich have invariably brought about the Adyar's challenges. This river, which is a very important part of the estuarine system that is South Chennai, boasted of leafy banks for a long time. The governors of Madras had their weekend retreat at Guindy, in a vast wooded estate that supported plenty of blackbuck and other fauna. Post-Independence, when, as we have seen earlier, this home away from home became the official residence of the governor and was styled the Raj Bhavan; part of its grounds was made over to the Guindy National Park and yet another slice went to house IIT. Deer still gambol

---

[31]V. Sriram, 'Kalaignar's Boating Jetties', *Madras Musings*, Vol. XXVIII, No. 9, 1–16 August 2018.

[32]Srivathsan, 'Down the Drain'.

[33]B. Aravind Kumar, '₹2000 crore scheme to clean Cooum', *The Hindu*, 21 September 2015.

[34]Srinivasachari, p. 272.

under the green cover, even as monkeys, peacocks, and other animal/bird life live on the trees. The Guindy Engineering College, the Alagappa College of Technology, and other institutions too line the river. At one time, in the absence of a bridge at Kotturpuram, students of all these institutions would boat down the river to board buses at Mandaveli. At the eastern end of the Adyar, on the southern bank, is the Theosophical Society, home to a religion that has its world headquarters in Chennai. This area is also known for its green cover. Politicians have eyed this prime piece of potential real estate for a long while but the Theosophists have asserted themselves repeatedly. If these are all naturally wooded precincts that have managed to retain their trees, the southern bank of the Adyar is also home to the Kotturpuram Tree Park, testimony to what social awareness can do to green an area which is entirely due to an NGO named Nizhal (shade).

All of the above create a green cover on the southern bank of the river. The northern bank, which till 1947 had formed the boundary of Madras city, was where the well-to-do European residents built enormous garden houses for themselves, first as weekend retreats and later as residences. Some of these still exist. The oldest among the buildings on the Adyar still survives and that is Mowbray's Cupola, now the property of the Madras Club.[35] Another is Brodie's Castle, built by James Brodie and now occupied by the Tamil Nadu Government College of Music. Some of the other old residences along the river have private boating jetties, indicating a long tradition of boating on the river. Indeed, one of the many tragedies that periodically visited itself on the occupants of Brodie's Castle was death by drowning in the Adyar. But that did not deter other rowers, and it was in 1867 that the Madras Boat Club was formed. Rowing initially took place at Ennore on the Kosasthalaiyar, on the Cooum, and the Long Tank of Mylapore, but eventually, with all of those water bodies degrading, Adyar became home to the activity. The club moved into rented premises, which it still occupies, in 1891, and gave its name to the entire area.[36]

The Boat Club area and its immediate neighbourhood may be verdant but the river is faced with indiscriminate dumping of industrial effluents, encroachments by hospitals, IT companies, and educational institutions, and steady choking through garbage dumping further south. The continued

---

[35]S. Muthiah, *The Ace of Clubs: The Story of the Madras Club*, Chennai: The Madras Club, 2002, p. 9.

[36]S. Muthiah, *Down by the Adyar: The Story of the Madras Boat Club*, Chennai: Madras Boat Club, 2010.

draining of the Pallikaranai Marsh for real estate development has only added to the river's woes. Boat Club Road itself has been subject to serious flooding in recent times, chiefly because of the way the Adyar has been encroached upon elsewhere. The construction of the airport's new runway has also altered the flow of the river. Discharge of city waste and silting up has constricted the flow area by more than 30 per cent in some places. The Adyar also has industrial estates by its side and many of the factories there think nothing of hiring tankers to dump their waste into the river, this chiefly to avoid the expense of installing and running an effluent treatment plant.[37]

The Adyar, and possibly the Cooum, may see better days but ruined beyond redemption is the Buckingham Canal, which, unlike the rivers which move west to east, flows from north to south. It is, in fact, a national asset though those in charge of it do not appear to think so. In its full glory, it traverses the states of Andhra and Tamil Nadu, links several important rivers and finally flows into the sea near Cuddalore. The brain that envisaged such a waterway, to facilitate movement of goods between the city and areas to the north of it, was that of Basil Cochrane, an EIC official. The first edition of the canal, 18 kilometres of it, was between the city and Ennore, where the saltpans were. This, completed in 1806, was unofficially known as Cochrane's Canal though it was named after Edward, second Lord Clive, governor of Madras between 1798 and 1803. Soon thereafter, it was extended by a further 20 kilometres or so, to reach Pulicat. The government saw the potential in the waterway and, in 1837, acquired it. Work began on extending it all the way to the Krishna River in the north. This became the North Canal. At the same time, a canal from Madras to Cuddalore was dug. When completed, the waterway ran 315 kilometres north and 103 kilometres to the south of the city. Significantly, the two canals were not connected and stopped at the outer bounds of Madras.[38]

The waterway eventually flowed through the city owing to a massive famine that rocked Madras Presidency between 1875 and 1878. The Dhatu and Iswara varusha panjam, as it came to be known in Tamil, would go down in song and literature but when it lasted, it was terrible with over 6 million people dying. There was a huge migration to the city and the local government, led by the Duke of Buckingham and Chandos, then governor, was faced with the task of feeding them and keeping them gainfully employed.

---

[37]'Sidco Industries dump chemical waste into Chennai's Adyar River', *New Indian Express*, 10 October 2018.

[38]Muthiah, *Madras Rediscovered*, pp. 186–188.

Sadly for them, Viceroy Lord Lytton, did not even believe that there was a famine and when on a visit to the city wrote mockingly of the refugee camps.

The local government went ahead regardless with a food-for-work scheme—digging across the city and connecting the two canals. Work continued till almost the end of the nineteenth century and despite protests from various quarters such as the Madras Cricket Club and the residents of Mylapore, the canal snaked its way across Madras. It was named after the duke.

An engineering marvel, the canal runs 1 kilometre inland from the sea. It tapped the water during the high tide and a series of locks running all along its length, facilitated the movement of boats, chiefly country barges bringing salt, jute, pottery, and rice from upcountry. In response to this came up the Tanneer Turai (waterside) market in Mylapore. The brainchild of Sir Vembakkam Bhashyam Iyengar, the first Indian to become advocate general, Madras High Court and also later a judge, he put together a trust that built a market along Royapettah High Road. Goods were brought in by boats and then traversed the short land route to the market by hand-drawn carts. Further north in Triplicane were built warehouses for firewood. Old Firewood Bankshall Street by the canal commemorates this. The word Bankshall is from the Tamil Pandaga Salai (Goods Warehouse). It would travel from Madras to Calcutta where the Magistrate's Court is even now on Bankshall Street.

An entire administrative set-up monitored the operation of the locks, the hiring of boats, and the maintenance of the jetties of the waterway. The canal was not very deep and much of the navigation was by means of towing, this being done by boatmen who walked along on the banks. When the water level was high, this did not demand as much effort as in summer when the canal had very little water. Boat fares therefore went up exponentially in hot weather. Within the city, the waterway proved to be an alternative means of public transport. You could hire a boat and travel from Adyar to Mamallapuram, a night journey that took fourteen hours or so. Two contrasting works, both of poets, survive of boat trips. The first is of Edward Lear, who travelled to Madras in 1873 and left behind a typical Raj-styled memoir, full of complaints, racist comments, and patronizing remarks. The boat journey, according to him, was beastly, made up only by the grandeur of the shore temple at Mamallapuram.[39] In sharp contrast is the beautiful poem on a similar journey in the twentieth century by Bharathidasan. The work takes in all the scenic beauty by day and moonlit night, but it does

[39]Ray Murphy (ed.), *Edward Lear's Indian Journal*, London: Jarrolds Publishers, 1953, p. 178.

not ignore the labours of the boatman and his assistant, towing the vessel along the banks.

A few decades earlier to Bharathidasan's trip, his role model and national poet, Subramania Bharati, evaded arrest for his 'seditious writings' by escaping to French Pondicherry by train. Within a month of his arrival, the publication *India* that he wrote for, relocated from Madras to Pondicherry, its first issue coming out on 10 October 1908. The printing press for the publication was brought in pieces by its owners Mandayam Srinivasachariar and S. N. Tirumalachariar via boat to Pondicherry and reassembled there. The journey was made at night on the Buckingham Canal. Indeed, the waterway could have been tailor-made for this journey—it ran along Triplicane where the publishers lived and from then on to Mylapore, Adyar, and then straight to Pondicherry via Mamallapuram!

The canal remained a navigable waterway till 1965 when a severe cyclonic storm damaged its banks—an integral part of its operation. It could have still been restored but the land by its sides became more convenient for use as slum settlement colonies. The areas surrounding the locks had anyway housed the less well-off and were known as Lock Cheries (slums). These became Lock Nagars and later, as they increased in population, Ma Nagars. There were periodic talks about restoring the canal to all its glory but nothing came of it. Then, in the 1980s, the government committed an unpardonable blunder. The Mass Rapid Transport System (MRTS) was planned and much of its route was on the canal, with the massive piers being sunk into its bed. With that, restoration of the canal, at least within the city, became impossible. It remains a gutter. Ironically, a central government funded initiative is now restoring the canal all along its length, outside Chennai. Has the government learnt its lesson? No. For work is ongoing on an elevated road along the Cooum, with pillars in the riverbed.

A symbolic marker of the Buckingham Canal's demise within the city was the closure and sale of the Tanneer Turai market property. With no goods coming by water, this became just another vegetable market, with commodities arriving by truck and causing enormous traffic jams in the area. In the early 2000s, a real estate developer began systematically buying off each of the trustees of the market. Some protested but eventually complied. The market was demolished to make way for a block of flats. The area is still referred to as Tanneer Turai but many of the newer residents have no idea as to why it is so.

Outside of Chennai limits, the Buckingham Canal remains a navigable waterway, with plenty of greenery along its banks. But it has had to contend with rapid urbanization. Its course runs parallel to the IT corridor of the city. Large apartment complexes and commercial establishments have begun discharging untreated effluent and sewage into the canal. The waterway is shrinking rapidly and is quite likely to end up the way it has in the rest of the city. From there to building on it is but the next step. This is also being aided by the dumping of garbage along its banks. Rather ironically, this narrowing of the canal has come about after the state government has spent a considerable amount of money in widening it to 100 metres along a distance of almost 13 kilometres. Originally planned to be 32 metres wide, it is at many places less than 6 metres. The depth, which was to be maintained at 2.5 metres, is less than a metre now.[40]

On paper, the state is committed to protecting its waterways. It is forever in river-cleaning mode, spending billions of taxpayers' money and all the while its own agencies, departments, and undertakings continue to pollute and impede the rivers as much as they can. This is the feeling that you get when you read the recent orders of the National Green Tribunal (NGT) when it came down heavily on state-owned power utilities for continuing to pollute the city's waterways.

India is a signatory to the Ramsar Agreement that aims to protect water bodies. The Ramsar Convention is an international body that aims to identify, conserve, and make wise use of wetlands. The treaty embodies the commitments of its member countries to maintain the ecological character of their wetlands of International Importance and to plan for sustainable use of all the wetlands in their territories. To what purpose are such agreements if they are not to be implemented at ground level? Of course, Chennai can take comfort in that it is in no way different than any other Indian city; almost all of them have degraded the rivers by the side of which they grew. But it is nevertheless an opportunity lost—these were all small and highly manageable streams which we have ruined.

[40]'Buckingham Canal clean-up to be focus', *The Hindu*, 19 May 2019.

6 | THE SEPTIC TANK

The waterways of the city are presently mere drains as we've seen, therefore, it is appropriate that we look at the sewers as well. As in almost all metros of the world, Madras too began life with open sewers, all of them draining into canals, which, in turn, poured forth their contents into the rivers, which dumped everything into the sea. This was fine as long as the waste was principally biodegradable and in manageable quantities. But even in the initial years of the British settling in, there were problems; the most common occurrence being the mixing of waste with ground water, resulting in epidemics. In fact, the challenge of the drainage of the city emerged long before that of providing protected water supply to it. It is a problem that the city is yet to solve in a satisfactory manner.

Not far from Chennai, in fact, well within the Chennai Metropolitan Area is Uthiramerur, an ancient village that boasts tenth-century inscriptions, which clearly indicate how advanced local area management was at that time. Under the Chola ruler Parantaka I, the villages had the right to elect their representatives and these candidates had to fulfil certain criteria to be eligible for elections. There were departments within the administration that took care of water, waste, roads, sanitation, and gardens.[1] It is ironic that with such a model available, centuries later, the city has not yet come to grips with its problems of sanitation.

We do not know how the villages that eventually formed the city managed sanitation issues in the era after the Uthiramerur inscriptions faded and were forgotten pending rediscovery. The poetry of the intervening years does not speak of such subjects. It would be safe to assume that all waste water drained through open sewage lines, with due care being taken to ensure that these did not contaminate freshwater sources. The rivers must have continued to receive food and other wastes. These were all essentially agrarian villages and therefore took care that food waste was used as manure. Open fields served as toilets and human excreta eventually mixed with the soil. It all sounds good on paper but in reality, there must have been outbreaks of water-borne epidemics in the summer and rainy seasons.

The problem of sanitation must have multiplied manifold once the concept

[1]Romila Thapar, *Early India: From the Origins to AD 1300,* Los Angeles: University of California Press, 2004, p. 377.

of a city, whose population was vast and not dependent on agriculture, grew. Unlike the royal cities of Thanjavur, Madurai, and other places, Madras grew in an unplanned fashion, adding, as we saw, villages to itself over a span of several centuries. Planning for drainage and sanitation therefore took place in several fits and starts, more often dictated by some immediate problem or the other. The same trend has unfortunately continued post-Independence. However, that being said, the history of sanitation and drains in the city is quite interesting, involving some celebrities and several unknown and unsung scavengers.

One of the biggest challenges that Madras posed to those concerned with its drains, and there were certainly very few who lowered themselves to worry about such matters, attention being more on making money for the EIC and themselves, was its flat terrain. Nevertheless, early in the nineteenth century, when Madras had expanded beyond the fort and Black Town, the city did have open channels of masonry in the crowded inner core and earthen drains on the outskirts.[2] Much of the surrounding area, barring the populated villages, was swampy, estuarine land and so eventual disposal of sewage posed no trouble.

The most famous among the open drains was the large channel that divided Black Town into Peddanaickenpet and Muthialpet. This received the sewage of the most populous area of the city and carried it on to the sea, entirely by gravity. Known in its heyday as Pedda Kalvai (Large Canal),[3] it had a history. This was once swampy land named Edapalayam, meaning a village of shepherds, indicating a pastoral past. Over a period, its name was corrupted to Attapallam. Stephen Popham, a British politician and solicitor of the city, acquired the entire patch of land in the late 1700s. People mocked this as a foolhardy acquisition. But Popham had the last laugh. He convinced the government that a high ground named Hoggs Hill was a security risk to the fort and needed to be flattened. The soil, thus dug out, was brought to Edapalayam and used to fill the bog that Popham had bought. The sand was rammed into the space to form a firm foundation and so some of the area became known as Mann (sand) Adi (ram). Popham had the land developed as Broadway (now called Prakasam Salai) and long into the 1800s, it remained a fashionable district of the city.[4] Alongside this space he constructed cross and main drains, all of them open sewers, for taking away the waste of Black

[2]Love, *Vestiges of Old Madras*, Vol. 3, pp. 160–163.

[3]Administration Report of the Madras Municipality, 1865.

[4]Muthiah, *Madras Rediscovered*, pp. 408–409.

Town to the sea. The main drain was the Pedda Kalvai.

Over time, this sewer became notorious. *Our Chronicle*, which was the monthly publication of the 67th (South Hampshire) Regiment of Foot stationed in Madras, in its issue of 1 November 1876, carried a humorous story of a conversation between an army officer and a rat that infested the drain. It claimed that the sewer was 'one of the oldest, most time-honoured and most cherished institutions of the city and materially aids in giving to Madras that pre-eminence it holds over the most odorous of cities'.[5] Submitting a proposal for a comprehensive drainage scheme for Madras, Captain Henry Tulloch in 1865, stated that the drain was a 'mere cesspool, from which sewage cannot possibly escape' and lamented about 'the abominable stench from the mouth of the sewer at the north-east angle of the Fort, which drains a portion of Black Town only. No description can convey to those who have never lived within the influence of the smell of this sewer its overpowering offensiveness while the outlet is open. The fort would hardly be habitable from October to February, or while the north-east winds prevail, if this outlet were kept open the whole day. Fortunately, the sewer is large enough to hold all the sewage which flows into it, for a day or two, so that it is unnecessary to open the mouth, except for about a couple of hours during the night. This is done, too, at a time when the wind is blowing from the city so that the smell may be driven out to sea'.[6]

Topping the mouth of the drain, at the point where it met the sea, was a curious structure. This, according to *Our Chronicle*, was named Kelly's Scent Bottle and was a 'short stoutly-built chimney-looking structure, situated on the Esplanade close to the north-east angle of Fort St George, and not so far distant from the beach'. Which probably means it was close to the present location of Evening Bazaar Road and Raja Annamalai Manram. According to the publication, the structure was the idea of a Dr Kelly, who planned it as a ventilating shaft to carry away the foul smells of the drains of the town. Unfortunately, through want of confidence in the doctor's theory or from other causes, the shaft was curtailed to one-fourth of its intended dimensions. 'The consequence is that under certain circumstances, the area is tainted with the vilest odours in the most concentrated form it is possible to imagine. Various efforts have been made to remove this nuisance but all

[5]V. Sriram, 'Kelly's Drain, Where was it?, Lost Landmarks of Chennai', *Madras Musings,* Vol. XXI, No. 4, 16–30 June 2011.

[6]Hector Tulloch, *Report on a Project for the Drainage of the Town of Madras*, Madras: Gantz Bros, 1865, p. 75.

have been unsuccessful. It seems sacrilege to meddle with it or disparage it in anyway'.[7] The article goes on to state that it was the regiment that was in the fort that suffered the most and one gallant officer decided to bring it to the notice of the governor in a rather dynamic fashion. He bribed the officer-in-charge of the scent bottle to open it when the governor and 'his council were transacting business in the Council Chamber in the Fort, whereupon such a stench arose that the Governor broke up the Council with all haste and betook himself away as far as he could'.[8]

Another account, that of Isaac Tyrrell, has it that Kelly's Drain was the main sewer north of the fort and was also known as Kelly's Folly. According to him, everyone took good care to remain on the windward side when the drain was opened, except Bishop Fennelly who said 'chaffingly that he did not think there was any harm in the smell, but that on the whole he rather enjoyed it'.[9]

In 1906, Kelly's Drain overflowed its banks. The stink, figuratively speaking, reached Westminster, for The *House of Commons Report* for that year records that 'owing to the nuisance caused by the overflow of sewage into the Kelly's Drain the matter was given preference to all other drainage proposals and a satisfactory scheme was under active preparation'. It appears that this scheme went the way of several of its predecessors and successors, for in 1927, G. A. Natesan in *The Indian Review*, Volume 28, was still lamenting that Kelly's Drain, 'familiarly known as Kelly's Scent-Bottle' was not connecting with the drainage through the Cooum 'rightly styled the Cloaca Maxima of Madras'. Evidently, by then, using rivers for discharging effluents and sewage was an accepted practice.

That Kelly's Bottle survived long into the twentieth century is clear from the reference above. By then Madras had a covered drainage system in place, almost entirely due to the efforts of the indefatigable Florence Nightingale. In 1864, she, with the help of some old India hands, put together the Indian Sanitary Report. Among its recommendations was that the cities of India be equipped with drains. For some reason, Madras became her favourite city in this regard. She invited Robert Staunton Ellis, president of the Madras Sanitary Commission (and later chief secretary, government of Madras) to be her guest in London. He was made to visit barracks, hospitals, and institutions

---

[7] *Our Chronicle*, published by the 67th South Hampshire Regiment, 1873.

[8] Ibid.

[9] Isaac Tyrell, *From England to the Antipodes and India–1846 to 1902 with Startling Revelations*, Madras: ALV Press, 1904, p. 144.

to see how the drains were laid.[10]

It was largely at her bidding that Captain Tulloch was sent to Madras to put together a comprehensive scheme for laying drains. The Tulloch Report became Miss Nightingale's favourite weapon in her battle to get Madras its sewage system. By then Madras was very much a benighted province with funds being allocated to it only after Calcutta and Bombay had been satisfied. Thus, while Calcutta and Bombay got their drains by the late 1860s, there was no sign of them here. Ellis' death in 1877 robbed Miss Nightingale of her ally, but she did not give up. She besieged the governors of Madras, their wives, viceroys, and vicereines, prime ministers of England, and even the royal family with letters on the subject.

In Prime Minister Lord Salisbury she had a doughty opponent. He asked her why Madras needed drains. Constantinople had none, he said, and 'managed perfectly well with dogs'. The Madras government, he told her, had funds 'only for imperious necessities'. Articles by her on the terrible plight of Madras in terms of its public health, sanitation, and hygiene poured forth. The government responded that the matter was under consideration. She retorted and demanded immediate action, 'Had it not been so for twenty years? The crime of past governments is to have dallied with these questions for so long and allowed the evils to continue unabated.'

By 1881, she was despondent, as she had no faith in the then governor, Sir Mountstuart Elphinstone Grant Duff. 'God Bless poor Madras,' concludes a letter. But she had a friend in Viceroy Lord Ripon. That year, at his prodding, the government finally ordered work on drains to begin 'at once'. There was another cause for this—in 1875, as we saw earlier, the then governor, Lord Hobart, died due to typhoid. Investigations revealed that the infection had spread due to the open drains near Government House infecting the water supply.

Work on covered drains commenced in George Town and continued at a snail's pace for twenty-five years. 'At once,' Miss Nightingale joked, 'was clearly measured in periods of Indian cosmogony.' Her parting shot was a simple formula for keeping Madras hygienic—'cleanliness of houses, of compounds and cattle stalls, removal of cattle out of houses, cleanliness of streets, but above all—protecting water from pollution.' She also felt that it would never do to mix rainwater with sewage. If only we had listened.[11]

---

[10]Gerard Vallee and Lynn McDonald, *Collected Works of Florence Nightingale on Health in India*, Waterloo: Wilfred Laurier University Press, 2006, p. 525.

[11]V. Sriram, 'How Florence Nightingale got Madras its drains', *The Hindu*, 8 January 2013.

Independent of Ms Nightingale, some efforts were made regarding the open sewers. Thus in the 1870s we read of the sides being lined with cement and plaster, and the bottom being glazed, to aid in the flow. This was the era when dry latrines were making their appearance in private residences. Knowing full well that much of the population would think nothing of throwing its excreta into the drains, houses in the more affluent parts of the city were provided with covered iron pails into which all human refuse had to be placed. These were emptied twice a day by specially constructed carts. In the poorer areas, cleaning was by scavengers—the city's long tryst with manual scavengers had begun. Despite all this, the city remained one of the worst drained, 'with the consequent death rate being among the highest in the country and the rest of the world. The municipality regretted that "nothing" had been done to improve the drainage, "a crying evil which will brook no further delay" and called for "immediate action".'[12] Arriving as a wide-eyed thirteen-year-old in 1886, Dr K. N. Kesari noted that, 'there were no proper gutters to drain out the dirty water. Rainwater which collected in roads had no way of draining out except to dry in the sun. Once in a way, the municipality took necessary steps to let out the dirty water by making gutters in the middle of the roads and covering them. During the rainy season, water overflowed and the roads were filled knee deep with water.'[13] Clearly in the 1880s, gutters were created in an ad hoc fashion, depending upon necessity. This was what Florence Nightingale and Captain Tulloch were striving to change.

Nightingale approved of the report Tulloch wrote which even today is one of the master documents on the city's sewerage system.[14] It made careful note of how the metropolis was essentially flat and just between three to six feet above mean sea level, making it one of the most difficult places to have a drainage system. Having taken into account all the challenges, it called for localized drainage systems, wherein each area would have a sewerage network that would let out all the fluid collected into a nearby swamp that would eventually be developed into a farm. The report, contrary to expectations, did not meet with universal approval. There were some on the corporation council who felt that it was too radical an idea and Tulloch had to defend it.

The report would most likely have been shelved had it not been for

[12]For an excellent summary of the history of municipal services in the city, see Menon, 'Municipal Services', in S. Muthiah, *Madras Rediscovered*, pp. 103–11.

[13]Menon, *Life and Times of Kesari*, p. 34.

[14]Tulloch, *Report on a Project for the Drainage of the Town of Madras*.

the arrival of pumping technology to lift the water. The construction of the Madras Harbour had begun in 1875 and huge pumps had been brought in for the initial work. These were now made available to the corporation and installed at Royapuram. The vice president of the corporation, J. A. Jones, produced a plan based on Tulloch's, with one important addition—pumped water could now be used to flush the drains. Massive sewers were laid in the three principal streets of Black Town: First Line Beach aka North Beach Road (now Rajaji Salai), Broadway, and Wall Tax Road (now V. O. Chidambaram Salai). All of these connected to a main 'where steam pumps will lift the sewage and discharge it by means of a closed pipe and afterwards, of an open channel to a large sewage farm to the North of the Town.' The Royapuram Pumping Station became operational in 1884.[15]

One of the sidelights of this new technology and the creation of sewage farms was the birth of some historic parks in the city, all of them fed by the drains. The Royapuram Pumping Station birthed the Robinson Park. Begun in 1879 and named after Sir William Rose Robinson, the Inspector General of Police, who also laid the foundation stone for the park, it had a fine botanical garden and a large fernery presented by A. Armoogam Mudaliar. It was in this park that on 18 September 1948, Annadurai declared the formation of the DMK. The park is now, therefore, named after him.[16] A park that came up almost entirely because of a sewage farm is May Day Park at the intersection of Chintadripet and Anna Salai. It began life as Napier Park, named after Governor Lord Napier and was entrusted to the municipality in 1879 when improvements were effected with flowerbeds and gravel paths. A favourite resort for the residents of Chintadripet, a congested division of the city, its swimming pool, now long gone, was also popular with the local children. The park was the venue for several labour union meetings, abutting as it did one of the biggest employers of the city—Simpson & Company. It was named the May Day Park in the 1970s. Pumping Station Road, which runs by the side of Napier Park, commemorates the sewage that fertilized the plants and lawns here.[17] But by far the biggest beneficiary of sewage farms was People's Park, now a mere shadow of what it once was.

Madras being a 'city of vast open spaces' the idea of building parks came up as early as in the 1850s, when Governor Sir Charles Trevelyan developed

---

[15]Menon, 'Municipal Services', p. 107.

[16]For more on Sir William Rose Robinson and the park, see V. Sriram, 'From Civilian to Police Chief', *Madras Musings*, Vol. XXVII, No. 5, 16–30 June 2017.

[17]V. Sriram, 'Chennai's Park with a Past', *The Hindu*, 19 April 2014.

the People's Park. At its height it spanned 116 acres, eleven ponds, 5½ miles of track, two swimming pools, and a bandstand. Its entire management was transferred to the municipality in 1866. At the geographical centre of the city, some of its portions housed 'zoological and ornithological collections [and] reserves for football, tennis and other games'. By 1878, a gymnasium had been started inside the park near the Vepery Gate. A band played twice a week at the bandstand, with attendance on Saturdays being 'invariably numerous'. The Madras Fair was held for the first time that year and managed by a Committee of Municipal Commissioners. The park's heydays were undoubtedly in the 1920s, especially during Christmas, when numerous events would take place in its commodious grounds. From 1921, its management was vested with the Health Officer. The Music Academy held its annual conferences here between 1930 and 1935. Far noisier and attracting huge crowds was the Park Town Fair and Carnival organized by the South Indian Athletic Association (SIAA) which occupied the Moore Pavilion and later the Victoria Public Hall, both in People's Park, for several years. The SIAA's fair, notwithstanding a devastating fire in 1886, was an annual feature in the city's social calendar. Chief attractions were Gunboat Jack, who performed daredevil stunts on a motorcycle in a barrel-like enclosure, boxing bouts with King Kong, and last but not the least, a local attraction—rekla (two-wheeled cart) race. The fair was a feature till the 1970s.[18]

People's Park was also home to the zoo, said to be the country's oldest. It was begun thanks to Edward Green Balfour, director of the Government Museum, Madras, who in 1854 persuaded the nawab of Arcot to hand over his menagerie to the museum. The zoo was founded officially a year later in the museum premises. Its specimens expanded to 300 in number within a year. In 1863, the zoo was shifted to People's Park, where it was to remain for almost 125 years.

A gruesome record was that for years the stray dogs of Madras were rounded up by the corporation, killed, and the meat given to the carnivores in the zoo! This was abandoned only in the 1970s following protests by animal lovers when sterilization rather than the culling of strays was adopted.

Located as it was on just 11 acres of land, the zoo began to get congested even in the 1940s. Around the time of Independence, Governor Sir Archibald Edward Nye offered 100 acres of the Guindy Raj Bhavan Estate for the zoo. While this eventually developed as the Guindy Park, the zoo stayed put. Nye's successor, Krishna Kumarsinhji Bhavsinhji, the maharaja of Bhavnagar, was an

[18]Muthiah, *Madras Rediscovered*, pp. 448–49 and p. 453.

animal lover and it was thanks to him that the zoo got several specimens, including lions, tigers, and macaws. The centenary of the zoo was celebrated with éclat in 1955 with a special souvenir and a new entrance in art deco style—the Darwin Gate.

Right through the 1940s, 50s, and 60s, the zoo was a favourite cinema setting. Perhaps its best representation was in the otherwise poor film *Kakkum Karangal* (1965) where an entire song was set in it. A decade earlier, the American film director Ellis R. Dungan did a whole photo feature of the zoo for the corporation.

In 1976, with increasing traffic noise, and the demand for People's Park land for other services, the zoo had to shift. The Forest Department generously gave 1,265 acres of land in the Vandalur Reserve Forest. Work began in 1979 and was completed in 1985 when, on 24 July, the then chief minister MGR declared the zoo open in its new location and named it Arignar Anna Zoo—after his mentor Annadurai. With a further 230 acres land being added to it subsequently, the zoo is one of the largest in Southeast Asia and is a great attraction in the city.[19]

Over the decades, People's Park had to give way to 'development'. On its fringes came up the Central Station, Moore Market, Victoria Public Hall, and Ripon Buildings, all magnificent edifices no doubt, but constructed at the cost of green cover. By the 1970s, the railways wanted more land and there were other demands as well.[20] People's Park vanished, leaving behind just the small but exquisite and quaintly spelt My Ladye's Garden—once the Mayor's garden where the incumbent hosted tea parties and conducted the annual flower show. All that is gone now but My Ladye's Garden still survives, a stunningly beautiful space with some elegant statues titled Prosperity, Flora, Letter Writer, and Venus.

All of People's Park was fertilized by a sewage farm and this had a beneficial side effect—growing of grass for sale. There were doubts initially as to whether grass grown on sewage was good for animals. A report from Bombay was quoted to the effect that not only was it beneficial but milk and butter from cows fed on hay made out of sewage-grown grass was excellent.[21] Thereafter, People's Park became a centre for sale of grass. A huge scale was erected for the weighing of the bales and this was as much

---

[19]V. Sriram, 'Madras Landmarks, 50 Years Ago', *Madras Musings*, Vol. XXIV, No. 11, 16–30 September 2014.

[20]Muthiah, *Madras Rediscovered*, p. 449.

[21]Administration Report of the Municipality of Madras, 1882.

a sight as the animals in the zoo and the birds in the aviary. Tamil songs on People's Park, composed early in the twentieth century, invariably mention this.[22] The grass was cut by prisoners serving terms in the Central Jail just opposite. The sewage farms were a success as long as waste was non-toxic and essentially biodegradable. The largest of them all was between Perambur and Purasawalkam, spanning 37 acres and producing vegetables, the best of which were the ones closest to the sewage lines.[23]

Not everyone was happy, most notably Sir Pitti Theagaraya Chetty who objected to a sewage farm being set up at Tondiarpet, near his home. Twenty years later it was still a bone of contention when Molony sorted it out by remarking to Sir Theagaraya that he was a fine example of good health despite living next to a sewage farm. The veteran let out a hoot of laughter and never referred to it again.[24]

Sewage farms had a fine run for years in the city. *The Madras Gazette*, which had an excellent entry by Shobha Menon on the working of the city's corporation, has this to say:

> In 1949, at the instance of Government of India, Dr R Talati, Sewage Utilisation Officer, visited the city and formulated a scheme where a portion of sewage collected at the main pumping station at Purasawalkam was diverted through a case iron pumping main to the Kodungaiyur sewage farm for which the required land was acquired by the Corporation. 'From 1957, grass, paddy etc. has been remuneratively cultivated in about 200 acres of this farm', a 1978 record stated, noting a Rs. 920,000 income. The scheme for growing grass started in October 1953 on a small two acre plot at a Korukkupet dumping ground. The experiment proving a success and it was gradually increased to seven acres. Grass, guinea and buffalo grass, and lucerine leaves for zebras, deer and birds in the zoo were grown. But with time and with wastes becoming increasingly toxic, waste treatment plants became essential.[25]

The success of the sewage farms notwithstanding, Madras remained 'a town site more favourable to the production of disease. Hutting grounds and slums had been built over tanks and low-lying places reclaimed with street

---

[22]*People's Park Vazhi Nadai Chindu*, Chennai: Chakravarthy Acchukoodam, 1915.

[23]V. Sriram, 'Caring For Chennai, a 100 years of Ripon Buildings', Corporation of Chennai, p. 63 (unpublished).

[24]Molony, *A Book of South India*, pp. 154–55.

[25]Menon, 'Municipal Services', p. 111.

sweepings. Thousands of bodies buried near houses and wells added their quota to the general pollution.'[26] In the 1890s, work began on connecting sewers directly to houses thereby eliminating leakages. In the early 1900s, a more comprehensive scheme was drawn up by J. W. Madeley, which involved the setting up of pumping stations at various areas in the city. This scheme was adopted and work continued in fits and starts, right until the 1970s and beyond. World Wars I and II put the brakes on the implementation and there were budget constraints post-Independence. The city did not exactly help by expanding in areas not envisaged by Madeley in his scheme. The population grew manifold, adding to the strain on the drainage system.

The newly developed areas of the city were the worst off, with housing colonies coming up long before sewerage lines were laid. When the CMWSSB began laying sewerage lines in these new areas, there were problems of space, poor design, and faulty execution. This is why such areas are in a perpetual state of being dug up. There are some other areas that have problems of another kind. Edward Elliots, now Dr Radhakrishnan Road, is an arterial thoroughfare connecting Mount Road, Royapettah, and Mylapore to the beach. This was the route that Chief Ministers M. Karunanidhi and J. Jayalalithaa took to and from office every day. As a consequence, it was termed a VIP road and no sewerage lines could be repaired on it from 1991 to 2015! It helped that this was an area with old and, therefore, well-laid drain lines that required minimum maintenance.

As of now, the city has four disposal sites for its sewage. Of these Kodungaiyur, Nesapakkam, and Koyambedu are densely populated areas and the local residents are up in arms. The fourth is in Perungudi, located close to the ecologically sensitive Pallikaranai marsh. Each of these locations has three sewage treatment plants, making it twelve in all for the city as a whole. The first of these was opened in 1958 at Kodungaiyur. Around 250 pumping stations all across the city deliver the sewage to the disposal site closest to them. Chemical treatment is undertaken at these places with the methane gas produced being recycled into the running of the sewage treatment plants. The sludge produced is stored in site and this is now a major problem as the four centres are running out of space. The water that emerges is treated for faecal coliform and released into the Cooum, Adyar, and Buckingham Canal.

It is not as rosy as it sounds. The city is divided into fifteen zones and of these only eight have underground sewage lines. Therefore, only a part of the sewage is actually collected by the drains and delivered via pumping

[26]Ibid.

stations to the disposal sites. And then there is the sheer lethargy of the establishment. How else do you explain the lack of underground drains in old areas such as Ambattur and Thiruvottiyur? Areas such as these make do with septic tanks or, worse, just dump their untreated wastes into the nearest water body—be it a lake or the two long-suffering rivers and the canal. They, therefore, end up polluting the subsoil water, which is what the city depends on for its daily use![27]

Tulloch, in his scheme, had made it clear that Madras as a city needed to separate its sewage from the storm water. It will be recalled that this was also Florence Nightingale's recommendation. As a consequence, the surface rainwater was always meant to drain via local channels to the nearest water body or the sea. This scheme was never properly implemented. Today, the storm water channels have become convenient outlets for the dumping of raw sewage by residential buildings and office blocks that have come up without official permits and so lack the necessary drainage connections. Others have decided that this is how they can save on payments of Metro Water charges and so have continued to survive without proper drainage. 'How can a city that is so dependent on rainwater not conserve its stormwater by letting it into the nearest lake or tank,' asks Sekhar Raghavan of the Rain Centre. 'It is nothing but sheer carelessness.' As per Raghavan, most streets of Chennai never had access to storm water drains, this being restricted to just the main roads.

It may have ceased to be a navigable waterway, but Buckingham Canal remains a lifesaver when it comes to draining surface run-offs. During the tsunami of 2004 it acted as a crucial buffer that broke the impact of the seawater. When it rains hard in Chennai, the canal serves as a storm water drain. As do the Cooum and Adyar. There are as many as forty-four minor canals, most of them of lengths not exceeding 3 kilometres, which serve the same purpose. Some are named after the localities through which they flow, such as Mambalam and Nungambakkam. Others have more exotic names such as Captain Cotton and Ainsley Canals, the origins of such nomenclature being lost in time. All of these perform the role of storm water drains. But we as people have not reciprocated with similar kindness to these waterways. All of them are encroached upon, dumped with plastic waste and construction debris, and have their inlets and outlets blocked off due to faulty planning. Some have vanished almost in their entirety, aided by those long drought

[27]Priyanka Thirumurthy, 'Where does Chennai's poop go? The stinking truth', *News Minute*, 3 May 2017.

years when it did not rain or flood and so the utility of these canals was not so manifest. The Mambalam Canal was taken over by a misguided NGO in the 1990s, which planned to block off parts of it and construct a football ground on it, so that children from a slum close by could play. That this did not happen was only a miracle of sorts though the canal remains a picture of neglect. The Nungambakkam Canal is now more or less under the control of a private hospital that has built parking lots on it. The Okkiyam Maduvu, a major drain channel in the new OMR area, was meant to flow into the Buckingham Canal. It functioned well as long as the city did not creep up to its vicinity. Now it is a water hyacinth-choked waterway and local residents, who of course did nothing to prevent its degradation, are up in arms, demanding that the authorities do something about it. The Maduvu, like many of its counterparts in other areas of the city, also played a major role in groundwater recharge.[28]

Areas without underground sewage lines depend on septic tanks—underground pits in which the waste is stored. Much of new Chennai gets by on this but it has its own drawbacks. These tanks fill over a long period of time and need to be cleaned out. This is often done by manual scavenging, resulting in death due to asphyxiation caused by noxious gases. Larger establishments with septic tanks are expected to get them cleared by tankers that are then to deliver the collected sewage to the local treatment plant. Many building owners avoid this by getting the tankers to dump everything in the closest water body. It also helps that this is actively encouraged by the real estate lobby. Sludge thrown near a lake constricts it thereby causing it to dry up, eventually allowing for the development of a housing colony on the site.[29] Sekhar Raghavan views it as yet another instance of the builder-bureaucrat-politician nexus. 'The tankers that suck out the contents of the septic tanks are all owned by politicians,' he says. 'Everyone is happy—the builder saves money by not spending on proper drains, the politician has a long-term revenue model.'

Cleaning septic tanks and blocked drains has traditionally been the task of the Arunthathiyar community in Tamil Nadu. The Corporation of Chennai employed several of these people who suffered, apart from the ignominy, several physical and psychological scars owing to their profession. There were huge risks, of death due to asphyxiation, drowning, and electrocution. Most deaths happen because septic tanks are rarely of a standard size, many owners

[28]K. Lakshmi, 'Clean up Okkiyam Maduvu', *The Hindu*, 4 March 2017.

[29]Thirumurthy, 'Where does Chennai's poop go? The stinking truth'.

opting to dig deep to increase volume and therefore reduce the frequency of cleaning. Most scavengers worked with their bare hands to clear drains in the absence of equipment. The trauma of literally swimming in refuse and night soil made many alcoholics. Skin diseases were rampant and some confessed to a sense of being unclean even after bathing in antiseptic after going home each day.[30]

'The very concept is casteist and endemic to cities,' says Venkatachalapathy.

'Manual scavenging is a by-product of urbanization. In the villages, everyone went to the fields. It was when cities developed that such practices came about. And they are inhuman to say the least. Cleaning up someone else's refuse is left to a group of people who are considered beyond the social pale. It is this same callousness that makes our residents throw garbage on to the streets.'

The Supreme Court banned manual scavenging in 2013 but that has not eliminated this terrible practice in Tamil Nadu and, more particularly, in Chennai. The state tops in manual scavenging deaths nationally and around one-third of that tally is in Chennai city.[31] Interestingly, it was in Gobichettipalayam, a town in southern Tamil Nadu, that manual scavenging was first done away with. That was in 1953 when the Gandhian G. S. Lakshmana Iyer was the chairman of the municipality.[32] The capital city of the state evidently did not consider it worthwhile to emulate the smaller town. The corporation denies employing any manual scavengers, though the city reluctantly admits that there are still around 300 doing the rounds for want of any other employment. But NGOs such as India Change Foundation and the Safai Karmachari Andolan put the figure at least ten times this estimate. The compensation for scavenging deaths is fixed at ₹10 lakh by the Supreme Court of India but the city has had a poor record of making such pay-outs. It simply refuses to accept applications by bereaved families. After all, manual scavengers don't exist—on paper.[33]

If the drains are a severe challenge, the problem of garbage disposal is yet another. On an average, the city, according to corporation statistics,

---

[30]Divya Gandhi, 'The first robots clean India's sewers, 25 years after manual scavenging was outlawed', *The Hindu*, 1 September 2018.

[31]Ram Sundaram, 'Stop killing us: Kin of dead manual scavengers', *Times of India*, 25 October 2018.

[32]Akila Kannadasan, 'Remembering a Great Man', *The Hindu*, 25 January 2012.

[33]Simran Bajaj and Anjali Venugopalan, 'The Missing Manual Scavengers of Tamil Nadu', *The Wire*, 16 August 2018.

generates 5,400 metric tonnes of garbage every day. This is transferred, without segregation of any kind, to landfills in what was once the outskirts of the city. Today, these are all well-populated areas. The accumulated garbage is often burnt, leading to protests from the local residents. The city still depends on a pretty rudimentary system of garbage collection and disposal. There is no segregation at source and all the garbage is thrown into neighbourhood bins from where it is emptied twice a day by conservancy workers. In reality, very little garbage is actually thrown into the bin by residents. Rather in the manner of basketball players, people tend to aim for the bin while on the move—walking, riding two-wheelers, or driving. The garbage tends to spill all over and becomes a feast for foraging dogs and cows. It is interesting to note that this attitude of keeping public spaces dirty even while cleaning up one's home is not new. Molony, commissioner of the corporation in the early 1900s wrote of how people would tip rubbish out into the street within minutes of the conservancy cart passing by.

> The output of rubbish from an Indian house is truly amazing. In Europe people accept it as an indisputable regulation that the householder should collect his rubbish into a dustbin, and empty that either into a public receptacle, or into the rubbish cart as it halts before his door. The Indian householder thinks otherwise. Sweepers, who handle dustbins and rubbish carts, are low-caste people, and high-caste people must keep away from that which the sweeper has defiled by his touch. Accordingly, the Madras householder, having collected his rubbish from the home, was wont to fling it into the street. The winds of Heaven blew the fragments hither and thither, and the sweeper chased them. I raged against the practice when I saw the householder emerge five minutes after the rubbish cart had passed his door and redecorate with ashes and plantain leaves the street which the sweeper had just swept clean.[34]

Not much has changed since Molony's time but yes, the nature of garbage has—the leaves and ashes have been joined by a lot of non-biodegradable and hazardous waste.

The collection of garbage was first privatized in the 1880s and since then we have been wondering about its efficacy. There have been long periods when the corporation tried handling it but this was never effective, what with much of the staff supposedly on its rolls being fictional. In the 1990s, conservancy in three zones of the city was privatized amidst much

---

[34]Molony, *A Book of South India*, p. 144.

fanfare but there is, in reality, very little to distinguish between private and corporation-handled collection. The city remains messy. Molony's analysis of the sweepers has remained true for all time, 'They swept well enough so long as I, or someone else in authority looked after them; but I do not think that it occurred to them that there was any reason, other than the whim of an insane master, to sweep at all.'[35]

Of course, this is pan-Indian and not unique Chennai behaviour, but for a city that forever wants to be Singapore, this may not be the path to that nirvana.

We next come to the question of what historically has been known as committing public nuisance, namely, the problems of defecating/urinating in public. This has had a rather interesting and fairly well-documented history in Chennai. In 1860, the city had 160 public conveniences but it was reported that these were hardly used, the citizenry preferring the wide-open spaces. The English did have lavatories but these were what were euphemistically known as thunder boxes—wooden commodes whose pan would be emptied by scavengers. Indian houses soon began having dry latrines—all night soil and excreta would be placed in a covered iron pail outside the house for the 'toties' to take away in the morning.[36]

But defecation in the open continued nevertheless. Addressing the council of the Madras Corporation in 1925, Mahatma Gandhi expressed his horror of the city thus:

> I am not a stranger to Madras. I have lived off and on several occasions in Madras, sufficiently long to enable me to study and understand the sanitation of your city; and it has always grieved me whenever I have walked through your streets early in the morning to see them disfigured.... I cannot help remarking upon the condition of your streets because I think that more than any other city of India, the streets of Madras were at that time disfigured even by grown-up elderly men. It was a sight to which I must confess I was unused before I came to Madras, and often did I feel like taking a broom myself and cleaning up every nook and corner of the streets through which I passed.[37]

In 1930, the government gave orders for every house in the city to be fitted

[35]Ibid.

[36]Menon, 'Municipal Services'.

[37]*Collected Works of Mahatma Gandhi*, Vol. 26, Publications Division, Ministry of Information and Broadcasting, Government of India, New Delhi, p. 240.

with flushed toilets. The majority of the population pleaded its inability to comply, citing non-affordability. The corporation introduced an instalment system of payment and went ahead. By 1933, around three thousand flushes were in place and an interesting corollary was the sharp decrease in deaths owing to diseases caused by water contamination. Rather inexplicably, the corporation stopped attending to public conveniences in the city and their numbers had dwindled to thirty-three by 1942, of which fifteen had been constructed just that year. The one on the Esplanade was described as an architectural marvel in harmony with the magnificent public buildings in its neighbourhood. Three years later, the neighbourhood was protesting about the toilet and especially the stench.[38]

The 1940s, thanks to energetic commissioners such as Shenoy and Narasimham, saw a renewed battle against open defecation. Public toilets were spruced up, provided with water supply, and cleaned twice a day. The police was roped in to round up people committing nuisance in the open and this became a routine sight, providing plenty of material for jokes and cartoons. The practice was given up in 1954.[39]

The number of public toilets rose to 905 in 2013 for a population of 8.6 million. The corporation then began an initiative to install urinals at various public places. These did not survive for long, losing first their doors and, in some cases, the porcelain fittings themselves. In 2018, Dhagam Foundation, an NGO, did a survey of public toilets as part of its Kakkoos-a-Kanom (the toilet is missing) Initiative. The results showed a complete inadequacy in terms of safety, hygiene, and facilities.[40] Clearly, the city has a long way to go. Incidentally, the colloquial term for toilet in Chennai-speak—kakkoos—is a loan word from the Dutch kakhuis (poop house). It is a throwback to the time when the Dutch had quite a presence in coastal Tamil Nadu.

[38]Administration Reports of the Corporation of Madras, 1930–35.

[39]Ibid., 1955.

[40]'Pee in Public Toilets? No Thanks', *New Indian Express*, 30 July 2018.

7 | TO AND FRO

One of the choicest terms of abuse in Chennai-speak, aka Madras bhashai, is the 'vootle sollikinu vandiya' (Have you informed your family before leaving the house?), which, however solicitous it may sound, in reality, drips with sarcasm. It implies—have you told your loved ones that you will not come home. This is asked of anybody—be they on foot or a vehicle—if they cross the path of another amidst traffic. It basically means the offender has decided not to return home, thereafter. Poromboke is a close second—it is old Tamil for land that is common to all but has come to mean anyone who is useless. Saavu graakki (death customer) is another endearing term that, according to the author Ashokamitran, had its origins in days when the city depended on hired horse-drawn carriages, jutkas, for its transport. Most of these vehicles would line up outside the Central Station each morning awaiting passengers alighting from trains. Also, opposite the Central Station is the General Hospital (GH), now named for no earthly reason the Rajiv Gandhi Government General Hospital. Jutkas would also be hired for taking home bodies of departed relatives from the mortuary of the GH. Dead, as opposed to live fare, was termed saavu graakki by the jutka drivers. This became a term of abuse for any person who violated traffic rules, which is practically everybody in Chennai. It is therefore axiomatic that if you drive/walk around in Chennai, you would have been addressed as saavu graakki at least once, if not several times. For that matter, you could have been called several other names as well. If you thought Delhi was the place for verbal abuse and swear words, the Tamil equivalents are pithier. In summer, the heat spurs people to greater road rage and therefore greater heights of creativity in abuse.

With traffic lights invariably switched off and not working owing to poor maintenance, Chennai's traffic manages by itself, the policemen on duty preferring to look the other way and surfacing only if there is a collision. In any case, there are so many traffic violations happening every minute that taking action on them all is an impossible task. The position of the police constable on traffic duty is also an unenviable one—subject to pollution of every kind, bad weather for most of the year, the demands of VIP vehicles as they careen by, and the apathy to traffic rules of the general public. Most drivers have no awareness of any traffic rule, the issue of licences mandating this only on paper. Going by the high decibel levels on the road, you would assume that most Chennai drivers know only how to hoot the horn.

It was, of course, not always like this. There was a time when Madras was a city of vast open spaces, 'its size out of all proportion to its population'.[1] That leisurely age was that of the horse carriage, with the jutka being the most common. There are plenty of accounts of travel by this means, most them highly critical.[2] There was no legroom and the vehicle had no springs. The term jutka (jolt) summed up the experience and many have written about how it felt as though all the joints in the passenger's body were coming apart. The drivers were rude and treated the horses most cruelly. To a child, however, riding in one such vehicle was the ultimate pleasure. The former editor of *Ananda Vikatan*, T. S. Sridhar, who wrote plays under the name of Marina and travelogues as Bharanitharan, describes in his memoirs the joy of travelling by jutka:

> If anybody in the house wanted one, I would run to Gangadhiswarar Koil Street and fetch a vehicle. Riding back I would proudly wave to my friends if I spotted them. True, the dirty sacking made my skin itch but the smell of the grass below it would kindle in me a desire to go on a long journey.[3]

His cousin, the celebrated novelist R. K. Narayan, also spent his childhood at the same residence in Purasawalkam. He wrote about how a temporary grass market sprang up near his home 'for the benefit of jutka drivers, and all through the evening hot exchanges went on over the price of each bundle, the grass-selling women shrieking at their customers and trying to match their ribaldry while transacting business.'[4]

The jutka has long vanished. Triplicane, one of the older areas of the city, has a spot referred to by locals even now as Bandy Mandapam (Pavilion for Carriages), though of vehicle or shelter there is no sign. Just opposite Central Station is where you will still see a few horse carriages, all of them ornate, meant for special occasions and not the humble jutkas that ferried passengers from the station to their destinations in the city. These surviving

---

[1]Molony, *A Book of South India*, p. 146.

[2]See, for instance, the brilliant compilation of travelogues from Tamil Nadu in the nineteenth and early twentieth centuries, *Tamizh Nadu, Noorandukalukku Munthaiya Payana Katturaikal*, A. K. Chettiar (ed.), Chennai: Sandhya Publications, 2012, pp. 62–72.

[3]Marina, *Chinna Vayathinile*, Chennai: Vikatan Prasuram, 2007, p. 62.

[4]R. K. Narayan, *My Days*, Chennai: Indian Thought Publications, 1979, p. 16.

carriages stand at a spot that was bequeathed to them by Lodd Govindoss, a Gujarati magnate of the late nineteenth and early twentieth century.

Meant to be shared, the jutka was in a way the first mode of public transport in the city. The phaeton was yet another vehicle available on hire and evidently a favourite with children, if Marina is to be believed. At the rear of the coach was a wooden platform on which they could crouch, unseen by the driver, and hitchhike. But if noticed, a sharp lash of the whip was the punishment. To avoid this nuisance, many phaeton drivers had nails driven into the plank, the sharp end facing upwards![5]

Bullock carts and horse carriages were the popular means of travel for the well-to-do. Kesari recalls the twentieth-century dubashes and businessmen, most of them Telugu Naidus and Chettys, 'riding in Rekla carts. These have two wheels. There is a seat and children can sit leaning back on the driver. It is light in weight and can pick up great speeds.' Kesari lists several other modes of conveyance, 'Three-wheeled carts were also there. Middle-class people owned these. Rich people, besides using horse-drawn carriages, also used three-wheeled carts for short rides to the market. Then came the Madras Coach, the Brougham, the Bombay Coach, and the Phaetons. Later came Landaus, Landaulets, and Dogcarts (so called because there was a box for dogs at the rear), with two and four wheels.' Kesari spanned the entire set of conveyances as he went from being a young man with no prospects to a prosperous medical practitioner. In the initial days, he walked; then bought a 'Madras Coach, then a Bombay Coach, and thereafter a Phaeton, a Landaulet, and a Landau. I also used the Velur Jatka and a cart drawn by two horses. I bought Australian horses and later sold them for a good price.'[6] Being an avid gardener, he prized horse dung as manure and notes that the best specimens were available at the jutka stand opposite his house on Royapettah. This was just next to the Royapettah Hospital Mortuary—the saavu graakki evidently had some side benefits.

Horse-drawn trams, on 11 miles of track made their entry in 1874.[7] This enterprise failed by 1888 but the idea was not given up. Electric trams were then suggested and a new company was registered in London in 1892. Tracks were laid by 1894 following which the trams became operational, a

---

[5]Marina, *Chinna Vayathinile*, pp. 70–71.

[6]Menon, *Life and Times of Kesari*, p. 38.

[7]Kartar Lalvani, *The Making of India, the Untold Story of British Enterprise*, London: Bloomsbury Continuum, 2016, p. 303.

year later.[8] Chennai was one of the earliest cities in the world to have this facility. The builder baron Thatikonda Namberumal Chetty greatly interested himself in this means of transport and, under his guidance, the network greatly expanded from 1904 onwards, connecting various parts of the city.[9] It rapidly became a popular service, much in demand among the working classes as a cheap means of travel between the suburbs and George Town, which was, by then, the commercial hub of the city and also close to the high court and Fort St George. Among the many who took the tram to the high court was Alladi Krishnaswami Aiyar. While his many co-passengers gossiped, he read law books. In later years, by when he was knighted and had served as Advocate General of Madras for a long time, he would recall his early years when he had put his time in the trams to good use. Sir Alladi would wind up an illustrious career by being a key member of the committee that drafted the Indian Constitution.

The Reverend C. W. Ranson, who ministered in Madras in the early twentieth century and penned deeply insightful essays on the city wrote:

> The city is provided with a rather limited electric tramway service. There were in 1932, 8¾ miles of double track and 7¼ miles of single track over which trams operate. The two main routes run from the south to the north of the city and there are a few minor routes, which operate towards the west over strictly limited tracks. The tramways are used by large numbers of people, but they are quite inadequate to serve the needs of a city, which has spread far and beyond the range of the present tramway system. It may be doubted whether, in a city where many of the streets are inconveniently and often dangerously narrow, tramcars are, under modern conditions, a suitable form of transport at all.[10]

The tram, like the railways, brooked no segregation by caste though, as per anthropologist Stephen Hughes, there was a protest by the upper castes against the employment of Adi Dravidas as conductors in 1908. The Madras Electric Tramway Company promptly capitulated and had them replaced by men from more acceptable castes.[11] But by and large, the trams created a

---

[8]S. Muthiah, *A Madras Miscellany: A Decade of People, Places and Potpourri*, Chennai: East West Books, 2011, pp. 1136-37.

[9]Chettiar, *Tamizh Nadu*, p. 118.

[10]C. W. Ranson, *A City in Transition, Studies in the Social Life of Madras*, Madras: The Christian Literature Society, 1938, p. 21.

[11]Venkatachalapathy, *Chennai, Not Madras*, pp. 39–48.

new social order based on economic status and not circumstances of birth. That it was not so easy is evident when you read that a lottery scheme, based on ticket numbers, had to be introduced to lure people to get rid of their caste and religious biases.[12]

The opportunity for trying out motor vehicles came in 1921 when the employees of the Madras Electric Tramway Corporation struck work. Trucks were pressed into service, plying on the Mylapore-George Town route and this marked the beginnings of bus transport.[13] In the initial years, the service was entirely privately run and that did not mean it was not subject to the usual ills of state-run enterprises. Articles of the era are rife with complaints as to how the bus operators focused only on profits, packed the vehicles with more passengers than admissible, paid scant attention to maintenance and facilities, and raised fares in an arbitrary fashion.[14] But they proved faster than the trams and eventually sounded the latter's death knell.

The tram service bled continuously from inception, more so after the 1920s when the Electric Supply Corporation divested the business and set it up as an independent entity. With money being scarce for upgrades, the service became increasingly ramshackle and by the early 1950s the owners of the Madras Electric Tramway Company became increasingly worried. That it was an English-managed entity only added to their concern. The tram service was suspended suddenly one morning in April 1953.[15] The government responded by pressing more buses into operation. But it was not so eager when a suggestion was made in the Madras legislative assembly that it take over the trams and operate it under a state-run entity.[16]

In the midst of all these advancements came the rickshaw, first hand-pulled, then mechanized, and finally in a new avatar as the motorized autorickshaw. All three had one common feature—the public made use of them and yet complained bitterly about the service, though, in all three cases, the fault lay more in the system. The hand-pulled rickshaw was essentially an idea borrowed from the Far East. It soon became a popular mode of transport, Chennai residents quickly stifling any stirrings of conscience over sitting in a vehicle pulled by a fellow human. Kothamangalam Subbu's *Vaitheekar Pattana*

---

[12]Lalvani, *The Making of India*.

[13]S. Muthiah and K. N. Gopalan, *Moving India on Wheels, The Story of Ashok Leyland*, Hinduja Group, 2008, p. 16.

[14]Chettiar, *Tamizh Nadu*, p. 131.

[15]'Trams Go Off The Rails', *Economic Weekly*, 25 April 1953.

[16]Dr P. Varadarajulu Naidu, *Swatantra*, Vol. 9, 1954, p. 46.

Pravesam is a droll story dating to 1940 and deals with the first impressions of Madras on Vembanna, an orthodox villager. Subbu receives him at the station. Vembanna is shocked at the prospect of boarding a hand-pulled rickshaw.

'What is this,' he asks. 'No bullock or horse and with such a short yoke! Does a turkey pull it?' On being told that a human pulls it, he assumes it was used for the transport of goods. When he is told it is meant for transporting people, he is shocked.

'All right, for the rickshaw puller it is a question of survival,' he says. 'But can a passenger agree to this?'

On being told it is acceptable in the city, Vembanna remarks that like the monkey in the crocodile story of the *Panchatantra* fame, it is best that rural folk leave their hearts behind in the village before coming to Madras.[17]

Fights over customers were common among rickshaw pullers and quarrels with customers over fares were legendary.[18] The rickshaw pullers were capable of some sharp practice too. Subbu's magnum opus, *Thillana Mohanambal*, the novel he wrote under the pseudonym of Kalaimani, has a scene where Dharman and Muthurakku, percussionists in the nagaswaram ensemble of the hero, Shanmugasundaram, accompany him to the city for his medical treatment. Having admitted him to the General Hospital they decide to visit Moore Market. They hail a rickshaw, not knowing that the market is just opposite the hospital. The rickshaw puller charges them a rupee, a mammoth sum for the 1930s, the period in which the novel is set, takes them on a roundabout route and finally deposits them at the market.[19]

Being a rickshaw puller was not easy. 'The rickshaw is a small two-wheeled gig, pulled by a coolie and it is not uncommon to see a wretched coolie struggling along with two heavy adults in his vehicle,' wrote Ranson. 'It is a cheap but slow method of transport and involves a type of human labour which is open to serious criticism. A sensitive person can hardly ride with comfort behind the strained and sweating back of a fellow human being, or feel justified in thus employing him as a beast of burden.'[20]

Rickshaw pullers lived on the fringes of society, earned a pittance, and ruined their health pulling the vehicle. To top it all, there were harassments

---

[17]Kothamangalam Subbu, *Vaitheekar Pattana Pravesam*, Pa Zha Athiyaman (ed.), *Chennaikku Vanden*, pp. 100–104. Translation provided by author.

[18]For a perfect enactment of this see N. S. Krishnan's *Kinthan Charittiram* from the film *Nalla Thambi* (1949).

[19]Kalaimani, *Thillana Mohanambal*, Chennai: Palaniappa Bros, 2000, p. 578.

[20]Ranson, *A City in Transition*, p. 21.

from policemen. In the 1940s and 1950s, rickshaws needed two licences to ply, one each from the police and the corporation.[21] You can imagine as to how the poor men were made to run from pillar to post to get the precious documents.

By the 1960s, the cycle rickshaw made its appearance. This was a more dignified vehicle, for the driver could remain seated and pedal instead of pulling his load. The government began encouraging rickshaw pullers to switch over to the new vehicle. It gave interest-free loans and made efforts to get the rickshaw drivers to form cooperatives. Progress was slow. In 1969, however, when Karunanidhi became the chief minister of Tamil Nadu, among his first acts was to ban the hand-pulled rickshaw and give cycle rickshaws as replacements for free. It was a revolutionary move for its time. The heydays of the cycle rickshaws were the 1970s. Many families had fixed arrangements with cycle-rickshaw drivers for dropping children at school, taking the lady of the house shopping, or the elders to the temple. The rickshawkaran became a family member over time. MGR, who in the late 1950s, had famously gifted 6,000 of these men with raincoats,[22] acted as a rickshaw puller in the 1971 film *Rickshawkaran*. Posters of the hero pedalling away can still be seen at the rear of some rickshaws. The DMK having just then banned the hand-pulled variety and MGR being a staunch member of the party, it was a topical subject and the film was a huge hit.[23]

But competition was already creeping up by way of the three-wheeled autorickshaw, the creation of Navalmal Kundanmal Firodia, and made in India by Bajaj Auto Limited. By 1970, the city had 200 of them.[24] In 2019, there were around 100,000.[25] As the city expanded, it became difficult for cycle rickshaws to offer anything beyond local rides and this restricted their scope. There were besides many hazards associated with the vehicle, owing to its design and its slow speed. The autorickshaw overtook the pedalling variety by the 1980s.

The city is hugely dependent on this mode of transport and yet, the autorickshaw drivers are perhaps the most vilified section of Chennai society. They are held up as all that is lawless. They pay scant heed to traffic rules, are rude, and do not charge as per the meter. They are also often associated

---

[21]Narasimham, *Me and My Times*, p. 136.

[22]R. Kannan, *MGR: A Life,* Gurgaon: Penguin Books, 2017, p. 25.

[23]Ibid., p. 154.

[24]Madras State Administration Report, 1970, p. 240.

[25]Ram Sundaram, 'Auto makes a comeback', *Times of India*, 11 September 2019.

with criminal gangs and come in very handy for politicians and gang lords to send their henchmen to settle scores. The most dreaded example of this was Auto Shankar, a serial killer of the 1980s, who was finally hanged at Salem Central Prison in 1995.[26] He was in many ways symbolic of all that was wrong with the auto driver's world. It was said that he was, in reality, a front for some politicians who were involved in the flesh trade but that was never conclusively established. You name any illegal trade and Shankar was in it. And yet, in the residential colony of Periyar Nagar, just off Thiruvanmiyur where Appar once sang of the bees and flowers worshipping Shiva, Shankar is remembered as a helpful man and loving husband, though nobody denies his hand in the murder of several people. In sharp contrast to Auto Shankar's image is the one portrayed by Rajinikanth in the 1995 hit film *Baashha*. It depicts a golden-hearted auto driver Manikkam (Rajinikanth), and the song 'Naan Autokaaran' (I am an auto driver) has since become an anthem of sorts for the men in the profession. But here, too, there are shades of grey, for the peace-loving auto driver, Manikkam, is, in reality, the underworld don, Manik Baasha, of Mumbai who, for the sake of harmony, fakes his death in that city and escapes to Chennai.

It is true that there have been some auto drivers who have worked towards changing the image of their ilk. K. Kumar is one such person and in 1998 he founded the Goodwill Auto Drivers' Union. An auto driver since 1978, he formed the union chiefly to dispel commonly held notions about auto drivers. Goodwill Auto Stands came up in different parts of the city and members of the union have helped conduct public safety and health campaigns. The city newspapers also carry reports of honest auto drivers who return bags with valuables that have been left behind by passengers. Many families hire autos on a contract basis for taking their children to school and dropping them back. But overall, the image remains that of a rough and ready lot who do not abide by any rules.

The problem lies elsewhere. Auto drivers rarely own their vehicles. They rent them from lawyers, policemen, and politicians, and hence are assured of protection. At the same time, being an auto driver is no cushy job. A 2010 study by the Chennai City Connect Foundation revealed that the ratio of hired to owned autos is 7:3. The fares are revised once in several years and are, therefore, not aligned with the fuel and depreciation costs of running an autorickshaw. As a consequence, drivers never use the meter and charge

---

[26] 'Auto Shankar's Reign of Terror: The incomplete story of the man who shook Madras', *News Minute*, 19 April 2019.

what they feel the market can bear. The meters have their own problems, often functioning erratically. While banks do offer loans for auto purchase, the documents and proofs they require are rarely with auto drivers and so the few that purchase their vehicles do so by borrowing in the informal market at high rates of interest. They eventually end up earning only to pay the moneylender. The same study also revealed that an auto driver needs to carry at all times a total of sixteen documents if he is to avoid harassment by the police! Bribing often becomes the only way out. This is where being in the pay of a lawyer, policeman, or a politician becomes useful.[27]

In many ways, containing the autorickshaw menace brings to mind a similar challenge that existed in Chennai between the seventeenth and nineteenth centuries—that of the masulah boat operator, who was in every way the autorickshaw driver's ancestor. Our city did not have a natural harbour, with the surf near the coast being particularly dangerous. Between 1639 and 1875 or so, all ships dropped anchor beyond the surf, at a distance of almost two miles from the coast. This spot came to be known as Madras Roads. The only vessels that could brave the surf and ply to and fro between the ships and the coast were the native masulah boats. Passengers and goods had to use this form of transport when they landed at Madras or embarked on a sea voyage. Over time, given this monopoly, the boatmen became a law unto themselves.

The two-mile ferry service on the native boats to the shore was fraught with risks. As an account put it, 'the boatmen waited for a big wave, came in on the crest of it till it was spent, paddled hard to get past the breaking place of the next wave so as to be carried by it right up to the beach. And as they waited outside the surf for a good wave they bargained with their passengers.' Those who did not accede to the boatmen's demands could be pushed over by means of an accidental rocking of the boat and their goods could also be roughly handled.

For years, the government tried its best to rein in the boatmen but as a writer put it, 'they were a gang of rapacious scoundrels who knew themselves to be indispensable and traded on it.' In 1839, the government tried to end the monopoly of a few boatmen who controlled the service by throwing open the supply of boats to public competition. But the boat cartel ensured that no newcomer came forward. In 1842, the government passed an Act by which it was compulsory for boats to be licensed. None

[27]Study on the Autorickshaw Sector in Chennai, available here: https://www.yumpu.com/en/document/read/12317543/autorickshaw-study-chennai-city-connect/.

of the boatmen applied for it and went on a strike! They 'defied the law and plundered property under the very eyes of the watching peons.' The government kept enhancing the rates and also published rate cards to bring some control but to no avail. In the 1860s, it even enacted a rule that every boat should have a policeman on board, no doubt to ensure safety of the passengers and goods. It all sounds terribly familiar, doesn't it?

It was finally technology that put an end to the boatmen. The ships became bigger and steam driven, enabling them to brave the surf. And the harbour works began in 1856, concluding in the early 1900s, enabling ships to dock safely. The boatman and the masulah boat became a thing of the past.[28]

Technology may eventually rein in the autorickshaws as well. The arrival of transport network companies such as Ola and Uber has eaten into their hold over public transport. Ola services now extend to autorickshaws as well. Besides these, there are aggregators such as Namma Auto and Makkal Auto that focus only on autos. Their impact has been limited but not insignificant. The autorickshaw will not vanish like the masulahs and it should not either, for it will continue to play an important role in last mile connectivity, between bus/train stations and eventual destinations. It will eventually need to network with mass public transport systems in the city of which at present we have quite a variety, though they are not entirely effective.

For years, the most visible of the government-run transport services were the buses. Post-Independence, Madras was the first city of India to nationalize bus services, till then the purview of private operators. The decision was taken in October 1947 and the process completed by July 1948. The running of the service was now entrusted to the State Transport Department, which had, as its headquarters the handsome Transport House at the edge of the erstwhile governor's Bodyguard Lines on the Island. With the governor and his bodyguards moving away to Guindy, the space also came in handy for a large bus depot behind Transport House. Thereafter, bus services in the city steadily expanded. In 1972, the DMK government announced the formation of the Pallavan Transport Corporation, which from that time ran the city transport service. Transport House became Pallavan House. The DMK ushered in a naming spree, for transport corporations were formed in other cities and districts of the state, each commemorating local heroes, freedom fighters, historic dynasties, and political leaders. But there were always more candidates for the names than the number of transport corporations. This led to protests and rioting. More and more transport corporations had to

---

[28]V. Sriram, 'The autorickshaw's ancestor', *The Hindu*, 22 November 2014.

be created to appease the various factions. Thus Chennai saw its transport services bifurcated between the older Pallavan and the later Dr B. R. Ambedkar Transport Corporation. It was in 1994 that the government, with the DMK in power once again, decided that the only way forward was to bring in functional nomenclature. The two companies in Chennai were renamed as Metropolitan Transport Corporations (MTC) I & II respectively.[29]

The MTC bus service is said to be one of the more efficient ones in the country. Buses arrive at their regular stops on time. Around 55 lakh people travel by the service every day, which is quite an achievement.[30] But all of this comes at a cost. The city has routinely topped in accident statistics when it comes to collisions caused by state-run buses. In 2012, the number of fatal accidents involving a public transport bus was thirty per year in Mumbai, eighty-three in Delhi, and 112 in Chennai. In 2015/16, the number of accidents (not fatalities alone) involving MTC buses was 1,500 as compared to around 750 by other state-run entities across India. The MTC got around this by claiming that it had a very transparent reporting mechanism which the other transport corporations did not have. In 2018/19 there was a marginal decline in the accident and fatality statistics.[31]

One of the most common reasons for accidents is over-speeding on the part of the MTC buses. Using their sheer size to their advantage, these vehicles do not seem to obey any traffic rules. They jump signals, bulldoze their way through traffic, and pay scant heed to the protests of other road users. The police, long frustrated in their attempt in bringing any errant MTC driver to book, have chosen to give up and watch with indifference. One of the most scary experiences in the city is to stop at a traffic light and suddenly realize that an MTC bus is inches away from your rear, with a driver honking impatiently, asking you to move. Action against drivers rarely happens, as the powerful unions make sure their members are protected. Other cities have installed speed-governors in their buses, which set off alarms each time the bus exceeds 50 kmph in speed. In Chennai too these were installed amidst much fanfare but they are functioning on very few buses now. In short, being inside an MTC bus is perhaps the safest option. Not everybody, however, gets to be inside the bus. Managing with a fleet

[29]History of metropolitan transport corporation Chennai, *Shodhganga*, available here: https://shodhganga.inflibnet.ac.in/jspui/bitstream/10603/123588/9/09_chapter%202.pdf/.

[30]Aruna Natarajan, 'Why MTC ridership in Chennai fell by 20 crores in a year', *Citizen Matters*, 31 August 2019.

[31]Ram Sundaram and R. Aditi, 'MTC cuts accident rate', *Times of India*, 12 July 2019.

of 4,000 vehicles to carry 55 lakh passengers is no easy task[32] and this results in overcrowding during peak hours, resulting in footboard travellers. There are others who do this for cheap thrills. Fatalities are common in both instances. Most MTC buses tilt to one side almost all the time, owing to overcrowding.

The maintenance of most MTC buses is said to be abysmal; a famed instance of a bus toppling over the city's iconic Gemini Flyover was attributed, at least by the driver, to a sudden buckling of his seat even as he negotiated a sharp bend. A recent report had it that the MTC has fared very poorly in recruiting technical staff. Against a prescribed ratio of 1.25:1 of technicians to buses, MTC manages with 0.8:1 and some depots have only two technicians when the required number is twelve. Added to this is the high salary structure of the MTC, which translates to ₹3,000 per bus per day. That leaves very little for maintenance. And with buses during peak hours carrying two to three times the permitted number of passengers, breakdowns are more frequent. Despite receiving central government aid for upgrading its maintenance facilities, MTC has very little to show for it.[33]

MTC bus drivers and conductors are legendary for their rudeness, which of course is partly due to the daily stress they face dealing with overcrowding. And there are irate passengers who often vent frustrations from elsewhere on the crew. Besides these, the staff faces other situations—eve teasing, picking of pockets, spontaneous quarrels, and even the occasional rushing to hospital of a woman passenger who goes into labour or an elderly traveller who develops heart complaints. On one occasion, a newly-born baby was discovered in a gunny sack inside a bus. Political protests often target MTC buses—they can be stoned or even set on fire. Being on duty when such incidents happen can be nerve-racking. And then there were the dreaded Bus Day celebrations—a unique Chennai phenomenon. What had ostensibly begun as a thanksgiving by students to MTC drivers and conductors for ferrying them to and from college became, over the years, an opportunity for display of rowdy behaviour. It had become the practice among students of the Arts College, Nandanam, Vivekananda College, Mylapore, Presidency College, Chepauk, Pachaiyappa's College, Chetput, and the Law College, Esplanade to hijack buses on Bus Day, force passengers to get off, and then direct the driver to take the bus

[32]Horeb Moses, 'Chennai Transport-Related Agencies', Citizen Consumer and Civic Action Group, 10 July 2019.

[33]'First in Bus Accidents, a dubious status for Chennai', *Madras Musings* Vol. XXII, No. 7, 16–31 July 2012.

on a route of their choice. Many would clamber on to the roof of the bus, shout slogans, make obscene comments at women passers-by, and bring traffic to a halt. Closely allied to the Bus Day celebrations, and often the biggest cause of unrest was the concept of Route Thala—the informal election of one student as the alpha male of the bus route, based on his prowess to take on others in combat.

There were many calls for a ban on such events but with the police turning a blind eye owing to political support, nothing was done. The police would in fact escort the buses along the entire route, ostensibly to regulate traffic but more to keep an eye on the students and ensure that the situation did not get out of hand. In 2011, the celebration turned violent at one of the colleges and the high court took notice, following a PIL. The court came down heavily and banned Bus Days thereafter.[34] Of course, this was not to the liking of the students who took it as an affront to their freedom. Pachaiyappa's College witnessed unrest in 2016 even as students 'flayed the bus ban'. One of those in the forefront attempted suicide—a standard Tamil protest tactic—and was rushed to a hospital and declared stable.[35]

It is no wonder that the health of many MTC drivers is in a precarious state. Many work overtime as well with very little scope for rest. In 2018, driver Sundararaj, started on his route from Avadi with forty passengers on board. Within minutes of suffering a heart attack en route, he steered the vehicle to safety before dying.[36] The same fate befell Sarveswaran a year later.[37] Both were victims of lifestyle and occupational stress.

Bus journeys can also be occasions for warmth and affection. Regular passengers form friendships with drivers and conductors. The residents of Melappedu near Avadi have been organizing an annual event for years now where they honour the drivers and conductors of route 61A, the only bus service that covers their colony. The bus is cleaned by the locals on the day of the event and new clothes are given to the crew, purchase of which is crowd-funded.[38]

Unlike Mumbai, Chennai does not have a train service forming a sort of transport backbone. The local trains skirt the periphery of the city but

---

[34] A. Subramani, 'High Court bans bus day celebrations', *Times of India*, 3 March 2011.

[35] 'Pachaiyappa's students flay Bus Day ban', *Daily Thanthi*, 6 July 2016.

[36] 'MTC driver suffers heart attack while driving, manages to halt safely', *Deccan Chronicle*, 7 March 2018.

[37] Vivek Narayanan, 'Driver who always went the extra mile', *The Hindu*, 12 February 2016.

[38] D. Madhavan, 'This MTC bus takes centre stage', *The Hindu*, 27 October 2015.

serve over 11 lakh people—a mere fraction of what they could have catered to had the network kept pace with the city. In sharp contrast is the Mumbai suburban, whatever its drawbacks, handling 75 lakh passengers a day. The first city in India to have an electrified suburban railway network, Chennai's system began in 1931, chiefly to cater to people travelling between the harbour and the then southern periphery of Tambaram. Since then the railway network has grown but it has not managed to keep up with the city's expansion. As a consequence, its usage has actually dropped over the years. Lack of interconnectivity between the railway services has also been a major bane. The three rail corridors—Chennai Beach to Tambaram, Chennai Central to Tiruninravur, and Chennai Central to Minjur—are completely independent and in no way connected to road transport, a throwback to the 1930s when roadways were considered a competition to the state-controlled railways.[39] If that is a tragedy of history, what is sad is that the Mass Rapid Transport System (MRTS), developed in the 1980s, was planned the same way, with no interconnectivity of any kind with bus transport networks.

The MRTS, originally planned to link Beach Station, Velachery, St Thomas Mount, Villivakkam, and Ennore, was conceptualized in the 1970s. Work, however, did not begin till 1984 and proceeded thereafter at a leisurely pace till 2007, with much escalation of cost. Today, it runs between Velachery and Beach Stations, the fate of the extension to St Thomas Mount being uncertain owing to land acquisition issues and the rest of it abandoned owing to the Metro Rail project. When planned, it was estimated to carry 6 lakh passengers a day but at present handles around 1 lakh chiefly because of several deficiencies in its execution—the most important being the lack of last-mile connectivity with other forms of transport.[40] It, however, enjoys the distinction of being India's first elevated rail network and therefore has the other distinction—of being the only functioning transport service when the city was almost submerged in 2015.[41]

If the MRTS is a well-planned service that was bungled in execution, its stations are another matter altogether. When the MRTS stations were built, the CMDA had retained the right to develop the 'air space', that is, the space above the station structures, which were the responsibility of the railways. In 2007, the CMDA announced that it was preparing plans with the help of

---

[39] B. Anbuselvan, 'MTC's loss not big gain for suburban railway', *New Indian Express*, 11 May 2019.

[40] 'Waiting for the MRTS Metro Link', *Madras Musings*, Vol. XXV, No. 24, 1–15 April 2016.

[41] 'Chennai Floods, MRTS a lifeline to many', *The Hindu*, 6 December 2015.

consultants to develop at least one lakh square feet of space above each of the three stations at Taramani, Perungudi, and Velachery. These were to house IT offices and shopping malls. It was reported that the CMDA was basing its plans on cities such as Hong Kong and Tokyo where similar services are provided above railway stations. Nothing has come of these plans so far and the stations, built as large structures, no doubt with a view to accommodate these ambitions, are mere shells, lacking even the most basic amenities. They also suffer from horrible maintenance. Rusted railings, staircases that lead nowhere, elevator shafts that are unguarded, lack of signage, and very poor illumination are their hallmarks.[42]

Perhaps having learnt from this, the Metro service, partly underground and partly above, has very well-designed stations, though purists have found fault with their execution as well. The service is still in its early days, with only Phase I in operation, but it may well hold the key to a well-integrated transport system for the city. But even the Metro will need to integrate itself with other transport systems if it needs to become truly effective. At present, however, the service has other problems—even in its first phase it is quite some years behind schedule. That has pushed up the cost of tickets which has in turn affected patronage. With work yet to begin on Phase II, it may be a decade before the city has an effective metro rail service, by which time the population may have gone up considerably.

It was with a view to enable linking up of all the transport systems in the city that the Chennai Unified Metropolitan Transport Authority (CUMTA) was set up following legislation in 2012. Two years later, it was announced that the CMDA would be in charge, which, going by the past history of that august body, meant that no earth-shaking changes could be expected. The mandate was, however, truly impressive. The state government wanted Chennai to follow the London model. The CMDA, on behalf of CUMTA commissioned a study on integrating the multiple modes of transport in the city. Four international consultants were brought in to study this, which included all modes—train, bus, and the metro. On the anvil was the setting up of a common ticket and fare structure to facilitate seamless commuting, something that is in existence in most world-class cities today. Nothing emerged thereafter and the various transport systems operate in independent silos. Presently the tussle is about who can head CUMTA. The CMDA wants its chief planner to do so but the bureaucrats cannot imagine reporting to someone who is not from the IAS. There matters rest, several years after

[42]Liffy Thomas, 'MRTS stations suffer for want of maintenance', *The Hindu*, 12 March 2013.

the body was mooted.[43]

It is because of this lack of coordination that the dependence on private vehicles is very high in the city. Around 1,500 new vehicles, cars and two-wheelers, get on to the road in Chennai every day. Overall, the city has around 55 lakh vehicles and the number is only increasing. With road space remaining the same, especially in the core city and the newer areas not planned any better, traffic speeds have decreased and are now at around 12 km/hour on an average. Vehicular movement being the most visible aspect of traffic management and private vehicle owners being the most vocal in their criticism on social and mainstream media, the management of road space is completely skewed in their favour. Pedestrian walkways have shrunk where they have not vanished altogether. Many roads now sport flyovers or grade separators that only serve to shift the congestion from one end to the other. The spaces beneath and on the sides of these structures are neglected and often become rubbish dumps.[44]

Cycling, a popular mode of transport from the 1920s onwards, received a boost with the setting up of the Murugappa Group's TI Cycles in Ambattur in the 1950s. Today, only the most intrepid, or those who have no other option, cycle in the city. Every once in a while, the government announces plans to launch cycling tracks all over the city. There are also plans to launch cycle banks at various stations from where they can be hired and used on furnishing of a smart card. These have now made a beginning but suffer from want of exclusive cycle lanes. Cycling to spots outside Chennai, however, is now a popular mode of recreation with people forming groups and setting out each weekend, on stylish bikes and in the latest protective gear. They travel to Pulicat, Mamallapuram, Sadras, and other places and return, pleasantly exhausted. It is an elitist activity, more for recreation than with a purpose but there is always the one interesting exception. Cycling Yogis, founded by Ramanujar Moulana, is as interesting as the combination of the two words that make up his name. This group documents the places it visits and has, over the past four years, been publishing booklets that map cycling trails within the city and outside.

The common people walked from the very early days till at least the 1960s. In the *Vaitheekar Pattana Pravesam* story by Kothamangalam Subbu, the two characters proceed to a bus stop where they wait for ages.

[43]'Creating Urban Transport Chaos', *Madras Musings*, Vol. XXIX, No. 18, 1-15 January 2020.

[44]'Expansion alone will not reduce congestion', *Madras Musings,* Vol. XXVII, No. 21, 16–28 February 2018.

Vembanna: 'What are we waiting for?'
Subbu: 'For a motor.'
Vembanna: 'How far is your house?'
Subbu: 'About a mile.'

'It is no use blaming you. It is the company you keep that has corrupted you, making you wait for a bus when you should be walking briskly in the morning. Come along, you lazybones,' Vembanna thunders as he proceeds on foot, his luggage perched on his head.[45]

There are plenty of *Vazhi Nadai Chindus*—poems that describe the sights and sounds of the city. The *Arubathu Moovar Chindu,* for instance, describes the journey of a man and his beloved, who, having set out from Mullah Sahib Street in George Town, walk all the way to Mylapore to see the famed, eighth-day procession of the Kapaliswarar Temple's annual festival.[46] The nineteenth-century Sanskrit work *Sarva Deva Vilasa* shows Madras as seen by two poets, Vivekin and Ativivekin, as they walk around the various localities and attend soirees at the residences of dubashes.[47] The dubashes themselves travelled in some style, either on caparisoned elephants or in horse carriages or borne in palanquins. Some were given the privilege of being accompanied by drummers and having umbrellas being held over their heads.[48] Historically, it was customary for really important people to be escorted by torchbearers, no matter whether it was day or night!

In the last couple of years, the government, having realized that it had pushed pedestrians to the very edge of the road, so to speak, has been trying to make amends. Work is ongoing on reclaiming pedestrian spaces, with an attempt at creating a non-motorized transport network in the core city. Footpaths are making a comeback. But Chennai today is still a walker's nightmare. Shops, electric transformers, and junction boxes, hawkers, kiosks, and vehicles encroach upon the sidewalks. The pedestrian, therefore, walks on the road, competing for space with vehicles. Crossing roads is a greater challenge, most people taking a chance whenever they see a break in traffic

---

45 Subbu, *Chennaikku Vanden*, pp. 100–4. Translation by the author.

46 V. Sriram, 'The Ballad of Arupathu Moovar', *Madras Heritage and Carnatic Music*, 5 April 2012.

47 Dr V. Raghavan, *The Sarva Deva Vilasa: Edited with critical introduction and notes*, Madras: The Adyar Library and Research Centre, 1958.

48 A. R. Ingram, 'Mayor and the Corporation of Madras', *The Madras Tercentenary Commemoration Volume*, p. 179.

flow. With pedestrian crossings being few and far between and very few vehicles stopping to let people walk across, most pedestrians take the shortest route, often climbing over four-foot-high barriers to get to the other side. Which is why 'vootle sollikinu vandiya?' is heard so often.

8 | HIGH ART TO HUMDRUM

'Are there public buildings in this city that we can be proud of, that are worth visiting or showcasing in postcards?' The truth is, not many. The list of worthy civic buildings in Chennai is as short as a lizard's tail—and includes only buildings from the past' thundered an article in *The Hindu* in 2012.[1] The situation has not changed for the better since. But we did begin very well.

The ancient villages that made up Chennai followed the conventional pattern of central temple or two, standing at the edge of a tank, with the houses fanning out in concentric streets. There were well-demarcated areas for shops and professional services. Some of the localities that retained this character till recent times were Mylapore, Triplicane, Thiruvottiyur, and Thiruvanmiyur. The houses invariably had tiled or thatched roofs, mostly of one storey. Access from the street was by a narrow and short flight of steps onto a transverse passage, the veranda, which had raised stone platforms. This was where most visitors were met with. Then came the main entrance, usually richly carved and made of teak or rosewood. A vestibule, that ran till the rear entrance of the house, began from here and cut across a central courtyard that was open to the sky. Being naturally ventilated, it cooled the house—a vital necessity at a time when air-conditioning was unheard of. Important family events—coming-of-age ceremonies, weddings, funerary rites—took place in this courtyard. In the nights, the courtyard and the vestibule doubled up as communal sleeping areas, for the concept of private bedrooms did not exist. There was one bedroom for the head of the family, and there was the other bedroom, which sons and their respective wives could retire to as per a rota system that the mother-in-law had absolute control over. To the rear of the courtyard were the domestic offices and then came the backyard, with the well, a small patch of garden, and a covered bathroom alongside. The toilet was situated some distance away, at the rear end of the house, with a door opening on to the backstreet. The first floor, if it existed, was accessed by two narrow flights of stairs, one from the entrance passage and the other from the middle courtyard. The upper storey largely repeated the pattern of the ground floor, with a veranda in front and a large central room, which overlooked the courtyard below. There was usually no construction beyond this on the first floor. Such houses shared common walls and it was possible

[1]A. Srivathsan, 'A dearth of well-designed buildings', *The Hindu*, 29 October 2012.

to leap from building to building and reach the end of the street. The top terrace was reached by a ladder opening on to a hatch in the tiled roof. The upper storey facade invariably sported decorative motifs—a pediment or a dormer window or the plaster frieze of a favourite deity. The merchant princes of Black Town too followed the same pattern in their residences, with one important change—the street-facing section of the lower storey was made over to shops or warehouses. No matter how wealthy the owner was, the houses remained spartan in style.

All walls were painted white, a necessity in such a hot climate, with the wood painted green or varnished. The buildings were made of lime mortar and the finish, known as Madras chunam, was a fine plaster that when polished was as smooth as marble and had a shine like it.[2] The floors were of local stone and some rooms were finished with red/green/blue oxide pigment. The ceiling, if flat, was of the Madras terrace variety—wooden joists resting on steel girders and the spaces in between filled with brick and plaster. The timber in the roof kept the temperature down, as did the plaster. This was how houses were constructed in this region for centuries and almost till fifty years ago. Today, much of the materials referred to above cannot be had for love or money. As for such building techniques, they have long been forgotten.

Temples abounded but unlike the present skyline where it is hard to imagine a shrine without a tower, most of the temples of the city appear to have been constructed along simple lines—single or double circumambulatory passages with a rectangular arched doorway leading to the flagstaff and the inner sanctums. The last named were capped with domed vimanas surrounded by statuary in stucco. Barring the ancient temples, later constructions were funded through local patronage. In the early days this meant the dubashes; later it was members of certain communities or residents of a particular area. Most temples expanded gradually, even as devotees endowed the precinct with more sub-shrines. In the twentieth century, increasing prosperity made sure most old temples acquired soaring gopuras. The Kapaliswarar Temple's east-facing tower was constructed in 1910 during the trusteeship of the noted playwright Pammal Sambanda Mudaliar. Much of the money for this came from public donations.[3] Those living in the newer areas built temples as well. Sadly, many of the new shrines are nothing but encroachments on public space, a pliant administration being reluctant to take any action.

---

[2]Dr A. Raman, 'Marble-like chunam in Madras Presidency', *Madras Musings*, Vol. XXIX, No. 20, 1–15 February 2020.

[3]Pammal Sambanda Mudaliar, *En Suyacharitai*, Sandhya Publications, 2012, p. 53.

The nawabs and their kin brought in the mosques. Triplicane, Mount Road, and Saidapet areas abound with shrines endowed by Muslim nobility. Of these, the Big Mosque in Triplicane, built in 1795, is perhaps the best known. Constructed with granite and lime mortar, it is a single-storey structure with a multi-arched entrance leading to the prayer hall. A flat roof, topped with a squat dome and two minarets completes the ensemble.[4] Inside the prayer hall is a chronogram written by Raja Makhan Lal Khirad, the Hindu minister of Nawab Muhammad Ali Wallajah.[5] The Thousand Lights Mosque on Mount Road is now thoroughly modernized in the Dubai style but the neighbouring prayer hall is a thing of beauty. The name, however, remains a mystery.

Surprisingly enough, there are no edifices such as palaces or administrative offices in the city from an era preceding colonial times. This is true of much of Tamil Nadu—there are no vestiges of such structures from the time of the Pallavas, Cholas, or Pandyas. The common explanation given is that these edifices were probably built of perishable material. But this posed a huge challenge to succeeding conquerors when they searched for suitable idioms that they could appropriate to establish the legitimacy of their rule. The medieval rulers, as is evident from the Nayak and Maratha palaces in Thanjavur, Madurai, and Gingee, used an amalgam of Hindu and Islamic elements. But the search for acceptable styles that exuded power became more acute once the British came along.

Given the wealth of Tamil building traditions and those of the Muslims from further north, the English adapted them for the more utilitarian constructions. The houses within the fort were all of brick and lime plaster, the residences of the more wealthy being on the eastern face where they could enjoy the sea breeze.[6] The soldiers camped in wretched barracks on the western side, with very little scope for ventilation. The warehouses in the fort were all built with high ceilings supported by tall pillars. Some of these structures survive even today, often denied even basic maintenance. They are testimony to the skills of the native builders and artisans who worked under British supervision. In the fort is St Mary's Church, begun in 1678 at the behest of Governor Streynsham Master. It is the oldest Anglican church east of the Suez Canal. Designed by William Dixon, its most impressive features

---

[4]K. Kalpana and Frank Schiffer, *Madras, the Architectural Heritage: An INTACH Guide*, Chennai: INTACH, 2003, p. 242.

[5]V. Sriram, 'Northern Origins of a Southern Temple', *The Hindu*, 29 August 2014.

[6]Sriram, *A Guide to Fort St George*, pp. 84–88.

are its four-feet-thick walls, meant to withstand cannonade. The roof, which is wagon-vaulted, is also meant to be cannon-proof.[7] Most of the EIC structures of this era follow the same pattern—thick walls, masonry roofs, and minimum use of wood from fear of fires. That this style of construction survived well into the 1830s is evident from Ice House, built near the beach in 1838 to store ice brought all the way from the United States of America. Over the years, much has been added to it. Today, it is a memorial to Swami Vivekananda who spent a week in it in the 1890s, at which time it was a private residence.

The construction of the Ice House marked the apogee of the EIC, that had eliminated all threats to its success. The increasingly confident English began moving out of Fort St George, building enormous garden houses for themselves in far-flung areas of what would eventually become Madras city. Very often, entire roads had to be laid to reach just one stately home and these were named either after the building or its best-known occupant. Thus Mowbrays (now TTK) Road, which stretches all the way from the Music Academy to Raja Annamalai Puram, took its name from the fact that it stopped just short of George Mowbray's residence, now the Madras Club. Wheatcroft's Road in Nungambakkam was named after a house that stood there. Wallace Garden in the same area takes its name from a vast residence that still stands there, hemmed in by later constructions. These houses, set in enormous gardens, were technically bungalows but very few sported the curved eaves that define that name. The garden houses, as they were also known, had flat or sloping roofs and, as for the façade, classicism became the norm, with large verandas and porte-cocheres sporting pillars with Ionic, Doric, Corinthian, or composite capitals. It was almost as though the conquerors were trying to distance themselves from local idioms, all of which they had so enthusiastically embraced just a few decades earlier. But even here, the mode of construction was entirely Indian—the material used was local timber, plaster, tile, and brick.

Public buildings began to be constructed in the prevailing styles of Europe, with some concessions to local climate. This is best illustrated in the building of St Andrews Kirk in Egmore. The architect, Major Thomas Fiott de Havilland, had to transplant the James Gibbs design of St Martin-in-the-Fields, London, to Madras, but he had to rely on local techniques to build it. The design of the kirk called for a dome. The technology of putting up such a structure was fairly alien to those in charge and it was felt that

---

[7]Ibid., p. 63.

a wooden dome with a metal covering would be more than adequate. It speaks volumes about the prevailing attitudes that none in the establishment thought Indians were capable of constructing such domes and could be consulted! A century earlier, a more consultative atmosphere had prevailed. It was de Havilland who revived the concept of using local techniques. In 1818, fresh from the success of building St George's Cathedral on Cathedral Road, he persuaded the authorities to go in for a brick dome at the kirk, confident of the abilities of the native masons to produce one. He argued that a timber structure was subject to the depredations of white ants and would wear out soon in the harsh climate of Madras.

To convince the patrons, de Havilland had a test dome built by native masons in his garden on Mount Road. To ensure its success, he modified the dimensions of the dome from the original Gibbs design and made it shallower and smaller in circumference. He also increased the number of columns to support it. This was later copied in full when the church was finally built. The laying of well foundations for St Andrews Kirk is an oft-quoted story. De Havilland opined that 'the time immemorial Madras method of well sinking' be used for overcoming the problem of soft soil on the site.[8]

The kirk was built on a foundation of 150 brick and terracotta wells, all sunk by local artisans. The columns of the edifice came up on these. Finally, the dome was constructed. An inherent trust in the native method of building however meant that acoustics had to be ignored, resulting in a dismal echo in the kirk, which still persists. The service could scarcely be heard but de Havilland conveniently blamed it on the 'age of the reverend!' When completed, everyone praised the designs and sagacity of de Havilland but not much attention was paid to the well sinkers who made it possible.[9] Sadly, contemporary Chennaiites too do not reflect on the Indian labour that went into it, branding the neo-classical kirk a colonial edifice.

Neo-classicism and an attitude of 'let's show the natives' prevailed till 1857 when it came to style, though in matters of technique, local expertise was used. Thus when Pachaiyappa's School[10] had to be built in 1844, it was more or less mandated that it had to be modelled on John Goldingham's Banqueting (now Rajaji) Hall, which stood on the banks of the Cooum, by

[8]Pillai, *Imperial Conversations*, pp. 82–107.

[9]Ibid.

[10]This school later morphed into the eponymous college located elsewhere in the city.

the side of the Government House. Captain Ludlow, an officer of the Madras Engineers came up with the new design, based on the Temple of Theseus and in the classical style for the assembly hall. To its rear came up the school proper and this is a tiled roof structure, completely Indian in design.[11] This magnificent building, where Annadurai studied, is now in a pathetic state.

The year 1857 changed perceptions. India came under the British Crown and several concessions were made, particularly in architectural motifs. If the natives were to admire a building, there had to be local elements in it. Moreover, it became necessary for the Raj to establish its continuity with the earlier ruling elite—the Nayaks. It became imperative to incorporate elements from their buildings as seen in the palace at Chandragiri, for example, in the public buildings of Madras. Interestingly, the first such attempt had been made in the 1760s, when the contract to build a palace for the nawab of Arcot was given to the notoriously corrupt Paul Benfield. Whatever be his faults, he built something unique—the first British structure in the Indo-Saracenic style, which combined various elements of Indian and Turkish architecture to produce what the Europeans considered to be a true representation of the Asian exotic.[12] At that time it was considered a fitting residence for an Indian ruler but ninety years later, it became the style that exuded the power of the British Raj.

Indo-Saracenic was resurrected for use in the 1860s, first in designing the University of Madras buildings. Land for the Presidency College and a University Senate House was allotted by 1865. But two years prior to this, the Government of Madras had, for the first and only time in its history, announced an architectural competition for the design of these two buildings. With ₹3,000 being offered as the prize, it was a prestigious affair and by 1865, seventeen designs had been received. Robert Fellowes Chisholm, an engineer in the Puri Division of the PWD, Government of Bengal, won the contest.

He was, accordingly, transferred to the Madras government in 1866, his arrival in the city coinciding with that of the new governor, Lord Napier. The latter was a man with a high imperial vision and in Chisholm he was to find someone who could translate his schemes into reality. Napier also began a new tradition, one that rulers of independent India have continued—putting up new facades for older buildings or replacing them altogether to reinforce the new dispensation in power. No doubt Chepauk Palace, that

[11]Pillai, *Imperial Conversations,* p. 136.

[12]Muthiah, *Madras Rediscovered*, pp. 192–95.

glorious symbol of nawabi rule on the beachfront, irked Napier and so, among Chisholm's first contracts was building the offices of the PWD, on the eastern face of the palace, thereby hiding it from public view.[13] Post-independence governments in Tamil Nadu have completed what Napier began. Buildings came up on the northern and western sides of the palace, thereby completely blocking it from view.

It is significant that none of Chisholm's early works in the city or in the Presidency were examples of the style for which he would eventually become famous. In his early years, he experimented with the Scottish-baronial (the PWD building), the severely classical (the Madras Club buildings as they stood, till recently, on Express Estates, and the Buckingham and Carnatic Mills at Pulianthope), and the Italianate (Presidency College and Lawrence Asylum which later became the Lawrence School at Lovedale, Ooty). When a suitable residence had to be found for the nawabs of Arcot, the Police Courts in Royapettah were selected and Chisholm was asked to convert the precinct into a royal residence. He chose to model it on the lines of Queen Victoria's Osborne House on the Isle of Wight. Thus came into existence Amir Mahal, a vast preserve in the heart of Royapettah. To most people, the only familiar part of it is its gateway, topped by a traditional Naubat Khana from which drums are played on ceremonial occasions. It does not prepare you for the European building within that is the residence of the prince of Arcot, the title and pension finding a place in the Constitution of India, along with the rank of a cabinet minister. Maintained by the PWD, this magnificent building is now occupied by the present holder of the title—the jocular Nawab Mohammed Abdul Ali—the eighth of the titular princes. 'The British took everything we had and left us this,' he smiles. Under him, Amir Mahal has repeatedly been opened up to visitors and for social events. Eid celebrations here are legendary. The nawab maintains an active social profile and it has been customary for dignitaries from India and abroad to beat a path to his door. Chisholm's creation lends grandeur and dignity to all the events that are held at Amir Mahal.

After his work on this stately home, there came two projects that would transform Chisholm's ideas forever. The first was a commission from Napier to restore the Thirumalai Nayakar Mahal in Madurai. Chisholm grumbled

[13]Ibid., p. 222.

about the heat and dust of travel by bullock cart but when he arrived at the site, he fell in love with the palace, particularly the polychromate work and the plaster statuary. Back in Madras, he reworked his ideas for the University Senate House, incorporating into it several elements from the mahal. He also added ideas and designs that had inspired him in other places such as Bijapur, Mahabalipuram, and Ajanta. As a consequence, Senate House, completed in 1878, emerged as a curious but beautiful amalgam of various styles that became a new genre by itself—the Indo-Saracenic. To fill the interiors of Senate House, Chisholm began working on a bewildering variety of stained glass, mosaics, and painted canvases. These were all done at the Madras School of Art (now the Government College of Arts and Crafts, Poonamallee High Road) of which he became the principal in 1868.[14]

In 1872, Napier sent Chisholm to Travancore where a museum was to be built. There he saw the Kerala style of roofing and concluded that it was 'a very beautiful form of domestic art'. Even as he designed the Napier Museum in Trivandrum, he began work on a General Post Office (GPO) for Madras and this incorporated his new fascination—the Travancore roof. The GPO on First Line Beach was completed in 1884.[15]

By this time, Chisholm was a very busy man, designing jails, courthouses, offices, and much more. Some of the other buildings in the city that bear his stamp are the Victoria Public Hall, the tower of the Central Station, and the main offices of P. Orr and Sons. Napier had long left the city and Chisholm worked with his successors. In 1887, he resigned from service and after completing some of his private projects in Madras, moved to Baroda to complete the construction of Lakshmi Vilas, the grand palace of the Gaekwar.

Then he retired to England, where he passed away in 1915. He was largely unknown in his home country. Indeed, of his works, only two or three are outside India. But, by the time of his death, his style was popular in the entire subcontinent. All the Raj edifices would follow the path he had laid down. The construction of New Delhi was to be its grand finale. Sir Edwin Lutyens detested the Indo-Saracenic style and was in favour of building a capital city in the classical style. But Chisholm was around to caution such a move—the architecture had to be something the native population associated with authority, he wrote. A phalanx of old India hands and even Queen Mary applied pressure on Sir Edwin and Indo-Saracenic won the day.[16]

[14]V. Sriram, *Fifty Historic Residences of Chennai*, Chennai: Kalamkriya, 2008, p. 41.

[15]Pillai, *Imperial Conversations*, p. 244.

[16]For further details, see Robert Grant Irving, *Indian Summer: Lutyens, Baker and Imperial*

Chisholm's successor in Madras, Henry Irwin, came in a blaze of glory, for he had just completed the gothic Viceregal Palace and several other buildings in the imperial summer capital of Simla. But once in Madras, he realized the importance of adhering to the Indo-Saracenic style and went on to design several buildings here, the high court, the Connemara Public Library, and the Victoria Memorial Hall (now the National Gallery of Art) being the most important. There were several other architects of the same vintage who also left their stamp on the Indo-Saracenic façade of Madras. These include Norman Robert Pogson (the Spencer Showroom), G. S. T. Harris (the YMCA Building), and J. H. Stephen (the Kardyl, now Bharat Insurance Building).

A running thread through much of the constructions of this style is the life of Diwan Bahadur Thatikonda Namberumal Chetty, the civil contractor. It was he who gave form and shape to what the architects designed. A legend in his lifetime, Namberumal and his wealth are spoken about even today in the city. Also remembered is his kindness to Srinivasa Ramanujan, the mathematician, who terminally ill and ostracized by many in his community for having crossed the seas, found in Namberumal a father figure. It was in Gometra, one of Namberumal's several houses in Madras, that Ramanujan passed away. And it was Namberumal who lit his pyre.

What makes the Indo-Saracenic style stand out is that it marks the first conscious use by British architects of Indian craftsmen in the construction of public buildings. Chisholm, while working on the Napier Museum in Trivandrum in 1872, conceded that his 'objective was to control the main forms of the building but in all else, in finishing, in elaboration, and in ornamentation, I would leave the native artisan entirely unfettered'.[17] Likewise, Chisholm was also 'fascinated by the famous Madras plasterwork or bulpum'. He described it enthusiastically: 'Applied in three coats—the first comprising river sand and shell lime, the second ground quartz sand and shell lime and the final the same mixture ground very fine to a consistency of cream which was trowelled on and polished with agate,'[18]—it gave a finish that was akin to marble. Chisholm had realized 'rather early on that by using Indian labour and materials he could initiate remarkable building programmes without excessive

Delhi, Yale University Press, 1983.

[17]Pillai, *Imperial Conversations*, p. 276.

[18]Ibid.

expenditure. It was a rare luxury.'[19] Here was Mughal vision combined with truly British financial prudence. At the same time, in typical colonial fashion, Chisholm boasted of resurrecting Indian art and architecture, thereby giving an impression that they would have died out had it not been for him.

The idiom of Chisholm and Irwin faded thereafter and neoclassicism was the rage by the early 1910s, as is evident in constructions of that period such as the iconic Ripon Buildings, headquarters of the city's municipal corporation and the Mercantile Bank (now HSBC) Building on First Line Beach/Rajaji Salai. Also in the same style are the inter-war years constructions such as the Freemasons Hall in Egmore and the annexe to the Presidency College, both designed by the firm of Jackson and Barker. Cinema theatres were coming up in the more crowded parts of the city and these too followed this style. It was almost as if the freedom struggle was once again distancing the colonial masters who saw no reason to incorporate Indian elements in what they were building. In the 1930s came art deco, inspired by visions of American success and the image of England being a major sea power, and it had a long hold over the city though, sadly, very few specimens remain. The first of these was, undoubtedly, the Laxman Mahadeo Chitale designed Oriental Insurance Building, Armenian Street.[20] It set the trend for many more such structures to come up in the same style in the China Bazaar/ NSC Bose Road area. In 1939/1940 came up Dare House, the headquarters of the Murugappa Group, at iconic Parry's Corner.[21] Other structures such as the State Bank of Mysore Building designed by B. R. Manickam and constructed by C. R. Narayana Rao,[22] later the progenitor of a firm of architects still flourishing in the city, the Bombay Mutual Building, the National Assurance Building, the Southern India Chamber of Commerce Building, and the Tamil Isai Sangam are magnificent examples of art deco in the same area. In keeping with international trends, many cinema theatres were built in this style though just one, the Kamadhenu, now a wedding hall, survives. Many residences in the newer areas of the city were art deco in design too, with smooth curves, round windows, iron grilles, and concrete mouldings. There are very few left.

---

[19]Ibid.

[20]V. Sriram, 'Madras Landmarks, 50 years ago', *Madras Musings*, Vol. XXIV, No. 24, 1–15 April 2015.

[21]Hilton Brown, *Parry's of Madras: A Story of British Enterprise in India*, Madras: Parry & Co, 1954, pp. 279–80, pp. 304–5.

[22]V. Sriram, 'Art Deco in a crowded city', *The Hindu*, 15 April 2014.

The trend of designing iconic public buildings continued. Jackson and Barker became Prynne, Abbot, and Davis; the firm created many striking edifices, perhaps the best example being the University Centenary Building, meant to harmonize with Chisholm's Senate House and yet make a bold architectural statement of its own. But the times were changing and after 1947, it became necessary to create visible images of an India embracing modernity.

These included the works of R. R. Sarma, whose Reserve Bank of India Building is a lovely modernist landmark, as also the factory buildings he designed for the TVS Group in Padi. Another was Srikrishna Chitale, son of L. M. Chitale, already referred to above. The firm of Jackson & Barker's later partners, Bennet Pithavadian and the Australian Kiffin Ray Peterson, designed some unique residences in various parts of the city, particularly the original Binny Bungalows on Boat Club Road and Adyar Villa, the residence of M. A. Chidambaram, business, turf baron, and the man who single-handedly ensured that the city got a cricket stadium at Chepauk.[23] The M. A. Chidambaram Stadium is by itself an example of modernism—a concrete bowl inspired by the works of Le Corbusier in Chandigarh. But if there is to be a prize for the best modernist structure in the city, it would probably go to the TTK Auditorium of the Music Academy, Madras. Designed by G. M. Bhuta of Bombay in the 1950s, it has served its purpose of a home to culture most admirably for more than sixty years.[24] The LIC Building on Mount Road was another. Conceived by M. Ct. M. Chidambaram Chettyar as headquarters for his United India Insurance, work began on this Mount Road landmark in 1953. Sadly, he died in an air crash a year later. Work on the eighteen-storeyed building designed by Brown and Moulin of London continued nevertheless, with Coromandel Engineers as the contractors. The nationalization of insurance and the absorption of United India's life insurance business into the newly created Life Insurance Corporation of India stalled the construction. When resumed, it was decided that the building would be restricted to fourteen storeys and that is how it remains. Many in Chennai consider it the tallest building in the city though that is not true at all.[25]

---

[23]Sujoy Gupta, *Vision Unlimited: The Outstanding Legacy of M. A. Chidambaram*, Chennai: MAC Public Charitable Trust, 2005, pp. 137–61.

[24]V. Sriram and Dr Malathi Rangaswami, *Four Score and More: The History of the Music Academy*, Madras: East West Books, 2009, pp. 119–28.

[25]*The Unfinished Journey: The Story of M Ct M Chidambaram Chettyar*, Chennai: M. Ct. M. Chidambaram Trust, 2004, pp. 242–43.

With the arrival of the Dravidian parties, the search began for a new architectural idiom, shorn of all the trappings of the past. It was true that when the DMK swept to power, it vowed to bring back the glories of ancient Tamil rule but when it came to symbols, it found itself drawing a blank. The problem was chiefly that all surviving icons from ancient Tamil times were religious in nature and these would not do for a party that at least outwardly swore by atheism. The Dravidian style made its entry with the construction of Valluvar Kottam in the 1970s. It was the brainchild of Karunanidhi, who, in the aftermath of Anna's death, became the chief minister of the state in 1969. The Kalaignar (artist) as he was known, desired a fitting memorial for Thiruvalluvar, the circa fourth century BCE to fifth century CE philosopher who composed the *Thirukkural*, a collection of 1,330 couplets divided into ten chapters of 133 verses each, which speak on ethics, matters temporal, and love. It was part of a grand plan 'to dot important sites in Tamil Nadu with monuments that commemorated or projected the Tamil past'.[26]

The area selected for Valluvar Kottam was part of the erstwhile Nungambakkam Tank. Envisaged as a memorial, a meeting hall, and a research and learning centre, the monument 'comprises a large public hall of 67 by 30 metres. At the end of the entrance axis is located a 30-metre-high temple car. There is a Valluvar statue on the first floor level.'[27] The irony was that the plan largely resembled a temple and the superstructure was modelled on the famed Azhi Ther of the Thyagaraja Swami Temple, Tiruvarur, Karunanidhi's constituency. The entire complex was designed and executed by sthapathis—traditional architects who designed temples. 'It is ironic that a rationalist party had to take to religious symbolism when it came to building a monument,' says Venkatachalapathy.[28]

The Kalaignar had planned a grand inaugural ceremony for it but that was never to be. In 1976, when Valluvar Kottam was just half-finished, the DMK government was dismissed and the party remained in Opposition till 1989. The structure was completed by the succeeding AIADMK government, with many of Kalaignar's cherished features given the go-by and inaugurated in a ceremony to which he was not invited.[29] Not surprisingly, when the DMK came back to power in 1989, it held its swearing-in ceremony at

[26]A. Srivathsan, 'Politics, Architecture and the City', *Chennai: Not Madras*, p. 55.

[27]Ibid., p. 56.

[28]Interview with the author, Chennai, 12 March 2020.

[29]Srivathsan, 'Politics, Architecture and the City', p. 61.

Valluvar Kottam.[30] But sadly thereafter, the party did nothing for the place, even though it kept returning to power in every alternate election till 2012. Valluvar Kottam suffers from poor maintenance and is let out for exhibitions of crockery and garments, a far cry from the memorial and research centre it was meant to be.

But it did showcase Dravidian architecture. By boldly breaking away from European/American and North Indian styles that abounded in the city by way of the neoclassical, Indo-Saracenic, art deco, and Modernist, it tried to establish a new order. Some elements of it were certainly incorporated into memorials for leaders such as Kamaraj and Rajaji, all located near the Raj Bhavan but that was all. Those who swore by the old order, and this included Raj apologists and those who belonged to the Congress or detested the DMK for its anti-upper-caste ideology, declared themselves appalled by the new order of architecture. But it cannot be denied that it was a bold statement of change, which continued what all earlier regimes had done—namely create visible symbols and edifices of power.

Since then, the degradation in style has been quite drastic. The taste in today's government buildings is essentially kitsch. Anna's memorial, an elegant, tall, black, granite-clad, obelisk-like structure, fronted by two tusk-like constructions forming an archway, later came to be masked from view by something copied from the Arc de Triomphe. The neighbouring M. G. R. Memorial had a sweeping archway that was inspired by his party symbol of two leaves. This later came to be fronted by yet another gateway in classical style, with a gold-coloured phoenix rearing out of it. Other gateways and memorials dot the city, all suffering from an excessive usage of polished granite and very doubtful aesthetics. And the tendency to ape Western monuments, with none of their class or finish in execution, has since come to stay. The contrast is striking—the colonials used indigenous styles, techniques, and material. The new rulers look to the West for everything—even the latest Jayalalithaa memorial claims to be inspired by the phoenix, a bird borrowed from European myth.

That even the Kalaignar came to be influenced by the new order was evident in the way his last pet project, and like the Valluvar Kottam, destined to be abandoned, was executed. This was the new Legislature and Secretariat for the Government of Tamil Nadu. It was true that the facilities at Fort St George were limited, with the chief minister reportedly sitting in a section that dated to the 1690s. Modernization was needed and the fort offered

---

[30]Ibid.

very little scope for that. Government Estate, across the Cooum, which contained Rajaji Hall, the old Government House that was the residence of the governors of Madras till 1947, and Kalaivanar Arangam, an auditorium once designed as the assembly, was selected as a suitable site. The existing heritage buildings, with the exception of Rajaji Hall, were all demolished, the Government House having to be imploded.[31]

The ₹450-crore project got underway thereafter, with a German architect in charge. By the time it neared completion, the Kalaignar and his spin managers were at great pains to explain how the structure had elements of Dravidian architecture—such elaborate statements were necessitated by the fact that nobody could see any connection with local traditions in the construction.[32] Muthiah, the chronicler of Madras, likened the curving façade to the oil tanks that stood in the harbour. Jayalalithaa said the building resembled a circus tent.[33] The dome had a marked likeness to the German kaiser's helmet, though the official explanation was that it was inspired by the Valluvar Kottam. There was, however, one redeeming feature—the edifice was business-like and showcased what India and Tamil Nadu wanted to be—liberalized economies attracting worldwide investment.

The complex was still incomplete when it was inaugurated by the then prime minister of India, Dr Manmohan Singh, in 2011. But in the next general elections, Jayalalithaa's AIADMK swept to power and she ordered the shifting of the secretariat and assembly back to Fort St George. Kalaignar's dream was converted into a multi-speciality referral hospital. It still remains, a gloomy edifice, on Mount Road. The bureaucracy, which would probably have ensured that the style of governance remained the same no matter which edifice it occupied, shifted its files and filing cabinets back to the old secretariat in the Fort.

If at all there is a part of the city that can boast of a lovely skyline incorporating almost all the styles of architecture referred to uptil now, it is the beach. Starting from the San Thome end, you cross the All India Radio Building, an elegant structure that incorporates several Dravidian motifs in its

---

[31]'Threat to Rajaji Hall from new Assembly?', *Madras Musings*, Vol. XVIII, No. 15, 16–30 November 2008.

[32]See for instance 'Tamil Nadu's New Legislative Assembly Building - World's First Green Assembly Building', Modern Green Structures and Architecture, available here: https://www.mgsarchitecture.in/architecture-design/projects/507-tamil-nadu-s-new-legislative-assembly-building-world-s-first-green-assembly-building.html/.

[33]Gopu Mohan, 'New CM, old seat of power', *New Indian Express*, 15 May 2011.

façade. Next comes the office of the Director General of Police. Known in the service as Chief Office, it began life as a Masonic Temple in the 1840s before being handed over to the police in the 1860s. Splendidly restored, its classical façade is a thing of beauty.[34] Thereafter comes the vast campus of the Queen Mary's College, South India's second such facility for women, begun in 1914. Its core, Capper's House, has disappeared, but what remains, especially Stone House, Jeypore House, and Pentland House, are beautiful. The campus however suffers from poor maintenance. After this comes the Lady Willingdon Institute of Advanced Study in Education, an art deco structure that has as its neighbour, the quaint Ice House, now Vivekanandar Illam.

The domed and red brick University Examination Hall follows, and next to it is the vast Presidency College Cricket Ground. Thereafter are three of Chisholm's creations—the Italianate Presidency College Building, the Scottish PWD Building, and the Indo-Saracenic University Senate House. This is followed by the University buildings, all of which complement Senate House in their skyline and layout.

On the opposite side of this long walk by the beach are several statues to Indian leaders and those who contributed to the development of the Tamil language. Of these, the one of Mahatma Gandhi and a second titled Triumph of Labour, inspired by the landing of the American troops at Iwo Jima, are the works of Debi Prasad Roy Chowdhury, master sculptor and principal of the Madras School of Arts.

A similarly impressive route is the beginning of Poonamallee High Road, where a quick walk takes you past the Madras Medical College's old campus including its red brick Anatomy Block, the Lady Hope Hostel for Nurses, Memorial Hall, the General Hospital, the headquarters of the Southern Railway, the Central Station, Victoria Public Hall, Ripon Buildings, the Raja Sir Savalai Ramaswami Mudaliar Choultry, and Siddique Serai. If you have enough energy, you can walk on past the art deco Jaya Mansions to the Government College of Arts and Crafts, Egmore Station, and the St Andrews Kirk.

A third walkway to feast the eyes on is NSC Bose Road and Rajaji Salai. Apart from the art deco buildings listed earlier, you can see the Armenian Church, Pachaiyappa's School building, Madras High Court, Dare House, Law College and on making a turn to the left, Harbour Police Station, the State Bank building, the GPO, the HSBC building, the Government Stationery

[34]V. Sriram, *Chief Office, Headquarters of the Tamil Nadu Police,* Chennai: The Director General of Police, Tamil Nadu, 2019.

Depot, and the Metropolitan Magistrates Court.

All very well, no doubt, but all these buildings are of a sound vintage dating back to the British Raj. Chennai has not been able to create an architectural vision of its own. Which is why, most films still show the LIC building, the Central and Egmore Stations as symbols of the city. We also have another icon in the Gemini flyover—the city's first grade separator. Constructed in the 1970s, it was named after Annadurai but is even now known as the Gemini flyover because of the eponymous studio that once stood beside it.

To be fair to those who have been unable to create the kind of skyline that Chisholm did, a vital ingredient—namely space—is now completely lacking in Chennai. How then is any bold statement even to be attempted? But even when space was not a constraint, as in the case of the Legislative Assembly and Secretariat building, what was finally constructed did not touch a chord with most. When faced with a lack of space, the new rulers have come up with the next best—put up new buildings in place of old heritage structures or erect giant towers by their side, thereby ruining the ambience for good. There are numerous examples of these—the Ripon Building Annexe (named Amma Maligai) and the new Police Commissioner's Office in the city are just two examples—and all these are buildings that could be in any part of the world, all plate glass and concrete. From having a unique character by way of its architecture, Chennai is fast becoming commonplace.

To construct new buildings that perpetuate a ruling dispensation's memory by way of names and foundation/inaugural plaques in granite and gold lettering, it has been necessary to do away with older heritage structures. It was in the 1980s that the government decided that it needed to pull down Bentinck's building, a lovely neoclassical building of the early nineteenth century which had housed for long the Chennai Collector's Office. There was a protest from heritage activists and someone managed to get the then prime minister's ear. A letter from her to MGR, then chief minister, halted all talk of demolition. But the building was emptied of all its offices and left to the elements. Within a few years, denied all maintenance, it became decrepit. The engineers of the Corporation of Madras gave a certificate qualifying the building as unsafe for habitation and that was that. The building was demolished but not all that easily. It transpired that it was not so structurally weak after all. But brought down it was and, in its place, rose Singarevar Maligai, a drab and shapeless creation.[35]

[35]V. Sriram, 'Going, going, but not yet gone—the story of Chennai's Heritage', available

Chennai, like Simla, holds a record of sorts when it comes to heritage buildings that have burnt down. The list is long—Moore Market, Spencers, the Anjuman-e-Islam, Gandhi Illam, Chepauk Palace, the old Mint, the GPO, and the State Bank building are some of the famed victims. In most cases, the fire was probably premeditated. In Moore Market, it likely was, the Railways wanting the land and the occupants of the market refusing to vacate.[36] Of course, in many others, poor maintenance, haphazard wiring, old timber, and water seepage made for a perfect formula for a short circuit. In the early years, bringing down what was left after the fire and putting up a high rise in its place was a simple matter, as it happened in Moore Market and Spencers. But with increasing awareness, brought on principally by the writings of Muthiah and the steady building up of a activist brigade, it has not been so easy to do away with heritage. The government has had to commit to restoration in the case of the Chepauk Palace and the National Gallery, whose dome had been sporting a crack for a long time.

Almost the first instance that heritage activists had their way was when it was decided that the headquarters of the Director General of Police on the Marina should be brought down to make way for a ten-storey structure. The certificate for demolition was easily obtained, for the chief minister had blessed the project. The police top brass was, however, not so enthused, for Chief Office was dear to them. The Indian National Trust for Arts and Cultural Heritage (INTACH) mounted a signature campaign among the public and filed a petition in court. The judges ordered an independent panel of experts to examine the structure and assess its stability. The report was wholeheartedly in favour of retention and restoration. Chief Office was repaired and is today one of the most beautiful buildings on the Marina. The chief minister, however, took it as a personal affront.[37] She was equally incensed when her plans to take over Queen Mary's College campus for building a new assembly and secretariat was foiled by student protests and a loophole in the land ownership clause. The buildings inside were denied funds for even basic maintenance thereafter and are steadily crumbling.[38]

---

here: https://www.youtube.com/watch?v=gCB79DrqKDQ/.

[36]Aloysius Xavier Lopez, 'The fire that changed the face of Chennai Central', *The Hindu*, 2 June 2015.

[37]A. X. Alexander, DGP of Police, Tamil Nadu, 2005-2006. Interview with the author, Chennai, January 2019.

[38]'Caring a fig for heritage campuses', *Madras Musings*, Vol. XXV, No. 20, 1–15 February 2016.

The central structure, Cappers House, collapsed and was replaced with a new building that seemingly blends in with the older structures by its side.

Not all of INTACH's petitions have been as successful. In 2012, the NGO had its powers severely curtailed by a judgement in a case pertaining to demolishing a part of the historic P. Orr and Sons to make way for Chennai Metro Rail.[39] Those in office have come to view activists and agencies such as INTACH to be enemies of progress and development—these latter being measured in terms of the number of multi-storeyed buildings that come to replace old heritage structures, all of which are branded colonial and therefore unwanted. What is forgotten is that much of the construction involved Indians and local techniques that are now lost. In bringing these structures down, we are killing our heritage.

There has been the odd silver lining. Disposing of a batch of litigations concerning heritage buildings, Justices Prabha Sridevan and PPS Janarthana Raja, in a landmark judgement in 2010, ruled that around 460 structures in the city be protected and a Heritage Conservation Committee (HCC) be formed by the CMDA to assess these and make sure that they are given due recognition under law.[40] The heritage lobby was jubilant. But the bureaucracy made sure that it had its way. An HCC was put together in which nominees of the government and its agencies were in the majority. The only private member was from INTACH and therefore the NGO's voice was in a perpetual minority.[41] In 2012, the P. Orr and Sons case terminated the membership of INTACH in the HCC, which has since become a somnambulant body. The government, thereafter, proceeded to demolish with impunity several structures listed in the high court judgement. The biggest lot comprising Cooum House, Gandhi Illam, Government House, the bandmaster quarters, Kalaivanar Arangam, and the ornate gate posts of Government Estate was demolished to make way for the ill-fated new assembly and secretariat.[42] Thereafter, Metro Rail claimed a couple of buildings. In short, the well-meant judgement was emasculated by vested interests. And a Heritage Act for the city and the state as demanded by the court has remained a pipedream.

And yet, all is not lost. A growing awareness has come about. Chepauk Palace is being restored after the fire. A day after the conflagration, a minister

---

[39]WP 7076 of 2012, The High Court of Madras.

[40]WP 25306 of 2006, The High Court of Madras.

[41]'Urgent Need to Bestir Itself', *Madras Musings*, Vol. XX, No. 11, 16–30 September 2010.

[42]'Threat to Rajaji Hall from new Assembly?', *Madras Musings*, Vol. XVIII, No. 15, 16–30 November 2008.

did declare that the edifice would be brought down[43] but the statement was later retracted and work began on restoration.[44] Victoria Public Hall, its restoration halted to allow for Metro Rail work, will soon get a facelift. Ripon Buildings was heavily impacted by deep drilling for the Metro and yet was not allowed to fall apart, being deemed a symbol of the city. The restoration of the National Gallery, a five-year-project, is nearing completion. The high court has a committee that is active in conservation and restoration. Senate House was restored owing to a spirited campaign by the then vice chancellor S. P. Thyagarajan, supported by Muthiah and INTACH. His successors have deemed it fit to lock up the building again but it cannot be denied that it is now in good shape. The old reading room of the Connemara Public Library too is splendidly restored. The Raja Sir Savalai Ramaswami Mudaliar Choultry was not demolished to make way for Metro Rail. And the latter, when it came to stations in heritage areas did listen and come up with sympathetic designs. We have also had the strange case of the Anna Nagar arches—not particularly great examples of architecture but, nevertheless, markers for that vast colony in West Chennai for more than fifty years. Threatened with demolition to make way for a grade separator, they were saved by Chief Minister Jayalalithaa, the route of the proposed flyover being altered.[45]

As can be seen, the government's record in heritage conservation is improving. That cannot be said for buildings in private hands. It is true that they are not rewarded in any way for protecting heritage structures and land values are forever increasing, but how does that explain a cash-rich entity such as the Life Insurance Corporation of India waiting for iconic Bharat Insurance Building to collapse so that high-rise can replace it? Private residences have perhaps been the biggest casualties, vanishing en masse for blocks of apartments, the majority of which give aesthetics the go by. Rather interestingly, most multi-storey residential complexes have the most anglicized of names—Manderley, Wuthering Heights, Wingate Gardens, Notting Hill are a few—giving an illusion of space and nature, the very elements that were sacrificed in their construction. There is also the promise of a swimming pool—in a water-starved city. Above all, when we now have the freedom to experiment with Indian styles, better suited to the climate and environment,

[43]G. Pramod Kumar, 'Chennai outraged: 224-year-old Chepauk palace gutted in fire', *Firstpost*, 18 January 2018.

[44]'Chepauk Palace fire, Amma to take final call', *New Indian Express*, 28 January 2012.

[45]Deepa Ramakrishnan, 'How the Anna Nagar arches stood their ground', *The Hindu*, 6 September 2012.

the preferred idiom is wholly Western for private buildings—glass, concrete, and boxed in, with no scope for natural light and ventilation. And as for the material used, practically everything is imported, for that is what is in demand.

There was a time when you could practically identify which locality of the city you were in by the buildings that you saw. That is not possible any longer. The same ill-designed multi-storeyed structures greet you everywhere. You could be in any locality. Or you could be anywhere else in India.

9 | CREATIVE CITY

In November 2017, UNESCO recognized Chennai as one of its 180-strong creative cities network. The metropolis was honoured for its contribution to music. There was a spate of congratulations, from the chief minister, prime minister, defence minister, and several others. The chief minister thanked the prime minister for congratulating the city. It was all rather ironic, given that the creative arts had always flourished here entirely due to private initiative.

'The cities in the network work together towards a common objective: placing creativity and cultural industries at the heart of their development plans at the local level and cooperating actively at the international level,' said the UNESCO on the key objective of this network.[1] There was a minor debate among the intelligentsia on whether the city was really deserving of the recognition. At its heart was the nagging fear that Carnatic music, the classical art form of South India, now more or less the fiefdom of the Brahmin community, would overwhelm the Creative City recognition. 'Music must leave the auditorium,' thundered an activist who was known more for the good work he does on environmental issues.[2] A year later, all of it was forgotten. Nobody knew what to do with this tag anyway. Music in Chennai is something everybody takes for granted. And we have many varieties of it, each with its own adherents. There is a dedicated band of Hindustani music aficionados, who still sigh over the memory of Pandit Ravi Shankar performing each year at the Music Academy on New Year's Eve, and ending his performance with a New Year greeting. That, by the way, is an exaggeration. The maestro performed only sporadically at the Academy, but he did have a large fan following.

Film music, as anywhere else in India, has a large fan base and is divided between those who love only Hindi film songs, others who swear by Tamil, and some who like both. And we also have within these, sub-groups—for some, there has been no good film music since the 1960s. For others it began thereafter. There are Western classical music performers such as the pianist Anil Srinivasan and there is Musee Musicals, the shop on Mount

[1]'Namma Chennai gets "creative city" tag from UNESCO', *New Indian Express*, 9 November 2019.

[2]Nityanand Jayaraman, 'For Chennai to truly be a Creative City, music must leave the auditorium and fill the streets', *Scroll.in*, 11 November 2017.

Road specializing in music instruments and representing the Trinity Music College of London here since 1901! There are die-hard fans of rock and roll, jazz, punk, rock, heavy metal, and just about any kind of new-age music.

Chennai has its own version of blues—the Gaana. The term itself is a Hindi import, meaning song. Gaana began as music in the poorest sections of society, from North Chennai. Its origins are obscure but it probably evolved as a medium of self-expression, for it deals with day-to-day life in the city. A large number of songs also deal with those who have passed on, thereby indicating that it has a strong association with the genres of lament. But, today, Gaana also stands for social reform. It is the voice of the Dalits demanding equal status in society. The words are colloquial, the instruments used are contemporary, the pace fast, and the volume loud. Gaana is gradually making space for itself.

But it is Carnatic classical music, which despite its miniscule fan base, that has the highest profile. Which is why perhaps many were uncomfortable with the Creative City tag. And there is Bharatanatyam, which is the classical dance form of Tamil Nadu. For both, Chennai is now the heartland.

Perhaps the first to describe the arts scene in the city is the nineteenth-century Sanskrit work *Sarva Deva Vilasa*. As its chief characters Vivekin and Ativivekin wander around the city, they describe the soirees 'convened by rich patrons, at fixed intervals or whenever there was festivity or the celebration of a happy event'.[3] Termed sadas, these gatherings 'provided occasions not only for witnessing the dance or listening to music by well-known artists, but also for the presentation of new songs by the composers'. *Sarva Deva Vilasa* mentions several patrons, all dubashes, by name, as also the various artistes in their retinues. It speaks of a gathering of scholars in a coconut grove just outside the walls of old Black Town.[4]

With so much music happening around them, the British realized the importance of musicians and dancers for ceremonial occasions. Descriptions of several processions have survived, one of these mentioning 'a great number of the Inhabitants of the Gentue Town, all in Armes, bringing with them also Elliphants, Kettle Drums, and all the Country Musick'. This was in 1685, on the occasion of the accession of King James II to the throne. The arrival of the charter of the Madras Corporation in 1688 was a similar event. The diaries of the Pondicherry dubash Ananda Ranga Pillai are likewise replete

[3]Dr V. Raghavan's preface to the *Sarva Deva Vilasa*, Madras: Adyar Library and Research Centre, 1958.
[4]Ibid.

with references to processions featuring Dupleix and other high-ranking Frenchmen, all attended by dancers and musicians. Since then, processions of this kind have only become bigger in Chennai, the only difference being the gradual disappearance of classical music and dance and the increased use of the Kerala Chenda Melam for sound in recent years.

Temple processions were long and elaborate affairs, with the nagaswaram, the traditional South Indian woodwind instrument, being played to the accompaniment of the tavil, the double-headed drum. In an era when ambient noises were low, the sonorous nagaswaram and the explosive tavil alerted the neighbourhood about the hours of worship, the specific service being done at any point of time, and processions at the temple. They also performed at weddings, the ensemble being considered auspicious. And yet, the nagaswaram and tavil performers were denigrated on account of their caste. While admired for their skills, they were not allowed to enter a home, being made to stand outside the front door or in the backyard. They were the last to eat at weddings and they had to go about bare-chested, their upper cloth tied around their waists. The fight for recognition and social equality for the nagaswaram community gained ground only in the twentieth century, with performers such as T. N. Rajarathinam Pillai leading the protest. Today, though there is no overt discrimination of the kind that was in vogue earlier, the nagaswaram itself is facing lean times. It doesn't find appreciative listeners where it is played. And being an outdoor instrument it has hit a few snags on the concert platform. It has had to conform to the concert format while it was in reality meant for free-ranging exploration of ragas. As a consequence, even in music festivals, it has been relegated to curtain-raiser performances that signify auspiciousness.

Sarva Deva Vilasa also documents the use of two instruments probably unique to the Chennai region—the surya parai and chandra parai. Shaped respectively like the sun and the moon, these had stands that sat on the head of the performer so that he could beat the instrument by raising his hands overhead even as he accompanied processions. Today, the two parais are relics, samples of which can be found in the Sangita Vadyalaya, a forgotten government-run museum on Anna Salai, which the authorities are trying to get rid of by transferring the collection to Delhi. It is an age-old story—someone (in this case it was the venerated professor and musicologist P. Sambamoorthy) builds a collection which is then acquired by the government that then relegates it to an inaccessible location and does nothing after that. No change of display is ever attempted, no information on the exhibits is made available and no publicity is given to the collection or the museum.

Over the years, the visitors dwindle to zero, the venture is branded as loss-making and eventually closed.

The dubash patronage for classical music continued for over two centuries. With the end of EIC rule and the Raj taking over, the hereditary role of dubashes ended and the merchant class became patrons for classical music. In this, the role of two hereditary business communities, the Telugu-speaking Arya Vaisya Chetties and the Tamil Chettiars, was particularly noteworthy. The British contributed, too, albeit inadvertently. Their orchestras used the clarinet and the violin, both of which became Carnatic music instruments. The former gained acceptance as accompaniment for the dances of courtesans. The violin had a far greater impact. It was Indianized by the talented Dikshitar brothers—Muthuswami, Chinnaswami, and Baluswami—all of whom had come with their father Ramaswami from Thiruvarur and settled at Thiruvottiyur in the 1700s at the invitation of the dubash Manali Muthukrishna Mudali. Within a few years, no Carnatic concert could be imagined without violin accompaniment.

The Dikshitars were perhaps the forerunners of the trend of musicians leaving their native villages and towns upcountry and moving to Madras city. From the late 1700s, with the kingdoms of South India becoming subservient to the British, migration to Madras became the norm. It was, however, necessary to establish pedigree and most performers retained the names of the towns of their origin as prefixes. Thus the family of Tanjore Kamakshi, a renowned courtesan who migrated to the city in the early 1800s, retained that town's name as its prefix till well into the twenty-first century.

By the late 1800s, patronage was no longer restricted to just a few rich people. Sabhas, social organizations for the promotion of arts, came into existence, funded by several prominent citizens or certain communities well-disposed to the arts. Historically, the word sabha may have meant a congregation of people but in modern parlance it has come to mean any organization that supports the performing arts. It began as a uniquely Chennai phenomenon and spread to other parts of what was then Madras Presidency and later to the rest of South India. Today, Carnatic music and Bharatanatyam performances depend entirely on the sabha network and, to a lesser extent, temple festivals and social gatherings such as weddings for performance opportunities. A very egalitarian form of entertainment was the Harikatha, which involved the telling of a moralistic or religious story to the accompaniment of music and dance. These recitals involved multiple languages and plenty of emotion of which humour was the dominant element. Not surprisingly, this found great favour with the public and the first few sabhas of Chennai were formed keeping the Harikatha in mind.

In the initial years, the sabhas did not ticket the performances they held, instead they circulated a salver among the audience encouraging voluntary contributions, the money collected being handed over to the artistes. But by the late 1880s, tickets had become the norm, though this met with stiff resistance, initially from patrons and performers. Large sections of Carnatic music audiences and almost the entire viewership for dance performances even today do not believe in purchasing tickets for performances. 'Is it an all are welcome concert?' is a frequently asked question by even the most well-to-do patron. Most classical art patrons expect to get their entertainment free, the artistes, by the same inference, being expected to live on nothing but air. Some learned members of the audience even believe that for an artiste to be good, he/she needs to be poor.

People began to feel the need for auditoria from the 1880s, the arts having managed till then in temples, school buildings, parish halls of churches, and the homes of the wealthy. The Madras Jubilee Gayan Samaj, modelled after the Poona Gayan Samaj and adding to itself the word Jubilee to commemorate Queen Victoria's Golden Jubilee, met at Pachaiyappa's Hall. This was a unique organization, for it had British and Indian members, with one of Queen Victoria's sons, Prince Arthur, the Duke of Connaught and Strathearn being its patron, though it is quite likely that His Royal Highness had never even heard of such a body. The samaj featured instrumental music and before each programme it was customary for an Indian, usually a high-ranking personage such as a judge, to present a paper on the arts. This was to help the westerners in the audience understand the proceedings.[5] By the early 1900s, concerts largely began to be held in enclosed spaces such as the McConnaughy Hall in the YMCA building, the Gokhale Hall built by Annie Besant on Armenian Street, the Soundarya Mahal, Govindappa Naicken Street, and Mani Iyer's Hall, belonging to the Theosophical Society and located in Raja Hanumantha Lala Street, Triplicane. These were all spaces in their individual right, used for varied congregational purposes, of which classical music was also one. It is interesting to note that the McConnaughy Hall, which belonged to the YMCA, was at one time home to over eight sabhas, including the only one run by a woman, this being Muthialpet Sri Venkatesa Bhakta Sabha, founded by Alamelu Jayarama Iyer, the wife of a prominent

[5]*Hindu Music and The Gayan Samaj: Published in aid of the funds of the Madras Jubilee Gayan Samaj*, Bombay: Bombay Gazette Steam Press, 1887, available here: https://archive.org/details/in.ernet.dli.2015.221500/.

lawyer in the city.[6] Another space used for performances was the St Mary's Parish Hall, Armenian Street.

With the demand for Carnatic music performances on the rise, more sabhas came into existence. Over the years, some vanished too. One survivor from that era is the Sri Parthasarathy Swami Sabha, set up in 1900. Today, it is the oldest sabha in the city. Mylapore, which became the centre for Carnatic music at this time, was rather late in having its own sabha. But by 1905, Luz and its environs had developed into a posh residential locality with several top-ranking lawyers and judges building their palatial residences there. The Mylai Sangeetha Sabha came up in response to this elite audience in 1919. Despite its high-profile clientele, it was a rather rough and ready venue, operating out of the Vanniyar School on the narrow Nadu Street. The thatch-roofed assembly hall of the institution was the venue for concerts held every Sunday afternoon. The atmosphere was informal, with members of the audience shouting out requests and the musicians obliging them. By 1924, making a name at the Mylai Sangeetha Sabha was considered very important among the artiste fraternity. The venue was not without its perils, for the thatch housed a family of scorpions, members of which would fall on the assembled throng causing much uproar.[7]

Concerts did not necessarily have to be at formal venues. The Jagannatha Bhakta Sabha, a highly respected organization that many artistes aspired to perform at, was in reality the veranda of Veda Vilas, a palatial house belonging to a prominent lawyer. Seating was on the floor and palmyrah fans were provided when the weather turned oppressive, which was for most of the year in Chennai. But the space was known for the discerning appreciation of its audience who would not let anything distract them from the music.[8] So much so that when a woman of the family went into labour during a performance, she was hurried into an anteroom and delivered her baby while the concert went on uninterrupted.[9] The homes of several businessmen of George Town doubled up as venues. Courtesans kept open house on certain days of the month. On Fridays, a chosen set of twenty or so would silently creep up a narrow stairway to Veena Dhanam's first-floor room where the

---

[6]V. Sriram, 'Feminine Touch to Sabha Culture', *The Hindu*, 29 December 2016.

[7]V. Sriram, 'The Sabha Culture of Chennai', *Madras Heritage and Carnatic Music*, 18 November 2011.

[8]R. Rangaramanuja Ayyangar, *Musings of a Musician: Recent Trends in Carnatic Music*, Bombay: Wilco Publishing House, 1977, pp. 18–19.

[9]Lakshmi Devnath, *Mrs YGP: A Class Apart*, Chennai: PSBB Alumni Association, 2005, p. 1.

old lady, blind and perennially acid-tongued, performed on her instrument for an hour. Nobody could make a sound—sneezes, coughs, exclamations of appreciation, and loud keeping of time were all banned—for otherwise the performance would halt abruptly. Far more accommodating were singers such as Bangalore Nagarathnamma, Coimbatore Thayi, and Salem Godavari, who had congregational music performances at their residences on some auspicious days. These bhajan sessions were much looked forward to by the musically minded.

There were, moreover, venues built specifically for the performances of bhajans. And this was the art form that really made music broad based. These structures were endowed by the wealthy, and singers and instrumentalists congregated on certain days stipulated by the donor and performed. Mint Street, in particular, had several of these bhajanai mandapams, most of which have, over time, morphed into temples with active worship, the musical element long forgotten. North Madras that had a large labour force and areas such as Triplicane and Mambalam where the lower-middle classes lived, had many such mandapams, some of which have been abandoned. It was at one such, the Venkatesa Gunamritha Varshini Sabha in Perambur, that workers of Binny Mills used to gather at lunchtime for some respite from their labours. The hosts, Venkataramanjulu Naidu and Selavapathi Naidu, overheard a conversation during a performance between two men about the harsh conditions at the mill. The matter was referred to Annie Besant and her two associates, B. P. Wadia and G. S. Arundale. The result of all this was India's first workers' representative body—the Madras Labour Union, founded on 13 April 1918.[10]

The early twentieth century saw classical music move from the public spaces to venues specially meant for performances. The formation of the Music Academy in 1928, following a resolution passed at the All India Music Conference that was held the previous year in Chennai, saw a new type of sabha. Supported largely by professionals in various fields, it pioneered the concept of a registered body with by-laws to foster the arts. The Academy viewed itself as a cut above the sabhas, with a serious focus on documenting the arts, showcasing performances in a manner it opined was the right way, presenting lecture sessions, collecting music books, and conducting teacher training classes. The Academy's membership was high profile and eclectic from its inception—it included freedom fighters, landholders, musicians,

---

[10] D. Veeraraghavan, *The Making of the Madras Working Class*, New Delhi: LeftWord Books, 2013, p. 86.

writers, publishers, singers, senior government officials, top-ranking lawyers, businessmen, and a maharaja or two.

The Music Academy pioneered the concept of a December Music Season timed to coincide with Christmas Week, when the high court, government offices, business establishments, schools and colleges were largely closed, thereby ensuring full attendance at its concerts. The mornings were devoted to deliberations on the theory of music and its practice and the evenings to performances. From the first year, the Academy's inaugural evenings became a high point in the Madras social calendar, with much of the city's bigwigs and, more importantly, their wives being in full attendance, dressed in the height of conservative fashion. The inauguration, each years was by a celebrity—a minister, a judge, a business baron, a vice chancellor, a maharaja, or a zamindar. Most often, it was not a personality known for any involvement with the arts. But their participation ensured a high profile for the organization. More importantly, and this is something very few realize or recognize, the Music Academy did not hibernate for the rest of the time. It held programmes throughout the year, its research wing under the redoubtable Dr V. Raghavan brought out several books, and it lobbied hard for music to be made a part of college curricula. Queen Mary's College had begun teaching music as an elective subject in 1917 and partly due to the Music Academy's prodding, began a two-year intermediate course in music from 1928. The Academy's Teacher's College of Music started functioning from 1931 and the University of Madras began a Department of Music in 1932. As the graduates from these institutions began teaching music at various places, they, along with the waning traditional gurukulams, did much to make the city a vibrant centre for music.[11] Others who graduated went into research, inspired by scholars such as V. Raghavan and Professor P. Sambamoorthy. All at once, the study of Carnatic music theory, which was largely looked down upon even till ten years earlier as suitable only for those who could not sing, became fashionable. The Music Academy's December deliberations provided a venue for presenting papers and began attracting interest from overseas scholars as well.

The Music Academy also championed the cause of classical dance, which until the 1920s, was performed only by women of the devadasi or courtesan community. The practice of dedicating girls to temples had been an age-old tradition in South India. The women were considered to be the custodians of the arts and, during the reigns of powerful kings, were well looked after

---

[11]V. Sriram and Dr Malathi Rangaswami, *Four Score and More: History of the Music Academy*, Chennai, East West Books 2009.

by the state. An entire community (later called the Isai Vellalars) came into existence, with the women taking to music and dance and the men to percussion, nagaswaram, and nattuvangam (teaching and conducting dance). Over the years, with the decline of native states, support for the devadasis was wanting and many took to living with patrons who provided much-needed financial security.

The first years of the twentieth century witnessed the spread of English education in South India and with it came new ideas of morality that were popular in Victorian and post-Victorian England. The devadasi tradition came under attack as it was mistakenly understood to be a euphemism for prostitution. Several social reformers sprang up to cleanse South India of this practice. All of them had one objective in mind—the outlawing of the devadasi system. There was never any talk of social and economic rehabilitation of the members of the community.

In 1927, the Madras Legislative Council passed a resolution moved by Dr Muthulakshmi Reddy, a leading medical practitioner of Madras, and the daughter of Chandramma, a devadasi of Pudukkottai, recommending that the local government take up legislation against the system. The Hindu Religious and Charitable Endowments Act was amended in 1929 to enable temples to disenfranchise the devadasis of their roles and take back the manyam (gift) lands given to them. Several women and their families were brought to the streets. The wealthy patrons abandoned the women in haste, further bringing about their financial ruin. The devadasis, under the leadership of Bangalore Nagarathnamma, banded together to form the Association of Devadasis of Madras Presidency to fight their case, but this was to no avail. In 1930, Dr Reddy tabled a motion in the assembly demanding the banning of dance performances in temples. The bill led to a bitter fight in the columns of the *The Hindu* and debates elsewhere between the pro-art and the anti-nautch lobbies.

The Music Academy, led by E. Krishna Iyer, its secretary, felt that the dance form had to be looked at as an independent entity vis-à-vis its hereditary practitioners. Deciding that if the art form was to be saved, it must be pulled out of the closet of private parties, the Academy began holding a series of performances from 1931. These events helped to showcase the beauty of dance to the general public and stemmed the tide of disapproval. By 1936, women outside the devadasi community, such as Rukmini Arundale, Lakshmi Sastry, Balachandra, and Kalanidhi Narayanan (nee Ganapathi) took to the art and the Academy saw its efforts bearing fruit. Somewhere along the way, though, this has never been clearly documented, classical dance was renamed

Bharatanatyam, 'to rid it of its association with the Devadasi system'.[12]

With the upper castes taking to dance, the future of Bharatanatyam became secure. But the traditional dance community was left embittered and frustrated especially when the law banning the Devadasi system was finally passed in 1947. The succeeding generations of the community took great care to hide their past. There was a general feeling of having been let down by the upper castes. The social stigma was hard to bear and soon the entire community of Isai Vellalars exited from classical music and dance. Those who remained were relegated to play minor roles. The anti-nautch movement thus marked the beginning of the alienation of a large section of society from the classical arts.

Fast on the heels of the anti-nautch debate came the Tamil Isai Movement. To audiences of today, the idea that Tamil was once accorded second-class status as a language for classical songs may be a surprise but this was so until the 1940s. Those who loved the language expected the Music Academy to correct the situation but that was not to be. The largely Sanskrit and Telugu-loving patrons of the Academy and its rival establishment, the Indian Fine Arts Society, did not pay much heed to this. It was left to Raja Sir Annamalai Chettiar, the merchant prince who had founded the Annamalai University in Chidambaram, to stir things up by calling for a series of Tamil Music Conferences and, in 1943, forming the Tamil Isai Sangam. This body, which had sound financial backing, soon became a worthy competitor to the Music Academy, which rather regrettably clung to its preconceived notion that songs in Carnatic music were preferable in languages other than Tamil.

The Sangam copied the Academy model of a music festival during Christmas week, from 1943 onwards, with songs presented in it to be largely in Tamil. The music community was faced with hard choices—performing at one venue brought retribution from the other. Thus, M. S. Subbulakshmi was dropped by the Academy for singing at the Sangam. The divide was also caste-based, the Academy's largely Brahmin-dominated patrons pitting themselves against the Sangam's Chettiar, Mudaliar, and Pillai clientele. It was only in 1950 that the two organizations recognized the virtues of the other. Rather interestingly, the Sangam hardened its stance thereafter and resolved only to present Tamil songs on its platform while the Academy softened and encouraged more Tamil songs in the bill of fare. But Carnatic music was now divided by caste—the next lot was ready to leave the fold. This was

[12]V. Sriram, *The Devadasi and the Saint: The Life and Times of Bangalore Nagarathnamma*, Chennai: East West Books, 2008.

also when Periyar's Self-Respect Movement and the Dravida Kazhagam were gaining ground, as was rationalist cinema. The non-Brahmin community was greatly attracted to these ideas, given that religion and the largely religious Carnatic music had Brahminism as their most visible symbols. Thereafter, music has remained essentially with the Brahmins. True, it is unidimensional because of its association with one community, but the community must be given credit for keeping the art form alive. In recent times, we often hear the claim that Brahmins acted as gatekeepers of music and appropriated the art form. However, an objective study of art history will reveal that the large-scale loss of popularity of classical music was due to macro factors as discussed above.

The same logic, however, cannot be said to hold good for dance, whose history is more complicated. The accusation of (mis)appropriation is valid to a very great extent there. The very same society that objected to dance performed by devadasis began to welcome upper-class girls and a few boys performing the same pieces. The first generation of gurus were the men and women of the devadasi community—gradually they found their hold over the art slipping away. Within a few decades of the legislation banning dance from temples, the Chidambaram Natyanjali festival came into existence, with scores of dancers making their way to perform at the temple.

There were, however, some positive outcomes during the bitter decades of controversy. In the immediate aftermath of Independence, when traditional patrons such as maharajas and zamindars faded away, it was the sabhas that stepped in to provide support to arts. This was also when the Academy and the Sangam, and other lesser sabhas, worked hard to build permanent locations for themselves, ensuring thereby that Chennai had several performing venues. The first of these was the Rasika Ranjani Sabha, Mylapore, founded in 1929, which built itself a beautiful little auditorium that served it well for years. A little maintenance would have enabled this heritage structure to survive but the management decided they wanted a grandiose edifice in granite and marble. By the mid-1940s, the Tyaga Brahma Gana Sabha built Vani Mahal in T. Nagar, which too has been modernized but more sensitively. The Tamil Isai Sangam, funded by Chettiar money, came up on the Esplanade by the late 1940s and still remains, splendidly maintained, a great landmark. The Music Academy, for all its high-profile image found the going slow. It hurt that the Sangam had built a home for itself as had smaller sabhas. But it was meant for bigger things.

Borrowing money was and is still largely anathema to the conservative South Indian mind. The Tambrahms on the board of the Academy were all for buying 2,400 square feet of space in Triplicane. But they had not contended with Basheer Ahmed Sayeed, a brilliant lawyer who later became judge of the Madras High Court. 'BasheerAhmedSayeed', as he was referred to by much of Madras long before hashtags became popular, was a man who believed that any institution worth its salt had to be backed by large parcels of land. The Music Academy, he argued, was such an institution, which needed space that matched its ideals. In this he was ably supported by Kasturi Srinivasan, editor of *The Hindu* and, like Sayeed, a vice president of the Academy. The rest of the committee gritted its teeth, fell in line, and the Academy borrowed money and purchased a large tract of land on Edward Elliots Road, now Radhakrishnan Salai. The old building on it was brought down and, in 1955, Jawaharlal Nehru laid the foundation stone for the Music Academy's auditorium. Money for the new building came by way of numerous fund raising performances by M. S. Subbulakshmi, who was brought back into the fold after the Academy ate crow. Other major contributors were T. T. Krishnamachari, then union minister and after whom the auditorium would eventually be named, the dancer Kamala Lakshminarayanan, and several industrialists.

The auditorium was complete by 1962 and remains a striking city landmark. Having built it, the Academy almost lost it by defaulting on its loan repayments. That was when T. S. Narayanaswami and K. S. Narayanan, founders of India Cements, worked with a will and got several industrialists to donate money copiously. The Academy was saved. Not everyone was happy, most notably the newspaper baron Ramnath Goenka who had planned to add it to his real estate portfolio.

After the Academy's auditorium there has been only one more—the Narada Gana Sabha—which managed to complete one of its own, on TTK Road. This came about thanks to fundraisers by the film star and dancer Hema Malini, the actor Sivaji Ganesan performing plays, and the musical seer Swami Haridhos Giri conducting several bhajan sessions. That was in the 1980s. Since then, while all sabhas claim that they will eventually build an auditorium, they know it is a pipedream. The audience for Carnatic music remains in the core city areas of Mylapore, Alwarpet, T. Nagar, and Adyar. Land prices here have made it impossible for a music organization to even contemplate such an idea. Most make do with wedding halls, school auditoriums, and open-air sites. The acoustics are a casualty but it doesn't seem to bother the aficionados, speakers set at full volume being considered ample compensation. The obsession with amplification has sounded the death knell for the veena, which is an instrument that requires careful listening. On the other hand, the strident nagaswaram has also become a casualty. What was once a sonorous outdoor instrument has since been forced indoors, emasculating its true potential. Today's audiences would be hard put to believe that the classical arts were meant at one time for performances in the open. The last such attempt by musicologist Ludwig Pesch resulted in an open-air auditorium at the Island Grounds. That has since vanished. Today, temple concerts do provide some idea of what the ambience was like for such performances but are marred by deafening artificial amplification.

It was also during its running battle with the Tamil Isai Sangam that the Music Academy, led by its martinet of a president, Rao Bahadur K. V. Krishnaswami Aiyar, thought hard over how to differentiate itself from other organizations. The first was the introduction of an award, the Sangita Kalanidhi, to be conferred on a top-ranking musician each year, which personage would also preside over the annual December music conference. Other sabhas copied the idea later but the Sangita Kalanidhi still remains the highest recognition that a Carnatic musician can aspire for. Ninety-two artistes have been so far conferred this title, M. S. Subbulakshmi being the first woman to get it. Most of the awardees deserved the accolade, though some lobbied hard for it and at least one got it by threatening to commit suicide in the Academy premises if ignored. But the list of those who missed it is equally illustrious.

The second innovation was the introduction of a season canteen, which Krishnaswami Aiyar brought about in 1939 when the Academy, then a peregrinating organization, met at the University Senate House. More on that is in the chapter on food in the city.

There is always a considerable amount of Carnatic music and Bharatanatyam in the city at any point of time in the year. The big sabhas do have their monthly concerts but a bigger contribution to this year-long activity is that of the smaller sabhas. Many do not have premises of their own and hire venues. For years, the Srinivasa Sastri Hall, on the first floor of the historic Ranade Library in Mylapore, was the favourite location. Countless stars in Carnatic music cut their performing teeth at this venue where a discerning audience led by veteran musicologist and musician Dr S. Ramanathan would gather. In more recent years, Raga Sudha Hall, just a stone's throw from Sastri Hall, has become the venue of choice. And it is today run by a woman—Jaya.

She is not the first, for, as we've seen, Alamelu Jayarama Iyer, wife of top-notch lawyer K. S. Jayarama Iyer had run the Muthialpet Sri Venkatesa Bhakta Sabha even in the 1930s, with a unique model—concerts of senior performers were ticketed and revenue went to fund junior artistes whose recitals were not. From 1970, Parimala Srinivasan ran Raga Tarangini, a sabha managed entirely by women. Later came the Sarvani Sangeetha Sabha, also founded by women. Raga Sudha Hall that Jaya runs was however founded by her father, S. V. Krishnan (SVK).

'Appa was a successful builder in Coimbatore,' begins Jaya in a soft voice as she perches on the edge of the stage that has over the past twenty-three years provided Chennai with some outstanding music. 'While there he became involved with concert organizing and gave it his fullest support. Artistes would be received at the station, hosted at our home, and then post-concert dropped back. This gave Appa and the rest of us plenty of opportunities to closely interact with artistes. Appa felt that live concerts and in particular chamber performances were the best, given the way artistes and audiences bonded. He soon began running a sabha named Raga Sudha in Coimbatore. Later when he shifted to Madras, he continued running it for a while, even as he began conducting performances in Madras at the Sastri Hall. Later he chose to focus on this city and when the opportunity presented itself, purchased land and built this small auditorium, with his residence above. The place was run as per his principles; it was run entirely by him, and he sold no tickets.'

SVK was quite a character—a man with bright eyes, a wide smile, a short and slim frame. He would prowl round and round the venue, ensuring audience discipline, yet taking in music at the same time, often humming the song being performed, always slightly offkey. At the end of the concert, he would sum it up in his characteristic fashion—no beating around the bush about perceived faults, and praise for all that went right. Many people detested SVK for this but you could not deny the service he was rendering music by providing a venue where everyone could come. When SVK died suddenly in 2007, his redoubtable wife R. Vijayalakshmi ('She was the one who managed all the finances even as Appa was the visionary,' says Jaya) suggested to her children that they ought to try carrying forward their father's vision. That is what Jaya and her brother did. Today, Jaya is the public face of Raga Sudha and the music organization that it hosts, Nada Inbam. The venue is let out for commercial events, that brings in the revenue that funds the concerts. It is a labour of love.

Carnatic music has been lucky in that it has always had its share of volunteers. Sabhas have been run everywhere from cow sheds to the terraces of hotels. There have been delightfully eccentric organizations as well such as the Fifty Fifty Club, so named because membership was for couples. You attended a concert and then sat down to a sumptuous dinner after. At least

50 per cent of the members came for the music, was the wry comment of one of the founders, S. Y. Krishnaswami, ICS.

Despite year-round performances, it is in December that the art reaches its peak. What began as a conference run by the Academy during Christmas week has now expanded to include several sabhas, each conducting its own festival. The logistics of making do with hired venues necessitates much planning and so the December Music Season now begins effectively mid-November and goes on till mid-January. It is estimated that around sixty organizations put up around 2,000 performances but nobody has precise numbers. That said, the December Season is impressive, especially if you consider the miniscule audience that follows it. The December Season is often described by naysayers as a case of too many performers running after too small an audience but this is true of any classical art the world over. The other criticism is that a large proportion of the audience consists of the elderly. This is true enough, though, of late, plenty of youngsters do attend, especially the dance performances.

Contrary to what would be expected with such a mega festival, the total number of people who attend these performances probably does not exceed 20,000 people, at most. The same faces can be seen attending concerts at multiple venues, sabha-hopping being an integral aspect of the season. This is also the only time of year when Chennai weather is passable. The world is in holiday mode and so work pressures ease enough that people are able to steal out of office and take in a performance or two. This is the time of year when the NRIs come back home and get their fill of music and dance performances. These migratory birds keep the Carnatic music world's economy going, for it is only from the 1990s, when travel became easier and the number of overseas Indians coming back in December increased, that the Music Season too became bigger. For the NRI, attending concerts is also talent-spotting time. Artistes are invited for concerts to the US; Skype and in-person classes are fixed for children. Over the years, the number of Indian children living in the US and who want to become Carnatic artistes has increased. Making an entry into the Chennai music circuit is not easy but there are a few who have done it.

Above all, Carnatic music has remained a meritocracy. The first performance opportunity may be cadged from a sabha secretary who is known to the family but thereafter, bringing in the crowds depends on the artiste and his/her capability. Public relations exercises do not work beyond a point and while those who fall by the wayside may blame their failure on nepotism, there is not one instance of a performer who made it big by sucking up to sabha officials alone. Ultimately, the audiences need to come.

The same, sadly, is not true of dance. It has always been a poor cousin of Carnatic music in several aspects. First, sabhas view the two the same way and remunerations for dancers are more or less what it is for musicians whereas the expenses involved are much higher. That deters most aspirants. Second, dance has become more of a social qualification—the affluent send their daughters to learn dance and this usually ends in a high-profile debut performance complete with expensive invitations and a dinner party held out as a carrot for the invitees to attend the recital itself. Thereafter, nothing is ever heard of these dancers, who are praised to the high heavens in the promotional brochures. The few that survive to pursue the art as a career know that they can never earn sufficiently from it. Most performers who remain in the circuit come from families with deep pockets. It is an open secret that sabhas are often paid money for performance opportunities. The quality of the art has declined sharply as a consequence. A decade or two ago there were many Bharatanatyam greats. The same cannot be said today. But in terms of numbers there are many middling and sub-par performers.

One of the interesting features in the growth of the classical arts in the city is the way technology has come to their aid in the last 200 years or so. Printing came to Carnatic music in 1856 with the publication of the *Sangita Sarvartha Sara Sangrahamu* by 'Vina' Ramanuja. Thereafter, the city became a major source for music books. Initially the books had the lyrics but, by the late 1800s, notation in a rudimentary form began being printed. This was revolutionary, for Carnatic music had till then remained a strictly oral tradition. The songs were reduced to European or Staff notation in the 1890s by A. M. Chinnasamy Mudaliar, a Roman Catholic who ruined himself in the venture, spending his government servant's salary and pension for it. But it was because of him that Subbarama Dikshitar, an orthodox musician living in distant Ettayapuram, was convinced to bring out a magnum opus—the *Sangita Sampradaya Pradarsini* in 1904, with a hugely refined notation system that (with some improvements) is still being used.

Next came recording. In keeping with the classical arts flourishing in Chennai, the city also became a major recording centre. Carnatic music had been recorded even late in the nineteenth century on wax cylinders. However, the first attempt at recording professionally was during the recording tour of William Sinkler Darby of the Gramophone and Typewriter Limited (GTL) in 1904–05.

International players saw a big opportunity in Madras and several went into exclusive representation agreements with local companies. The most prominent among these were the tie-ups between Columbia Records and P. Orr and Sons in 1931 and the German Odeon Records and A.V. Meiyyappa Chettiar's Saraswathi Stores in 1932. By 1934, the number of companies in the recording business in Madras had jumped to nine, with a few having their own recording studios in the city. Madras had a local brand as well, Broadcast, begun by the jewellers Surajmal's. The recording boom of the 1930s led to gramophone song books flooding Madras as well, with the series of C. Candiah Pillai of the Federated Malay States being the most popular. These featured selections from various records and gave their lyrics and notation. Gramophone records were also reviewed in the popular press and broadcast by Corporation Radio from 1935.

The radio played an important role in the propagation of South Indian classical music in the city as well. Madras was the first location in India where broadcasting of any kind was attempted, with the Madras Presidency Radio Club (MPRC) coming into existence in 1924, founded by C. V. Krishnaswami Chetty, son-in-law of builder baron T. Namberumal Chetty, and an electrical engineer with the Corporation of Madras. The transmission initially comprised gramophone records and later moved to live performances of various kinds, including Carnatic music. To ensure that the broadcasts reached a wide audience, loudspeakers were installed in public places such as the Marina Beach, Robinson's Park, and Panagal Park. The last named still sports its radio house, a round building right at the centre. With the MPRC folding up, the Corporation of Madras stepped in and began the Corporation Radio, taking over Krishnaswami Chetty's transmitter. Concert performances were broadcast live from the studio at Ripon Buildings. Then in 1936 came All India Radio (AIR). Its Madras station was an important centre for classical music and recorded and broadcast several artistes' performances. AIR also transmitted the concerts of some performers during the December Music Festival, the privilege being still proudly held by the Music Academy and the Tamil Isai Sangam. In addition, AIR Madras began tutorial lessons in Carnatic music. Prominent musicians would be invited to conduct mock classes, with a disciple or two, and these would be faithfully followed by listeners and learners from their homes. To aid the tutelage, AIR's monthly magazine, begun in 1958 and stopped in 1987, published the songs to be taught with notation. The 1950s, 60s, and 70s were decades when all of these efforts brought classical music into homes and ensured a wide listener base. Strangely enough, when Doordarshan attempted the same tactics, it was not as successful, probably owing to the visual nature of the medium.

The Carnatic music world was dominated by 78 rpm discs for very many years along with the 33 rpms which came in the 1940s and the 45 rpms which came in the 1950s. HMV ruled the roost during these years with many recordings being made at its Madras studio. Production of 78 rpms ceased in 1974. In the 1980s came the cassette boom and then by the 1990s came the CDs. Carnatic music kept pace with all of these. And then, when YouTube and iTunes and the rest of them transformed the music experience, the art was at the forefront here as well. At the time of writing, it is on Spotify, SoundCloud, and just about any internet platform. The art has moved on to video formats as well, with concerts being screened in film theatres. This niche art has remained alive by reaching out to evolving audience tastes.

Technology has not been all boon to Carnatic music. In the process of making itself available on all media, the art has chosen to ignore a key feature and income generating means for classical arts in the rest of the world—IPR and copyright. Nothing is sacrosanct in Carnatic music when it comes to recording and sharing of performances. It would not be incorrect to say that the art has grown only because it is free of this, no matter how badly it affects the musicians themselves. Over the years, musicians have come to accept this as a fact of life. And it must also be admitted that we have concert recordings of several artistes of the past chiefly because of these surreptitious recorders. There are websites today where entire concerts are available for download within minutes after a live performance. At concerts, it is a familiar sight to see people holding up mobile phones, recording bits and pieces (and at times entire chunks) of a performance and simultaneously 'going live' on Facebook or uploading to a YouTube channel. Some artistes have protested but it is now more or less accepted. How does the musician benefit? More publicity, of the right kind, means more performance opportunities. Today, with digital media providing much of Carnatic music for free, earnings for musicians are restricted to live concerts. The concept of royalty is non-existent. Why then do people still perform, especially when remuneration in Carnatic music is far less than what is received by artistes in the Hindustani idiom? Love for the art is the only explanation possible.

10 | SCORING A CENTUM

The word 'centum' could well be part of the Tamil lexicon, given the number of times it is regularly thrown at Chennai children when it comes to academics. It could also rank among the most hated words if you were a normal child that believed fun and games are an integral part of growing up. Not so for the elders in any middle-class family. Centum, or getting full marks in all subjects, was and is their idea of nirvana. We are a very academically-oriented lot and if you are a Chennai kid, it is likely your entire childhood is spent in going from one coaching class to the other, ferried there by your parents who have not stars but centum in their eyes. Scoring a centum and making your way into one of the IITs or the top-ranking medical colleges of India is the goal that most children need to contend with.

It is, therefore, in eternal search of that centum that most children of Chennai spend much of their day and part of the night. It is no wonder that the pressure on children is intense, leading to suicides peaking among the juvenile population just before examinations or after results are declared.[1]

The parents add for good measure a whole host of non-academic classes, no doubt to relieve the child's tedium—lessons in everything from cricket to swimming to archery to music to dance are the norm. All of these, inadvertently, add to the pressure but they assuage parental conscience—most argue that they would like their children to avail of opportunities they never had while growing up. Nowhere is this vicarious way of reliving their childhood more evident in parents than in the swimming coaching camps where they walk up and down by the pool shouting instructions to their wards who huff and puff down the lanes.

Given such an academic bent, it is perhaps no wonder that Chennai regularly ranks somewhere near the top in nationwide surveys on literacy, gross enrolment ratio in higher education, and the number of professional courses on offer. The downside is of course that the arts courses are considered inferior and, therefore, the refuge of those scoring low in subjects that matter—mathematics, physics, chemistry, biology, and accountancy. Schools are generally ranked on their ability to ensure high ranks for their students in the public examinations that are held at the end of the twelfth standard. Chennai has plenty of such schools, all of which are in a perpetual state of

[1]K. V. Navya, 'TN stays second in suicide rates', *New Indian Express*, 9 September 2018.

demand for seats. To be on the boards of such schools counts for much. To know someone who is related to or is close friends with someone on the school boards ranks next in order of importance. At the time of writing, Sishya School, which is where much of Chennai's uber rich sent their kids till international schools came along, has put up a notice on its website that applications to the kindergarten level is open for three years hence. This means you ought to have applied just after having delivered the child. Chennai's school system thrives on a perpetual shortage, driven more by the search for excellent academic results. Parents will not think twice before sending their wards to an excellent institution several kilometres away from their homes, rather than consider another one close by that is quite good in its own way but is not so academically driven.

Looking at it positively, Chennai has always been in a virtuous cycle when it comes to education—demand and supply keep reinforcing each other, demand always being far in excess of supply. Historically, Chennai has been an education centre. Being a Presidency city helped, for the city's academic infrastructure grew along with Mumbai's and Kolkata's, invariably at the expense of other cities and towns in the hinterland. But what is of interest is that even in the ninth and tenth centuries CE, this was a centre of learning, with the villages of Thiruvottiyur, Mylapore, and Thiruvanmiyur having several monasteries and religious establishments that taught language and scripture in Tamil, Sanskrit, and Telugu.[2] The historic Thiruvottiyur Tyagarajaswami Temple had a pavilion exclusively for the teaching of Sanskrit.[3]

The ancient system of thinnai (forecourt) schools wherein students sat on the front steps of the residence of the teacher or at a public building such as a temple clearly survived in Madras well into the eighteenth century. This is evident from the writings of the Rev Dr Andrew Bell, who arrived here in 1787 as chaplain to several of the regiments stationed in the city. While he was here, he amassed considerable wealth and also had ample time to closely watch the way Indian schools ran. He found that the teachers taught with the aid of senior disciples and hence, could simultaneously monitor classes of considerable variation in levels of learning. The students who taught also became better at their subject, for the questions of the juniors and the necessity to repeat the same course material for their benefit enhanced understanding. Returning to England in the late 1790s, Rev Bell wrote *The Madras School or Elements of Tuition*, which included a 'sketch of a national

[2]Raman, *Early History*, pp. 203–8

[3]Ibid., p. 204.

institution for training up the children of the poor'[4]—the Madras system used fewer teachers, the students performing that role gratis and so could easily be used for setting up low-cost schools across the country and enable the less affluent to afford education. The system was implemented to good effect in England during the nineteenth century. Dr Bell's school building in Leith, Scotland, is even today a preserved structure. Paradoxically, this was when the traditional school system waned in Madras and the rest of India, even as parents began to seek admissions in institutions following Western patterns of teaching. However, thinnai schools survived for a while longer at least in the older parts of the city. As late as the 1940s there are accounts of a 'Dadi Vadyar' (bearded master) Thinnai School in Mylapore.[5]

In the early years, the English were hard pressed to find a good teacher for the Eurasian children they were siring at Fort St George. This is quite clear from the haste with which they forced Father Ephraim de Nevers, who had strayed into the city en route to Indonesia, to stay on. He consented, and among his first acts was to begin a school in Fort St George in 1642, just three years after the British set up base here.[6] By 1678, we read the name of Ralph Ord, 'schoolmaster for the White Town of Fort St George', with a salary that was equal to a junior member of the Council.[7] His was a free school, open to English, Portuguese, and Indian children, though it is not clear as to how many of the last actually enrolled. The EIC's direct involvement with education was fleeting, and thereafter it restricted itself to funding institutions such as asylums. The management was invariably left to the chaplains, through the seventeenth, eighteenth, and at least the first half of the nineteenth centuries.

Thereafter began a period of great change. Firstly, the government began to see the necessity for its involvement, both in lower and higher education. Secondly, simultaneous lifting of restrictions on missionary work in India enabled the start of several schools under the auspices of the London Missionary Society, the Society for the Promotion of Christian Knowledge, and similar bodies. Thirdly, Indians were gradually also realizing their responsibility in the setting up of educational institutions both at the school and college levels. Some other factors contributed too—Indians, both Hindus and Muslims, found

[4]Dr Andrew Bell, *Sketch of a National Institution for Training up the Children of the Poor, Extracted from the Madras School*, London: J. Murray, 1808.

[5]G. Ram Mohan, *Pelathope Days*, Chennai: Akshaya Publications, 2010, pp. 64–9.

[6]Love, *Vestiges of Old Madras*, Vol. 1, p. 49.

[7]Ibid., p. 397.

themselves being employed in professional capacities within the echelons of the government and so could influence official thought; some emerged as legislators and therefore played a more direct role in influencing the spread of education. Lastly, this was also the time when women began to take greater interest in public affairs.

Early in the nineteenth century, we see schools being set up by the various churches in operation. In Chennai, you can always identify an EIC-sponsored/British/church-established school. These always have large campuses. Not so the others. But they served an enormously useful role—education was open to all, irrespective of what their caste or religious background was. The same could not be said of the Hindu/Muslim equivalents. In time, the mission schools, notwithstanding the evangelical reasons for their being set up, ensured that education percolated to classes who would have otherwise had no hope of ever seeing the inside of a school.

In 1838, the Catholic church founded its first school in the city, in Armenian Street. It still functions from there, as the St Mary's Anglo Indian Higher Secondary School.[8] Even older is the Scottish presence, the St Andrews Mission School being founded in 1835 on the campus of St Andrews Kirk, Egmore. This later became the Madras Christian College School, functioning off Harrington Road in a vast campus, with its famed principal of thirty years (1931–1962)—Kunnenkeril Kuruvila Jacob, taking it to great heights and also leaving an impact on school education systems in other institutions of the city.[9] The Wesleyan presence is of older vintage, for it was in 1817 that the mission opened here, with two schools, one in Royapettah and the other in Black Town. The former is the Wesley Higher Secondary School, on Westcott Road.[10] We have several other mission/missionary-founded schools in the city, most dating to the nineteenth century.[11]

But there is one much older, not in the news, but still functioning, and that is St Paul's Higher Secondary, Vepery. It stands apart from most of

---

[8]Muthiah, *Madras Rediscovered*, pp. 437–8.

[9]Joshua Kalapati and Ambrose T. Jeyasekaran, *Life and Legacy of Madras Christian College, 1837-1978*, pp. 7–8.

[10]Muthiah, *Madras Rediscovered*, p. 440.

[11]Some of these include Bishop Corrie (1834), Lady Bentinck Higher Secondary (1838), Christ Church Anglo Indian (1842), Northwick Higher Secondary (1847), ELM Fabricius (1849), Monahan Girls Higher Secondary (1851), Doveton Corrie Boys and Girls (1853), the Anderson Mint Middle, and the Anderson Rajagopal Higher Secondary (1870), St Peter's (1870s), St Patricks (1875), Kellet Higher Secondary (1889), and the St Columban's High (1899).

the other schools mentioned above for two reasons. The first is its year of founding, 1716, which clearly makes it the oldest school of the city founded outside the Fort. But more importantly, it was perhaps the first missionary school to teach Tamil. And that was due to its founding fathers who were from the Tranquebar (Tharangampadi) Mission. This is a tiny village near Nagapattinam on the Coromandel Coast, famed in history as the headquarters of the Danish East India Company. The mission here was established in 1706, by the Rev Bartholomaus Ziegenbalg and Heinrich Plutschau, both from Halle, in Germany. They made it their goal in life to learn Tamil and in this they succeeded to an extent where they translated the Bible into that language and also pioneered its printing. In 1716, Johann Gründler of the same mission was given permission to set up two schools in the Vepery area, one for Eurasian children to learn Portuguese and the second, the Malabar Charity School, for poor native children to learn Tamil. This latter eventually became St Paul's in 1912, its core still a building dating to 1835.[12]

St Paul's may be considered an aberration, for teaching of Tamil and any other Indian language or subject remained the purview of the traditional gurukulams, funded by charities of rich benefactors. That was to change following the death of Pachaiyappa Mudaliar, one of the richest dubashes of Madras, in 1794. His will, after making provisions for his two wives, an infant daughter from the second, and a nephew who is described as an idiot in the document, left the bulk of the vast estate to various good causes, chiefly the conduct of certain rituals and celebrations at various temples and monasteries. This was not to the liking of the nephew, who proved to be not so much an idiot as an arch schemer. The various factions quarrelled violently over the spoils and dragged the matter to court. Several twists and turns later, with the law taking its own time and all the litigants dying like so many characters in a Shakespearian tragedy, the government was left with an interesting problem—an estate that continued to make money, with nothing to spend it on. Enter George Norton, advocate general, Government of Madras. It was he who suggested that the charities stipulated by Pachaiyappa be first isolated and the money endowed for their conduct be ring-fenced. The balance, of which there was quite a bit, it was decided, would be used for education.

It had taken forty-eight years after the death of Pachaiyappa to reach this decision. In 1842, the newly constituted Pachaiyappa's Charities to be administered by the government established the Pachaiyappa Middle School,

---

[12]Ibid., p. 460.

with Tamil and Telugu as the mediums of instruction. A magnificent school building in the Esplanade area, designed by Captain Ludlow and based on the Temple of Theseus, was constructed in 1850.[13] By 1880, the school became a college, which in 1940, moved to a sylvan campus in the Kilpauk area.[14]

In the nineteenth century, Pachaiyappa's Charities, what with its running being under the watchful eye of the government, was viewed as the best and most trustworthy recipient for all donations by the well-to-do and the well-intentioned. Dubash Araneri Govindu Naicker gave the bulk of his fortune in the 1860s and a school in his name began functioning from the Esplanade campus in 1865.[15] The dubash P. T. Lee Chengalvaraya Naicker left his fortune to it in 1874. That money came in useful when Sir Pitti Theagaraya Chetty of the Justice Party and later, the first Indian president of the Corporation of Madras, pushed for the starting of a polytechnic for Indians. That became reality in 1908 when the P. T. Lee Chengalvaraya Naicker Technical Institute was set up in Vepery. It was the city's first skills-based educational institution.[16] In the 1990s, the Chengalvaraya Naicker bequest was separated into an independent trust. Notwithstanding this bifurcation, Pachaiyappa's Trust remains one the biggest of its kind, controlling much real estate across Tamil Nadu and running several educational institutions. But it remains in the news chiefly for the (bad) behaviour of the students of its college and the litigations that the trust is forever embroiled in.[17]

The Pachaiyappa's School began a trend among Indians to start educational institutions either collectively or in their individual capacities. Many were founded to teach in the principal languages of the city—Tamil and Telugu, and were located in the older parts of the city. The Samskrita Andhra Dravida Pathashala, as the name suggests, had three mediums of instruction—Sanskrit, Telugu, and Tamil. Founded in 1847 in George Town, it is today known as the Muthialpet Higher Secondary School, its building much modified, the classroom where the first Carnatic music sabha of Madras functioned from long gone. The Thondaimandala Thuluva Vellalar School was a community-based one and had Tamil as its medium of instruction. Founded in 1854, it expanded to include a branch in 1951, named after the famed doctor

---

[13]Srinivasa Pillai, *Pachaiyappa Mudaliar Charittiram*, Chennai: Sethuselvi Pathippagam, 2015.

[14]*Pachaiyappa's Trust Centenary Volume*, Madras, 1942.

[15]Ibid., p. 65.

[16]Ibid., p. 62.

[17]'Chennai college gang fight spills on to the streets, two Pachaiyappa's students attacked', *News Minute*, 24 July 2019.

and principal donor, M. R. Guruswami Mudaliar.[18] In the old building is a classroom in which at a religious discourse, the talents of the nineteenth-century versifier, seer, and social reformer, 'Vallalar' Ramalinga Swamigal, were first discovered.[19] Not far from here is the Hindu Theological, now Higher Secondary School, begun in 1887. This was the dream child of Shivshankara Pandya, a lawyer turned educationist who literally walked door to door seeking donations for the institution.[20] Its campus is historical, for it has had visits by Swami Vivekananda and Mahatma Gandhi, besides being the place where C. Saraswathi Bai performed a Harikatha and showed the bigots that a woman was equal to if not better than many male performers. Most of the older 'native' schools of the city were community or linguistic identity based and, in many ways, their locations reflect the ethnic character of that area's population.

But there were schools that catered to students irrespective of their caste or religious affiliation. This was also the era when Indian royalty began showing interest in school education, though it must be admitted that much of this was to curry favour with, and appear progressive to, the British. The raja of Ramnad funded much of the plans of the Progressive Union School, founded in 1888. The maharaja of Vizianagaram was one of the early worthies and he took special interest in two schools in Triplicane—the Dravida Pathashala and the Hindu Andhra Balura Pathashala, founded in 1852. Later they would merge to form the Hindu Higher Secondary School, located in two beautiful Indo-Saracenic buildings on Big Street.[21] The same ruler also funded the Vizianagaram Maharaja Girls School in Mylapore in 1869, which kept changing its name over the years depending on who was the patron of the moment, ranging from the maharaja and his son, his sister, the redoubtable Rajakumarika Appalakondayamba Bai Saheba, maharani of Rewa, V. Krishnaswami Iyer, Annie Besant, and others. In the 1940s, the school was going through a financially tough patch when Sir P. S. Sivaswami Aiyar, former advocate general of Madras, sold his palatial house in the upmarket Edward Elliots Road (now Radhakrishnan Salai) area and donated the bulk of the proceeds to it. When he died, the school changed its name once

[18]See TTV Group of Schools website, available here: http://www.ttvschools.org/ttvhss.asp/.

[19]Ibid.

[20]V. Sriram, 'One small meal for children, one giant leap for literacy', *The Hindu*, 26 June 2012.

[21]See Hindu High School website, available here: http://www.hinduhighschool.net/history/index.htm/.

again, to Lady Sivaswami Aiyar Girls School, in memory of the donor and his equally bountiful wife. It was for long the school of choice for all of Mylapore gentry and has since gone on to cater to the less affluent.[22] Its new creation, Sivaswami Kalalaya, caters to the well-off. The early twentieth century saw several other lawyers and judges endowing schools with their wealth. One of these was Pennathur Subramania Iyer, whose estate went to create the PS Group of Schools, beginning in 1905.

The merchant princes of George Town established schools too, the role of the Calavala brothers being particularly noteworthy. Dewan Bahadur Calavala Ramanujam Chetty and his wife, Ethirajamma, were interested in a school run by teachers since 1891 in the Puraswalkam area. When Ramanujam Chetty died in 1916, the school was named after him. In 1929, the school was taken over by Sir M. Ct. Muthiah Chettiar and after his death, was run by his son Chidambaram Chettyar, who also renamed it after his father. The M. Ct. M. schools for boys and girls are major presences in the Purasawalkam area today. The other brother, Rao Bahadur Calavala Cunnan Chetty, proved to be no less generous and lived up to his title of Dharmamurthi. Schools in his name now function from the Perambur and Pattabhiram areas, the latter having an arts college too.[23]

The modern-day corporate houses of the city have continued this tradition. The Murugappa Group runs many schools through its AMM Charity Foundation. The Rane Group supports the Ganapathy Iyer Higher Secondary School in Gopalapuram and helped the Meenakshi College greatly in its early years. The Sanmar Group manages the Indian Education Trust that runs the two Sankara schools, one each in Adyar and Thiruvanmiyur. To list all such institutions would be an impossible exercise.

Late in the nineteenth century, women began taking an interest in the education system prevailing in the city. To further this, the government set up a school in 1870, where upper-class women of Madras could train to become teachers. Begun in the Presidency College campus and named the Presidency Girls' School, it moved to Egmore where it trained women to teach in English, Telugu, and Tamil mediums. It later became the Presidency & Secondary Training School (P&T), remembered chiefly for its star pupil—'Sister' R. S. Subbalakshmi. Born in 1886, she was, in keeping with the times, married while still pre-pubescent and lost her husband shortly thereafter. Her father did not bow down to custom which demanded that her head

[22]V. Sriram, 'From Vizianagaram to Mylapore', *The Hindu*, 20 May 2016.

[23]Sriram, *Fifty Historic Residences*, p. 54.

be tonsured and she be consigned to the backyard of his house forever. On the other hand, he dreamt of educating her and making her a useful contributor to society. This was easier said than done. Subbalakshmi was admitted after much difficulty to the P&T School, Egmore, where she passed with honours in every subject. Post-schooling, she enrolled at the Presentation Convent, George Town, where she completed her First in Arts intermediate degree, winning two gold medals. The next step was to enrol at the Presidency College, Madras, where she planned to graduate in mathematics.

Orthodox Madras was aghast. People lined the streets and showered abuse on her as she made her way to college in a rickshaw. This coupled with the comments of fellow students, all male, could have scared her off but she graduated, scoring the highest marks in the presidency. Showered with job offers, many with high salaries attached, Subbalakshmi turned them all down, resolving to becoming a sister for widows and prefixing the word to her name thereafter. In 1912, she established a Brahmin widows' home, under the auspices of the Sarada Ladies Union, a society formed by the well-to-do women of Egmore. The three girls who enrolled were sent to the P&T School where 'Sister' was employed as a teacher. Gradually the number of widows increased leading to the home having to shift several times. The government purchased the Ice House on the beach and handed it over to her in 1915 to establish the Widows' Home there. Realizing that the women had to train at a school and the P&T in Egmore being some distance away, the government set up the Triplicane Government Secondary and Training School (TGSTS), by transferring the Tamil section of the P&T to it.

Sister, who received the Kaiser-i-Hind medal from the government, was not alone in her battle to give her wards a new life. Her widowed aunt, Valambal, was of immense help as were women members of the Education Service—Miss Christina Lynch (later Mrs Drysdale) and Miss Mildred Prager. In 1920, Sister set up a school for the children of the fisherfolk who lived near the beach. The Kuppam School as it was called, began in the Ice House. It was renamed the Lady Willingdon High School after the then governor's wife, who in her forceful and often highhanded way, did much to further women's interests in Madras. In 1922, this school moved into the premises next door to the Ice House, where it still functions from. Sister, in 1927, established the Sarada Vidyalaya in neighbouring Venkatarangam Pillai Street. In 1938, this was handed over to the Ramakrishna Mission, which shifted the school to Mambalam and later to T. Nagar. Her last creation was Vidya

Mandir School, Mylapore, in 1956. She also served as a member of the Legislative Council from 1952 to 1956.[24]

Sister showed the way and several other women followed, many as teachers and some as founders. Vidya Mandir, referred to above, was co-founded by the Mylapore Ladies Club, a social organization for the women of the area. Children's Garden School, located in Mylapore on the same street where Sister once lived, came up in 1937, due to the vision of Ellen and Dr V. N. Sharma. This German lady and her scholar husband envisaged a school that would impart education to children from low-income families. Today, this government-aided school is part of the Children's Garden School Society that has spawned several educational institutions across the city, all with the same motto of affordable education.[25]

In 1922, a few years after Sister began her journey of reform, another child widow, but belonging to the Arya Vysya community, Andalamma, was married off to Mutha Venkatasubba Rao, a lawyer with bright prospects. It was a revolutionary move for bride and groom. Both were socially committed and as he rose higher in the profession, becoming judge of the High Court of Madras, being knighted and appointed Agent to His Exalted Highness, the nizam of Hyderabad and Berar, they used their clout and wealth for the benefit of the less fortunate. In 1928, when the Women's Home of Service begun by the Women's Indian Association was put on the block, the Venkatasubba Raos acquired it and renamed it the Madras Seva Sadan. This home for destitute girls was, unlike Sister's institution, open to all castes, and a record was set when, in the 1930s, the first Dalit girl was admitted. By then Seva Sadan had moved into Shenstone Park on Harrington Road, a vast tree-studded garden with a bungalow in the middle. It became the birthplace of two educational institutions, apart from social welfare organizations. These are the Madras Seva Sadan Higher Secondary School for Girls and the Lady Andal Higher Secondary Matriculation School, which rather ironically, has now become the preserve of the rich and famous. In the same complex is one of the city's finest auditoriums, named after Sir Mutha Venkatasubba Rao. He also has a school in his name in T. Nagar. In addition, two schools in Tambaram are also run by the same group.[26]

The arrival of Maria Montessori, the pioneering educationist from Italy, in 1940, at the invitation of the Theosophical Society (TS) world headquarters

---

[24]Monica Felton, *A Child Widow's Story*, New Delhi: Katha, 2003.

[25]See Children's Garden School website, available here: http://childrensgarden.in/.

[26]Randor Guy, *The Madras Seva Sadan Saga*, Chennai: The Madras Seva Sadan, 2008.

in Madras, brought a new wave of thinking into the city. The TS, which in 1894 had begun the Olcott School in the hamlet of Urur on the banks of the Adyar for the benefit of Dalit children, had, in 1935, set up the Besant Memorial School within its sylvan campus, named after Annie Besant. Montessori made it into an institution that followed her system of education. The lady was in the event to have a long stay in India, what with the British government putting her under house arrest in Kodaikanal on the grounds that she was from an enemy country, this being the time of World War II. She put her tenure here to good use, imparting training on her system to several people. The Besant School, later renamed the Besant Theosophical School, and a second institution, The School, founded on the same campus by the Krishnamurthy Foundation of India, have remained true to her methods.[27]

Just as Vidya Mandir was founded by the Mylapore Ladies Club, the Padma Seshadri Bala Bhavan (PSBB) chain of schools came up thanks to the Nungambakkam Ladies Recreation Club. It was, in particular, the vision of one member—Rajalakshmi or Rashmi or Mrs Y. G. Parthasarathy or Mrs YGP, as she was variously known. She remained the prima donna of the education world of Madras till her passing in 2019, when she was well into her nineties. The PSBB schools, named after the wife of the first benefactor, began in 1958 with rather appropriately the first and only woman mayor of Madras, Tara Cherian, lighting the lamp. Today it has several branches in the city and outside, handling over 12,000 students.[28]

Right through the early twentieth century, mission schools continued to be set up. St Kevin's came up in Royapuram in 1905,[29] followed by St Bede's in San Thome,[30] better known for its vast cricket grounds, in 1907. The Don Bosco chain of schools established by the Salesian Brothers came up in the 1950s[31] as did the famed Rosary Matriculation School for girls.[32] This was also the time when the Presentation Convent expanded, from its North Madras base, to establish a spacious campus off Mount Road, where

[27]K. V. S. Krishna, 'Maria Montessori Recalled', *Madras Musings*, Vol. XXI, No. 2, 1–15 May 2011.

[28]Devnath, *Mrs YGP*.

[29]See St. Kevin's Anglo-Indian Higher Secondary School website, available here: www.stkevinsaihs.com/.

[30]See St. Bede's school website, available here: http://www.stbedeschennai.org/.

[31]See Don Bosco Matriculation School website, available here: https://dbegmore.com/history-of-the-school/.

[32]See Rosary Matriculation School website, available here: https://www.rosarychennai.com/chennai/school/.

its Church Park school caters to the girls of well-heeled families, even as its St Ursula's, which has a history going back to 1810, enrols the less well-off.[33] Having its origins in the 1880s as the St Anthony's School in San Thome, Holy Angels Anglo Indian Higher Secondary School made a name for itself only in the 1930s, when under its present name, it shifted to five acres of land in the then new and upcoming area of T. Nagar.[34]

Hindu missions set up schools too, the most famous being those of the Ramakrishna Order. The Ramakrishna Mission Boys' Home was started in 1905 in Mylapore by Swami Ramakrishnananda, one of the senior disciples of the saint, as a place where poor students could be provided accommodation, food, and education. Nurtured by the cousins C. Ramaswami (Ramu) and C. Ramanujachari, it acquired a beautiful building in the same area where it still functions from, handling 600 students and three institutions—a residential high school, a residential polytechnic, and a day school.[35] Elsewhere in the city, the mission runs schools for boys and girls.

Chennai also has several educational institutions set up by some of the religious and linguistic minority communities in the city. The Madrasa-i-Azam is arguably the oldest of the Muslim schools, tracing its origins to a facility established by Muhammad Ali Wallajah, the nawab of Arcot in 1761 to educate the boys of the royal family. His successor, Umdat Ul Umrah, widened the student base to include the sons of nobility but it was under Nawab Ghulam Muhammad Ghouse Khan, who wrote poetry under the name of Azam, that the school was thrown open to all and took his pen name in gratitude, becoming the Madrasa-i-Azam. In 1849, the government took over the school, renaming it the Government Madrasa-i-Azam. The school initially functioned from Chepauk, but early in the twentieth century moved to Umda Baugh, a nawabi palace on Mount Road, which had by then come into the possession of the Gujarati Lodd family, who were happy to part with it for a nominal price. The school continues to function from this campus though Umda Baugh itself, whose design probably inspired Falaknuma Palace in Hyderabad, was neglected and allowed to collapse.[36]

---

[33]S. Muthiah (ed.), *The School in the Park*, Chennai: The Sacred Heart Alumni Association, 2009.

[34]Holy Angels Anglo Indian Higher Secondary School, available here: https://en.wikipedia.org/wiki/Holy_Angels_Anglo_Indian_Higher_Secondary_School/.

[35]Su Na Chokkalingam, *Ramakrishna Mission Manavar Illam Thotramum Valarchiyum*, Chennai: Ramakrishna Mission Manavar Illam, 1998.

[36]S. Muthiah, 'Education beyond religion', *The Hindu*, 27 November 2017.

There were, besides this institution, traditional madrasas as well, the oldest in the city being the Madrasa-i-Sayeedia established in 1872 and closing down in 1995.[37] There are several others of later vintage, functioning even now.

Education of Muslim girls began with the founding of a lower primary school in Royapettah, which later became the Government Hobart School in 1873, named after the then governor of Madras. It moved into its present campus, a lovely but now badly neglected palace opposite the Express Avenue Mall, late in the nineteenth century. It is now a higher secondary school.[38] The thrust for the education of Muslims has since been admirably given by the Anjuman-e-Himayath-e-Islam. This was begun in 1890 by a few prominent Muslims of the city, led by His Highness Muhammad Munawar Khan Bahadur, prince of Arcot. Registered in 1894 under the Literary, Scientific and Charitable Societies Registration Act, it began life in the Wallajah Mosque, Triplicane, under the guidance of Shamsul Ulama Moulvi Haji Ghulam Rasool Sahib. It was chiefly meant to be a hospice for poor and orphaned Muslim boys who came to the city for education. But over time it became an institution for formal education. In 1948, the Anjuman shifted to its present campus on Boag Road. The foundation stone was laid by the then Governor General of India, Rajagopalachari. A magnificent mosque was inaugurated on the premises in 1969. A boys' home was also built here, and this was inaugurated by Annadurai, chief minister of Tamil Nadu. The Anjuman owed much of its growth to T. Abdul Wahid, a dynamic business personality of Madras.[39] Interestingly, the Muslims of Madras were not swayed by Jinnah's blandishments and preferred to work closely with the Hindu community here. An example of this is Nawab C. Abdul Hakeem's Hindu-Muslim Higher Secondary School in George Town. The same donor also set up a high school in Triplicane.[40]

The Punjabis of the city, through their association, began the Adarsh Group of schools. Likewise, the Sindhis began their Model Schools, starting with one in Kilapuk in 1975. The Telugus' need for instruction in their medium was met by Dr K. N. Kesari, who set up in 1944 the first of the schools

---

[37]S. Anvar, *Islam, Madras: The Land, The People & Their Governance*, Chennai: Palaniappa Bros, 2008, p. 150.

[38]Ibid.

[39]V. Sriram, *When Mercy Seasons Justice: The Life and Times of Habibullah Badsha*, Abdul Jabbar Suhail, 2018, p. 130.

[40]'Hundred Years of Melvisharam Muslim Educational Society (1918-2018)', Melvisharam: Melvisharam Muslim Educational Society, pp 1–21.

that would bear his name. Several schools, particularly in north Chennai, owe their existence to the prominent business communities of the city—the Gujaratis, Marwaris, Jains, Tamil Chettiars, and Telugu Chetties.

The Dalits of the present day were beyond the pale with regard to education in any of the institutions listed above, barring those run by missionaries. This imbalance was set right in a small but significant way by the reformer Ayothi Das Pandithar, who along with the Theosophist Colonel H. S. Olcott, set up schools for what was then known as the Adi Dravida community. Pandithar also approached the government and impressed upon it the necessity to have special schools for the community. This resulted in the setting up of Adi Dravida Welfare Schools which over a period of time spread all over Madras Presidency.[41] In the city, these came under the care of the Corporation of Madras.

No story of education in the city can be complete without detailing the role of the corporation in this field, and unlike its record in matters such as drains and roads, its performance in this aspect is exemplary. The civic body's involvement began in the 1870s when it started aiding elementary schools under private management. By 1879, 200 such institutions with over 7,000 students were being supported. The corporation opened its first school in 1906 and this was at Chetpet, for the benefit of Dalit students. By 1910, the civic body had decided to undertake the building of 'forty model elementary schools at the rate of four schools each year, cost of each building with necessary equipment not exceeding ₹10,000'. Money was hard to come by and it was able to construct only twenty-six schools and maintain four others in rented buildings within the prescribed period. In 1920–1921, a beginning was made to provide free elementary school education exclusively for girls. In 1923, the corporation, for the first time, earmarked a part of property tax collected exclusively for education. Thereafter, it began introducing free and compulsory education progressively in all its wards, the first of the high schools coming up in Nungambakkam in 1926. Attendance Committees soon began to function in each Division and did commendable work, 'bringing children to school and in watching the progress of those who joined the schools'. It was recorded in 1931 that 'as a result of these measures, the average attendance at Corporation Schools rose from 76.9 per cent to 81.4 per cent, and it was hoped that by these arrangements, the poor parents will be greatly encouraged to send their children to schools instead of to work. Conductors and conductresses escorted pupils safely along routes of heavy

[41]Gauthama Sannah, *Ka Ayothidasa Pandithar*, New Delhi: Sahitya Akademi, 2012, p. 50.

traffic, bullock carts conveyed (purdah-observing) Muslim girls from home to school and back, and guardians were interviewed and prevailed upon to send their wards to school. Notice was also issued against them for default.'[42]

The Corporation Education Department also arranged special courses on subjects like agriculture, gardening, bee-keeping, poultry-rearing, road sense and safety-first, history, geography, language-teaching, and music. The services of the Agriculture Department, police officers, and specialists were availed of for this purpose. There was even a course in scouting, for male and female teachers. With a view to wiping out illiteracy gradually, attendance checkers were appointed in 1945 to organize an intensive drive to enforce rules.[43]

Madras realized very early on that students from very poor families could be induced to attend school if there was one hot, healthy meal offered to them each day. The Dalit leader Ayothi Das Pandithar is said to have introduced it in 1909 or thereabouts in a school for his community. In 1918, Kurichi Rangaswami Iyengar arranged for it at the Hindu Theological School, Mint Street. In 1923, Thamarapakkam Sundara Rao Naidu, who would later become mayor, inaugurated the experiment of providing tiffin 'to secure continuity and regularity of attendance of pupils' at the Corporation School at Thousand Lights and this was subsequently extended to the pupils of the Corporation Schools at Mirsahibpet and Chetpet. The Corporation of Madras started a scheme for the supply of midday meals to poor and deserving children in all corporation primary and middle schools in 1925. Pupils were given the benefit of midday meals and reconstituted milk, taught cleanliness, and given free baths, supplied with soap, oil, comb, and towel. While this was done in order to improve attendance in schools, the supplementary diet to children ensured healthy growth, and helped them pay more attention to their studies. On 1 August 1930, with the council sanctioning ₹25,000 from general funds, supply of midday meals to poor pupils in schools began. In 1947, the scheme was reorganized with supply through three midday meals centres (North, Centre, and South Ranges) with cooking done in central kitchens maintained by the corporation. This inspired Chief Minister Kamaraj to take it to several schools in the state in the 1950s. The programme in the city, which started on a modest scale with 500 beneficiaries, was gradually extended from time to time and, by 1978, it covered 60,000 children. Private and state government contributions were also made. In 1983 came the Chief Minister's Nutritious Noon Meal Scheme to poor and deserving children.

[42]Menon, 'Municipal Services', pp. 118–9.

[43]Ibid.

Food sourced from 336 schools' cooking centres was sent to 375 primary and middle schools. The brainchild of the then chief minister, MGR, it has today received praise and has been implemented in several nations of the world.[44]

The Corporation of Madras today manages several higher secondary schools, high schools, an Urdu High School, a Telugu High School, middle schools (Tamil, Telugu, and Urdu), primary schools and thirty kindergarten schools with an overall enrollment of around 100,000 students and 4,000 teachers.[45]

To benefit pupils of the backward classes living in slums, the Corporation of Madras soon decided to run branch schools. Education was brought 'to the very doors of the slum'. There are also several nursery schools functioning under the auspices of the corporation across the city. In the past few years, the methodology of teaching and studying has completely been overhauled. The corporation schools now have the flexibility to adopt activity-based learning and some use the Montessori system in junior classes as well. Maths labs have come up in some schools. The emphasis on bringing in more children to achieve 100 per cent literacy continues. Students are given geometry boxes, scholarships, and special programmes are extended to girls.

Despite all this, to be seen attending a corporation-run school is considered infra dig and only the poor admit their children there. This is partly owing to faulty methods in teacher selection, which results in poor quality of faculty members. The corporation has also not been able to sufficiently market itself in the face of the private institutions, and the glamour these latter have with their English-speaking staff and students. A vicious cycle grips the corporation schools—they get poor teachers, and so only poor students join. The government continues pumping in money to build infrastructure and it is a pity when these are not put to good use.

One of the key drawbacks of the corporation schools as per many parents is their 'low standard'. This can imply anything—a view that students and teachers are drawn from the lower levels of society, the consistent lowering of standards which is across the entire administration in the state, or a view that corporation schools do not provide skills that can enable children to handle complex tasks later. There is yet another, and more important belief—the corporation schools follow the State Board when it comes to syllabus and this is not comparable in standard to the Central Board of Secondary Education

[44]V. Sriram, 'Caring for Chennai, a hundred years of Ripon Buildings', Corporation of Chennai, 2013, p. 84 (unpublished).
[45]Ibid.

(CBSE), which is the most popular school certifying board in India.

Education is a state subject as per the Constitution and Tamil Nadu guards this prerogative jealously. Begun in 1910, the Tamil Nadu Board of Secondary Education has four certifying streams under it for all classes up to the tenth standard. These are the Anglo-Indian, the Matriculation, the Oriental School Leaving Certificate, and the Secondary School Leaving Certificate examinations. The eleventh and twelfth standards have a common board—the Higher Secondary Certificate. Over the years, the state has been caught in a dilemma—should it focus on getting more and more enrolments and higher pass percentages or should it look at raising the standard of education so that the bar is set higher, more or less on par with the CBSE? Successive state governments have preferred the former and the State Board has come to rank below the CBSE when it comes to standards of education. Nobody really complained. In fact, it helped everyone—CBSE schools induced less gifted children to leave and join State Board schools where it would be easier to score high marks, a prerequisite for seeking college admissions. Parents also preferred the State Board for the same reason—scoring marks was easier and so admissions to colleges in the state was more or less assured.

In 2010, the Karunanidhi-led DMK government brought in the Tamil Nadu Uniform System of Education Act, which normalized standards across all state-run boards and, in the eyes of critics, lowered it to the lowest common denominator. It was decried as a dumbing down of education to suit the masses. The government had sound logic behind its move—there was of course the matter of electoral advantages, but it also had the potential to get more children to achieve pass marks. The principal Opposition party, in keeping with the recent legislature traditions in the state, chose to remain silent but when it came to power a year later, scrapped the scheme. With textbooks already printed but prevented from being released to students, schools and parents became a worried lot. The matter went to court, which ruled that the scheme had to be implemented. Known as Samacheer Kalvi, it came into effect in 2011, much to the distress of its detractors. It must be emphasized here that the problem did not affect the more affluent. They simply moved elsewhere, to CBSE-run schools or those following international boards, several of which had come up in the OMR area. For those of the middle classes and below, Samacheer Kalvi was, at best, a mixed blessing.

While it helped with scoring in the board exams, it did not help in coping with undergraduate studies. Not every student passing out of schools following the Tamil Nadu boards was assured of admission within the state. Some had to move out and when they did, they found themselves struggling when compared with fellow students who had qualified in the CBSE or other State Board examinations. Once this became known, schools in Chennai and elsewhere in Tamil Nadu, which were affiliated to the State Board found demand for seats dropping, in some cases by as much as 50 per cent.[46]

Compounding their woes was the National Eligibility & Entrance Test (NEET), a common examination across India for admissions to all medical colleges, private and state run. Tamil Nadu reacted on predictable lines when this came into effect in 2018—perceiving it as an affront on the state's rights on education. But there was no way it could be avoided, with the courts upholding the validity of the examination. The state did badly in the first year, with only 39 per cent of its candidates passing.[47] At least one of those who did not make it, Anitha, committed suicide, an unfortunate occurrence that the government could have easily prevented.[48] A year later, Tamil Nadu showed a marked improvement—48 per cent cleared the exam, making it the state with the fastest growth on NEET scores.[49] Learning from the Anitha episode, for she had failed because her parents could not afford coaching classes, the state introduced free coaching classes for students in rural areas, to help them qualify NEET.[50] This was despite its official stance of protesting against the examination.

At a fundamental level, Tamil Nadu's concerns over NEET are genuine. Loaded as the examination is in favour of those who come from the Central Board and also from the more privileged strata of society, NEET will end up discouraging aspirants from rural areas and backward castes from appearing for it. These have traditionally been the candidates who, on qualifying and graduating, fill the state's public healthcare, its hospitals, and its medical centres in rural areas, in short, the backbone of the health industry of which Tamil Nadu and Chennai are so proud. What will happen if they shy away in large numbers from NEET? At the same time, the state cannot keep lowering its standards while the rest of the world is moving in the opposite direction. Samacheer Kalvi has had its impact on engineering as well, with just one

---

[46]'Has Tamil Nadu plateaued?', *Madras Musings*, Vol. XXV, No. 15, 16–30 November 2015.

[47]'Tamil Nadu Among States With Lowest Pass Percentage In NEET 2018', *NDTV Education*, 4 June 2018.

[48]R. Rajaram, 'Girl who filed case against NEET commits suicide', *The Hindu*, 1 September 2017.

[49]'Tamil Nadu betters NEET results by 9 per cent, city girl gets 57th rank', *DT Next*, 6 June 2019.

[50]'Tamil Nadu To Provide Free NEET Coaching To Government School Students', *NDTV Education*, 13 May 2020.

student from the Tamil Nadu Board schools ranking in the first 100 at the IIT JEE exams in 2019.[51] For a state that has always boasted of high standards of education and literacy, this is a tough challenge.

But there is good news—a survey conducted by ASSOCHAM shows that Tamil Nadu has 100 per cent enrolment in primary and upper-primary education—we did manage a centum, after all.

[51]'TN yet to improve performance in IIT JEE', *New Indian Express*, 15 June 2019.

11 | BACHELORS AND MASTERS

'Learning promotes natural talent' is the motto of the University of Madras, which for almost a century defined higher education in the state of Tamil Nadu and, therefore, of Madras city as well. A brief history of that institution may be the right note to start this chapter with but long before the university was the College of Fort St George, a unique experiment put together for the EIC's servants to learn Indian languages. In the process, it brought to light several local talents and many classical works. It also set in motion a long line of political thought, albeit unwittingly, which still continues to dominate Tamil Nadu.

College Road is an upmarket thoroughfare in the Nungambakkam area. Most Chennaiites would assume that the road is named for Women's Christian College, which functions from one end. But the road remembers the College of Fort St George, which once existed here on a vast tree-studded campus, now home to the Directorate of Public Instruction, a body that seems quite determined to stamp out what little heritage there is in the place by building bigger and bigger office blocks, all of very doubtful architectural merit.

The closing years of the eighteenth and the early years of the nineteenth century saw many Europeans taking an active interest in Indian antiquities, history, and culture. This saw the setting up of the Asiatic Societies in Bengal in 1784 and in Bombay in 1804 respectively. Madras did not have one but officials here who had the same interests corresponded with the societies in Calcutta and Bombay, eventually forming a local equivalent—the Madras Literary Society, in 1817 or thereabouts. Five years prior to this, rather on the lines of a similar institution at Fort William, Calcutta, the College of Fort St George came up in Nungambakkam. It was, as mentioned earlier, chiefly to teach officers of the EIC the principal languages of South India—Tamil, Telugu, Kannada, and Malayalam, as well as Sanskrit and Arabic/Persian. In the process, it recruited as teachers several scholars in each of these languages. Such an institution needed a syllabus and this was structured on Western lines with oriental content. There were examinations and the candidates that did well were not only given performance bonuses but also fast-tracked in their careers at the EIC.

The college also became the centre for much research activity, studying the grammar of various languages. The findings were published and within a short while, a stream of books began coming out. These included Beschi's

'Low Tamil' Grammar, an eighteenth-century work by the Italian linguist, *A Brief Exposition of Tamil* by Chidambara Pandaram, Head Tamil Master at the College of Fort St George, *Andhra Dipika* by Mamidi Venkayya, *A Grammar of Teloogoo Language Commonly Termed the Gentoo* by A. D. Campbell, John McKerell's *Canarese Grammar,* and Rev C. M. Whish's *Malayalam Grammar and Dictionary*—all of them among the first printed books in the respective languages.[1]

Among the moving spirits behind the college was Francis Whyte Ellis, who had come to Madras in 1796 as a writer in the EIC. He had risen steadily, becoming in 1810, the collector of Madras. All the while, even as he focused on his work, Ellis studied Tamil and Telugu, becoming in the process, an ardent admirer of Thiruvalluvar and his *Kural*. This and his awareness of local traditions were to see him at his best in the final eight years of his life, for Ellis died when he was barely forty-two, of food poisoning/cholera while on a tour of Ramnad district. But the legacy of those eight years lives on.[2]

Ellis involved himself in the revival of several temple festivals. The Panguni Uththiram of the Kapaliswarar Temple in Mylapore was funded by the EIC when its hereditary trustees fell out with each other. He developed a great attachment to the Egavalli/Pidari Amman Temple in George Town, declaring the goddess to be the tutelary deity of Madras. The processional icon would come once a year to the North Gate of Fort St George and be received with all honours by Ellis.[3] When Madras faced a severe drought in 1818, Ellis dug twenty-seven wells, surmounting them with a quote from the *Kural* that lauded such acts. One of these inscriptions survived for long on the wall of the Periyapalayathamman Temple in Royapettah. Among Ellis' numerous responsibilities was the Madras Mint and in that capacity he struck a gold coin bearing the effigy of Thiruvalluvar.[4]

By far the biggest legacy of Ellis was, however, his recognition of the Dravidian languages being independent of Sanskrit. The Telugu grammar penned by A. D. Campbell, a protégé of Ellis', had him writing the foreword. In it, Ellis, for the first time, postulated what is now known as the Dravidian

---

[1]For a detailed and excellent account of the college, see Thomas R. Trautmann (ed.), *The Madras School of Orientalism: Producing Knowledge in Colonial South India*, New Delhi: OUP, 2009.

[2]V. Sriram and Karthik A. Bhatt, *Brotherhood and Benevolence: The History of English Freemasonry in South India*, Chennai: The District Grand Lodge of Madras, 2017, p. 51.

[3]Ibid., pp. 90–91.

[4]Muthiah, *Madras Rediscovered*, p. 517.

proof—that Tamil, Telugu, and Kannada had roots outside of Sanskrit. That evidence would grow under people like Bishop Caldwell and later acquire gargantuan proportions on account of the Dravidian movement in the twentieth century. It would take its time to crystallize, the sudden death of Ellis no doubt slowing down further progress, but its time would come.[5]

The EIC closed down the College of Fort St George in 1854, for by then, there were few officers of the calibre of Ellis or Campbell. Most believed that India had nothing to offer by way of thinking and learning. The teachers went their separate ways but a glimpse of what the place was in its heyday is offered by U Ve Swaminatha Iyer in his biography of his guru, Meenakshisundaram Pillai. He lists a veritable galaxy of Tamil greats in the employment of the college in the 1840s and gives a brief description of the research and publishing activities of the Tamil department.[6] The closure of the college however did not affect the Madras Literary Society, which had functioned as its library and research centre. Under its auspices, a journal, the *Madras Journal of Literature and Science* (MLS), was published for years.[7] The MLS also birthed the Madras Museum, the country's oldest. Today, the MLS survives as the city's oldest library, housed in a beautiful heritage structure within the erstwhile college campus, struggling to keep together a vast collection of antiquarian books. A young team of dedicated volunteers strives to keep the society going.

The death of the college meant but a small setback for higher education in the city, for within three years, Madras had its university, set up along with counterparts in Bombay and Calcutta, by the Act of 1857. But work on setting up institutions of higher education in the city had been in progress for two decades. Sir Thomas Munro, governor of Madras between 1820 and 1827, was a man with a vision, who even foresaw a time when the British would have to leave India and advised them to do so with grace when that came to pass. During his tenure as governor, Munro, who was very familiar with Madras Presidency, declared that a school ought to be established in every collectorate and taluk, and towards this end set up a Committee of Public Instruction. This naturally began functioning from the campus of the College of Fort St George and the office of the Director of Public Instruction

---

[5]Sriram and Bhatt, *Brotherhood and Benevolence*, p. 51.

[6]U Ve Swaminatha Iyer, *Sri Meenakshisundaram Pillai Avargal Charittiram*, Chennai: Dr U Ve Swaminatha Iyer Nul Nilaiyam, 2013, pp. 55–71.

[7]N. S. Ramaswami, *Madras Literary Society: A History, 1812–1984*, Madras: The Madras Literary Society, 2018.

(DPI), formally established in 1854, has been here ever since.

Macaulay's famed Minute of 1835 that advocated English as the language of education, administration, and jurisprudence speeded up matters. Advocate General George Norton, he of the Pachaiyappa Trust fame, led a signature campaign in 1839, of 70,000 'native inhabitants' wherein the need for an English college in the city was highlighted. Replying to this, the governor, Lord Mountstuart Elphinstone, decreed that two institutions would be set up—first a high school that taught English literature, a regional language, philosophy, and science, and, second, a college that provided instruction in the higher branches of the same subjects. The school was the first to come up, in 1841, with Eyre Burton Powell, a Cambridge Wrangler, as the headmaster. The faculty comprised successful lawyers, journalists, and men about town of the city. The graduates were termed Proficients and among the early ones were Calamur Viravalli Ranganatha Sastry, later to become a judge of the Court of Small Causes, and (later Sir) Thiruvarur Muthuswami Iyer, first Indian to become a judge of a high court. By 1855, the high school was upgraded and became the Presidency College. It moved into its present Chisholm-designed buildings on the Marina in 1870/1871. When the University of Madras was formed, Presidency was the first college to be affiliated. It became an autonomous institution in 1987.[8]

A few colleges that taught professional courses also predated the formation of the University of Madras. The Madras Medical School was founded in 1835 and by 1851 had become the Medical College.[9] In 1855, the Government Law College began in the premises of the Presidency College. It moved to its magnificent but now sadly neglected buildings at the edge of the Esplanade in the 1880s.[10] In 1997, this became the Tamil Nadu Dr Ambedkar Law University, a naming that the Constitution-maker of India may not have been very comfortable with, given his caution against idolization in a democracy. An institution that regularly makes it to the news for protests by its students, many of whom aspire for a career in politics and not the practice of law, it nevertheless has a glorious past.

Beating the university's creation by a few months was the teacher-training institute, the oldest in the country, later to become the Government College of Education and affiliated to the University of Madras. It became

[8] *150 Years of Excellence: A Pictorial History of the University of Madras*, Chennai: University of Madras, 2006, pp. 7–15.

[9] Ibid., p. 16.

[10] Ibid., p. 179.

autonomous in 2005.[11] The College of Engineering, Guindy, now a part of Anna University, traces its origins to the Survey School begun in 1794 which in 1861 became a college.[12] The Government College of Arts and Crafts, now a part of the Tamil Nadu University of Fine Arts, was founded as a private school in 1840 and became a college in 1961.[13] The Agricultural School was begun in Saidapet in 1868 and this shifted as the Agricultural College in 1906 to Coimbatore. It was for long affiliated to the University of Madras before becoming the Tamil Nadu Agricultural University in 1971.[14] The Madras Christian College, the origin of whose school we saw in the previous chapter, came into existence in 1867.[15] The Pachaiyappa's School became an eponymous college in 1880.

It was with these institutions in place that the University of Madras came into existence in 1857. It, thereafter, guided higher education in much of what was Madras Presidency and neighbouring princely states till the twentieth century.

Thus it was from the University of Madras that there emerged universities of Mysore (1917), Osmania in Hyderabad (1918), Andhra (1926), and Travancore, now Kerala (1937).[16] In 1929, the university also saw to the birth of one of India's first public universities set up by private initiative. This was the Annamalai University, founded by Raja Sir Annamalai Chettiar, the business baron from Chettinad.[17] Independent India saw yet another Chettiar magnate lavishing funds for the creation of colleges across Tamil Nadu, specializing in science and technology, the best-known in the city being the A. C. College of Technology, now a part of Anna University. This was K. V. Al. Rm. Alagappa Chettiar and eventually an entire university came to be named after him.[18] Several others have since emerged from the University of Madras. These include the Bharathiyar and Bharathidasan universities, located in Coimbatore and Trichy respectively, both begun in 1982.[19] In 1989, the Tamil Nadu University of Veterinary and Animal Sciences was set up, its core

[11] *150 Years of Excellence,* p. 17.

[12] Ibid., p. 167.

[13] Ibid., p. 178.

[14] Ibid., p. 65.

[15] Ibid., pp. 20–21.

[16] Ibid., p. 73.

[17] Ibid., p. 75.

[18] K. Vairavan, *Dr R. M. Alagappa Chettiar: The Life and Legacies of a Visionary*, New Delhi: Sai Amartya, 2014.

[19] *150 Years of Excellence*, p. 107.

being India's first veterinary college, set up in 1903 under the University of Madras.[20] All of these hived-off entities have not diminished the stature of the mother institution, which today has sixty-eight departments that are divided into seventeen schools, seven campuses, and has ninety-eight colleges affiliated to it. In 2005, the university was accredited at the five-star level by the National Assessment and Accreditation Council (NAAC).[21]

Women's higher education has had a long history in the city, the first steps towards it being taken late in the nineteenth century. But it was only in the early years of the twentieth century that concrete action was contemplated. In 1914, the Madras College for Women was established, a farsighted British educationist, Miss de la Hey, being the first principal. Her brother was the principal at the same time at the Newington College—an institution for the sons of the zamindars of Madras Presidency, located at Teynampet, a suburb of the city. His murder by shooting at point-blank range on the night of 15 October 1919 saw the college closing down, the death being an unresolved mystery till date.[22] His sister, however, had a long and respected tenure in Madras as principal of Madras College for Women, which, in 1915, changed its name to Queen Mary's College (QMC).[23] QMC remained for long the premier institution for women in the city and much of Tamil Nadu. Its historic campus by the Marina boasted of several heritage structures and a swimming pool for girls long before such facilities became commonplace. QMC today caters to girls from less affluent backgrounds. A casual walk around the campus shows that the college, now autonomous, has seen better days.[24]

A year after QMC's establishment, the city got its next women's college with assistance from twelve inter-denominational American church organizations. Named Women's Christian College, it moved in 1916 to its 16-acre campus on the banks of the Cooum, in Nungambakkam, next to the erstwhile College of Fort St George precinct.[25] Stella Maris College, easily the best known among higher education institutions for women in the city, began at the Rosary Matriculation School campus on 15 August 1947. It later moved to its present campus on Cathedral Road and became

---

[20]Ibid., pp. 18–19.

[21]Ibid., pp. 20–203.

[22]Randor Guy, *Crime Writer's Case Book*, Chennai: KK Books Pvt Limited, 2007, pp. 155–75.

[23]Nithya Balaji, Gita Narayanan, and S. Anandalakshmy, *Celebrating a Century: Queen Mary's College, Chennai 1914-2014*, Chennai: The QMC Alumnae Association, 2014.

[24]V. Sriram, 'Will they team together to clean it up?', *Madras Musings*, Vol. XXI, No. 19, 15–31 January 2012.

[25]*Women's Christian College: A Hundred and Counting*, Chennai: WCC, 2016.

an autonomous institution in 1987.[26] The famed lawyer V. L. Ethiraj gave Madras its next women's college in 1948, named after him and endowed with much of his wealth and real estate.[27] In 1975, the Meenakshi College for Women was founded, the brainchild of Professor K. R. Sundararajan. It became reality largely due to the Ganapathy Educational Trust funded by the Rane Group of Companies.[28]

But even before these high-profile colleges came up, a woman of the city had made up her mind that her wealth would be donated to furthering education. This was Chellammal Gramani. Born in 1867, she was married off to Mylai Vadamalai Gramani, who, despite his inclination towards an ascetic life, became a very successful businessman. The couple was childless and when Vadamalai died in 1911, Chellammal decided to donate his wealth to the cause of education. Her will, made in 1913, stipulated that after certain charities, the remainder of her estate had to be handed over to Pachaiyappa's Trust. This was duly done and several years later, in 1971, the city saw the establishment of yet another educational institution for women—Chellammal's College, located at Guindy in what was once the donor's property. The benefactress herself remains buried in an unkempt grave, located deep in the midst of a slum off Avvai Shanmugam Salai (Lloyd's Road).[29] At around the same time as Chellammal, another woman, and a celebrity at that, the courtesan and singer Salem Godavari too placed a large chunk of her savings at the disposal of Pachaiyappa's Trust.[30]

In 1984, the University of Madras set up a unique institution—the Mother Teresa Women's University in Kodaikanal, which promotes research in all aspects of women's studies. It is a university run by women, for women. At a more functional level, the University of Madras also began encouraging education through correspondence from 1985, through its Open University system. This has helped several thousands of aspirants, the majority being women, to acquire degrees without formal school education as a prerequisite.[31]

The Muslim Educational Association of Southern India (MEASI) is a

[26]See Stella Maris College website, available here: https://stellamariscollege.edu.in/.

[27]Randor Guy, *Anraiya Chennai Pramukargal*, Vol. 1, Chennai: Manivasagar Pathippagam, 2002, p. 42.

[28]V. Sriram, *The Rane Story: A Journey of Excellence*, Chennai: Rane Holdings Pvt Limited, 2011, p. 280.

[29]See Chellammal Women's College website, available here: https://chellammal.edu.in/?page_id=666/.

[30]*Pachaiyappa's Trust Centenary Volume*, p. 113.

[31]*150 Years of Excellence*, pp. 108–9.

historic body, having its origins from a Muslim Educational Conference held in Madras in 1901 under the leadership of Sir Syed Ahmed Khan, the Islamic reformer and philosopher of the nineteenth century. The founder of the Mohammedan Anglo-Oriental College, which later became the Aligarh Muslim University, Sir Syed, was passionate about the spread of education in the modern sense amongst his community. It was as a result of his forceful arguments that some of the prominent Muslim men of Madras founded this body. Under the guidance of a galaxy of Muslim worthies, the MEASI grew. Soon it had in Basheer Ahmed Sayeed (who ensured that the Music Academy bought its present property) a dynamic leader. One of India's oldest minority education institutions, the MEASI now runs multiple-level educational systems ranging from schools to colleges and institutions that offer post-graduate research courses. Its most well-known creations are the New College in Royapettah (named after the eponymous institution at Oxford) and the Institute of Architecture located on the same campus.[32]

In later years, Sayeed opted to break away from the MEASI and set up a clutch of educational institutions where, as per his wishes, admissions were not restricted to just Muslims. The South Indian Educational Trust (SIET) that administered these first founded the SIET College in 1955, which has since been renamed Justice Basheer Ahmed Sayeed College for Women. Located in a vast campus in Teynampet, (Sayeed endowed all institutions he founded with copious real estate to ensure their stability), the SIET has birthed several schools and associated institutions.[33]

It was in 1919 that the Mohammaden College came up on the premises of the Madrasa-i-Azam referred to in the previous chapter and it remained a premier institution for Muslims. By 1938, it had a 25 per cent quota for students of other religions as well. In the immediate aftermath of Partition it became the Government Arts College.[34] In 1975, the institution divided into two, the Men's College moving to Nandanam while the Women's College remained behind, renamed after Quaid-e-Millath Muhammad Ismail, a leader of the Muslim League.[35]

Two years prior to this move, yet another Government Arts College came up, in Vyasarpadi in North Madras, in response to a long-standing request

---

[32]Sriram, *When Mercy Seasons Justice*, pp. 129–30.

[33]See Justice Basheer Ahmed Sayeed College for Women website, available here: https://www.jbascollege.edu.in/article/about-jbas.html/.

[34]Sriram, *When Mercy Seasons Justice*, p. 25.

[35]Ibid.

from the residents there for a suitable institution in their area. Later renamed after Ambedkar, it offers science, commerce, and arts courses now.[36] Women have a college for arts in North Chennai as well, named after the national poet, Subramania Bharati. Located in what was the civil debtors gaol during EIC days, on what is still known as Old Jail Road, this general degree college was founded in 1964.[37] But, by far the oldest college in the north is the Sir Theyagaraya College. Begun in 1897 as the North Madras High School in Washermanpet where the Pitti family had enormous landholdings and business interests, it was nurtured by two scions—Pitti Theyagaraya Chetty senior and his eponymous but knighted junior. After the demise of the patrons, the school changed its name to incorporate theirs by way of thanksgiving. It continued to be nurtured by other members of the family even after the management was made over to a broader board. In 1950, the institution upgraded itself as the Sir Theyagaraya College, focusing on arts and science.[38] Another famed arts and science college, and one that is now autonomous, though coming under the University of Madras, is Loyola, founded in 1925 by the Jesuits. Its magnificent campus, situated on what was once the Nungambakkam Tank, is now home to several departments and institutes that the college has spawned.

That Chennai, given its affinity for classical music, has several educational institutions for the performing arts should be no surprise. As we saw in the chapter on music and dance, Queen Mary's College was the first to offer music as a subject and this later expanded into a full-fledged degree course, from 1930. The Music Academy started a Teacher's College of Music in 1931 with 'Tiger' Varadachariar as its first principal. The college was meant for students who aimed to teach music. In 1937, the college was granted recognition by the Director of Public Instruction, Madras, and a three-year course was formulated. In 2010, the college was transformed into the Advanced School of Carnatic Music, which now runs a three-year course.[39]

The Department of Music, Madras University, came into existence in 1932 and 'Tiger' Varadachariar left the Teacher's College at the Music Academy to become its first Head of the Department. In 1937, he was succeeded by the eminent musicologist Professor P. Sambamoorthy, who remained in office

---

[36]See Dr Ambedkar Government Arts College website, available here: http://www.daga.co.in/.

[37]Muthiah, *Madras Rediscovered*, p. 398.

[38]See Sir Theagaraya College website, available here: http://sirtheagarayacollege.com/history/.

[39]See The Music Academy website, available here: https://musicacademymadras.in/academics/advanced-school-of-carnatic-music/.

till 1961. During his tenure, he published a series of books that became the official course curriculum for most Carnatic music degree courses in India. The Madras University Music Department now offers MA, MPhil, and PhD degrees in music.[40] The Kalakshetra founded by Rukmini Devi Arundale has done its bit for music too. Set up as the International Centre for Arts in the Theosophical Society premises in 1936, it later became Kalakshetra, India's premier school for South Indian classical dance and today an institution of national importance run by the Government of India. It began offering a course in music in 1944. Those graduating from it were given the degree of 'Sangita Shiromani'. However, the institution has always been better known for its activities in the dance arena, with several talented dancers qualifying from it each year.

The Tamil Isai Sangam too runs its own Tamil Isai Kalluri, which was started in 1944 and functions from the Raja Annamalai Manram. The college offers a full-time course of three years and part-time courses in music (vocal and instrumental), and percussion. The degree of 'Isaikkalaimani' is conferred on those graduating from this college.[41]

In 1949, the Government of India appointed Sambamoorthy as special officer to look into the setting up of a Central College for Carnatic Music in Madras. This was set up the same year with Musiri Subramania Iyer, the well-known singer as the first principal. The college which began functioning from Bridge House, Adyar, later shifted to Brodies Castle, from where it continues to function. It was later taken over by the Tamil Nadu government and renamed as the Isai Kalluri. It offers a two-year course in music with the degree of 'Isai Mani'.[42]

Chennai is home to colleges and institutions specializing in languages as well. If French, German, Japanese, and Korean are taught at facilities set up by organizations of the respective countries or their trade bodies, mention must be made of two institutions, one focusing on Arabic and the other on Sanskrit. The Madrasa Jamalia was founded in 1900 at Perambur by Jamal Moideen, a leather merchant. Under the guidance of his son, Haji Jamal Mohamed Rowther, this later graduated into the Jamalia Arabic College, the medium of instruction being that language.[43] Younger to it by

[40] *150 Years of Excellence*, pp. 142–3.

[41] V. Sriram, *Nurturing Music and Fine Arts: A Historical Perspective*, Chennai: The Tamil Nadu Dr J. Jayalalithaa Music and Fine Arts University, 2021, pp. 203–13.

[42] Ibid., pp. 119–27.

[43] Anvar, *Islam*, p. 151.

five years is the Sanskrit College, founded and endowed by that dynamic lawyer V. Krishnaswami Iyer. With 'Mahamahopadhyaya' Kuppuswami Sastri, after whom a research institute later came up on the premises, as principal, the college grew in leaps and bounds. Aided repeatedly with donations from many philanthropists and grants from the central government, the college remains a hive of activity in the Sanskrit language.[44]

Besides this, the University of Madras has had a long tryst with languages, Indian and foreign. The Oriental Faculty of Comparative Philology with special reference to Sanskrit, Tamil, Arabic, and Persian came up 1914. This graduated into the Oriental Research Institute in 1927, at which time departments for Telugu, Kannada, Malayalam, and Hindi were added. The School of English and Foreign languages had its origins in 1926, when French and German began to be taught at the university. It now has departments for Russian, Korean, Italian, and Spanish as well.[45]

Languages come under skill development and so do polytechnics, which are diploma-offering engineering institutes. Chennai has any number of these, the oldest, as mentioned in the last chapter, was the P. T. Lee Chengalvaraya Naicker Technical Institute in Vepery. The British were not so keen on these, preferring Indians to acquire degrees that made them fit for the clerical grade. But as industries around Madras grew, there was need for skilled hands and polytechnics came into existence. The Leather Institute came up in the early 1900s. Within a decade of its founding, it had become the Madras Trades School and by the 1940s was offering courses in civil, mechanical, electrical, sanitary, print, cinema, and sound engineering, all of them having classes at the old jail campus where the Bharathi Women's College moved in later. But with the Guindy Industrial Estate coming up in 1958, the school, renamed the Central Polytechnic (CPT), moved to a 3,000-hectare campus in Taramani where it constructed its main offices, an auditorium named after Jawaharlal Nehru, India's first prime minister, and several hostel blocks.[46]

Several institutions came out of the CPT and now share its campus. The department of printing technology became the Institute of Printing Technology in 1958. The cinematography section, which was begun in 1945, became the Institute of Film Technology in 1961. It is India's oldest. Today, it is named after MGR, one of Tamil Nadu's charismatic chief ministers who also had a flourishing career in films. Till the early 2000s, there was

[44]Golden Jubilee Souvenir of the Sanskrit College, 1956.
[45]*150 Years of Excellence*, p. 163.
[46]Sriram, *Nurturing Music and Fine Arts*, pp. 155–6.

also a vast space behind this institute known as the MGR Film City. This was let out for film shoots. But much of that has now been swallowed by IT offices and buildings. Some other departments of the CPT that are now independent organizations include the Institutes of Chemical, Leather and Textile Technology.[47]

Other institutions located within the CPT campus include the Asian College of Journalism (ACJ), founded in 1994 by the Indian Express Group. It came under a not-for-profit trust in 2000 and was housed initially at 100, Mount Road, once the home of *The Hindu*.[48] In the last decade, the ACJ shifted to Taramani, where it has in its campus, the city's first mic-less auditorium.[49] Also located close to it is the Press Institute of India which amalgamated into itself the Regional Institute of Newspaper Development (RIND). Not far from here is the Institute of Mathematical Sciences, the brainchild of mathematician Alladi Ramakrishnan and modeled on the Princeton Institute. Inaugurated in Mylapore in 1962 by Nobel laureate Subrahmanyan Chandrashekar, it shifted to Taramani in 1969. Matscience, as it is popularly known, came under the Department of Atomic Energy, Government of India in the 1980s.[50] At the other end of OMR, in Siruseri, is another institution dedicated to maths—the Chennai Mathematical Institute. Founded in 1989 as part of the SPIC Foundation, it became autonomous in the 1990s.[51]

Also in Taramani is the M. S. Swaminathan Research Foundation founded in 1988 by India's best known agricultural scientist, Professor M. S. Swaminathan, with proceeds from the Food World Prize that he won in 1987. The organization uses science and technology to address problems faced by the rural population in the areas of agriculture, food, and nutrition, besides carrying out research on subjects such as climate change, biodiversity, and food security.[52]

Close by is the Regional Technical Teachers' Training Institute, one of four campuses across India. The one in Chennai is the oldest, coming up in

---

[47] Ibid.

[48] See Asian College of Journalism website, available here: https://www.asianmedia.org.in/.

[49] V. Sriram, 'Can Carnatic Music cope with a "mic-less" auditorium?', *Madras Musings*, Vol. XXVIII, No 16, 1–15 December 2018.

[50] See The Institute of Mathematical Sciences website, available here: https://www.imsc.res.in/1961_2/.

[51] See Chennai Mathematical Institute website, available here: https://www.cmi.ac.in/.

[52] See M. S. Swaminathan Research Foundation website, available here: https://www.mssrf.org/.

1964. It was set up chiefly to create a pool of teachers who could impart education at the various regional engineering colleges and polytechnics across India. The Chennai institute came up with technical collaboration from Huddersfield College of the UK. In the 1980s, this campus pioneered the concept of using television as a teaching aid in India.[53] The National Institute of Fashion Technology set up in 1986 in Delhi, later created a Chennai campus in Taramani. The institute is very much in demand for its degree course in textile design.[54] Not far from here is the National Institute of Ocean Technology, established in 1993 under the Ministry of Earth Sciences.[55]

The CPT and its child institutions helped in creating a technically skilled manpower pool when industries came flocking to Madras from the 1950s onwards. That was also when a new wave of engineering colleges came about. For years, the College of Engineering (CEG), Guindy, was the only such institution in the city. In 1944, the AC College of Technology, endowed by K. V. Al. Rm. Alagappa Chettiar, came up next door to it, specializing in leather, textile, and chemical technology. Five years later, distant Chromepet saw the establishment of the Madras Institute of Technology (MIT), funded by industrialist C. Rajam and specializing in aeronautical and automobile engineering, Dr A. P. J. Abdul Kalam being its most famous alumnus.[56] It was later to be helped enormously by the eminent lawyer M. Subbaraya Iyer, who similarly fostered two other educational institutions—the Ramakrishna Mission Vivekananda College founded in 1946 and the Vidya Mandir Senior Secondary School.

The CEG, AC College, MIT, and the Madras School of Architecture and Planning, which began in 1957 as the Department of Architecture of the University of Madras, all combined in 1978 to form Anna University, Tamil Nadu's engineering university. Opposite the Anna University campus is that of the Indian Institute of Technology, Madras, IIT-M as it is known. One of the premier technical institutions of India, it was set up on 617 acres carved out of the Guindy National Park in 1959. Some of India's best young minds study in this campus, sharing space with much flora and some

[53]See National Institute of Technical Teachers Training and Research website, available here: https://www.nitttrc.ac.in/.

[54]See National Institute of Fashion Technology website, available here: https://www.nift.ac.in/chennai/.

[55]See National Institute of Ocean Technology website, available here: https://www.niot.res.in/niot1/index.php/.

[56]Dr Prema Srinivasan, *A Visionary's Reach: C. Rajam and the founding of the Madras Institute of Technology*, Chennai: Madras Institute of Technology, 2013.

fauna including blackbuck and monkeys. IIT-M is internationally renowned and its alumni have gone on to name and fame in various walks of life.

All of these institutions, together with the premier medical colleges in the city—MMC, Stanley, and Kilpauk—made Chennai a higher education hub by the late 1970s. This, despite the number of graduates in engineering and medicine not exceeding 4,000 a year. All of these were subject to state and central quotas for reservation and that had its benefits in terms of social inclusivity while at the same time promoting intense competition and much heartburn, many breakdowns and depressions, for those coming under the general quota. Thus, while India and, within, it Tamil Nadu and Chennai were going about creating an educational ecosystem, it was one plagued by shortages, with higher education institutions entirely controlled by the government and the number of seats on offer each year miniscule vis-à-vis the demand. By the early 1980s, reservation had become a burning issue, the upper castes protesting against discrimination and the lower castes fighting to increase the quota for themselves. Every community desired to be declared backward and get a certain number of seats assured for itself. Caste and community-based politics, always lurking in the background, now came to the fore, marking the beginnings of blatantly casteist and many communal outfits and leaders. Tamil Nadu by then 'had a staggering 174 castes listed as backward and there was 50 per cent reservation in educational institutions and government jobs'.[57]

In 1983, MGR, then chief minister, a master of flamboyant gestures, suddenly announced that the state government was seriously considering extending reservation to all castes, based on economic backwardness. This caused a furore. Arch-rival Karunanidhi immediately denounced it and said that the Constitution recognized only education and social backwardness and financial status had no place. K. Veeramani of the Dravida Kazhagam said he would fight the move in courts of law. Four years earlier, MGR had stoked the fires when he suggested that reservation ought to be available only to backward-caste families that earned less than ₹9,000 a year. Protests had forced him to backtrack and he had, as a conciliatory gesture, raised the reservation percentage from 31 to 50.[58] While the state roiled in controversy once again in 1983, MGR changed his mind. With a view to placating those he had alienated, he raised the reservation percentage to 67 in educational institutions

[57]S. H. Venkataramani, 'Tamil Nadu CM MGR stirs a hornet's nest with his concessions for all proposal', *India Today*, 15 January 1983.
[58]Ibid.

and government jobs. At the same time, he threw open the higher education sector to private enterprise. Gone were the days when pillars of society set up colleges, now anyone who had money could do it. These would of course conform to the same quotas of reservation, but the remaining seats, classified as management quota, would be granted only on payment of capitation fees, which was the chief attraction in starting such institutions. In short, seats would now be available for those who could afford them.

The chief minister's closest associates were the first to jump in. N. P. V. Ramaswami Udaiyar, the liquor baron, founded India's first private medical educational institution in 1985—the Sri Ramachandra Medical College, named ostensibly after the bow-wielding deity but in reality the chief minister. It is now a deemed university. Another factotum, Jeppiaar, who had begun life as a police constable but later grew to become a key figure in the AIADMK, set up the Satyabhama College of Engineering (Satyabhama was MGR's mother's name) and later several other institutions. He was known for running his colleges with an iron hand (Girls-Girls talk, Boys-Boys talk, but no Girl-Boy talk was a motto often attributed to him).[59] Others soon followed suit.

MGR would not live to see it but his decision paid rich dividends to Tamil Nadu and Chennai, in addition to high returns to the founders. By 2014, the state had 552 engineering colleges—a record for the country—of which only twenty-eight were government-run/aided or autonomous colleges. Anna University became the apex body for all of these institutions, which collectively churn out around 70,000 engineering graduates each year. Similarly, the number of medical colleges, at forty-eight, is also the highest in India. They all come under the Tamil Nadu Dr M. G. R. Medical University.[60]

Quantity had certainly been achieved. And it also managed what Sridhar Vembu, the founder of Zoho Corporation, an IT major in Chennai, calls the placebo effect—the confidence it gives its graduates. The quality is highly variable—at one end are the really impressive private institutions such as the Sri Venkateswara Engineering College, replete with all facilities and at the other, are colleges merely in name, with a shell for a building. And yet, students from both get degrees from Anna University as do those who qualify from the hallowed CEG, Guindy! Ultimately, how employable a candidate

[59]Divya Karthikeyan, 'The life of Jeppiaar: MGR's Man, who turned educationist and anti-cupid to Chennai's engineers', *News Minute*, 19 June 2016.

[60]List of Affiliated Institutions, The Tamil Nadu Dr M. G. R. Medical University, available here: https://www.tnmgrmu.ac.in/index.php/news-events/2-uncategorised/1704-list-of-affiliated-institutions.html/.

is depends on the individual, for the system gives no guarantee of churning out graduates of uniform standard.

Despite this drawback the scheme worked, and did well, for over two decades. The Y2K problem, the dotcom boom, the body shopping business, and the outsourcing model all saw Chennai, together with Hyderabad and Bangalore, ride several IT waves. Entire new areas came up, with IT and Knowledge Parks, gated communities, shopping malls, and a whole new generation of consumers. And what was more, they were from all over India. Students came to study in Chennai and then stayed on when they were absorbed by one of the many IT companies that had set up base here. From the late 1990s, there was a manufacturing boom as well, with many engineering and automotive majors moving to Chennai. They cast their net and raked in all the engineering graduates they could find. MGR's scheme was a success many times over.

And yet there were always undercurrents of dissatisfaction—the system was wrong, recruits had to be practically trained from scratch once they joined and they were an itinerant lot, jumping jobs at the drop of a hat. There was a time when much of Madras considered a job to be for life; that was no longer the case. But as long as the system could absorb all the graduates, everything went well. That all of this could not last forever became manifest when automotive component and vehicle manufacturers found their margins squeezed in the face of international competition. Automation became the new mantra, which meant only one supervisor was needed to manage a line that once employed fifty and more. The world of IT was also changing—coding, in which much of Chennai had specialized, was now uniform, with much of it available as blocks for free off the web. The demand was for specialists in mobile technology, the internet of things, and artificial intelligence—subjects in which none of Chennai's engineering colleges had much to offer. Here too, the bigger institutions managed to bridge the gap but not so the understaffed and underequipped lesser players. This, coinciding with a sharp reduction in recruitments in the IT industry, saw graduates facing an uncertain future.

Suddenly engineering did not appear such a good idea after all. Students, brought up with the idea that careers in technology, medicine, accountancy, and law were all that mattered, found exciting alternatives in visual and mass communication, hotel management, and a whole host of courses for the various service industries that were developing. The great success of M. O. P. Vaishnav College for Women founded in 1992 and specializing in visual and mass communication courses is a shining example. The demand for engineering college seats fell by more than 50 per cent from 2017 onwards.

That year, twenty-two private colleges applied for closure. In 2019, the Anna University, waking up to the fact that it had a problem on hand, sent out inspection teams to all its constituent colleges. Ninety-two of them were made to cut their intake of students, some by as much as 50 per cent, on the basis of the infrastructure they offered.[61] This struck at the very viability of such colleges, fewer seats meant less capitation fee and so less returns. It is likely that more colleges will close, leaving the better-equipped ones to survive. Will that mean there will again be a situation when demand will outstrip supply? Unlikely, for the demand for engineering seats has weakened. But it had a good run while it lasted. Medicine, on the other hand, by the simple expedient of not facing such a glut, continues to be in demand but the numbers are fewer. And it has its own issues of quality of students.

Chartered Accountancy is a third profession much in demand in the city. The Institute of Chartered Accountants has its southern chapter here and the CA Institute, as it is known, is famed for the quality of coaching it offers to prepare aspirants for the exceedingly tough examination that qualifies candidates as chartered accountants. Students from all over India come here to attend the classes either at the institute or at one of the many private teaching facilities that flourish here.

In the midst of all this, the liberal arts and humanities have taken a beating. They remain the courses that nobody will dare to take. Today, it is surprising to even think that there was once a Madras Art Movement, begun at the Government College of Arts and Crafts, led by Debi Prasad Roy Chowdhury, its first Indian principal. A sculptor, body builder, and much else, he fashioned the localization of the arts syllabus. His successors K. C. S. Panikker and S. Dhanapal took this further and between the 1960s and 1980s, Madras had a vibrant art movement, based on local traditions and practices.[62] Panikker established the Cholamandal Artists Village in 1966 as the largest artists' commune in India, where practitioners could live freely, work, and also exhibit their work.[63] Today, it is less in the news but it does remain one of the few successful artist-driven initiatives in the country. But that it did not encourage more to take to it is a tragedy.

Likewise, between the 1930s and 1970s, Madras produced some outstanding historians—K. A. Nilakanta Sastri, S. R. Balasubramanyam, T. A.

[61]A. Ragu Raman, '92 engineering colleges of Tamil Nadu told to cut intake due to lack of infrastructure, faculty', *Times of India*, 14 May 2019.

[62]Sriram, *Nurturing Music and Fine Arts*.

[63]Ibid.

Ramachandra Dikshitar, T. V. Mahalingam, K. K. Pillay, R. Nagaswamy, K. V. Raman, and Cadambi Minakshi, the first woman to get a doctorate from the University of Madras. But this did not encourage more people to take to the course. There is a stern practical streak in the people of Chennai. They prefer mainstream courses that are much in demand in the job market. Even an institution such as IIT-M introducing a five-year humanities course has not cut much ice with the local people.

12 | THE WHEELS OF COMMERCE

One of the most fascinating aspects of Chennai is the way it developed as an industrial centre. For a city that was practically written off by the British after they saw the riches of Bengal and Bombay, it has come a long way. It did not have much going for it in terms of traditional raw materials—not being in proximity to the mining centres of India like Calcutta nor being a financial capital like Bombay. And yet the city held its own. Today, while it is home to practically all kinds of industries including finance, it is best known for being an automotive hub, a leather major, and an IT centre. The last named is recent history and one still in the making. It had much to do with the burgeoning of engineering colleges, as seen in the last chapter. The other two, of the brick-and-mortar variety, have a much longer association with the city and are still thriving. Let us see what led to their success in Chennai.

Bhakti poetry of the region indicates that between the fifth and ninth centuries this area was known for all the trades associated with seacoasts. Precious stones appear to have been dealt with, as also coastal and deep-sea fishing. Pottery was and is an abiding tradition. The presence of Nagarathars or Chettiars, the principal business community of Tamil Nadu, in the coastal town of Mylapore and the northern village of Thiruvottiyur, attests to these being centres of commerce. As per Kanakalatha Mukund, agriculture and trade were the two principal activities with salt, pearls, conches, and dried fish being the chief commodities along the sea.[1] Eventually, the Nagarathars, being seafaring traders, established bases all along Malaysia and Indonesia.

But cloth was what this coastal region of India was known for, supplying this commodity even to the ancient Romans and the Chinese. From Orissa downwards, the Coromandel Coast was a centre of excellence for cloth weaving. Writing in the thirteenth century, Marco Polo waxed eloquent on how 'in this kingdom are also made the best and most delicate buckrams, and those of the highest price; in sooth they look like tissue of spiders' web!'[2] By the time the Vijayanagar Empire reached its height, several villages

[1]Kanakalatha Mukund, *The Trading World of the Tamil Merchant: Evolution of Merchant Capitalism in the Coromandel*, Hyderabad: Orient Longman Pvt. Limited, 1999, p. 15.

[2]Dr Rajkumar, *Encyclopedia of the Untouchables: Ancient, Medieval and Modern*, New Delhi: Kalpaz Publications, 2008, p. 241.

that would eventually become Madras, were well known as weaving centres, Mambalam, in particular, being famed for its 'paintings' (Kalamkari) and block prints.[3] San Thome, known as Badshah Bandar in later years, was the port from which much of the cloth was traded.[4] The area's ancient links with cloth weaving is also attested to by the legend that Thiruvalluvar, the composer of the *Thirukkural* and supposedly a resident of Mylapore, was a weaver.[5] Even larger than San Thome and classified as the major port of the Vijayanagar Empire, was Pulicat, the saltwater lagoon just north of Chennai.[6]

Unlike the west coast of India, where the spice trade attracted Europeans, it was cloth that brought them to the Coromandel Coast. The Dutch were the first to arrive, setting up base at Pulicat in 1610.[7] This was not to the liking of the Portuguese who did their best to thwart the newcomers but the latter proved tenacious. By the late seventeenth century, the Dutch had a series of factories—places from where they sourced and exported cloth—all along the coast.[8] The success of the Dutch brought the English, who too set up base in Pulicat, following a peace treaty in Europe.[9] This was not successful, and a subsequent settlement, at Armagaon (Durgarayapatnam) further up on the Pulicat lagoon met with the same fate. Then, in 1639, Francis Day arrived in Madras, where he found 'Excellant long Cloath, Morrees and percalla and better Cheape by 20 per cent.'[10]

In the initial years the English modelled themselves on the Dutch, and built a network of agents or dubashes. Indeed, the first dubash they hired was Malayappa Chetty, who was dubash to the Dutch too.[11] Over the years, the English prospered while Dutch interests in the region waned. Between 1639 and 1750 or thereabouts, the cloth trade was the principal business in the city. Financing the activity was quite a challenge and this brought in the native moneylenders or shroffs–Gujaratis, Marwaris, Chettys, and Chettiars.[12]

---

[3]Love, *Vestiges of Old Madras*, Vol. 1, p. 77.

[4]Numerous references to Badshah Bandar can be found in Dr M. Rajendran and Dr A. Vennila (ed.), *The Private Diary of Ananda Ranga Pillai* (12 vols.), Thiruvannamalai, Akani Veliyeedu, 2019.

[5]Gopalkrishna Gandhi, *The Tirukkural*, New Delhi: Aleph Book Company, 2015, p. xxxvii.

[6]Mukund, *Tamil Merchant*, p. 46.

[7]For a detailed account of the trading activities of the Dutch, see Mukund, *Tamil Merchant*.

[8]Ibid.

[9]Ibid.

[10]Love, *Vestiges of Old Madras*, Vol. 1, p. 20.

[11]Mukund, *Tamil Merchant*, pp. 62–65.

[12]V. Sriram, *Championing Enterprise: 175 Years of the Madras Chamber of Chamber of Commerce*

If the EIC's rulebook had been followed strictly all imports to and exports from Madras would have been channelled only through it. But in reality everyone was involved in trade. The EIC paid very low salaries, which encouraged its servants to indulge in what was termed 'private trade' and the higher one climbed in the company's hierarchy, the more the opportunity. The governor was supposed to accept a commission for virtually everything, ranging from goods supplied to the company—from arrack or betel leaf to cloth that was being exported.[13] This is why most administrators of the EIC were termed nabobs and returned to England with enormous riches. Some of Elihu Yale's pickings in Madras even went to fund a college in America, which later became a famous university in his name.[14] Even the few women in the fort were said to be in business and according to one source, some were 'so forward as to have invoices, accounts current etc in their own names.'[15] The most notorious among these was Mrs Nick, a woman who was considered close to Governor Yale; she made money at a galloping pace.[16] To hide any indication of their direct involvement company servants encouraged their friends and relatives to come over from England and set them up as free merchants.[17] These were, as the name suggests, allowed to trade in a set of commodities not controlled by the company.

Over time, the number of free merchants in Madras increased, as it did all over India. As British control over the country strengthened, the atmosphere became more conducive for business and free trade prospered often at the expense of the EIC. At least two household names of Madras Presidency began business as free merchants. Thomas Parry, a Welshman, came to Madras in the 1780s and set himself up in trade.[18] The second was John Binny, who came from a family that already had a powerful link with the city. He came armed with a letter of recommendation from his uncle Charles, who had been secretary to Nawab Wallajah.[19] A huge financial scam, that of loaning money to the Nawab of Arcot at usurious rates of interest and channelled

and Industry, Chennai: The Madras Chamber of Commerce and Industry, 2011, p. 9.

[13]Ibid., p. 10.

[14]Hiram Bingham, *Elihu Yale: The American Nabob of Queen Square*, New York: Dodd, Mead & Co., 1939, pp. 316–35.

[15]Sriram, *MCCI*, p. 10.

[16]Bingham, *Elihu Yale*.

[17]Sriram, *MCCI*, p. 10.

[18]Sir Gerald Hodgson, *Thomas Parry: Free Merchant, Madras, 1768–1824*, Madras: Higginbothams Limited, 1938.

[19]F. Desouza, *The House of Binny*, Madras: Binny Limited, 1968.

via the contractor Paul Benfield, flourished in the late eighteenth century and Parry and Binny were active participants in it. The exposing of the fraud and the nawab's inability to repay his debts would have far-reaching consequences. Many business houses collapsed and eventually the whole of the Arcot kingdom would fall into the EIC's lap.[20]

In the early nineteenth century, a rather unusual business prospect was the import of ice, brought all the way from the United States of America. This was a monopoly in the hands of the Tudor Ice Company, founded by by Frederick Tudor, who it is said, dreamt of such a prospect when he was just thirteen! Harvesting ice from the east coast of the US and sending it swathed in pine dust (a waste product of the lumber industry), all the way to India became business, which lasted till mechanized refrigeration ended the dream run.[21] The sole vestige of that venture in Madras is the Ice House, a round structure on the beach, which, as we've seen, later expanded into a residence and is now a museum to the memory of Swami Vivekananda.

In an effort to decongest the fort, the administration moved the Customs House from there to a disused granary to the north, on the way to Royapuram. The road leading to it developed as North/First Line Beach Road (present-day Rajaji Salai). The business houses too moved, Parry being the first, setting up their offices at a spot that is even today known as Parry's Corner. Others—Arbuthnot & Co, the Bank of Madras, Binny & Co being some—followed and built offices all along the same thoroughfare.[22] These companies banded together in 1836 to form the Madras Chamber of Commerce, India's second-oldest surviving representative body for businesses, being just one week younger than its Bombay equivalent. This was begun as a British-only body but the governor of the time, Sir Frederick Adam, withheld permission insisting that some Indians be brought in. Two of them were made members and the chamber got going.[23]

For all its anti-Indian stance, it must be acknowledged that the Chamber fought hard for the city's infrastructure, albeit to serve the interests of its members. Post and telegraph networks were expanded, the GPO coming up on First Line Beach, the railway terminus was built at Royapuram, at the end of the same road.[24] The Chamber protested the imposition of income

[20]Sriram, *MCCI*, p. 13.

[21]Ibid., pp. 18–19.

[22]Ibid., p. 25.

[23]Ibid., pp. 21–29.

[24]Ibid., pp. 49–67.

tax, which came to India following the uprising of 1857.[25] It lobbied for lowering of tariffs. But by far its biggest achievement was getting the powers-that-be to begin work on a proper harbour for the city.

As has been mentioned earlier, this was considered a technical impossibility, given the city's coast, its violent surf, and the tendency of cyclones to occur in any month of the year. Moreover, the successful ports of Calcutta, Colombo, and Bombay were against Madras getting a harbour. But the Madras Chamber of Commerce did not give in and it eventually had its way. In 1856, a screw pier was laid from land to the clear water two miles distant, where ships then anchored. This was battered by cyclones, and in 1875, work finally began on a proper harbour, which culminated in 1914 or thereabouts, with Sir Francis Spring, the dynamic chairman of the Port Trust, declaring that the project was a 'challenge flaunted in the face of Nature.'[26]

The harbour changed the face of Madras business. Oil was brought in by ship and stored by the seaside. More importantly, car and bus chassis began coming in. Prominent Madras business houses—Addisons and Simpsons being two of the pioneers that are still household names in the city—initially retailed these. They made their fortunes building customized bodies on the chassis and selling cars to the rich and buses and lorries to operators. Mount Road became the retail hub, with other British firms, involved in various trades, building offices, and showrooms. These companies banded together in the 1880s to form the Madras Trades Association.[27] There was bitter rivalry between the Madras Chamber of Commerce and the Madras Trades Association with the former's members, considering themselves industrialists, looking down on the latter, who were mere traders. But both were united in keeping Indians out as far as possible.

The natives were, however, learning, and quite fast at that. They set up showrooms alongside the British companies and proved that they were second to none when it came to the car trade. Names such as Rane, Union Motor Company (now the UCAL Group), and Rajagopal Motor Works (now the Rayala Group) were some of the Indian names that made it big in this business from the 1920s onwards. Many of the erstwhile dubash families moved into trade, importing 'piece goods' (an umbrella term that included everything from stationery to clothing to clocks) and selling them here. Some such as Raja Sir Savalai Ramaswami Mudaliar and the Calavala Brothers even took

[25]Ibid., pp. 40–47.

[26]Ibid., pp. 87–93 and pp. 124–128.

[27]Ibid., pp. 33–36.

over failing British firms and managed them successfully.[28]

Indians also began getting into finance and banking following the crash of Arbuthnot & Co in 1906. One of the biggest business houses of the city, the bulk of its money came from its financial services and in its heyday the firm was considered unshakeable. When the collapse happened, Indians were caught unawares with several thousands being rendered insolvent. The British establishment tried its best to protect the promoters but the times had changed. Indians had taken to law and there were even then several native vakils of extraordinary brilliance practising in the Madras High Court. If the defence was led by Eardley Norton, the prosecution saw V. Krishnaswami Aiyar leading the pack. Having an Indian judge—Sir S. Subramanya Iyer—helped. Sir George Gough Arbuthnot was sentenced to two years, rigorous imprisonment. Left to pick up the pieces, prominent Indians of Madras did not sit idle. They formed the Indian Bank and that opened the floodgates for indigenous banks.[29] The M. Ct. family-promoted Indian Overseas Bank soon followed, its focus, as its name suggests being more on tapping the money of Indians settled or doing business overseas.[30] Indians became active in stock broking as well, with the Madras Stock Exchange, when it was begun in 1937, having Indian firms as members. Insurance became yet another activity that saw many Indians; indeed, the formation of Indian insurance companies was considered a sign of being swadeshi. The biggest in Madras was the M. Ct. M. family-promoted United India Insurance.[31]

The British businesses dominating the Madras Chamber were in for a shock when the Indian Bank purchased the erstwhile headquarters of Arbuthnots and moved in. It was even more galling when from the 1930s many Indian companies in financial services began buying up land all around Rajaji Salai and constructed their buildings.[32] That did not alter the Madras Chamber's sense of superiority. In its centenary volume, published in 1936, it noted with some pride that it still had only two Indian members, the same number as at inception.[33] But this was in no way reflective of ground reality. The number of Indian-run businesses was sharply on the increase. They had formed their own Chamber—the Southern India Chamber of

[28]Ibid., pp. 94–103.

[29]Ibid.

[30]*Unfinished Journey*, pp. 98–139.

[31]Ibid., pp. 48–97.

[32]Sriram, *MCCI*, p. 144.

[33]*Centenary Volume*, Madras Chamber of Commerce, Madras, 1936.

Commerce (SICC). It was perhaps indicative of true Indian shrewdness that among the early acts of the SICC was to move out of the offices of its patron, the Indian Bank, and construct a splendid office for itself on the Esplanade.[34] The Madras Chamber, on the other hand, happily remained a tenant of *The Madras Mail* and later the Mercantile Bank, and still later, Parry & Co. In later years it would struggle to find office space for itself, eventually managing it only in the 1990s.[35]

Manufacturing, as opposed to trading, came late to Madras. The first major employer was the Perambur Workshop of the Madras Railway Company, established in 1856.[36] Then in the 1860s, Binny & Company promoted first Buckingham and later, the Carnatic Mills, to produce yarn and cloth. The factories located at Pulianthope, close to Perambur, soon began employing a vast labour force of various castes and creeds, the number being as many as 20,000 by the 1920s. Three villages were created for workers to live in, while the bosses had their exclusive residential quarters at the Buckingham and Carnatic Gardens, and that quintessential British facility—the CarnBuck Club.[37]

The Government of Madras, probably realizing that it had to hawk what was produced here to stand a chance against Calcutta and Bombay, began organizing industrial exhibitions from the 1850s, the first in 1855 was a first for India.[38] From then on, these events were regularly held and did much to boost interest in local produce. The government also leaned heavily on the Madras Chamber and asked it to get its members to create manufacturing facilities and not remain content with just exporting raw materials to and importing finished goods from England, selling them locally at huge prices. The response was half-hearted at best.

In 1899, the Government of Madras roped in Alfred Chatterton, of the College of Engineering (now at Guindy) to study the possibility of setting up industries in the province. Chatterton, upon discovering vast deposits of bauxite near Mettur, suggested aluminium extraction and making of vessels as a cheap replacement to brass, bronze, and copper. The local companies

---

[34] *A Journey of Excellence and Enterprise*, Chennai: The Southern India Chamber of Commerce and Industry, 2012.

[35] Sriram, *MCCI*, pp. 226–27.

[36] Somerset Playne in *Southern India, Its History, People, Commerce and Industrial Resources*. Arnold Wright (ed), London: The Foreign and Colonial Compiling and Publishing Co., 1915, p. 651.

[37] Desouza, *The House of Binny*.

[38] Official and Descriptive Catalogue of the Madras Exhibition of 1855.

being reluctant, Chatterton went ahead and demonstrated the viability of such a facility at the Madras School of Arts and Crafts. The government suggested the formation of a commercial entity and thus was created the Indian Aluminium Company, later Indal.[39] In 1908, largely at the prodding of Chatterton and Frederick Nicholson, ICS, the Government of Madras created a Department of Industries, the first in the country. Its mandate was to set up small manufacturing entities, make them viable and then sell them off to Indian entrepreneurs. The Swadeshi movement, which aimed at Indians being self-reliant, was in the air. V. O. Chidambaram Pillai had floated his shipping venture in direct competition to British shipping interests and such ideas were anathema to the establishment. The Madras Chamber and its constituents howled in protest and got the Department of Industries closed by 1910. But they were behind times—Indians were by then members of the central legislature in Calcutta and protested the closure. The Department of Industries was reopened in 1914[40] and celebrated this with yet another exhibition of Madras products.[41]

Chatterton and Nicholson had not been idle in the interim. The former openly sided with the Swadeshi movement, declaring it 'a good sign for India to develop her industrial life' and 'Madras to rid itself of its character of an overstocked market of literacy employment.' The latter went a step further, stating that in the matter of Indian industries, 'we are bound to consider Indian interests—firstly, secondly and thirdly—I mean by firstly, that local raw products should be utilised; by secondly that industries should be introduced and by thirdly, the profits of such industry should remain in the country.'[42] Nicholson went on to establish the Fisheries Department and the Lalita Soap Works. Chatterton began the Madras Pencil Factory at Korukkupet. Wood was imported from East Africa but graphite was sourced locally. Taking inspiration from Horatio Nelson, Chatterton released advertisements that said: 'India Expects Every Man To Do His Duty; So does the Madras Pencil Factory'. The going was tough for a couple of years but by 1918 the unit was in the black and auctioned. The business house of V Perumal Chetty & Sons bought it and for nearly a century kept Indian students well stocked with writing materials.[43] Both Chatterton and Nicholson were knighted

[39]Sriram, *MCCI*, p. 148.

[40]Ibid.

[41]*The Book of the Madras Exhibition, 1915-1916*, Madras: Madras Government Press, 1916.

[42]Ibid., p. 151.

[43]V. Sriram, 'Made in Madras', *The Hindu*, 16 November 2014.

for their efforts, this despite going against the grain of establishmentarian thought. Getting into manufacturing, however, was to remain out of reach for most Indian entrepreneurs till Independence. Getting finance was well-nigh impossible with most banks being British-run and therefore not supportive of Indian interests. The Imperial Bank of India, which had been formed by the amalgamation of the Banks of Madras, Bombay, and Bengal in 1921, was a typical example. Post-Independence, the successful-entrepreneur-turned-Union Industries Minister, T. T. Krishnamachari (TTK), would describe the institution as typical of 'all that was wrong with the colonial economic policy. The Bank with its tentacles spread around the country's economic life, had not only been deliberately discriminating in favour of the European companies but also strangled Indian business over the years. It (the Bank) is cent per cent European-controlled, and packed with Indians whose desire to please the European is psycho-pathological; the shareholders control over the institution is a farce. Even the Government's control over it is unreal.' TTK went on to say that it ought to be every finance minister's goal to destroy the Imperial Bank.[44] It was eventually taken over by the government and became the State Bank of India.

It was no wonder that by the time of Independence, there was hardly any industry in Indian hands. 'Most of the Englishmen then working in India were on the make,' says M.V. Subbiah, former chairman of the Murugappa Group. 'Today they are all romanticized but they were in my view as exploitative as the East India Company before them. Almost all of them spent company money on their pet fancies and hardly ever bothered about what would happen in the future. Which is why these companies barely survived into the 1980s.'

On the eve of Indian Independence, there was considerable nervousness among the British business houses and many went up on sale. Among the few companies that had planned the transition with great foresight was Simpsons. In 1930, the directors had been sufficiently impressed with an employee of their auditors, Fraser & Ross (then the leading accountancy firm of Madras and set up by Best & Co.) and had got him on board as company secretary. This was S. Anantharamakrishnan or J, as he was to be known within the company. J's rise in Simpson was meteoric thanks to his financial wizardry, his capacity for hard work, and his innate business skills. Owing largely to J, Simpson was able to weather World War II and the pressures that independence brought to European-controlled businesses. In 1939, largely at J's

[44]Sriram, *MCCI*, p. 179.

initiative, Simpson formed a holding company, Amalgamations Limited, with the express intent of 'acquiring and supervising any business which could be complimentary to the expansion of the business of Simpson & Co or to help further the industrialisation and development of Madras and its Presidency'. The new entity began a slew of acquisitions, which would make it one of the biggest industrial houses of that time in Madras. Among the noteworthy establishments that became part of Amalgamations Limited at this time were Addison, George Oakes, and three from Spencer's stable—Higginbothams, Associated Printers, and *The Madras Mail*.[45] It was said that J had sought the help of Fraser & Ross in the last acquisition but that firm had not helped. He went ahead and then retribution fell on the accountancy firm—for Simpson changed its auditors. It was a jolt to the European business establishments of Madras which had till then always operated on the basis of the old school tie. J then went on to shake things up further. In the 1940s, Simpson was having a tough time with the National Bank, one of the crusty British establishments. Business was difficult and managing liquidity was not easy. But the bank was proving to be non-cooperative. It insisted that Simpson sell off its extensive landholdings to meet its requirements. J travelled to London to reason with the National Bank's Board and was denied the courtesy of an appointment. He immediately decided on a change of bank for Simpson and Amalgamations. The choice was a bank run by Indians—the Central Bank of India. The National Bank was most contrite. It sent out conciliatory letters to J but he remained unmoved.[46]

It was around this time that the city's first major Indian industrial group was in the process of formation. The family of Dewan Bahadur Murugappa Chettiar had, like so many other members of its community, invested heavily in Burma. 'But by the 1930s, my father, uncles, and grandfather had the foresight to realise that they would never probably be able to repatriate the principal they had sunk there,' says M. V. Subbiah. 'It was therefore decided that profits had to be invested in India as a safety net. Beginning first with estates in South India, the family began contemplating industry. We began with steel cabinets—assembling imported components at Thiruvottiyur in 1940 or so. That marks the origins of the Murugappa Group as an industrial entity.' Subbiah does not mention it, but the land for the Ajax Products Limited factory was acquired from the Calavala Cunnan Chetty Trust, named after

[45]S. Muthiah, *Getting India on the Move: The 150 Year Saga of Simpsons of Madras*, Madras: Higginbothams Limited, 1990, pp. 98–114.
[46]Sriram, *MCCI*, p. 178.

the Arya Vysyas who had once taken over a failing English company and set it on the road to profit.[47]

The first decade after Independence also saw the first stage of growth of Madras as an automotive hub. Cars, buses, and trucks had always been big business in the Presidency and the city. By 1947, Simpson and its holding company, Amalgamations, were both further committed to the automotive business. In 1948, Simpson ushered in the diesel revolution. The breakthrough came when a lorry operator on Walltax Road agreed to the conversion of his truck to a Perkins diesel engine. From then on, after a lot of hard work, diesel engines came to be the norm for heavy vehicles. Simpson initially began with importing engines from Perkins and then graduated to assembly of engines from CKD kits.[48] The government had, in the meanwhile, decided that it would encourage the manufacture of cars. This saw Ashok Motors being incorporated for the assembly and sale of Austin cars. The facility was to come up near Ennore, close to Madras. When Austin developed cold feet, this venture was given up and Ashok Motors decided to switch over to trucks, signing up with Leyland of England. This marked the birth of Ashok Leyland Limited.[49] Manufacture of two-wheelers came to India for the first time with Enfield India Limited being set up in Madras by the entrepreneurs Easwara Iyer and Sundaram Iyer, who headed the Easun Group, a business entity that had begun its existence trading in cycles.[50]

The setting up of these major vehicle manufacturers, all of whom had committed to indigenization, meant a need for ancillary industries as well. J was the pioneer here too, setting up India Pistons in 1950, long before the government began to demand indigenization.[51] Addisons, which had lost out in the race for cars owing to government intervention, made over their factory to the development of machine assembly and cutting tools. Later, J would found Tractor and Farm Equipment Limited, in collaboration with Massey Ferguson. Today, it is one of India's largest tractor manufacturers. One can only wonder what else J could have accomplished had he lived longer. Sadly for him, his health suffered and T. T. Krishnamachari's dislike for him did not make life easier—the latter was by then union minister for Industries. J passed away just shy of sixty, in 1964, but his creations prospered

[47]Muthiah, *Looking Back from Moulmein*, p. 52.

[48]Muthiah, *Simpsons*, pp. 137–54.

[49]Muthiah and Gopalan, *Moving India on Wheels*, pp. 41–63.

[50]'The Easun Legend', *Maddy's Ramblings*, 18 January 2018.

[51]Muthiah, *Simpsons*, p. 121.

and lived to tell his tale.

More and more auto-ancillaries and component manufacturers began plants around Madras, right through the 1950s and 1960s. The Murugappa Group was striking out in a slightly different direction. In 1949, it tied up with the TI Group of the UK for the manufacture of bicycles. The area of Ambattur was selected for the new company—TI Cycles of India.[52] Here too the government insisted on indigenization in a phased manner and that resulted in several group companies and ancillaries being set up in the neighbourhood. Ajax, the Murugappa Group's first manufacturing foray referred to earlier, had also diversified. It had imported from America a complete plant that made abrasives and set it up in Thiruvottiyur. In the 1950s, this company tied up with Carborundum Company, Manchester, and the Universal Grinding Wheel Company of New York to form Carborundum Universal of Madras, India (CUMI).[53]

With the TVS Group getting into the manufacture of auto components, Chennai's future as an auto hub was more or less assured. In the late 1950s, the four surviving sons of T. V. Sundaram Iyengar, the man who had found success in automobile and auto spare parts retailing in Madurai, decided that the future lay in setting up manufacturing facilities in Madras. Four companies, respectively into the manufacture of wheels, brakes, auto-electricals, and clutches, were developed at Padi near Ambattur between 1962 and 1965. Wheels India, Brakes India, Lucas TVS, and Sundaram Clayton Limited and their parent company, T. V. Sundaram Iyengar and Sons would later spawn several successful auto component companies.[54] The Rane Group was yet another conglomerate that came into existence at this time. But unlike Amalgamations and TVS, which retained their trading activities even as they moved into manufacturing, this group made a leap of faith, its prime mover L. L. Narayan giving up all its earlier businesses when he set up plants.[55] Another giant that took its first steps in the 1950, was MRF Limited, its first tyre facility coming up at Thiruvottiyur.[56]

All these enterprises were coming up at a time when the heavy vehicle industry dominated the automobile market. Purchasing of trucks and buses

---

[52]AMM Arunachalam, pp. 100–15.

[53]Ibid., pp. 146–59.

[54]V. Sriram, *Sixty Years of Trust: The Sundaram Finance Story*, Chennai: Sundaram Finance Limited, 2014, pp. 97–101.

[55]Sriram, *The Rane Story*, p. 53.

[56]Sriram, *MCCI*, p. 190.

had to be funded in full by those wishing to enter the business, for most banks would not dream of loaning money to transport operators. This was where T. S. Santhanam, one of the TVS scions, saw a major opportunity. He founded Sundaram Finance Limited in 1954 and it soon emerged as one of India's most respected non-banking finance companies, a position it enjoys even today. Santhanam and the Sundaram Finance Group, as it became over time, with ventures in insurance and mutual funds, even influenced legislation to assist the truck and bus business, all of which would have a major impact on transportation across the country. Yet another entity that made its name here is the Shriram Group, whose NBFC flagship, Shriram Chits, is one of the largest in the country. Its founder R. Thyagarajan believed in a very Indian style of management—no frills and a paternal interest in employee welfare above all else. Chennai can also take credit for pioneering the leasing industry in India, with the appropriately named First Leasing Company, now in deep hot water, taking the lead. Similarly, the first mutual fund of India was also from here—Kothari Pioneer, which later became Franklin Templeton. But then, the first nidhi, or chit fund, known as the Sudder Court Fund, was also started here, in 1858! Since then Chennai has been sadly known more for the regular collapse of many fly-by-night nidhis, though some solid ones have continued for years.

Financial adventurers are thankfully few and far between in Chennai but not so men of deep financial acumen. The CAs from here are always in demand across the world with Chennai being the city of choice for all of the World Bank's back offices. And the largest of India's mutual fund processing agencies, CAMS, is also located here.[57]

The industrial story of Chennai is not just of automobile and auto component manufacturing. Several defence-related establishments came to Avadi, a suburb of the city. Between 1965 and 1966, two giant facilities—Madras Refineries and Madras Fertilizers were set up as joint ventures between the government and American and Iranian companies. The plants came up at Manali and made that suburb of the city a chemical hub. There were, besides these, other industrial houses that established corporate offices in the city even as their factories came up elsewhere. A notable example was the India Cements Group, now owned by N. Srinivasan, better known for his cricketing interests, but founded by S. N. N. Sankaralinga Iyer, whose grandson N. Sankar

[57]For further details on this low profile but key service, see V. Sriram, *An Eye for Detail, The Chronicle of CAMS*, Chennai: AcSys Investments Pvt Limited, 2016.

would later create the chemicals and engineering conglomerate Sanmar.[58] Similarly, M. Ct. Chidambaram Chettyar began Travancore Rayons, which was the country's first venture in synthetic yarn, long before the Ambanis.[59]

Much of this heady growth was fuelled by a very progressive government. Kamaraj was chief minister between 1953 and 1963 and pushed for the industrialization of Madras, aided by stalwarts such as R. Venkataraman and C. Subramaniam in the state cabinet and TTK at the centre in his capacity as minister for Industries and later, Finance. 'Kamaraj was the visionary,' says Subbiah. 'And we were lucky that he had people like R. Venkataraman and C. Subramaniam who would deliver.' South India's first industrial estate came up in Guindy in 1958, followed by the one at Ambattur in 1964.

The 1970s proved difficult. There was a crippling power shortage and labour was militant, with the Dravidian leaders supporting the latter. 'This was also when we saw for the first time, government interference in the way we managed labour,' recalls Subbiah. 'But they were always amenable if we held firm.' He illustrates with his experience at the TI Cycles facility. 'There was violence and I ordered the closure of the factory. The Government of Tamil Nadu tried to pressurize us into reopening the unit but we held firm that we would not do so unless we were allowed to sack all those who had attacked our executives. They finally had to agree. We went ahead and then reopened the factory. But this also made us realize that it was perhaps best not to concentrate all our manufacturing in Madras. We began looking at other places in Tamil Nadu.' This was the beginning of a trend, when most industrial houses of the city, alarmed at the labour situation, began to open new plants in districts designated backward by the government. In a way, it was the city's loss, but the rest of the state gained. 'While that was the net outcome, I would regard much of the 1970s and 1980s as lost decades,' says Suresh Krishna, Chairman of Sundram Fasteners Limited (SFL) and one of the most senior members of the TVS family.[60]

The 1980s brought the first winds of change. The economy was being slowly opened up. There was greater exposure to Japanese technology with Maruti cars becoming visible on the roads. Chennai's auto component manufacturers saw the opportunity that Maruti was and became vendors. This was no easy task, for it involved being certified as per international standards. In 1993, Sundram Fasteners of the TVS Group became the first

[58] V. Sriram, *Integrity and Excellence: The Sanmar Story*, Chennai: Kalamkriya, 2019.

[59] *Unfinished Journey*, pp. 140–79.

[60] Interview with the author, Chennai, 24 February 2020.

company in India to get qualified for ISO.[61] 'Today this may seem a fairly straightforward process but in the 1990s nobody knew anything about it,' recalls Suresh Krishna. 'I still remember the way it all happened. Local growth had tanked and I realized that the only way we could survive was by exporting. This was not easy as India was a protected economy, our currency was artificially shored up and our prices were nowhere near what overseas competitors were selling at. Our first orders were in fact executed at a loss. Then one day, one of my managers came and told me that something called ISO was the new buzzword abroad and we had to have it if we needed to survive. We had to look for a consultant and there was none available in the country, nor for that matter were there certifying houses. We had to get them all from abroad but because the company was strong in systems, the certification became a straightforward process.'

SFL's ISO certification made waves in industrial circles and began a scramble for the same. The company then went on to notch other significant firsts. In 1993, it bagged the contract for moving a radiator cap facility of General Motors to India. 'I insisted and obtained permission for stamping each cap with the TVS logo,' says Suresh Krishna. 'The purchase department at GM was most reluctant but we held firm. It remained for long the only component in GM cars to carry a vendor's logo.' In the 1990s, when India was just liberalizing, this was a major ego boost for the whole country. So was SFL's repeated bagging of best vendor awards at GM. In 1998, SFL became the first company in India to obtain Total Productive Maintenance (TPM) certification for all its plants. Later, SFL would achieve another record—becoming the first Indian company to set up a manufacturing facility in China that is still going strong.[62] If described today as the poster boy of India's post-economic liberalization scenario, Suresh Krishna just smiles and waves it off. But the significance of SFL's benchmarks cannot be brushed aside.

Others followed. Another TVS company, Sundaram Clayton Limited, bagged the Deming Prize for companywide quality control in 1998. It was the first non-Japanese company and fourth entity worldwide to qualify in the award's fifty-year history. The auto-component manufacturers of Chennai had become dominant in the Madras Chamber of Commerce, by then renamed the Madras Chamber of Commerce and Industry. They were also prime movers in the Confederation of Indian Industry. L. Lakshman, former chairman and

---

[61]V. Sriram, *The Nuts and Bolts of Excellence: Fifty Years of Sundram Fasteners*, Chennai: Sundram Fasteners Limited, 2017.
[62]Ibid.

present director, Rane Holdings Limited, recalls presentations were made at both centre and state levels, pitching hard for Chennai and its surroundings to be considered for foreign investment.[63] By 1995, Ford opted to have a manufacturing base just outside the city. This was followed by Hyundai and, over the years, practically every international vehicle manufacturer wanted to be in and around the city.[64] Today, Tamil Nadu is one of the top ten auto hubs in the world. The city is now referred to as the Detroit of Asia and produces a vehicle every three minutes. It manufactures 30 per cent of India's vehicles and 35 per cent of auto components.[65]

An interesting side effect of the auto boom in the city is the number of expatriates—Americans, Germans, Koreans, and the Japanese—who now call it home. But for Chennai this is nothing new—remember that in the seventeenth century, the Dutch, British, and Portuguese were all in the city. A hundred years later, the French occupied it briefly and the Armenians established businesses here. The Germans ran the missions with a Swede or two thrown in for good measure. There was an American representative for trade here from the 1790s. And in the immediate aftermath of Independence, we once again had an influx of businessmen from Europe and the US, keen to enter into collaboration with industrialists here. It was only in the socialist 1970s that the expatriate presence faded somewhat but by the 1990s it was back.

It also needs to be documented here that the boxwallah companies of pre-Independence largely died out by the 1990s, unable to keep pace with the demands of a new India. Those that survived, such as Parry, did so because of the way they were transformed by those that acquired them, in this instance, the Murugappa Group. Subbiah, who is responsible for much of the turn-around at Parry, still considers the company's acquisition to be a mistake. 'I argued long and hard with the family that it ought not to be touched. But when the elders insisted I go and correct the situation, I did. We were brought up that way.' Subbiah's handling of the company is the stuff of legend—he just bulldozed his way through the senior executive rank and file. Most preferred to resign on hearing that he was taking charge. But Parry did flourish and is now an integral part of the Murugappa Group. Many other companies closed down and sold off their assets for a song. As

---

[63]Sriram, *MCCI*, p. 231.

[64]Ibid.

[65]Automotive Components, available here: https://en.wikipedia.org/wiki/Automotive_industry_in_Chennai#cite_note-4/.

for their executives, that flock of gilded peacocks, and their world of old-school ties vanished forever from Chennai's skyline.

Chennai is not just an auto city. A major industry that is hardly ever mentioned is in leather. The state of Tamil Nadu accounts for 70 per cent of India's leather output and 40 per cent of its export, and Chennai is one of the major production centres, its volume usually running neck-and-neck with that of Kanpur, Uttar Pradesh. This also being the principal port city of the state, it handles all the leather exports from Tamil Nadu. The commodity had a long history in the region, with the English eyeing Madras as a centre for leather almost from the early nineteenth century. By the early 1900s, many of the established business houses of Madras were involved in the leather industry—principally the export of raw and tanned hides. A thriving set of leather companies founded by Indians came up in parallel, in George Town, later moving to Periamet, just abaft the Ripon Buildings.

Madras leather came into its own in three distinct phases. The first was during World War I when there was huge demand from England. The Indian manufacturers were not yet into tanning while the British companies were well established in it and so the Government of Madras very cleverly imposed a ban on the export of raw hides so that all of it could be diverted to those who had tanning facilities. There was great conflict between the two lobbies but the British interests represented by the Madras Chamber of Commerce had their way. To counter this, Indian merchants banded together to form the Southern India Skin and Hide Merchants Association (SISHMA), in 1917, which in 1978 became the All India Skin and Hide Tanners and Merchants Association. The pre-Independence years were tough on the association, for most government legislation favoured the British companies.

Help came from Sir Alfred Chatterton, who, apart from his pioneering work in aluminium and helping Indians set up industries, also did considerable research into the chrome tanning process. To facilitate dissemination of the latest methods and also to create a workforce for the industry, the government, largely at Chatterton's bidding, founded the Leather Trades Institute in 1915 at Washermanpet. The Madras Chamber and its members were most cynical about it, preferring older techniques, but not so the members of SISHMA, who took to it readily. Rather ironically, it was G. A. Chambers, one of the Madras Chamber members and among the most strident critics of Chatterton, who established the biggest leather factory in the city's outskirts, his Chrome Leather Company giving its name to an entire locality—Chromepet, though there is nothing left of the factory. Chambers Road commemorates the founder in the same area.[66]

The inter-War years saw the Indian leather lobby growing more powerful, with SISHMA, on occasion, joining hands with the Madras Chamber to fight for reduction in export duties of raw hides. The second phase of growth came during World War II when, once again, demand peaked for Indian leather. Madras being one of the few ports on the eastern side not to be threatened by the advance of the Japanese, much of the leather export happened from here, with the South Indian Export Company, not surprisingly a British business house and a member of the Madras Chamber, being entrusted with checking the quality of leather sent from here. SISHMA swallowed its pride and complied, but its heyday and that of the leather industry, in general, was just around the corner.[67]

It was in 1942 that Y. Nayudamma returned to his village of Yelavarru in present-day Andhra, from Benares Hindu University, with a degree in Industrial Chemistry. That got him nowhere and so he moved to Madras to study law. But, within a month he had joined the Leather Institute as demonstrator. It was in this same year that the Government of India founded the Council for Scientific and Industrial Research (CSIR) in Delhi. In 1946, the CSIR recommended that a Central Leather Research Institute (CLRI) be set up in Madras for furthering the cause of the eponymous industry. As a precursor to this, Nayudamma was selected to go to England for further training. Once there, he did complete the course but realized that an MS degree from an American university would be better.

This was a man who usually achieved what he aspired for and, sure enough, he not only obtained admission to the Leather Technology Course at Lehigh University, Pennsylvania, but also managed to convince the authorities in Madras to fund his tenure there. Returning to India in 1951, he was appointed assistant director at the CLRI, the foundation stone for the institution having been laid three years earlier. Those working with him got an inkling of his dynamism, when a few weeks before the formal inauguration of the CLRI, in 1953, Nayudamma, dejected at the desolate vision the garden presented, managed to scoop up entire lawns and full-grown trees from elsewhere and got them relocated. TTK, the chief guest, was most impressed and showered praise. Rivals at the CLRI became worked up and they managed to get the bills for the laying out of the garden held up on technicalities. Nayudamma

---

[66]K. Chandrahas, *The People's Scientist: A Biography of Dr Y. Nayudamma*, Bengaluru: Prism Books Pvt. Limited, 2013.
[67]Sriram, *MCCI*, pp. 152–3.

snatched the papers, had them shredded, and declared that he would settle the dues himself. He had to borrow from his father but he did pay up. The man was unstoppable.

From there to becoming director was but a step, a powerful lobby comprising Dr Sir A. Lakshmanaswami Mudaliar, Vijayalakshmi Pandit, whose son was a fellow student at Lehigh, and Professor Thacker, director general for Scientific and Industrial Research throwing their support behind him when the incumbent retired in 1954. Nayudamma was all of thirty-four when he became numero uno at the CLRI.

He worked hard to transform the leather industry. His approach was bottom-up, for he chose to address the needs of the traditional leather workers, who occupied the lowest rungs in the Indian social order. CLRI employees were sent to live in villages where skins and hides were dealt with and study the methods used. These findings were then channelled into discussions on how these practices could be improved upon. Much thought went into the modernization of the leather industry as a whole and finally expos were planned to showcase Indian leather. The first International Leather Fair was held in January 1964 at the CLRI premises. For several years thereafter, it remained a high point in the social calendar of Madras, with fashion shows and the participation of several film stars. On a less publicized level but probably of greater consequence was the Tanners' Get-Together, which has since been renamed the Leather Research Industry Get-Together. The CLRI under Nayudamma also became a regular stop in the travel itinerary of international visitors and that only added to its image.

His associates in the industry such as A. Nagappa Chettiar and T. Abdul Wahid lobbied hard for the setting up of a leather export promotion body. The central government accepted the recommendation and, in 1956, the Leather Export Promotion Council was founded, with its headquarters in a beautiful heritage structure, Marble Hall, in Periamet. That building has since given way to drab high-rises but the organization, now merged with a parallel body in the north and renamed the Council for Leather Exports, is still headquartered in Chennai and fulfilling its mandate.[68]

Looking back, Chennai had many things going for it at the right time. The construction of the harbour was certainly the beginning but thereafter, the belief that the resident entrepreneurs had in their immediate ecosystem was a huge contributor. Not only did they teach the British-run businesses

---

[68]J. Prasad Davids, *Leather King Padma Shri A Nagappa Chettiar: Inspiring Legacy of His Success*, Chennai: Nagappan Foundation, 2015.

a lesson or two but also stepped in to the vacuum created by the latter's exit after 1947, and created large enterprises that provided employment to several thousands. That, in turn, would lead to an influx of aspirants into the city, a trend that has not declined ever since. Today, Chennai is a destination for many not just in Tamil Nadu but across India.

Why then are industrial houses in the north far bigger than what we see here? One reason is, as L. Lakshman, director of Rane Holdings Limited puts it, that companies remain focused on core specializations. The second reason is conservatism—most industrial houses here prefer to keep their shareholding private, and their borrowings from banks and institutions to a minimum. The emphasis is more on doing well in what they have chosen to do rather than on growing enormous and unwieldy.

13 | THE HEALING TOUCH

At the 2016 Health Summit, the Confederation of Indian Industry brought medical professionals, capital market players, businessmen, and government officials under one roof to discuss and explore the opportunities in the fast-growing healthcare sector. It predicted that within ten to fifteen years, the healthcare sector would also boom like IT in the 1990s. A key observation made during that meet was that 'Tamil Nadu can become the global benchmark of healthcare in India... [The state] has its unique advantages—best in terms of health parameters like mortality rates, a robust public healthcare system, largest and strong private provider base, a hotbed for innovation and emergence of non-profit and other institutions delivering outstanding services.'[1]

If that is true of the state on the whole, Chennai too scores high when it comes to the medical industry. The city also happens to be the healthcare capital of India, attracting much of the 40 per cent share[2] that Tamil Nadu enjoys of the US$ 6 billion Indian medical tourism industry.[3]

The term 'medical tourism' conjures up an image of hospital chains run with an underlying profit motive and certainly Chennai has several of those. But it cannot be forgotten that the backbone of the city's reputation for excellent healthcare comes from a long line of historic institutions that focused on making it affordable to all sections of society. They ensured Chennai was a medical capital even in the nineteenth century, when a steady stream of patients came to the city from all over India for treatment. Such institutions are largely forgotten in the glamour and glitz of private healthcare.

The city has had a long tryst with healthcare, the first modern hospital being set up in 1664 in Fort St George. General Hospital (GH) is still around, at the edge of Park Town; a location that it has been functioning from since 1772. GH was a whites-only hospital till 1842, when Indians were allowed in.[4] Next to it is the Madras Medical College (MMC), founded in 1835 as

---

[1]'Healthcare as an Industry', *Madras Musings*, Vol. XXVI, No. 4, 1–15 June 2016.

[2]'40% of the medical tourists to India visit Tamil Nadu: Minister', *The Hindu*, 27 September 2019.

[3]'Medical tourism companies turn to telemedicine in wake of Covid-19', *Hindustan Times*, 16 May 2020.

[4]V. Sriram, 'A brief history of the General Hospital—a Chennai landmark', *Madras Heritage and Carnatic Music*, 23 February 2013.

the Madras Medical School, one of India's oldest educational institutions.[5]

GH is forever in the news for its shortcomings but it cannot be denied that it is the first rung of affordable medical help, a place to which thousands flock. Along with others of its kind such as the Royapettah Hospital, begun in 1911, the Stanley Medical College and Hospital which originates from the Madras Native Infirmary established in 1799, and the Kilpauk Medical College and Hospital, which began life as the School of Indian Medicine in 1925, it is among the best-known institutions of the city, run by the government and catering to the non-affluent.

While the above hospitals built a reputation for overall treatment, they also have interesting histories. GH, for instance, was where the first recorded post-mortem was done in India. That was in 1693, performed by Dr Edward Bulkley, who lies buried in a large tomb just outside GH.[6] He also issued the first medical certificate to enable hospitalization to avoid arrest. That was for his friend John Nicks, who was facing charges of corruption.[7] This has since become par for the course for most Tamil Nadu politicians—they go to hospital, not jail, when arrested. Stanley Hospital is also known as 'kanji thotti aspithri' most probably due to the neighbouring Monegar Choultry, a hospice for the poor and homeless, where a gruel distribution centre functioned each time famine struck Madras, which was quite often during the British era. Monegar Choultry and Stanley Hospital have a working relationship, for the bodies of inmates who die in the former are donated to the latter for medical research.[8] Attached to Stanley Hospital is the Raja Sir Savalai Ramaswami Mudaliar Lying-in Hospital, named after the business baron who donated funds to it in the late nineteenth century. It is one of the earliest maternity hospitals of the city.[9] Not far from Stanley is Christina Rainey Hospital, founded in 1888 by Scottish missionaries and named after a teacher who helped enormously in raising funds.

Several path-breaking developments in the medical world took place in Madras. Charles Donovan, the co-discoverer of the kala-azar causing micro-organism worked at GH,[10] while Sir Ronald Ross, who later acquired

---

[5]Muthiah, *Madras Rediscovered*, p. 417.

[6]V. Sriram, 'The Bulkley Tomb Resurfaces', *Madras Musings*, Vol. XXII, No. 12, 1–15 October 2012.

[7]V. Sriram, 'Mystery of a Missing Tombstone', *The Hindu*, 12 September 2012.

[8]Muthiah, *Madras Rediscovered*, pp. 412–13.

[9]Ibid., p. 457.

[10]Dr S. Tharakaram, 'Donovan of MMC', *Madras Musings*, Vol. XX, No. 18, 1–15 January 2011.

international fame for identifying the role of the mosquito in spreading malaria, worked at Royapettah Hospital, his research benefiting hugely from the drawings of his assistant, Amy Skelland, a Eurasian whom he acknowledged.[11] Not so well known is Dr W. J. Niblock, who documented in India the first successful gastrojejunostomy for gastric outlet obstruction due to peptic ulcer at the GH on 2 March 1905. He also wrote a widely-quoted article 'Epidemology of cancer in India' as early as 1902.[12]

Such pioneering work was not restricted to just English doctors. Even in the pre-Independence years, many Indian medical professionals had begun making a name for themselves. The first Indian to receive a medical degree overseas was from here. This was Senji Pulney Andy, who, in 1860, qualified from MMC and then went on to pursue an MD at St Andrew's University, Scotland.[13] Dr S. Rangachari, Dr Sir A. Lakshmanaswami Mudaliar, and Dr M. R. Guruswami Mudaliar are all famed names, commemorated in street names and statues. While Rangachari went about in a Rolls Royce and flew his personal aircraft so that he could reach his patients faster, Lakshmanaswami Mudaliar was a famed gynaecologist whose Mudaliar-Menon Regime for Eclampsia, a condition when pregnant women suffer fits owing to high blood pressure, was followed all over India for years. He also served as the vice chancellor of the University of Madras for a record twenty-five years, from 1942 to 1967. Dr Guruswami Mudaliar was a master of the percussion method of diagnosis, at a time when tests for all possible conditions were neither available nor in vogue.[14] Better remembered today for being an ardent follower of Swami Vivekananda but, in his time, a prominent doctor who counted Subramania Bharati and Sarojini Naidu as his friends was Dr M. C. Nanjunda Rao of Mylapore. He is commemorated in a street name in that locality.[15]

Another famed personality from the medical world was Dr U. Rama Rau, who became well-known for his malaria cure, being a firm believer in quinine. This doctor, who was also a freedom fighter, ran an open-air Swadeshi Hospital, where those who were beaten by the police during rallies were

---

[11]See here: https://aim25.com/cgi-bin/vcdf/detail?coll_id=12246&inst_id=20&nv1=search&nv2/.

[12]V. Sriram, 'Madras Landmarks, 50 years ago', *Madras Musings*, Vol. XXIV, No. 21, 16–28 February 2015.

[13]Sriram and Bhatt, *Brotherhood and Benevolence*, p. 114.

[14]For further details on their lives, see *Chennai Pramukargal*, Vols. 1 & 2.

[15]Dr M. C. Nanjunada Rao Malarvannan, *Swami Vivekanandarin Chennai Cheedar*, Sri Ramakrishna Math, 2013.

treated free of cost. He founded the Indian Medical Association in protest against European doctors getting preferential treatment and, together with his political opponent, Dr Taravath Madhavan Nair, brought out a medical journal, *The Antiseptic.*[16]

The trend of several great doctors emerging from Chennai continued post 1947. Dr B. Ramamurthi, considered the father of neurology in India, set up a department for this branch of medicine, in 1950, in GH and later in the Institute of Neurology at the Voluntary Health Services, Taramani, of which more to follow. Likewise, the success of Stanley Medical College and Hospital in the reconstruction of the hand owes much to Dr R. Venkataswamy, who set up the Institute for the Research and Rehabilitation of the Hand and the Department of Plastic Surgery there. This was a case of one man rising to meet a felt need—North Madras was where most industrial establishments were developing, ever since the Perambur Workshops of the railways came up there in the 1850s. Workers often injured themselves while operating heavy machinery, the hand being the first casualty. They were often maimed for life, which made the victim unemployable. The nearest hospital being Stanley, Dr Venkataswamy made it his life's mission to ensure that those who came received the best possible attention, with the treatment ensuring minimum loss of digits.[17]

In more recent times, Chennai has had the distinction of being the first in the detection of HIV positive cases in India. That was due to the work done by Dr Suniti Gaitonde Solomon, a graduate of MMC who, after post-graduation and work abroad, returned to Chennai as she felt the city needed her services. Working as a professor in the Institute of Micro Biology at the MMC, she studied papers connected with the discovery and research into AIDS and decided that it was time to check if sex workers in India had the same disease. That was in 1986 and the test revealed six of the hundred samples received to be HIV positive, which was India's first such documentation. There was disbelief all around but a retest at the Johns Hopkins University in Baltimore confirmed the same. Thereafter, Dr Solomon made it her mission to spread awareness about HIV and AIDS among the most vulnerable communities—homosexuals, sex workers, and drug addicts who injected themselves. A result of this was India's first comprehensive

---

[16]V. Sriram, 'A Great-grandfather of many parts', *Madras Musings*, Vol. XVIII, No. 14, 1–15 November 2008.

[17]Swami Subramaniam, *Healing Hands: The Inspiring Story of the Surgeon who set up the world's largest hand injury service*, Bengaluru, 2019.

HIV/AIDS facility. Named the AIDS Resource Group, it was founded by Dr Solomon in 1988. The Y. R. Gaitonde Centre for AIDS Research and Education, named after her father, was set up in 1993. She became well-known across the world for her work in AIDS thereafter, collaborating on numerous research papers and studies. Dr Solomon passed away in 2016 but her work lives on.[18]

The city has a record to be proud of when it comes to mental health. For years, going to Kilpauk was a euphemism for disorders of the mind and that is because of the Regional Institute of Mental Health, which completed 225 years in 2019.[19] This institution and some of its well-known doctors went on to establish Chennai as a centre for mental health; one of the pioneers being Dr J. Dhairyam who served as superintendent and, in the 1950s, set up one of India's first private health facilities for mental illnesses.[20] Within a short while, this clinic and its hospice located en route Mamallapuram became very popular, attracting patients from all over India and abroad.

Work by other organizations in recent years has only enhanced Chennai's reputation in the area of mental health. Most interestingly, these have all been women-led initiatives. The first was Shanthi Ranganathan, who in 1979 lost her husband, a scion of the TTK family, to alcohol-related issues. She was just thirty. Encouraged by her in-laws, she chose to go abroad and train herself so that she could set up a de-addiction centre in Chennai on her return. A day-care centre for addicts came up in one of the family properties in 1980. Along with a few colleagues, she began visiting various factories and establishments to counsel people on the effects of alcohol. In 1987, funded largely by the TTK Group, Shanthi set up the TTK Hospital, a sixty-bed facility dedicated to de-addiction. It was India's first and helped many realize that alcoholism was a treatable condition, classified as mental illness. The hospital is now managed by the T. T. Ranganathan Clinical Research Foundation and has also brought drug addiction into its ambit. Shanthi, who holds a doctorate for her thesis on addiction, now resides mainly in the village of Manjakudi, but the institution she founded continues to bring several addicts back into the mainstream.[21]

It was in 1984 that Dr M. Sarada Menon, India's first woman psychiatrist

---

[18]Vishwas R. Gaitonde, 'Remembering Dr Solomon', *The Hindu*, 1 December 2015.

[19]Shobha Menon, '90 + and still going strong', *Madras Musings*, Vol. XXVII, No. 4, 1–15 June 2017.

[20]WP No. 229, High Court of Madras, 1965.

[21]'A Tribute to Shanti Ranganathan's Work', *The Hindu*, 21 February 2020.

and first woman superintendent of the Institute of Mental Health, Kilpauk, founded the Schizophrenia Research Foundation (SCARF) along with colleague Dr R. Thara. This has now emerged as India's premier institution for research, treatment, and creating awareness about schizophrenia. Recognized as a collaborating centre for mental health and training by the WHO, its nucleus is the centre at Anna Nagar, which, apart from rehabilitation and treatment, also has residential facilities for patients. The institution is also known for its outreach programmes, particularly in slums and economically depressed areas of the city.[22]

Chennai is one of the suicide capitals of India—this dubious distinction has a long history, what with Tamil traditions celebrating suicide, particularly in situations when the choice is between honour and life. In more recent years, political parties have all but openly encouraged suicides as a form of protest and this can be for anything from social issues to the death or illness of a beloved leader. The obsession with academic performance and the inability to cope with less than top marks in competitive examinations, coupled with fear of the future drives many to commit suicide. Such incidents are usually reported in the newspapers and *The Hindu,* in particular, has made it a practice to always add a line to the effect that suicides are avoidable and those who have suicidal thoughts ought to contact Sneha Suicide Prevention Centre, the numbers being provided alongside. Dr Lakshmi and her husband, Dr Vijayakumar, founded this volunteer-based counselling organization in 1986 after a visit to Austria opened their eyes to such facilities in Europe. Sneha offers anonymous emotional support via its helplines and counsellors, at all times, at no cost. Several lives have been saved this way. The organization has also advised the government and the public so as to avoid situations that can lead to suicide, and this includes influencing the way examination results are announced.[23]

The Banyan is the fourth initiative from Chennai in the area of mental health. And what makes it unique is that unlike SCARF and Sneha, it was begun by two women—Vaishnavi Jayakumar and Vandana Gopikumar—who were not qualified psychiatrists but recognized the crying need for providing mental healthcare by way of holistic and not illness-based solutions. Begun essentially as a facility for women, it has since expanded to include men. The Banyan offers a gamut of services right from the rescue of the mentally ill to

[22]Priyamvada Chugh, 'This 95-YO Padma-Awardee Psychiatrist Changed The Way We View Mental Health', *The Better Home*, 2 December 2018.
[23]Vijayakumars, available here: http://www.vijayakumars.com/about-us-4/.

their treatment and perhaps most importantly—their rehabilitation. The last named includes setting up some of the treated patients in clustered-group homes where they divide the work among themselves and learn to co-exist in a family-like environment. Home Again is yet another model where individuals form affinity groups and together with a community worker, set up a home. The Banyan also recognized early on that incidence of mental illness is far higher in the poorer sections of society and focuses chiefly on that stratum. Today, Banyan has urban clinics in Chennai, a chapter in Trichy, and has spread to Maharashtra and Kerala as well. Its success has been recognized by several awards and its model is upheld as one worthy of emulation by other states of India.

Madras had a hospital exclusively dedicated to the eye as early as 1819. The 'kann aspithri' as it is referred to, though its real name is the Regional Institute of Ophthalmology and the Government Ophthalmic Hospital, is the second oldest in the whole world, after the facility in Moorfield, England. This hospital, located in Egmore, is housed in a heritage structure, well cared for and containing what is probably the only museum dedicated to the eye.[24] Not so lucky is the Government Hospital for Women and Children, set up in 1844, for its main edifice, constructed in 1881 and shaped like a female pelvis, has just been demolished in the name of modernization. The institution, nevertheless, is a centre of excellence and houses the Regional Institute of Obstetrics and Gynaecology.[25] Ob-Gyn is also the main focus of the Kasturba Gandhi Memorial Hospital, colloquially referred to as 'gosha aspithri', as several of the women who come here are orthodox burqa-clad Muslims. This was the brainchild of Mary Dacombe Scharlieb, an Englishwoman who, in the 1880s, forced Madras Medical School to throw its doors open to members of her sex, becoming the first student herself. Begun in 1887 as the Victoria Caste and Gosha Hospital, its red-brick buildings take you to another era but the medical practices are all up-to-date.[26]

India's first radiology facility came up at the GH in 1905, five years after Roentgen discovered x-rays. In 1920, a technician was sent out to Madras to begin a new x-ray facility. This was Captain T. W. Barnard who became so good at his work that he was considered a doctor and eventually honoured in 1934 with the Institute of Radiology and Cancer being named after him.

---

[24]Muthiah, *Madras Rediscovered*, pp. 421–22.

[25]Ramya Raman and Anantanarayanan Raman, 'Women Doctors and Women's Hospitals in Madras', *Madras Musings*, Vol. XXIX, No. 16, 1–15 December 2019.

[26]Ibid.

It is today known as the Barnard Institute of Radiology and Oncology.[27] Cancer however began receiving focused attention when Dr Muthulakshmi Reddy, the pioneering social reformer, set up the Cancer Institute under the auspices of the Women's Indian Association in Adyar in 1954. This is today, a world-famous institution, run for many years by Dr Reddy's associate, Dr V. Shanta, who passed away in 2021.[28]

The TB Institute was set up in Madras in 1916 and has been continuously upgraded ever since, becoming the National Institute for Research in Tuberculosis. The first facility to treat patients in isolation, however, was the Tambaram Sanatorium, founded in 1928 by Dr Chowry Muthu, a Tamil Christian who graduated in medicine from England, ran a health centre there, married an Englishwoman, and treated the mathematician Srinivasa Ramanujan during his tenure in Cambridge. The sanatorium was acquired by the government in the 1930s and repeatedly expanded upon.[29] A smaller facility with the personal touch of the founder was Dr Mathuram Santosham's Sanatorium, also at Tambaram, begun in 1945. This institution and its feisty doctor who had a parallel career in politics as a staunch supporter of Rajaji's Swatantra Party, played a key role in the Madras Experiment, which, in the 1950s, funded by the WHO and under the auspices of the Tuberculosis Research Centre, Madras, studied whether sanatoria were at all required for the treatment of TB, given the availability of modern drugs. Dr Wallace Fox from England conducted the study and aiding his efforts was Dr Santosham who knew that the findings would go against the continued use of sanatoria for TB. Sure enough, the Madras Experiment demonstrated that there was no difference whether a patient was treated at home or at a sanatorium and it spelt the end of such facilities across the world. Dr Santosham, however, ran his sanatorium for many years, remarking rather jocularly that it gave him a return on investment of 1.5 per cent per annum.[30]

The history of TB treatment in the city would be incomplete without mention of the controversy that was generated when BCG, the vaccine, was introduced. Unlike in the rest of India, it was not accepted as a matter of faith. Tamil Nadu has had a dedicated public health cadre since 1939

[27]See Barnard Institute website, available here: https://www.barnard.in/about-bir.html/.

[28]Dr T. Muthu Kannappar, *Dr Muthulakshmi Reddy Vazhkai Varalaru: Vizhippu Unarthiya Veeranganai*, Chennai: Gangai Puthaka Nilayam, 2002.

[29]V. Sriram, 'The Story of a Sanatorium', *The Hindu*, 7 February 2013.

[30]V. Sriram, *Goodness and Mercy: The Life and Times of Dr Mathuram Santosham*, Chennai: The Santosham Hospital Public Trust, 2013.

when legislation was passed to that effect. This comprises a whole workforce including doctors, paramedics, village-level midwives, and others, and ranks the best in India. The state remains one of the very few in the country to have such a service in place and has reaped dividends.[31] Mass immunization programmes were most effective with such a large team available and, in the 1950s, the same network was pressed into service for BCG vaccinations. Former chief minister Rajaji was not a votary of BCG. He ran a consistent campaign against the vaccine, essentially based on the writings of A.V. Raman, his close friend and former sanitary engineer of the Madras Corporation, claiming it to be 'worthless quackery'. He was concerned that the government had begun a mass-immunization campaign with this vaccination, at a time when BCG was still in its infancy and its permanent effects had not been gauged. Combating Rajaji on this was Dr K. S. Sanjeevi, an eminent physician of the city who had served as director of the TB Institute, among other positions.[32] The city's suspicion of vaccines was not new. In the early 1800s when W. S. Swamy Naik, the then superintendent of vaccinations went about his business, syringe in hand, he was waylaid and attacked by a group of Armenians. He was not deterred and went on to become the chief medical practitioner, Department of Vaccinations, and retired in 1829. A memorial to him stands near where his house once was, in Komaleeswaranpet.[33]

The opposition to BCG died down and Sanjeevi went back to his pet mission—creating health centres in the outskirts of the city and in villages so that medical help was available to the poorest of the poor. The Voluntary Health Services (VHS), at Taramani, was his creation. Founded in 1958 with public donations, it became a hospital in 1961 with Nehru laying its foundation stone. It is today a 400-plus-bed hospital with several community centres in the periphery of the city fulfilling the vision of its founder.[34]

Making it big in cardiac surgery was the Railway Hospital, Perambur, now known as the Southern Railway Headquarters Hospital. Founded in 1925 to cater exclusively to the employees of the Madras and Southern Mahratta Railway, it soon extended its services to the general public, charging very

[31]Sanjiv Kumar, Vinay Bothra, and Dilip Singh Mairenbam, 'A Dedicated Public Health Cadre: Urgent and Critical to Improve Health in India', *Indian Journal of Community Medicine*, Oct-Dec 2016.

[32]V. Sriram, 'Madras fights Tuberculosis—3/When we opposed BCG', *Madras Heritage and Carnatic Music*, 3 April 2020.

[33]V. Sriram, 'Memorial to a Vaccinator', *The Hindu*, 17 April 2012.

[34]See The Voluntary Health Services website, available here: https://vhschennai.org/aboutus.php/.

low fees. It built up a formidable practice and by the 1970s had emerged as a referral centre across India for cardiac surgeries, its Dr K. M. Cherian performing the country's first successful coronary bypass surgery in 1975.[35] It also became a hunting ground for private hospitals that lured away many of its doctors, in particular its cardiac specialists. Another unsung institution is the Communicable Diseases Hospital, Tondiarpet, which was set up as an Isolation Hospital in 1924. It played an important role in the eradication of smallpox, which regularly visited the city with terrible consequences till the 1960s. The vanquishing of this scourge was due to Dr A. Ramachandra Rao, public health officer and Superintendent of the Tondiarpet Hospital in the 1960s. Dr Rao, who had begun recording cases of smallpox, identified that it broke out in three-year cycles. Noticing in 1964 that yet another epidemic of smallpox was brewing, Dr Rao, contrary to accepted medical practice, insisted on all infants in the hospital being inoculated against the virus. This was at a time when it was believed that infants below three did not benefit from vaccination. It was noticed that all the injected children became immune to smallpox, thereby proving that inoculation could be done at any age. With that, the dreaded disease was eradicated from India. In 1972, Dr Rao wrote a monograph on smallpox. By then he was a consultant at the WHO and had trained several doctors around the world on handling the virus.[36] Sadly, he is not remembered in Chennai.

The United Nations declared 1978 the International Year of the Child and that was the year in which Madras got its Child's Trust Hospital, founded by Dr M. S. Ramakrishnan, a well-known paediatric surgeon, who dreamt of an integrated facility where all medical requirements could be met, at affordable costs, for children. It was a first for South India. The institution, in later years, was acquired by the Kanchi Mutt and is now known as the Kanchi Kamakoti Child's Trust Hospital.[37]

In 1978, Sankara Nethralaya, the not-for-profit hospital dedicated to eye-related diseases, was founded in the city by Dr S. S. Badrinath. Today, it is internationally renowned and despite thousands of people who come seeking treatment, pushing its main block and branches to their very limits, it remains true to its founder's philosophy of affordable eye care.[38] At Sankara

[35]Shahid Akhter, 'Interview with Dr KM Cherian', *Economic Times*, 27 October 2015.

[36]V. Sriram, 'The Slayer of Smallpox', *The Hindu*, 20 June 2014.

[37]See Kanchi Kamakoti CHILDS Trust Hospital website, available here: https://www.kkcth.org/about-us/history/.

[38]V.V. Ranganathan, George Skaria, and Meera Prasad, *In-Sight: Sankara Nethralaya's Passion*

Nethralaya you will find a virtual Tower of Babel, with patients from all over India and other countries, several on their maiden journey to Chennai. The staff speaks several languages and a spirit of extending tender loving care pervades the whole oragnization.

Sankara Nethralaya is a great leveller, for you will find the well-heeled being treated along with several less fortunate people. Here is an institution that, owing to its excellence, draws people from all strata of society. The Cancer Institute is also similar in this regard. Also worthy of commemoration are numerous doctors of the city who made affordable treatment their life's mission: Dr A. S. Thambiah in dermatology, Dr K. V. Thiruvengadam and Dr C.V. Krishnaswami in diabetology, and Vyasarapadi's Dr V. Thiruvengadam who charged ₹2 as consultation fee till his passing in 2020, are a few examples. Catering to the needs of the more affluent were several private hospitals and nursing homes across the city, the bulk of them being on Poonamallee High Road, which in the 1950s, 60s, and 70s was known as the Harley Street of Madras. At the upper end of this spectrum of private hospitals was the Lady Willingdon Nursing Home that was funded and founded in the 1920s by and for the exclusive use of the senior employees of the British companies in the city.[39] With healthcare facilities multiplying all over Chennai in the 1990s, this hospital, whose managing trust was by then in the hands of Indian conglomerates, found its clientele waning. The facility was closed and the property was acquired by Sankara Nethralaya, with much of the funding for this coming from the Amalgamations Group. It uses the place only for treatment of the poor. The trust, renamed the Chennai Willingdon Corporate Foundation, now uses the money generated from the sale of the property for a whole host of charitable causes.[40]

Matching Sankara Nethralaya in terms of brand identity and recall is Apollo Hospitals, the conglomerate that redefined healthcare as a service that can also make profits. It was not the first, for that record is held by HM Hospital, founded by Dr H. Mehta in the 1960s, now no longer in existence.[41] Dr Prathap C. Reddy, founder of Apollo, worked at HM but his dream was much larger. In 1983, he set up Apollo's flagship hospital in Nungambakkam. This was an era when no financing was available for such businesses and Dr Reddy had to meet successive prime ministers and

---

for Compassion, New Delhi: Lone Tree Books, 2012.

[39]Sriram, *The Sanmar Story*, p. 414.

[40]Ibid.

[41]Muthiah, *Madras Rediscovered*, p. 425.

governors of the Reserve Bank of India, to convince them of such a need. Laws had to be amended to allow for hospitals to raise finances thereafter.[42]

'I acknowledge that I did have a major role in setting up India's first corporate hospital,' says Dr Reddy. 'But I would be failing in my duty if I do not mention others who shared my vision. Prime Minister Indira Gandhi brought about changes in legislation and helped me in introducing high-end tertiary care. R. Venkataraman, when he was union finance minister granted corporate status to Apollo and allowed listing of the company. It was Pranab Mukherjee, who succeeded him and amended existing rules to enable the funding of hospitals.' [43]

What he does not say is that it needed a man of his vision to get them all to act.

Inaugurated by the then president of India, Giani Zail Singh, who repeatedly exclaimed that an American hospital had come to India, Apollo has always been high profile—be it the personality of its founder, the doctors who work for it, and also some of the patients who come for treatment. It helped that within a year of inauguration, the chief minister of Tamil Nadu, MGR, was brought in, in a very precarious condition. In the old days, leaders were treated at the GH but with MGR, all that changed. Sure, it was risky housing him, given the mass hysteria his illness aroused but the hospital could hardly have refused. It bore the brunt of misplaced public anger when MGR's condition worsened and he had to be flown to the US for further treatment. Much of the credit for keeping him alive goes to Dr M. K. Mani, the tough-talking no-nonsense nephrologist at the hospital. MGR returned, lived on for three more years and then died at home.[44] Not so his protégé Jayalalithaa, who as chief minister was similarly brought in and had a prolonged stay at Apollo, subject to some hush-hush treatment, and eventually died in the premises. The subsequent commission of enquiry on her death is one of the many crises that Apollo has weathered, but they all add to the conglomerate's brand recognition.

Apollo today is a ₹6,000-crore business entity with a network of hospitals and pharmacies across India and abroad. Not everyone has agreed with its mode of functioning but it cannot be denied that it placed Chennai on the medical map of the world. Several other hospital chains have attempted to

[42]Pranay Gupte, *Healer: Dr Prathap Chandra Reddy and the Transformation of India*, New Delhi: Penguin Books, 2013.

[43]Interview with the author, Chennai, 25 January 2018.

[44]MGR, pp. 339–42.

emulate it, but rarely met with that kind of success. But then, not every doctor is a P. C. Reddy—a unique combination of doctor and businessman. An interesting side benefit as it were from the Apollo story was the pressure it brought on other private facilities in the city to ramp up, in matters of infrastructure, certifications, equipment, and doctors. This went a long way in transforming the good base that Chennai had into a revenue generation proposition, making the city the medical capital of India.

Corporatization of healthcare is increasingly the trend in Chennai but some have remained steadfast to the mission of providing treatment at affordable costs. Sundaram Medical Foundation, begun by Dr S. Rangarajan, son of TVS scion T. S. Santhanam, runs on a different policy from Apollo's but with the same goals as far as the quality of care is concerned—its capital costs are met by the TVS Group of companies and Santhanam's independent creation—the Sundaram Finance Group. Patients are therefore charged only for running costs, thereby keeping bills low.[45]

Chennai has a number of other charitable hospitals running on the same principles. One of the most successful is the Public Health Centre (PHC), West Mambalam. Developing as it did in the shadow of the upmarket T. Nagar, and populated largely by the lower-middle class and the poor, this part of the city was grossly neglected. In 1952, T. T. Krishnamachari, while out campaigning, remarked that West Mambalam lacked every possible amenity, including health facilities. Listening in the audience was M. C. Subrahmanyam, a journalist who resolved to build a health centre for the people of Mambalam, funded by them. Armed with pamphlets, appeals, and receipt books, MC, as he was known, went from house to house. People volunteered and in 1953, PHC was inaugurated by the chief minister of Madras State, Rajagopalachari. Doctors volunteered their time and services and medicines were sold at subsidised rates. The demand always exceeded supply and soon it became clear that maternity facilities were of the utmost need. The government was appealed to and land adjoining PHC was granted. Gradually, with funding largely from the TTK and TVS Groups, PHC expanded and is today a multi-disciplinary hospital, catering to the lower-income groups.[46] A very similar story is that of the Hindu Mission Hospital, started by D. K. Srinivasan for the benefit of people residing in Tambaram and its environs. Known as the ten-paise hospital after what was charged for examining patients in camps that were

[45]Sriram, *Sundaram Finance Story*, pp. 244–49.

[46]Shobha Menon, 'A Memorial to a Life of Service', *Madras Musings*, Vol. XXII, No. 18, 1–15 January 2013.

set up under trees, it is today a 200-bed facility with several branches of medicine being practised under its roof.[47]

Some of the corporate houses of the city have been at the forefront when it came to setting up hospitals, especially in the vicinity of their factories. Just two instances would suffice to illustrate the work done by them. It was in the 1950s that the Murugappa Group began expanding in the Ambattur area, land for its factories coming up on what was once a camp for refugees from Malaya. The group set up its cycle and other allied plants here, the principal collaboration being with the Tube Investments (TI) Group of the UK. The population in the surroundings began to grow and the Murugappa Group began to plan amenities—the Sir A. Ramaswami Mudaliar School, named after one of the two famed Arcot twins and the man who introduced the Murugappas to TI, was set up. A hospital was next and when plans began, it was decided to consult the other Arcot twin, Dr Sir A. Lakshmanaswami Mudaliar, who was then the vice chancellor of the University of Madras. The well-known gynaecologist strongly advised against making the facility free, emphasizing however that charges needed to be kept low. Upon coming to know of the proposed hospital, Sir Ivan Stedeford, Chairman of TI UK, expressed his delight and donated £5,000. He arrived in person to inaugurate the hospital in 1966. Funded and nurtured by the AMM Foundation of the Murugappa Group, Sir Ivan Stedeford Hospital is now a 200-plus-bed facility that handles a whopping 450,000 patients a year.[48]

Similarly, it was the Rane Group's dynamic chairman, L. L. Narayan (LLN), who in the 1960s gave the suburb of Nanganallur its first health facility. The area, coming as it did under the Alandur Municipality where Rane's Engine Valves Limited (EVL) was established, was a remote suburb of Madras in the 1960s, known more for its disproportionately large number of temples than anything else. With many of the EVL staff being drawn from the same locality, LLN became aware that there were hardly any medical facilities in the area. In 1966, he wrote that 'it is advisable to provide a maternity home with 4/5 beds and a family planning clinic in the Saidapet/Guindy/Alandur area to cater to the needs of 400/450 families of our group of factories.' The board, however, demurred and the matter was pigeonholed.

Not one to give up so easily, LLN persisted. In the early 1970s, residents of the area formed the Ganesh Mandali, a trust for charitable causes. EVL

[47]T. Atul Swaminathan, 'I dedicate the award to my family, doctors and staff', *The Hindu*, 30 January 2016.

[48]Muthiah, *Looking Back From Moulmein*, pp. 256–62.

donated ₹20,000 towards the setting up of a health facility by the trust and made sporadic contributions thereafter. In 1974, the Mandali wrote to EVL requesting funds for the setting up of a hospital in the area. They estimated the cost at ₹2 lakh. EVL decided to fund the construction in full. The hospital was completed by late 1976 and was ready for inauguration when Sidney and Margaret Lewis, long-time collaborators of LLN and Rane, arrived on a visit from the UK in January 1977. LLN convinced the trust that the hospital ought to be named after his close friends. The Margaret Sidney Hospital was declared open by Mrs Lewis on 15 January. On their return to England, the couple sent a large donation to the hospital. Given the stringent tax laws that governed UK at that time, it took all of Sidney's well-known powers of persuasion to convince the tax authorities to ensure that the amount reached India in full without suffering deductions. In time, the trust was renamed the Ganesh Mandali Engine Valves Trust and continues to govern the hospital.[49]

The Corporation of Chennai, usually the subject of much criticism for its functioning or lack of it, has been extremely effective when it comes to its public welfare initiatives in healthcare. With its clinics, family welfare centres, and specialist hospitals dealing with chest disease, maternity, leprosy, infections and dental care, the corporation has kept infant and adult mortality at very low levels consistently over several years. It has also used this formidable network to conduct mass immunization programmes and tackle epidemics at the very outset.

Hospitals and doctors would have found the going tough had support services by way of nursing and pharmacology not existed. Here, too, Chennai was at the forefront. There was a Madras Midwifery School in 1843. By the 1870s, courses in nursing were available at the GH, Gosha Hospital, and Hospital for Women and Children.[50] Those who joined were essentially from the Eurasian and Dalit Christian communities. As early as in 1904, the Lady Ampthill Nurses Institute had been founded. This and the South India Nurses Association founded in 1920 largely comprised European nurses who came down to cater to the British population in the city. These, in turn, were absorbed into the Lady Willingdon Nursing Home referred to earlier, when that body was set up in 1920.[51] The Indian nurses of the city had their own

[49] Sriram, *The Rane Story*, pp. 279–80.

[50] See http://nursingandmidwifery.gov.in/nursinghistory.html#.YFxhUi0Rq_w/.

[51] V. Sriram, 'Where stood de Havilland's twin castlets?', *Madras Musings*, Vol. 21, No. 10, 1–15 September 2011.

association and building in Vepery, both of which reached their peak in the 1940s under the redoubtable Hanen Angelo, a Eurasian who not only became a councillor of the Madras Corporation but also unsuccessfully contested the Legislative Council elections.[52] Today, over twenty nursing schools and forty colleges in the city offer three- and four-year nursing courses.[53]

Madras was the pioneer in training chemists and druggists, the course beginning at the MMC in the 1870s. One of the early graduates, Mohideen Sheriff, would, in 1891, bring out the *Materia Medica of Madras*, listing the drugs used in medical treatment in the city that were not documented in standard pharmacopoeias of the time.[54] In 1925, largely at the bidding of Wilfred Pereira, a pioneering city pharmacist, the country's first professional association for pharmacists was established in Madras. The Pharmaceutical Society of India, as it was called, was later amalgamated with the Indian Pharmaceutical Association, Varanasi.[55]

Running in parallel to the allopathic story of the city is an equally interesting thread concerning native medicine—Ayurveda, Siddha, and Unani. The first and second were essentially ancient Indian medical practices while the third, as the name suggests, had to do with Greek medicine, which came to India via the Persians and Arabs. In the early years of Madras after the arrival of the British, it is quite likely that most residents of the city took recourse to one of these streams of medicine. Those were the years of cordial stones and potions. When Shivaji the Maratha came within calling distance of Madras, he ordered the EIC to send him just those medications, not once but twice. He also offered to pay but the terrified British were happy to gift them to him as long as he did not invade the city. They did, however, mournfully note that the presents had cost them sixty pagodas.[56] The Italian Niccolao Manucci, author of the famed *Storia do Mogor* (Story of the Moguls), which he wrote while in Madras, practised as a native doctor here in the 1680s. He had learnt Indian techniques and the secret of his

[52]S. Muthiah, 'When the Postman Knocked', *The Hindu*, 29 August 2015.

[53]T. Rajagopalan, 'Not the happiest of nursing scenes', *Madras Musings*, Vol. 28, No. 18, 1–15 January 2019.

[54]Dr A. Raman, 'Pharmacy Education evolves in Madras', *Madras Musings*, Vol. 28, No. 23, 16–31 March 2019.

[55]V. Sriram, 'A Pharmacy that helped found a Society', *Madras Musings*, Vol. 28, No. 20, 1–15 February 2019.

[56]J. Talboys Wheeler, *Madras in the Olden Time: Being a History of the Presidency*, Madras: Higginbothams & Co, 1882, pp. 49–55.

success was 'Manoch's Stone'—slivers of cinnabar made into liquid medicine.[57]

By the nineteenth century, prospects for Indian medicine had dimmed, what with several doctors qualified in allopathy setting up practice. It was left to Pandit D. Gopalacharyulu, who came from a family of hereditary Ayurvedic practitioners in Andhra, to set right the imbalance. Nominated as the first principal of the Sri Kanyaka Parameswari Devasthanam's Ayurvedic Hospital, he soon attracted a large clientele. With a whole host of patent medicines that were advertised as cures for influenza, plague, menstrual problems, and anaemia, all made at his Ayurvedasrama in George Town, Pandit Gopalacharyulu became a national figure, raking in much money and several awards and titles. In later years, he came to be known as Bhishangamani, Ayurveda Marthanda, and Vaidya Ratna D. Gopalacharyulu. His Ayurveda Pracharini Sabha acted as a publicity organ for his medicines and also spread awareness about Ayurveda. Gopalacharyulu was not yet fifty when he died, in 1920. His work was carried on by Dr A. Lakshmipathi, a qualified eye surgeon from the MMC, who chose to make his career in Ayurveda instead. Having apprenticed under Gopalacharyulu, he later took over the Ayurvedashrama after the founder's death. He began marketing the ashrama's products through retail outlets across the country as well. He and his assistants regularly went on Arogya Yatras—journeys to conduct medical camps in villages. This came to the notice of Mahatma Gandhi who invited him to do the same at Sevagram. In 1926, he purchased a few hundred acres near Avadi, a suburb of the city, and began a charitable health farm named Arogya Ashrama. Most significantly, it was open to all, irrespective of caste, religion, or financial status. In the 1940s, the government requisitioned the lands for setting up defence establishments.[58] The money that came by way of compensation was used to help his son-in-law, Dr B. Ramamurthi, set up the Neurological Department at GH and, years later, the Institute of Neurological Sciences at the VHS as well. Entire blocks at the GH and the VHS commemorate Dr Lakshmipathi today.[59]

A breakaway from Gopalacharyulu was Dr K. N. Kesari, whom we have met earlier in this book. He set up the Kesari Kuteeram Ayurveda Oushadhashala in 1900. After initial tribulations, this became hugely successful, with his Lodhra tonic, in particular, meant for women, being much in demand. To cater to his female clientele, Dr Kesari turned publisher, bringing out a

[57]S. Muthiah, 'The Italian in Madras', *The Hindu*, 26 November 2016.

[58]Bishag Ratna Dr Achanta Lakshmipathi, *Autobiography*, Madras: The Arogya Ashrama Samithi, 1994.

[59]Ibid., pp. iv–v.

Telugu magazine, *Grihalakshmi*. The publication changed hands after he passed away in 1953 but Kesari Kuteeram still flourishes, run by his grandson.[60] Gopalacharyulu was also to leave his impression on the brilliant vakil and later judge of the High Court of Madras and still later a member of the governor's Executive Council, V. Krishnaswamy Aiyar. Arriving for a visit in 1904, Aiyar was enthused to establish the Venkataramana Ayurveda Dispensary in Mylapore the very next year, and it has remained in operation ever since.[61]

'Desoddharaka' Kasinathuni Nageswara Rao Pantulu, commemorated in Mylapore's famed Nageswara Park, was not a medical man but he invented one of Chennai's most enduring brands—the pain balm, Amrutanjan. Rumour had it that he came up with the product to cure the headache caused to the readers of his *Andhra Patrika*, but it is true that he distributed the product as a publicity gimmick in the early years at Carnatic music concerts. Nageswara Rao Pantulu would later turn patriot and a staunch Congressman but he kept an eye on his business, which still functions from his erstwhile residence in Mylapore.[62] Like him, another native name still remembered is Jammi Venkataramanayya, who, in 1949, came up with Jammi's Liver Cure to help children tide over chronic diseases of the liver and spleen. His native products later extended to cover whooping cough, digestive disorders, and a whole host of other diseases. The company still functions from a vast art deco structure named Jammi Buildings, a landmark in the Royapettah area but a poorly maintained rabbit's warren of offices.

Ayurveda is essentially a science whose treatises are in Sanskrit and its followers are largely members of the upper castes. Tamil Nadu had its native medical techniques, grouped under what is known as Siddha medicine, based entirely on locally available herbs and minerals. This was generally considered the preserve of mystics who meditated in remote hills where plenty of medicinal herbs grew. Over time, some products came to be commercially marketed, one of the best known being Abraham Pandithar's Korosanai Pills.[63] In Madras, one of the hereditary families that practised Siddha was that of Ayothi Das Pandithar. He is chiefly remembered today for his anti-caste activities and is considered the progenitor of the Dalit Movement. It is interesting to reflect that the history of inclusivity in Tamil Nadu, and the

---

[60] Menon, *Life and Times of Kesari*.

[61] K. Chandrashekaran, *V. Krishnaswami Iyer*, Chennai: Kuppuswami Sastry Research Institute, 1998, p. 38.

[62] Sriram, *Fifty Historic Residences*, p. 90.

[63] Wright, *Southern India*, pp. 486–91.

state can rightfully claim to be the first in India in this regard, which begins with a Siddha doctor, namely Pandithar, later grew as the non-Brahmin movement under two allopathic doctors—C. Natesa Mudaliar and T. M. Nair.[64] It was entirely apt that in 2005, when the central government set up the National Institute of Siddha in Tambaram, on land once occupied by Dr Chowry Muthu's sanatorium, its adjunct hospital came to be named after Ayothi Das Pandithar.

Unani medicine came to Madras with the nawabs of Arcot, one of the earliest practitioners being Hakim Ahmadullah, medical adviser to Nawab Mohammad Ali Wallajah in the eighteenth century and author of a number of Persian treatises on medicine. In 1900, the city got its first Unani facility in the Unani Medical Hall, begun by A. S. Hakim Mohammad Shamsuddin, descendant of a family that had treated the rajas of Tanjore. The Unani doctors were the first among native practitioners to realize that all government support was for the allopathic system and so began the Eastern Medical Association of South India. This body established in 1913 the Khuddusia Tibbi School, an institution to teach the Unani system of medicine and later, in 1919, upgraded it into a college. Three years later, a dispensary was opened. In 1925, the association organized a Unani conference, the first in the country. The then premier of Madras, the raja of Panagal, inaugurated it and was so impressed that he offered to open an Indian School of Medicine, with government support, and even offered his property, Hyde Park Gardens in Kilpauk, for the institution. The school was upgraded to a college in 1957, thanks to the intervention of Rukmini, wife of Dr Lakshmipathi, referred to earlier, and a freedom fighter in her own right, who was by then minister for Health in the Rajaji cabinet. But in 1960, the government decided to close down the college and gave away the land to the Kilpauk Medical College.

However, as is common with the government, there was a rethink years later, and the College of Indian Medicine reopened, at Palayamkottai, near Tirunelveli. This, in the 1970s, relocated to Anna Nagar, Chennai. It is, as its name suggests, a place where equal representation is given to Ayurveda, Siddha, and Unani. There is in fact a Unani Medical College on the campus.[65] This, however, is not the only institution dedicated to Indian forms of medicine. As early as 1944, Captain G. Srinivasamurti, an allopathic doctor who had studied Ayurveda as a hobby and become deeply immersed in it, formed the Indian Medical Practitioners Co-operative Society (IMPCOPS). It is an

---

[64]For further details see Guy, *Anraiya Chennai Pramukargal*, Vol. 1 & 2.

[65]Anvar, *Islam*, pp. 151–52.

interesting matter of trivia that he headed the Indian School of Medicine when it was in Kilpauk and his statue is still there, though the former has no connection with the KMC that now functions from that campus. He is also commemorated with a statue at IMPCOPS in its nine-acre plot in Thiruvanmiyur, which was purchased in 1949. IMPCOPS today has a membership of 12,000 practitioners from all over the country, and makes Ayurvedic, Siddha, and Unani medicines and tonics.[66]

In retrospect, it would appear that Chennai had all the right breaks when it came to the medical industry. The fact that it was a presidency capital meant it had institutions established in it from early on—both colleges and hospitals. Some path-breaking research did help but more important was the sheer continuity of the institutions—some, as we saw, have been around for centuries. Missionary activity and the founding of the Christian Medical College, Vellore, not far from the city gave an added fillip. Several well-known physicians and surgeons helped put Chennai on the world medical map. But here Dr N. Varadarajan, the city's first vascular surgeon, who is now in his nineties and has seen healthcare grow over seven decades says:

> ...when I embarked on my chosen field, it was to Bombay that I went to observe surgical practices and train. But yes, we [Chennai] did score in the number of hospitals and nursing homes that were begun. For a long while we had the great government-run institutions and private nursing homes, just enough for the city's needs. Then came private speciality hospitals, providing outstanding service. All of that pushed Chennai far ahead.[67]

With such a vibrant eco-system for the practice of medicine, it is no wonder that Chennai is a medical capital. In fact, the city repeatedly tops tourism statistics, beating even the golden triangle of Delhi–Agra–Jaipur for the simple reason that medical tourism figures are also included in the computation. It also possibly explains why the state's Tourism Department is one of the most poorly run and highly complacent set-ups, with no effort being taken to market any of the attractions in the city. Their attitude appears to be that when people are visiting even without any promotions, why bother?

---

[66]Muthiah, *Madras Rediscovered*, p. 470.

[67]Interview with the author, 12 March 2020.

14 | THE SPORTING SPIRIT

There is no doubt that when we think of a sport-rich city of India it is Kolkata that first comes to mind. Before the IPL craze and team CSK hogging the limelight, it is unlikely that Chennai was even thought of as a sports centre. But the city has been quietly notching up its records. In classic Chennai fashion, the city does not flaunt its achievements. In this city you are always taught to be wary of the evil eye that can destroy anything you boast about.

Organized sports as we recognize them today came to the city with the British but we have very few accounts of what was played. Hawking appears to have been practised from 1654 onwards[1] and as for the taverns in the city, of which there appear to have been plenty, almost all of them had billiard tables from the early days.[2] Gambling at cards and otherwise was common, and the EIC, namely the directors in England, frowned on the practice but not with any great success.[3] A bowling green was put up in the early years at the EIC's garden, on the Island, and so we do know that bowls were played.[4] There is sadly no clue as to what the Indians played.

From then on, Chennai has developed in its own way in sports. While it may not be possible to cover all the various activities that come under this head, some that have had a significant history here do need some detailing. Horse racing was perhaps the first sport to develop here, for there is mention of it as early as in 1775, making it the oldest track in India.[5] The 'old Guindy racecourse and the assembly rooms, its "grandstand" where entertainments were also frequently held,' were depicted in an aquatint by Thomas Daniell in 1792. The assembly rooms were demolished in the 1990s but the Madras Race Club, which emerged in 1887[6] from the early attempts at racing, is going strong, both for the sport and as a social entity. The heyday of racing in Madras was undoubtedly the pre-Independence era, when going to Guindy became synonymous with betting on horses. 'Guindy is the place where races

[1]Henry Dodwell, *The Nabobs of Madras*, London: Williams & Norgate Limited, 1926, p. 225.
[2]Ibid., p. 217.
[3]Love, *Vestiges of Old Madras*, Vol. 3, p. 501.
[4]Ibid., Vol. 2, p. 61.
[5]Dodwell, *The Nabobs*, p. 225.
[6]Muthiah, *Madras Rediscovered*, p. 319.

are held at stated seasons of the year,' wrote S. V. Vijayaraghavachariar (SVV), the noted humourist, whose columns appeared in *The Hindu* in the 1930s.

> On race days the whole city gets empty and congregates at the course, from HE the Governor of Madras down to Muniammal the vegetable seller. A racecourse is the most democratic place in the world. It would be nothing surprising if a Secretary to Government should take Muniammal aside and request her to whisper in his ears the name of the winner. And mind you, Muniammal knows the birth, upbringing and idiosyncrasies of every horse that runs in the race even better than the owner himself. It is really staggering what an amount of money passes from the hands of the visitors through the small apertures of the ticket-selling windows. Guindy is the bottomless sink into which all wealth, earned or borrowed in the city, disappears without a trace.[7]

The scandals associated with racing in Madras were many, as were tales of families that were once well-to-do but came to ruin owing to the addiction of betting on horses. Post-Independence governments frowned on this form of gambling and tried their best to control it. In 1974, the Karunanidhi-led DMK government brought in an ordinance banning horse racing in the state. This was ostensibly to protect the poor from squandering all their earnings in a colonial sport while market rumour had it that the barons of the turf had offended the powers-that-be. Almost within a month, the DMK government commissioned a pair of statues, of a rearing horse being reined in by a muscular man wearing a veshti. These were erected on either side of the Anna Flyover, the city's first-grade separator, with plaques proudly declaring that they commemorated the end of horse racing. The turf club challenged the ordinance in court and, within four years, was back in operation. The statues remain where they are, 'marvellously irrelevant pieces of art', as historian K. R. A. Narasiah describes them.[8]

Racing does continue at Guindy but it is no longer as popular. Chennai did have its first family of racing—the descendants of Raja Sir Annamalai Chettiar, namely his son, M. A. Chidambaram, and grandson M. A. M. Ramaswami, who were barons of the turf. Their passing has created a void in the racing scene that will remain unfilled for long, though Chidambaram's son A. C. Muthiah, having inherited the horses of his cousin Ramaswami is interesting himself

---

[7]Rangaswami Parthasarathy, *A Hundred Years of The Hindu: The Epic Story of Indian Nationalism*, Madras: Kasturi & Sons, 1978, p. 427.

[8]'Symbol of Racing off the high horse', *Times of India*, 15 August 2016.

once again in the turf.[9] An institution that Chidambaram helped set up is the Madras Polo & Riding Club (MPRC), which, coming out of the Madras Riding School in the 1960s, has for long been promoting equestrian events in the city, conducting them at the Officers' Training Academy, Pallavaram.[10] The club earlier held its matches at the Raj Bhavan, Guindy, whose grounds housed the Madras Riding School but found that the gambolling blackbuck and deer often held up the game. The MPRC also hosts matches for the Kolanka Cup, instituted by the raja of that principality. At 6 feet tall and made of solid silver, it holds a world record for being the largest trophy.[11] Muthiah, a keen polo player, today rues the vanishing of the vast green spaces where this game once flourished. The family estate of Adyar House at Kotturpuram once boasted a polo ground but that has made way for real estate. He also laments the vanishing of the marshes to the south of the city where bird shooting was common at one time. Much of it is has been given over to high-rises.

The Daniells, during their stay here in 1792, also executed a painting of a cricket match in progress, at the Island. The game, however, had to wait for fifty-four years, till 1846, before an organization was founded to promote it—the Madras Cricket Club (MCC). The MCC, like many other social clubs of the city, was founded in the rooms of the Madras Club, then located off Mount Road. The prime mover behind the MCC was Sir Alexander Arbuthnot, chief secretary to the government. The early years saw matches being played at the Island and it was only in 1865 that the governor in council gave permission for a circular piece of land at Chepauk to be marked out as a cricket ground. This marks the beginning of the continued association of cricket with Chepauk in Chennai.

The MCC did not own the land, it being leased from the government. That would result in trouble hundred years later but in the nineteenth and early twentieth centuries the MCC looked at a secure future, when it was a whites-only club.[12] But Indians had already come to appreciate the wonder that was cricket. The credit for ensuring that they also had facilities to play the game goes to M. Buchi Babu Naidu of the family of 'Dare House' Naidus.

Moddaverapu Dera Venkataswami Naidu, the patriarch, was dubash or

[9]In conversation with A. C. Muthiah.

[10]Gupta, *Vision UnLimited*, p. 151.

[11]Interview with the author, Chennai, 14 October 2020.

[12]S. Muthiah, *The Spirit of Chepauk: The MCC Story, 150 years of a Sporting Tradition*, Chennai: East West Books, 1998.

agent to Parry & Co (whose HQ was 'Dare House') in the nineteenth century and hence the family name of Dera. He became enormously wealthy and acquired 20 acres in Luz, building the family home, Lakshmi Vilas, there in the 1830s. He subsequently built Luz House on the same property in the 1850s. He also owned shops and houses in Triplicane in the vicinity of Big Street. One of the by-lanes off Big Street is Dera Venkataswami Street.

Venkataswami Naidu had only one daughter who bore five sons, the eldest of whom was Venkatamahipathi aka Buchi Babu. He was adopted by Venkataswami Naidu. Buchi Babu and his brothers were brought up in the best English tradition which included British nurses and governesses, all of whom inculcated a great love of cricket and all other sports, in general, in their wards. In time, Buchi Babu became a fine cricketer and a pillar of the Madras United Club (MUC) which he founded and to which cricket-playing Indians owed affiliation.

Buchi Babu ensured that Indians were given proper kits and trained to play well. He also persuaded the MCC to have an annual match between Madras Indians and Europeans. But he died in 1908, a few months before the first match, the early widowhood of his daughter and the subsequent death of his wife sapping his will to live. Buchi Babu Street, also branching off Big Street, commemorates this sportsman. The match that he instituted became an annual fixture and the MUC instituted the Buchi Babu Trophy in his memory, which, for unknown reasons, is no longer played.

Buchi Babu's three sons, Venkataramanjulu (Bhatt), Baliah, and Ramaswamy became great cricketers and carried on the family tradition. With Independence and subsequent legislation against vast landholdings, the family was forced to sell its surplus lands. Baliah Avenue came up on Luz and is today a thriving colony of houses with the gates to Luz House at one end. Lakshmi Vilas has long since vanished.[13]

Buchi Babu's legacy was carried forward by others and by the 1930s, a Madras Cricket Association (MCA) had been formed, which was an Indian body, to counter the MCC. There was much rivalry between the two, and it hurt the MCA that it had to seek permission from the MCC to play its matches at Chepauk and this was not always forthcoming. At a time when this rivalry was at its height, a new body, with pretensions to becoming a national entity for cricket was registered in the city without much fanfare.

[13]Raja and Suri, *Buchi Babu (Father of Madras Cricket) and his Sporting Clan*, Madras: M. Suryanarayan, 1993.

We know of it today as the Board of Cricket Control in India![14] Post-Independence, the MCC and MCA had several common members, many being Indians as well, but this did not make matters easier. When the lease for the Chepauk ground came up for renewal in the 1960s, the MCA clearly had the upper hand in negotiations with the government. The new agreement leased the space occupied by the clubhouse and some more to the MCC while the actual playing area went to the MCA, which in 1971 became the TNCA. This body erected the MA Chidambaram Stadium by 1975, the name commemorating the sports administrator who single-handedly ensured that the structure became reality, extending a personal guarantee to enable banks to loan the necessary funds.[15]

Cricket interest in the city has spanned all forms of the game—the five-day tests, the ODIs, and the T20s. The first of these, especially the international matches, played till the 1990s, largely in the winter months, invariably had the Chennai test during the Pongal break in January. These were social occasions as much as sporting ones. The upper echelons of society were there en famille, women in silk Kanjeevarams and jewellery, and the food being served out of the family car. Tales abound of West Indian cricketers in particular taking a shine to some Mylapore mamis. You had singing sensations such as M. L. Vasanthakumari and D. K. Pattammal watching avidly, unmindful of an evening concert looming. Film stars turned out regularly and they organized matches too, often as fundraisers for causes such as war, natural calamities, and special government projects. Those leisurely days are long gone, with tests rarely happening in the city, while the ODIs and T20s continue. Till very recently a niche attraction was the annual Youth Association for Carnatic Music cricket match. It was interesting to see many Carnatic musicians, most of whom have been historically cricket crazy, change from their veshti and kurta to cricket gear and wield bats and balls.

Cricket in the city was never confined to just the MCC or the TNCA. The Corporation (now Jawaharlal Nehru) Stadium, constructed in the 1950s had its share of cricket lore,[16] though looking at it now that would be hard to believe. All over Chennai, several cricket clubs came up, to support local teams. These were played at the Marina or at one of the many open fields that Chennai once had in abundance. Many of these clubs are now nearing

---

[14]Muthiah, *The MCC Story*, p. 212.

[15]Gupta, *Vision UnLimited*.

[16]V. Sriram, *175, Not Out! 175 Years of the Madras Cricket Club*, Chennai: Madras Cricket Club, 2021, pp. 98–99.

a century in age and are part of the Tamil Nadu league, with matches taking place year-round. Some of the grounds too are as legendary as Chepauk. These include the ones at Vivekananda College, St Bede's in San Thome, the Presidency on the Marina, and the IIT-M at Guindy. Several of these are maintained by corporate houses, which also maintain their own teams apart from sponsoring local cricket teams. The Sanmar Group, for instance, maintains the IIT ground, has its own teams, and supports the Alwarpet Cricket Club and the Jolly Rovers.[17] The last named has had a continuous association with the controlling family of the Sanmar Group for over fifty years, having been supported by *The Hindu* family prior to that. The newspaper has also had a continuous association with cricket for years, reporting on the game from the 1890s.[18] Another instance of corporate interest in cricket is the MRF Pace Foundation, begun in 1987 at the Madras Christian College School campus, in collaboration with international legend Dennis Lillee. It trains aspiring fast bowlers, several of whom have gone on to represent India.[19] It is interesting to note that Lillee convinced an early aspirant not to join and focus on his batting instead. That was Sachin Tendulkar.[20]

Chennai, associated with cricket for so long, also brought infamy to the game. The first was the reconstruction of the Chidambaram Stadium to make it more ergonomic, in the first decade of the present century. Necessary permissions from the statutory authorities were not taken before the construction. A change in the political regime in the interim did not help and three stands of the stadium remained locked for years till matters were resolved in 2020.[21] There was also the infamous betting scandal in the Indian Premier League (IPL) matches, involving the Chennai Super Kings team, which, however, has survived the ignominy. Lastly, we did see petty political considerations over the never-ending water disputes between Tamil Nadu and Karnataka resulting in the IPL series of 2018 bypassing Chennai altogether, and matches being held in faraway Pune instead. Whatever be the reason, there is no denying that the TNCA remains in the news. And several of its members such as M. A. Chidambaram, A. C. Muthiah, and N. Srinivasan have gone on to play key roles at the national level. And while

[17]Sriram, *The Sanmar Story*, p. 389.

[18]Parthasarathy, *Hundred Years of The Hindu*, p. 87.

[19]Pace Foundation website, available here: https://www.mrftyres.com/pace-foundation/.

[20]'Tendulkar lauds MRF Pace Foundation', *The Hindu*, 21 August 2015.

[21]Sriram, *MCC 175*, pp. 303–10.

Chennaiites may have divided loyalties when it comes to Test cricket or ODIs, their team in the T20 league is Chennai Super Kings with the boys in yellow led by the 'city's own' MS Dhoni. The way Captain Cool, as he is known, has been adopted by Chennai is amazing, given the city's normally cool response to anything or anybody from the Hindi heartland.

There are also some cricketing families of Chennai that will remain forever associated with the sport. Foremost is perhaps that of A. G. Ram Singh, the Sikh who made Madras his home. Legend has it that on arrival here in the early part of the twentieth century, he was asked his initials, for there is no concept of a surname in Tamil Nadu. When he said he had none, the locals helpfully fashioned it for him, out of the names of his hometown and guru. Thus, he became Amritsar Gobindsingh Ram Singh. A first-class cricketer for many years, he was an even more beloved coach. Of his sons, A. G. Kripal Singh and A. G. Milkha Singh played test cricket for India while A. G. Satwinder Singh was prevented from doing so owing to an accident.[22] The next generation has continued playing the game as well. The grandsons of Justice P. R. Sundara Iyer, of whom there were many, were into cricket. Their descendants include V. Ramnarayan, V. Sivaramakrishnan, and the latter's son, Vidyut. Chennai is also home to several star cricketers such as S. Venkataraghavan, L. Sivaramakrishnan, and of course the colourful and ebullient Krishnamachari Srikanth or Cheeka as he is known to friends. In recent years, Ravichandran Ashwin has joined this galaxy.

Tennis came to the city in the 1880s, when the MCC allotted space within its premises for courts. The first lawn tennis tournament in the whole of South India was organized at the club in 1887. It remained for long a whites-only sport, Indians becoming interested in it only from the 1920s. Thereafter, there was a surge in the sport's popularity, particularly with the arrival of Governor and Lady Willingdon. By the time they left in 1924, there were enough tennis clubs in the city to form a Lawn Tennis Association, which they did, in 1926. Other clubs in the city that had facilities included the Madras United and the Chennapuri Andhra Maha Sabha located at the Victoria Public Hall. Women got their courts early in the twentieth century, with facilities in the Queen Mary's College, the Egmore Ladies Recreation

[22]Ramachandra Guha, *The States of Indian Cricket: Anecdotal Histories*, New Delhi: Permanent Black, 2005, p. 125–9.

Club,[23] and the Mylapore Ladies Club.[24] It was a common sight to see Indian women playing in six- and nine-yard sarees at these courts.

Tennis still remained a game to be played in the privacy of homes, colleges, and clubs. It was in 1946 that the city acquired its first public tennis courts. This was entirely due to J. P. L. Shenoy, then commissioner of the Corporation of Madras. A keen tennis player, Shenoy decided that the city needed a public tennis court. He chose the Egmore playground set up by the corporation in 1928 as a suitable site. The military was roped in to complete the construction quickly. Under the supervision of corporation engineer M. Meeran, work on the stadium began on 10 November 1946 and was completed on 30 December the same year. The facility, with three tennis courts and concrete galleries that could seat around 1,000 people was declared open on 31 December 1946 by the Gaekwar of Baroda in the presence of Mayor T. Sundara Rao Naidu. The Madras (later Tamil Nadu) Lawn Tennis Association moved into the clubhouse that was built alongside.[25]

It was here that the Davis Cup matches were played in the 1950s, all of them featuring the Madras-based international tennis legend Ramanathan Krishnan. 'FULL-THROATED roar from the huge gathering at the Egmore Stadium in Madras (at) a grand match when a tall and lithe Australian, Roy Emerson by name, went down in the fifth set to the Indian genius, Ramanathan Krishnan,' began an article in *The Hindu's Sport & Pastime* in 1964.[26] That, incidentally, was perhaps India's first magazine exclusively dedicated to sports. It ceased publication in 1968, two years after its prime mover, S. K. Gurunathan passed away. In 1978, *The Hindu* launched *Sportstar*, which in 2015 became an online magazine.

By the late 1960s, with crowds increasing, Davis Cup tournaments began to be held at a makeshift facility on the Island Grounds. The Egmore Stadium continued to be used for training—this was where the Amritraj brothers were taught the nuances by famed coach T. A. Rama Rao. The rear of the stadium was where football, hockey, and volleyball were played. With the Sports Development Authority of Tamil Nadu constructing a modern stadium

---

[23]V. Sriram, '100 years of a 'ladies only' club', *Madras Musings*, Vol. XX, No. 24, 1–15 April 2011.

[24]V. Sriram and Karthik A Bhatt, *Brick by Brick: The Vidya Mandir Story*, Chennai: The Vidya Mandir Senior Secondary School, 2016, pp. 9–10.

[25]V. Sriram, 'Taking Tennis to the People', *The Hindu*, 9 January 2015.

[26]V. Sriram, 'A Tennis stadium sans Tennis', *Madras Musings*, Vol. XXVIII, No. 19, 16–31 January 2019.

at Nungambakkam in the 1990s, tennis moved away from here forever. A vast hockey stadium was constructed at the rear and named after former mayor M. Radhakrishna Pillai. It overshadows the old tennis stadium, parts of which, along with the clubhouse, have been taken over by the Tamil Nadu Volleyball Association.

What is left could do with better maintenance as part of our sports heritage. A dense overgrowth hides much of the access to the tennis court. The cement stands are chipped. The court, surprisingly, is well-maintained. It is used as a walking track early in the morning by several locals of Egmore. Below one of the stands is a forlorn plaque. A close scrutiny reveals it to be the foundation stone—Shenoy's dream come to life.

Mention has already been made of Ramanathan Krishnan, the self-effacing sporting legend, and the only Indian to qualify as a semi-finalist in the mens' singles at Wimbledon. Outside the portals of the city clubs, it was his father T. K. Ramanathan who made tennis a very popular sport, coaching several youngsters the same way as he did his son. Ramanathan Krishnan's son, Ramesh, won the boys' singles title at both the Wimbledon and the French Open in the 1970s. He reached three Grand Slam quarter finals and was also part of the Indian team that reached the Davis Cup finals in the 1980s. Ramesh, who later became captain of the Davis Cup team from India, ran till recently the Krishnan Tennis Centre where several young hopefuls were coached in the game. The city is also home to the famed Amritraj brothers–Vijay, Anand, and Ashok, all three international tennis players.

Says Ramanathan Krishnan, 'My father first saw tennis when he worked in Madras briefly in the 1930s. He was cycling to work when he saw Englishmen playing in a court. He was fascinated. That evening he made arrangements with the marker there to play after the sahibs had left. He became very good at it. When I was two or three, that is towards the end of the 1930s, we shifted to Delhi where his skill was noticed to an extent where the Viceroy Lord Linlithgow extended a standing invitation to him to play at Government House (now Rashtrapati Bhavan) courts. Later we shifted to Tenkasi and then returned to Madras.'[27]

By that time, Ramanathan had trained his son.

'Father was a martinet—no relaxation. If it was hot, I wore a cap and practised. In Madras of those days, we of the middle class had no club facilities. I began playing in a ladies' club in T. Nagar, where men and boys were allowed, in the mornings. The Chennapuri Andhra Maha Sabha located

[27]Interview with the author, Chennai, 13 March 2020.

in VP Hall was another place that encouraged sports and had courts. Later Father purchased a plot in Raja Annamalaipuram. He first put up a tennis court and in whatever space was left over, he constructed the house.'

Krishnan recalls vividly the excitement that was generated when he, all of thirteen, won the Stanley Cup at a tournament at Loyola College—his first major win.

'I was initially not even allowed to participate on account of my age but they later relented. As I inched my way to the finals, everyone took notice. On the final day, Loyola College was unprepared for the crowd—they usually got around 80 people but this time there were 800—seated in chairs, perched on branches of trees and standing around, cheering me. When I won, the principal of Loyola whispered into my ear that there was a seat for me in the college as and when I completed school.'

The success of his son made Ramanathan a popular coach. He trained several players of the city including N. Sankar, later the founder of the Sanmar Group, who played a mean game for years; N. Srinivasan of India Cements, TNCA, and BCCI fame; and Lakshmi Mahadevan, often described as the poster girl of Indian tennis, who won the Asian Championships in Calcutta in 1964 and was ranked Asia number one, thereafter, for quite a while.

'But the lack of suitable facilities always was an issue,' says Krishnan. 'We made do with what was there—drinking water in a pot, changing behind trees and making sure we left home with empty bladders and bowels.'

By the time Ramesh came on the scene, the exclusive British clubs had been open to Indians for several years and there were more courts, especially in the homes of the well-to-do. 'Land prices were low and people could afford to buy extra space just for tennis,' says Ramesh. 'It helped that the city had plenty of open areas, which encouraged games such as a cricket, football, and hockey. Tennis was different but there were enough courts around to play in so that, as a student, I did not waste time travelling long distances to play a match. That is not the case today when open spaces have shrunk but then clubs are aplenty and have made up with their tennis courts.'[28]

The hosting of the South Asian Federation Games (SAFG) in Chennai in 1995 saw sports facilities improving, with many specialized stadia coming up. The one for tennis was built in Nungambakkam—a world-class stadium that Krishnan regrets being too old to play in. While it lasted, the Chennai Open tennis tournament, played at this venue, which was great, for it brought some international stars to our city. It began life as the McDowell Open in

[28]Interview with the author, Chennai, 11 March 2020.

1996 in New Delhi and moved to Madras the next year as the Gold Flake Open. In 2002 it was renamed Tata Open and then in 2005 it became the Chennai Open, in which name it held its annual tournament here till 2017 before moving to Pune.[29] When this tournament was held, the tennis stadium filled up, thereby indicating the enthusiasm for this game in Chennai.

The other racquet sport—squash—has been steadily growing in the city. The MCC was naturally the pioneer and still has the best facilities in the city for this energy-consuming sport. The Squash Rackets Federation of India has a major presence in the city by way of its Indian Squash Academy, set up in association with the Tamil Nadu Squash Racquets Association. The India Cements Limited, known more for its association with cricket, especially the IPL, sponsored the academy's initial construction in 2006. Many Indian champions have trained here. Asian titleholders such as Joshna Chinappa and Saurav Ghosal are both products of this academy. In recent years, the Express Avenue Mall has become the venue for many squash tournaments.[30]

The 1990s were a good time for sports infrastructure in the city—the Jawaharlal Nehru (formerly the Corporation) Stadium was modernized to global standards in time to host the Nehru Football Cup in 1993. The SAFG of 1995 saw the Mayor Radhakrishnan Hockey Stadium being renovated, and the tennis stadium in Nungambakkam and the aquatics complex at Velachery being built.[31] Since then much of these remain grossly underutilized, a sad reflection of how Chennai is rarely the venue for national or international sporting events. But once a year, the hockey stadium comes into its own, hosting as it does the MCC Murugappa Gold Cup Tournament. The MCC initiated the Madras Challenge Cup in 1901 and the Murugappa Group, the Murugappa Gold Cup in 1962. In 1996, the two came together and have remained so ever since, with the MCC managing the logistics and the Murugappa Group taking care of the financials. Olympic star Munir Sait is the livewire who puts much of it together. Teams from all over the country come to participate at the astro turf of the hockey stadium. Sadly, not many come to watch this sport but V. Chokkiah and Barkat Ali are usually there, cheering the teams. As reported in *Sportstar*, these fans have been regulars since 1978. They were once part of a larger group that would pool money together and buy a gift for the best player in the series—an evaluation that

[29] Sriram, *The Sanmar Story*, p. 388.

[30] Sriram, *MCC 175*, pp. 214–27.

[31] Partab Ramchand, 'Sports-loving Jayalalithaa remembered', *Madras Musings*, Vol. XXVI, No. 17, 16–31 December 2016.

they did themselves. Now the others have passed on but the duo still return, and to the same seats![32]

The British introduced other sports to Madras such as rowing, yachting, flying, and football, each having a champion in one club of the city or the other. The Madras Boat Club (MBC) may date itself to 1890 but the first rowing contest in the city was as far back as 1867. In the early days, rowing took place on the Long Tank, that vast water body that was so short-sightedly filled in in the early 1900s to make way for T. Nagar. The contests began at Cathedral Point, at the edge of Nungambakkam High Road near the Anna Flyover, and ended at Saidapet. Boating also took place on the Cooum and at the Ennore Creek but later came to settle on the Adyar, by the side of which the MBC built its clubhouse. Rowing now happens from the club to the Kottupuram Bridge. The long-standing tradition of dunking the winning team in the waters of the Adyar is no longer followed, given the level of pollution.[33] Yachting or sailing takes place at the harbour, the Royal Madras Yacht Club (RMYC) functioning from there. The RMYC began in 1911 and was only for whites initially, the 'Royal' prefix being conferred by King George V in 1926. It is now a very active place, especially over weekends, when several of the well-heeled members sail their vessels.[34]

Flying in Madras began with hotelier D'Angeli who piloted a locally-made aircraft using the Island Grounds as his airstrip. The aeroplane was manufactured by Simpson & Co. Some more exhibition flights did take place, including one by J. W. Madeley, the waterworks engineer.[35] The next attempt was immediately after World War I when the Madras Chamber of Commerce was approached by aircraft manufacturer Sopwith to explore if there was a market in the presidency. The chamber did not respond; such a service ought to be run by the government, it felt.[36] In 1915, the house of Tatas began the Karachi–Madras airmail service, putting the city on the aviation map.

Rather ironically, several members of the Madras Chamber went on to be pioneering aviators. In 1930, the Madras Flying Club (MFC) was founded with William Maurice Browning of Burmah Shell as its first president. He

---

[32]Samarntah Soory, 'Meet V. Chokkaiah and Barkat Ali, the fans who will never give up on hockey', *Sportstar*, 12 September 2019.

[33]Muthiah, *Down by the Adyar.*

[34]Muthiah, *Madras Rediscovered*, p. 366.

[35]Ibid., p. 164.

[36]Sriram, *MCCI.* p. 135.

was ably assisted by (Sir) Gerald Hodgson of Parry. Soon the sahibs of other British-owned companies, especially those that had far-flung industrial establishments, such as Beardsell and Binny, joined. It is significant to note, however, that there were at least fourteen Indians as MFC members even at its inception; the Chettiar community, in particular, having a strength of three in the list.[37] The MFC's stars were pilot G. Vlasto, flight instructor, Flight Lieutenant H. N. Hawker, Chief Flying Instructor Tyndale Biscoe, and Chief Pilot Instructor Mohammed Ismail Khan. In 1936, Captain V. Sundaram became the first Indian to get a commercial pilot's licence from Madras, and he flew a De Havilland Dove from Karachi to the city.[38] Four years prior to this, J. R. D. Tata's solo flight in a De Havilland Puss Moth from Karachi to Bombay was further continued to Madras via Bellary by Neville Vincent.[39]

World War II saw the Royal Air Force moving in, commandeering much of the MFC's resources, and making full use of its facility of which there was nothing more than an airstrip near St Thomas Mount. By 1939, the top brass of the government and several Indian leaders were flying into Madras. In 1948, Madras became headquarters to K. V. Al. Rm Alagappa Chettiar's Jupiter Airways, which operated a Madras–Delhi service. The airstrip expanded to become the Meenambakkam Aerodrome, India's first post-Independence terminal and named after the village near it. For years, a hamlet continued to remain in occupation in the triangle formed by the runways and it was only after considerable effort that those in residence were convinced to move.[40] With aircrafts being few and far between, the runway was also used for the races conducted by the Madras Motor Sports Club before it shifted to Sholavaram in 1955.[41] In later years, the MFC made a conscious effort at getting the middle classes interested in flying by offering lessons at affordable rates. It continues to function though it has seen better days.

It was only in the 1930s that table tennis came to India, and when it did, it was via Madras, the pioneer being P. S. Viswanatha Iyer, ICS, who learnt the game while appearing for the civil services exam in England. The first match was held in Coimbatore, where Iyer was posted. From there he

[37]Muthiah, *Madras Rediscovered*, p. 162.

[38]Captain V. Sundaram, *An Airman's Saga*, Mumbai: Bharatiya Vidya Bhavan, 1998, p. 28.

[39]See https://www.indianairmails.com/official-southbound.html/.

[40]V. Sriram, 'Madras Landmarks, 50 years ago', *Madras Musings*, Vol. XXIV, No. 14, 1–15 November 2014.

[41]Ibid.

brought it to Madras, where for years afterwards, the tournaments were held at the Young Men's Indian Association, Gokhale Hall, and the Chennapuri Andhra Maha Sabha. Iyer was tragically killed in an air crash in the 1950s, while he was serving as Industries secretary, Government of Madras.[42] Women took to table tennis in a big way in the city, the Egmore Ladies Recreation Club and the Mylapore Ladies Club featuring many women playing the game in sarees. The national championship in the game for women still awards the Jayalakshmi Cup, named after Viswanatha Iyer's wife.

But the city's greatest player in this sport also had the greatest ill-luck, which would change his life. This was Venugopal Chandrasekhar, who by the age of twenty-five, was a national champion making a mark in the international arena. A niggling knee problem required minor surgery and he was admitted to Apollo Hospitals in 1985. An error in the application of anaesthesia left him near blind, brain damaged, and not in control of his limbs. The hospital denied any mistake on its part and he had to be flown abroad for further treatment, the money for this being crowd sourced, which included a Kapil Dev-led benefit match. On return after partial recovery, Chandrasekhar sued Apollo for medical negligence. The case dragged on for eight painful years, at the end of which the High Court of Madras awarded him ₹20 lakhs in damages. This was contested in the Supreme Court but the hospital opted to settle after a couple of years. Still not in full control of his limbs and with weak eyesight, Chandrasekhar worked at a bank and ran a table tennis academy till his passing in 2021.[43]

In 1895, *The Sketch: A Journal of Art and Actuality* published in England noted that football was making rapid progress in Madras despite being practically non-existent till a couple of years earlier. 'Last year, a few ardent devotees came together and decided to make a start. The game found support at once, and when, at the General Meeting of the Gymkhana Club a request was made for a tournament cup to be played under certain conditions, a uniform consent was accorded,' it said, thereby dating the advent of football in our city to 1894. The Gymkhana Club, founded nine years earlier, may be more of a social club today but in its youth was very much the place for all kinds of sports barring cricket, which of course had its home on the other side of the Cooum, at the MCC.

The first tournament in the city was held in 1894 with ten teams from all over the country participating. The entire list of members of the Gymkhana

---

[42]See http://simpli-city.in/app/articledetail.php?aid=748.

[43]V. Chandrashekar, *My Fight Back from Death's Door*, Chennai: East West Books, 2006.

Club who played a match in that tournament against the 5th Field Battery of the Royal Artillery is still available. From 1895, the Gymkhana Club hosted an annual tournament, which became a fixture; the winning team being awarded the EK Chetty Cup. The governor of Madras was an honoured invitee to the finals, Lord Willingdon being a particularly committed patron between 1919 and 1924. By then, Indians had begun to take to football elsewhere in the city. The South Indian Athletic Association instituted the Jatprole Cup Tournament. The EK Chetty Cup of the Gymkhana Club regularly went to regimental teams until 1933 when the Pachaiyappa High School became the first Indian and non-military team to win it. Another powerful contender was the Minerva Club. The Gymkhana Club fielded all-European teams till 1940, when for the first time an Indian—S. K. Swaminathan—played for the club.

In 1934, the Madras Football Association (MFA) was formed owing to the efforts of the MUC. Other clubs of the city, including the Gymkhana Club, became members of the MFA, which began conducting First Division League football matches from 1936, the Second Division beginning in 1937. In 1972, the MFA became the Tamil Nadu Football Association.[44]

The Gymkhana Club also brought rugby to the city and in 1914, Somerset Playne noted that the club's fifteen-member team regularly travelled to Calcutta and Bombay, winning cups everywhere.[45] Arriving in Madras in January 1929 as a young, covenanted officer of Best & Company, A. W. Stansfeld, was summoned to meet the director of the firm—Sir Robert Denniston. He was quite apprehensive as to what it was all about only to be told to sign up as a member of the Gymkhana Club immediately. The club had to play a rugby match against a team from a visiting ship—HMS *Emerald*, and was one man short! Stansfeld left his impress on Madras sports and in business, for he rose to become a director at Best.[46] World War II ended the Gymkhana Club's interest in football and allied sports. With several playing members opting to fight at the front and never returning thereafter, the club last hosted its football tournament in 1941. But it ensured an everlasting legacy—our city's love for the game.

Viswanathan Anand is synonymous with chess the world over and Chennai takes pride in the local boy. Anand owed much of his initial success to his

---

[44]V. Sriram, 'When football came to Madras', *The Hindu*, 19 June 2014.
[45]J. Somerset Playne, *Southern India: Its History, People, Commerce and Industrial Resources*, London: The Foreign and Colonial Compiling and Publishing Co., 1914-1915, p. 420.
[46]Sriram, *MCC 175*, p. 84.

mother, who saw the spark and ensured that he received requisite training.[47] But the city too played a great role, for, by the mid 1970s, it had emerged as a major chess centre, the Russians (then Soviets) being responsible in large part. The Mikhail Tal Chess Club began in 1972 at the Soviet (now Russian) Cultural Centre, Cathedral Road, with Manuel Aaron, the chess legend as the secretary. The club became the training ground for several talents including Anand but it cannot be forgotten that eleven years prior to its being set up, it was Aaron who brought glory to Chennai, by becoming India's first International Master. In many ways, his success made many youngsters in the city take to chess.[48] In 2019, Chennai's Gukesh became the world's second youngest grandmaster.

The Young Men's Christian Association (YMCA), or Y as it is referred to, has had a long association with the city, establishing a branch here in 1890. Its first general secretary, David McConnaughy, founded the National Council of YMCAs in India, in the city. By 1895, the first of the YMCA buildings in the city, a lovely sandstone-clad edifice on the Esplanade, was well on its way. The McConnaughy Hall in it, apart from hosting boxing and oration contests, became busy as a concert hall for many sabhas, the Music Academy being inaugurated here on 18 August 1928. But it is the Y's contribution to Chennai's sports that is most noteworthy. That was due to Harry Crowe Buck, who came to Madras in 1919 to work at the Y and within a year had founded, at Royapettah, the YMCA College of Physical Education, Asia's first such facility. It later moved to Nandanam, where under Buck's recruit, P. M. Joseph, a leather technologist turned sports administrator, the college grew in leaps and bounds. Between them, Buck and Joseph did much to draft the National Policy for Physical Education and set up schools for this in Bombay and Gwalior. When the Indian Olympic Association was formed in 1924, Buck, who by then was keenly encouraging sports and athletics in the city, became a member. The Nandanam facility was where the Indian Olympics team of 1924, of which Buck was manager, trained. The 1948 Olympics team sprinter, Eric Prabhakar, trained here, and after a distinguished career in the IAS became the chairman of the board that administered the Y's Nandanam College. It is a buzzing space today, full

[47]Viswanathan Anand with Susan Ninan, *Mind Master, Winning Lessons from a Champion's Life*, Gurugram: Hachette India, 2019, p. 22.

[48]Manuel Aaron, 'An Inspiration for Madras chess players' (sourced from Adyar Times), *Madras Musings*, Vol. XXIV, No. 22, 1–15 March 2015.

of varied sporting activities.[49] Once in two years, its vast acreage is put to a diametrically opposite use—the Chennai Book Fair when thousands of bookworms descend on the place.

The Y played a major role in propagating volleyball in the city and the rest of the country. Introduced most likely by American troops who flooded Chennai during World War II, and taken further by Buck, the sport was sufficiently popular for the first national championships to happen in the city in 1952. In later years, the media baron Sivanthi Adithan more or less made the sport his own and the Indian Volleyball Federation was headquartered in the city.[50] The other American import, basketball, came very early to India, in the 1900s, just a few years after it was invented. The Y's director, Duncan Patton, is credited with introducing it here. But it was Buck who took it further. When the Basketball Federation of India was formed, it was C. C. Abraham, then principal of the YMCA College at Nandanam, who became its first president.[51]

The Y's record in athletics and sports often overshadows that of a coeval institution, which today is practically dead. This was the South Indian Athletic Association (SIAA), founded in 1901. It functioned for years from the Moore Pavilion, a lovely tile-roofed two-storey structure in People's Park behind Ripon Buildings. The SIAA encouraged football, tennis, billiards, and cricket besides being accredited as the birthplace of boxing in India. Each year it hosted the annual Park Town Fair during Christmas Week, at People's Park, and this was a high point in the social calendar of Madras. Track events, boxing matches, and rekla (two-wheeled horse carriage) races were held. The fair ceased to be held after 1971. The SIAA itself had to move out of Moore Pavilion into Victoria Public Hall and has since been evicted from there as well. Its sporting association is now a thing of the past. As for Moore Pavilion, named after Sir George Moore, once president of the corporation, it is now completely cut off from all access, being walled in. A visit ten years ago revealed a building with several snakes, and some chipped marble plaques that recorded the winning teams of the SIAA in various events.[52]

Talk of a Motor Sports Club began in the city sometime in the late 1940s and fructified following a race between two men, Rex Strong and K.

---

[49]S. Muthiah, 'Builder of the Spirit of Sport', *The Hindu*, 31 October 2010.

[50]See Tamil Nadu State Volleyball Association website, available here: https://www.tnsva.in/.

[51]See C. C. Abraham Memorial Letter website, available here: https://cdm16122.contentdm.oclc.org/digital/collection/p15370coll2/id/5640/.

[52]V. Sriram, 'Where the sporting spirit still haunts', *India Today*, 21 January 2008.

Varugis, from Chesney Hall, Egmore, to the Catholic Centre, Armenian Street, in 1952. Today, such a competition will be impossible, given the congestion on the roads. The Madras Motor Sports Club (MMSC) came into existence a year later, the watchful presence of M. A. Chidambaram ensuring it had a set of by-laws and constitution right from the beginning. The Sholavaram air strip, built during World War II, became the venue for the races and the first such event was held in October the same year. The heydays of Sholavaram were undoubtedly the 1970s, when the MMSC, together with its counterparts in Calcutta, Coimbatore, Bombay, and Bangalore, formed the Federation of Motor Sports Clubs of India (FMSCI), headquartered in Chennai.

The first two weekends of February each year, right up to the 1980s, were when over 50,000 people would cram themselves into makeshift casuarina stands, to watch the races. The events included cars and motorcycles and a total of 800 or so of them would participate year after year. In an era when India did not have televisions and so did not get to see racing in other parts of the world, this was the place to experience the thrill. The state government arranged for buses to take the fans to Sholavaram and the place had a carnival-like atmosphere. Glamour was there in plenty—Vijay Mallya was of course the star, but also in attendance was the last of Indian royalty—Gondal, Pithapuram, and others of their kind, living out the craze that their ancestors had once exhibited for horses. Film stars were there, as were some foreign contestants too. Combining flamboyance with seriousness in racing were others such as Vicky Chandhok and S. Karivardhan. In 1987, Kari, as he was known, envisioned the Formula Maruti, for which the eponymous company gave at his request thirty-five mechanical kits and gearboxes of its popular Maruti 800 model. At a curtain-raiser held at the Taj Coromandel, twenty-eight cars were snapped up by various corporates who sponsored the drivers too. Formula Maruti became a huge success. It would bring in a whole new generation of racers—Narain Karthikeyan, Karun Chandhok, and Armaan Ebrahim, all from South India.

In the 1980s, the FMSCI decided that it needed to structure its facilities better, in tune with changes in international motor sports. Thus the Madras Motor Race Track at Irungattukottai came about, inaugurated in 1990. The races continue in a more professional environment, but the crowds have disappeared. It is a serious sport now but the fans prefer to watch international races either at the respective foreign venues themselves or over television or the internet.[53]

---

[53]Abhishek Takle, 'Why did 70,000 fans flock to a town in Tamil Nadu to watch motor

When compared to all the sports that developed among the more well-to-do and then trickled down, carrom in Chennai grew chiefly in the industrial suburbs. Associated essentially with the workers' unions, where a table, a board, and strikers were all the investment needed, carrom was a hugely popular sport in Perambur, Wimco Nagar, Pulianthope—workers' colonies and the nearby slums. Film stars such as MGR, M. R. Radha, and S. S. Rajendran were avid fans of the game and provided all the support even after they attained fame. But it was an unsung hero, B. Bangara Babu, who took the sport to international level. A man who came to Chennai from neighbouring Andhra, he literally lived for the sport, going to the extent of naming his house Carrom Villa. Through the 1980s, Babu struggled hard, networking with other players across India and finally succeeded in forming a national federation for the sport, even convincing Bengal, which had stayed aloof as it had a different style of playing, to join in. He then went abroad to rope in Asian and European countries, and by the late 1980s, had formed the International Carrom Federation, which in 1991 hosted the first World Cup in Delhi in 1991 where Chennai's Anthony Maria Irudayam was the champion. Irudayam has gone on to win the World Cup a second time and now coaches in North Chennai. But it is Babu who is referred to as the father of carrom, not just in Chennai or across India, but worldwide.[54] Chennai's love for carrom has made it to films as well—Kamal Haasan's *Pammal K. Sambandam* (2002), set in North Chennai, repeatedly features it; a film that focused entirely on the carrom ethos is *Striker* (2010)—it came in for critical acclaim though it was not a commercial success.

Who would have thought that pigeon racing was a big sport in Chennai? Lucknow or perhaps Hyderabad or Kolkata may have been the first choices if one were to guess. But it is apparently Chennai that has become home for what was once a sport for the more leisured classes. As early as in the 1930s there are mentions of a Madras Pigeon Racing Club but it did not survive very long.[55] Associations formed in the 1970s met with the same fate but not so the New Madras Racing Pigeon Association, founded in 1984. Today, there are over thirteen clubs in the city, 200 pigeon fanciers, each with around 100 pigeons. Races happen between January and April, usually ending with the longest and most gruelling, flying between Nagpur

racing in the 1970s?', *Scroll.in*, 14 July 2017.

[54]R. S. Prasad, 'Chennai slums, boardrooms of carom', *Times of India*, 18 June 2015.

[55]Directory of Madras and South India, Madras: Directories and Agencies Limited, 1934, p. 652.

and Chennai, a distance of 925 kilometres![56]

Swimming is perhaps the last sporting activity that could be associated with a water-starved city but Chennai has its fair share of enthusiasts in this as well. The name of Kutraleeswaran springs to mind—he was just thirteen years when he swam across six international channels in one calendar year. The city's clubs had their swimming pools as did hotels such as the Connemara and a few colleges from quite early on. The public used the now defunct Royal Swimming Pool at the People's Park and the still functioning Anna Swimming Pool by the beach. Then, in 1995, the city got its magnificent aquatics complex at Velachery, just in time for the SAFG, which Chennai hosted that year.

Surfing is the new entrant to Chennai's sporting scene. The long coastline has always deterred swimmers owing to perpetual currents, but surfing has caught on of late. Kovalam, just off Chennai, is the centre for this. The youth of the village taught themselves by watching foreigners and with help from the NGO Earth Sync and industrialist Arun Vasu, have formed a training school that has a large clientele.[57]

Taken overall, Chennai has an impressive record in sports. And it contrasts strangely with the usual perception of its citizens being bookish, career-minded people who are all work and no play.

---

[56]'Flights of Fancy', *Madras Musings*, Vol. XXVII, No. 1, 16–30 April 2017.

[57]Shoba Narayan, 'The Surfer and the Sportsman: Murthy Megavan and Arun Vasu', *Mint*, 28 July 2017.

15 | MEALS READY!

Chennai may not be a food capital like Lucknow or Indore but it does have a culinary reputation. After all, even those who have not set foot in the city do know that it is synonymous with the idli and the dosa (which is pronounced with a soft d). For years, people in other parts of India have puzzled over how the idli of Tamil Nadu is softer and the dosa crispier than any that they make. In just the same way, Tamilians have despaired over rotis and poha. The secret, as any Tamil cook will tell you, lies in kai manam, literally legerdemain. The other secret is that Chennai in reality is neither the best place for idli (Madurai is better) or the dosa (Mysore far surpasses it) but it would rank high for both dishes.

Today, visions of idli and dosa bring to mind Saravana Bhavan—the worldwide chain of fast-food restaurants set up by P. Rajagopal, better known as 'Annachi'. He was from the Nadar community, whose lifeblood is retailing. But Annachi dared to be different. Having seen some success in running a provisions store at K. K. Nagar, he launched an eatery by the name of Saravana Bhavan, the name inspired by his favourite deity, Murugan, and his preceptor in matters spiritual—the savant Kripananda Variar. That was in 1981, at a time when most people in Chennai did not believe in dining out. But tastes were changing. The economic liberalization of the 1990s brought with it many transformations and one among these was fast food, chiefly pizzas and burgers. People were no longer content with home-cooked food and began to flock to restaurants. This was where Annachi saw his opportunity—he would be in the business of South Indian fast food and within a decade he had emerged as the leader.

In retrospect, what Annachi achieved was nothing short of remarkable. A chain of eateries came up all over Chennai and its immediate environs. They were identical—down to framed depictions of the deities from the six most famous Murugan temples of South India and the photo of Annachi standing reverentially beside Kripananda Variar. The sambar and chutney supplied by a central kitchen, tasted the same at all the outlets. The staff wore paper hats and used plastic gloves—standards of hygiene never seen before in eateries of this kind. And then, there was the coffee! A statement attributed to T. Sadasivam, the husband of M. S. Subbulakshmi, had it that good coffee had to be dark as night, sweet as love, and hot as hell.[1] At Saravana Bhavan it was. In fact, it became the chief attraction for many and when they came, they rarely stopped with coffee. It was said that once they realized this, Annachi and his sons avoided increasing the price of this beverage for a long time, even as the prices of other items on offer kept inching steadily up.

The late 1990s and early 2000s were Saravana Bhavan's heydays. The menu steadily expanded to include North Indian dishes and milk shakes, which tasted like what they were—alien recipes handled by good Tamil hands, but the patrons remained faithful. Going to a Saravana Bhavan at peak hour required planning. You had to be prepared for a long wait and once seated, eat in record time.

At a time when India was waking up to Western styles of management, Annachi proved to be far ahead of his times, all of his ideas evidently fuelled by common sense. He took good care of his staff and the incentive schemes in place meant that tips/gratuity were frowned upon as a matter of policy. Personnel who went above the call of duty were rewarded with trips abroad for the full family. It was no wonder that his employees loved Annachi and it showed in the way they worked. The demand for Saravana Bhavan grew so much that the chain went international, even opening branches in the US.

And then came the downfall, at least for the proprietor. Briefly put, Annachi was advised by an astrologer to marry again and he selected a woman who was not interested, she being happily wed to someone else. For a man of his clout, it was simple enough to do away with the spouse but the chosen bride proved tough. She tenaciously pursued the matter of her husband's murder through due process of law. The high court sentenced Annachi to life in 2009, eight years after the crime. He was sent to jail but released later, pending an appeal in the Supreme Court. With that, Saravana Bhavan's image took a severe beating. It did not help that several competitors—Adyar Ananda Bhavan (A2B), Sangeetha, Vasantha Bhavan, and Murugan Idli had come up in the meantime. This also coincided with a sudden lack of interest in menial jobs by the local population. There were several reasons attributed to it. The government said it was because of rising education levels and the preference of people for other avenues of employment. The detractors opined that the continued offering of freebies by successive governments of Tamil Nadu, combined with the vending of liquor by the state had sapped the city's work culture and Tamilians were taking to an easy life. Whatever be the truth, the vacancies had to be filled in by people from elsewhere. This

[1]T. J. S. George, *MS: A Life in Music*, New Delhi: Harper Collins, 2004, p. 224.

did not go well at Saravana Bhavan. The chain was pushing its staff to the front without adequate training. Suddenly, you found bare hands handling vadas and the coffee was mediocre at best. Today, Saravana Bhavan is still a force to reckon with and is a case study for business schools, but it is no longer what it was. The Annachi story came to an end in 2019, when the Supreme Court confirmed his life sentence. He surrendered reluctantly, being quite ill and died within a month. It was an ignominious end for a trailblazing career, one that even *New York Times* was tracking.[2] Several rival restaurant chains released obituary ads in his honour, for it cannot be denied that he showed them the way.[3]

What was eating out like before Annachi arrived on the scene? For a long while Chennai did not believe in this concept. The middle classes frowned on it, for it was a sure sign that the woman of the house was not a good cook or was incapable of managing the kitchen. Brahmins-only hotels flourished, however, where patrons had to display their sacred threads before entering, this pernicious practice being finally stopped by Periyar E.V. Ramaswami Naicker, who ran a spirited campaign against such establishments, often picketing on their doorsteps. The most prolonged battle was at Murali Café in Triplicane's Bharathi Salai, with the proprietor holding out till HH Chandrasekharendra Saraswathi, the pontiff of the Kanchi Math, advised him to move with the times.[4]

During the days when the Brahmins-only hotels flourished, bachelors from other castes found the going tough, and by the early 1900s, eateries began making their appearance, especially in the George Town area. Here again, caste had a role to play and care was taken to ensure that the kitchen was under the control of Brahmins. Within this community, the best cooks came from the Udupi region of present-day Karnataka. One among these was Kadandale Krishna Rao, who came to Madras in the 1920s and worked as a grinder of idli batter at an eatery in George Town. The owner was impressed with his diligence and entrusted the management of another eatery in a neighbouring street to him. Success in this venture emboldened Krishna Rao and by 1926, he had opened a restaurant on Mount Road—Udupi Sri Krishna Vilas, thereby starting off the Udupi revolution in Chennai. Several of

---

[2]Amie Tsang, P. Rajagopal, 'Restaurant Mogul Convicted of Murder, Dies at 71', *New York Times*, 25 July 2019.

[3]Swaminathan Ramasubramaniam, 'Annachi, Humble Beginnings, Global Presence and an Ignominous End', *Madras Musings*, Vol. XXIX. No. 8, 1–15 August 2019.

[4]'Memories of a Violent Movement led by Periyar', *Times of India*, 25 June 2016.

his compatriots would follow, all of them setting up imitation restaurants and achieving a modicum of success. The masala dosa was essentially an Udupi creation which is now synonymous with South Indian cuisine.

But Krishna Rao was meant for bigger things. In 1938, the raja of Ramnad leased Woodlands, his palace on Royapettah's Westcott Road, to a contractor from Bangalore who turned it into a hotel. This was not a success and Krishna Rao took the place on a sub-lease. He would wait at the railway station each morning and solicit custom from first-class passengers. Other marketing techniques helped—Woodlands hosted the December Music Season of the Music Academy in 1937 and was also the venue for sale of used cars. The hotel became a roaring success leading to the Bangalore contractor being tempted to run the place himself. When he proved difficult to deal with, Krishna Rao opted to move out, identifying property on Mylapore's upmarket Edward Elliots Road (now Radhakrishnan Salai) where he built his New Woodlands and from there embarked on a successful chain. It withstood the onslaught of the Saravana Bhavans of the world and is still a successful hotel with restaurants.[5]

Not so fortunate was Krishna Rao's other creation—Woodlands Drive-in Restaurant, located inside the Agri-Horticultural Society gardens on Cathedral Road. Established in 1962 in the midst of a vast acreage of greenery, this was where much of Chennai went of an afternoon. You drove up, placed your order and the food arrived, delivered on trays that were fixed to the car window! Woodlands Drive-in was famed for its rose milk, masala dosa, and coffee. You also got a glimpse of several celebrities, including playback singer and composer P. B. Sreenivas, turbaned and ever surrounded by a sheaf of handwritten notes. This unique restaurant closed in 2008 when the government decided to take over the space and develop it as a green reserve, named Semmozhi Poonga.

Dasaprakash was the creation of another Mysorean, K. Seetharama Rao, who in the 1920s gave up a lowly government job and turned restaurateur. Modern Café in Mysore was the first and then came similar restaurants in Madras, including one near the swimming pool by the Marina. All of this however paled into insignificance in the face of Dasaprakash, the hotel and restaurant that he set up in 1954 on Poonamallee High Road. An art-deco dream, it had rooms to stay in and its restaurants offered Udupi fare, as well as ice creams and milk shakes. Rooftop dinners on moonlit nights were an

[5]S. Krishnan, *Host to the Millions: The Story of Krishna Rao of Woodlands*, Madras: New Woodlands Hotel, 1983.

added attraction as was the jewel of an auditorium where music and dance performances took place. Honoured guests included Jawaharlal Nehru, the maharaja of Mysore, and J. K. Galbraith. Seetharama Rao went on to establish Dharmaprakash, an upmarket wedding hall, next to his hotel and, after his demise in 1968, his sons set up a Dasaprakash in Ooty, and then hotels in North India and the US.[6] But back home, the original edifice was crumbling. Differences within the family led to the closure of Dasaprakash and the sale and subsequent demolition of the iconic building. The memory of its cuisine was carried on for some time by AVM's Dasa, a lovely restaurant in a beautiful heritage building on Anna Salai, whose leasehold was with the AVM Group. It closed to make way for a hideous glass and steel structure.[7] Today, the cuisine of Dasaprakash is a mere memory but some of it survives in Kapila Dasa in the Express Avenue Mall, run by Tulsi Reddy, a granddaughter of Seetharama Rao. Also gone are many Udupi hotels of the city, including the one that began the trend—Krishna Vilas. In that long line of extinguished eateries we need to include Pankaja Café of Purasawalkam, immortalized in the writings of the playwright Marina.[8] Several of Chennai's famed 'lunch homes', which specialized in traditional midday meals served on banana leaves, have also shut shop. The best remembered is Ramakrishna Lunch Home on NSC Bose Road, for years the mainstay of middling lawyers and their clients, when the high court took its midday break. The genial proprietor was V. R. Ramanatha Iyer, who also served as mayor of the city. VRR's other entity was Shankar's Café, also on the same stretch, which, rather ironically, after having been a jeweller's showroom, is now Saravana Bhavan's George Town branch.

Vegetarian food in Chennai does not mean just South Indian fare. The streets and lanes of George Town, peopled as they are with Gujaratis, Marwaris, and Jains, have plenty of eateries in them, serving delectable North Indian food. The humble Gujarati Mandal in Gunvanti Bhavan on Broadway is known for its thalis while Kakda Ram Prasad, close by, is famed for its snacks, especially jalebis. Just outside it, and bringing a whiff of Varanasi is Anmol Lassi Bhandar, a kiosk where a wrestler pours out lassis. Agarwal Bhavan in the same area is the place to go to for North Indian sweets.

Each December, Chennai has some added options when it comes to dining out on vegetarian food—the sabha canteens. Many of the core rasikas may

[6] V. Sriram, 'Lost Landmarks of Chennai—Dasaprakash', *Madras Musings*, 10 April 2014.

[7] V. Sriram, 'The Store that brought Music into Homes', *Madras Musings*, Vol. XXVIII, No. 16, 1–15 December 2016.

[8] Marina, *Chinna Vayathinile*, p. 67.

argue that the eatery is but a fringe element in the December Season, but its role in making the music festival a lively affair over the years cannot be denied. Had it not been for World War II, restrictions would not have been imposed on gatherings at outdoor spaces in Madras. Had that not happened, the Music Academy would have happily continued hosting its conferences and concerts in 1939 in the gardens of Woodlands Hotel, Westcott Road, as it had the previous year, to great success.

But with World War II breaking out in September, the Music Academy and its dynamic president, KVK, were faced with the task of finding an enclosed precinct in which to conduct the music festival. Being a member of the University Syndicate, KVK, with some help from S. Satyamurti, who was mayor of Madras that year, managed to get the University Senate House for the series. Not everyone was happy. The acoustics were bad and to the conservative Carnatic crowd, it was a lonely spot, especially in the evenings.

KVK had an answer for everything. The acoustics at Senate House were improved by draping sacks across all the windows and doors. Special buses transported music lovers to and from the venue.

But the new complaint that emerged was that Senate House had no eatery in the vicinity. The next year, 1940, with the series being held once again at Senate House, KVK went a step further. An eatery would function from the premises itself—Ambi's Café of Broadway being the caterer. This was evidently a great success.

The next year's festival was also at Senate House and the Tanjore Lodge of Mambalam won the contract. In 1942, the last year that the Senate House hosted a concert, Bharath Café of Mount Road, Mambalam and Mylapore, was the canteen operator. From then on, a canteen at the academy became de rigueur.

The canteen history of other sabhas is not so well-documented but it is clear that the Tamil Isai Sangam had a subsidized kitchen functioning even in the 1950s, which still operates from the premises. The Indian Fine Arts Society souvenir too has advertisements of caterers from the 1950s. Thereafter, the other sabhas followed suit.

Through the 1950s and 1960s, when the Music Academy operated from the RR Sabha and the PS High School, its canteen was run by Appaswami Iyer. Among his specialities was a badam halwa that had S. Y. Krishnaswami, the music-loving ICS officer, waxing eloquent. Not so appetising from its description, but equally in demand was a preparation of dry coconut scrapings and crystallized sugar that was sold in small paper packets. The canteen contract was an entry into high society for Appaswami Iyer and he was soon in demand for weddings.

His successor at the Music Academy was Krishnamurthy, who had at one time presided over the kitchen fires at M. S. Subbulakshmi's Kalki Gardens. He was to bring the same grace and hospitality that embellished that stately home to the canteen. His speciality was kasi halwa and the news that it was ready would spark off an exodus from the auditorium. Even Semmangudi Srinivasa Iyer, that top draw among musicians, it was rumoured, timed his concerts to avoid the exodus when the halwa was prepared.

Others have come and gone since then at the Music Academy, but the canteen magic is now broad-based—'Arusuvai' Natarajan, 'Gnanambika' Jayaraman, 'Meenambika' Kannan, 'Mount' Mani, 'Mint' Padmanabhan...the list goes on, the prefixes being the names of their catering business ventures. They are as much stars as the artistes who perform within the auditoria. A few weeks before the season, artistes are besieged with fan mail requesting that they sing some favourite song or the other. Similarly, entire WhatsApp groups are formed and messages sent to caterers requesting certain dishes.[9]

Like the canteen specialists who cashed in on the December Season, Grand Sweets & Snacks, founded in 1982 by G. Natarajan, carved a niche in catering to special preparations associated with one Indian festival or the other. Having started at Gandhi Nagar, Adyar, Grand released topical advertisements, each centred on an imminent festival. It described the logic behind the celebrations and then listed out the snacks to be prepared for the same. It then asked patrons to come over to Grand and taste them. This was when most joint families had broken up, with nuclear outcomes often comprising working couples. Women found it difficult to prepare the savouries and sweets for festivals and Grand was the saviour. At the outlet, rather like the ice-cream parlours abroad, patrons were encouraged to taste the latest preparations, placed in leaf cups and described as prasadam (offerings to the divine). Many filled their stomachs with these, and Grand never counted what was consumed thus. But hardly anyone left without buying something or the other. Inside, women, mostly from disadvantaged families, manned everything—from the kneading and preparation of ingredients, the actual cooking, the counters, the packaging, and the serving. All of them wore uniform sarees, overcoats, and caps. Some of them became stars in their own right, known for one item on the menu or the other. Rukmini Mami, for instance, was the queen of the poli. NRIs soon began flocking to Grand and its preparations became the gift items of choice to take abroad. Murukkus, thattais, cheedais, maladus,

[9]V. Sriram, 'Three Cheers to Super Chefs', *The Hindu*, 18 December 2014.

and other items just flew off the shelves. Natarajan died in 2001, by then recognized as one of Chennai's highest taxpayers for several years.[10] His descendants did not see eye to eye and split Grand into two entities, both sharing the same name. A wall came up, dividing the Gandhi Nagar outlet, with identical eateries coming up on both sides, serving up the same dishes and preparations, handled by women in mustard-coloured saris. But internally, there was strife. Rukmini Mami ended up on one side of the wall, while her handpicked assistants were on the other. Quality suffered but the twin Grands multiplied, opening outlets across the city. Some patrons aver that it is not the same as in Natarajan's time but the crowds still line up, especially around the time the 'prasadams' emerge piping hot.

Talking of prasadams and the more genuine versions of these, prepared at temples, some of these are famous too. The Parthasarathy Temple in Triplicane is, perhaps, best known for its sakkarai pongal, rice sweetened with jaggery, to which plenty of dry fruits have been added. Its tamarind rice is equally famous. The Kapaliswarar Temple in Mylapore, though it does have a sale counter that always has customers, cannot lay claim to any particular dish that is in demand. But its ven pongal (the South Indian khichdi), dripping with ghee and distributed piping hot early in the morning during the month of Margazhi (Dec/Jan), is something worth queuing up for.

Following more or less on the same lines as Grand is Sri Krishna Sweets, which originated in Coimbatore in 1948 but moved to Chennai in the 1990s. It focused entirely on sweets and its piece de resistance is its Mysorepa, a variant of the more famous Mysorepak, a sweet made from generous helpings of ghee, gram flour, and sugar. The brownish-yellow delight, packed in trademark white plastic boxes with blue lettering is a familiar sight on most festive occasions. Also in trademark white is one of the scions of the family—M. Murali, who is known as Krishna Sweets Murali. A patron of the arts, he is known to extend his generosity to several deserving causes.

Chennai has had its famed non-vegetarian restaurants too. Harrison's of Broadway was extremely popular between the 1890s and the 1950s, despite the name not being Indian. Founded by G. Varadarajulu Chetty in 1891, it later passed into the hands of P. Nammalwar Naidu, with whose family it remains, morphing into Queen's Hotel in Nungambakkam, the name being inspired by the property having been the residence of Her Highness Vidyawati Devi Saheb, the colourful maharani of Vizianagaram. Today, Queen's Hotel has given way to Harrison's Hotel, which, in an interesting twist, also houses

---

[10]Malathy Sriram, 'A Sweet and Savoury Tale', *Bloncampus*, 10 March 2017.

Eden, Chennai's only continental vegetarian restaurant whose original outlet still functions in Besant Nagar. Harrison's specialized in 'Butler Cuisine', a term that comprised Indianized British, Dutch, Portuguese, and Goan recipes. This was also the speciality of Spencer's, the retail and hotel chain that ran the catering department of the South Indian and later Southern Railway, for long.

But for years the mecca for non-vegetarian food was A. M. Buhari's eponymous restaurant on Mount Road, begun in 1951. An article in *The Hindu* in 2014 noted that Buhari who 'brought the mildly spiced, fragrant biryani from Colombo, was a pioneer of sorts. Whether it was a boiled egg nestled in a bed of saffron-infused rice or Chicken 65 fried to perfection—called thus after the year it was created in, he set himself apart in the restaurant business early on.'[11] The restaurant on Mount Road soon gave birth to several branches, now run by the third generation of the family. In its day, Buhari boasted of Sivaji Ganesan, Raj Kapoor, and other film stars as its patrons.

Chennai had a rather strange term for eateries that specialized in non-vegetarian Hindu fare—military hotels. This was because in a largely vegetarian city, it was believed that only those in the army ate meat. Hotels they were certainly not, for they offered no accommodation, but they were always referred to as such. The entrances to these places often featured paintings of men in army uniform, lavishly endowed with moustaches. The food here was spicy. Velu Military Hotel on Eldam's Road was probably the first, begun in 1951. Today, most military hotels refer to themselves as Chettinad specialists and it is interesting that the first of these, Anjappar's, dating to 1964, began as a military mess. There are several more Chettinad eateries today, but the leader of the pack is the Thalapakatty chain, which having begun in Dindigul in 1957, moved to Madras later and has around thirty outlets in the city. Unlike Saravana Bhavan, which has rarely bothered about clones who sometimes use very similar-sounding names, Dindigul Thalapakatty has zealously guarded its trademark and won landmark litigations too.[12]

There are other lesser-known locations for special dishes—attukkaal paya (lamb trotters) in various forms are available in many eateries, including at the most expensive, but the best can be had only in the small corner outlets located along the older parts of the city such as Triplicane and George Town. And yes, the city has had no problems with people eating beef or pork, for

---

[11]Evelyn Ratnakumar, 'A gastronomic journey with biryani', *The Hindu*, 13 August 2014.

[12]R. Sivaraman, 'Dindigul Thalappakatti biriyani wins trademark row', *The Hindu*, 6 April 2013.

that matter. These are available everywhere with the shacks around Vyasarpadi offering the most delectable preparations.

On the vegetarian front, there are a few humble establishments and their bills of fare that have attained immortality in the city's food history. Mylapore has its Kalathi's shop where rose milk can be had at certain times of the day before it runs out. Equally hallowed is Mami's Mess on Pichu Pillai Street just opposite. Then there is Jannal Kadai, which as the name suggests, is just a window in a wall, from where the most delectable savouries are sold, for a short while each day. Not far from here is Rayar's Mess on Arundel Street—with seating for just sixteen patrons. There is always a long queue outside, with people waiting patiently to choose from the limited but delectable menu of standard South Indian fare—idlis, vadas, sambar, and chutney. There is no paper bill; instead, after the batch clears out to have coffee in the open, the proprietor ambles along and asks each person what he or she ate and informs them of what they need to pay. Of similar vintage but more spacious and with greater variety is Geetha Café in T. Nagar—the floor is ancient mosaic, the table tops marble, and the chairs hard wood and when it comes to closing time, the last named will be lifted and placed on the tables. Rathna Café is the place to be in if you are in Triplicane. The sambar is said to be the secret that brings people back and it is served here not with a ladle but poured out from spouted tureens. Founded in 1948 by Triloknath Gupta from Mathura, it is now run by his kinsmen who have since expanded the scope to include catering. Of similar vintage is New Prakash Bhavan on NSC Bose Road, its small interior teeming with patrons at all times of the day.

Blessed with such a large beachfront, it is no surprise that Chennai is also home to much seafood. But before we move on to that, we have to mention some snacks associated with the beach. Thenga manga pattani sundal is fried peas mixed with raw mango, grated coconut, and chilli powder sold at the beach by vendors for decades. Also associated with the beach is raw mango, cut into slivers and spiced with a dash of curry powder. Sea food in Chennai largely means crab, shark, and local fish and these can be had at a wide variety of eateries, ranging from the upmarket ones to wayside kiosks near the beach. Fresh fish in the city is sold all along the coastline, though the biggest fish market is located at Chintadripet and has been functioning for a century. And Chennai has its Chinese food fans too, who swear by restaurants such as Mainland China, Golden Dragon in Taj Coromandel, and China Town. And there are the one-offs such as Benjerong on TTK Road, known for its Thai food, while frontier cuisine is brought in by Peshawari, once in Chola Sheraton (now Fortune) and later moved to ITC Grand Chola. Korean cuisine made its appearance in the city shortly after Hyundai opened its factory here but it still remains an acquired taste. Burmese food has its presence too, though the best of this variety is available only in the 'atho kadais' that come up each night at the Second Line Beach, close to Burma Bazaar.

There are very few accounts of how cakes and breads were made in old Madras but by 1884, when Colonel Arthur Robert Kenny-Herbert's *Sweet Dishes: A Little Treatise on Confectionery and Entremets Sucres* was published, these were commonplace items made at the clubs, homes, hotels, and standalone bakeries. He was also the first person to document the recipe for mulligatawny, the soup that the Madras Club claims was invented in its premises. The colonel was its secretary for years and that lends some credence to the claim.

'The native cook is a fairly good hand at sweet things,' the colonel grudgingly wrote, while at the same time cautioning that 'Ramasami's repertoire of presentable sweets is somewhat limited',[13]—the name being his generic moniker for all Indian servants. It is interesting that many Indians set up bakeries from almost the time that the book was published, the oldest in operation today being Smithfields, named after the brick kilns in Purasawalkam/Perambur by the side of which it came up in 1885.[14] Mylapore's Crown dates itself to 1905 and was known for years for its wood-fired oven, where neighbours could bring their dough and mixes and bake for themselves.[15] The city's oldest-running confectionery chain, McRennet, is also Indian in origin, dating to 1903, when Manikkam Pillai literally pulled out an English-sounding name from his hat and got into the baking business. There are over thirty McRennet outlets in the city today.[16] Another hallowed name, Bosotto's, was, however, Italian in origin, beginning in 1906 as D'Angeli's in a hotel of the same name located on Mount Road. When Giacomo D'Angeli quit the country in the 1920s, his business was acquired by fellow countryman Attillio Bosotto, who renamed the hotel and bakery after himself. Under Bosotto, his eponymous businesses prospered, the bakery honoured with an 'appointment to His Excellency, the Governor of

[13]'Wyvern', *Sweet Dishes: A Little Treatise on Confectionery and Entremets Sucres*, Madras: Higginbothams & Co., 1884.

[14]Priyadarshini Paitandy, 'Flour power', *The Hindu*, 17 May 2017.

[15]Karthik Subramanian, 'The bakers of Bazaar Street', *The Hindu*, 7 August 2014.

[16]Mythreyee Ramesh, 'Mcrennett: The original Chennai bakery with an English name but a Tamil heart', *News Minute*, 3 June 2016.

Madras', whose Mount Road residence it faced. When Independence came, the Italian, like so many other Europeans, was not so keen on staying in India. The bakery was sold to his erstwhile vendor of dairy produce—Muslappa Chowdhury, whose descendants continued running Bosotto's bakery from the same hotel, which, unlike the former, changed hands and names over the decades. The bakery's apogee was when it supplied a cake to celebrate Queen Elizabeth's birthday when the British monarch visited Madras in the 1960s. But by 2012, all that was a distant memory.[17] The hotel's latest owners decided to demolish the building and with that the bakery had to move, now functioning from a nook in Nungambakkam. Its erstwhile premises that included a restaurant where the lyricist Kannadasan is said to have penned some of his best works is a shell awaiting development.

In recent years, the Hot Breads chain has far outstripped other confectionary stores and chains by the sheer breadth of its vision. The founder, M. Mahadevan, even while teaching at the University of Madras, began a Chinese eatery and went from strength to strength, finally establishing the Hot Breads chain and Copper Chimney restaurants all across the city. The former then went international, opening outlets in West Asia, Africa, and Europe. Combined with his strong commercial instincts was an equally powerful charitable streak in Mahadevan. He began training the poor in baking, giving them employment in his outlets, and encouraging them to dream of a future.[18] And then came Writers' Café, yet another chain, which combined books with coffee, cakes, and snacks. The heart-warming aspect in this is that the staff largely comprises burn victims and acid-attack survivors, for which Mahadevan has collaborated with the International Foundation for Crime Prevention and Victim Care. Going to a Writer's Café outlet takes a deeper meaning, given this aspect.[19] Mahadevan today spends much of his time in the Middle East pursuing the restaurant business there while his son, Tarun, handles the many chains and eateries in India.

Going out for a drink was never an option in orthodox Madras. According to the more conservative elements, that was something the Europeans and Anglo-Indians did. In reality, the city probably never lagged behind other metros of India in its consumption, only it was a more surreptitious activity as

[17]V. Sriram, *The Rayala Story: The Legacy of MR Rajagopal Naidu*, Chennai: Rayala Corporation Pvt. Limited, 2015, p. 47.

[18]Bishwanath Ghosh, 'The world on a table', *The Hindu*, 23 May 2014.

[19]Kayalvizhi Arivalan, 'Chennai's Writer's Café Empowers Burn Survivors And Victims Of Abuse', *Femina*, 18 September 2020.

compared to anywhere else. Who would believe that the famed liquor brand McDowell's had its origins in Madras? Founded in 1825 by Angus McDowell, a Scot, the company was greatly successful and later came into the Eurasian family of Coleman, before becoming a private limited company in the early 1900s. In 1951, it was acquired by Vittal Mallya and the rest is history.[20] Soda, a close associate of the liquor industry, had its special Chennai brands for years. In the pre-Independence years, McClures was the rage, as were McDowells and Spencers. Today, these have all left the market to international brands. Also not so popular these days is the goli soda—carbonated water sold in cod-necked bottles and once the mainstay of political meetings in the city, and used to revive those who went into religious trances and as a cure for dehydration, indigestion, and gas.

In the pre-Independence years, alcoholic refreshments could be had at the posh hotels that had bar licenses, clubs, departmental stores such as Spencers, and railway refreshment rooms. Entry was invariably restricted at most of these places. But in 1936, the city and the presidency went dry. That was when Rajagopalachari was elected premier of Madras and headed the first Congress ministry. The British hemmed and hawed but could do nothing other than obediently apply for permits to drink, ostensibly for medical reasons. A few Indians managed this as well. Thereafter, Madras State remained dry for a long while, barring a couple of brief interludes when prohibition was lifted. This was when neighbouring Pondicherry and Bangalore became very popular weekend getaways. It was only in 1971 that the Karunanidhi-led DMK government, much to the disappointment of Rajaji who had campaigned for the party, removed all curbs on alcohol consumption, the excise earned on the sale of liquor being revenue that the government could ill afford to lose. Prohibition was, however, back in 1974, only to be lifted again in 1981, when MGR was in power. Two years later, his government created the Tamil Nadu State Marketing Corporation (TASMAC), the public sector entity that would henceforth be responsible for the wholesale vending of liquor. The state flirted briefly with prohibition thereafter too but liquor had come to stay.[21] The money earned through sales and the auctioning of licences for retail outlets was an attraction; in addition, liquor kept political cadres happy. Outwardly, all parties profess to be in favour of an outright ban on the sale of alcohol, especially during the run-up to an election but

[20]V. Sriram, 'Indian Charivari—3, Making McDowells a liquor brand', *Madras Heritage and Carnatic Music*, 10 July 2017.

[21]Sriram, *The Sanmar Story*, pp. 58–65.

in reality very few would like to implement it. The net result is that liquor is freely available and though Chennai still ranks low in terms of alcohol consumption, it is fast making up for lost time during the prohibition years.

There is no word in Tamil for ice—the nearest equivalent is pani, which means dew. The commodity was unheard of in the city and for that matter all of Tamil Nadu, for the idea of frozen water was alien to the place. By the nineteenth century, artificial means of freezing water had become well known in Europe and what could have been India's first attempt at chemically making ice took place in Chennai, in 1802, at the residence of Benjamin Roebuck, now a part of the Women's Christian College campus. Later, as we saw earlier, the Tudor Ice Company supplied the commodity from America. It folded up in the 1860s, artificial refrigeration having arrived in India by then. Through the next few decades, before ice-making became popular at homes, several English, Anglo-Indian, Indian, and Parsi firms tried their hand at running ice plants in the city. A major player was P. Venkatachellum (PV), who, from 1901, after reportedly having worked in the kitchens of Government House, perfected recipes for curry powder and pickles. PV's condiments and sauces became world-renowned, being sold all across the British Empire, with agents in even faraway locations such as Australia. The heyday of the business, which spanned three generations of the family, saw the acquisition of much real estate and a successful ice factory as well. A shrinking world and change of tastes, coupled with descendants who were happier managing land saw the business wane, and today, PV's is a minor name. But in its time, the controlling family was powerful enough to fund government illuminations across the city for Queen Victoria's Golden Jubilee, and PV's was probably the first Indian curry brand to make it big across the world.[22]

Of the more upmarket hotels, Chennai always had just a few. The old Connemara, named after a first lady of Madras who separated from her husband and stayed at the hotel for a few nights before embarking to England from where she fought a bitter divorce case,[23] is still going strong, managed by the Taj Group. Dating to 1854 when it started life as the Imperial, it is lovingly tended to, and has had a complete overhaul in 2018, having been closed for three years after the floods of 2015. In Connemara is The Verandah, known for its breakfast and Anglo-Indian cuisine, while Raintree, named after a giant samanea saman that graces its courtyard, is famed for Chettinad

[22]Wright, *Southern India*, pp. 711–16.

[23]V. Sriram, 'Tale of the Connemara', *The Hindu*, 16 April 2013.

cuisine.[24] Of equal renown is the Crowne Plaza's (formerly Adyar Club Gate and later Welcomgroup Park Sheraton Hotel and Towers) Dakshin, which is thirty years old. This specializes in South Indian cuisine, in general, its chef Thanikachalam having been with it since its inception. But the bigger attraction in the early years was Iyer, the man who poured degree coffee by the yard—that distance separating the tumbler and davara, the two vessels that make up the standard South Indian coffee set. Iyer's trolley in the restaurant commemorates him till date.

Can any account of food in Chennai be complete without dwelling on coffee? The social impact of this beverage is best analysed by A. R. Venkatachalapathy in his essay 'In Those Days There Was No Coffee'. It was a late arrival among the local population in Chennai, the British having long enjoyed it; the first coffee tavern opening in Fort St George as early as the seventeenth century. Early in the twentieth century, coffee began entering Indian homes, especially those of the upper classes. There were many doubts expressed about its suitability. The hidebound sections of society denounced it as the mother of all evil, attributing every possible illness including nervous disorders and impotence to it. It was considered particularly bad for women.[25] Nevertheless, coffee made progress, more in particular after Indians became involved in growing and blending it, the brand Narasu's, begun in 1926, being one of the oldest. Coffee-making became a ritual of sorts at most houses, the beans being roasted and ground and the decoction being prepared just before it was served, with plenty of milk and sugar. There was pecking order to serving coffee too—honoured guests were served in silver or at least bell metal tumblers and davaras while the less exalted got it in brass or stainless steel. The tumblers had flattened rims so that the orthodox did not have to sip the coffee and could pour it down their throats. By the 1960s, Chennai was a full-fledged coffee city, many of its residents declaring themselves unable to begin their day without it. Sadly for coffee, Chennai began mixing chicory into it very early on. This, according to many, gave body to the drink but it destroyed the very flavour of coffee as did the adding of extra milk and sugar. But that became the Chennai way.

Tea, surprisingly, was accepted very slowly and rather grudgingly by Chennai. Coffee was always considered socially superior, while tea was what

[24]S. Muthiah, *A Tradition of Madras that is Chennai: The Taj Connemara*, Chennai: S. Muthiah, 2006.

[25]A. R. Venkatachalapathy, *In Those Days There Was No Coffee: Writings in Cultural History*, New Delhi: Yoda Press, 2006, pp. 11–28.

servants and menials drank. World War II saw much tea advertising in the city but to very little effect.[26] It was only in the new millennium that tea became fashionable in Chennai, with growing awareness of multiple varieties, blends, and flavours.

Like tea, wheat too struggled to gain acceptance, though much was done, especially in famine years to get the Madras population to accept wheat. Arriving in the city as part of his father's drama troupe in the 1920s, the young 'Avvai' T. K. Shanmugam recalls being served poori and masal (the Chennai term for semi-dry potato curry flavoured with onions) and hating the combo. The caterer was sent out to get what everyone wanted—idli![27] Following the setting up of the All India Women's Central Food Council in New Delhi in 1951, Madras got its own state unit, managed by the Guild of Service under the leadership of Mary Clubwala Jadhav. This entity ran Annapurna Cafeterias in the city where wheat preparations were offered on sale.[28] It did, however, allow plenty of opportunity for jokes in the vernacular press, the best one being an *Ananda Vikatan* cartoon where the husband holds up a chapatti and asks his wife if wheat is used for making glue as well. The cafeterias folded up by the 1970s but their task was done—Madras was waking up to wheat and families began using it as an alternative but never as a full replacement to rice. Today, the city thinks nothing of trying all kinds of cereals—millets being the latest craze.

But rice remained and continues to be the principal ingredient in most traditional Chennai food preparations. This is made most evident by a perusal of that enduring South Indian cookbook which came from Chennai—*Samaithu Par* (*Cook & See*). This was the work of Meenakshi Ammal, a widow in the 1940s who had to take care of an infant son, a seven-year-old brother-in-law, and an aged mother-in-law. Noticing her culinary skills, her uncle, K. V. Krishnaswami Aiyar of the Music Academy fame, suggested that she pen her recipes and publish the compilation. A second volume of recipes followed and then a third—dedicated to recipes for festivals and special occasions. Couched in homely language but with a scientific precision in measures that was amazing, *Samaithu Par* has remained in print ever since. Thanks to Meenakshi Ammal's son, Sankaran, it was later published in English, as *Cook*

[26]Sriram, *MCCI*, p. 173.

[27]Avvai T. K. Shanmugam, *Enathu Naadaga Vaazhlkai*, Chennai: Vanathi Pathippakam, 1972, p. 84.

[28]V. Sriram, 'The Cafeteria that offered alternative grains', *Madras Musings*, Vol. XXVII, No. 21, 16–28 February 2018.

& See. It is now in electronic format as well. Rice is king in *Samaithu Par*. Meenakshi Ammal would have probably sneered at wheat but in the hands of later cookbook writers, it has received its due share. Today, Chennai is willing to try everything, including quinoa.[29]

That is probably a reflection of the way the city has opened up post liberalization of the Indian economy. Coffee today does not mean just the filter variety. We know all about latte and mocha and espresso. Chennai abounds in garden cafes today, the two best examples, perhaps, being Kiran Rao's Amethyst and S. Gomathy's Kipling. The former is in the heart of the city while the latter is on the East Coast Road but both have seats in vast open spaces. Kiran was undoubtedly the pioneer in this, first setting up Amethyst in a heritage bungalow her aunt owned. From there, she moved to a disused warehouse off Anna Salai where the surrounding area under her green fingers has become a verdant garden. Kipling is in a naturally green part of town. The food at both places is essentially European and Far Eastern. The clientele in both places is young.

But despite all the fancy cuisine available in the city, ask any Chennaiite what their idea of soul food is and the answer is most likely to be thayir sadam—curd rice. This can be in many varieties though the basic content is the same—rice mixed with curd. In the past, this was what defined lunch for most households, across all layers of society. The poorest had watery buttermilk mixed with rice for lunch and for breakfast it was the fermented rice of the previous night, to which a dash of salt and buttermilk was added. In the wealthier households, buttermilk was replaced by thick curd, made from buffalo's milk, the animal most often reared in the backyard. On festive occasions, curd rice was seasoned with curry leaves, diced green chillies, and some spices. The tendency to introduce fruits such as grapes and pomegranates is an abomination but many like that too. The best thayir sadam is said to emanate from orthodox Iyengar households. The secret is to cook the rice with milk and add a dash of curd to it as it cools. The milk gradually ferments into curd even as the rice blends in.

Whatever be the formulation for curd rice, it has come to typify the end of a satisfying meal in Chennai parlance. In fact, in Tamil culture, dessert is always served before curd rice. And Chennai needs its curd rice. This explains why you will always find it a standard item on hotel menus, even if the rest of the cuisine is Continental or Chinese.

---

[29]Vidya Raja, 'In 1951, this housewife wrote a cookbook that made her a legend in Tamil Nadu', *The Better India*, 19 March 2019.

16 | THE GREAT SOCIAL WHIRL

'Nothing ever happens in Chennai' was a frequent lament heard from children from elsewhere who were forced to spend their holidays in this city. The same sentiment was echoed by adults when they came visiting, especially from Bombay and Bangalore. A stand-up comic recently declared that the most happening place in Chennai is Bangalore. Yet, Chennai's ideas of entertainment are all its own and some can be quite quirky.

Our weddings are important. They are the reason why we save money and invest in gold, of which we cannot have enough. Our jewellery is of the solid variety, not for us flaky filigree work and, as for gemstones, we prefer them in close setting and not the open way of the north. That way, our diamonds and emeralds will not fall off. And we like our diamonds polished and not left uncut. What is the use of having diamonds if they don't sparkle? Anyway, we love buying jewellery and legend has it that the day after the floods of 2015, the only shops that were open were jewellery stores. The other items we stock up on as part of the trousseau are low on beauty but rank high on utility—stainless-steel vessels, except we refer to the metal as eversilver, no doubt after some long-forgotten brand name.

Coming to the actual event, we splurge on it, hiring wedding halls, featuring live classical or light music performances that nobody listens to, and catering by some of the best-known names in the business. Venues are clear social markers—there are certain locations that automatically make weddings held there as must-attends, and this does not mean five-star hotels alone. Places such as AVM Rajeswari (Mylapore), Kuchalambal (Chetpet), Anna Arivalayam (the DMK headquarters has a huge wedding hall attached to it), Raja Muthiah, and Rani Meyyammai Halls (if it is a true-blue society wedding, these venues located contiguously in Egmore will both be hired) belong to this class. And then there is the Ramachandra Convention Centre in Thiruvanmiyur, which is the place to get married in if you expect a significant chunk of Chennai's population to attend.

After the location, the next important qualification for a wedding is its choice of caterer. As a Sanskrit verse goes—the bride desires a handsome groom, the mother wealth, the father learning; the relatives look for pedigree while the rest of the guests are there only for the food.[1] Gossip on how bad

[1]Kanyaa varayate rupam, maataa dhanam pitaa shrutam Bhaandhavaaha kulam icchanti, mishtaannam itare janaah.

food was at a certain wedding can linger for years. And talking of guests, invitations and the mode of inviting are taken very seriously indeed. The more important guests need to be invited in person and entire weeks can be spent in calling at homes, falling at feet, handing over of gifts and re-iterating that their presence is of the essence. Those in an immediate lower rung can be invited by snail mail followed by an obligatory phone call. Emails are strictly for the least important. WhatsApp messages are frowned upon.

A Tamil wedding can be of two types—those blessed by a priest or officiated by an elder, often a politician. The latter variety is referred to as a reformist wedding, which came up in the 1940s in reaction to the older practice that was dominated by rituals. Both are grand spectacles, complete with videographer who keeps getting his wires entangled around everyone's legs. The original Tamil wedding was probably just a morning event but we then added layers to it. It can now range anywhere from a day to a week, with such essentials as mehendi, baraat, and sangeet thrown in. Prenup photo shoots too have become de rigueur, the more discreet ones showing them as videos at an evening prior to the wedding while others think nothing of putting up flex banners featuring these pictures just outside the venue.

All of the above does not necessarily pertain to the Hindu or upper-class weddings alone. These practices, often permanently draining the family exchequer, have now spread to all classes and communities. It is interesting that at a time when dowry demands have come down drastically, the wedding expenses themselves have become so exorbitant as to make up for it. 'We are nothing but a city of show people,' says M.V. Subbiah. He laments over the loss of simplicity even though he belongs to the Chettiar community, well known for its grand marriages and stupendous dowries. 'But there is an important difference,' he states. 'In the old days people spent based on what wealth they had. The richer families organized grand spectacular weddings but don't forget that it helped the village or local community's economy. Every ethnic community, caste, and social group was involved. It was a way to help the locals. Today there are wedding planners and much of the money goes to some retailer in China who supplies what is wanted. But even worse than this are the destination weddings where nobody local benefits. The same set of jetsetters travel to each of the marriages and return.'

Subbiah is a minimalist, and after stepping down from corporate affairs, is focused on going back to the roots, contributing to the community, and helping the spread of education. Not everyone may agree with his assessment but there is much truth in what he says. Marriages, however, pale into insignificance in the face of the puberty rite, once a family event, then dropped as a purely age-related matter but now back as a public spectacle. Families think nothing of hiring community halls, putting up flexboards, hiring music bands, and celebrating this entirely biological phenomenon. The more politically-inclined may also feature their beloved leader on the banner. All of these along with other celebrations such as sixtieth, seventieth, and eightieth birthdays, and countless other family events, all important in their own way, is what Chennai spends on.

Subbiah rues this tendency to spend what he says is often borrowed money, especially when the celebrants are from the economically weaker sections of society. And he blames the well-off for this, 'There was a time when Chennai society was unostentatious. Then the rich changed. That has had a cascading effect. People feel that it is necessary to spend, taking loans for this. It is expected of them.'

But, by and large, what Chennai truly enjoys is a funeral. The city's idea of Page 3 is the obituary column of *The Hindu*, which is what we wake up to, along with the obligatory cup of coffee and M. S. Subbulakshmi's 'Suprabhatam'. The list is scanned and if there is someone who has departed who, as per the local expression, is near and dear, then an immediate visit is mandated before a morning bath. Sunday mornings in Chennai and to a lesser extent, Thursdays, are busy, for that is when you catch up on condolence visits missed on the day of the funeral. For some reason, it has become de rigueur to serve coffee on such occasions, with many now emphatically stating that it is part of ancient custom. You will invariably find some mourners murmuring about the quality of the beverage in a deeply critical vein even as they mouth platitudes about the departed. The last journey by itself is a pageant, often in a flower-bedecked bier, people scattering flowers and a group of intoxicated individuals dancing before the cortege. The police will obligingly divert traffic for such processions and vehicles that may hesitate before an ambulance will immediately give way. Posters announcing the person's passing miraculously make their appearance and thereafter they re-appear on the tenth, sixteenth, and fortieth day after the death and on anniversaries. Chennai's walls are awash with posters of such proclamations, apart from those of the cinema and political worlds.

Chennai also spends an equal if not greater amount of time, effort, and money on shopping, which is why the city is a retail hub. Sari shopping perhaps tops the list and within a square mile in T. Nagar you will find every retailer worth its name starting from Nalli's, the first among equals. While several others such as Kumaran, Raasi, Pothy's, and RMKV have since established themselves, Nalli remains a unique brand and that has much to do with the image of its proprietor, Kuppuswami Chetty. Avuncular, soft spoken, and always clad in white shirt and veshti, Chettiar, as he is referred to, is an icon of the city. Society matrons take pride in knowing him personally and to call at the headquarters on Nageswaran Road, be met by the proprietor himself and, above all, being pressed to have coffee ('the milk is from our cows', he will say with quiet pride) even as diverse minions bring saris to the sanctum itself for your selection, counts for much. Musicians and dancers too make a beeline to Chettiar, for he is the patron of numerous sabhas in the city, president of some, and a liberal donor to several others. True, his attempt at taking over the Music Academy backfired but he is still the most popular personality in the world of arts.[2] A fixture at many cultural events, Chettiar is also a man of letters, being the author of several books, ranging from the history of his neighbourhood of T. Nagar to interpretations of philosophy and thought. Nalli Chettiar personifies his brand and keeps it flying high. A couple of years back, the garment retailers, particularly those dealing in silk, indulged in a price war, offering all kinds of discounts. Nalli countered it with a hoarding that said it offered no discounts. The headquarters of Nalli is a period piece—art-deco architecture, wood panelling, and mosaic flooring from the 1950s—all maintained perfectly. At the rear is the owner's house and somewhere further behind are the cows that provide the milk that makes his coffee so popular. He and his environment are in perfect sync and that makes for good business.

Not far from Nalli is the retail hub of Ranganathan Street and Usman Road, where Chennai flocks to satiate its appetite for shopping. Both thoroughfares are a civic nightmare but a shopper's delight. Here you will find Saravana Stores, the biggest branch of the retail chain, which began in the 1960s. This multi-purpose store is where you will find everything you want, from electronic goods to buckets, mops, and pans, at fabulously discounted prices. The outlet at Ranganathan Street, T. Nagar, is flooded with customers day in and day out, at all times of the year, rising to an impossible influx during Deepavali, throwing traffic out of gear and giving much stress to the city's police force. How does Saravana manage its pricing? Wholesale purchasing and a very sharp buying department are obviously key. Employment policies at the retail outlet also focus on keeping costs low. The floorwalkers are hired in their thousands from the rural hinterland, made to stay in cramped shared quarters, and work for long hours. And yet, the lure of working in the city is strong. In 2010, Director Vasanthabalan's

[2]Sriram and Rangaswami, *Four Score and More*, pp. 247–53.

Angadi Theru (Market Street) released and was met with critical acclaim for its authentic portrayal of the life of the staff at Saravana Stores. All of that has, however, not made much difference to the way Chennai's shoppers see the place. The crowds have only increased. Kishore Biyani, of Big Bazaar fame, has gone on record to state that Saravana Stores was the inspiration behind his nationwide chain of shops that promised a plethora of goods at unbelievable prices.[3] Saravana Stores later branched into jewellery as well, under the brand Saravana Thanga Nagai Maligai (Gold Jewel Palace) and that too draws crowds at all times.

Around festival time, the newspapers of Chennai are assured of some full-page advertisements, chief among them being from Saravana Stores, whose young owner likes to feature as the model. He is rivalled in this aspect only by his equivalent at Lalitha Jewellery, a rival of Saravana's jewellery outfit, who also releases full-page advertorials, featuring as the model. Both are lampooned mercilessly by the city's humourist Krishṇa Shastri Devulapalli but that has had no effect. In the face of these jewellers, and later ones such as Joyalukkas and Kalyan Jewellers, Chennai's older establishments such as Vummidis, Nathella, and Vecumsee have found the going tough. Not everyone can be a Nalli. Malls too have not dented the crowds at Nalli and Saravana. The draw of the malls has more to do with the air conditioning they provide, their food courts, and their multiplex cinemas than with actual shopping.

Staid Chennai has its share of nightlife too. Cabaret shows made their appearance in the city with the American soldiers stationed here during World War II. Interestingly, the Guild of Service, an organization for social upliftment run by the redoubtable Mary Clubwala Jadhav, was responsible for putting up these shows for the army, often at the Connemara.[4] The first disco was Nine Gems, at the basement of the Safire Theatre complex, alas, now a mere plot of land on Mount Road. Its heyday was in the 1960s and a young singer by the name of Usha Iyer performed there. Later, she was contracted by the Savera Hotel to sing at its nightclub and from there, as Usha Uthup, she moved to Bombay and Calcutta to everlasting fame.[5] In recent years, Hell Freezes Over at the Quality Inn Aruna was a popular discotheque but it incurred Jayalalithaa's ire when she was in power, as

---

[3]Kishore Biyani, *It Happened in India*, New Delhi: Rupa, 2007, p. 116.

[4]Rukmini Amirapu, *Guild of Service (Central) Seva Samajam: Spreading Hope and Happiness*, Chennai: Guild of Service, 2019, p. 31.

[5]Chitra Deepa Anantharam, 'Savera, Chennai's first four star hotel turns 50', *The Hindu*, 23 January 2018.

Dayanidhi Maran of the DMK owned it. It had to close and the hotel too wound up later.[6] Today's enthusiasts go to Pasha at The Park—the hotel that stands on what was once part of Gemini Studios. The disco-goers are probably jiving where T. R. Rajakumari once performed her drum dance for the 1948 film *Chandralekha*.[7]

Chennai's calendar is full of temple festivals and religious observances. January is when we have the harvest festival of Pongal, the Tamil equivalent of Makar Sankranti. There was a time when this was a two-day event, the added excitement being the test matches that were held at this time at Chepauk. Over the years, with successive political regimes adding to the days off, this has become a week-long break, rather in the manner of Durga Puja in Kolkata. In recent times, Pongal holidays are when *The Hindu* hosts its literary festival, Lit For Life. For three whole days, all the literati, bibliophiles, and intellectuals descend on the Sir Mutha Venkatasubba Rao auditorium, to listen to panel discussions, talks, presentations, and debates. For a few years, DMK's Kanimozhi conducted a traditional arts festival—Chennai Sangamam—in January, which created quite a buzz.

February has Masi Makham, when deities are traditionally taken to the sea for a ceremonial bath. March is when the Panguni Uthiram festival, lasting ten days, takes place at all Shiva temples, complete with processional outings for the deities, twice daily. This is also the month when, in the first new moon night after Maha Shivaratri, the fishermen community observes its worship of Angala Parameswari, the goddess having her shrines close to cremation grounds in all the coastal villages that became part of the city. Central to the celebrations is the Mayana Kollai—the midnight raid conducted on the crematorium by the goddess and her faithful assistant Pavadairayan to fish out demons. In the olden days this involved the faithful feeding on the unburnt parts of corpses but this has since tempered down.

April has, apart from Ram Navami, the birth of Ram, the Tamil New Year, which most Chennaiites stubbornly stick to, despite Karunanidhi's efforts to get Pongal to be observed as the beginning of the Tamil New Year. May is sacred to Murugan, when festivities break out at all temples dedicated to this Tamil deity, later absorbed into the Vedic pantheon as the son of Shiva and Parvati. July is when the mother goddess has her month-long celebration. This is considered so sacred that no weddings or purchases happen during this

[6]'Chennai's popular discotheque Hell Freezes Over closes shop', *India Today*, 25 June 2001.

[7]Ashish Rajadhyaksha and Paul Wellemen, *Encyclopaedia of Indian Cinema*, New Delhi: OUP, 2004, p. 310.

time. This Tamil month of Aadi therefore sees a lull in retailing activity and to revive this, shops come up with huge discounts. The Aadi sales have since achieved what they were meant to. August is a month of festivities—there is Avani Avittam when Brahmins don new sacred threads, Janmashtami, and Ganesh Chaturthi. The last named was once a domestic affair—families making small clay idols of the deity, worshipping and then ceremoniously immersing them in the well in the backyard. In recent years, Chennai has taken a leaf out of Mumbai's book. Large public celebrations are organized and the day of immersion, at sea, normally coinciding with Muharram, is fraught with tension. Triplicane is particularly stressed, with immersion processions vending their way to the sea via the Big Mosque. Not far from here, however, is a scene that unfolds each Muharram—Muslims immersing their taziyas at the Kapaliswarar Temple tank. That is a part of the city's history, for the land for the tank was gifted by the nawab of Arcot, whose descendants receive traditional honours on the day of the temple's float festival till date. 'I look forward to that invite each year,' says Nawab Mohammad Abdul Ali. 'I have attended the float festival and enjoyed it. To me it is symbolic of all that is joyous in the city.'

In September, Chennai has a small but unique celebration. This involves the offering of a traditional umbrella made by artisans in Chintadripet, to Lord Venkateswara at Tirumala. The pilgrims set out just after the start of the Tamil month of Purattasi (Sep/Oct), sacred to Vishnu. On that day, much of North Chennai shuts down and the umbrella is taken, accompanied by music and chanting, over five days to the lord on the hill.

Speaking of dance, Chennai has taken to the dandiya in recent years and this becomes the rage especially during Navaratri and Deepavali which are observed in the months of September and October. It is in a way a reflection of the increasingly cosmopolitan nature of the city. But deep in the lanes of George Town, dandiya is serious business. Come Navaratri, Gujaratis from all over the city congregate there on each of the nine nights. Under gorgeously decorated pandals, the goddess is enshrined and after prayers have been offered, the community begins dancing, continuing till the wee hours of the morning. Rather surprisingly, the city is fast forgetting its traditional group dance forms—the kummi and kolattam—the latter, in particular, being the Tamil equivalent of the dandiya, complete with the usage of short sticks. Card parties during Deepavali have also, of late, become the craze, introduced largely by the Gujaratis and Marwaris who have settled here. This has, in a way, brought about a difference to the way Deepavali was traditionally celebrated in the city. Unlike the rest of India, this is an early morning festival here, with the Brahmin community, in particular, having an oil bath—applying oil all over the body and washing it off with shikakai (powdered *Senegalia rugata* bark), which is a natural exfoliant. New clothes are worn before sunrise and crackers are burst immediately thereafter. Sweets and savouries are served and along with it what is known as lehyam—a paste-like herbal preparation that tastes like flavoured mud—which serves as an aid to digestion. Lighting of lamps along housetops was never part of Chennai tradition and has only made its appearance in recent times. That happens during a uniquely Tamil festival in November known as Karthikai, associated with the temple at Thiruvannamalai, where Lord Shiva is worshipped as fire.

Festivals like Deepavali are important in Chennai, as is Navaratri, when households put up displays of clay dolls, collectively referred to as kolu—a Tamil and Telugu word that means pageant. It was customary for women to go from house to house, sing songs before the kolu and receive sundal (a lentil preparation), sweets, betel leaves, and areca nuts. Of late, these have become huge social occasions, replete with expensive invitation cards and hosts throwing in lavish high teas, which are nearly dinners. A surfeit of sundal can cause gastric problems, and it makes you wonder as to why the Deepavali lehyam is not distributed during Navaratri as well. The dolls on display too have become bigger and often tasteless. Some families have treasured old clay dolls, graceful in features and colour schemes. Very few also have Gowri dolls—wooden ones with moveable hands and legs that can be arranged in various postures. But by and large, aesthetic kolus are things of the past. Thematic kolus however are an interesting feature where the entire display is based on a central idea.

Apart from the feasting and socializing, Navaratri, Ram Navami, and Janmashtami was the time for much music before the December extravaganza upstaged them. Performances are hosted even now, at this time, in temples, sabhas, and most importantly at the Ramakrishna Mission, Mylapore. What started off as a fund raiser for the boys' home has endured.[8] Inmates attend the festival along with music lovers. Navaratri is also the time when all the shrines dedicated to the goddess in her various forms will have special worship, the processional icon being decorated lavishly on each of the nine nights and kept on display on various mounts. Makeshift stalls selling clay dolls come up around some of the more popular temples such as in Mylapore, with shoppers thronging the streets. Basement bargains are struck on the day

[8] *A Palace for the Poor, Centenary Commemoration Volume, 1905-2005*, Ramakrishna Mission Students' Home, pp. 121–27.

after Navaratri when the vendors begin leaving. These dolls, purchased at throwaway prices, are kept in store for the next year's Navaratri. Clay doll shopping also happens in more refined surroundings at places such as the government-run Kuralagam on the Esplanade, the Khadi Gramodyog Bhavan, and the Victoria Technical Institute, both on Anna Salai.

The ninth and tenth days of the Navaratri are celebrated differently in Tamil Nadu. The former is observed as Ayudha Puja, when all implements of trade are worshipped. Machinery in factories, vehicles at commercial establishments and homes, computers in IT companies, for instance, will be given the day off, cleaned thoroughly and worshipped with flowers, the application of sandal paste and kumkum, and the waving of camphor flames. This is also Saraswathi Puja, when the Goddess of Learning is worshipped—books, geometry boxes, musical instruments, pens, erasers, scales and just about everything else will be taken to the puja room, formally arranged and prayed to. The next day, Vijaya Dashami, all the books will be taken out once again. Factories and places of work will hum with activity—unlike the rest of India, the tenth day of Navaratri is not a holiday here; indeed, it is considered auspicious to work on this day and begin new projects. Young children take their first steps in learning on Vijaya Dashami and this is also the day when a round is made of all gurus, which in Chennai can be considerable, for the average child here, apart from going to school, will attend a couple of tuition classes for academic subjects, learn classical music or dance, take coaching lessons in swimming and some other sports. All these teachers are necessarily called upon on Dashami day, propitiated with gifts, and their blessings taken. While most such relationships drop off as the student grows older, calling on the music teacher alone remains a lifelong commitment. Students who have long stopped learning music will still make that annual visit to the guru's residence to receive blessings.

Soon it is time for December (Margazhi in Tamil), the sacred period for Vishnu and Shiva, when the deities are propitiated with music. Once again, no transactions or weddings take place but there is no Margazhi discount festival to revive retail sales. A very beautiful aspect of Margazhi, lost in the glamour of the music festival, is the concept of bhajan groups setting out early in the morning and going around temples singing songs. The shrines at Mylapore and Thiruvallikeni, in particular, see many such groups during this month. The composer Papanasam Sivan was a fixture in the Mylapore bhajan sessions between 1931 and 1972. His daughter Rukmini Ramani and grandson Ashok Ramani now continue the tradition.

To the above set of festivals you need to add Easter, Christmas, Bakrid,

Eid-e-Milad-Un-Nabi and other such events to get a very interesting mosaic.

If the above descriptions make Chennai appear a hyper-religious city, it is no exaggeration. One of the most visible elements of the metropolis is its profusion of religious edifices—temples and churches being the maximum, followed by a lesser number of mosques, a gurudwara, and a Parsi fire temple thrown in for good measure. It is customary to build small niches for Ganesha, the remover of obstacles, especially at the intersection of three streets whereby the temple becomes one of the many hurdles for the pedestrian. Of late, we have similar shrines to Christian saints as well. What begins mostly as a tiled image of the deity to prevent urination on the wall soon morphs into an idol in an alcove, which gradually enlarges to become a temple. With so many shrines and deities, it is no wonder that Chennai is, forever, in a frenzy of worship.

All of this is observed despite the fact that political parties with strong roots in atheism have dominated Chennai for years. Sometimes it would appear that the people view political ideology as completely different from religious affinities. Even politicians appear to think that way. Many, such as MGR and Jayalalithaa, were openly religious. As for the DMK, opinion is sharply divided. While the patriarch, Karunanidhi, and his children have claimed to be atheists, it is a well-known fact that other family members are intensely religious. Detractors have it that even the avowed rationalism of the leaders is but a sham. Certainly, nobody has been able to explain as to why Karunanidhi suddenly switched to donning yellow shawls, abandoning the DMK's regulation black. Most ironically, Chennai is the city where you will find the maximum number of statues for the social reformer Periyar. And under most of these, the first inscription on the pedestal is 'Those who believe in God are fools.' Just a few metres away from his statue near the Government Estate is Bodyguard Muniswarar Temple. This was once a small shrine set up by the Hindu sepoys in the governor's bodyguard when the official residence was Government Estate. A Governor's Bodyguard mosque nearby was meant for the Muslim sepoys. With the governor moving to Guindy after 1947 and the concept of an exclusive bodyguard becoming redundant, both temple and mosque became open to public worship. Somewhere along the line, Bodyguard Muniswaran became a deity who, by virtue of his name, protects people from accidents involving vehicles. It has, therefore, become customary for people to bring newly purchased buses, trucks, cars, scooters, and motorcycles to this shrine and perform elaborate pujas. On full moon and new moon nights, the massive crowds that gather here can block off all access to the Central Station. You often wonder as to what Periyar would have made of it all.

The arrival, stay, and departure of various religious heads—be they the ochre-wearing orthodox or the English-spouting modern holy men and women—will see hundreds lining up for darshan. And then, occasionally, the gods too have some fun at Chennai's expense. It was in the early 1970s that a Ganesha idol suddenly manifested itself on an empty plot of land in T. Nagar. It soon became a sensation. Thideer (Sudden) Pillaiyar (Ganesha) was deemed a miracle. Thousands came to see the icon which was immediately declared to be a million years old. Even as the police mustered force to ensure that people lined up in an orderly fashion, the higher echelons of the government were racked with worry. Police Commissioner Vaikunth was asked to investigate. 'It transpired that the land, which abutted the T. Nagar police station, was allotted for a mosque,' he smiles in recollection. 'This was not to the liking of die-hard Hindus and the Ganesha was planted, by of all people, a constable in the same police station. The idol was removed in the dark of night and the policeman suspended.' But the elephant-headed God was back in the news, this time in all temples dedicated to him, when on 21 September 1995, Chennai, along with the rest of India, believed that the idols were drinking the milk that was offered to them.

As to how gullible the city can be when it comes to matters of religion was demonstrated in the 1990s by the magazine *Ananda Vikatan*. A crudely sculpted statue of a deity was buried at midnight on the beach and the next evening, as walkers and sightseers thronged the place, a woman, in reality an employee of *Vikatan*, went into a trance and, pointing to a spot, said that a goddess was lying buried there. Within a short while a vast crowd had assembled to watch the impromptu excavation. There was a gasp when the idol surfaced. A priest materialized out of nowhere and worship began, the lady who had identified the spot now seated alongside the icon, with people falling at her feet for blessings. By nightfall, the goddess, named Pacchamman, had a makeshift temple as well. It took the *Vikatan* team quite some effort the next day to explain that it had all been a prank.[9] At the same beach, a different kind of religious meet drew thousands for several years. These were by evangelists at the Seerani Arangam, an open-air stage that had once been built for entertaining the public. It was said that Annadurai was the one who conceptualized it for getting cadres to become socially responsible. However, frenzied preaching with simultaneous translation and the sudden occurrence of miracles were the features here with most Sunday evenings being given

[9] *Vikatan Pavazha Vizha Malar: 1926-2002*, Chennai: Vikatan Publications, pp. 60–62.

over to such sessions. That was until 2003 when at the behest of then Chief Minister Jayalalithaa, the structure was demolished overnight.[10]

Religion is the great social leveller in Chennai, no matter how hard Periyar tried to make us understand rationalism. This is the one activity where you will find the billionaire and his wife walking barefoot along with commoners, offering gruel at the local Mariamman Temple. It can also be the great divider, for Chennai, despite being a haven of peace across religions, is greatly stressed within each one. Thus you have the maximum number of castes and sub-castes, almost all of them desirous of declaring themselves backward, within the Hindu community. The Muslims do not fare much better, there being sharp divides between the Sunni and the Shia communities and more so between the Tamil and Navayati Muslims, who pride themselves on their Persian origin and, hence, consider themselves superior. Christianity too is not immune, populated as it is largely with converts from Hinduism. They carry their castes en masse into the new religion and so churches come up in the city accordingly. Even within churches, there are gradations based on caste.

But, by far the great divider, sharply segregating the haves from the have-nots is club membership. There are several examples of this purely British creation dotting the city. Many such as the Boat Club, the Race Club, the Gymkhana Club, and the Cricket Club came up to provide sports and recreational facilities to their European members and remained exclusively white long after Independence, opening themselves to Indians only when survival became a question. At the top of this list is the Madras Club, the second oldest such facility in the country, founded in 1832.[11]

By the early twentieth century, Indians too had begun founding clubs of their own. The Cosmopolitan Club established in 1873 was perhaps the first of this kind, where both Britishers and Indians could become members.[12] The Madras United Club founded by Buchi Babu in 1888 was the first exclusive sports club for Indians in the city.[13] In those days, there were two powerful cliques in the High Court of Madras, the Egmore lobby dominated by non-Brahmins (and a few Iyengars, including the founder of *The Hindu*) and one

[10]Arun Ram, 'Tamil Nadu Government knocks down Seerani Arangam', *India Today*, 25 August 2003.

[11]*The Madras Club*, pp. 8–9.

[12]V. Sriram, 'The Cosmopolitan Club—a brief history', *Madras Heritage and Carnatic Music*, 2019.

[13]Raja and Suri, *Buchi Babu*, p. 54.

at Mylapore comprising Brahmins, chiefly Iyers. The former, dominating at the Cosmopolitan, kept the latter out of the club, which led to disgruntled elements such as V. Krishnaswami Iyer, Sir C. P. Ramaswami Iyer, and others to found a rival club in their stronghold. However, the Mylapore Club, begun in 1905, never managed to attain the social elevation that the other did, despite its illustrious founders.[14] By the banks of the Adyar is yet another such institution—the Alumni (aluminium in local parlance) Club, meant for graduates of the Anna University.

Almost all the city clubs have long waiting lists, not so much for the facilities they offer, which are considerable and at a fraction of what they would cost at hotels, but for the social prestige that such membership bestows. Getting in is not easy at all, and much depends on the condescension and grace of a committee member or two. Blackballing is rife and those who can, derive considerable pleasure in exercising their powers. The rules of admission are often cloaked in nearly Masonic secrecy and can be changed at will, depending on the exigencies of the moment. Getting in is not the end of the story, for the member passes through various stages of elevation, the first being long-term temporary, followed by invitation and then finally, full membership with voting rights. The first two stages can be extended forever, at the pleasure of the executive committee. Sometimes, when the club needs money, which is fairly often, these waiting periods can be shortened, leading to several people getting membership, the old and diehard members immediately bemoaning the quality of new entrants and lamenting the collapse of society as they knew it. The world of clubs has sometimes benefited by these discriminatory practices. Thus four rundown clubs in the city received a fresh lease of life when a membership war erupted between two rival Chettiars who were formerly brothers-in-law. Thwarted from becoming a member at the Madras Club, the rebuffed man swore to uplift four other clubs and make them equal in stature to the one he could not get into. That did not happen, but the four became prosperous social institutions.

Most of the clubs have dress codes that go back to the heydays of the Raj. Shirts with collars (for some reason, Chinese collars are frowned upon) and shoes are de rigueur for men, while women are let off lightly, being asked to be 'decorously attired'. The Madras Club is perhaps the most finicky of the lot, with different dress regulations depending upon the time of the day and the part of the vast property the member happens to be in. But

---

[14]Chandrashekaran, *Krishnaswami Iyer*, p. 56.

dress regulations are strictly not legal, as the clubs of Chennai discovered much to their chagrin. They had in the past made it to the news for refusing entry to a VIP or two for not being dressed as per their rules but, when in 2014, a sitting judge of the High Court of Madras was asked to leave the Tamil Nadu Cricket Association Club (TNCA) for being dressed in a veshti, the government took notice. There was uproar in the assembly and Chief Minister Jayalalithaa decried what she termed the tendency of the TNCA towards 'sartorial despotism'. It did not help that Amma was not fond of the TNCA's big boss, N. Srinivasan, who was known to be close to the rival DMK. The assembly, largely at her prodding, enacted a law immediately to the effect that national dress, including the veshti, had to be allowed in all places.[15] The clubs of the city were disappointed but they have, however, managed to keep informal restrictions in place.

Another ticking bomb for most clubs is the ownership of the large tracts of land they occupy. Barring a few such as the Madras Club and the Cosmopolitan Club, most occupy leasehold properties in the possession of the government and the latter extracts its pound of flesh each time the agreement comes up for renewal. Old and long forgotten cases can be resurrected, violations are suddenly discovered, and huge penalties imposed. These are all par for the course for the clubs and they somehow survive. But some have suffered—the MUC for instance lost a large chunk of its cricket grounds, which had done much to foster the love of the game among Indians, to the Broadway bus terminus. The Madras Race Club routinely gives up land for various public projects and the Mylapore Club, on lease from the Kapaliswarar Temple, has seen parts of its grounds being taken away. The Madras Cricket Club remains forever on edge over its lease renewal as does the Madras Golf Club in Nandanam. The Gymkhana Club operates at the mercy of the army.

The old British clubs, however, remained male bastions for long and it is only in recent years that some have allowed women to become members in their own right. Women began forming their own equivalents, the first being the Ladies Recreation Club founded in 1911 with both European and Indian members. It was here that many Madras women, clad in six- and nine-yard sarees, learnt to play tennis. The first lady of the presidency was the patron and in the 1920s it greatly helped that the incumbent was the redoubtable Lady Willingdon, who participated in all the club activities, bringing her high energy levels to every event. It was she, who through

[15]'India's Tamil Nadu state rules on club dress code use', *BBC News*, 12 August 2014.

a donation from Raja Sir Annamalai Chettiar, managed to get the club a vast property in Egmore, its ownership vested in a trust named after Lord Willingdon. The club flourished till the 1980s, when the temptation of real estate development came on the controlling body. The huge compound with its tennis courts were turned into high-rise buildings and the club reduced to a card-playing facility occupying two measly rooms. Elsewhere in the city, women formed clubs of their own, those in Nungambakkam and Mylapore making way for the Padma Seshadri and Vidya Mandir schools. The Anna Nagar Ladies Club still flourishes, located at one corner of Tower Park, in the Thai Pavilion, so named for it was home to exhibits from Thailand during the World Trade Fair held in 1968.

It is indeed ironic that a women's club should be located in a building commemorating Thailand, a country where the sex industry is a significant contributor to the GDP. Perhaps that irony is lost on Chennai, a city that chooses to sweep sex under the carpet. But it cannot be overlooked and sex as entertainment has had a long and significant presence in the city. Polygamy and the practice of maintaining several households by rich men was an accepted and, indeed, expected attribute. The richer the man, the more the number of wives and mistresses was the maxim. The nineteenth-century *Sarva Deva Vilasa* lists three famed courtesans of the city—Nachiyar, Manga, and Veera, each in the retinue of a famed dubash.[16] *Natakadi Vidyala*, the longest song in Carnatic music and the work of Ramaswami Dikshitar, speaks, among other things, of the love that women in his retinue had for Manali Venkatakrishna Mudali, a dubash of the EIC.[17]

The English were quick to get with this custom and in the early years of Fort St George, in particular, when it was largely a bachelor establishment, maintained several Portuguese mistresses. The founder, Francis Day, it was said, maintained a woman in San Thome, who he passed on to Henry Greenhill, one of his juniors. Elihu Yale was notorious in this regard, maintaining apart from his legal wife, Catherine, two other women—Catherine Nicks, who was nominally wedded to his best friend, and Heironima de Paiva, the widow of a rich Jewish merchant of the city. Post-Independence Madras has had its share of colourful leaders who openly lived with two wives and had children from both. The second establishment even has an accepted code word in Madras-speak—chinna veedu or small house. The film industry of Chennai, which provided the political world with its leaders, had any number of

[16]Raghavan, *Sarva Deva Vilasa*, p. 49.

[17]I thank T. R. Aravindh for this.

these small houses—heroes, directors, producers, lyricists, and writers having a tendency to marry starlets. The tendency of the heroines of Tamil cinema, many of them fiercely independent in their careers, to settle down as second wives, is a never-ending source of amazement. Was it a quest for social or financial security?

Prostitution has always been a thriving business in the city, though unlike Kolkata or Mumbai, it has rarely been concentrated in any one district. Till early in the twentieth century, Vodacaul Street in George Town, near the harbour, was the red-light area, but it has long since faded away.[18] Its heart, an old market called Chengam Bazaar has, however, given rise to a term—Chengam sarakku (material)—which is a euphemism for a harlot. Chengam itself is a village off the temple town of Tiruvannamalai and its association with the flesh trade in the city is not clear. Thereafter, with the rise of Kodambakkam as a film hub, the lodges around it were in demand. The film and sex industry nexus has however continued unbroken. The arrest in 2009 of Bhuvaneswari, a small-time actress, for prostitution, would have hardly made the news had it not been for her statement that several others, far bigger in stature, were part of the same trade. The scandal sheet *Nakkeeran* carried this news on its front pages. The next day, several of those named descended on the police commissioner's office and demanded action against the offending magazine. *Dinamalar*, another popular publication, did get into trouble for publishing the names of the others she had alleged were in the same business.[19] In 2018, the arrest of TV actor Sangeetha Balan on the same charges, however, only goes to reinforce the fact that sex is a fact of life in Chennai as it is elsewhere.[20]

During the 1980s, Malayalam films with lurid titles were all the rage in Chennai and the actress Seema of *Her Nights* fame became a star. Film festivals that took place regularly in the city were also much in demand chiefly for their Western titles that promised a dose of titillation. Chennai has since moved to the internet for its delights. The city reportedly ranks second in India in its viewership of online pornography, though its 6 per cent of the country's viewership is a small fraction when compared to Delhi's whopping 40 per cent.[21] Another indicator of the city's sleazier side is the number of

---

[18]V. Sriram, 'Some X-rated heritage', *The Hindu*, 24 July 2015.

[19]'Tamil daily editor held for defaming actors', *India Today*, 8 October 2009.

[20]'Tamil actor Sangeetha arrested for allegedly running prostitution racket: Reports', *Scroll.in*, 3 June 2018.

[21]Syed Mohammed, 'Delhi tops in porn viewership', *Times of India*, 7 April 2016.

SMSs the average cell-phone subscriber gets, with invitations to try massage parlours (four-hand wine massage, with two trained women therapists) and escort services (fun with high class female in direct meeting offer. No fake, no chepness (sic), 100 per cent safe and earn).

In short, there is something for everyone in the city.

17 | STAGE LIGHTS

Any observer of the Indian political scene will vouch for the fact that Tamil Nadu is different. It has a tendency to oscillate between the two Dravidian parties, ignoring the claims of any entity from the north. Those outfits, if they do have any ambitions in the state, need to tie up with one or the other of the two big parties here and hope that whichever one they are piggybacking on is the one the electorate has decided to favour in that election. It can be a demeaning experience for any national leader, used to waves in his/her favour and being idolized elsewhere. There is an added factor in Tamil Nadu—a stint in cinema helps enormously in political careers here, such being the hold of the medium over the masses. Most Tamil politicians have had some connection or the other with the film industry at least from the 1950s. And then, finally, there is the matter of pride in the Tamil language—rightfully so, for this is an ancient language with a rich corpus of work in music, literature, poetry, and theatre. A strong identification with the language has also been one reason why no national party has been able to strike roots here. This and the following chapters look at all these aspects.

Much before cinema, however, was theatre. Now essentially a forgotten category of entertainment, its apogee was in the late nineteenth and early twentieth centuries. It flourished in particular around the labour-dominated areas of North Chennai with many famed locations being nothing more than tented facilities where audiences, often running to several hundreds, could watch plays. Theatre, though a popular mode of entertainment, was considered terribly lowbrow, at least till the late nineteenth century. As film historian Randor Guy writes, 'A play began at 9 pm and went on till almost dawn. The average theatre-goer preferred quantity to quality! [The] professional troupes had both male and female artistes generally drawn from the lower strata of society. Such men and women created their own world of licentious living—and loving—and took to drinking and debauchery without any thought of the morrow. Often, artistes of both sexes were drunk on stage and indulged in bits of business and acting not in the script. Vulgarity on stage was indulged in freely, often with the raucous encouragement of the audience. Lyrics were deliberately given a daub of obscenity, under the guise of making people laugh.'[1]

[1]Randor Guy, *Starlight Starbright: The Early Tamil Cinema*, Chennai: Amra Publishers, 1997, p. 2.

Two great reformers appeared on the scene in the 1880s. The first of these was Pammal Sambanda Mudaliar, who came from an aristocratic Madras family and looked down on all forms of theatre. But this perception was corrected when he witnessed a play performed by a Kannada troupe. Their professionalism made such an impression on him that he and seven other friends of his, all university graduates, formed an organization to present Tamil theatre very much in the Western style. This was the Suguna Vilasa Sabha (SVS), founded in 1891. The initial years saw plays largely lifted from Shakespeare; later several of Mudaliar's creations were staged and SVS introduced many changes. It brought in evening and matinee shows, with all-night performances becoming a thing of the past. Taking a leaf from Parsi theatre, which was noted for perfection in stage management and moving of props, SVS brought in the same, introducing two intermissions, then a novelty. Tamil audiences were unused to tragedies in the Shakespearian sense and yet, SVS boldly staged them. In time, the sabha was so successful that its membership was bursting at the seams with lawyers, judges, government officers, and aristocrats. Its abode and staging venue was the Victoria Public Hall, the Gothic creation of R. F. Chisholm. This was where it held its fancy dress competitions, its famed Navaratri display, and its charity fundraisers. By the 1930s, SVS had become prosperous enough to buy property of its own, on Mount Road. Rather ironically, this coincided with the decline of theatre and the rise of cinema and with that the sabha became a social club, its office bearers still using designations such as director, prompter, etc.[2]

SVS was an all-male entity, with men performing the roles of women, dressing to the nines in brocade sarees and jewellery especially during Navaratri, when they handed out the auspicious betel leaves and flowers to women guests.[3] The sabha felt it could keep out licentious behaviour in theatre by keeping the troupes all-male. Of the same view was Sankaradas Swamigal, who came from the opposite end of the theatrical world—that of the itinerant drama troupes comprising poverty-ridden actors. Swamigal, this prefix being an honorific that the theatre world gave him in gratitude, came onto the stage in 1891 as an actor. His plays soon became very popular, staged under licence by various troupes. With a view to reforming theatre, he hit upon the concept of 'Boys Companies'—troupes comprising pre-pubescent boys who would be moulded into fine actors by him. His Bala Meena Ranjani

[2]Pammal Sambanda Mudaliar, *Nataka Medai Ninaivukal*, International Institute of Tamil Studies, Chennai, 1998.
[3]Ibid.

Sangeetha Sabha was the first of this kind. Unlike SVS, which frowned on music, Swamigal's plays were full of songs, he being a fine composer and lyricist.[4] The arrival of the pedal harmonium and the perfecting of the violin and clarinet for South Indian music allowed plenty of scope. The boys were trained in various nuances of acting and the plays became greatly successful.

Boys Companies became the norm thereafter. But there were problems that Swamigal had not foreseen. Guy gives us a glimpse of what went on behind the scenes:

> At least ninety per cent of the boy actors had run away from their homes due to grinding poverty or ill-treatment by drunken fathers or selfish stepmothers. These were exploited to the hilt by troupe-owners and their managers, many of whom were sadists. Sexual exploitation was also rampant. Letters from home and the boys' letters were severely censored and often destroyed by the bosses. If a letter contained any complaints against the bosses, the boy was beaten black and blue and starved for days. Some were even branded with hot irons. When parents came to meet their sons, the meetings were held with a barred window separating them and a man standing guard and overhearing every word and whisper. It was frankly a case of child labour and exploitation in the name of art.[5]

Other memoirs, such as those of Avvai Shanmugam and film actor and director S. V. Sahasranamam, highlight other problems—the embezzlement of profits by theatre owners and managers, boys being habituated to alcohol at an early age, and the trauma of adolescence when voices broke and the boys were no longer right for the parts.[6]

Besides these, if the memoirs of the likes of Dr K. N. Kesari and 'Tiger' Varadachariar are to be believed, the streets of the city were at one time alive with theatrical entertainments. They list a bewildering variety such as Veethi Natakam, Koochipudi Bhagavata Street Drama, and Chenchu Natakam.[7] These forms of street theatre were considered lowbrow by many but Varadachariar appreciated the quality of music presented in them.

In any case, the Boys Companies defined theatrical entertainment and

---

[4]Guy, *Starlight Starbright,* pp. 2–4.

[5]Ibid., p. 5.

[6]Shanmugam, he tells of many such episodes in this book.

[7]See Dr K. N. Kesari, pp. 134-6 and also *Tiger Varadachariar Birth Centenary Commemoration Volume,* The Tiger Varachariar Birth Centenary Celebration Committee, Madras, 1977, p. 33.

the late 1800s were their heyday. One of the troupes based out of Madras was that of C. Cunniah, who staged several plays very successfully in the city. In the early 1900s, a new concept emerged—that of theatre stars who would contract themselves to various troupes. The scripts of Swamigal and Mudaliar being standard works, it became easy for freelance stars to fit into any troupe and play the central role.[8] At this time, women also started finding their feet in theatre, the undoubted pioneer being Kumbakonam Balamani Ammal, who ran an all-woman troupe that was best known for its erotic play, *Tara Sasankam*, concerning the moon god's seduction of his preceptor's wife, Tara. The highlight of the play was Tara giving Sasanka an oil massage and even though it was two women who performed the role, hundreds thronged to witness it,[9] leading to the railways running what were known as Balamani Specials to facilitate fan movement. Within a few years, more stars were born—'Golden' Saradambal, S. D. Subbulakshmi, and K. B. Sundarambal. The last was a bold personality who overcame financial privations to reach the top quickly and run an all-woman troupe as well. There were many male equivalents but there was one superstar and that was S. G. Kittappa—actor and master singer who, had he not succumbed to alcoholism in 1931, would have gone on to become a great film star.[10]

'The origins of cinema's involvement in Tamil politics goes back to the days of theatre, in particular the time of KB Sundarambal and SG Kittappa,' says actor Mohan Raman, who in the past decade, has emerged as a serious analyst of Tamil cinema. 'Their combined star value did not go unnoticed by S. Satyamurti—lawyer, theatre enthusiast (he was a member of SVS), fine speaker, and Congress activist. He soon hit upon the idea of getting them to attend public meetings, as a means to attract crowds. The duo deeply venerated him and enthusiastically agreed. They took to wearing khadi offstage and Sundarambal in particular began recording patriotic songs. There are gramophone discs where there is a song by Sundarambal on one side and a speech by Satyamurti on the other.'[11]

Publicity posters announcing Congress party meetings at places such as Marina beach, for instance, made mention of Kittappa and Sundarambal

[8]Guy, *Starlight Starbright*, p. 94.

[9]Veejay Sai, *Drama Queens, Women Who Created History on Stage*, New Delhi: Roli Books, 2017, pp. 22–37.

[10]Pa Chozhanadan, *Kodumudi Kokilam K. B. Sundarambal Varalaru*, Chennai: Rishabham Pathippakam, 2002, p. 42.

[11]Interview with the author, Chennai, 14 February 2020.

being in attendance. Large crowds came to listen to their favourite stars sing patriotic songs and stage numbers as a prelude to the meeting proper. On certain occasions, the duo went out among the assembled throng, selling khadi cloth. Kittappa's fountain pen was auctioned once, fetching a handsome sum for the Congress.

Music being an important component of the plays, it became necessary to introduce new songs to infuse variety into what were otherwise standard scripts. It was here that songwriters such as Madhurakavi Bhaskara Das became vital. A resident of Madurai and its environs, he maintained a diary for most of his life and these give a clear idea on how the world of theatre functioned in Madras and the rest of the Presidency in the early twentieth century.[12]

The success of the plays led to the actors/singers being sought by gramophone recording companies for release of discs comprising popular songs as well as sections of dialogue. The comic songs of 'Buffoon' Shanmugam became the rage. The recording facilities existed mainly in Madras and this is where most of the artistes had to come, from Madurai, which was then the heartland of theatre. Most of them were drafted into the Congress as part of its propaganda machinery.

Most Tamil plays continued to be staged at open-air venues that had tents erected for the shows. The Empress, the Grand, and the Royal, for all their high-sounding names were all tent theatres. Even the famed Parsi theatre of Balliwala and Company, which had such an impact on its Tamil counterpart, performed in the open in front of the Madras High Court. That the situation had not changed by 1929 is evident from the Mylai Sangeetha Sabha refusing to countenance the staging of plays or allowing nagaswaram performances at the Vanniyar Sangam School premises from where it functioned. That resulted in a split and the formation of the Rasika Ranjani Sabha in neighbouring Sundareswarar Street, complete with stage, proscenium arch, and chairs for the audience.[13] In the meanwhile, the Wall Tax Theatre on the eponymous road had emerged as the location of choice. The road had got its name from the fact that a protective wall for the city of Madras had originally been proposed, to be funded by a tax. The citizenry had protested but old Black Town did finally get a wall, which by the twentieth century remained in bits and pieces along Wall Tax Road. This meant that no houses could be

[12]Cha Murugabhupathi, *Madhurakavi Bhaskaradasin Natkurippukal*, Bharathi Putthakalayam, Chennai: Bharathi Putthakalayam, 2009.

[13]See V. Sriram, 'Remembering the Sabha Part 1', *Madras Heritage and Carnatic Music*, 16 January 2014.

built along the side on which the protective wall ran and so the road was named Otrai Vadai (one-sided). The theatre too came to be known as the Otrai Vadai.[14]

The Wall Tax Theatre is long gone and even its location cannot be traced. And yet it was here that much of Tamil theatre history was written. The place was a favourite for talent scouts, among them film producers and directors. It was said that the movie offers for stage stars such as M. K. Thyagaraja Bhagavathar, S. D. Subbulakshmi, and T. P. Rajalakshmi, South India's first woman actor, producer, and director, were made here after their stellar performances on stage. The Wall Tax Theatre was also in many ways a crucible of the Dravidian movement and, in the 1960s, even hosted conferences of various such parties. It had its bit of sinister theatre history too.[15] This was where, it was alleged, Thyagaraja Bhagavathar and N. S. Krishnan (NSK) plotted the murder of Lakshmikanthan, a muckraker who ran the scandal sheets *Indunesan* and *Cinema Thoothu*.[16] The deed was done by hirelings one dark evening in November 1944 at the double bend on General Collins Road, Vepery. Lakshmikanthan died of the wounds within a couple of days and on the basis of some detailed investigations, the police arrested Bhagavathar and NSK, then Tamil cinema's leading hero and comedian respectively, and others. The trial dragged on for three years before the Privy Council in London acquitted all the accused.[17] Once released, life was never the same for Bhagavathar or NSK. Unlike the former who saw a sharp decline in fortunes, the latter worked in many films post release, invariably paired with his talented wife T. A. Mathuram. He even sang a song in one of his movies on the joys of prison life. While he was incarcerated, his wife, along with associate S. V. Sahasranamam had kept the home fires burning by staging plays. These also enabled the collection of funds for NSK's appeal at the Privy Council.[18]

NSK's plays focused on social reform, before and after his tryst with prison. He espoused several causes including widow remarriage, the doing away of blind beliefs, and the evils of alcohol (of which he was ironically

---

[14]Guy, *Starlight Starbright*, p. 6.

[15]K. A. Natarajan, *Dravida Manava Munnetra Kazhakam Podu Manadu*, Chennai: Dravidian Students Progressive Federation, 1970, p. 24.

[16]See *M. K. Thiagarajan vs Unknown*, available here: https://indiankanoon.org/doc/244689/.

[17]Guy, *Starlight Starbright*, p. 102.

[18]S. V. Sahasranamam, *Thirumbi Parkiren*, Chennai, 2012: SVS Centenary Committee, pp. 153–61.

an addict). Others troupes too began toeing the same line, and plays with social reform as the central theme began to gain ground. Several actors wore only khadi offstage and began to incorporate messages of social relevance such as abstinence from alcohol, avoiding of gambling, respect for women, and eventually Indian independence as well. The scripts that had, till then, largely focused on religious topics and stories involving kings and queens in mythical kingdoms gave way to plays set in the contemporary social context. The government, which had so far ignored Tamil theatre, began to take notice. The Dramatic Performances Act of 1876 became a convenient tool for gagging any performance that was considered unsuitable. It became mandatory for the script of a play to be submitted to the commissioner of police, Madras, three weeks before its staging and obtain permission. This was withheld or granted at the last minute, leading to great stress in what was already a profession fraught with tension. Theatre companies, which needed to publicize their plays by means of considerable handbills, posters, and announcements using drums and megaphones borne on bullock carts on the day of the premiere, incurred expenses without knowing if their play would be allowed at all. Thus, in 1922, when permission to stage T. P. Krishnaswamy Pavalar's play *Khaddarin Vetri* (Khaddar's Victory) was denied, the author had to use his contacts to meet Governor Lord Willingdon and obtain sanction just a few hours before the curtain went up.[19]

There was close networking among the various drama troupes then and news of withholding permission for a play by a troupe would invariably lead to another applying for the same, under a different title. Thus, when in 1931, the government banned the staging of *Banapurathuviran*, the Madurai Sri Bala Shanmukhananda Sabha run by the TKS brothers (comprising Sankaran, Muthuswami, Shanmugam, and Bhagavati) decided to present it under the name of *Desa Bhakti*. The play, though set in mythical times, incorporated a song in praise of Gandhi. This being around the time Bhagat Singh, Sukhdev, and Rajguru had been hanged, it included verses on them as well. Permission was somehow obtained but it was customary for police informers to attend the staging and a complaint was registered that the play was seditious and it was banned. This naturally got the Congress party interested and Kamaraj, then a rising leader, made it a point to meet the troupe and encourage them to keep going. The next production was *Gomasthavin Penn*, (the Clerk's Daughter) which focused on the travails of women. Given such a focus on society's problems, it was no wonder that the TKS brothers' troupe also came

[19]Guy, 'He took Khadi to Wembley', *Madras Musings*, Vol. XVIII, No. 18, 1-15 January 2009.

to be known as the Reformist Drama Company. But T. K. S Shanmugam was best known for his portrayal of Avvaiyar, the legendary Tamil poetess.

The motto of their company, significantly, was 'Workers of the World, Unite!' The brothers took reform of the theatre very seriously. Shanmugam was the founder of, perhaps, the only Tamil tabloid exclusively meant for the theatre fraternity. *Arivucchudar* (Illuminating the Brain) had stories, articles, political news, snippets, explanations of the *Tirukkural*, and letters to the editor. The tabloid didn't last very long. Shanmugam, undaunted by its failure and distressed at the high levels of ignorance in his fraternity, founded Arivu Abhivrutti Sangam, a club in Madurai where artistes could read magazines, be taught languages, and listen to speeches by several leaders.

C. N. Annadurai saw the *Clerk's Daughter* and wrote a glowing tribute to the script and the quality of the production, apart from dwelling on how it held up a mirror to society. That marked the beginning of Anna's involvement with the theatre folk, a relationship that his party, the DMK, would utilize to the hilt to gain office several years later.[20]

The trend set by social dramas of the 1930s would continue through the 1940s. Music in theatre too began to fade away with the focus being completely on word play and dialogue. At the same time, it is quite interesting to see how eclectic the audience and artistes' tastes were. Those who knew no language other than Tamil flocked to see Kannada plays staged by troupes from Bellary. Parsi Theatre, with plays in Persian or Arabic settings and featuring Urdu songs were also popular and setting Tamil songs to Parsi tunes led to a new genre known as Parsi music.[21] Madras also appears to have had its favourite Parsi theatre troupe—the Victoria Company.[22]

Anna turned playwright at this time, his first work *Chandrodayam* (Moonrise), a social satire on religious establishments written as a fundraiser for his party's weekly, *Dravida Nadu*. Several more plays followed—*Velaikkari* (The Maidservant), *Or Iravu* (One Night), *Kadal Jothi* (The Flame of Love), and *Sorgavasal* (Gateway to Heaven). These attacked a variety of problems—feudalism, the condition of widows, hypocrisy, and caste. Anna even wrote a play lampooning the practice of marrying off young women to far older men. *Paavayin Payanam* (The Maiden's Journey), when staged, was understood to be veiled criticism of his mentor, Periyar E.V. Ramaswami Naicker, marrying

[20]Shanmugam, *Enathu Naadaga Vaazhlkai*, p. 330.

[21]P. S. Ramulu Chetti, *Gandharva Kalpavalli*, Nabu Press, pp. 121–48.

[22]Kathryn Hansen, 'Tamil Drama in Colonial Madras: the Parsi Theatre Connection', *South Asian History and Culture*, 2020, doi: 10.1080/19472498.2020.1816414.

Maniyammai, a woman far younger than him. It is most unlikely that Periyar, who considered cinema, plays, devotional concerts, and music records to be far worse than 'toddy shops, harlot, prostitute and courtesan homes and the loots of Marwaris and Chettys', ever watched the play, but there is no doubt he would have heard all about it.[23]

With the coming of Independence, the Dramatic Performances Act of 1876 was given a quiet burial, but it came back in Madras State as the Madras (later Tamil Nadu) Dramatic Performances Act of 1953, chiefly to gag one man—M. R. Radha. Though never a card-carrying member of any political party, this versatile actor, who had as much flair for comedy as he did for villainous roles, both of which he essayed in cinema to much acclaim, was a rationalist and a staunch supporter of Periyar. His *Ratha Kanneer* (Tears of Blood) remains an immortal stage and cinematic production. But it was his *Keemayanam*, which was an eternal work-in-progress satire of the Ramayana that attracted the ire of the administration. As early as in 1948, it, along with several other works of the Dravidian authors and playwrights, was banned by the Congress-led government of Madras, for containing incendiary material.[24] It was an early indication of the ruling party's insecurity when it came to the rise of regional, and, at that time, separatist entities.

But that did not deter Radha from staging it as a play. His *Keemayanam* repeatedly drew full houses, Anna himself stating that he cared only for the acting talent of two artistes—Radha and Sivaji Ganesan.[25] In 1953, the government enacted its law on dramatic performances. Henceforth, all plays would need police permission before being staged.[26] 'But Radha was equal to this,' chortles Mohan Raman. 'He never applied for permission to stage *Keemayanam*. One of his other works would be submitted and approved and also advertised for. During the actual performances, scenes from the *Keemayanam* would be introduced, much to the delight of the audience...often in the second half of the staging, after the police informants had left.' Radha would later bring ignominy on himself for attempting to shoot matinee idol M. G. Ramachandran after which his career more or less petered out.[27] But the Dramatic Performances Act of 1953 remained in effect until 2013 when, following a suit by the

[23]Kannan, *Anna*, pp. 72–98.

[24]Ibid., p. 174.

[25]*Asian Survey*, Vol. 13, University of California Press, 1973, p. 296.

[26]For a detailed account of Radha's struggles with the law, see Sudhangan, *Suttacchu Suttacchu: MGR vs MR Radha*, Chennai: Kizhakku Pathipakkam, 2004, pp. 92–106.

[27]Ibid.

writer Gnani, the High Court of Madras struck it down.[28]

The golden age of Tamil theatre extended till the 1960s when with some support from cinema, artistes could manage a living from the art. The big troupes of that era were Krishnan's NSK Nataka Sabha, Sahasranamam's Seva Stage, and those of 'Nawab' Rajamanikkam and R. S. Manohar. The last stubbornly clung to mythologicals, replete with grand sets and elaborate props and in his own way propagated Dravidian ideals—he chose to project characters considered negative in Brahminical lore.

Beginning with the 1960s, it was the time for amateurs, the ones with day jobs who did theatre out of passion. Poornam Viswanathan, who announced the birth of a new India on 15 August 1947 over AIR Tamil, was a professional broadcaster who took to the stage.[29] Similarly, Kathadi Ramamurthy, who got onto the stage while a student at Vivekananda College in the 1950s, launched his Stage Creations in 1965, and juggled a busy career in the corporate world while continuing stage and occasional film presence. The same era saw the rise of Cho Ramaswamy, the noted Tamil satirist and playwright, later film comedian, and still later editor of the magazine *Thuglak*. Cho became the mainstay of Viveka Fine Arts, an amateur troupe of which his brother was a founder. His plays, in which he acted as well, were sharp social satires, highlighting corruption in every aspect of daily life. The best-known play remains *Thuglak* which later became the name of the magazine he launched. In an era when atheism was gaining popularity, Cho remained a staunch believer, one who promoted Brahminical thought, that later made him an anchor of sorts for Jayalalithaa as well as the Tamil Nadu branch of the BJP, when that party began attempting inroads into the state. It is no surprise therefore that after Cho's death, his magazine is now run by BJP-supporter S. Gurumurthy. It is in many ways a precipitous comedown for a magazine that once dared to stand up to the excesses of the Emergency. Another popular troupe of the same vintage was United Amateur Artistes, founded in 1952 by Y. G. Parthasarathy and his wife Rajalakshmi, who as Mrs YGP would one day trailblaze as an educationist.[30] It still stages plays, managed by the founders' son, Y. G. Mahendra.

Writing in 1983, the author Ashokamitran squarely blamed cinema for the dismal state of Tamil theatre. He recalled how in 1953, the Moral Rearmament Army came to the city and staged plays such as *Jotham Valley* and *Forgotten*

[28] *N. V. Sankaran Alias Gnani vs The State Of Tamil Nadu*, WP No. 11311 of 2012.

[29] '"Poornam" Viswanathan passes away', *Rediff.com*, 2 October 2008.

[30] *Mrs YGP.*

Factor using minimal sets and yet creating a magical impact. But he laments that they were enjoyed as plays and not as something to learn from. He then goes on to acknowledge that by the 1980s, several local troupes were experimenting with themes that focused on social upliftment.[31]

The 1970s and 1980s were when serious plays by writers such as Indira Parthasarathy and Vietnam Veedu Sundaram became good material for staging. While the former worked on a wide range of subjects from theology, history, and social issues, the latter focused on the here and now, which made some of his scripts ideal for films as well, most of them starring Sivaji Ganesan. The Tamil magazines of the era serialized plays and these were staged by amateur troupes. *Ananda Vikatan*, the veteran Tamil weekly now in its ninth decade, was perhaps the pioneer in this. The works of Devan (R. Mahadevan) and Marina (T. S. Sridhar), both of whom worked for the magazine, became hugely popular. They portrayed humorous plots set in typical middle-class Brahmin families. A parody of Tamil Brahmin wedding customs was *Washingtonil Thirumanam*, a novel by Sa. Viswanathan that speculated on what it would be like if such a wedding were to be conducted in the American capital, Washington. In the 1960s, it was a novel idea and, when staged as a play, it became a huge success. Today, of course, Indian weddings in the US are a dime a dozen. But even so, *Washingtonil Thirumanam* remains a quaint but charming work.[32]

Humour remained the bedrock of Tamil theatre thereafter with specialists in that genre such as Crazy Mohan and S.Ve. Shekher making their appearances in the 1970s. The 1980s were their heyday when all their performances played to full houses. But the arrival of the television, and later the internet, and eventually the smartphone, has dampened enthusiasm for Tamil theatre. Today, it is only passion that keeps Tamil plays alive. Nothing illustrates the condition of Tamil theatre better than the Avvai Shanmugam Theatre inside the Local Library Authority compound on Anna Salai. This pink modernist structure was constructed in 1973. It was meant to commemorate T. K. Shanmugam of TKS brothers fame and after whom Lloyds Road was renamed Avvai Shanmugam Salai. It is now a dump yard.[33] Rather ironically, street theatre, which had gone into eclipse in the golden years of formal drama saw a revival at just about this time, with Veedhi Nataka Iyakkam calling for a serious discussion on theatre, which it said had been 'destroyed by films and sabha dramas'. It is interesting that the revival of Tamil street theatre

---

[31]Ashokamitran, *Bioscope*, Chennai: Kizhakku Pathippakam, 2006, p. 80–81.

[32]V. Sriram, 'A Tambrahm Wedding in Washington', *The Hindu*, 18 July 2014.

[33]Sriram, V., 'Theatre in Memory of a Thespian', *The Hindu*, 20 March 2012.

required Badal Sircar, the noted playwright from Calcutta, to come down and conduct workshops. Thereafter, several groups were formed, most of which drifted into the proscenium format. Those that remained emerged as powerful voices, speaking up on topics such as caste, gender, public health, and environment.[34]

It was in the 1980s that the links between Tamil theatre and cinema were broken for good. Beginning with 1931, when sound first came to Indian cinema, theatre had been the hunting ground for actors. Through the reformist 1940s and 1950s, play scripts were regularly turned into films, with the Congress initially encouraging it for the freedom movement and the Dravidian parties later adapting the same techniques for their messages to reach a wider audience. Many thespians of the silver screen took time off to act in plays—in their view it brought them face to face with audiences, something they could not experience in cinema. In the 1950s, K. Balachander, whose entry into theatre was via YGP's United Amateur Artistes, began a trend of social plays, most of which he wrote himself. These featured actors such as Nagesh, Sowcar Janaki, and Major Sundarrajan; most of them repeated their roles on screen when Balachander turned these plays into films. The wonder was that both versions drew full houses. As late as 1980, Balachander made *Thanneer Thanneer* (Water, Water) from Komal Swaminathan's play of the same name, which exposed bureaucratic ineptitude and apathy in solving water shortage in the rural areas.

But that all is not lost is evident in the way some of the troupes have kept going. There is Magic Lantern, which was founded in 1993 with the aim of taking contemporary theatre to newer audiences, beginning with schools and later bringing villages into its ambit. In 1999, Magic Lantern did what was considered well-nigh impossible till then—the staging of Kalki Krishnamurthy's magnum opus—*Ponniyin Selvan*, set in the Chola era and comprising a huge set of dramatis personae. It was received with great acclaim and resulted in a huge amount of goodwill for Magic Lantern. The play was re-staged in 2015 with the same response.[35] Another organization that has done yeoman service to drama is Sangeet Natak Akademi award-winner Na Muthuswami's Koothu-P-Pattarai (literally the smithy of theatre), which has been staging plays for over three decades. Its style, described as an intense physicality coupled with powerful ideas, focuses on bringing

---

[34]Mangai, 'Street Theatre in India, With special reference to Tamil Nadu', *Bring Down the House Lights: 50 Years of Madras Players*, P. C. Ramakrishna (ed.), Chennai, 2006, pp. 83–92.
[35]'Ponniyin Selvan returns in July', *The Hindu*, 11 June 2015

elements of folk theatre to contemporary stage.[36] Both Koothu-P-Pattarai and Magic Lantern have also consistently fought against the tyranny of the proscenium arch and have experimented with several other locations. There are also plenty of amateur drama groups in the city that keep staging plays at frequent intervals, though it must be admitted that very few draw full houses. Some of the sabhas in the city host theatre festivals in the summer, each year. Many of them, such as the Mylapore Fine Arts Club (MFAC) owed their survival to theatre. A breakaway from the MFAC is Karthik Fine Arts, which too takes its role as a patron of the theatre very seriously. Its Kodai Nataka Vizha (summer theatre festival) has a precondition—all plays staged under its auspices have to premiere at the festival.

English and Tamil theatre rarely ever ran into each other and the former too has had a long presence in the city. It owed its origins to the British. Amateur theatricals were obviously a good way to spend time but it is only in 1780, that we first hear of a proper playhouse, built by Provisional Governor John Whitehill in the Company Garden. The man was roundly criticized for focusing on this construction, but two years later, when Hyder Ali laid waste much of the surrounding country and there was a terrible famine, the theatre became useful for the staging of plays for fundraising.[37] By 1790 there was a Madras Theatrical Society in place and it began hunting for a suitable site on which to erect a theatre, the old one in Company Garden having been dismantled for military reasons. The new one came up on the Great Choultry Plain, present-day Anna Salai/Mount Road, and was known as the Little Theatre on the Plain. The funding was evidently through subscription and within a year the society is described as having been 'very fertile', staging several plays.[38]

English society in Madras continued its search for a suitable place for its amusements and eventually zeroed in on land in Egmore. By 1793, plans were afoot for the building of the Pantheon, which for the next thirty years or so became the place for all entertainments. There were rooms for balls, dinners, and card games apart from a theatre, which was constructed with the help of a stage manager who came all the way from England. The design and layout was Grecian as per a contemporary account though no visual depiction exists. A description in 1859 speaks of a fair degree of sophistication in the design of props and sets, all of which were mounted

[36]Kausalya Santhanam, 'Master of Avant Garde Theatre', *The Hindu*, 28 November 2008.
[37]Love, *Vestiges of Old Madras*, Vol. 3, p. 222.
[38]Ibid., p. 444.

on revolving triangular frames.[39]

By the late 1870s, with other locations being favoured, this theatre was evidently closed. The land on which the Pantheon stood was cut up and diverted to other purposes and, eventually, by the 1880s, the place was earmarked for the museum. On the grounds came up the Museum Theatre, presumably designed by Henry Irwin. A delightful piece of heritage, this semi-circular theatre, with its raked seats and richly embellished stage, has seen many theatrical and musical performances and continues to be used. Restored with care in recent years, it has evidently seen periods of poor maintenance as can be gleaned from an account dating to 1928 that speaks of bandicoots and bats running riot amidst flyblown doors, rotted floors, curtains torn, and wings forlorn.[40] The Museum Theatre was home to several performances of the Madras Dramatic Society, which came into existence in 1875 and actively put up plays till 1965 or so, when it ceased to exist. Sadly, there is practically no documentation on this body.[41] It did ensure a legacy of English theatre, sufficient for the Madras Players to be founded in 1955.

Today, this is the oldest English theatre group in the city and its origins can be traced to a group of students who constituted the British Council Play Reading Group. With no permanent office and not much money, the Madras Players has continued putting up play after play, initially those of English playwrights and later those of several Indian authors, writing in English and the vernacular. It was in many ways the launch pad for Girish Karnad.[42] In recent years, there have been independent directors who have used Madras Players actors to stage their creations. One among these is Prasanna Ramaswamy who carries on the social reform tradition of the old Tamil playwrights through her musical plays set in English. These espouse several causes—the oppression of caste, the destruction of the environment, and women's rights. The JustUs Repertory is yet another production house launched by writer Gowri Ramnarayan. It has used her works and also those of her illustrious grandfather Kalki Krishnamurthy, besides those of other authors from India for its plays. Coming from a rich musical background, M. S. Subbulakshmi being her grandaunt, Gowri also uses plenty of music in her plays.

---

[39] V. Sriram, 'The Pantheon, a name remembered', *Madras Musings*, Vol. XXVIII, No. 13, 16–31 October 2018.

[40] Shipley, *Madrassi Madrigals*.

[41] Muthiah, *Madras Rediscovered*, p. 183.

[42] Mangai, 'Street Theatre in India, With special reference to Tamil Nadu'.

Chennai has also been home to Sanskrit theatre. This was chiefly owing to the impetus given by Dr V. Raghavan, an extraordinary scholar who, by the time of his death in 1976, had dedicated over fifty years to the promotion of the language. He had been helping All India Radio and other organizations to produce Sanskrit plays for several years prior to his decision to set up the Samskrita Ranga in 1958, for the promotion of Sanskrit theatre. In the initial years, this was an adjunct to the Natya Sangh, a theatre training unit set up in affiliation with UNESCO. With Dr Raghavan as president and the redoubtable Mrs Y. G. Parthasarathy as secretary, the sangh conducted training workshops. The list of attendees is a veritable who's who—J. Jayalalithaa, Cho Ramaswamy, Major Sundarrajan, and Srikanth. The Samskrita Ranga staged several classics and was, for years, a fixture at the Kalidas Festival, Ujjain. Today, after completing sixty years and more, it is kept going by Dr Raghavan's son, R. Kalidas, and daughter, Nandini Ramani.[43]

Given the sharply bilingual focus of Chennai, it is only rarely that the city finds itself hosting theatre in other languages. But *The Hindu*'s Theatre Festival, which began in 2005 and has since spread to other cities, provides such an opportunity. For a long while, a festival of English plays only, it has since expanded its scope to include Tamil. The Hindu Metroplus Playwright Award, with prize money of ₹1 lakh, is awarded to the best English-language script. The theatre festival is more or less synonymous with the Chennai-based theatre group Evam, and here probably lies the seed for the future of drama in the city.

Evam focuses on light entertainment and brands its platform as the Happy Factory Model. The money comes from event management, theatre workshops, and ticket sales and all of it is channelled into theatrical productions. Founded by Sunil Vishnu and Karthik Kumar in 2003, Evam today is that rare entity—a profitable theatre group with a business model. This is path-breaking for traditional theatre in Chennai, be it English or Tamil or Sanskrit, has always looked to the generosity of patrons—be it royalty or the heads of corporate houses —to keep it going.

Evam has also been the pioneer in Tamil stand-up comedy, which is rapidly gaining ground. Its Stand-Up Tamasha started it all and today Tamilians are learning to laugh at themselves—their obsession with academic performance, the concept of arranged marriages, the appreciation of Carnatic music, the perennial hunt for good coffee, the necessity to end all meals with curd rice, the annual migration of grandparents from the city to take care of

---

[43]See: https://www.drvraghavancentre.com/sr-organization.html/.

grandchildren in the US—all of these and more are grist to the stand-up comedy mill. Today, Tamil is considered to be leading among all stand-up comedies in the regional languages.[44]

In keeping with dwindling audience attention span, Chennai has of late seen the Short + Sweet South India festival as part of a global initiative. Begun in Australia, it features a series of ten-minute plays with prizes to be won. It remains open to all languages and that, in itself, is a refreshing change. Chennai's theatre has long operated in language silos and perhaps it is time for it to come together, consolidate, and grow.

In 2020, theatre and all other forms of entertainment were faced with what could be done in the face of the Covid-19 pandemic. Many troupes have vanished but those that survived did so by adopting technology—plays were showcased on YouTube and other social media. Does that translate to ticket sales? But then Chennai theatre has, for long, managed only on sponsorship. So perhaps it makes no difference. The art form had come a long way from the time of the likes of M. R. Radha who viewed theatre as commercial art. This is best illustrated in his being firm that police officers who came to keep an eye on what he was staging had to purchase tickets to gain entry. When asked to explain to the authorities, he made it clear that his troupe needed to sell tickets to survive.[45] Today, performances cannot even hope to break even through ticket sales. What is inspiring is the will to keep the art alive.

One of the reasons for Chennai theatre's bleak scenario is its inability to improve production values. Historically, we came from a tradition of grand sets and slick backdrop changes. In the 1930s, we were probably as good as any vaudeville production in the West. But unlike what happened in Broadway or Westend, theatre here got side-tracked into message-bearing and ceased being pure entertainment. Technical aspects and presentation values of theatre stagnated at a tacky level. All of these are reflected in how the venues have hardly bothered to update themselves from the time they were built. In this, the Sir Mutha Venkatasubba Rao and Music Academy auditoriums are exceptions, but they are unaffordable for most local theatre groups and their seating capacity is far in excess of what any performance can hope to sell tickets for.

Ashokamitran's 1983 assessment that all serious change and evolution in

[44]Susanna Myrtle Lazarus, 'How Tamil stand-up is leading the regional comedy scene', *The Hindu*, 5 July 2019.

[45]M. R. Radha, pp. 97–98.

Tamil drama had happened when professional troupes held sway holds true even now. The amateurs he says, barring a few exceptions, did not have staying power. There is no getting away from the fact that Tamil theatre, which influenced the creation of Tamil cinema, ended up being overshadowed by it and never recovered.[46] Today, Chennai theatre is forever in a state of making do with less, and less, of both finances and audiences.

[46]Ashokamitran, *Bioscope*, pp. 80–81.

For all that it would one day take over the imaginations and lives of a majority of the people in Chennai and the rest of Tamil Nadu, cinema's entry was not auspicious. In December 1896, T. Stevenson, owner of the Madras Photographic Store, advertised the first cinematograph or animated photograph show, to be held over three nights. This was at the Victoria Public Hall, the standard venue for such novelties. Tickets were priced quite high: ₹3, 2, and 1 and if that was not a dampener, a cyclonic storm and the inauguration of the new buildings of the Madras Museum on the same day diminished attendance even further. But Stevenson did hold his screening, which comprised ten short films (including the ones titled *The Czar's Entry into Paris* and *Donkey Riding*) amidst a magic lantern slide show. There were technical flaws in the screening too.[1] Despite all this, Stevenson was not disheartened and went on to become a salesman of silent cinema, introducing them to Hyderabad, Dhaka, and Calcutta, where he eventually settled.[2]

It would appear that the first initiatives in the city after this were sporadic and dealt more with exhibition of films than actual production. The theatres, therefore, began coming up long before the studios. Thus, in the first decade of the twentieth century, we hear of the Lyric, which was a playhouse that doubled as a cinema.[3] There were plenty of tent cinemas—makeshift facilities with projector and screen. It was also at this time that cinema with sound of some kind was attempted, the pioneer being Raghupathy Venkiah who imported a chrono-megaphone—a projector with an attached gramophone player. This made it seem that the sound was emanating from the screen. The screening was done at tent houses, set up near where the Raja Annamalai Manram stands today.[4]

The first permanent movie theatre of the city was The Bioscope, on Popham's Broadway, then a fashionable part of George Town. Begun in April 1911, it ran continuous shows every evening from 6 to 11 p.m. The proprietor was Mrs Klugg, of whom nothing is known. She was perhaps India's first woman in the film exhibition business. The theatre probably

[1]Stephen P. Hughes, 'In Search of Beginnings', *The Hindu*, 13 February 2010.

[2]Ibid.

[3]Muthiah, *Madras Rediscovered*, pp. 77–78.

[4]Guy, *Starlight Starbright*, p. 13.

wound up after Mrs Klugg's departure from the city in October 1911.[5] In 1913, Warwick Major, an impresario who had had a successful run in Sri Lanka,[6] relocated to Madras and built the Electric Bioscope. The first facility built for screening films, Mrs Klugg's being a pre-existing building that was modified for projection, the Electric remained in operation for around two years before the Department of Posts took it over. Unlike the purpose for which it was built, the structure has had a long life, now being used as the philatelic bureau and rather well maintained at that.[7]

The first theatres that began in the silent era and continued long thereafter were the creations of the father-son duo Raghupathy Venkiah and Prakash. Between them they set up the Crown in Mint Street, Globe (later Roxy) in Purasawalkam, and Gaiety off Anna Salai on Blackers Road.[8] In the meanwhile, the old Lyric had burnt to the ground and made way for Elphinstone on Anna Salai.[9] This, in turn, moved across the road in 1916 and became the New Elphinstone, famed in later years as much for its English movies as for its soda fountain and Jaffer's ice creams.[10]

In the meanwhile, Tamilians were becoming familiar with film production. The pioneer was R. Nataraja Mudaliar, a successful dealer in automobiles, who, having seen India's first feature film—Dadasaheb Phalke's *Raja Harischandra* (1913), decided that this was the field to be in. Having trained with an expert in Pune, Mudaliar promoted the India Film Company in 1916. After consultations with Pammal Sambanda Mudaliar, the father of modern Tamil drama, he chose to film an episode from the Mahabharata—*Keechaka Vadam*. With actors trained by the members of the Suguna Vilasa Sabha, shooting progressed. Mudaliar felt that the humid climate of Madras was detrimental for film processing and so this was done in Bangalore. The tri-lingual title cards for this silent film were written by a famed trio—English by Dr Guruswami Mudaliar, noted physician, Tamil by Thiruvengada Mudaliar of Pacchaiyappa's College, and Hindi by Devadas Gandhi, the Mahatma's son. The film was a huge success and so were several other silent films that he made thereafter. Unfortunately, a fire gutted Nataraja Mudaliar's studio at Tower House, Millers

---

[5]Stephen P. Hughes, 'Our Tryst with Celluloid Magic', *The Hindu*, 14 August 2010.

[6]Mudaliar, *En Suyacharitai*, p. 445.

[7]Muthiah, *Madras Rediscovered*, pp. 77–78.

[8]V. Sriram, 'Not much Gaiety in its history', *Madras Musings*, Vol. XXIX, No. 23, 16–31 March 2020.

[9]Muthiah, *Madras Rediscovered*, p. 79.

[10]Ibid.

Road, Purasawalkam and that ended his dream run.[11] 'Some day I hope to find the exact spot on Miller's Road where this building stood,' says Mohan Raman. 'We need to put up a plaque there commemorating Nataraja Mudaliar. I also hope to get the road renamed after him.'[12]

The success of Nataraja Mudaliar did not go unnoticed and soon Raghupathy Venkiah sent his son, Prakash, to England for training in motion-picture making. On his return, the duo founded the Star of the East Studio in Purasawalkam but their poor financial skills led to insolvency for the father and the auctioning off of the facility after a few releases.[13] Prakash then branched off on his own, with some Andhra aristocrats bankrolling the setting up of a studio in Tondiarpet. This too closed down for the same reasons as the Star of the East but not before Prakash had imparted his skills to several men who stayed on in the industry and contributed to it.[14]

A. Narayanan, who bought the Tondiarpet studio from Prakash in 1929 was one of his protégés. For a while he made silent films, but then in 1931, sound came to Indian cinema, with Ardeshir Irani's *Alam Ara*. That led to the first Tamil film—H. M. Reddy's *Mahakavi Kalidas*, made in the same year.[15] Narayanan, realizing that sound was the new thing, quickly ramped up. His new studio, in the Kilpauk area, was named Sreenivasa Cinetone but was known as Sound City. His wife, Meenakshi, whom he trained, became India's first woman sound recording engineer. Their first movie, *Srinivasa Kalyanam*, released in 1934, was a runaway hit but Narayanan who was addicted to alcohol did not make much headway thereafter, dying in 1939. Rather ironically, *Dharmapatni*, one of the films he made and probably Tamil cinema's first social, dealt with the problems of alcoholism.[16]

The silent era was plagued with certain problems uniquely Indian. Audiences in the country (Tamilians were no exception to this), were used to watching theatre with plenty of music and excellent dialogue. Harikatha—the monoact art of storytelling with plenty of emotion, music, and drama—was also at the peak of its popularity at this time. While action situations as depicted on screen were viewed with interest and applauded, stories when

---

[11]Guy, *Starlight Starbright*, pp. 20–25.

[12]Interview with the author, Chennai, 14 February 2020.

[13]V. Sriram, 'Not much Gaiety in its history', *Madras Musings*, Vol. XXIX, No. 23, 16–31 March 2020.

[14]Guy, *Starlight Starbright*, p. 18.

[15]Aranthai Narayanan, *Tamizh Cinemavin Kathai*, Chennai: New Century Book House Pvt. Limited, 2002, p. 42.

[16]Guy, *Starlight Starbright*, pp. 26–33.

depicted in silence were not appreciated. Story cards in English made no sense to an audience unfamiliar with the language. To overcome this, some theatre owners had live orchestras seated in the pit, and sometimes incorporated a commentator who explained what was taking place on screen. The second and bigger problem was the recruitment of actors. Theatre veterans such as the TKS brothers sneered at silent cinema.[17] Getting women to act on screen was even more difficult and the only ones ready to do so were Eurasians, several of whom were given Hindu names to make them more acceptable.[18] With the arrival of sound, this problem became even more acute—Eurasians could not speak high-flown Tamil. Secondly, they could not sing Indian classical music, which filmmakers realized was a vital ingredient for the success of their productions. Everyone sang in theatre, as did the solo performer in Harikatha, and they had to do so in cinema as well. For quite a while thereafter, in cinema, the ability to sing ranked higher than the ability to act. There was a third challenge—no studio in Madras could handle sound, until Narayanan's Sound City came up. And so between 1930 and 1933, there was no option but to take the entire cast and crew to production centres such as Calcutta, Bombay, and Kolhapur.[19]

The solutions gradually fell into place. Classical music performers began to make a beeline to the new medium, the first being Prabhat Studio's *Seetha Kalyanam*, featuring S. Rajam, who would later become famous as a singer, a musicologist, and a painter. Thereafter, most Carnatic musicians took to films. Very few could act but that did not matter. In the early years, songs dominated everything else. The music of the first decade of sound was heavily classical and so lyricists and composers came with Carnatic training. The rise of Papanasam Sivan as a respected composer of classical music had much to do with films, beginning with *Seetha Kalyanam*.[20] He and others of his kind, such as the versatile Harikesanallur L. Muthiah Bhagavathar—composer, scholar, India's first musician to receive a doctorate, and much else, restricted themselves to the tunes, leaving the orchestration to others. The 1934 film *Pavalakkodi*, starring M. K. Thyagaraja Bhagavathar and S. D. Subbulakshmi, had fifty songs, all composed by Papanasam Sivan.[21] The era of classical musicians in cinema survived well into the 1950s, even after the

---

[17]Shanmugam, *Enathu Naadaga Vaazhlkai*, p. 292.

[18]Guy, *Starlight Starbright*, pp. 14, 24.

[19]Guy, *Starlight Starbright*, pp. 47, 88.

[20]Ibid., pp. 72–73.

[21]Ibid., p. 74.

refining of playback singing reduced the demand for them. Some such as M. L.Vasanthakumari became successful as playback singers, even while managing their Carnatic music careers in parallel. Songs have since reduced in number in Tamil cinema but they are still an integral feature, so much so that the first movie in Tamil sans songs, *Andha Naal* (That Day), was made only in 1954 and is still remembered for this novelty. 'Is it not ironic that the first Tamil movie without a song was directed by the brilliant veena maestro S. Balachander?' asks Mohan Raman.

Songs in films made in Madras Presidency were used to propagate the freedom movement in several subtle and a few direct ways. The review of the first talkie film, *Kalidas*, appearing in the *Swadesamitran* dated 29 October 1931, stated that several of the songs had a nationalist tint and extolled the virtues of Gandhi, the Swadeshi movement, and the charkha.[22] Lyrics for the songs sung by actors T. P. Rajalakshmi and Narasimha Rao, were all taken from the works of the poet Madhurakavi Bhaskara Das whose songs of the nationalist genre had become very popular in South India from 1915 onwards. The 1933 *Valli Thirumanam*, produced by Samikannu Vincent of Coimbatore, which was hailed as the first big hit in Tamil, having run for ten weeks in Madras, was based on the eponymous popular play. The film starred Rajalakshmi as Valli and C. M. Dorai as Murugan. Using Bhaskara Das's songs once again, it had Valli shooing away 'shameless white cranes' from her fields in the song 'Alolam Alolam'. Similarly Murugan, while trying to entice Valli into marriage, pretends to be a bangle seller who sells only 'Hindu Swadeshi' bangles in the song 'Valaiyal Vangalayo'.[23]

In 1928, the Government of Burma, then part of British India, banned the singing of Subramania Bharati's verses and the same took effect in Madras as well.[24] This led to film makers thinking up ingenious ways to propagate them. The film *Menaka* (1935) used Bharati's songs for the first time and this was publicized openly as such by the producers Tirupur Shanmukhananda Talkies, the director, Raja Sandow, and the actors comprising the TKS brothers' troupe.[25] By 1937, however, with the new Congress government in power in Madras, censors began concentrating on removal of scenes with sex and violence, and patriotic songs were left untouched. The film *Vimochanam*

---

[22]Aranthai Narayanan, *Suthanthira Poril Tamizh Cinema*, serialized in Dinamani Kathir.

[23]Ibid.

[24]A. R.Venkatachalapathy, *Who Owns That Song? The Battle for Subramania Bharati's Copyright*, New Delhi: Juggernaut, p. 30.

[25]Shanmugam, *Enathu Naadaga Vaazhlkai*, p. 292.

of 1938 had songs of Subramania Bharati as well as a song praising Rajaji for his attempts to make Salem a dry district.[26] The ban on Bharati was effectively lifted in 1948, after Independence.[27] It was only in 2000 that a film was finally made on the national poet, which received critical acclaim.

Theatre artistes began to see a new future in talking films. As mentioned in the chapter on drama, the stage was one of the regular suppliers of actors for films. Most of the men who acted in cinema right up to the end of the 1960s were from a theatrical background and this included big names—M. K. Thyagaraja Bhagavatar, N. S. Krishnan, MGR, Sivaji Ganesan, T. S. Baliah, V. K. Ramaswami, M. R. Radha, S. S. Rajendran, Nagesh, and M. N. Nambiar, to name just a few. Some of the women artistes too were from theatre—mention has already been made of T. P. Rajalakshmi. There were others such as the comedienne Manorama and the character actress M. N. Rajam. All of them, male and female, had some hallmarks of theatre—clear diction and a loud voice, both absolutely necessary on stage, performed at venues where at times amplification was unavailable or acoustics poor. They were also multi-skilled—most could perform acrobatics (at least while they were lissom and slim which was not for long in Tamil cinema), sing, dance, and had a remarkable sense of timing in dialogue delivery. Almost all of them had great flair for comedy. It was therefore no wonder that the stage artistes soon began outshining their Carnatic counterparts, especially after playback rendered a good singing voice redundant for actors.

Knowledge of classical dance, the item numbers of the early years, was an advantage when it came to women. Thus, the film world increasingly looked to the descendants of the courtesans, whose entire community had been outlawed by the Anti-Nautch Bill passed by the Madras Legislative Council in 1927. Though initially reluctant to face the camera, women from the community took to acting, chiefly as a means of sustenance. Some such as T. R. Rajakumari, she of Gemini's *Chandralekha* fame, rose to great heights. She eventually became a producer and theatre owner apart from being a top-ranked heroine and vamp. Males of the community were in demand as dance masters to choreograph the various dance sequences in films. The classical music and dance era in films saw many noted names such as Vazhuvoor Ramaiah Pillai, Muthuswami Pillai, and Vempatti Chinna Satyam train artistes.

---

[26] Randor Guy, 'Vimochanam', *The Hindu*, 25 March 2010.

[27] The details of how this happened are the subject of a book. See Venkatachalapathy, *Who Owns That Song?*

As the popularity of dance began spreading among women outside the Devadasi community, it became easier to select heroines. In fact, the increase in popularity of dance itself was due to one of the new recruits—Baby (and later Kumari) Kamala. Her talents were recognized as early as when she was five or so, for she was cast in 1938 in a Tamil film.[28] Learning Kathak from Lachhu Maharaj and later moving to Madras to train under Kattumannarkoil Muthukumaraswami Pillai and Vazhuvoor Ramaiah Pillai, Kamala began to be frequently engaged to perform dance numbers in films. Later, she would turn heroine for a while too, but it was her dance that held audiences enthralled. Suddenly, everyone wanted their daughter to dance like Kamala. Clay dolls for Navaratri were modelled after her, as they were after the other famed child artiste Baby Saroja, and many girls were named after one or the other. Kamala's success would pave the way for many other dancers to try their luck in films. Some of the big names were Vyjayanthimala and the Travancore Sisters (Lalitha, Padmini, and Ragini). As late as the 1960s it was dance that brought Jayalalithaa to the silver screen.[29] It was not as though ability to dance or a striking screen presence was the only requisite for a heroine. The 1950s would also see several talented actresses making their way to the top. There was P. Bhanumathi Ramakrishna, actress, director, producer, singer, and studio-owner, who was respected and feared in equal measure. Savithri, who displayed immense talent, also directed films.

It was mentioned earlier that most Tamil films made in the early 1930s were produced outside Madras. But from 1934 onwards, studios began making their appearance here, the initial ones coming up in remote locations such as the banks of the Adyar river and in the vicinity of Kilpauk.[30] The Motion Pictures Producers Combine (MPPC) of Director K. Subrahmanyam was located on a vast and densely wooded property just off the intersection of Mount Road/Anna Salai and Nungambakkam High Road. From 1937, the studio made at least three thought-provoking films—*Bala Yogini* that dealt with class conflicts, *Sevasadanam* (M. S. Subbulakshmi's debut film) which focused on talented but penurious young women condemned to marry rich, old men, and *Thyaga Bhoomi*, based on Kalki Krishnamurthy's eponymous novel that dealt with untouchability and the freedom struggle. The last film

[28]Two films featured her in 1938: A. N. Kalyanasundara Iyer's *Valibar Sangam* and Sohrab Modi's *Jailor*.

[29]1962 film *Man Mauji* in a 3-minute dance sequence with Baby Naaz.

[30]Meenakshi Cinetone by the Adyar (later Sathya Studios) and Newtone in Kilpauk were two examples.

was distributed by S. S. Vasan but it ran into trouble with the government which banned it.[31] To compound matters further, the MPPC caught fire and burnt to the ground.[32]

It was left to Vasan to salvage the situation. Having bought the place in the auction that followed the conflagration, he set up Gemini Studios on the site. For the next forty years or so, this would remain the most famous film production facility in the city. Employing over 600 people in its heyday, Gemini was known for its ponderous pace of production, most of its films involving mega budgets.[33] It was not for nothing that Vasan was known as the Cecil B. DeMille of India. A man of great energy and charm of manner beneath which was a fair degree of ruthlessness, he made many hits, among which the film still talked about is *Chandralekha* (1948), best known for its climactic drum dance. Vasan spent lavishly on the film and its publicity, staking all, as per most accounts, and reaped rich dividends.[34]

The success of Gemini brought more studios to Madras. And they all set up base at Kodambakkam, then a suburb of the city, access to which was, for years, via a railway level-crossing whose gates would be locked for hours on end. Spotting film stars in full makeup waiting patiently in their cars for the gate to open was a pastime for many film-crazy fans. That was until the Kodambakkam overbridge solved the traffic problem but removed much of the thrill in waiting at the railway gate. Nobody is very clear as to why the studios preferred to locate at Kodambakkam but the most common reasons given are cheap land, relative remoteness of the place, and the abundance of electric power owing to a newly-erected electric sub-station. The first to come up there was Star Combines in the mid-1940s[35] and then came Vauhini and AVM Studios, both in 1948/1949. At the height of the studio system in Chennai during the 1960s, there were as many as seventy-seven production floors spanning twelve studios in Kodambakkam, according to actor Mohan Raman. 'The studios, especially the big ones such as Gemini, Vauhini and AVM, were microcosms of India', he says. 'They made films in as many as seven Indian languages, with Tamil and Telugu dominating. Kannada, Malayalam, Tulu, and the occasional English being the rest. The

[31]Contrary to what is claimed by Subramaniam's biographers, the film was banned only four years after its release.

[32]Guy, *Starlight Starbright*, pp. 242–43.

[33]Ashokamitran, *Fourteen Years with Boss*, Gurgaon: Penguin Books, 2016.

[34]Guy, *Starlight Starbright*, pp. 244–51.

[35]Ajai Sreevatsan, 'Heritage Walk around Old Studios', *The Hindu*, 22 August 2011.

seventh came when Vasan's *Chandralekha*, dubbed in Hindi and released in the north, was very successful and that encouraged him to remake several of his earlier Tamil/Telugu hits in Hindi and release them across India.'

This made other Tamil producers sit up and soon, Hindi films made in Madras were hugely successful. In order to reach Tamil audiences, many Hindi producers began to dub their films in the former language and release them here and this too met with a good response.[36] Raj Kapoor's *Aan*, Dilip Kumar's *Naya Daur*, and the Naushad-produced Dilip Kumar, Nimmi, and Suryakumari-starrer *Uran Khatola* were just a few. But these were not a patch on the success that Tamil producers enjoyed in Hindi cinema. The same can also be said of the heroines who went from here to the North. The trend continued well into the 1980s.

The necessity for Hindi-knowing scriptwriters, directors, actors, music directors, and lyricists meant a steady stream of Bollywood visitors to Madras, many of whom stayed on in near-permanent suites at the Connemara or the Oceanic.[37] Writer Ashokamitran in his book on Gemini Studios mentions how Indian Airlines flights would be kept waiting for actors to finish their shoots and rush to the airport, in full make-up. The occasional gift to the pilot or an invitation en-famille to witness shooting was evidently enough to get this goodwill.[38] Dilip Kumar was such a frequent visitor to the city and he developed such rapport with Vasan and B. Nagi Reddy that he even contemplated buying a house in Madras. In his memoir, *Dilip Kumar: The Substance and The Shadow*, he refers to it as the most erudite and culturally wealthy city of India.[39]

'Most studios of Madras were multicultural and a perfect instance of a pluralistic society,' sighs Mohan Raman. 'Gemini, for instance, employed Bengalis, Gujaratis, many from the Hindi heartland, Kannadigas, Telugus, Malayalis—and among these Hindus, Muslims, Christians, and Anglo-Indians.' Lording over them all was an American—William Moylan, who was the general manager of the studios.[40] It is no wonder that even a non-Tamil knowing director, Ellis R. Dungan—could fit in and make several successful

---

[36]Ashokamitran, *Bioscope*, Chennai: Kizhakku Pathippakam, 2006, p. 175.

[37]See Vasan, *Centenary Volume* and Dilip Kumar's autobiography, *Dilip Kumar: The Substance and The Shadow*, New Delhi: Hay House India, 2014.

[38]Ashokamitran, *Years with Boss*, p. 99.

[39]Kumar, *Dilip Kumar: The Substance and The Shadow*, p. 237.

[40]Ashokamitran, *Years With Boss*, p. 46.

films in the language.[41] The studios hosted many an international visitor—heads of state, actors, poets, writers—all keen to see how cinema worked in India. Employees in the studios more or less unknowingly developed a sense of cosmopolitanism and were liberal in their thinking.[42] On the flip side, women never had an easy time in most of these places, with the notorious casting couch more or less a permanent presence.

The studios were also centres of excellence. Nothing but the best in production techniques, equipment, and technicians would do for the Madras studios, which is why they became such important production centres. A. V. Meyyappan, for instance, had as early as 1945 mastered at his AVM Studios the process of post-synchronization, wherein songs later recorded by a professional playback singer were synchronized with the lip movements of an actor.[43] Nagi Reddy and A. Chakrapani's *Maya Bazaar* (1957), made at their Vijaya Vauhini Studios is spoken of with awe for its special effects even today.[44]

The studios began to lose their sheen in the 1970s. The death of Vasan in 1968 had robbed Gemini of much of its dynamism.[45] But a bigger problem, according to Mohan Raman, was the withdrawal of Hindi and other language films from the city. Beginning with the 1960s, the Shiv Sena in Bombay demanded a boycott of films made in Madras on the grounds that they robbed the locals in the former city of employment. If that gave Bombay actors and others cold feet, the anti-Hindi agitation of 1967 in Madras compounded matters. Soon Hindi cinema began to be made only occasionally here. Worse was to follow.

For very many years, Tamil cinema and Kollywood (a portmanteau of Kodambakkam and Hollywood), in general, had employed a number of Telugu-speaking people and the financing too had come from several rich zamindars and businessmen from the area. The linguistic division of states and the later creation of Andhra Pradesh by amalgamating the nizam's erstwhile dominions with the Telugu-speaking areas of the old Madras Presidency meant Hyderabad became the new focal point for films in that language. By the 1980s, that city had five film studios and the numbers only increased with

[41]The best introduction to this filmmaker is the Karan Bali documentary, *An American in Madras*, 2013.

[42]Ashokamitran, *Bioscope*, pp. 201–11.

[43]Guy, *Starlight Starbright*, p. 144.

[44]Vamanan, 'Enduring magic of Maya Bazaar', *DT Next*, 30 March 2017.

[45]Ashokamitran, *Years With Boss*, p. 161.

time.[46] 'The first to move was A. Nageswara Rao,' says Mohan Raman. 'He was followed by N. T. Rama Rao and that began a flood.' The stoppage of Telugu-film production in Madras, combined with Kannada and Malayalam films moving away as well, hit the Kodambakkam studios hard. But this was just the beginning of many more troubles to come.

Steady improvements in dubbing technology reduced the importance of the studios. It was no longer necessary to shoot in a place insulated from external sound. Technological advances in cameras made them lighter and therefore easier to take outdoors. There was a sudden spurt in location shootings—K. Balachander, for instance, shot in middle-class homes. In the 1970s, the arrival of director Bharathiraja and others of his ilk shifted focus to stories in rural settings. Units went on shoots to far-flung places and stars such as Kamal Haasan, Rajinikanth, Sridevi, and others trooped to those locations.

Studios also found it tough to retain talent. While in the 1940s it had been de rigueur for studios to have an entire complement of staff including music directors, script writers, lyricists, dance masters, and playback singers, most became freelance artists over time. Vasan had probably begun the trend with his *Insaniyat* (1955), whose entire crew was from Bombay.[47] By the 1960s, even the technical personnel came to be on hire. And yet, at the same time, it was difficult to retrench staff, given the prevalent labour laws. With that studios became mere shells where films were made.

The closure of Gemini Studios in 1976 was nevertheless a shock. B. Nagi Reddy of Vijaya Vauhini wrote a heartfelt tribute since he adored Vasan and was sorry to see the latter's creation disappear. But it had become more or less necessary, for Gemini had bled for some time. The vast property would transform into a rabbit's warren of buildings amidst which is the Apeejay Group's The Park, which in a genuflection to Gemini made the theme of its hotel cinematic.[48] Within a decade or so, and even during Nagi Reddy's lifetime, his studio went defunct as well, to be replaced by wedding halls and hotels. AVM chugged along for much longer but large chunks of it have been made over to real estate development. Today, there are fewer than five production floors in the whole of Kodambakkam. But Tamil cinema is still referred to as Kollywood. In terms of volume of production, Chennai would still be significant. And the city did enjoy around twenty years of technical

[46]Mohan V. Raman, 'Where it all began', *The Hindu*, 12 May 2012.

[47]Ashokamitran, *Years With Boss*, pp. 93–110.

[48]V. Sriram, 'Lost Landmarks of Chennai-Gemini Studios', *Madras Heritage and Carnatic Music*, 6 August 2014.

supremacy, chiefly from the late 1980s to the early 2000s when anything related to graphics was executed here for cinema across India. But then, with cloud technology and the internet, Chennai is only as good as any other city.

The rise and fall of cinema theatres was coeval with that of the studios. We have already seen the history of Raghupathy Venkiah's facilities—Crown, Gaiety, and Roxy. From the 1940s, a series of theatres came to be built, and their plans and layouts varied considerably based on where they were located. Thus, the early ones such as the Prince of Wales Theatre and its twin, Kinema Central (later Murugan Talkies), Select, Minerva—all in George Town and the Star in Triplicane, Lakshmi and Saraswathi on New Farrens Road, did not have any parking facilities. The ticket counter was accessed from the road and patrons walked in to the foyer and from there to the theatre. The clientele here was all working class and no cars were expected to be parked in the compound. And yet, many of these were prestigious locations as far as releases were concerned. Kinema Central, since demolished but which held the record of having screened the first talkie in 1931, was, as Murugan Talkies, the theatre that regularly premiered MGR films and was, hence, frequently visited by the matinee idol.[49] Minerva, now Batcha, located on the first floor of a transport godown dates itself to 1916 when it was launched as the coolest and most comfortable theatre in the city. From the 1930s, it had an exclusive contract for a long while with Paramount Pictures for the screening of their films. An open veranda that runs along one side was where refreshments were served. The theatre was one of the earliest to incorporate air conditioning but today screens reruns keeping its doors and windows open. The clientele is chiefly manual labourers and rickshaw pullers.[50]

In sharp contrast to the George Town theatres were the ones on Mount Road and its vicinity. Near Blackers Road were Gaiety, Casino, and Chitra of which only the second survives, its beautiful art-deco frontage now having given way to some horrendous modernization. On the other side, and within Wallajah Road was Paragon. Along the main road itself were New Elphinstone, Plaza, Globe (later Alankar), while tucked just inside General Patters Road was Wellington with Midland and Odeon (later Melody) a short distance away. Returning to Mount Road, there was Shanti, owned by Sivaji Ganesan, Anna, Sun and close to Saidapet—Noorjahan. Multiplexes may be all the rage

[49]Mohan V. Raman, 'End of another edifice', *The Hindu*, 19 December 2011.

[50]V. Sriram, 'Some Theatres in George Town', *Madras Heritage and Carnatic Music*, 23 June 2010.

today but Chennai foresaw this decades back, when its Safire/Blue Diamond/Emerald complex with three screens came up in 1964. The promoters were the Veecumsee family that traded in precious stone and hence the names. The basement had the city's first discotheque—Nine Gems. Safire was the biggest and one of the earliest 70mm screens in India. Blue Diamond offered continuous shows and featured mainly English films. Soon other multiplexes came up in the vicinity—Anand and Little Anand, and the Devi Complex comprising several screens.

Between the 1960s and the 1980s, going to see a movie on Mount Road was Chennai's idea of an outing and the public thronged the area. With so many theatres in close proximity, non-availability of tickets in one meant you could try your luck with another. Pongal and Deepavali were special, for movies were released to coincide with the festivals. Such was the draw of the Mount Road/Anna Salai theatres that building such facilities in the suburbs was not a viable proposition. But some did come up—Pilot in Royapettah was India's second theatre to offer Cinerama screening technology, Mylapore had Kamadhenu and Kapali while Adyar had Eros. There were others further afield but most specialized in reruns. The T. Nagar theatres, Rajkumari and Nagesh, named after the film stars who promoted them, fared better.

Today, very few of these theatres survive. None of the single-screen ones on Mount Road remain, barring Casino which too does not screen films any longer. The Devi Complex continues in business while the two Anands have given way to several new constructions. The loss of Safire/Blue Diamond/Emerald is still felt very keenly by the older generations. The property was acquired by the AIADMK in the 1990s to build its headquarters and the theatres were demolished, but then Vastu considerations intervened and so the site remains empty and overgrown with weeds.[51]

Why did the theatres fade out the way they did? The arrival of television and later videos and then CDs killed all enthusiasm to travel to a theatre. Tamil cinema has been plagued with video and CD piracy, allegedly promoted by politicians. Every once in a while, crackdowns by police netted a big haul but the actual perpetrators were never apprehended. For being such a movie-crazy city, Chennai happens to levy the highest tax on cinema tickets. Local Body Entertainment Tax along with the GST imposes a hefty burden on the ticket value.[52] Maintenance costs have also spiralled over the decades and refurbishment is prohibitively expensive with the returns not

[51]'End of the Road for Safire', *The Hindu*, 20 December 2014.

[52]'TN Govt reduced LBET tax to 8%', *Business Standard*, 13 October 2017.

commensurate with the costs. With real estate prices in the city shooting skyward, most theatre owners in Chennai have deemed it good business sense to close, demolish, and develop the space or sell outright to builders.

And yet there is the one exception. Osborne House in Royapettah was the city residence of the rajas of Venkatagiri. The family members were ardent devotees of Sathya Sai Baba of Puttaparthi and he had often stayed at this large garden bungalow and conducted bhajan sessions. In the early 1970s, the then raja decided to demolish and build a theatre on the site. The Royal Theatre came up here in 1974 and by 1980s changed hands, becoming part of the SPI Cinemas Group, who renamed it Sathyam Cinemas, in memory of the association with Sathya Sai Baba. Over the years, Sathyam became a multiplex that people flocked to, given the continued investments the promoters made in infrastructure and screening technology. It had the advantage of scale, for SPI ran theatres in various parts of the country. With considerable competition in recent years from multiplexes in various malls of the city, Sathyam has still been able to hold its own. As this book goes into print, Sathyam is going through another change in ownership, the buyer being the pan-Indian PVR Cinemas.[53]

In the midst of this chronicling of commercial cinema theatres in the city, it is also necessary to document the story of its Children's Theatre. The Madras Presidency was governed by a legislative council lorded over by the governor from the 1860s onwards. This body steadily expanded, Indians being nominated to it, and by the 1920s, had a Council Chamber in Fort St George. In 1936, the Presidency acquired its elected lower house, the legislative assembly. Space was needed to house this and while it initially sat at the University Senate House, work began on Government Estate for a suitable House of Legislature. But with World War II intervening, progress was slow. By the time the building had been completed, India had become independent and the states had been divided linguistically. The legislative assembly now had fewer seats, with Andhra having gone, and occupied the erstwhile Council Chamber in the fort, from where it still functions. The less important upper house, the legislative council, was relegated to a smaller chamber in the fort and functioned from there till Tamil Nadu became unicameral in the 1980s.

In the meanwhile, work continued on the new legislature building. But by the time it was inaugurated in 1952, there was no use for it, so it

---

[53]Sreedhar Pillai, 'SPI Cinemas CEO Kiran Reddy on why they chose to sell their business to PVR over other multiplex operators', *Firstpost*, 16 August 2018.

was notified as the Children's Theatre where films for the young were to be shown. That rarely happened and it morphed into Kalaivanar Arangam, an auditorium for government events and named after 'Kalaivanar' N. S. Krishnan.[54] Early in the new millennium, this building, along with several of its neighbours, was demolished to make way for Karunanidhi's dream—the new assembly cum secretariat. When that was scuttled by Jayalalithaa, work began on a new Kalaivanar Arangam, which emerged as a work of artistic and architectural merit. It, however, remains sparingly used.

Despite the drastic fall in the number of theatres, having films release on the big screen remains important and so the action has shifted to the multiplexes. Gone however are the days of silver, golden, and platinum jubilee hits, with M. K. Thyagaraja Bhagavatar's *Haridas* standing out for having run for three full years. Today's Tamil films hope and pray that the pirates don't get to them before or immediately after release even though the era of CDs has ended. Screen runs are for a week or two at most, with returns being maximised by simultaneous release across the world.

Through all these ups and downs, the star system more or less remains intact. Tamil film stars, especially if male, are idolized, though that word hardly manages to describe the levels of adulation. Fans can go to any extent for their hero, including maiming or killing themselves. Beginning with MGR, it has been customary for leading men to nurture and encourage rasikar manrams (fan clubs), which in reality function as well-oiled propaganda machines. MGR utilized the system to the hilt to further his political career, though it cannot be denied that he was a man with a great amount of goodness in him. Heroes after him have nurtured similar ambitions though very few, such as Vijayakanth, have actually taken the plunge. Some such as Rajinikanth, sat on the fence for decades, before deciding against seeking public office. But that is a subject for a more detailed narrative when we look at Tamil cinema and its political connection.

The other abiding feature of stardom in Tamil cinema, once again applicable to the heroes alone, is that there is always space at the top only for two of them—one playing the superhero and the other taking on myriad roles. For almost three decades we had Sivaji Ganesan and MGR while others such as Gemini Ganesan and S. S. Rajendran ranked second. Sivaji essayed numerous roles while MGR stuck to safe and narrow roles of the defender of the good and the weak. Then came the Rajinikanth–Kamal Haasan era,

---

[54]V. Sriram, 'Lost Landmarks of Chennai—Kalaivanar Arangam', *Madras Heritage and Carnatic Music*, 3 October 2014.

which lasted for two decades or so. It must also be added here that male heroes never really fade out in Tamil cinema and their stardom, like some exponential graph, takes a long, long while to reach near zero. Thus chances are that there are still Sivaji or MGR fanatics who consider later arrivals as trash. MGR, apart from numerous statues to himself, has a temple too, just outside the high court. And though he acts only sporadically now, we can be sure that Rajinikanth's fan following is more or less intact.

There may have been makkal thilagams (the crest jewel of the people—MGR) and nadigar thilagams (crest jewel among actors—Sivaji Ganesan) but there is only one superstar as far as Tamil cinema is concerned. Nothing in him was the stuff that superstars are made of—his looks were below average, his skin colour was dark and he did nothing to mask it, which was surely the route to failure in fair complexion-obsessed Tamil Nadu. Even his gait was not right and as for his acting, it would have ranked as subpar by any standard. And yet, Rajini made it, and how! There was a time when Rajini essayed a variety of roles, including those with negative shades, but somewhere along the way, he morphed into a superhero who rises from being an underdog to a super-noble superman, in multiple films. This is in sharp contrast to the way Kamal Haasan's career graph has played out—he has essayed numerous characters and acted in a variety of films and he is definitely the greater actor, but charisma is what Rajini has.

Though Rajini played the same role in various films, the audience never tired of it. To them he meant hope that everyday people like them could also succeed and rise above problems that fate placed their way. His films are said to be hits even in Japan. Stories about his religiosity circulate all the time, his attachment to Raghavendra Swami of Mantralayam, whose biopic he acted in, and his almost saintly detachment from day-to-day matters are the stuff of legend.

After Rajini and Kamal's active days on screen, it has been the turn of Vijay and Ajith—the former Thalapathy (commander) to the latter's Thala (head). Once again, Vijay's films follow a formula of a fun-loving, slightly crooked character who sets out to avenge evil, while Ajith's roles have had greater variety. The former's fan associations have been urging him to step into politics and pronouncements by him in some of his films seem to point in that direction. Ajith has not shown any interest in life outside films and is said to be a very private individual. Most refreshingly, he encourages no fan associations and if any are formed and function in his name, it is without his support. That cannot be said of most heroes today who think nothing of distributing money to these associations on the eve of releases and make them buy tickets in bulk and attend the premieres, giving hugely laudatory reviews at the end of the show, chiefly to create the momentum that could make the film a hit.

What of the women? The era till the 1980s did see some very powerful actresses and films that had them as the central character. But, by and large, it has remained a male-dominated industry with heroines playing increasingly subservient roles in recent times. The other interesting aspect is that the Tamil audience has rarely been enamoured by physical fitness on screen. Most screen heroes ran to fat and flab, with MGR and, later, Kamal to an extent being exceptions. In recent times, the six-pack ab has been flaunted by actors such as Surya but the fad never really did catch on. As for heroines and the vamps, the Tamil audiences like them curvy and light-skinned. The derogatory term 'thunder thighs' was probably coined for what passed off as sexy in Tamil cinema. Size zero is a long way from Kollywood. This is probably the reason why in recent years many women from the North have come to Chennai and met with reasonable success in films. That none of them know any Tamil is masked by the excellent dubbing, with many former actresses offering their voices for this. This marks the reversal of the trend in earlier years when clear voices and a good diction were essential for the Tamil cinema industry. The long line of women coming down south also shows how times have changed. Till the 1970s, it was Kollywood that supplied many heroines to its Bombay counterpart.

Cinema in Chennai spawned an entire genre of journalism devoted to the industry, a few in English but the majority in Tamil. Some were serious journals, with in-depth articles on the state of the industry, emerging technologies, and analyses of performance at the box office. Predictably, these did not fare well. *Sound and Shadow* was perhaps the first, published in the 1930s.[55] *Talk-a-Tone* was its successor and it had, among other features, a gossip column penned by 'Studio Guy'.[56] But the hardcore yellow journal was *Cinema Thoothu* and its successor *Indunesan*, both brought out by C. N. Lakshmikanthan referred to in the chapter on drama. The early magazines had short runs in comparison to *Gundoosi* and *Pesum Padam*, both of which began in the late 1940s.[57] Of these, the latter was around for quite a while,

[55]Sriram V, 'Where music and dance flourished', *Madras Musings*, Vol. XXVII, No. 17, 1–15 December 2017.

[56]Swarnavel Eswaran Pillai, *Madras Studios: Narrative, Genre and Ideology in Tamil Cinema*, New Delhi: Sage Publications, 2015, p. 238.

[57]See https://rec.music.indian.misc.narkive.com/rBnlMQm8/pre-1947-news-papers/for a

closing down late in the twentieth century. In recent years, there have been attempts to establish film magazines in English devoted to Tamil cinema but these have not been successful. For years, newspapers and magazines had sections devoted to cinema, *The Hindu*'s Friday supplement featured reviews almost till the 1990s, when these were moved to the Metroplus section. *Indian Express* had its *Cinema Express*, which began in 1980 and closed down in 2016. Among the Tamil magazines, *Ananda Vikatan*, given its Vasan connection, was one of the earliest to devote space to films, its critics' ratings being notoriously strict (only three have scored more than 60 per cent in all these years).[58]

We left the musical aspect of filmmaking in the 1940s when it was still in the grip of the classical genre. But gradually, studios and independent filmmakers began to look at other forms. It was Saluri Rajeswara Rao, then of Gemini Studios, who first introduced Western tunes into Tamil cinema, this being Carmen Miranda's 'I, I, I, I like you very much' from *One Night in Rio* in the film *Mangamma Sapatham*. Chennai was no stranger to Western classical music and so large chunks of it began to make their way into song and dance sequences. Light classical as a genre held sway over Tamil films from the mid-1950s to the mid-1970s, the acknowledged kings in this being the duo Viswanathan–Ramamurthy and after their split in 1965, M. S. Viswanathan alone. It was a great combination—lyrics by the immortal Kannadasan, music by the duo or Viswanathan alone, and playback singing by T. M. Soundararajan and P. Susheela, Tamil cinema's own lady in white, but mercifully with none of the monopolistic tendencies of her counterpart in Bombay. Between them, this quartet occupied centre stage for over three decades. There were other great voices, lyricists, and music directors, but none commanded the fan following of these greats.

Beginning with 1976, there was a change. That was the year the film *Annakili*, a story in a rural setting, hit the screens and started a trend that lasted for ten years and more. The music was as much a factor in its success as was the superb direction by the duo Devaraj–Mohan and the acting by Sujatha, Sivakumar, and 'Phataphat' Jayalakshmi, who formed the lead triangle. Lyrics by Panchu Arunachalam were great but what was superlative was the music by Ilayaraja, then an unknown name in the film industry. Thereafter it was Ilayaraja all the way, till the 1990s. Like Rajinikanth, he

comprehensive listing.

[58]Talk by B. Srinivasan, MD of Vikatan Publications at Madras Week celebrations, 9 August 2019.

too became a larger-than-life figure, referred to respectfully as Isaignani (one who is knowledgeable in music). Much has been written of his saintliness, his deep love for philosophy, and his talents in setting ancient Tamil poetry to delectable music.

If the 1970s and 1980s belonged to Ilayaraja, the succeeding years were those of A. R. Rahman. By then film music itself had changed quite a bit—it had become more rhythm-oriented with lyrics being relegated to the status of a non-entity. It was left to Rahman to make melody with such requirements and he rose to the challenge. His music has gone places and has also won him an Oscar. And in more recent times we have had the only-rhythm song, 'Why This Kolaveri Di'. Conceptualized in 2012 for the thriller *3* by Anirudh Ravichandar and sung by actor Dhanush, it became a hit on social media long before the film released and sank without a trace. But the song trended for quite a while, winning awards from YouTube and getting an invitation for the singer to meet the then prime minister of India, Dr Manmohan Singh.[59]

That makes us wonder if the film song is the single and most enduring legacy of Tamil cinema. The actors may be forgotten and the film invariably vanishes from memory but what remains are the songs. Suddenly, late in the evening, when all is dark and quiet, on hearing a song from a neighbourhood television or a radio, you find yourself momentarily transported to an era which will not return. That kind of make-believe is, after all, the stuff that makes for good cinema.

[59] 'Kolaveri star Dhanush dines with PM', *India Today*, 29 December 2011.

19 | 'TAMILAN DA!'

Chennai is the capital of Tamil Nadu and, therefore, is also a Tamil city. But is it really? True, the bulk of the population here speaks Tamil but the city evolved with several languages contributing to it. Tamil, however, remains constant, from ancient times. Many classics in Tamil are associated with this area. The *Thirukkural* by Thiruvalluvar, who according to Kamil Zvelebil's analysis, lived between the fifth and sixth centuries CE,[1] was composed at Mylapore. Some of the Azhwars and Nayanmars were from villages that became parts of Chennai and they left behind their verses in praise of the deities at temples that are still functional.[2]

Tenth-century inscriptions regarding local area administration, arguably India's first on the subject, are in Tamil and located at the Vaikuntha Perumal Temple, Uthiramerur, just outside Chennai.[3] Sekkizhar, who in the twelfth century composed the *Periya Puranam*, the hagiography that contains the lives of the sixty-three Nayanmars, was from Kunrathur near Chennai.[4] Though Kamban was born at Therazhundur near Thanjavur, it was in Thiruvottiyur that he composed his famed Tamil version of the Ramayana in the twelfth century.[5] Three hundred years later, Arunagirinathar, the devotee of Murugan, spent his lifetime visiting temples to that god, and singing verses at each location—several of these shrines were in the region that would become Chennai.[6] Pattinathar, the philosopher and versifier whose timeline is agreed to be between the tenth and fifteenth centuries, spent his last days at Thiruvottiyur.[7]

Though it is believed that the Pallava and the Chola kings were of Telugu origin, there are practically no records of that language in and around the

---

[1]Thiruvalluvar, Wikipedia, available here: https://en.wikipedia.org/wiki/Thiruvalluvar/.

[2]Those born around here would include Peyazhwar, Thirumazhisai Azhwar, Vayilar Nayanar, and Kaliya Nayanar.

[3]Uttaramerur Inscription, available here: https://tnrd.gov.in/reports/Jain_Report/english/annex3.pdf/.

[4]N. Mahalingam, 'General Editor's Preface', *Periya Puranam in pictures*, Madras: International Society for the Investigation of Ancient Civilizations, 1993, p. iii.

[5]Preeti Zachariah, 'History etched in stone', *The Hindu*, 22 August 2017.

[6]There are verses on the following temples in and around Chennai: Thirumullaivayil, Thiruvalidayam, Thirumayilai, Thiruvanmiyur, Thiruvottiyur, and Madambakkam.

[7]A. Mahadeva Yogi, *Pattinathar Padal Mulamum Thattuvartha Vilakka Uraiyum*, Chennai: B. Rathina Nayakar & Sons, 1932.

city until the arrival of the Vijayanagar Empire from the fourteenth century onwards under the rule of its viceroys, the nayaks. But it was certainly the lingua franca when the British arrived here in 1639. That the area was already a melting pot of sorts as far as languages were concerned becomes evident when you consider that San Thome to the south was Portuguese and Pulicat to the north was Dutch. A few loan words would come into Tamil from both these languages—kakkoos has been mentioned earlier; similarly, a barrel is peepa in Tamil, from the pipes (pronounced peep) that the Portuguese stored their Madeira in. The first business transactions of the British here were in Portuguese, which was the language that translators or dubashes were familiar with. Gradually, these middlemen learnt to transact in English, Tamil, and Telugu.

In old Black Town, a Babel of sorts prevailed. In addition to the Tamil of everyday use, Gujarati, Marwari, and Telugu were heard. The first two communities set up base here chiefly owing to opportunities in money-lending and, more importantly, in money exchange, given that a bewildering variety of currencies and coinage abounded in the seventeenth and eighteenth centuries. With the nawab settling down in the city in the 1760s, Persian and Arabic too were added to the languages heard. The market that came up in Triplicane is even now known as Puli Bone Bazaar—a delightful amalgam of Puli (tiger–in both Tamil and Telugu), Bonu (cage in Telugu), and Bazaar (market in Urdu and Persian).[8] Kannada, Marathi, Bengali, and Malayalam-speaking people arrived here in search of employment from the mid-nineteenth century. Each of these communities and the castes within them set up societies and, at times, schools for perpetuating their language and their heritage. In addition to these, the College of Fort St George, which flourished between 1812 and 1854, as seen in the chapter on higher education, did much to encourage structured learning of the four principal South Indian languages. It must however be remembered here that all of them had clear rules of grammar and were already repositories of a rich wealth of prose and poetry.

The city was caught up in a publishing boom from the 1850s and that did much to propagate the principal languages spoken here, with Tamil, in particular, being a great beneficiary. In fact, it holds the world record for being the first non-European language to be printed. That was in 1554, when much of India was still recording on palm leaf, cloth, wood, metal, and stone. The printing took place in Lisbon and, thereafter, for some time

[8]V. Sriram, 'The Tiger of Triplicane', *The Hindu*, 23 September 2016.

in the sixteenth century, extremely limited print runs of Tamil books, for use by missionaries, were undertaken at Goa.[9]

These were at best sporadic attempts and the first serious efforts at printing Tamil happened at the Tranquebar (Tharangampadi) Mission early in the eighteenth century. In 1716, the missionary Johann Grundler founded the Society for the Promotion of Christian Knowledge (SPCK) in Madras and to this came Johann P. Fabricius, in 1761. He set up printing facilities in the city and this became the Diocesan Press, which functions as the Christian Literature Society Press even today.[10] The government was quick to see the benefits of printing and soon its notifications were all printed at the Diocesan.[11] In its heyday, which was early in the twentieth century, this press printed just about anything, including the statement of accounts for the annual Tyagaraja Aradhana![12]

The Diocesan Press set off a printing boom. The business savvy Chetties of George Town soon took to it and in and around Mint and Govindappa Naicken streets, several printing presses came up, churning out calendars, books, invitations, and leaflets in various languages, Tamil and Telugu being the most in demand. That this coincided with the growth of schools and colleges in the city meant there was a wide readership that encouraged printing. Bookshops too began coming up in the city of which Higginbothams, in its magnificent showroom on Mount Road, is now India's oldest, dating to 1844. This store, which is headquarters to a chain that spread across South India, with outlets at many railway stations, had its own press that published books and now focuses on government security papers. Close by was the Male Orphan Asylum Press (now defunct), which between the nineteenth and twentieth centuries churned out the *Madras Almanac*, which was a sort of annual compendium on the city. Hoe & Company of Stringer's Street run by V. Perumal Chetty & Sons, was another hallowed name, famed for its annual diaries.

The increase in literacy meant the rise of print media as well. Madras has had a long tradition of English newspapers, its history littered with

---

[9]A. R. Venkatachalapathy, 'This Great Benefit: Print and the Cultural Encounter in Eighteenth Century Tranquebar', *Beyond Tranquebar: Grappling Across Cultural Borders*, Esther Fihl and A. R. Venkatachalapathy (ed.), Hyderabad: Orient Blackswan, 2014, pp. 476–77.

[10]Muthiah, *Madras Rediscovered*, pp. 459–60.

[11]Ibid.

[12]The Sri Thyaga Brahma Vaibhava Mahotsava Sabha account statement, 1909, copy with author.

names such as the *Madras Courier* (1785), the *Madras Gazette* (1795), *The Spectator* (1836), the *Madras Times* (1859), and the *Madras Mail* (1868).[13] Of these, the last two had fairly long runs, merging in 1921 after which the combined entity was called *The Mail*, an eveninger which eventually closed in 1981.[14] Of more durable stuff is *The Hindu*, founded in 1878 by a few angry young men protesting against the British establishment being unhappy over the appointment of an Indian, Thiruvarur Muthuswami Iyer, as judge of the High Court of Madras. The initial years were full of turbulence when it came to viability and it was only when Kasturiranga Iyengar acquired it in 1905 that a semblance of stability came about.[15] Since then, *The Hindu* has come a long way, fondly referred to as the Mahavishnu of Mount Road, owing to the controlling family being Vaishnavites. In its time, the daily has seen several ups and downs. It was an ardent nationalist newspaper during the pre-Independence years[16] and then became a staid publication, catering to the state during the Emergency. In the 1980s, it came out with all guns booming to expose the Bofors scandal[17] and in recent times, it has taken a strong stance against communalism and sectarian violence. That, in turn, means it has sacrificed the orthodox among its readers, which has happily not made the paper soften its views.

If at all a newspaper made its name for being consistently anti-establishment, it is the *Indian Express*. The publication was begun in 1931 by Varadarajulu Naidu, an Ayurvedic doctor often described as the Tilak of South India for his fearless views. The paper changed hands a few times and eventually was acquired in 1939 by Ramnath Goenka who transformed it into a national chain whose finest hour was during the Emergency, which it firmly opposed. In later years, the *Indian Express* would take over the Bofors exposes from *The Hindu* and carry on.[18] Its fiery proprietor is now dead but some of the old fire still lingers. 'Loss to the Nation: ₹1760000000000' was how the paper announced the 2G scam to the country. In recent years, *The Hindu* and the *Indian Express* have seen competition from the *Times of India* and, to a much lesser extent, from others such as the *Deccan Chronicle* and *DT Next*, the English paper of the Dina Thanthi Group.

[13]Muthiah, *Madras Rediscovered*, pp. 61–74.

[14]Ibid.

[15]Ibid.

[16]Ibid.

[17]Ibid.

[18]Ibid.

Research has revealed that there were Tamil periodicals and dailies brought out from Chennai as early as in 1812.[19] However, the first Tamil newspaper from Chennai which had a long career was the *Swadesamitran*, founded by G. Subramania Iyer, the same man who began *The Hindu*.[20] Begun in 1899, it remained the only Tamil newspaper till 1916 when the pro-British and anti-Congress paper, *The Dravidian* began its journey. *Swadesamitran*'s heydays were when C. R. Srinivasan was its proprietor and editor, between 1928 and his death in 1962. Thereafter, the paper declined slowly, closing in 1985. Today, it is chiefly remembered for the fact that Subramania Bharati was its associate editor for a brief while. Unwillingness or inability to change from its Brahminical content to cater to a larger reading public that had come about owing to the spread of education was the paper's nemesis. This was something that *Dinamani*, promoted by the Express Group, had foreseen even in the 1930s. And then came the biggest of them all—*Dina Thanthi*, founded by C. P. Adithanar in 1942, in Madurai, later moving to Madras from where it has since spread extensively. *Dinamalar*, begun in 1951 but moving to Madras only in 1979, is more of a middle-of-the-road paper.

Chennai has also had its share of papers exclusively meant for members of a particular community or political persuasion. Perhaps the first was the *Azdarar*, the world's first Armenian newspaper, established by Father Harutyun Shmavonyan in 1794. Though it lasted only for around two years, it is deemed a big landmark in Armenian history. A memorial to the founder stands inside the Armenian Church and a postage stamp has been released in commemoration by Armenia. What is probably the world's only handwritten Urdu paper still comes out from Chennai. *The Musalman* was established in 1927 and is published in the vicinity of the Big Mosque.[21]

Among the earliest in Tamil to espouse Dalit rights was perhaps *Dravida Pandian* begun in 1885 by Ayothi Das Pandithar along with Reverend John Ratnam. Pandithar's next creation, *Oru Paisa Thamizhan* begun in 1907 was a greater success.[22] Thereafter came *Justice*, of the anti-Brahmin party, the South Indian Liberation Front (SILF), which was founded in 1916. The *Andhra Patrika*, of 'Desoddharaka' Kasinathuni Nageswara Rao Pantulu was

---

[19]For a fascinating account on the history of Tamil dailies and periodicals, see A Ma Sami, *19-am Nootrandut Tamizh Ithazhgal*, Chennai: Navamani Pathippagam, 1992.

[20]Ibid.

[21]Navmi Krishna, 'The World's only handwritten newspaper is 91 and sells at 75 paise', *The Hindu*, 14 April 2018.

[22]Sannah, *Ayothidasa Pandithar*, p. 50.

begun in 1908 and it catered to the Telugu-speaking, upper-class, Congress-supporting readers of the city.[23] Annie Besant's *New India* catered to Brahmins and others who supported the Home Rule Movement and had Theosophist leanings. There was also the *Indian Review*, founded by G. A. Natesan in 1900, which was a Congress supporter.[24] It was therefore no surprise that when the Dravidian parties began emerging from the SILF, they all began newspapers and magazines to spread their ideals and thoughts among their followers. Periyar ran *Kudi Arasu* and *Viduthalai*, while Anna had his *Dravida Nadu*.[25] As early as 1942, Karunanidhi had begun his *Murasoli* as a handwritten newspaper. It is today the mouthpiece of the DMK.[26] MGR was no litterateur but his party, the AIADMK, came out with its *Dr Namadhu MGR*. The trend continued with the advent of private TV channels. The Sun TV network was for long the backbone of the DMK before differences forced the party to come up with its Kalaignar TV. The AIADMK has had less success but keeps its Jaya TV going. The Pattali Makkal Katchi of Dr Ramadoss runs Makkal TV while Vijayakanth has his Captain TV.

There are, besides the above newspapers and channels, a host of periodicals in Tamil. *Ananda Vikatan,* now in its nineties is probably the oldest survivor. Begun by Puthur Vaidyanatha Iyer, its fortunes took a turn for the better when it was acquired by S. S. Vasan in 1928. Under his careful nurturing and marketing, it soon became the leading weekly in Tamil. The *Vikatan*, with its logo of a grinning and tufted elderly man, catered to a largely Brahmin clientele but its mix of humour, features, competitions, and novels held it in good stead for many decades. The periodical saw the launch of some great writers, with 'Kalki' Krishnamurthy being the best known.[27] Differences between Vasan and Kalki saw the latter leaving the fold in 1941 and he, together with T. Sadasivam, M. S. Subbulakshmi's husband and the erstwhile advertising manager of *Vikatan*, set up *Kalki*. The world of *Vikatan* and *Kalki* received a jolt in 1948 when *Kumudam* was launched by S. A. P. Annamalai. Writing in the language of the common man, it soon cornered a vast readership, remaining the leading Tamil periodical for almost five decades.[28]

---

[23]Sriram, *Fifty Historic Residences*, p. 88.

[24]S. Muthiah, 'The House of Natesan', *The Hindu*, 25 October 2009.

[25]Kannan, *Anna*, p. 32.

[26]Ibid., p. 70.

[27]Muthiah, *Madras Rediscovered*, pp. 112–15.

[28]Ibid., p. 115.

It took time for *Vikatan* to make changes but when it did, it returned with a bang. The magazine, now a Group, launched a series of special-interest periodicals, all of which became hugely popular. As early as in the 1990s, *Vikatan* decided to go online with its content but with a difference—subscribers would have to pay for it. Today its online revenues far outpace its print revenue. *Vikatan* is once again Tamil's leading magazine and India's second-largest magazine in circulation.[29] Also going strong is Cho Ramaswamy's *Thuglak*, which initially seen as a platform for social and political satire, has now become one-sided.

In these days of SMS, WhatsApp, Facebook, Twitter, email, and other forms of communication, it is difficult to think of a period when news and messages to the public were transmitted by the medium of songs sung at crossroads and other important locations. And this was not very long ago. The practice existed right up to the 1940s after which it faded away. And when the government disliked the message being shared, it reacted much the same way as it does in present days—by attempting to clamp down—but with far less success.

This 'street corner literature' has been the subject of research for Dr A. R. Venkatachalapathy, the well-known scholar. The songs were important documents of the city's history, much of them social and cultural rather than political, from the common man's point of view. Refreshingly, it is a genre that looks at history not from the point of view of the victor alone The modus operandi was simple. Any significant news or event of the day would be turned into a song set to the tune of a popular theatre number or of a folk mode such as venba, kalitturai, viruttam, kummi, chandam, chindu, vannam, oradi, kalivenba, tazhisai, and kirtanai and sung. Pamphlets containing the lyrics would then be sold. These pamphlets also indicated the tune in which the song was to be sung. Compilations of several such songs would also be sold in the form of booklets. The prices of these books rarely exceeded ¼ or ½ anna and so these were also called Kaalana or Arayana Paatu Puttagams. Most of the printing presses that churned out these books were located around the Guzili Bazaar area near the Central Station. The verses therefore came to be known as Guzili songs.

Almost anything and everything appears to have been grist to the songsters' mill. There are songs structured as debates, to be sung as a duet, with each singer taking up one point of view. Thus there are discussions on castor oil vs kerosene, rice vs wheat (a new import to Chennai during the years of food

---

[29]Talk by B. Srinivasan, MD, Vikatan Group, 21 August 2019.

scarcity), and coffee vs tea. Some songs even had a third party sitting in as judge. Thus, in the song on coffee and tea, rice gruel appears as the judge. The more popular variety involved news on murders and this spawned a new genre of songs called the kolai (murder) chindu. There are songs ranging from an unknown Rajambal who was murdered in the Bangalore Mail to the sensational murder of C. N. Lakshmikanthan of *Indunesan* fame. There is even a song on the collapse of the Arbuthnot Bank. Nationalist songs were also very common and, among the patriots, it is Bhagat Singh who emerges as the most popular choice. It was the freedom theme that brought the songs, their authors, and their publishers under the British government's scanner for some time and there were frequent attempts to arrest those involved in writing and circulating such literature.

Composing, typesetting, and printing on a shoestring budget must have always been a challenge and recycling of blocks containing illustrations were very common. Similarly, the recycling of poetic material was also done. Almost all songs began with a prayer to a favourite deity in true theatrical style. The haste with which the pamphlets had to be prepared led to errors in printing and very often the language used was not as per the tenets of composition. Not surprisingly, intellectuals such as Subramania Bharati, A. Madhaviah, and T. K. Chidambaranatha Mudaliar looked down on such literature and wrote disparagingly about them. Notwithstanding that, Guzili art appears to have flourished for over fifty years.

To any historian of the city, the songs on Madras are perhaps the most important takeaway from this genre. There are pieces on People's Park, on temple festivals such as the Arupattu Moovar of the Kapaliswarar Temple and Vedarperi Mahotsavam of the Kandasami Temple at Rasappa Chetty Street. There is a song on a great fire that broke out in the 1890s at the SIAA's annual fair at the People's Park and there are songs on important incidents such as the arrival of the *Emden*. Unlike so many other art forms, Guzili literature has largely survived. This is chiefly because the imperial government confiscated chunks of what it perceived as seditious content and the chapbooks remained stored in the archives for years, yielding a treasure trove for researchers.[30]

Any city that has such a large range of publications to choose from must necessarily be a reading city as well. Evidence of that is the number of libraries. The Madras Literary Society Library, begun in 1818, is one of India's oldest. The Mohammedan Public Library was begun in 1850 and

[30] A. R. Venkatachalapathy, *Mucchandi Ilakkiyam*, Nagercoil: Kalacchuvadu Pathippakam, 2004.

still exists, after a fashion, its beautiful heritage home demolished to make way for an ugly replacement. The Connemara Public Library, established in 1897, is one of the six national libraries of India. In the late nineteenth and early twentieth centuries, many rich patrons established reading rooms across the city, some of which still survive and have regular visitors. But of greater consequence has been the concept of district libraries run by the government.

Madras was a pioneer in this and the movement began in 1927 when, during the Congress session that saw the establishment of the Music Academy, resolutions were also passed to initiate the establishment of a Madras Library Association (MALA). K. V. Krishnaswami Iyer (KVK), the man who helmed the Music Academy for thirty years, was also MALA's first president and it had several of his committed lieutenants, such as the writer P. N. Appuswami Iyer (Pe Naa), and (later Justice) Basheer Ahmed Sayeed on board. MALA made the propagation of libraries in rural areas its main focus and towards this, the first mobile library, in a bullock cart, was instituted in 1929.

It was due to MALA and KVK that the father of Library Science, S. R. Ranganathan (SRR), then librarian at the University of Madras, got due recognition. The need to improve school libraries was recognized and a series of lectures on the subject by SRR was organized at the Teachers' College, Saidapet. This blossomed into a course for librarians and was taken over by the University of Madras in 1931. It is now a full-fledged degree course.

SRR had developed the colon classification system for libraries. KVK was to recognize the genius in this method and it was given due publicity. MALA also began a publications division. The first book to be brought out was *Essays by Diverse Hands*, a selection from writings by eminent personalities. The second was SRR's *The Five Laws of Library Science*. His *Colon Classification: Classified Catalogue Code and Library Administration*, also published by MALA, was to become famous all over the world and became the basis on which libraries began classifying their books. Under KVK, MALA lobbied the Madras government hard to get a Libraries Act passed. It took twenty years but it was ultimately successful in 1948 with Madras becoming the first province to have such legislation in place. Under this legislation, it became necessary for every town/village with a certain population to have a public library. These were to be under the Local Library Authority (LLA) for which funding was from a cess levied on local taxes. The Connemara Public Library became the State Central Library. Overall administration of the LLA was to be under a library committee headed by the Minister for Education. The Act, now the Tamil Nadu Public Libraries Act, remains in force, though its libraries are a far cry from what KVK and SRR envisioned.[31] But nevertheless, they exist and even today, despite competition from the internet, have a dedicated clientele visiting each day.

Circulating and lending libraries may today be on the decline with much-loved Eloor in T. Nagar closing shop[32] but others of its kind and far older, such as Eswari begun by T. N. Palani in 1955, are still going strong. With a collection of over 400,000 books (just 100,000 short of the Connemara) and eleven branches, this chain shows no signs of fading away. Also surviving are countless and nameless second-hand bookshops all along the Luz Corner and Triplicane, several of them nothing more than a wooden box on which books are displayed during the day and then stored within at night. The best known among these is Alwar's, taking its name from the sage-like elder who ran it on the footpath outside the Mylapore Club. His partners were Iyer, a heavily myopic and emaciated individual who knew every title and Mary, Alwar's wife. All three have passed away but the bookshop still survives, under tents, run by the founder's children.

The extension of libraries to the districts by the 1950s saw most Chennai-based Tamil magazines being made available across the state. As the author Ku Azhagirisami once commented, it was possible to write poetry in the village but if it had to be printed and distributed so that others could know of it, then the city was the only place that provided the opportunity and the means.[33] Beginning with the 1930s, when *Ananda Vikatan* began drawing talents such as Kalki Krishnamurthy, authors began flocking to Chennai in droves. By the mid 1950s, the city was the hub of a teeming literary movement. Several magazines were being brought out and though very few survived in the long run, they shone a light on prodigious talents during their lifetimes. The money was a pittance, but the satisfaction of seeing one's work in print was immeasurable. The works between the 1930s and 1950s largely dwelt on Brahminical and upper-caste themes, this stratum being the principal readership. But as time went on, this changed. Perhaps it is Jayakanthan who best exemplifies the new style—he focused largely on the underbelly of the city. It is also noteworthy that as early as 1925, Tamil had its first woman publisher—the author, freedom fighter, and singer Vai Mu Kothainayaki Ammal.[34] Beginning with her publication, *Jaganmohini*, there

[31]V. Sriram, 'KVK and his public causes', *Madras Musings*, Vol. XXII, No. 23, 16–31 March 2013.

[32]Meghna Majumdar, 'Chennai's Eloor Library in its final chapter', *The Hindu*, 4 January 2018.

[33]*Chennaiku Vanthen*, pp. 43–51.

[34]Tiruppur Krishnan, *Kothainayakiyin Illakkiya Pathai*, Chennai: Vanathi Pathippakam, 1999.

has been a long line of magazines exclusively dedicated to women, which have not only promoted independent thought, but also encouraged their writing talents. *Saraswathi*, a magazine that existed in the 1950s, ran a series featuring authors narrating how and why they first came to the city. Titled *Chennaikku Vanden* (I came to Chennai), this was compiled as a book by author Pazha Athiyaman in 2008—all the narratives, deeply individual and varied in treatment, had a common thread—the writers had been attracted by the intellectual stimulus that the city offered.[35]

Hindi was a late entrant, making its way in chiefly with the Congress, which by the 1920s, had a good hold over the city. It was useful to know the language to understand what leaders from the North were saying in their speeches. In 1918, Mahatma Gandhi inaugurated the Dakshin Bharat Hindi Prachar Sabha (DBHPS) to teach South Indians Hindi, his son Devadas being among the first pracharaks. Initially, a wing of the Congress and an independent organization from 1927, its avowed mission was to ensure that non-Hindi speaking people learnt the language so that as and when India became independent, it would have one common national language. The DBHPS, which began life in George Town, moved later to Mylapore and Triplicane, before acquiring seven acres of land in T. Nagar and settling there. It introduced examinations in Hindi as well, initially up to three levels and later increasing to six. Each had a degree prefixed by the term Rashtrabhasha, which clearly showed what the intent was—the creation of a common Indian language. It became fashionable thereafter to learn the language, especially among the upper classes, with many stating with pride that they were qualified up to the Prathamik, Madhyama, or Visharad levels. Ambujammal, the staunch Gandhian, became proficient enough to translate Munshi Premchand's novels into Tamil.

Madras was used to multiple languages, being capital to a vast presidency that comprised in the 1930s, Orissa, the whole of present-day Andhra, parts of Karnataka, and Kerala. Orissa was the first to leave the fold, becoming a separate province in the 1930s. And the Andhras had already begun to dream of a state of their own. The broad outlines of such an entity were drawn up in Madras city in the 1930s, at Sri Baugh, the vast residence of 'Desoddharaka' Kasinathuni Nageswara Rao Pantulu. The Sri Baugh Pact, as it was known, was to get the diverse Telugu-speaking regions of Madras Presidency and outside of the nizam's territories to agree on the formation

---

[35]Ibid.

of a state when the time came.[36] Hindi was a minor matter when compared to such momentous happenings, or so it seemed.

Beginning with the early twentieth century, a movement had begun to restore Tamil to its classical status by purging it of all words of Sanskrit origin. Adherents to this school of thought even changed their names. Thus, the poet Surya Narayana Sastry became Paruthi Mal Kalaignar[37] and N. C. Vedachalam became Marai Malai—the replacements being the exact Tamil equivalents of the Sanskrit words. They also supported the self-respect movement and its opposition to Hindi. In this, they were one with Periyar whom they differed with on matters concerning religion.[38]

In 1937, Rajaji, on becoming premier, made it mandatory that all schools in Madras Presidency teach Hindi. In this, he was toeing the Congress line. Satyamurti warned him of the inadvisability of such a step but the premier proved obdurate and went ahead. Periyar sternly opposed the step. In his view, it was the tool by means of which upper-caste North Indians would eventually come to rule over the Tamils. In this, he also included Tamil Brahmins, who, given their familiarity with Sanskrit, were at the forefront of learning Hindi. Periyar saw this as that community's way of ensuring its success in Independent India. The protests that he and Anna fanned against the language eventually came to engulf Sanskrit and Telugu as well. A deep divide was emerging—the Brahmins were largely supporters of Sanskrit and Hindi, while the Andhras were championing Telugu. Tamil supporters were banding together to fight for their rights.

Fasts, protests, and unrest followed in the Tamil-dominated areas. Stalin Jagadeesan announced his intention to fast unto death for the sake of Tamil. He became a role model for protestors with Anna announcing that if Jagadeesan were to die, he was prepared to take his place and die for the cause. In the event, Jagadeesan did not die and called off his fast after ten weeks, amidst rumours that he had been taking refreshments on the sly. A far more serious matter was the death of two men in police custody, following their arrests for participating in the agitation. These were Thalamuthu Nadar and Natarajan. Interestingly, both were illiterate but were filled with an abiding love for Tamil. Arrested at separate places, they had both refused to accept certain

---

[36]Sriram, *Fifty Historic Residences*, p. 88.

[37]V Sundaram, *Scholars and Savants: Portraits of Selected Tamil Scholars*, Chennai: Vanathi Pathippakam, 2010, pp. 28-30.

[38]For further details see Marai Thirunavukkarasu, *Maraimalai Adigal Varalaru*, Chennai: Banu Pathipakkam, 2007.

conditions for their release and died in custody. While the government gave out the usual medical reasons for their death, for the anti-Hindi agitators, they were martyrs to the cause. An emotional Anna declared that their deeds ought to be inscribed in gold. With matters coming to a boil and Rajaji remaining unmoved, Governor Lord Erskine was at his wits end. But World War II unexpectedly solved matters. Gandhi ordered all Congress governments in India to resign in protest against Viceroy Lord Linlithgow's unilateral decision to drag India into the conflict. The Rajaji government quit and Lord Erskine rescinded the order on Hindi education.[39] Peace returned but the attitude of the people towards Hindi had crystallized. It was perceived as a tool by which North India would dominate and destroy Tamil culture. Extending this argument further, Periyar declared that it was far better to be subservient to the British than to subject the Tamil-speaking regions to North Indian rule. He began a demand for Dravidistan, comprising areas where the four southern languages were spoken. Anna supported him on this. But even he was not willing to toe Periyar's line that 15 August 1947 be observed as a day of mourning by the Tamils.[40]

The question of Hindi's proposed status as national language was hotly debated in the Constituent Assembly and it was decided that the K. M. Munshi–Sir N. Gopalaswami Iyengar formula would prevail as per which there would be no national language for fifteen years, with Hindi in Devanagari script being one of several official languages of the union. English would remain in use for fifteen years (until 26 January 1965) and a language commission would be set up to investigate how it could be phased out in favour of Hindi over the period.[41] The question of national language simmered, thereafter, but did not reach flash point. The death of Nehru in 1964 saw Lal Bahadur Shastri succeeding him at the centre and powerful factions in the union cabinet immediately began lobbying hard for Hindi to be made the national language in 1965 as agreed in the Munshi–Iyengar formula. In Madras, this was met with public protests. The DMK was at the forefront of the agitation and students joined en masse, boycotting classes and leading protest marches. Congress politicians from Madras such as Kamaraj too voiced their protests with those serving in the union cabinet even tendering their resignations. The surprising protester against Hindi was Rajaji. He was then heading the Swatantra Party, an entity opposed to the Congress while

[39]Kannan, *Anna*, pp. 50–62.

[40]Ibid.

[41]Ibid., pp. 271–84.

representing the interests of rich agriculturists, the business class, and erstwhile royalty. As astute at reading the wind and as Ashokamitran once wrote of him, a man who 'only gently lowered himself into water of the mundane or the ordinary when he could see bottom level',[42] Rajaji had seen what the future portended.

Unfortunately, Chief Minister M. Bhaktavatsalam saw all of it as a law and order problem. Colleges were closed indefinitely and protesting students were met with tear-gas shells and lathi charges. The centre eventually backed down but the damage had been done. In the 1967 elections to the state legislature, the DMK knew that it was winning. Rajaji announced that he 'would beat the Congress with the DMK shoe'.[43] That election saw the defeat of the Congress and it has never made it back to office in the state. Kamaraj was defeated by an unknown student leader in his constituency. Anna became chief minister. Among the first acts of the new government was to rename the state Tamil Nadu.[44]

It was serendipitous that a World Tamil Conference organized by the International Association for Tamil Research (IATR) was slated to be held in Madras in January 1968. The IATR was a body formed in 1964 at the twenty-sixth International Congress of Orientalists held in New Delhi.[45] The first of the conferences was held at Kuala Lumpur and it was Chennai's turn in 1968. With the DMK in power, it naturally became a grand celebration of the party's victory, though the conference had a serious academic side to it that is largely forgotten.[46] An integral part of the event was a procession involving a series of decorated floats down the Marina, extolling the virtues of Tamil culture, all put together by the studios of the city. Tamil identity, its glories—whether true or grossly exaggerated—and its culture had all become intertwined inextricably with cinema. Statues of Tamil scholars and iconic characters from Tamil literature were erected on the beach. Thalamuthu and Natarajan, who had sacrificed their lives for the Tamil cause in the 1930s would later be honoured with an important government precinct being named after them. Streets, subways, and parks would be named after others who martyred themselves through self-immolation during the 1967 agitations.[47]

[42]Ashokamitran, *Years with Boss*, p. 52.
[43]Kannan, *Anna*, p. 302.
[44]Ibid., pp. 334–38.
[45]Ibid., p. 319.
[46]Ibid., p. 320.
[47]V. Sriram, 'A Tradition of Political Martyrdom', *The Hindu*, 3 October 2014.

Tamil vis-à-vis Hindi has since remained a touchy subject in the state, even though the popularity of Hindi cinema has not diminished. But, by and large, Tamil Nadu has defended its right to its language. AIR, by virtue of its having been around in the city from the 1930s, has a powerful Tamil portfolio when it comes to programming. When Doordarshan (DD) began broadcasting from the city in 1975, certain changes were made keeping in mind the sensitivity of the local populace. If *Chitrahaar*, the programme that featured song and dance sequences from Hindi films was telecast all over the rest of the country, DD Chennai had its *Oliyum Oliyum* (light and sound), which featured Tamil songs. Hindi feature films were beamed on Sunday in the rest of the country with Saturday being reserved for local language films. In Chennai it was the other way round. As Hindi serials such as *Hum Log* and *Buniyaad* began to grow in popularity across the country, including Tamil Nadu, there had to be introductory précis by announcers on what was to follow. The mega serials such as *Ramayan* and *Mahabharat* had to be dubbed in Tamil. Those were days when attitudes hardened to such an extent that anybody speaking in Hindi would pointedly be asked to change over to English or Tamil. And yet, people from Chennai proved adept in learning the other languages of India, Hindi included, when they had to settle in other parts of the country. That was more than what could be said of their North Indian counterparts moving South. Not that it is easy. Unlike most other languages of India, there is a clear distinction between formal, spoken Tamil and what is heard on an everyday basis. The latter is easy to master, but the former can be quite a challenge. The AIR and DD years were marked by good, clear diction and excellent usage of the Tamil language. The arrival of the private channels has more or less dealt a mortal blow to Tamil, for, barring the news broadcasts, what is spoken is colloquial in the extreme, faulty in pronunciation, and Tanglish at best. In many ways, it follows the Tamil of Chennai, which is pidgin, evolving over time owing to various linguistic groups settling in the city. This is not Tamil but an entirely local language known as Madras bhashai.

It is to be noted here that when the political fathers changed the name of the city to Chennai, they did not want the language to be known as Chennai bhashai, for this is a dialect that nobody wants to own up to. Imagine a base of Tamil garnished with liberal helpings from Telugu and some toppings from English, Sanskrit, and Hindi, and you get Madras bhashai. It is in many ways a work in progress, for it has evolved over time. But some gems will always remain evergreen and hopefully survive the vicissitudes of time. An offender in traffic will always be a saavu graaki (customer of death), a drunk will always be 'full load', and a policeman 'mama'. Bribe is 'mamool', from the Telugu and Hindi term that stands for custom, showing that it has been an age-old practice in our country.

Tamil chauvinism has since had its funnier sides as well. M. Tamilkudimagan (literally means 'son of the Tamils'), whose original name was Sathiah, became minister for Tamil language and culture in the 1996 DMK cabinet and took his portfolio rather seriously. One of his diktats was that all commercial establishments in the city had to put up signboards that featured their names in Tamil prominently. This was taken by officialdom to greater heights when they decided to interpret his ruling to mean that all English words in names had to be translated into Tamil. There was panic in the corporate and commercial worlds as everyone scrambled to find equivalents in Tamil for English words they had used till then. To find Tamil words for ice cream, coffee, and pumps became a challenge. In the meanwhile, bands of implementers of the ministerial diktat wandered around markets and commercial districts, imposing fines on those who had not complied, occasionally tearing down signboards. Like everything else, this too lost steam after a while and Chennai went back to its old ways. In 2001, for reasons unknown, this Tamil champion and true scholar was denied a ticket by the DMK to contest elections, this despite the party's love for the language. He promptly defected to the AIADMK but Jayalalithaa did not offer him a ministerial berth, which is what he had hoped for so that he could implement whatever he had left unfinished. He died in 2004.

There has been progress in the development of the Tamil language as well. Serious research into Tamil is conducted at many places across the world. Chennai too has played its part. Scholars such as Marai Malai Adigal and U Ve Swaminatha Iyer worked in this city. The University of Madras contributed as well, its Department of Tamil embarking on a lexicon in that language in 1913, completing it in 1936, with S. Vaiyapuri Pillai, R. P. Sethu Pillai, and V. Venkatarajulu Reddiyar, all hallowed names, working on it. A further 20,000 words were added by 1939.[48] In 1954, a concise Tamil lexicon was brought out. The International Institute for Tamil Studies came up in 1970 in the city. In 1978, the then MGR government made some modifications to the script, chiefly to rationalize certain practices. These came to be accepted only in part and that too only in Tamil Nadu, with other Tamil-speaking countries preferring to stick to tradition. In 1981, the MGR government set up what had originally been proposed in 1925—a

[48] *150 Years of Excellence: A Pictorial History of the University of Madras*, Chennai: University of Madras, 2006, p. 77.

Tamil university, located in Thanjavur.

By the 1950s, research in Tamil had spread across the globe and it was the American scholars who pointed out a treasure trove that lay right in Tamil Nadu's midst. This was the collection of printed matter in Tamil painstakingly put together by 'Roja' Muthiah, a signboard painter in Kottaiyur, Chettinad. The prefix came about because he had a habit of signing all his artworks with a rose. He began his collection in 1950s and naturally acquired a lot of what was printed earlier as well. By the time of his death in 1992, there was a 100,000-strong collection of printed matter—periodicals, books, newspapers, posters, leaflets, and wedding invites. It had been put to good use by scholars the world over and when it came to be known that Roja Muthiah's descendants were planning to sell everything as scrap, there was consternation. The University of Chicago stepped in and purchased the entire lot and then decided that it ought to remain in Tamil Nadu. The collection was shifted to Chennai in 1994 and was housed initially in Mogappair East before shifting to the Central Polytechnic Campus in Taramani, where the government placed a building on long lease at its disposal. The Roja Muthiah Research Library has since grown to a 300,000-strong collection but its future remains uncertain, chiefly owing to lack of funds to carry on its good work. In the meanwhile, even as it manages a hand-to-mouth existence, scholars make a beeline to it. All that professed love for Tamil has not seen the state government extend much help.[49] And when it has offered help, the end result has often been counterproductive. Marai Malai Adigal's vast personal collection of books was, for years, housed in a library dedicated to his name, in North Chennai. This did not see much patronage but it was at least open to scholars. The Government offered to make it a part of the Connemara Library and when that happened the collection just became part of a large ocean, accessed with great difficulty.

Tamil has also often been used to suit political ends. The 'threat of Hindi' is revived each time an election is due. There are more visible markers as well. On 1 January 2000, then chief minister Karunanidhi unveiled a 133-foot statue of Thiruvalluvar at Kanyakumari, thereby setting off a race of sorts to erect giant statues all across the country by various political parties. In 2010, he decided to host yet another World Tamil Conference on the lines of what his mentor had done in 1968. The state government was increasingly in the news for the wrong reasons—corruption, nepotism, and its equivocation over the Sri Lankan government's final push in its battle against the LTTE.

---

[49]Muthiah, *Madras Rediscovered*, pp. 92–93.

The IATR, however, refused to grant its stamp of approval but the DMK went ahead, hosting what it labelled the World Classical Tamil Conference in Coimbatore and converting it into a political broadcast in every way.[50] The voters unfortunately were not impressed. But it did result in plenty of civic improvements in Coimbatore. In 2016, the Edappadi Palaniswami-led AIADMK government decided to score some brownie points by getting the Tamil diaspora to crowdsource a Tamil Chair at Harvard University.[51] It was pointed out by critics that the money could have been put to better use by improving facilities for research in Tamil in one of Tamil Nadu's many universities.

In the meanwhile, the rise of the BJP in national politics may yet bring Tamil to the fore. The party, branded as north Indian by much of Tamil Nadu, has seen that championing Tamil is necessary for breaching what is a bastion for regional outfits. The Rashtriya Swayamsevak Sangh (RSS), which is the ideological guide for the BJP has had Tarun Vijay, one of its pracharaks bone up on Thiruvalluvar and extol him at all available opportunities. He had a statue of the composer installed at Haridwar, campaigned for Tamil to be made the official language of the High Court of Madras and also lobbied to get Tamil recognized as a national language of India. Calling himself an adopted son of Tamil thai (mother), he had even held up a placard in the Parliament while he was a Rajya Sabha member, asking MPs disrupting the house to follow the path of Thiruvalluvar.[52] The DMK and others reacted warily to all this posturing, for it was after all appropriation of one of their key political weapons. But they need not have worried. In a TV interview, Tarun Vijay infamously remarked that India did not have any problem with racism, for after all did not the North happily coexist with the South, which was full of black people? He, the RSS, and the BJP have since rued that statement and are yet to live down the lampooning that followed.[53]

The ruling party at the centre has since made a couple of maladroit moves. In June 2019, it was reported that the draft education policy of the Human Resources Development Ministry of the Government of India has

---

[50]Noboru Karashima, 'IATR and the World Classical Tamil Conference', *The Hindu*, 23 July 2010.

[51]'TN Govt to create Tamil chairs in top global universities', *New Indian Express*, 29 June 2018.

[52]Prakash K. Dutta, 'When Tarun Vijay fought for Tamil', *India Today*, 7 April 2017.

[53]'Tarun Vijay lands in trouble with "black people" remarks, later apologises on Twitter', *The Hindu*, 7 April 2017.

recommended that Hindi be made compulsory as a third language in all non-Hindi speaking states. Stalin of the DMK immediately announced that Tamils had no Hindi blood in them and would wage a war to prevent this from happening. But will Tamils do that any longer remains a question. Chennai itself has changed quite a bit since the 1960s. It is now more cosmopolitan with the upwardly-mobile classes focusing on getting their children to speak English fluently, often at the expense of the mother tongue. It has been pointed out by critics that the children and grandchildren of DMK leaders attend international schools where the medium of instruction is English, with no Tamil being taught. Certainly, a working knowledge of English has become a vital necessity in today's connected world.

What of Hindi? That has become necessary in Chennai as well. For over a decade now, increasing prosperity has meant that the Tamils have, more or less, abandoned menial chores, leading to large-scale migration from North India to fill the demand. Cooks, carpenters, watchmen, masseurs, hairdressers, and nursing staff now come from states such as Bihar, Rajasthan, UP, Orissa, and the Northeast. Communicating with them requires a working knowledge of Hindi. One of the less appealing features of this is the tendency to address everyone as 'ji', in the fond hope that it makes the speaker appear to be fluent in Hindi. Karunanidhi and Anna must be squirming somewhere. But they need not worry. Much of Tamil Nadu and a large chunk of Chennai may learn Hindi but will never allow Tamil to be sacrificed in its favour. The quality of the Tamil, however, leaves much to be desired.

Interestingly, the best-known biography of Tamil is by David Shulman, an Israeli Indologist.[54] And we take pride in the fact that the man who edited the definitive anthology of modern Tamil fiction, *The Tamil Story: Through the Times, Through the Tides*, is Dilip Kumar, a Gujarati by birth and whose chosen medium of self-expression in writing is Tamil.

[54]David Shulman, *Tamil: A Biography*, Cambridge, Massachusetts: The Belknap Press of the Harvard University Press, 2016.

By virtue of being the capital of Tamil Nadu, Chennai has been at the centre of political developments in the state for long. The city is often seen by outsiders as a place that thinks differently, consistently voting for the underdog at the centre and always supporting one of the two regional parties in the state. No matter what be the political wave spreading across the rest of the nation, Chennai and Tamil Nadu have chosen to cast their lot with local leaders, for over fifty years. To many, the most abiding aspect of politics here is its close association with cinema and the principal roles played by a few individuals ever since Independence.

What is forgotten is that politics here began not so much as part of the freedom movement but as a struggle for equality. The nobility of that fundamental objective can never be doubted. 'Chennai is quite unique in the way the fight for social justice came together with other causes,' says Dr A. R. Venkatachalapathy. 'Elsewhere you had rationalist movements, struggles to establish social equality, efforts to reform theatre and cinema so that they represented burning issues. But all of them were in silos. Here in Chennai, it all came together, and that is why it had a lasting impact.'[1]

Probably because of a relatively better spread of education when compared to several other provinces of India, the struggle for equality started much earlier here than in other parts of the country. The beginning of social reform may be accredited to Gazulu Lakshminarasu Chetty, who in the mid-1800s was a thorn in the flesh of the British establishment. A rich merchant who spent generously on causes dear to him, Lakshminarasu began *The Crescent* in 1844, a newspaper devoted to the amelioration of the Hindus. It fought against proselytization, the torture of peasants who could not pay their dues, and unfair trade practices. He established the Madras Native Association, which could be considered the first political entity of South India. Lakshminarasu later made it to the Madras Legislative Council as well.[2] Though his initiatives died with him, the ideas endured, and several found voice in the Madras Mahajana Sabha (MMS), founded in 1884. This organization still survives but more as a social club. The MMS, along with the Poona Sarvajanik Sabha,

[1]Interview with the author, Chennai, 12 March 2020.

[2]Karthik A. Bhatt, 'An Early Madras Activist', *Madras Musings*, Vol. XX, No. 20, 1–15 February 2011.

the Bombay Presidency Association, and the Indian Association, is considered one of the progenitors of the Congress party. Indeed, some of its founders, such as P. Anandacharlu and P. Rangiah Naidu were early members of the Congress as well.

It may be a surprise to many that the idea of a Congress party was first mooted in Madras, at a house on R. K. Mutt Road, Mylapore. This was in 1884 at Krishna Vilas, then the residence of Dewan Bahadur R. Raghunatha Row, civil servant and dewan of Indore, where 'seventeen good men and true' met and resolved that 'a national movement for political ends' be formed. A plaque to this effect was affixed to a wall and survived until the property changed hands and became a high-rise.[3]

In the meanwhile, the spread of Western education was being taken full advantage of by the Brahmins who were also filling up the government jobs being thrown open to them. The other caste Hindus, Christians, and, to some extent, Muslims followed suit while the plight of backward classes, known as Adi Dravidas, remained more or less untouched. Education, largely made possible owing to Christian missionaries, caused a transformation, brought about by members of the community themselves. These included Ayothi Das Pandithar referred to in the previous chapter, and his brother-in-law, Rettamalai Srinivasan.

Born in 1859 at Chengalpattu near Chennai, Srinivasan studied accountancy in Coimbatore, where he noted that out of 400 students, 390 were Brahmins. Employed in tea estates in the Nilgiris, he thereafter devoted much of his life to the upliftment of the outcastes. He established the Paraiyar Mahajana Sabha in 1891 and two years later began a paper titled *The Paraiyan*. In December 1893, he held the first conference of Adi Dravidas, at the Wesleyan Mission Hall, Royapettah. In 1895, he organized a second meeting at the VP Hall, where he enlightened the gathered members about the rights of the community. A greater breakthrough was achieved when he hosted a welcome for Viceroy Lord Elgin in December 1895, in a public pandal put up at the intersection of Mount Road and General Patters Road. While detractors dismissed this as a stunt, it resulted in Srinivasan and his comrades being welcomed to the governor's house where they could confer with the viceroy in a one-on-one meeting.

It was Srinivasan who impressed on the British government of the times that the Adi Dravidas needed to be treated as a bloc apart from the Hindus, as members of the latter would never represent their interests. From this point

[3]Muthiah, *Madras Rediscovered.*

it became customary for the community to conduct its parallel welcomes and farewells to visiting dignitaries and serving governors of Madras. In 1898, the Paraiyar Mahajana Sabha sent its greetings to Queen Victoria on her completing sixty years as the reigning monarch. In many ways, this was the beginning of the path that would eventually lead to separate electorates for depressed classes in pre-Independent and post-Independent India.

Srinivasan and his association, likewise, opposed the Congress party's demand, made in 1895, that the ICS examination ought to be held in India as well, so that Indians could sit for it. It was the Adi Dravida contention that such a relaxation of rules would lead to wealthy, caste Hindus qualifying and then perpetuating their pre-conditioned notions in their official capacities. It was Srinivasan's view that it was preferable to be governed by English officers. The Congress withdrew its demand thereafter. This was the precursor to Periyar's opposing the Independence struggle itself, claiming that it would place the country squarely in the hands of caste Hindus.

Srinivasan went about achieving a lot more. A government order in 1893 had mandated that schools ought to be open to all and that if a set of seven students had been admitted, such an institution could get government recognition. Five years later, in *The Paraiyan,* Srinivasan exposed that this law had remained on paper as far as the Adi Dravidas were concerned. No caste Hindu would come forward to teach them, and no school would admit them. He then presented a memorandum seeking the establishment of Adi Dravida schools in Madras and elsewhere. The government acquiesced and these schools came under the purview of the corporation. In 1904, it was at one of these that Srinivasan's brother-in-law and fellow activist, Ayothi Das Pandithar, introduced the noon meal scheme (see chapter on education), which under Kamaraj and MGR would extend across the state, with monumental results.

Pandithar and Srinivasan did not see eye to eye on many matters, though they were united in their common goal. The former objected to the use of the word Paraiyan and filed a civil suit against the latter's paper in 1896, which resulted in a fine for the publication. The impact of Srinivasan's writings was displayed when members of the community filled the court hall and paid the money themselves. Likewise, Srinivasan did not agree with Pandithar encouraging the Depressed Classes to embrace Buddhism, something Ambedkar would take to later. The other Dalit leader from Madras, M. C. Rajah, opined that conversion was unacceptable and born as they were into Hinduism, the community members ought to remain in it. Srinivasan was of the view that the Adi Dravidas, being outside of the caste system, did not qualify as Hindus and so need not convert. This, however, did not affect his cordial relations with Ambedkar. Likewise, he disagreed with Gandhi referring to the Depressed Classes as Harijans and bringing out a paper by the same name, where he 'wrote whatever occurred to him, none of which applies to the depressed classes'.[4]

Between 1900 and 1923, Srinivasan travelled across the seas—his plan was to get to London. But he stayed on at South Africa, worked there, befriended Gandhi, and returned to India. Here he was nominated to the Madras Legislative Council as a representative of the Backward Classes, defending foremost their right of access to any road, well, temple, market, and public site. He demanded the closure of shops selling alcohol on festival days and Sundays, chiefly with a view to curtailing consumption among his community. In later years, he worked closely with Ambedkar and went to the Second Round Table Conference, achieving finally his dream of visiting London and meeting King Emperor George V, at Buckingham Palace. A question that the king asked remained with him—if a low caste man fell in a street, would a high caste man not go and help him? Srinivasan had to reply in the negative.

Richly decorated by the British with the Rao Sahib, Rao Bahadur, and Dewan Bahadur titles, Srinivasan lived a long and fruitful life, passing away in 1945.[5] By then much had changed in Madras. In 1916, the non-Brahmins had come together to form the South Indian Liberation Front (SILF), the architects of which were Dr C. Natesa Mudaliar, (later Sir) Pitti Theagaraya Chetty, and Dr T. M. Nair. This entity had a pan-south Indian membership, the dominating group being landholders from the Telugu-speaking regions of the presidency. Non-Brahmin lawyers of the city were yet another significant group, having suffered for long in their profession from the dominance of the Mylapore lobby (read Brahmins). The party's paper, *The Justice*, later gave its name to the way the entity was referred to by the public. It must be noted here that the Dalits remained largely out of the purview of the Justice Party, as they had suffered ostracization at the hands of the non-Brahmins as well.[6]

The Justice Party, which initially restricted itself to petitioning the imperial

---

[4]Walajah Vallavan (ed.), *Dewan Bahadur Irattaimalai Seenivasan Avarkalin Thanvaralaru*, Chennai: Tamizh Kudiarasu Pathippakam, 2009, p. 38. Translation provided by the author.

[5]For further details on this personality, see Walajah Vallavan (ed.), *Dewan Bahadur Irattaimalai Seenivasan Avarkalin Thanvaralaru*.

[6]Karthikeyan Damodaran and Hugo Gorringe, 'The DMK Has Been Two-Faced in Its Commitment Towards Social Justice', *The Wire*, 19 August 2018.

government for concessions towards its member communities, later opted to directly participate in governance. The establishment of diarchy under the Montagu–Chelmsford Reforms provided an opportunity and the party, unlike the Congress, contested the elections to the Madras Legislative Council in 1920, winning a majority of the seats. Its leader was invited to become the premier of Madras Presidency and under Sir P. Ramarayaningar, the raja of Panagal, who was the second incumbent to occupy the post, it enacted some path-breaking legislation. The first of these, popularly known as the Communal Governmental Order came about in 1921 and provided for caste-based reservations in government jobs and higher educational institutions. It was the first of its kind in the country. The same year it reversed a Government of India ruling that prevented women from becoming legislators. The party also legislated that terms such as Panchama and Pariah were derogatory and needed to be replaced with Adi Dravida—Ayothi Das Pandithar being the first to raise such a demand.[7]

There were several aspects of the party that were not palatable to the Congress and a larger public, notably its strong support of the British, to the extent of banning Subramania Bharati's songs from the presidency, its opposition to independence as a concept, and its acting as per the whims of the landed aristocracy.[8] There were divisions within as well, between the Tamil and Telugu-speaking members. Thus, when the Andhras began demanding a university where Telugu would be given importance, the Tamil members demanded a similar university for Tamil.[9] This was solved by the creation of the Andhra University in Vishakhapatnam and following an endowment from Raja Sir Annamalai Chettiar, the formation of the Annamalai University, which gave prominence to Tamil, in Chidambaram. There was also discontent among the Adi Dravida members. One of the chief reasons was the repeated labour trouble at Binny Mills and elsewhere, where there were riots between upper-caste workers and those of the Depressed Classes. The government repeatedly sided with the former.[10]

But it cannot be denied that the party had set Madras and the rest of the presidency on the path of social reform. By the time it was eventually

---

[7]GO 217, 25 March 1922.

[8]P. G. Sundararajan, *Life of S Satyamurti*, pp. 19-43.

[9]B. S. Baliga, *Madras District Gazetteers, Pt 1-2, Thoothukudi District*, Madras: Superintendent, Government Press, 1957, p. 170.

[10]Dilip Veeraraghavan, *The Making of the Madras Working Class*, New Delhi: LeftWord, 2013, pp. 136–37.

defeated by the Congress in 1934, leading to Periyar walking out with a significant chunk of its membership and forming, in 1941, the Dravida Kazhagam, the entire region had changed character. Voices of all communities were being heard, albeit in various strengths.

Language politics reared its head in the city immediately after Independence. The Sri Baugh Pact (see chapter on language) for a separate Andhra was resurrected and an agitation began in Madras. Potti Sriramulu, a high-strung Congressman, was induced to fast-unto-death for the cause.[11] It was his misfortune that the chief minister of undivided Madras State at this time was Rajaji. The man who had time and again declared that he was an outsider in politics and a sanyasi not interested in office, had by then served as governor general of India, governor of West Bengal, and minister for Home Affairs, Government of India. He was living in self-imposed retirement, one of his many, when the first elections to the states of independent India were held. In Madras State, as it was then known, the Congress barely scraped together a majority and it was believed that any government it formed would hold together only if there was a leader of stature. Kamaraj was available but he was unacceptable to the Telugus and so Rajaji was induced to become the chief minister. He had refused to stand for elections and so a pliant governor, Sri Prakasa, nominated him to the upper house, for his contribution to literature.[12] It was considered by many to be the first instance of the subversion of democratic process in forming a state government in India.

Once in, Rajaji proved to be a tough administrator and refused to countenance any division of the state to form Andhra Pradesh. Meanwhile, Potti Sriramulu fasted, some say reluctantly, hoping that Rajaji would come around. The situation in Mylapore where Sriramulu was then living was tense. But it was nothing compared to what it was in the Telugu-dominated areas of the state. Sriramulu eventually passed away and riots broke out everywhere. Made aware of the gravity of the situation, Nehru was horrified. Work began at once on the linguistic division of the states, with Andhra Pradesh being carved out of the Telugu-speaking areas of Madras Presidency. The question of what was to be done with the city of Madras arose. 'Madras Manade' (Madras is ours) cried the Telugus while the Tamils would not part with the city. Rajaji once again proved a tough negotiator and refused to give in.

---

[11]Venkatachalapathy, *Chennai, Not Madras,* pp. 9–18.

[12]Significantly, Rajaji's grandson, Rajmohan Gandhi, titled this chapter in his biography of Rajaji 'Downfall', *Rajaji, A Life,* New Delhi: Penguin Books, 2010.

The city remained with Madras State.[13] As any map will show, Chennai is at the extreme northern tip of the state, while it is in the geographic centre of what was once Madras Presidency.

The agitation to ensure Madras city remained with the Tamil-speaking regions was led by Dravidian stalwarts such as Anna and Periyar. The two had enjoyed a very close friendship that soured to an extent when the latter, late in life, married Maniammai, a lady several years his junior. Her ascendancy in politics saw Anna moving out and forming the DMK, its first meeting taking place in 1948 at the Robinson (now Arignar Anna) Park in Royapuram. Anna's charismatic leadership attracted several people and Periyar was relegated to the position of an ideologue thereafter.[14] The two leaders remained on the closest of terms, however, united in their vision of a Tamil country freed of caste and religious divide, but Periyar's Dravida Kazhagam became, at best, a fringe outfit.

This was however the Congress's heyday and none believed that the DMK would one day take its place. But that rise did happen owing, in part, to the hold that cinema had over the people. But before that we need to document the rise of the Congress in the state. We last saw Rajaji when he took over as chief minister. Once the dust had settled on the formation of Andhra, he launched a pet scheme of his—modified elementary education wherein schools would run in two shifts, the first involving conventional classroom teaching and the second at home, where students learn the skills of their parents. The Opposition, with some egging on by Kamaraj, who never got on with Rajaji, was quick to cry foul. Periyar dubbed the scheme casteist, for, in his view, by making children learn what their parents did, Rajaji was ensuring that a potter's son would remain a potter and so on. The chief minister proved adamant, and chose to resign rather than back down.[15] The Congress immediately elected Kamaraj, who along with colleagues R. Venkataraman and C. Subramaniam in the state and T. T. Krishnamachari at the centre, embarked on industrialization in a big way. By the late 1950s, the position of the Congress appeared unassailable, such being the progress of Madras State. And yet, the DMK was steadily progressing too with the help of cinema.

Most theatre artistes began their political journey as ardent Congressmen

[13]Venkatachalapathy, *Chennai, Not Madras*, pp. 9-18.

[14]For much of what follows on Anna and Periyar, see, Kannan, *Anna*.

[15]D. Veeraraghavan and A. R. Venkatachalapathy (ed.), *Half a Day for Caste? Education and Politics in Tamil Nadu, 1952-55*, New Delhi: LeftWord, 2019.

as far as Indian Independence was concerned and as ardent Anna followers when it came to the fight against social inequalities.

'It must be remembered here that Periyar was uncomfortable with actors,' says Venkatachalapathy. 'But his dislike was more than countered by Anna, who made them welcome. He had the vision to foresee their ability to influence public thought.'

Gradually, they became more attached to the Dravidian ideology. With Satyamurti's death in the 1940s, it became evident that Rajaji and Kamaraj had no great love for the film and theatre world, ensuring that most artistes moved to the camp of the Dravidian movement. By the late 1940s, Anna was much in demand in Tamil cinema as a scriptwriter and his films carried strong messages for the masses. His reformist plays were hugely successful and it was but natural that film producers would make a beeline to him. Gone were the days of dialogues in Brahminical language and plots that dealt with mythological themes. Anna's scripts, such as for the film *Velaikkari*, were situated in current times, dealing with the day-to-day problems of the people. The language was Tamil at its finest—every line was crafted to perfection. By the early 1950s, Anna's trusted lieutenant M. Karunanidhi too became a scriptwriter. His film *Manthiri Kumari*, starring future matinee idol MGR, made waves, though the central characters in the movie were its villain and his quick-thinking wife. In 1952, Karunanidhi wrote the script for AVM's *Parasakthi*. It starred V. C. Ganesan, an unknown actor from the stage. Its dialogues, especially those delivered by Ganesan, made him and the movie a cult classic. It questioned the ways of the priestly and upper classes at every stage and that delivered a powerful social message. Making films of the *Parasakthi* kind became the new norm.[16]

Strangely enough, Ganesan, who would go on to be immortalized with the prefix Sivaji after he played the role of the Maratha ruler in a play written by Anna, had a relatively short association with the DMK and remained a Congressman till the end of his life.[17] It was MGR who would fill the void. Anna, taking a leaf out of Satyamurti's book, asked for the actor's presence in public meetings. MGR, who adored Anna to the point of deification, agreed and became the crowd-puller for the DMK. MGR became Makkal Thilakam (crest jewel of the people) and Pon Mana Chemmal (he of the golden heart) to the people. Though known to be ruthless in private, especially

[16]Theodore Baskaran, *The Eye of the Serpent: An Introduction to Tamil Cinema*, Chennai: East West Books Pvt. Limited, 1996.

[17]Kannan, *Anna*, pp. 218–19.

to those who dared cross him, his public persona was one of unbounded generosity, feeding everyone who came home, donating money to well-publicized charitable causes, and as the protector of women. Throughout his long, film career, MGR would be linked romantically to several women but all of that was overlooked when it came to the image of preux chevalier that the public invested in him. This was because of his films that always portrayed him that way—as a champion of the downtrodden.[18]

The irresistible combination of Anna, Karunanidhi, and MGR at the top, coupled with a disciplined cadre at the grassroots level meant that the DMK slowly began gaining ground. By July 1961, when the party held its third state-level conference in Madurai, its strength was visible to everyone. But it still had to contend with Kamaraj and, under him, a strong Congress. In the 1962 elections, while the DMK did emerge as the single largest Opposition party in the state, the Congress formed the government. Surprisingly, Anna was defeated in his hometown of Kanchipuram. He was later nominated to the Rajya Sabha.

It was here that Anna and the DMK faced a major hurdle—the party's stance on a separate nation called Dravidistan, with Madras as its capital. Nehru had set up a National Integration Committee headed by the brilliant lawyer and former dewan of Travancore, Sir C. P. Ramaswami Iyer. Kamaraj was a key member too. The two men from Madras, who were also close friends, their fondness for Satyamurti being a common bond, clearly had a critical role to play in making the recommendations of the committee. One of these was that those being elected to public office had to swear allegiance to the concept of a united India. Faced with the prospect of mass disqualifications for elected representatives of the DMK, Anna dropped the demand of Dravidistan. The Chinese aggression of that year proved a convenient excuse and in an impassioned speech at the Rajya Sabha, Anna declared that the DMK would henceforth opt for federalism—a principle on which the party has remained quite firm for decades.

The DMK would have found the going tough despite the groundswell of popularity had it not been for Kamaraj stepping down as chief minister to focus on party matters at the national level. His successor, M. Bhaktavatsalam, was in every way a lesser man. As explained in the chapter on language, his bungling of the anti-Hindi agitation was a key factor in the defeat of the Congress. Anna became the chief minister. He remained in office for a little more than a year, succumbing to throat cancer. V. R. Nedunchezhiyan, the

[18]Kannan, *MGR: A Life.*

next most senior in the party ought to have succeeded him but Karunanidhi was politically nimbler and became the chief minister. One of those unhappy with this was MGR. The two had started out in life as friends but their political proximity had caused friction. Karunanidhi was always wary of MGR's popularity while the latter had reasons to suspect that the former was feathering his nest and building a network within the party.

The bitter breakup happened in 1972, when Karunanidhi rather maladroitly got MGR suspended for anti-party activities. Though initially heartbroken, the matinee idol rallied. MGR floated his All India Anna Dravida Munnetra Kazhagam (AIADMK or ADMK for short) on a watered-down version of the DMK's Dravidian plank.[19] Kamaraj, on coming to know about it, rather presciently remarked that there was very little to choose between the parties, for they were both 'rotting timber from the same gutter'.[20]

The DMK should have known that it did not stand a chance against Pon Mana Chemmal. In 1967, MGR was shot at by fellow actor M. R. Radha and contested the election from bed. Posters all over the state depicted him with bandages around his neck. He won hands down. In 1976, his party swept to power and was not dislodged till his passing in 1987. Towards the end of his life, MGR suffered several health setbacks, and had to be rushed to the US for treatment. Elections were held and he won once again, this time with posters showing him receiving treatment. He came back to a tumultuous welcome—a massive public reception in the city. He was emotional but he could not express it for he had practically lost his ability to speak. But his presence was all that mattered.

In the latter half of his tenure as chief minister, MGR pondered over the question of a successor and handpicked his one-time heroine in films, J. Jayalalithaa. Once again it was a cinema star to the rescue though it must be acknowledged here that Jayalalithaa was a great orator, had a striking presence, was extremely well-read and was known to have an eidetic memory. She did not find the going easy; there was a rival faction led by MGR's wife, Janaki, also an erstwhile actor. When MGR died in 1987, Jayalalithaa was pushed off the gun carriage that carried his body, but in what was an indication of her inner strength, she stood her ground during the long lying-in-state. Machinations in the assembly ensured that Janaki became the chief minister and the AIADMK split. With the inevitable fall of the government,

---

[19]Much of the information here on MGR and his rule is from R. Kannan, *MGR: A Life*.

[20]Jeyakantan, *Cintayil Aayiram Karutturaigal*, Chennai: Sri Cenpaka Pathippakam, 2003, p. 765. Translation by the author from the original 'Ore Kuttayil Ooriya Mattaikal'.

it was time for elections and the DMK came back to power, after a gap of ten years. Jayalalithaa was leader of the Opposition and in characteristic fashion hardly put in an appearance in the assembly. This was a tradition that Karunanidhi had begun, for as leader of the Opposition, he rarely attended assembly proceedings during MGR's tenure.

On the one occasion that Jayalalithaa did attend, pandemonium reigned in the House. She later alleged that there had been an attempt to molest her in the assembly.[21] With pressure from the AIADMK and its ally, the Congress, mounting, the centre had to dismiss the DMK government. Elections were held in 1991 and Jayalalithaa's AIADMK was voted to power. Much was expected of the new chief minister and she did deliver on many fronts. However, her unpredictability, arrogance, and blind faith in a cabal led by her companion, Sasikala, proved to be her undoing. Veneration of political leaders had always been a Tamil tradition but under Jayalalithaa, it reached new heights, quite literally, for giant-sized cut-outs of her were put up wherever she went. In addition, flex banners extolling the great leader's virtues became the norm all along processional routes. Under Amma, as she was referred to, any outing became a pageant—even a routine visit to the AIADMK office or her daily journey to Fort St George and back. How much did she really notice as she rushed past? Nobody knows, but the party satraps, none of whom felt any sense of security in their posts, were quite sure that even if she did not, her companion, Sasikala, made note and suitable rewards or retribution would be handed out eventually.

It became the norm for ministers, MLAs, and others to prostrate before Amma. Personal meetings with her meant having to carry bouquets and flower baskets of a certain (regulation) size and the colours had to be her then current favourite—this varied over time but the one she consistently disliked most was yellow, that being the shade of Karunanidhi's shawl. Party men took to wearing white linen shirts through the translucent pockets of which Amma's laminated photograph would show. In his time, MGR had asked party men to tattoo the two-leaves symbol of the party on themselves but Amma had taken displays of personal loyalty to new heights.

That she was something extraordinary even by Tamil Nadu standards became manifest even in her first term in office. Citing threats from the LTTE, against whom she always took a firm stance, she was upgraded to the Z-category security status. Roads were cleared well in advance of her convoy emerging from her residence and the police even went to the extent

[21]Kavitha Shetty, 'Jayalalithaa emerges as a regional superpower', *India Today*, 15 July 1991.

of erecting cantilevered barricades on the principal thoroughfares, which could be lowered to block traffic as and when she went about. Veda Nilayam, her bungalow in upmarket Poes Garden, became a fortress of sorts, with barricades put up from the entrance to the colony. Amma would make periodic appearances on an upper-floor veranda and wave to the crowds, rather in the manner of British royalty at the Buckingham Palace.

High-profile neighbour and superstar of Tamil cinema, Rajinikanth, did make some noises about the disturbance[22] but nothing could stop the Amma juggernaut. In her first term in office, the security threat saw her take on a cape as part of her outfit. This was in the same material and design as the sari she wore for the day. For some time, Chennai watched in awe. Here was a relatively young chief minister, acceptable across all sections of society (even the Brahmins loved her, for after all, she was an Iyengar), with a clean personal background, and known to be a fighter. But the magic soon began to fade. Tales of corruption began being heard. Land grab rumours spread fast, a high-profile case of a bungalow in the Luz area being the first to make the rounds,[23] giving the Opposition something to protest about. Amma later gave them plenty of ammunition, the final straw being the lavish wedding of her foster son and companion Sasikala's nephew V. N. Sudhakaran to Sivaji Ganesan's granddaughter. A huge tract of land in the Chettinad Palace premises in the Raja Annamalaipuram area was cordoned off and a studio set of a wedding hall emerged on it. Many arterial roads were cut off to ensure easy access of guests to the wedding site. The highlight was Jayalalithaa and Sasikala, walking with the wedding procession, accompanied by other women relatives and adorned with jewels.[24] For years, Madras had spoken in awe of the pomp and circumstance with which movie mogul, S. S. Vasan, had conducted his daughter's wedding in the 1950s.[25] That had been an aesthetic display, with the bride's father spending his hard-earned wealth. Sudhakaran's wedding was considered a vulgar display and several questions were asked about the source of the money spent. Karunanidhi smiled.

The elections of 1996 saw the DMK win by a landslide, the AIADMK getting just four seats. Jayalalithaa lost at Bargur. But a new trend had crept in—that of several smaller players making off with the vote share and therefore

[22]Sadanand Menon, 'Can Rajini rescue this book?', *Outlook*, 31 March 2008.

[23]Shobha Warrier, 'The many homes of Sasikala Natarajan', *Rediff.com*, 1996.

[24]G. C. Shekhar, 'Jayalalitha's foster son married off amid extravagance and controversy', *India Today*, 30 September 1995.

[25]Ashokamitran, *Years With Boss*, pp. 126–33.

needing to be placated by the principal parties with a coalition arrangement. During the five years that the AIADMK had been in power, the DMK had split, with V. Gopalaswamy (Vaiko), forming the Marumalarchi Dravida Munnetra Kazhagam (MDMK). The Congress had split too, with G. K. Moopanar forming the Tamil Manila Congress (TMC). The DMK aligned with the TMC and, most crucially, Rajinikanth went on television to state that 'even God cannot help Tamil Nadu if the AIADMK was returned to power'.[26] That had swung the tide—Rajini was second only to MGR when it came to star power. The Congress hardly made any news, something that it had got used to in the state. The fringe players rarely made an impact, other than gnawing away at vote share.

The history of Tamil Nadu politics can thereafter be summed up as a seesaw battle between the two main players, the AIADMK and the DMK, both of them alternating in power. The electorate always voted overwhelmingly for one of the two parties, the other invariably being reduced to single digits. Amma's high-handedness was always her downfall, apart from her closeness to Sasikala. The DMK patriarch's weakness was his family, comprising two living wives, many children, several grandchildren, nephews, and nieces. It took just five years for the electorate to tire of one's failings and give the opponent a chance.

Tenures in power for both parties saw a common pattern—the leader of the Opposition stayed away from the assembly, allowing assistants to raise points of order. All projects begun in the previous regime were scuttled or at best denied funds. Corruption cases were foisted on the previous incumbent and both Jayalalithaa and Karunanidhi managed to send each other to prison for short stints. While Jayalalithaa's arrest was seen as unavoidable, given the charges of corruption against her, the DMK patriarch's arrest at midnight was a bungled affair. Sun TV's repeated broadcast of the leader being pushed around during his arrest, screaming in pain, gained him sympathy.

Officers perceived to have been close to those earlier in power would be summarily transferred. Those lower down in the rungs of the government machinery lived in mortal dread of chief ministerial retribution. Ministers and MLAs who were aware that their tenure in office was at best for five years made the most of it. In 2018, Transparency International ranked Tamil Nadu the third most corrupt state in India.[27] The state had certainly come

[26]'I had criticised Jayalalithaa and hurt her: Rajinikanth', *Times of India*, 12 December 2016.

[27]B. Sivakumar, 'Tamil Nadu third most corrupt State shows survey', *Times of India*, 12 October 2018.

a long way from the time of Kamaraj, upheld by admirers and detractors alike as an exemplar of honesty. The irony is that Tamil Nadu, and by way of being its capital, Chennai, remain well-administered entities. This is because the basic framework, set up years ago, remains strong. To give them credit, Karunanidhi, with his sharp understanding of what was required at the grassroots, and Jayalalithaa with her quick grasp of governance, were excellent administrators. The tragedy was that they delivered far less compared to what they were truly capable of.

Throughout their tenures in office, both the political leaders and their respective parties played important roles in national politics. This was the era of coalition governments at the centre, and the ability of TN leaders to contribute a block of seats counted for much. MGR, and later Karunanidhi, always maintained the most cordial of relationships with whoever was in power in New Delhi. Amma was more mercurial. She had, on occasion, kept leaders such as George Fernandes waiting for hours on end in Chennai, not confirming a meeting.[28] In 1999, she and her party withdrew support to the Vajpayee government at the centre, thereby causing it to fall.[29] That caused the DMK to tie-up with the BJP and gain several ministerial berths when the coalition subsequently came to power. Both the AIADMK and the DMK used their clout in the centre to good effect when it came to Tamil Nadu and Chennai. Major investment projects came here in automotive and other sectors.

For someone who entered politics with such a clean record, it was Jayalalithaa who had to face several charges of corruption. After winning the elections in 2001, she had to step down from office for a few months owing to one of these charges, placing her trusted lieutenant O. Panneerselvam in her place. She resumed office in 2002 but there was a disproportionate assets case that would hound her till the very end. It pertained to her first tenure in office and the lid was blown off it following complaints after her foster son's wedding. Raids conducted on her residence after she lost power in 1996 revealed huge quantities of gold, silver, jewellery, saris, shoes, and watches. The case was tenaciously pursued over eighteen years through the courts by opponents such as K. Anbazhagan, on behalf of the DMK, and Subramanian Swamy of the Janata Party. At one stage, fearing interference, the trial was moved to a special court in Bangalore.

---

[28]Jaya Menon, 'By George Fernandes! How Atal Behari Vajpayee's envoy waited endlessly for Jayalalithaa', *Times of India*, 30 January 2019.

[29]'Jaya may withdraw support today', *Business Standard*, 13 August 1998.

By 2011, with the 2G scandal, involving daughter Kanimozhi tarnishing his party's image and several other corruption charges within the state, it was Karunanidhi and the DMK's turn to sit in the Opposition. But the Amma who returned to office was not the firebrand of the past. The old haughtiness remained strong but she was physically ill. The special court in Bangalore delivered its judgment on 27 September 2014. Justice Michael D'Cunha was the fifth judge appointed by the Supreme Court and he found her and several of her accomplices guilty, making her the first ruling chief minister of a state to be so sentenced.[30] The punishment comprised four years imprisonment as well as numerous fines. Panneerselvam was back in the saddle. He spent his time making numerous journeys to the Parappana Agrahara prison to meet his leader. Judge D'Cunha's sentence came up for appeal at the Karnataka High Court and was overturned in May 2015, thereby releasing Jayalalithaa and enabling her to take office once again. Chennai witnessed scenes of jubilation. Thousands lined the route that Amma took to her residence and there was the usual display of the party faithful drumming, dancing, bursting crackers, and distributing sweets. But the woman who returned was not the same—the imprisonment had clearly been a severe shock and there was still a question mark, for the Karnataka High Court's judgement had been appealed against in the Supreme Court.

Amma was now quite ill and it was evident even in the way she walked. Her clout in the centre had also diminished considerably. For that matter, no regional party had a role to play, what with the BJP under Narendra Modi being sworn in with a majority. He and Jayalalithaa had a close, personal rapport and after much dithering in the 2014 general elections, Amma decided to oppose the BJP. Her calculation was that with a completely discredited DMK, her party would win the majority of the Lok Sabha seats in Tamil Nadu, which would come in useful, for nobody expected the BJP or any other party to get a majority at the centre. Her famed quote asking the electorate to choose Lady (herself) over Daddy (Karunanidhi) and Modi is remembered even now. And yet, the unpredictable happened. The BJP was able to comfortably form the government and though the AIADMK won all the thirty-seven Lok Sabha seats in the state, as Amma had predicted, it had no role to play.

In December 2015 came the famed Chennai floods when the city witnessed torrential rains. The administration, especially the Chennai Metrowater and

[30]'Jayalalithaa convicted, sentenced to four years in jail, 100 crore fine', *Economic Times*, 28 September 2014.

Sewerage Board and the PWD, was clearly caught unawares. The decision to release surplus waters in the Chembarambakkam Reservoir was delayed until too late, some say because the chief minister was incommunicado, and her ministers were unwilling to take a call. The floodwaters entered the city and caused untold misery and havoc, though with surprisingly very little loss of life. Chennai, which over the years had been consistently building over its lakes, wetlands, and reservoirs, was paying the price, but it could have been avoided under a more vigilant administration.

The floods, it was expected, would severely dent Jayalalithaa's popularity but that did not prove to be the case. Over the years, her image of being a tough administrator, her multiple legislations in favour of women, and her usurping the image of Amma or mother had struck a chord with most voters. And there was the usual Tamil sentiment of sympathizing with the one who had suffered, for after all, she had been to prison while several others who were no better when it came to honesty were free. In the 2016 elections, Jayalalithaa and the AIADMK were returned to office. It was a record since no ruling party had been re-elected since 1991.

But the victory had been hard won—at enormous expense to the exchequer. Both the DMK and the AIADMK had, over the years, become masters in announcing populist schemes on the eve of elections. If one offered mixers and cycles to everyone below a certain income level, the other upped the ante, showering laptops, cows, and goats on the electorate. The upshot was the Amma Canteen, subsidized food outlets run by the Corporation of Chennai, for the benefit of the poor. All of it had to be funded by the revenue collections of the civic body and that meant it hardly had any money for other schemes. The jury is still out on these schemes, after all, everyone, including Karunanidhi, had jeered at MGR when he introduced noon meals in schools. There is no doubt that they do have a trickle-down effect and help the downtrodden, freeing them of many drudgeries and enabling them to rise above their daily challenges. But are all such freebies warranted? Whatever be the eventual verdict, they have come to stay as essential features of Tamil politics.

Returning to office, Amma proved even more elusive than ever, working mainly from home and putting in an appearance when needed via video conferencing. Her favourite colour was now green and even flyovers in the city were painted in that shade. There were speculations galore about her state of health and that prompted questions about succession, though none could ask openly. In September 2016, she was rushed to Apollo Hospitals where an entire floor was emptied to accommodate her and her entourage, the faithful Sasikala dominating the situation. Thereafter, the treatment proceeded in Masonic secrecy. The conflicting statements given to the press and the sporadic updates that the AIADMK and the hospital gave were tailor-made for the rumour mills. Social media, in particular, was awash with memes on the situation. All of this contrasted quite starkly with the time when MGR had been admitted to Apollo Hospitals when the world at large was regularly informed about the nature of his illness and the treatment he had received. After several false alarms, Jayalalithaa died due to cardiac arrest on 5 December 2016.

Contrary to what was expected, the city and the state reacted with quiet grief. Unlike the immediate aftermath of MGR's death when mobs went on a rampage and a statue of Karunanidhi on Mount Road was smashed, there were no untoward incidents. Several small impromptu memorials were put up on street corners. The city closed for the funeral that was held the next day. Most surprising, and gracious, was the banner put up by the DMK:

You are no more
The brave adversary who stood before us
You are no more
Even if thousand leaders stand before us
Valiant maiden
How can they match you?
Everything you did
You desired to be ahead of our leader
But do you have to be the first one even in death?
Where will our commander go in search
For a rival like you?
In the battle of elections
We intended to face you as a gallant maiden
But in the heart of leader and commander
We always wished you a long life
Never had any other thoughts
Now, where can we find a worthy opponent like you?
Without you, we are at the peak of sadness.[31]

Chennai, and Tamil Nadu, instinctively knows what a state funeral involves. For years, the city had seen its political leaders making their last journey via

[31]Translation from the Tamil in K. Mugunthan, 'In death Jayalalithaa finds unlikely admirers in DMK cadre', *Business Standard*, 7 December 2016.

Rajaji Hall, once the Banqueting Hall for the British governors of Madras. In earlier days, the bodies of leaders were kept inside the huge hall but with crowds increasing over the years, the grand flight of steps became the venue. Annadurai had lain in state here and the funeral procession that followed went on to hold a world record for having the largest crowd. Anna was laid to rest by the beach, where his successor, Karunanidhi, planned a grand mausoleum for him.

In the meanwhile, other leaders such as Rajaji, Periyar, and Kamaraj passed away. Karunanidhi, then in power, took care to ensure that no other political figure was buried by the beach. Rajaji and Kamaraj had memorials built for them in Guindy, close to an earlier structure commemorating Mahatma Gandhi. To give him credit, Karunanidhi took personal interest in the design of each memorial, going to the extent of capping Rajaji's with a crown said to be inspired by that of Lord Rama, in recognition of his having authored the work *Chakravarthi Thirumagan*.[32] When MGR's time came, he too was interred on the beach, by the side of Anna. The leader was buried in full costume including his fur cap, black glasses, wig, and watch. The last, being battery-operated, ticked on for months, leading to a rumour that MGR was immortal and that his heart was continuing to beat. Thousands lined up to place their ear on the granite and marvel at the steady ticking. This ceased once the battery died out.

But over the years, there had been several petitions before the High Court of Madras seeking directions for the prevention of further burials by the beach. When Amma died, it was decided that her mausoleum would come up on the land occupied by the MGR memorial. She was consequently buried there, after a very cold and sad funeral. Despite the adulation from the masses, Amma died a loner. She was estranged from her family and Sasikala stood in as next of kin. After a Hindu priest played his part in what was manifestly a sham funeral rite and a nephew had gone through the motions, the coffin was lowered into the ground. Panneerselvam once again became acting chief minister.

With her death, it was expected that trusted aide Sasikala would manipulate the party so that she and her family would take over. She was elected general secretary of the party overnight. She took to dressing like Jayalalithaa—even wearing the Vaishnavite mark on her forehead. But the public was not taken in—such tactics might have worked fifty years earlier. There was an outpouring

[32]Sowmya Rajendran, 'Did Karunanidhi deny Rajaji and Kamaraj a Marina burial?', *News Minute*, 8 August 2018.

of hatred towards the cabal that had more or less ruled through Jayalalithaa.[33] This was when Panneerselvam staged a coup. After meditating one evening at Amma's burial spot, he announced that he could not serve under Sasikala. He became the hero thereafter but Sasikala was not to give in so easily. The party's MLAs were taken to a resort where they were kept incommunicado even as the city, the state, and the rest of India watched in amazement. The Supreme Court's judgement on the disproportionate assets case came about in February 2017 and it upheld the decision of the Special Court that had originally held Amma and her associates guilty. After keeping everyone guessing for a couple of days, Sasikala emerged from the resort, having made faithful aide Edappadi Palaniswami the chief minister. And then, after having delivered three powerful blows on Jayalalithaa's tombstone, whether out of rage at the former chief minister escaping prison or as an expression that justice will be meted out, she surrendered at the Bangalore Jail.

With her out of the picture, Palaniswami was quick to reach out to Panneerselvam. The party united under this duumvirate and much to the disappointment of the DMK, remained in power, with some support, it is said, from the BJP at the centre. This was quite ironical and a reversal of sorts, for it was the party in power in Tamil Nadu that invariably propped up successive tottering central governments till a decade ago. That all of this happened without the DMK trying to wrest power was an indication that the supremo Karunanidhi was ageing.

By 2018, it was his turn to fall ill. He was admitted to Kauvery Hospital and lingered for quite a while. Unlike what happened with Amma, there was never any mystery about his illness. And as he sank, the crowds gathered outside the hospital, just as they had when Anna, Periyar, MGR, and Jayalalithaa had died. That he was ninety-three years old and had remained more or less an invalid for a year did not prevent emotional men and women from crying out loud and chanting slogans, asking him to come back and rule over them. All the prayers notwithstanding, he too passed on and was laid out in state at Rajaji Hall.

Even as the mourners thronged past, the question uppermost in the minds of his family members and party seniors was his burial spot. They wanted the Marina but the ruling AIADMK, in a remarkable display of pettiness, considering that Jayalalithaa had just been interred there, refused permission. Recourse had to be taken to the law and permission obtained from the high court. The Kalaignar, it was decreed, could be buried close

---

[33]'Why is Sasikala hated so much?', *Swarajya*, 8 December 2016.

to where Anna was. No additional land would be taken from the beach.[34] And so, he too made his way to the Marina, where he now lies practically next to arch-rival MGR and bitter political enemy Jayalalithaa, with Anna keeping the peace over them. A memorial for Jayalalithaa, said to resemble a phoenix, has since come up over her sepulchre. As to how a convicted person merits a memorial is a matter that has troubled very few. Chennai is very forgiving of the dead. The Kalaignar, too, will eventually get a memorial.

Contrary to all expectations, the AIADMK government sans Amma completed its full five-year term and the state went to the polls in 2021 under the shadow of the Covid-19 pandemic. This was the first election in living memory when the two Dravidian parties were without star campaigners. The BJP piggybacked on the AIADMK and that eventually proved the combine's undoing. The DMK came to power with Karunanidhi's son M. K. Stalin ending his long wait in the wings and becoming chief minister. The AIADMK too did not fare badly, bagging a respectable number of seats and, more importantly, holding on to a significant vote share even in places where it lost. Tamil Nadu and Chennai are on the cusp of change but the dominance of the two regional parties will continue.

In the meanwhile, what of the Dalits whose cause the likes of Pandithar and Srinivasan espoused? To an extent, their lives have improved, given the successive governments and their welfare measures. But there is still a long way to go as far as real equality is concerned as has been pointed out by Thol. Thirumavalavan, leader of the Viduthalai Chiruthaikal Katchi, which positions itself as a social movement apart from being a political party. Opposition of all castes in the Hindu hierarchy and the unexpressed but similar opinions in other religions towards Dalits will have to be overcome. That may take a long while. In the meantime, Tamil Nadu and Chennai can take comfort in ranking high on most social and economic indices. That is an indication that taken overall, things have turned out not badly, after all.

[34]WP No. 20531 of 2018, High Court of Madras.

21 | HOW GREEN WAS MY CITY

Today, if you mention the word 'Tiger' in Chennai, the chances are that most people would assume you were referring to the two-legged variety from across the Palk Strait. But there was a time when our own Madras, or at least its environs, had plenty of tigers, and not all of them in captivity.

Perhaps the first instance is recorded on the base of the monument to Edward Winter, who was governor of Madras in the 1600s. The memorial, which is in St Mary's Church, Battersea, has on its pedestal a carving depicting Winter wrestling with a tiger on the seashore.This was apparently no hyperbole, for a Latin inscription confirms that this incident actually occured.[1]

Another account is as follows:

> A Detachment of the 1st Battalion of the 15th Regiment lay encamped at a village near Pollevaram hills. On the night of the 28th of December, a royal tiger came into the village and seized a bullock. After gorging on his prey, he retired to a house on the banks of the river, where he took up his quarters. Lieutenant Stuart being informed of it went with a Naig's guard to the place, where they saw the monster stretched in the cottage! They mounted on the roof of the adjoining hut, and by removing the thatch of that where he lay, disturbed him and he went out! After a few turns, he sprang at the party and settled on the roof close to them, but an instantaneous discharge of two or three firelocks wounded him and he fell to the ground but immediately got up and made a second attempt, when finding his efforts ineffectual, he made off under a pandal adjoining the house he first entered and could not for some time be found...[2]

The story does not end happily, at least for the tiger. Stuart walked along the edge of the river (most probably the Adyar) and, at a point where the bank rose steeply by 20 feet, the animal sprang at him. Stuart somehow managed to avoid tumbling down the bank and stabbed the tiger with his bayonet. The sepoys accompanying him did the rest and Stuart was warmly

[1]V. Sriram, 'A Winter's Tale', *Madras Musings*, Vol. XXII, No. 12, 1–15 October 2012.

[2]W. S. Seton Karr, Selections from Calcutta Gazettes of the years 1798, 1799, 1800, 1801, 1802, 1803, 1804, and 1805, Calcutta: Office of the Superintendent of Government Printing, 1868, pp. 299–300.

mentioned in despatches. The incident has been recorded in the *Madras Gazette*, dated 20 February 1802.

Then there's this from *The Old Forest Ranger* by Walter Campbell (1842): 'A Madras sepoy was killed some years ago whilst measuring a tiger which had just dropped, apparently dead. The expiring brute struck at him, and fractured his skull by one blow of his tremendous paw.'[3]

There is a record in 1812 of a party of officers, out shooting in the vicinity of Madras, who had sat down in the jungle to dine (no doubt in full dinner dress) when a tiger sprang out of nowhere and made off with a young midshipman who was waiting at the table. The officers pursued the animal but when it laid its victim down prior to killing him, they dared not shoot for fear of injuring the man instead of the beast. But the midshipman had presence of mind:

> On a sudden the hand of the midshipman moved lightly across the tawny side of his captor; and as the poor youth had hitherto lain motionless the horror-stricken spectators thought...this must be the last convulsion before death. The tiger fell 'plomb down' on the earth, and the midshipman leapt forward, waving his bloody dirk in triumph... The youth, it seems, took advantage of his position to draw his dirk, felt deliberately for the brute's heart and thrust his weapon into it, up to the very hilt... [4]

Not so lucky was Captain R. M. Humphreys of Madras. 'While hunting a tiger he ascended a tree, and on the tiger attacking one of the men, jumped down, when the infuriated beast sprang upon him and killed him on the spot.'[5]

By 1878, tigers were considered such a menace in the presidency that there was a reward of ₹100 for every tiger shot. Five years earlier, Captain Caulfield was appointed 'Tiger-Slayer' of Madras Presidency and he applied any method possible from strychnine to shooting.[6] This was a temporary assignment and, assisted by Inspector Mackenzie and A. Wedderburn, he managed to bring down the numbers significantly within the stipulated time period of six months.[7]

The Illustrated Magazine of Arts, London (1854), noted that in Madras it

---

[3]Walter Campbell, *The Old Forest Ranger*, London: How & Parsons, 1842, p. 432.

[4]William Pinnock, *The Guide to Knowledge*, London: Shepherd and Sutton, 1836, p. 271.

[5]*The Gentleman's Magazine*, 1835.

[6]'Tiger Killers and Tigers Killed', *Punch or the London Charivari*, 14 November 1874.

[7]*Journal of the Society of Arts*, 8 February 1878, p. 193.

was common for people to 'take round a tiger for exhibition, with a sheep or another animal to display its strength upon'.[8]

How would a tiger fare if today it wandered into Madras? It would be run over by a lorry or bus before it crossed Pallavaram. The closest that we can now get to a tiger, as Theodore Baskaran, former postmaster general of Tamil Nadu and an ardent conservationist, comments is 'in the Mudumalai Sanctuary 600 km away, where only a mere 25 manage to lead a precarious existence'.[9]

The tiger is not the only animal to have been frightened away from Chennai. Shakuntala Jagannathan, writing of her grandfather Sir C. P. Ramaswami Iyer's home The Grove, which is located at the intersection of Alwarpet and Teynampet, both teeming urban localities now, says that it had 'deer, jackal, palm civet, peacock and even a leopard'.[10] It is unimaginable to even think of such animals in such locations now. And yet, the memory that this was once a forest and not so long ago still lingers. Leopards, even now, put in an occasional appearance, the last sighting being of a healthy male somewhere near Chingleput in 2014.[11]

Among all the animals that Shakuntala writes of, the deer is the only remnant. That it has survived at all is due to a hospice in the Guindy National Park, once part of the governors' weekend retreat. Hived off as a 400-hectare expanse in 1947 when the rest became Raj Bhavan, this has since shrunk to 271 hectares, with land being repeatedly granted for various educational institutions. What remains is still impressive, for it is pristine coastal scrub jungle. Baskaran is not so impressed. He grudgingly acknowledges the jungle's survival, 'albeit in a degenerate form'. He writes of it as a:

> ...link with the ecological past of the city...the park, provides an idea of the heritage lost. It is also one of the last holds of the endangered antelope that is exclusive to India, the blackbuck, the fastest animal in India that can run 15km at a stretch at an average of 70 km/h, sometimes peaking at an astonishing 90 km/h! The park is also home

---

[8]'The Tiger and the Boa Constrictor', *The Illustrated Magazine of Art*, Vol. 3, 1854, p. 278. This story originally appeared in Oliver Goldsmith et al., *A History of the Earth and Animated Nature*, 1847.

[9]S. Theodore Baskaran, 'A Squandered Heritage: The Wildlife of Madras', *Madras: The Architectural Heritage*, Section H.

[10]Shakuntala Jagannathan, *Sir CP Remembered: To Thatha with Love*, Mumbai: Vakils, Feffer & Simons Ltd., 1999, p. 17.

[11]P. Oppili, 'Leopard caught on camera in Chingleput range', *The Hindu*, 18 July 2014.

to the spotted deer, but these are not original residents of the jungle. Besides other mammals such as jackal, Indian hare and monitor lizard, the park is also home to a variety of reptiles including the Star tortoise. More than a 100 varieties of birds, both migrant and resident, can be seen here. Noteworthy among these are the greenbilled makhola, a resident cuckoo that builds its own nest, and the forest wagtail a migrant bird the size of a sparrow with zebra markings on its grey body.[12]

Guindy National Park is a great attraction for school children, in particular, and many educational institutions bring them on excursions here. Inside is a smaller enclosure, inaugurated by Nehru in 1959 and named Children's Park. All around the park, and along the roads leading to it are signs that indicate that deer could be crossing. The deer have found a route that connects Guindy National Park to the Theosophical Society and from there they make it to the Kotturpuram Tree Park that Shobha Menon and the rest of Nizhal have created.

The brainchild of green activists Shobha Menon, S. Theodore Baskaran, Sekhar Raghavan, and G. Dattatri, first chief urban planner of the CMDA, Nizhal aims to sensitize government departments and private citizens about the importance of retaining what little green cover there is left in Chennai. Activism usually entails being at loggerheads with the authorities but Nizhal aims to influence by befriending them. It is a Gandhian way and infinitely more tiring than challenging the government in court but it has had a good degree of success. One of Nizhal's achievements is the Kotturpuram Tree Park. Impressed with what the NGO had done, the PWD gave it five acres housing a rubbish dump on the southern bank of the Adyar, near the Kotturpuram Bridge. The NGO was asked to create a park with public participation. Nizhal set to work creating 'a master plan thereby converting this land into a biodiversity hotspot and arboretum for indigenous tree species'. The NGO worked closely with the local community for creating the park. Those who came to walk in the space were asked to fill a pail from a hand pump and water a plant or two before leaving. These 'shramdans' had their effect. Green enthusiasts and volunteers planted the trees and watched them grow. Over 150 varieties of trees and plants found a home here, as did over a hundred species of birds and animals. This, on a piece of land where not even an earthworm once existed. The PWD made over the land to the corporation but the maintenance of the park is with Nizhal. It is a unique example of what can be done by voluntary effort.

[12]Baskaran, *Madras: The Architectural Heritage*.

Not far from here is Adyar Creek, which is where the river meets the sea, and was once a valuable wetland, teeming with birdlife. In the nineteenth century it even boasted of a tiger or two! In the twentieth century, it had signboards, albeit rusty, which declared the place, around 358 acres of it, to be protected for the sake of birds. Then came real estate greed and the government began steadily nibbling away at it—the first step being the construction of memorials and the dumping of garbage and debris. The Consumer Action Group (CAG) went to court over the matter and fought a long and bitter battle during which officialdom tried every trick in the trade. But the High Court of Madras in 2008 declared that the area had to be restored. The CAG continuously opposed any attempt at constructing permanent structures on the site. There was also considerable opposition to planting alien species of trees. A further worry was the government's commitment then to work on only 58 acres, which were separated from the water by the remaining 300 acres. It was feared that such isolated preservation would cut off the water from the park. But work went ahead nevertheless, and the first phase was declared complete in 2010. Thereafter, there was a change of heart and the government decided to go ahead with the rest of the project. The corporation has been asked to stop dumping debris and the Metro Water and Sewerage Board has promised to build storm water drains that will bring fresh water to the creek. Much of this is still on paper, which passes for progress but it cannot be denied that the restored first phase is teeming with plant and animal life. School children are allowed in for nature studies and their happy laughter combined with bird calls gives us some confidence about the future.

An outing to a proper zoo today means going to Vandalur in the extreme south of the city, once well beyond urban limits. In the 1920s, this was a station that was on the metre-gauge line from Madras Egmore to Rameswaram and the place where pilgrims got off to visit Sriperumbudur. It was also the place where the sahibs came to hunt hare and partridge and, in the cold season, plenty of snipe.[13] Today, you can reach within an hour by car but the animals, except those caged in the zoo, are elusive. Apart from its magnificent wide enclosures for animals and the natural beauty of the place, the Arignar Anna Zoological Park, as it is officially known, also has an enclosure for butterflies, making it one of the few zoos in India to have such a facility.

An attraction that is coming into its own these days is Pulicat, the saltwater lagoon to the north of the city. People also come here to see the launching of rockets from Sriharikota, which is an island in Pulicat. It

[13] *Illustrated Guide to the South Indian Railway*, Madras, 1926, p. 24.

was in this lake and on its banks that the colonial history of the region began, if you discount the earlier Portuguese presence in San Thome. The Dutch, who were the first traders, settled at Pulicat and a small graveyard, a battered church, and the ruins of a fort completely covered in scrub are all that remain. Also present are Shiva and Vishnu temples of Pandyan origin besides a couple of mosques. But it is the flamingos that camp here which attract visitors. An average of 15,000 of these birds come to Pulicat every year. There is rich biodiversity here and the water has a 'high biomass of fish, prawn, crustaceans and plankton, which form the principal source of food for the birds'.[14] 'The brackish water also attracts large congregations of greater and lesser flamingos, grey pelicans, painted storks, grey herons, ducks, teals, terns, herons, gulls and a number of waders, besides large numbers of migratory water birds.'[15]

And yet, all is not well with the region. Local rivers that empty into the lake dump insecticides and effluents. The mouth of the lake gets blocked owing to silt and this increases the salinity of the water, thereby affecting aquatic life. The Andhra and Tamil Nadu governments have made a beeline for the place, putting up satellite ports, industrial complexes, and power plants. Fishing has also increased alarmingly, with trawlers being pressed into service. There is also appalling poverty, with the locals' only hope of earning money limited to ferrying visitors on boat journeys, apart from fishing. Interestingly, boating is officially banned here. The government, rather than improving safety standards, opted to impose a blanket ban. Ironically, India is a signatory to the Ramsar Treaty and is committed to protecting sensitive water habitats such as Pulicat.

Yet another birdwatchers' paradise is Vedanthangal—the term thangal being an old Tamil word for lake, according to Sekhar Raghavan. It is India's oldest preserve for, at the request of the locals, Lionel Place, the first collector of Chingleput, declared it a protected area as early as in 1798 though official recognition came only in 1858, the year which is now being taken as the beginning of ecological conservation efforts in Tamil Nadu. Spread over 75 acres, the Vedanthangal Lake is an important source of water for the agricultural lands in the surrounding areas. It is also home to a bewildering variety of migratory birds.

There are some sylvan private campuses too—including IIT-M,

[14]'A Treat for Birdwatchers at Pulicat Lake', *The Hindu*, 6 January 2020.

[15]Jayapaul Azariah, *My Biography: Palliacatta The Pulicat, 1400-2007*, Chennai: Centre for Research on New International Economic Order, 2007, p. 4.

Theosophical Society, and Madras Christian College. Of these, the first is but an extension of the Guindy National Park. The Theosophical Society spans 260 acres across the Adyar and is a thickly-wooded estate. It is now home to the standard fauna of Chennai—snakes, mongooses, hares, spiders, jackals, and wild cats. The trees, including the 450-year-old banyan which is the single biggest attraction, are famous but it is worth pondering how many grew by themselves and how many were planted and tended to. This being a coastal region, scrub forest and mangroves were possibly the only vegetation that existed, apart from palm trees. It is very likely that William Huddlestone, who owned this estate in the nineteenth century, and the Theosophists who followed, planned the entire layout, including the forest.

The Theosophical Society does not have records of this but the Madras Christian College in Tambaram has excellent documentation on what its 390-acre campus was like when it moved in, in 1930. There were only a few palmyras growing at that time. The rest of the greenery that pervades the place now was due to the efforts of the professors and students. As a consequence, the campus today is home to over 120 bird species, several varieties of snakes, a whole lot of mammals, and plenty of butterflies. Beginning with Edward Barnes in the 1930s, a series of professors such as Gift Siromoney and P. B. Bonnel at the college have painstakingly documented the animal and bird life at the campus.[16]

Another sylvan lung that began as a barren piece of land is Kalakshetra—the temple of dance that Rukmini Devi founded within the Theosophical Society and later moved further south to a place from where the city burial ground was in view, as senior dance guru Professor Janardhanan remembered.

'I brought a small sapling of the great banyan in the Theosophical Society and on the 1 of January 1951 we had a small ceremony for planting it in our new campus,' said Rukmini Devi. 'Many friends from different parts of the world brought earth from their own countries for this ceremonial planting. The land was bare except for small saplings that we had been planting from time to time. It was a vast sandy beach with not a speck of green and only the sea to make us feel cool under the hot sun.'[17]

To quote the NGO Nizhal, Kalakshetra's 'spreading tree canopy and openness to the light and the breeze have ensured a spirit of reverence for

---

[16]Joshua Kalapati and Ambrose Jeyasekaran, *Life and Legacy of Madras Christian College: 1837–1978*, Chennai: Zha Communications, 2010, pp. 161-66.

[17]*Pidhana, The Canopy of Life*, Chennai: Kalakshetra Foundation, 2014.

learning and for the environment over the last many decades'.[18] The birds, animals, and insects live harmoniously here, though the same cannot be said of all the resident humans.

Much of what Chennai possessed by way of wildlife may have never come to be documented had it not been for M. Krishnan, the son of writer A. Madhaviah. Beginning from the 1940s, Krishnan, who, according to writer Tulsi Badrinath, 'believed that the identity of a country depended not so much on its mutable human culture as on its geomorphology, its flora and fauna, its natural basis,'[19] wrote regularly on these subjects pertaining to South India. The initial writings were in Tamil but he later switched to English, having a column titled *Southern Diary* in the *Illustrated Weekly of India* and another, more sporadic one in *The Statesman*. Krishnan was also a hugely talented photographer, capturing not just wildlife but plenty of the performing arts and architecture too. Had it not been for Krishnan, it is highly unlikely that Chennai would have woken up to the natural heritage that it possessed.

Not known for mincing words, Krishnan was brutally frank on what he perceived were the threats to ecology. He wrote in 1983:

> It is ironic, even tragic, but deplorably true that in the bad old days of colonial rule and despotic princely power the integrity of our vast and ancient land was much better safeguarded than in the past three decades. On detached consideration, it will be realised that to some extent this was inevitable. Not because of our newly evolved Constitution (though a major defect in it is that while it has many provisions for securing the interest of the people, there is nothing in it to protect the land) but since our population had increased enormously by the time it was enacted and has continued to increase, naturally at an accelerated tempo. To meet the growing demands of our burgeoning industries and our ever-growing populations, our governments (in sole charge of the land and with an acute awareness of their need to be popular) have, with hasty and uncoordinated wastefulness, depleted the country and eroded its physical entity. What is lost is lost, much of it irretrievably, but there is still enough left truly representative of the magnificent and varied natural richness of India for preserving its identity.

---

[18]Ibid., Foreword.

[19]Tulsi Badrinath, *Madras, Chennai and the Self: Conversations with the City*, New Delhi: Pan Macmillan, 2015, pp. 115–33.

He was equally scathing of well-meaning but misguided individuals or groups that got into conservation:

> I must not shirk mentioning another handicap our wildlife conservation effort suffers from—our experts. Many of them do not know enough to know how little they know, and therefore cannot be accused in their claims to expertise but these men are wholly harmless, others see through them. But regrettably, barring a few, the people who do know something about our wildlife have their interests sustained, not by their subject but only by the personal benefits and recognition they can get out of it, and are therefore pretentious, insincere and jargon-ridden in what they say or write. They even form mutual benefit coteries and cliques – by some form of poetic justice, these often result only in mutual recriminations and jealousies and anyway they get no joy from wildlife —nor does our wildlife get anything from them.[20]

Close on the heels of Krishnan came Harry Miller, who wrote on similar subjects for the *Indian Express*. Unlike Krishnan, who was rather a serious writer, Miller added plenty of humour to his writings and anecdotes. One of his most famous stories concerned his visit to the Ramanathaswamy Temple in Rameswaram where it is mandatory that men enter bare-chested, wearing a veshti. The temple elephant, which had probably never seen a white man before, simply extended its trunk and pulled off Miller's veshti. It was his everlasting regret that the photographer who accompanied him chose to shut his eyes in horror rather than capture that moment for posterity.[21] On a more serious note, Miller repeatedly drew attention to reptiles and birds in particular, by means of his writing. In a tribute to him, written in 2017, S. R. Madhu recalled:

> Miller was a naturalist and wildlife enthusiast, particularly knowledgeable about snakes. He wrote an article for *National Geographic* in September 1970 on 'The cobra, India's good snake'.
>
> For many years, Miller's home in Chennai was a two-acre house in Thirumullaivayal (in Thiruvallur District, near Avadi).Visitors to the house in this rural setting were varied—frogs, snakes (including cobras, kraits, and vipers), monkeys, pigs, mongooses, and many strange insects. Miller

[20]M. Krishnan, 'Saving India' in Theodore Baskaran (ed.) *Sprint of the Blackbuck: Writings on Wildlife and Conservation in South India*, New Delhi: Penguin Books, 2010, p. 112.
[21]S. R. Madhu, 'The Most Unforgettable Briton The City Has Known', *Madras Musings*, Vol. XXVII, No. 17, 16–31 December 2017.

frequently received frenzied SOS from neighbours about snakes intruding into their homes. Priests of the Vaishnavi temple in Thirumullaivayal depended on him to get rid of the snakes slithering in their compound. He kept a pet python in a cupboard, and once offered to garland me with it. I fled before he started insisting![22]

The house, incidentally, was named The Frog.

The writings of Krishnan and Miller did generate interest but there was more action with the arrival of Romulus Whitaker. An American by birth but having done much of his schooling in India owing to an Indian stepfather, Whitaker qualified in the US and later enlisted with the US Army. He then apprenticed at the Miami Serpentarium for two years and arrived in Madras in the 1960s. This was the time when there was growing concern over the fate of snakes in and around the city. Sighting them was quite commonplace at one time but by the 1960s, loss of habitat was playing havoc with their survival. Commercial interests too played a detrimental role. As Baskaran notes, 'in the late 1950s, a tannery near Madras was curing five to ten thousand snakeskins in just one day!'[23]

Snakes were, rather ironically, worshipped too. Most of the Mariamman shrines that dot Chennai city have come up on sites that originally had snake hills. In the historic Mundagakanni Amman shrine of Mylapore, it was customary to place milk and eggs in the hollow of a tree at the rear of the sanctum. Nobody had ever seen a snake here but sometime in the temple's long history there had been a resident cobra. The fisher folk too built a shrine to the goddess in the area now called Raja Annamalai Puram. Here, close to the sanctum which is dominated by a giant yellow-faced deity, is a tree, one branch of which is decorated in a yellow and red pattern by means of turmeric and vermilion, making it look like a twining snake. The author Tulsi Badrinath has memories of snake hills in Sastri Nagar in Adyar as late as the 1970s. She notes how swiftly they became places of worship.

One of my earliest memories of Madras is of oil lamps radiant in the dusk, just outside the compound of our house. There, on the other side of the hedge, visible during the day and worshipped at night, were several ant hills, low cones of mud with snake burrows underground. In the evenings passers-by lit oil lamps, poured milk and left eggs at the shrine of the snake gods. Warm flames flickered at dusk, rendering alive

---

[22]Ibid.

[23]Baskaran, 'The Architectural Heritage'.

> the primordial mounds adorned with red Kumkum and red hibiscus flowers. When it turned dark, the golden light wavered in the wind, conical shadows turned taller and there was a palpable sense of the mystic.
>
> I never saw the snakes.
>
> The anthills had sprung up recently, as also the shrine, similar to others scattered throughout the city, at the root of old trees in groves or those by the road. At some point, my father, irked by the increasingly large, noisy gatherings just outside our gate and the imminent possibility that they would encroach on public land and build a permanent shrine, or perhaps worried that there were indeed snakes so close to our home, ordered the hillocks to be razed. No one protested. The holes were filled up and that evening there was only absence, the darkness, and thwarted puzzled wayfarers who carried their offerings home.[24]

Snakes were definitely on the run in the city by the 1960s and even now are faced with a shrinking habitat. But they are better off than most other fauna, chiefly owing to the Snake Park, a creation of Romulus Whitaker, who became a close associate of Harry Miller. It was the latter who introduced him to members of the Irula tribe—expert snake-catchers. Whitaker was then working with the Bombay-based Haffkine Institute on a venom-extraction project and he enlisted the help of the Irulas. Their success in locating the snakes impressed him and thus was born the Snake Park in Madras, in 1966, at what was then Selaiyur Village, on the road to Tambaram. In this he was assisted by Natesan, an Irula. The park, located on one acre of rented land, had snake pits 'and talks were organised on identifying poisonous snakes. Entrance tickets were priced at just 25 paise. Soon the word spread and snakebite victims were often brought to the park.'[25] Encouraged by what it saw, the government came forward in 1972 to give one acre of land in the Guindy Park for this initiative. The Madras Snake Park Trust was thus formed and it administers what is now one of Chennai's biggest tourist attractions. The snake park has a library, a museum, and a research unit. It conducts awareness programmes and workshops, besides bringing out a quarterly journal titled *Cobra.*

Whitaker's next initiative had to do with sea turtles, in particular, the Olive Ridley. This is a species that returns to the same beach every year to nest, no matter how far away it is prior to the breeding season. The eastern coast of India is a favoured nesting ground and that includes the beaches

[24]Badrinath in Muthiah, *Madras, Chennai*, 'Introduction'.

[25]S. Theodore Baskaran, 'Wildlife' in Muthiah, *Madras, Chennai*, p. 66.

of Chennai. Nesting in groups, the females drop their eggs into pits they dig in the sand. The hatchlings know by instinct how to make their way to the sea. The turtles and their eggs were heavily poached, drastically reducing their numbers. In 1970, Whitaker began taking an interest in the animals. He planned turtle walks, with volunteers, supported by the World Wildlife Fund (WWF). The volunteers walk along the beaches, collect the eggs, and take them to hatcheries, set up initially by the WWF. This work is now carried on by the Students Sea Turtles Conservation Network. However, the nesting turtles are still poached in the belief that their blood is medicinal. Increasing filth and human activities at the beaches are major detriments. Commercial sea fishing and oil spills are bigger threats. Artificial lighting on the beaches is yet another challenge for the turtles that were earlier guided by moonlight. But the work goes on, with enthusiasts collecting the eggs, transferring them to temperature-controlled hatcheries and then taking the hatchlings to the shoreline. It is a magnificent initiative on the part of the people of Chennai.[26]

It was also in the 1970s, around the time that the turtle walks began to have an impact, that the Madras Naturalists' Society (MNS) came into existence. It was the brainchild of V. J. Rajan, a superintendent in the Telegraph Office, who had then recently taken to birdwatching. Forming a group of sixteen enthusiasts, he founded the MNS in 1978, under the leadership of V. J. Kunte. It first drew attention to the pathetic state of the Adyar Creek, which battle was then taken up by the Consumer Action Group. The MNS then successfully conducted a survey of blackbuck and chital in the Guindy Deer Park. In the 1980s, it undertook a survey of the coastline from Chennai to Mamallapuram, to protect the Olive Ridley turtle habitats. A year later, it began bringing out its quarterly journal, *Blackbuck*. Today, the MNS, with more than 600 members, fights to save the Pallikaranai Marsh.[27] It also conducts nature walks in the patches of greenery left—the Adyar Creek (now Poonga Park), the Semmozhi Poonga (once that part of the Agri-Horticultural Society which housed the Woodlands Drive-In), and in Guindy.

Romulus Whitaker's next brainchild was the Crocodile Bank, begun in 1976. A conservation and breeding centre for these reptiles, it is located on the East Coast Road. Over 6,000 crocodiles have been bred here and even now as many as 4,000 of them, across fourteen species, live here. The location has not been without its share of problems. At one time, this was located

[26]Ibid.

[27]Baskaran, 'Introduction', *Sprint of the Blackbuck*, pp. xi–xv.

outside city limits and so was a calm habitat. But the city kept expanding and now next to the Crocodile Bank is a hotel, whose late-night events began disturbing the reptiles, some of which began showing signs of stress. Whitaker was swift to protest and there was wide coverage in the media too. The hotel has since agreed to switch off all music and reduce noise by 10 p.m. In 1985, Whitaker's first wife, Zai, launched *Hamadryad*, a quarterly journal and this has become a publication of great repute.[28]

Whitaker has since become something of a legend in Chennai, a Padma Shri Award in 2019 being a richly deserved recognition. He has gone on to establish cooperatives for Irula women that helps them economically through various initiatives. Several serious researchers of India's animal life trained under him. Satish Bhaskar became the resident expert on turtles. Shekar Dattatri, another intern, is now famed as a wildlife photographer and documentary filmmaker.[29] In recent years, Whitaker's second wife, Janaki Lenin, has written a series of lively columns on life with the man and his love for animals. The couple lives at the edge of the Chingleput scrub forest. If life with Whitaker at the Crocodile Bank, surrounded by crocodiles, snakes, turtles, and lizards was not enough, their home has more 'pesky tree frogs, adamant Russell's vipers and a dog-eating leopard'. In addition, the farm has 'four dogs, a pair of emus, a flock of geese and a pig'. For Janaki, it is a 'childhood dream come true'.[30]

Mention of the Whitakers' emu brings to mind the time when in the early 2000s, rearing these flightless birds became popular in the whole of Tamil Nadu, owing to a Ponzi scheme that emanated from Erode. The perpetrators fashioned a multi-level financing set-up whereby people paid a deposit for procuring the emus, which they then reared. The incentive was that there was a ready market for every part of the bird, from its meat to its nails. Soon others joined the race, each company claiming that its emus were better than that of the others. The scheme flourished in Chennai too and these birds running into traffic on some of the side streets became a regular feature. The swindle was exposed in 2012 by the *Economic Times*—most companies were selling the emus to the latest entrants to the scheme and there was no real market. It all ended with the arrest of the biggest promoter and since then emus have become something of a rarity.

The insect life of Chennai has its own warrior in S. Venkataraman, who

[28]Baskaran in Muthiah, *Madras, Chennai*, p. 66.

[29]Ibid., p. 69.

[30]Janaki Lenin, 'Introduction', *My Husband and Other Animals*, Chennai: Westland, 2012.

is affectionately known as 'Poochi' (insect) Venkat. A grand-nephew of R. K. Narayan and R. K. Laxman, his interest in insects came through his passion for photography. That was something he took to even while in school and he set up a processing facility at home for friends. Later, Venkat moved on to sound engineering; he and his friends developing audio systems as a hobby. But photography remained a serious passion and the turning point came when someone gave him 200 slides of micro-fauna to blow up.

'I was quite amazed at this craziness—who would want to see blow up photos of insects I wondered even as I took on the assignment,' he says. Ironically, it caught Venkat's attention and he became a serious researcher on the city's insect life. An assignment in the Guindy National Park in 1998 saw the staff giving him the appellation of Poochi. Very few people know of his real profession—a video editor who has worked on several documentaries and at least one feature film. A couple of years back, Kalamkriya, the publication wing of the Sanmar Group published his book *Insects: Guardians of Nature*, which documents some of the city's arthropods and arachnids.

'Insects are not for the faint-of-heart,' warns Venkat. 'Their strange shapes and buzzing and colouring and stinging and creeping can make you a phobic... or a lover. In my relationship with these creatures, I have been bitten, stung, and infected.' Those attacks and even an allergy that lasted days have not deterred him.[31] Poochi Venkat deals with insects that we are not familiar with, even though they may be plentiful. The mosquito is an insect that has been documented almost from the time of Kamban, the twelfth-century creator of the Tamil Ramayana. One of the opening verses has him comparing his efforts to that of a mosquito being inspired to fly with the eagle that is Valmiki's Sanskrit version. In the colonial city, it was Mambalam that always took pride of place when it came to the mosquito menace, a cricket team eventually taking the name Mambalam Mosquitoes. The writer Ashokamitran recalls that in the 1950s, most Mambalam residents had frighteningly swollen arms and legs owing to the prevalence of the filarial mosquito. Nowadays, most areas of the city compete with Mambalam as far as mosquitoes are concerned, the presence of stagnant sewage in the rivers and canals providing fertile breeding grounds.

Chennai has plenty of crows and when movies were shot outdoors, a crow shooter was part of the team and acknowledged in the title credits. In the nineteenth century, the Madras Club employed a functionary 'who was

[31]Poochi Venkat, 'Introduction', *Insects: Guardians of Nature*, Chennai: Kalamkriya Limited, 2017.

known by several names. Archer, Bowman, Crowman, Intimidator of Crows and Shikaree were only a few of the names he was called. But there was little he could do to ensure the undisturbed slumber of many after 5.00 am.' The banyan tree in front of the bedrooms was the 'standing nuisance' responsible for this state of affairs. It was the roost 'of half the crows in Madras' and during the time when the fruit is ripe, the rest of the crows of Madras joined them. One member declared that it was 'impossible to eat, read, write or sleep in comfort during the better part of the day because of the fearful nuisance of these pests'.

The club, however, refused to cut the offending tree or any other, conceding at most the expense of maintaining a scarecrow. The Madras Club, now in Adyar, is a splendid green space and strangely enough still needs to employ intimidators to ward off dogs, buffaloes, crows, and snakes![32] Sadly, such an attitude is missing in the city now and with it, much of the green cover. The loss of trees has hit Chennai hard, for it has not only increased ambient temperature and reduced rainfall, but also taken away with it a whole host of smaller animals and birds, once so vital to the ecosystem. Not to be seen any longer is the house sparrow—its familiar habitat of wooden rafters and eaves not being used in modern construction. Its space has been taken over by the pigeon and multi-storeyed buildings, with their flat sunshades and window sills, are roosting grounds for these birds. Their proliferation also increases the risk of lung disease to humans but that does not prevent many from feeding them.

Another hardy survivor is the parakeet. They can be seen everywhere, from holes in the ancient walls of Fort St George to trees by the roadside. And each day, around 8,000 of them make their way to Triplicane, where Joseph Sekar feeds them. The birdman of the city, as he is often known, embarked on this journey in 2004, when, following the tsunami, two parakeets made it to his doorstep. All these animals, insects, and bird species thrive because of the tree cover and that is increasingly under threat in Chennai. Fighting this desecration is the NGO Nizhal, which we have already seen in other contexts earlier in this book. Its credo is to inform and educate, in a non-confrontational manner. Nizhal has, according to Shobha Menon, focused entirely on endemic tree species and advises people on how to work towards conserving what is left of the historic green cover. 'One of our earliest campaigns was Free the Tree—we worked towards removing nails and

---

[32]S. Muthiah, *The Ace of Clubs: The Story of the Madras Club*, Chennai: The Madras Club, 2002, p. 27.

signboards from them,' says Shobha. The NGO has since done remarkable work with prisons, government offices, and schools. It has all been very tiring work, according to Shobha, 'repeating the same thing over and over again, mostly to no effect, but some of the response is encouraging. In the initial days people thought they could simply alert us when a tree in the neighbourhood was cut. Nowadays they consult us but take the initiative to prevent such occurrences. More frustrating are those who chose to get involved in such exercises only for the optics.'[33]

Nizhal has compiled a book on endangered trees in the city that need protection. Published by Kalamkriya, *Living Landmarks of Chennai* has some sage advice in its preface:

> This book is a small effort to catalyse our collective respect and care so that the living landmarks flourish and continue to enrich our lives. With deeper appreciation, living in harmony with nature becomes a real possibility.[34]

[33]Interview with the author, Chennai, 3 March 2020.

[34]Nizhal, 'Introduction', *Living Landmarks of Chennai*, Chennai: Kalamkriya Limited, 2015.

EPILOGUE
A CITY UNITED

Why Chennai? This is a question that often arises. What makes this a living and thriving city, throbbing with life and energy? After all, let's face it, this is no Singapore, though our politicians would like us to believe that we are well on our way to becoming a clone of that city. 'Vandaarai Vaazha Vaikkum Chennai' is an expression that means this is a city that welcomes and gives hope and livelihood to those who come here. The city has lived up to its name several times over.

While we may not know what prospects this region held in ancient or medieval times, we do know that it gave much to the British. They may have come here to purchase cloth but they stayed on to become masters, not just of the Coromandel coast but the whole of India and beyond. In the wake of the colonial masters came Indians from all over and they gave the city its cosmopolitan character.

Chennai is not often associated with the word cosmopolitan, for that is chiefly believed to be an adjective that best describes Mumbai, especially during the first half of the twentieth century. In comparison to that city, ours was much smaller in every way. But in its quiet fashion, Chennai has displayed its egalitarian nature time and again. Let us see some instances.

'Charitable Chennai'[1] was how the savant Ramalinga Swamigal described the city in the nineteenth century. He would have known, for he was the living embodiment of charity. He believed all were equal; God was love personified, He manifested as light and had to be worshipped that way; and, finally, that devotion was best displayed by kindness to all living creatures. Much of what he preached was, in many ways, a prescient description of the path that Chennai trod.

I can see many readers scoffing. Chennai? Egalitarian? Is it not one of the most hidebound, reactionary, and conservative cities? Cinema of the mid-twentieth century, always found it convenient to portray the city as the den of the mean-minded, the Godless, and the profiteering.[2] While it may

---

[1]'Dharumamigu Chennai' is what he says in his song composed on the Murugan deity at Kandar Kottam in Rasappa Chetty Street, George Town.

[2]Such as 'Madras Nalla Madras' featuring Nagesh in the film *Anubavi Raja Anubavi* (1967) and 'Paarappa Palaniappa' featuring MGR in *Periya Idathu Penn* (1963).

be true to an extent, it cannot be an image for the city as a whole, for peppering its history are several examples of great generosity. In my view, these far outweigh the negatives that Chennai is saddled with. The city, in my opinion, got bad press.

In his article on how he first came to Chennai, writer Sami Chidambaranar speaks of certain traits, apart from writing skills, that are needed to become successful in the writing profession:

> Not everyone can make it to the forefront. You need to keep pushing yourself into the limelight. You need to make it to all events even if you are uninvited and keep publicising yourself. You need to please editors, publishers, broadcasters and media barons. Only then can you succeed.[3]

Going by this, Chennai would have made a very unsuccessful writer indeed. For years, it was simply the southern metropolis where nothing ever happened—occupied by that band of dark Madrasis who spoke a language called Madrasi and opposed Hindi. They said 'Ayyo' in response to everything and mixed tamarind in all their food. Illad was the name given to these people who came from Madras to other cities and snatched all the jobs in just about every sector. They saved and saved, bought gold, and, finally, on retiring went back to the Madras that they came from. But silently, during those 'dark' years, Chennai was moving ahead, at its own pace. Remember, a Chennaiite measures success on the basis of progress. Not for him or her the overweening ambition to become number one. Reaching the top spot always was accompanied by the risk of being toppled by a number two. Which is why Chennai even now happily accepts that its Marina beach is the second longest urban beach in the whole world. (Which is the longest? Nobody is sure. But none has challenged Chennai's claim of having the second longest beach). Chennai has progressed in that same fashion on many counts.

Today, in Chennai, it is almost impossible to set up housing segregated on the basis of caste, religious sect, or community. On an informal basis, this may take place in some pockets—Brahmins and other vegetarians are known to get together to prevent non-vegetarians from becoming tenants in their housing complexes; Muslims, especially the wealthier ones, have steadily built up almost exclusive colonies in certain parts of the city. But by and large this is not allowed and people rarely, if ever, bother as to what caste, community, or religion their neighbour belongs to. This is of course true of most Indian cities, but where Chennai is different is that equality was

---

[3]Subbu, *Chennaikku Vanden*, p. 57.

practised here in the 1700s when Chintadripet was planned! Today, if there are pockets where certain communities dominate, these are due to historic reasons and nothing has rent the fabric of harmony in any of these places.

Chennai was never a favoured city of the empire once it had been used to give the initial leg up. Kolkata was the capital and Mumbai the financial hub and so most resources were used on those cities and only what was left came to Chennai. The harbour came 240 years after the British established their base here. And when famines struck, the imperial government rarely bothered with sending aid. Chennai fended for itself! The city steadily built itself up as an educational hub, as an automotive centre, as a medical capital, and as a bastion for the leather business. Eventually, when the IT revolution came, Chennai was ready. It has always grasped whatever opportunities came its way and emerged trumps. All of these sectors have provided employment and made the city prosperous. It is a far cry from the Madras of the nineteenth century when shortages of every kind plagued the city. There too, the city survived owing to the munificence of kind souls. And not many of them were blessed with deep pockets. It was the desire to do good that prevailed.

The seventeenth, eighteenth, and nineteenth centuries saw severe food shortages in the city and its environs. Famines struck with alarming regularity, leading to the death of thousands of people. The worst came about in the 1870s when food riots ensued in the city. Standing in a corner of Nyniappa Naicken Street is a handsome building from the 1890s. This is the home of the Chennapuri Annadana Samajam. Moogallur Cunniah Chetty was just fifteen, studying at the Pacchayappa's High School, when the famine of 1877 struck the city. The horrors he witnessed made him resolve that when he had the means he would ensure that food was made available to all. But lack of financial means made him forego all ideas of college education and join the Telegraph Department in 1882 as a clerk. Yet, he never gave up his dream of feeding the poor. In 1890, he founded the Chennapuri Annadana Samajam. It began with feeding eight blind persons at an eatery on Iyyah Pillai Street each Sunday. By 1893, the owners of Lakshmi Vilasa Nataka Sala (the Walltax Theatre on the eponymous road) allowed the use of their premises for this purpose and the number of those fed increased to fifteen. Several businessmen and government officials living in George Town donated generously and soon it was possible to feed people twice a week.

The big break came when Raja Sir Savalai Ramaswami Mudaliar, the powerful dubash of Dymes & Co and a great philanthropist in his own right, became a patron of the institution. People from the higher echelons of society began to take interest in the samajam. The royal families of South

India donated liberally and it was a proud day for Cunniah Chetty when, owing to the efforts of leading solicitor J. R. B. Branson, the Gujarati magnate Lodd Krishnadoss Balamukundoss funded the construction of the samajam's permanent home. Governor Lord Wenlock inaugurated the building on 18 December 1895. Governor Lord Ampthill became a patron in 1904 and remained so till his death in 1934.

It had now become possible to feed the poor every day. Cunniah Chetty's dream had come true. In 1914, he took early retirement, so that he could focus on running the samajam. By then, the institution had taken on the task of providing noon meal schemes at thirteen schools in the city. Cunniah Chetty's services were recognized by the government and he was awarded the title of Rao Saheb in 1925. In the 1930s, an orphanage was added to the samajam by P. Chengalvaraya Chettiar, who succeeded Cunniah Chetty as secretary when the latter passed away in 1933. By the time the samajam celebrated its diamond jubilee in 1950, it was taking care of 150 orphans and feeding over 600 people daily.[4]

Today, such requirements have shrunk. But the samajam continues its work, silently. In an increasingly commercial world, it remains a beacon of humaneness. As are several other annadana samajams that dot the old city.

But there are other requirements, of shelter, succour, and love. The work of Udavum Karangal or Helping Hands is as inspiring as that of the samajam. Its founder Vidyaakar was inspired by Mother Teresa. A destitute himself, he tended to an accident victim at the age of thirteen and came under the care of the person he had saved. He decided that his life would be in social service. A graduate in social work who also trained at the Institute of Mental Health and the Greater Madras Leprosy Treatment and Health Education Scheme Hospital, he found his metier when he was entrusted with the responsibility of tending to an abandoned girl child. Thus was born Udavum Karangal in 1983. Today, it is an organization that has helped several thousand children and adults. As a matter of policy, Udavum Karangal stays away from government aid and relies entirely on donations from well-wishers from across the world.[5]

Women began taking an active interest in social welfare schemes from the 1920s, especially once they were able to join the legislature. The first set to avail of this opportunity had some connection with the Theosophical Society.

---

[4]V. Sriram, 'Food for all', *The Hindu*, 29 May 2012.

[5]Dr Shoma A. Chatterji, 'Udavum Karangal: A story of love and compassion', *India Together*, 13 November 2015.

The leader at this time of that new-age religion, whose world headquarters was in Madras, was the redoubtable Annie Besant. At her encouragement, the women of the Theosophical Society had been instrumental in founding the Women's Indian Association and several others, not Theosophists but with an ardent desire to do good for society, joined in. Prominent amongst them were Ambujammal, Dr Muthulakshmi Reddy, Lady Andal Venkata Subba Rao, Ammu Swaminadhan, Margaret Cousins, Radhabai Subbarayan, and Durgabai Deshmukh. Beginning with 1919, several became councillors of the Corporation of Madras, Ammu Swaminadhan, Lady Masilamoney Chellammal Devadoss, and Hanen Angelo, being among the first. With their presence, the civic body began pushing forward maternity and general healthcare facilities for women, all of which continue to exist today, in vastly expanded facilities. These efforts went a long way to ensure that women were healthy and later able to join the mainstream workforce.

The concept of active volunteer work, apart from donations by the elite ladies of Madras was conceived by Irene Waller, the wife of the then Bishop of Madras, in 1923, leading to the founding of the Guild of Service. Upper class, socially conscious British women voluntarily gave their time and money to underprivileged sections of society in the city of Madras. Initially, help was rendered in small ways, by visiting hospitals, engaging with sick children, writing letters, and distributing medicines. It is also a matter of interest that in the same year, Irene Waller's husband began the Madras Vigilance Association. A group of American women were staying as guests of the Wallers, and one evening, as they returned from an outing, were trapped by a mysterious group and taken to a notorious part of the city. The bishop mounted a rescue operation but it opened his eyes to human trafficking. He established the Madras Vigilance Association as a consequence. This body, in which he was ably supported by several prominent citizens of Madras, regularly helped the police conduct raids and rescue young women from brothels. By 1928, Bishop Waller had found an able lieutenant in Muthulakshmi Reddy. In 1934, the Vigilance Association set up Stree Sadhana, a rescue home for girls, located on Santhome High Road.

Mrs Waller was president of the guild till 1929. Though she and her husband were to have a much longer tenure in Madras, returning to England only in 1942, it is clear that she stepped back after giving the guild its initial impetus. Some of the activities the early members engaged in were conducting feeding programmes, taking care of the welfare of children and the aged, and providing medical service to the disabled. Every Saturday, at the Mental Hospital, a tea party would be held, with cakes being contributed by about thirty-five ladies. These cakes would also be distributed at the General Hospital, the Ophthalmic Hospital, and the Women and Children's Hospital. The women also volunteered and raised money for the Friend-in-Need Society, the oldest Anglo-Indian organization, and the Alms Home where the Child Welfare Centre was begun. The Salvation Army, the Red Cross, YWCA, the Girl Guides, and the St Georges' School saw the involvement of the guild members. In 1928, the TB Hospital was also included. The welfare of sailors was also looked into and a Stranded Travellers' Fund was started to help travellers return home.

World War II mobilized and energized the ladies of the guild to contribute towards war services. The volunteers received special nurse training from institutions like St John's Ambulance and found work in various hospitals as auxiliary nurses. The naval commander's wife encouraged the ladies to take courses in air-raid protection. They, in turn, were asked to teach the women in the slums and other institutions, especially in the harbour and George Town areas. The freedom fighter Ambujammal, who was deeply involved in the work of the Women's Indian Association, gives further details in her autobiography, *Naan Kanda Bharatham:*

> It was expected that Japanese troops would soon land in Madras and the Government was also apprehensive about aerial strikes. Air Raid Patrols (ARP) were formed and these had a women volunteer's wing as well. This was headed by Mrs Clubwala Jadhav. Classes were conducted to inform women on where and how to take shelter when the air raid sirens sounded. First Aid training was also given. My aunt Janammal and I attended these classes and then went to the more depressed areas of the city to train women there.

The Japanese infiltration into Burma (present-day Myanmar) saw thousands of refugees finding their way to Madras. The Hope Club was started to rehabilitate and assist refugees by putting them up in refugee camps. The ladies helped with clothing, feeding children, and meeting the refugees at the harbour or the Central Station, when they arrived by ship or train and brought them to the camps. We must turn to Ambujammal once again for a word picture of the prevalent situation then and the role that women volunteers played in rehabilitation. It also shows how institutions that went about helping those in distress had reached a critical mass in the city by then and witnessed sufficient networking between them:

With members of the public as volunteers, a refugee camp was put up by the government at a rented bungalow on Spur Tank Road. Councillors of the Corporation of Madras such as Chakkarai Chettiar and T. S. Ramaswami Iyer were at the forefront of the efforts. Women included Mary Clubwallah Jadhav, Manjubhashini, my aunt Janammal, my friend P. K. Kalpakam and myself. Each morning, armed with food, a flask of coffee and a container of water, we would leave in my car for the camp. It would be late in the evening when we returned.

The refugees came by foot to Chittagong and there segregated based on their ultimate destination and sent onwards. Those bound for Madras were routed via Calcutta. We would meet them at the station or at the harbour. The refugees were all sent by a special bus to the camp. Then having ascertained their ultimate destination we would arrange for their travel. During this time, they invariably narrated their harrowing experiences and gave vent to their grief on all they had lost—money, possessions, and family members. It was a heartrending experience. Many were ill, owing to malnutrition suffered during the two-month trek from Burma to Chittagong. We arranged for nutritious food. Several were sick and these were medically treated. Many came with wads of Burmese currency notes and these had to be converted into Indian rupees. But by far the most disturbing were the deaths and separation from family members. There was one instance of a family of five comprising father, mother and three children making it intact all the way from Burma to Chittagong to Calcutta to Madras Central, only to have the father die just as the train steamed into the station. Janammal and I had him cremated and brought his widow and children to our home. Having stayed with us for a few days, they then departed for Palghat where her sister lived and extended her a warm welcome.

In all this, the contributions of the Gujaratis of Madras was immense. They donated saris, dhotis, food packets and sweets generously. The families began departing one by one. But what of the orphaned children that numbered around thirty? These were taken in by Dr Muthulakshmi Reddy in her Avvai Home. The Government gave a stipend to each of these children. Similarly, there were around 50 women who had nowhere to go. The Ramakrishna Mission rented a bungalow in D'Silva Road and housed them under the care of Rajamma, a volunteer. Each woman was given ₹30 a month by the Government. We began literacy and tailoring classes for them. Gradually they became independent and moved out. There were some young girls as well and these were all taken in by the Madras Seva Sadan.

The entire process of rehabilitation lasted four months.[6]

It was during this same time that Lieutenant Colonel Gurdial Singh Gill welcomed partition refugees to Chennai. Unlike Delhi where the logistics of handling the influx was mindboggling, the numbers were much smaller here. But they were attended to nevertheless. Gill and his fellow Punjabis made it a point to go to the Central Station every day, receive those coming in, and ensure they were sheltered, clothed, fed, and finally given some occupation. Most went into auto parts dealership, setting up shop around the General Patters Road area.[7]

In later years, the Guild of Service, under Mary Clubwala Jadhav rose to great heights, birthing the Madras School of Social Work, running several hospices and schools under its Seva Samajam and being a beacon of hope to many.[8] Similarly, the Balamandir Kamaraj Trust, established in 1949 by S. Manjubhashini, in close coordination with K. Kamaraj, began as a hospice for destitute children and later expanded to include schools and a research foundation. It also sent out positive messages to marginalized sections on childbearing and rearing. The Balamandir, quite early in its life, enlisted the support of the corporate house Larsen & Toubro and that marks the beginning of commercial enterprises aiding such socially committed organizations in the city. In recent years, we have had the Madhuram Narayanan Centre (MNC) for Exceptional Children that handles those with autism and other related issues, supported by the Sanmar Group.[9] The Madras Dyslexic Association (MDA) is similarly a body that, thanks to its livewire President D. Chandrashekar, has grown from strength to strength, providing a new future to several children who have this disability.[10] Both the MNC and the MDA were founded by people who just wanted to make a difference. Support, when it came, was generous.

Durgabai Deshmukh is yet another hallowed name when it comes to the upliftment of women. Having joined the Congress when she was just twelve,

---

[6]S. Ambujammal, *Naan Kanda Bharatham*, pp. 218-222.

[7]V. Sriram, 'Gill of Kill Nagar', *The Hindu*, 4 June 2013.

[8]For more details on the Guild of Service and Mary Clubwala Jadhav, see Rukmini Amirapu, *Spreading Hope and Happiness*, Chennai: Guild of Service, 2019.

[9]Ranjitha Ashok, *A World of Difference: Madhuram Narayanan Centre for Exceptional Children*, Chennai: Madhuram Narayanan Centre, 2014.

[10]See Madras Dyslexia Association website, available here: https://www.mdachennai.com/about-mda/committee-members/.

Durgabai parted ways with her husband and migrated to Madras with her mother and brother, to study law. Even in her native village in Andhra, she had proved a tough fighter, banding the women together to challenge men who were alcoholic or abusive. A name and shame campaign reformed many. The urge to study law had come about while in prison for participating in the freedom movement. Having graduated, she enrolled in the High Court of Madras and practised her profession. But it was the championing of causes concerning women that she was best at and, having managed to get aristocratic Telugu women to donate, she formed what would become the Andhra Mahila Sabha (AMS). Today, the AMS is many things rolled into one, with healthcare, education and, above all, shelter being its main objectives. Durgabai would trailblaze a career, becoming a member of India's constituent assembly where she ensured her voice, concerning the women of India, was heard, and her words were written into the Constitution. She ended up marrying C. D. Deshmukh, former governor of the Reserve Bank of India and later union finance minister. Durgabai also served as the chairperson of the Central Social Welfare Board.[11]

There were others who did good work in their own way but are now no longer remembered. Ambujammal began the Srinivasa Gandhi Nilayam, dedicated to her 'biological and spiritual fathers' (Sriman Srinivasa Iyengar and Mahatma Gandhi) for ensuring women learnt skills to manage life on their own.[12] This still functions though in a very small way. Sadly defunct now is Mahatmaji Seva Sangam founded by the writer and freedom fighter Vai Mu Kothainayaki Ammal.[13]

While all of these were important initiatives in their own right, they did operate in their respective areas of interest and influence. The larger public weal, by way of creating a sense of equality, was brought about by the long line of reformers, beginning with Ayothi Das Pandithar and Rettamalai Srinivasan and culminating in Periyar. Their principles came to dominate the way successive governments went about administering the state. Reservation in government jobs and admissions to higher educational institutions steadily inched upwards in favour of the Backward Classes, with around 69 per cent of the total seats now being allocated to them. The Brahmins and other forward castes were understandably miffed, but they too have moved on, managing to survive in a changed environment.

---

[11]Durgabai Deshmukh, *The Stone that Speaketh*, Madras: Andhra Mahila Sabha, 1979.

[12]Ambujammal, *Naan Kanda Bharatham*.

[13]Krishnan, *Kothainayakiyin Illakkiya Pathai*.

That is one of the reasons why when in the 1980s, the rest of India burned following the Mandal Commission Report, Tamil Nadu and Chennai, remained calm. The flip side is that reservation itself has sharpened caste divides—Tamil Nadu probably has the largest list of castes today and most of them are in the Most Backward or Other Backward lists. Even within this, there is a tussle, with each caste aiming to increase its share of seats within the reserved percentage. There is also the issue of the creamy layer within these backward castes, comprising families who have already availed of the benefits of reservation and yet claim the same facility for successive generations.[14]

At least one step, said to have been inspired by Periyar's ideals, ended up as a joke, though its objective was noble. In 1976, MGR announced that all caste names featuring in street nomenclature would have to go.[15] C. P. Ramaswami Iyer Road became C. P. Ramaswami Road thereafter. This posed a major problem in places like George Town where there were streets named after Kasi Chetty, Kasi Mudali, and Kasi Naicken. All of them could not become Kasi Street and so they became Kasi (Che) Street, Kasi (Mu) Street, and Kasi (Na) Street respectively. An apocryphal story has it that somewhere in the city was a Telugu Brahmin Street, which, during the Potti Sriramulu fast, fearing violence against Telugus, truncated itself to Brahmin Street. This, in 1976, became Street.

That MGR was quixotic was more than evident to Jayalalithaa, who in the 1990s, out of political necessity to placate various caste outfits, each dominant in one part of Tamil Nadu or the other, began to bifurcate existing districts and rename the new ones after political leaders from each of the groups, complete with caste names. The DMK, which had begun the trend of naming bus transport corporations after caste leaders faced the brunt when it came to power after her in 1996. Everyone was happy with such honours being bestowed but when a Dalit leader in Virudhunagar was commemorated, the OBC communities were incensed. Riots ensued, leading to an all-party meet where the DMK proposed to do away with all caste names in district and bus corporation nomenclature. The districts were named after the most prominent town in their midst while the transport corporations became TN State Transport Corporations. Peace may have

[14] S. Venkatanarayanan, 'It's High Time Tamil Nadu Rationalises Its Quota System', *The Wire*, 17 August 2019.

[15] Divya Karthikeyan, 'What's in a name? Tamil Nadu's stormy past with caste names on street corners and institutions', *News Minute*, 2 September 2016.

returned but caste divides have not gone away.[16]

Will they ever go away? The initiatives of leaders like Periyar made people aware that all humans were created equal. But shedding the caste baggage and working together has proved more difficult, particularly when every government application form asks for these details and keeps reminding people of their origins. Feelings of equality need to come from within. Will that ever happen?

Chennai today is home to thousands of youngsters who grow up with no awareness of what caste their friends or colleagues belong to. The proliferation of the private sector, where employment opportunities are equal, has ensured that caste divides are negligible. The city sees hundreds of youngsters coming in on a daily basis, to work and eventually settle in the city. They join organizations, work with colleagues of both sexes not bothered about who is from what caste, but when it comes to marriage, most prefer to toe the line and tie the knot with someone from their own community. Inter-caste marriages have come to be accepted but only among some. There still remains a strong prejudice against stepping outside the caste barrier.

The film world, for long an egalitarian set up, brooks no caste and, indeed, very few would be interested to know what caste their favourite hero belongs to, until the time he enters politics of course. On the other hand, there have been endless discussions on depictions of caste in Tamil cinema. A screenplay has to be examined under a microscope to ensure that no particular community takes offence. Even in that there is a hierarchy—some communities can be laughed at. Others cannot. Some can take offence. Others cannot. Offence by some can initiate governmental action too—that depends on the size of the voting population in the offended community.

And despite many deep divides within, it is to be noted that there has never been a caste riot in the city. That is, if you discount seventeenth-century history when a vertical division in society between the left-hand (involved in manufacturing) and right-hand (involved in agriculture) castes, details which are hazy at best, caused many headaches to the British. This prompted the division of the Old Town on caste lines but not for long. Soon everyone was back coexisting happily. At least until now.

A few years ago, I would not have included that caveat for I was sure that Chennai had risen above divisions, at least in public. Now I am not so sure. Politicians, media, and above all social media, are spewing venom and, sadly, I see many Chennai people falling victim to this. All of a sudden, religious

---

[16]Ibid.

and caste divides have come to the fore. Where have people like Valliammal Muthiah who, after reciting *Kanda Sashti Kavacham*, would light candles at St Anthony's altar vanished? I am sure they are still around but their numbers have reduced. From a time when your religion was a personal matter in Chennai, we have degenerated to wearing it on our sleeves. Loudspeakers chanting prayers, evangelical speeches, and singing devotional music have just got louder, making me worry about the shape of things to come.

And yet, I see a lot of hope.

Every year, the festival at the Kapaliswarar Temple takes place for ten days in the month of Panguni (Mar/Apr). The number of devotees reaches a peak on the eighth day, when Lord Kapaliswara, accompanied by his consort, Karpagambal, and sons, Ganesa and Singaravela, comes out in procession. On this day the Lord is preceded by his sixty-three devotees, the Nayanmars, their bronze images mounted in palanquins. They face the Lord, their palms pressed together and as the Lord advances, they walk backwards, facing him the entire way. The press of devotees, numbering a lakh and more, is enormous and there is the heat too, for this procession begins in the afternoon and wends its way around the four streets surrounding the temple tank. It has been customary for donors and devotees to erect tanneer pandals (literally water-dispensing kiosks) all across the route that devotees take to come to the temple. Some are put up in places as far removed as Ambattur and Pulianthope. Buttermilk, water, biscuits, and cooked rice flavoured with spices are distributed. Some of these tanneer pandals have histories themselves, the oldest being put up by the same family year after year near the tank and having a record dating back to 1852! In the midst of all the chaos, I also see my office boy who every year collects money from everyone in my workspace to buy biscuits and distribute them to the pilgrims during this event. His name? Joseph. Why does he do it? He thinks it is a good deed, to tend to devotees. I have never asked him why he, a Christian, wants to do this. Such a doubt has arisen in my faction-ridden mind, not his. I am the one with this question despite posing to be a secular individual who believes that all are born equal. His thought process is clear. Why should I sully it? And so, every Friday, as I watch Joseph wave the camphor plate around the gods in my office as part of the obligatory puja, I am happy. I know there is hope. Yes, to be sure there are several others who shy away from festivals and celebrations of other religions. But there is also Joseph.

It is Eid. The nawab of Arcot has invited my wife and me to Amir Mahal for the celebrations. We go with much trepidation and excitement. What if only non-vegetarian food is served? What if we have to participate in the prayer? Do we know when to stand up and when to kneel? On reaching the place, our doubts melt away in the warm embrace in which the nawab enfolds me. We are led to a table where there is vegetarian biriyani. 'But you don't know what you are missing on the other side,' says His Highness with a twinkle in his eye. Two days prior to this, my friend Anwar led several people on a heritage walk down Triplicane. The walk ended just as the evening prayers concluded at the Big Mosque. It was the month of Ramadan and with this prayer, the day's fast could be broken. Anwar got everyone to join in the first meal of the day, nombu kanji, gruel, served to all irrespective of what religion they profess. Anwar just smiles at the wonder many of the participating Hindus express. His documentary *Yadum* on Tamil Muslims shows how in the annual Meenakshi temple festival in Madurai, an important role is played by Muslims. Yes, there is hope.

And that hope has pulled the city through its challenges, which, in recent years, have been rather often. As it did during the floods of 2015. On 2 December, even *The Hindu* had to suspend publication. Chennai was declared a disaster site and while the administration began coming to grips with the situation, the corporation and Vikram Kapoor, its commissioner, in particular doing a magnificent job, it was the people who rose to the challenge. There was no question of caste or economic status. There was a problem out there and help and succour had to be sent out to millions.

For over a month, Chennai worked as one mass of humanity. Film stars and radio jockeys managed social media—tweeting messages about where help was needed or where relief materials were located. Musicians, the December Music Festival notwithstanding, waded through water to reach slums and handed out food that they had, just a few hours earlier, prepared in community kitchens. Corporate houses donated money and also sent employees over to help. School and college buildings, wedding halls, community centres, and places of worship were thrown open to facilitate the preparation and packaging of relief material—medicines, food packets, clothes, and utensils. These were then picked up by relief trucks, often arranged by the volunteers themselves and delivered at various places. By the end of December, normalcy had been restored to an extent but there was still much to be done and outreach efforts continued for many months. And when all was done, people went back to what they had been doing before the floods, as quietly as they came. Periyar would have been delighted, as would Muthulakshmi Reddy, Mary Clubwala Jadhav, Moogallur Cunniah Chetty, and everyone else among that list of pioneers who had taught Chennai to give. Ramalinga Swamigal would probably have composed a verse in praise. Thiruvalluvar, who centuries earlier had exhorted people to give liberally, would have smiled.

A year later came cyclone Vardah, which battered the city on 16 December 2016. With wind speeds of over 65 mph, it uprooted over 100,000 trees, damaged roads, and cut electricity. The next morning, Chennai was back in action. Local area help groups cleared fallen trees and debris even before the corporation trucks began arriving. This was a new Chennai. There was a time when it was so insular that nobody looked at a neighbour's house, but now people were learning to come together and work for the common good. And there was no whining that the government had done nothing. Now there is talk of entire colonies segregating their waste, conserving water, and cleaning their streets. The beginnings of all this can be traced to the NGO ExNoRa, led by founder M. B. Nirmal in 1989, which encouraged housing colonies to tackle civic issues together. There was, however, no talk of caste. Or religion.

In January 2017, there was a different coming together. The festival of Pongal has always been associated closely with Jallikattu—the traditional bull-taming sport. Over the years, this event has caused loss of life to the spectators and also cruelty to the animals. The People for the Ethical Treatment of Animals (PETA) had challenged the validity of the sport and the Supreme Court had banned it. This was seen as an affront to Tamil pride. Here, it may be best to leave aside a debate on this topic. It is also not possible to dwell on the way in which the state government, then just recovering from the death of Jayalalithaa, circumvented the issue by passing a bill to amend the Prevention of Cruelty to Animals Act, thereby enabling the Jallikattu events to be held. But what stood out was the way in which people protested the ban.

Beginning from 8 January, diverse groups of young people, largely alerted through social media, began congregating at the Marina Beach. And they stayed there for sixteen days, staging a peaceful protest. Alyque Padamsee had once famously remarked that Madras was a city where it was all right for Murugan and Muthu to walk hand in hand on the Marina Beach but to do the same with their wives was not acceptable. Within three decades, the city had changed. Young men and women sat together and there was no incident of eve teasing. The government and the police reacted with maturity—nothing was done beyond appealing to the protestors to disperse. On the last day, after the enactment of the law by the assembly, the protestors were expected to leave, but there was chaos. This was later attributed to some miscreants who had infiltrated the group. But there was no loss of life and people went back to their lives. Gandhi, whose statue stood sentinel over these protestors, would have perhaps understood.

There were many who did not understand what the protest was all about. Some attributed the entire thing to be the work of missionaries. Very few realized that it was a matter of regional pride. Jallikattu was a matter of Tamil identity.

In 2020 came the pandemic. Suddenly, the entire country went into a lockdown. What then of those who survived only in a city where life was normal? What of the thousands of migrant labourers from Bihar, Rajasthan, MP, and UP, who had come to earn a livelihood in Chennai, knew only Hindi and now were faced with starvation? Once again the city rose to the occasion. Social organizations such as the Bhoomika Trust, Feed My Chennai, and the Chakram Foundation worked day and night, offering support via helplines, reaching food and vital provisions and eventually finding ways and means of sending these workers back to where they came from. It was a cathartic period for most of the volunteers, to realize on what slender threads the lives of these migrant labourers depended. And there were tears of joy when these workers reached their hometowns and called to inform the volunteers that they had made the journey safely.

True, many other cities did the same. But remember, it was Chennai that was considered hidebound, conservative, and insular. We had to fight bad press.

Six months later, much of the migrant workforce was back. Why did they come back? To earn a living, of course. But why Chennai, so far away from their hometowns and a place which speaks an alien language. 'There is shanti (peace) here,' said one. What more is there to say?

Where was caste or religion in all of this? Nowhere. People had reacted as people and not based on who or what they were. Today, despite all the ranting by bigots of every kind ranging from the rabid right to the loony left, Chennai's harmonious fabric remains intact, with the added colour of rising above divisions when it matters most. And to all of them, Chennai is oor, their native place, their home. True, they still have strong connection with their places of origin—what is called 'my native' in Chennai-speak. But there is no talk of going back there. Chennai is home, because that is where livelihood is and life is to be led. Vandaarai vaazha vaikkum Chennai.

That then, is Chennai—it never lets go of its traditions and it still follows certain established tenets of what is expected of good people. And it moves ahead, at its own pace. Most metros can be slotted into one of two categories—the kind that remains in the past, glorifying its decay, or the kind that moves ahead all the time, abandoning its heritage. Chennai has perfected the middle path—for every two steps it takes forward, it always looks back to make sure that it takes along that which is worthwhile in its culture and heritage. It may sometimes carry forward useless baggage as well, but then, that is a matter of individual perception.

ACKNOWLEDGEMENTS

And so, phew! It is done. As Bertie Wooster says after finishing his article titled 'What the well-dressed man is wearing', I now realize 'why author blokes have bald heads and faces like birds who have suffered'. But the important thing is that it is over. And I realize I did enjoy putting it together. And while researching further for this book, I learnt a lot anew.

All of this would not have happened without the help of several people. And my thanks goes to the following:

Nirmala Lakshman, Director, Kasturi & Sons, the Lady of *The Hindu*'s Lit Fest, as I like to think of her, for introducing me to David Davidar and suggesting this book.

David Davidar of the house of Aleph for readily accepting the idea and in good faith, goods unseen, as they say in commercial transactions.

S. Muthiah for having been guru, guide, philosopher, and friend (he did not like poetry and so I am leaving out poet) on matters Chennai for two decades and I am sure he is wondering from up there as to why I did not name the book *Madras: A Biography*.

Dr A. R. Venkatachalapathy, who I am sure will like the title of this book, though I do not know if he will like what is in it, for readily sharing his insights which are quoted in several places in the book.

His Highness Muhammad Abdul Ali, the prince of Arcot, for sharing his views on the city.

Suresh Krishna and M.V. Subbiah, captains of Indian industry who gave me their inputs on the industrial scenario.

Sekhar Raghavan and Shobha Menon who were my go-to people on matters concerning the city's natural heritage.

Mohan Raman for sharing his insights on the world of Tamil cinema.

Dr N. Varadarajan, who over dinner one evening, gave me a masterful survey of the city's healthcare scenario.

Madras Musings—that wonderful creation of S. Muthiah's which was, as expected, a treasure trove of information.

Karthik Bhatt, my right hand on Chennai's history, who read the manuscript thoroughly and set me right on several points.

Pujitha Krishnan of the house of Aleph who patiently put up with all my delays and made sense of what I had sent.

Sarada, my dear wife, who was, as always, the balancing factor and who took care of the one million other more important things in life, all of which will manifest themselves just when a book is on its way.

My colleagues at office who understood that the writerly life had taken over for a while and I would eventually return.

All the authors who wrote on Chennai and matters concerning Chennai before me, from whose material I have liberally quoted, with acknowledgments of course.

And finally, the people of Chennai, past and present, who made the city what it is.

INDEX